D0368548

HISTORY AND LITERATURE
OF EARLY CHRISTIANITY

Second Edition

ANCIENT MEDITERRANEAN

WEST

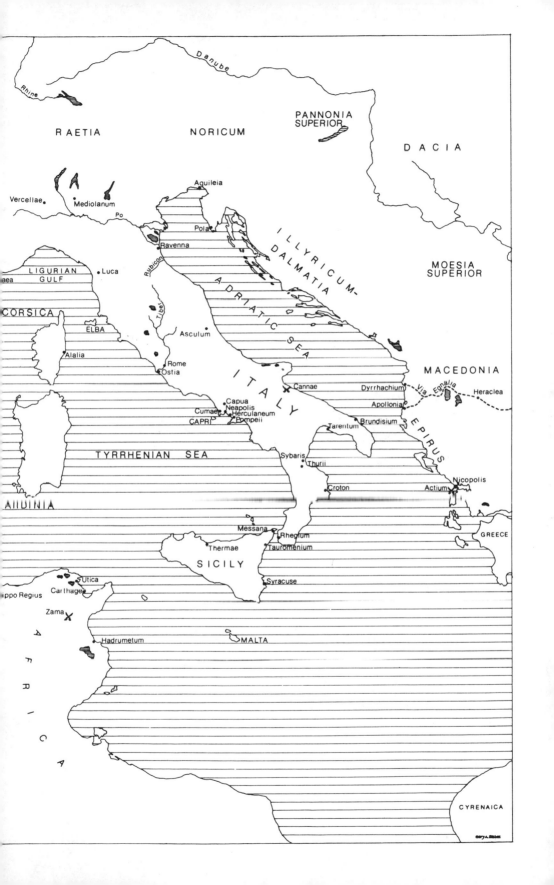

CASPIAN
SEA

COLCHIS

Trapezus

Amisus

ARMENIA

Tigranocerta

ADIAPENE
Nisibis
X Gaugamela

Ecbatana

ADOCIA

Samosata
Zeugma Apamea Edessa
COMMAGENE OSRHOËNE
LICIA X Issus
Tarsus

Euphrates

Tigris

PARTHIA

Rhossus
Seleucia Antioch
SYRIA
Aleppo

Dura Europos

MESOPOTAMIA

Laodicea Apamea
Orontes Epiphania

Palmyra

Seleucia Ctesiphon

Babylon

Byblos
Berytos Baalbek
Sidon PHOENICIA
Tyre Damascus

ARABIA

Uruk-Warka

Caesarea Philippi
Seleucia
tolemais-Ake Tiberias
Nazareth Gerias Bethsaida
reaMaritima Gadara
Samaria Scythopolis Bostra
Sichem Gerasa
Joppa Philadelphia
Jamnia Qumran
Jerusalem
Bethlehem
Ascalon
Gaza Masada
Raphia X

NABATEA

Petra

ANCIENT MEDITERRANEAN

EAST

GAB

Volume Two

INTRODUCTION TO
THE NEW TESTAMENT

HISTORY AND LITERATURE
OF EARLY CHRISTIANITY

Second Edition

HELMUT KOESTER

WALTER DE GRUYTER
NEW YORK • BERLIN

ABOUT THE AUTHOR

Helmut Koester is John H. Morison Professor of New Testament Studies and Winn Professor of Ecclesiastical History at Harvard University, Emeritus; Editor of *Harvard Theological Review* (1975–1999); Editor of *Archaeological Resources for New Testament Studies;* and Chairman of the New Testament Board of *Hermeneia,* a continuing critical and historical commentary on the Bible.

Copyright © 1982, 2000 by Walter de Gruyter & Co., Berlin

Library of Congress Cataloging-in-Publication Data
Koester, Helmut, 1926–
    Introduction to the New Testament / Helmut Koester. —2nd ed.
        p.   cm.
    Includes bibliographical references and index.
    Contents: v. 1. History, culture, and religion of the Hellenistic age
    ISBN 3-11-014693-2 (cloth : alk. paper). —ISBN 3-11-014692-4
(pbk. : alk. paper)
        1. Bible. N.T.—History of contemporary events.   2. Bible. N.T.—
Introductions.   I. Title
    BS2410.K613   1995
    225.9'5—dc20   94-47576
                                                                          CIP

Manufactured in the United States of America

10 9 8 7 6 5 4 3 2 1

TO THE MEMORY OF MY TEACHER
RUDOLF BULTMANN

Contents

§7 THE SOURCES FOR THE HISTORY OF EARLY CHRISTIANITY

§10. PALESTINE AND SYRIA

Maps

Photographs

Charts

Like the second edition of the first volume of the *Introduction to the New Testament,* the new edition of the "History and Literature of Early Christianity" is no longer dependent upon my earlier German book, *Einführung in das Neue Testament.* When my German work was written during the seventies—the first English edition was essentially a translation of that German book—I was, to be sure, very much aware of the newly discovered library of Nag Hammadi and I had already participated actively in the efforts of publishing and evaluating these new documents with respect to their impact upon a fresh understanding of the history and literature of early Christianity. That effort was then only in its beginning stages. During the last two decades, however, all of the writings of the Nag Hammadi Library have been published in critical editions and numerous monographs and articles have been produced on these important texts, thanks to the efforts of my friend James M. Robinson and the group of scholars he brought together under the auspices of the Institute for Antiquity and Christianity in Claremont, California. Moreover, the subsequent renewed interest during the same period in the wide-ranging corpus of writings generally designated as the "New Testament Apocrypha" has resulted in a number of new editions and translations of these works and intensified the scholarly scrutiny of their intent and value. Finally, a large number of learned commentaries on the books of the New Testament and the Apostolic Fathers have since appeared both in the United States and abroad—not to speak of the new flood of books on the historical Jesus. All this made it necessary to reconceive large portions of my book, although I have not been persuaded that I should change its perspective, approach, and overall structure. I remain committed to the methods of historical criticism, and to an interpretation of the early Christian writings and of the traditions that preceded them in the context of their own unrepeatable historical, theological, and social situations.

I am again indebted to my former student Philip Sellew, professor at the University of Minnesota, for his invaluable help in the arduous task of updating the bibliographies. He also graciously contributed the chapter "Narrative and Rhetorical Criticism" (§1.4e). My colleague Marianne P. Bonz read the entire manuscript, making numerous suggestions for improvements, and gave valuable advice for the chapter on Luke-Acts (§12.3e), for which I am grateful. I have learned much from my colleagues at Harvard, especially François Bovon, David Mitten, and Gregory Nagy, and also from my students; the close contact with these students and especially with my teaching fellows, Mark Kurtz, Melanie Johnson De Baufre, Anne-Marie Luijendijk, and Laura Nasrallah, was particularly valuable when I taught the course "Introduction to the New Testament" during my last semester of active service at Harvard University in the spring of 1998. I am, however, most indebted to the patience and moral support of my wife Gisela, who thought that I would finally retire and then had to discover that I was now devoting most of my time to the completion of this volume. My thanks also go to the staff of Aldine de Gruyter for the congenial and expert efforts in the editing and production of the book.

Looking back at the course that New Testament scholarship has taken over the now passing 20th century, there is little question that Rudolf Bultmann was the one who set its parameters and defined its tasks for more than a generation. It has been the most fortunate turn in the events of my life—be it called divine guidance or providence—that the U.S. army, in the fall of the year 1945, released me from a POW camp in Marburg, Germany. With no other place to go (of my parents, I knew only that they were somewhere in the Russian occupation zone), I decided to en-roll for courses in the theological faculty at the Philipps-University of Marburg, the oldest Protestant university in the world, founded in 1527 by Duke Philipp of Hesse. It was there that I soon became fascinated by the lectures of Rudolf Bult-mann, going to his seminars with fear and trembling, surviving his unrelenting crit-icisms, and being revived by his faithful encouragement in my efforts to write a dissertation. What I owe to him is expressed in the continued dedication of this work to the memory of the unrivaled master in the art of interpreting the New Tes-tament in its contemporary setting.

Helmut Koester

Lexington, Massachusetts
February 2000

The concept of an "Introduction to the New Testament" in the form of a history of early Christianity in its contemporary setting, including a survey of the political, cultural, and religious history of the Hellenistic and Roman imperial period, stems from the predecessor of this book, the *Einführung in das Neue Testament* by Rudolf Knopf (revised edition by Hans Lietzmann and Heinrich Weinel) in the series "Sammlung Töpelmann" (now succeeded by "De Gruyter Lehrbücher"). Thus, the *Introduction* presented here in its English version does not aspire to be an "Introduction" in the technical sense nor a "History of Early Christianity Literature" which treats the scholarship, date, integrity, and literary structure of each of the New Testament writings. To be sure, these questions are encompassed in the present work, but they are discussed within the context of a reconstruction of the historical development of early Christianity. My primary concern is to present the history of the early Christian churches, since it seems to me that the student of the New Testament must learn from the outset to understand the writings of the earliest period within their proper historical context.

It is obvious that this attempt to reconstruct the history of early Christianity requires one to relinquish some strictures of traditional introductions. I do not limit the discussion to the twenty-seven canonical books, but treat also sixty other early Christian writings from the first 150 years of Christian history, whether or not these writings are preserved fully or in fragments. These non-canonical works are witnesses to early Christian history no less valuable than the New Testament. A historical presentation of these materials requires that clear decisions be made about authorship, date, and place of each writing; in other words, the results of historical-critical inquiry have to be consulted fully in each instance. I have also made an effort to discuss the problems in making such decisions. If these issues remain controversial with respect to some parts of the New Testament, they are even more difficult for non-canonical literature: traditionally scholarly debate has focused on the canonical literature, whereas the so-called apocrypha and other non-canonical writings have received only scant attention. Furthermore, quite a few of the latter have been discovered only recently, and their critical evaluation has just begun. Nevertheless, it is much better to advance scholarship, and thus our understanding, through hypothetical reconstruction than to ignore new and apparently problematic materials.

In view of the present situation of New Testament scholarship, it would be misleading to suggest to the students of early Christian history that they can expect largely secure results. The New Testament itself furnishes evidence that the history of early Christian communities was a complex process, full of controversies and difficult decisions. Understanding this process requires critical judgment as well as the construction of trajectories through the history of early Christianity. The recent discovery of even more early writings not only demands a basic reorientation of our views, but will also enable the student to appreciate more fully the depths and riches of this formative period, especially as it is seen in the context of the general history of the culture in which Christianity began.

The scope of this book does not permit me to base my entire presentation upon the results of my own research. There are many topics in my survey of the Hellenistic and Roman world on which the specialist will have better insights and judgment. I am not only indebted to the published works of many scholars, but also owe much to my students at Harvard University, who have enriched this book in its various stages of writing and rewriting with their suggestions and criticisms, and equally to my colleagues, from whom I have learned a great deal during the last two decades in seminars and in discussions. I wish to express my special thanks to colleagues and friends: to Klaus Baltzer, of the University of Munich, and to Frank M. Cross, Dieter Georgi, George MacRae, Krister Stendahl, John Strugnell, and Zeph Stewart, all of Harvard University.

This book is the author's own translation of the German *Einführung in das Neue Testament,* published in 1980 by Walter de Gruyter, Berlin and New York. Only in a few instances has the text been changed; one chapter was added (§6.3d). However, a number of minor errors and a few major mistakes were corrected. For this, I am particularly indebted to Eckhard Plümacher's review of the book (*Göttingische Gelehrte Anzeigen 233* [1981] 1–22) and to the extensive notes which he kindly made available to me.

The bibliography has been redesigned so that editions and translations or texts are quoted first in order to encourage the student to read further in primary materials. English translations of texts are cited in the bibliographies wherever available. I am grateful to my colleague Albert Heinrichs of Harvard University for suggestions regarding the revision of the bibliography. The bibliography is not meant to be exhaustive, but is designed to emphasize what is, in my opinion, the most valuable and more recent material, and what will be best lead to further study. I have, however, included the most important "classics" which are still basic guides for scholarship today. For further reference, the reader should consult the standard reference works: *The Interpreter's Dictionary of the Bible* (especially its recently published supplement), *Reallexikon für Antike und Christentum, Der Kleine Pauly, Die Religion in Geschichte und Gegenwart,* and *The Oxford Classical Dictionary* (specific references to these works are normally not given in the bibliographies.

The English edition (as already the German work) would scarcely have been finished in such a brief time without the patience and interest of my wife and my children. Numerous persons have given their help in the various stages of translation and production of this work: Philip H. Sellew (editing, bibliography), Jonathan C. Guest (editing, copyediting, and proofreading), Gary A. Bisbee (maps), Pamela Chance (typing), Robert Stoops and Douglas Olson (bibliography). I am very grateful for their expert and untiring help. Rarely does an author enjoy such experienced and congenial production assistance as I had from my friends Charlene Matejovsky and Robert W. Funk of Polebridge Press at Missoula, Montana. Their dedication, care, competence, and advice accompanied every step of the book's production.

Inter Nationes, an agency of the government of the Federal Republic of Germany in Bonn, made a major grant to offset the cost of assistance for this translation. Thanks are due for this generous help.

This book is dedicated to the memory of my teacher Rudolf Bultmann. He encouraged me more than thirty years ago to deal more intensively with the extra-canonical writings from the early Christian period. His unwavering insistence upon the consistent application of the historical-critical method and his emphasis upon the investigation of the early Christian literature in the context of the history of religions must remain basic commitments of New Testament scholarship.

Helmut Koester

Harvard University
Cambridge, Massachusetts
May 1982

Acknowledgments

Grateful acknowledgment is made for the permission to use a number of photographs in this volume: to the Freer Gallery of the Smithsonian Institution, Washington, D.C., for the photograph of a page from Codex Washingtonianus (p. 29); to the Houghton Library and the Semitic Museum of Harvard University for the photograph of Oxyrhynchus Papyrus 655 (p. 155); and to the Institute for Antiquity and Christianity of the Claremont Graduate School for photographs of a page from Codex II of the Nag Hammadi Library and of the site of the discovery of the Library (pp. 215 and 233).

Additionally, the author wishes to present his thanks for permission granted him to take photographs used in this volume at the following institutions: the Byzantine Archeological Administration, Thessaloniki, Greece (p. 92); the Staatliche Museum Charlottenburg, Berlin (pp. 249 and 292), and the Pergamon Museum Berlin, German Federal Republic (pp. 121 and 341); the National Museum, Numismatic Collection, Athens, Greece (p. 81); the Museum of Ancient Ephesus, Selçuk, Turkey (p. 254); and the Corinth Excavations of the American School of Classical Studies, Athens, Greece (p. 129).

A final word of thanks is due to the research team for Religion and Culture of the Lands of the New Testament (Harvard Divinity School), which supplied the remaining photographs in this volume, as well as to Dr. Gary Bisbee, who drew the various maps.

Abbreviations: Serial and Journal Titles

AARAS	American Academy of Religion Academy Series
AAWG.PH	Abhandlungen der Akademie der Wissenschaften zu Göttingen. Philologisch-historische Klasse
AB	Anchor Bible
Abh.RWA	Abhandlungen der rheinisch-westfälischen Akademie
ADAI.K	Abhandlungen des deutschen archäologischen Instituts Kairo, Koptische Reihe
AGSU	Arbeiten zur Geschichte des Spätjudentums und Urchristentums
AHR	*American Historical Review*
AJP	*American Journal of Philology*
AKG	Arbeiten zur Kirchengeschichte
ALGHL	Arbeiten zur Literatur und Geschichte des hellenistischen Judentums
AnBib	Analecta Biblica
ANRW	*Aufstieg und Niedergang der römischen Welt*
ANT	Arbeiten zur neutestamentlichen Textforschung
APOT	*Apocrypha and Pseudepigrapha of the Old Testament* (ed. R. H. Charles)
APP	Ancient Peoples and Places
ASNU	Acta seminarii neotestamentici upsaliensis
ASP	American Studies in Papyrologyy
AThANT	Abhandlungen zur Theologie des Alten und Neuen Testaments
ATLABS	American Theological Library Association Bibliography Series
AVTRW	Aufsätze und Vorträge zur Theologie und Religionswissenschaft
BAC	Biblioteca de autores cristianos
BAR	Biblical Archaeology Review
BBB	Bonner Biblische Beiträge
BBR.NTS	Bibliographies for Biblical Research. New Testament Series
BCNH.ST	Bibliothèque Copte de Nag Hammadi. "Section Textes"
BETL	Bibliotheca Ephemeridum Theologicarum Lovanensium
BevTh	Beiträge zur evangelischen Theologie
BFChTh	Beiträge zur Förderung christlicher Theologie
BHTh	Beiträge zur historischen Theologie
BibOr	Biblia et orientalia
BJudSt	Brown Judaic Studies
BJRL	Bulletin of the John Rylands Library
BKP	Beiträge zur klassischen Philologie
BT.B	Bibliothèque de théologie, 3. Ser.: Théologie biblique
BWANT	Beiträge zur Wissenschaft des Alten und Neuen Testaments
BWAT	Beiträge zur Wissenschaft vom Alten Testament
BZNW	Beihefte zur Zeitschrift für die neutestamentliche Wissenschaft und die Kunde der alten Kirche
CB.NT	Coniectanea Biblica. New Testament Series
CBQ	*Catholic Biblical Quarterly*
CBQ.MS	Catholic Biblical Quarterly. Monograph Series
CChr.SA	Corpus Christianorum. Series Apocryphorum

CGTC	Cambridge Greek Testament Commentary
CNT	Commentaire du Nouveau Testament
ConB	Coniectanea biblica
CP	Classical Philology
CRBS	*Current Research: Biblical Studies*
CRINT	Compendia Rerum Iudaicarum ad Novum Testamentum
EdF	Erträge der Forschung
EHS.T	Europäische Hochschulschriften. Reihe 23: Theologie
EKKNT	Evangelisch-Katholischer Kommentar zum Neuen Testament
EPhM	Etudes de philosophie médiévale
EPRO	Etudes préliminaires aux religions orientales dans l'empire romain
ErJb	Eranos-Jahrbuch
ET	English translation
EtBib	Etudes bibliques
EtJ	Etudes Juives
EvTh	*Evangelische Theologie*
FC	Fontes Christiani
F&F	Foundations & Facets
FKDG	Forschungen zur Kirchen- und Dogmengeschichte
FRLANT	Forschungen zur Religion und Literatur des Alten und Neuen Testaments
GBSNTS	Guides to Biblical Scholarship, New Testament Series
GCS	Die griechischen christlichen Schriftsteller der ersten drei Jahrhunderte
GLB	De Gruyter Lehrbuch
GRBS	*Greek, Roman, and Byzantine Studies*
GTB	Van Gorcum's theologische bibliotheek
GWU	*Geschichte in Wissenschaft und Unterricht*
HAW	Handbuch der Altertumswissenschaft
HCS	Hellenistic Culture and Society
HDR	Harvard Dissertations in Religion
Hesperia.S	Hesperia Supplements
HeyJ	*Heythrop Journal*
HHS	Harvard Historical Studies
Hist	*Historia, Zeitschrift für alte Geschichte*
HNT	Handbuch zum Neuen Testament
HNT.E	Handbuch zum Neuen Testament. Ergänzungsband
HSCP	*Harvard Studies in Classical Philology*
HSM	Harvard Semitic Monographs
HSS	Harvard Semitic Series
HThK	Herders theologischer Kommentar zum Neuen Testament
HTR	*Harvard Theological Review*
HTS	Harvard Theological Studies
HUCA	*Hebrew Union College Annual*
Hyp.	Hypomnemata. Untersuchungen zur Antike und zu ihrem Nachleben
ICC	International Critical Commentary
IDBSup	*Interpreter's Dictionary to the Bible. Supplement*
Int	*Interpretation*
JAC	*Jahrbuch für Antike und Christentum*
JAC.E	Jahrbuch für Antike und Christentum. Ergänzungsband
JAL	Jewish Apocryphal Literature
JBL	*Journal of Biblical Literature*

JEA	*Journal of Egyptian Archaeology*
JHS	*Journal of Hellenic Studies*
JJS	*Journal of Jewish Studies*
JQR.MS	Jewish Quarterly Review Monograph Series
JR	*Journal of Religion*
JRomS	*Journal of Roman Studies*
JSHRZ	Jüdische Schriften aus hellenistisch-römischer Zeit
JSNT	*Journal for the Study of the New Testament*
JSNTSup	Journal for the Study of the New Testament Supplement Series
JSOT Press	Journal for the Study of the Old Testament Press
JSPSup	Journal for the Study of the Pseudepigrapha Supplement Series
JSS	*Journal of Semitic Studies*
JTC	*Journal for Theology and the Church*
JTS	*Journal of Theological Studies*
KAV	Kommentar zu den Apostolischen Vätern
KEK	Kritisch-exegetischer Kommentar über das Neue Testament
KIT	Kleine Texte für (theologische und philologische) Vorlesungen und Übungen
LBS	Library of Biblical Studies
LCL	Loeb Classical Library
LEC	Library of Early Christianity
LHR	Lectures on the History of Religions, Sponsored by the American Council of Learned Societies
MAPS	Memoirs of the American Philosophical Society
MBPF	Münchener Beiträge zur Papyrusforschung und antiken Rechtsgeschichte
MH	*Museum Helveticum*
MHGRW	Methuen History of the Greek and Roman World
Mn.Suppl.	Mnemosyne. Bibliotheca classica/philologica Batava. Supplements
MThSt	Marburger theologische Studien
MThZ	*Münchener theologische Zeitschrift*
NAWG.PH	Nachrichten der Akademie der Wissenschaft in Göttingen. Philologisch-historische Klasse
NF	Neue Folge
NH	Nag Hammadi
NHC	Nag Hammadi Codex
NHMS	Nag Hammadi and Manichaean Studies
NHS	Nag Hammadi Studies
NovT	*Novum Testamentum*
NovTSup	Novum Testamentum. Supplements
NS	New series; neue Serie
NTA	Neutestamentliche Abhandlungen
NTDSup	Das Neue Testament Deutsch. Supplementband
NTOA	Novum Testamentum et Orbis Antiquus
NTS	*New Testament Studies*
NTTS	New Testament Tools and Studies
NumenSup	Numen. International Review for the History of Religions. Supplements
ÖAW	Österreichische Akademie der Wissenschaften
OBO	Orbus Biblicus Orientalis
OCT	Oxford Classical Texts
OLZ	*Orientalische Literaturzeitung*
OTS	*Oudtestamentische Studien*

PBA	*Proceedings of the British Academy*
Ph.S	Philologus. Supplement
PMAAR	Papers and Monographs of the American Academy in Rome
PTS	Patristische Texte und Studien
PVTG	Pseudepigrapha Veteris Testamentis graece
RAC	*Reallexikon für Antike und Christentum*
RB	*Revue Biblique*
RechBib	Recherches bibliques
RechSR	*Recherches de science religieuse*
RGG	*Die Religion in Geschichte und Gegenwart*
RPS	Religious Perspectives (series)
RSR	*Revue des sciences religieuses*
RVV	Religionsgeschichtliche Versuche und Vorarbeiten
SAC	Studies in Antiquity and Christianity
SBAW.PPH	Sitzungsberichte der bayerischen Akademie der Wissenschaften. Philosophisch-philologische und historische Klasse
SBLDS	Society of Biblical Literature Dissertation Series
SBLEJL	Society of Biblical Literature Early Judaism and Its Literature
SBLMS	Society of Biblical Literature Monograph Series
SBLSBS	Society of Biblical Literature Sources for Biblical Studies
SBLSCS	Society of Biblical Literature Septuagint and Cognate Studies
SBLSP	*Society of Biblical Literature Seminar Papers*
SBLTT	Society of Biblical Literature Texts and Translations
SBS	Stuttgarter Bibelstudien
SBT	Studies in Biblical Theology
SC	Sources chrétiennes
SCHNT	Studia ad corpus hellenisticum Novi Testamenti
SD	Studies and Documents
SEÅ	*Svensk Exegetisc Årsbok*
SG	Sammlung Göschen
SHCT	Studies in the History of Christian Thought
SJ	Studia Judaica
SJLA	Studies in Judaism of Late Antiquity
SNTA	Studiorum Novi Testamenti Auxilia
SNTI	Studies in New Testament Interpretation
SNTSMS	Society of New Testament Studies Monograph Series
SÖAW.PH	Sitzungsberichte der Österreichischen Akademie der Wissenschaften. Philologisch-historische Klasse
SQAW	Schriften und Quellen der alten Welt
SQS	Sammlung ausgewählter kirchen- und dogmengeschichtlicher Quellenschriften
SSRH	Sociological Studies in Roman History
StANT	Studien zum Alten und Neuen Testament
StHell	Studia Hellenistica
STL	Studia Theologica Lundensia
StPB	Studia Post-Biblica
StNT	Studien zum Neuen Testament
STRT	Studia theologica Rheno-Traiectina
SUNT	Studien zur Umwelt des Neuen Testamentes
SUNY	State University of New York

SVTP	Studia in veteris testamenti pseudepigrapha
TANTZ	Texte und Arbeiten zum neutestamentlichen Zeitalter
TEH	Theologische Existenz heute
TF	Texte zur Forschung
ThBü	Theologische Bücherei
ThHK	Theologischer Handkommentar zum Neuen Testament
ThLZ	*Theologische Literaturzeitung*
ThR	*Theologische Rundschau*
ThZ	*Theologische Zeitschrift*
TSJTSA	Texts and Studies of the Jewish Theological Seminary of America
TStAJ	Texte und Studien zum Antiken Judentum
TU	Texte und Untersuchungen zur Geschichte der altchristlichen Literatur
UB	Urban-Bücher
VigChr	*Vigilia Christiana*
VigChrSup	Vigilia Christiana Supplement Series
VT	*Vetus Testamentum*
VTSup	Vetus Testamentum. Supplement
WBC	Word Biblical Commentary
WdF	Wege der Forschung
WMANT	Wissenschaftliche Monographien zum Alten und Neuen Testament
WUNT	Wissenschaftliche Untersuchungen zum Neuen Testament
WZ(J)	*Wissenschaftliche Zeitschrift der Friedrich-Schiller-Universität Jena*
YCS	Yale Classical Studies
YPR	Yale Publications in Religion
Zet.	Zetemata
ZKG	*Zeitschrift für Kirchengeschichte*
ZNW	*Zeitschrift für die neutestamentliche Wissenschaft und die Kunde der alten Kirche*
ZThK	*Zeitschrift für Theologie und Kirche*

Short Titles of Works Often Cited

Apophoreta
  W. Eltester and F. H. Kettler (eds.), *Apophoreta: Festschrift für Ernst Haenchen* (BZNW 30; Berlin: Töpelmann, 1964).
Armstrong, *Mediterranean Spirituality*
  A. H. Armstrong, *Classical Mediterranean Spirituality: Egyptian, Greek, and Roman* (World Spirituality 15; New York: Crossroad, 1986).
Barrett, *Background*
  C. K. Barrett (ed.), *The New Testament Background: Selected Documents* (London: SPCK, 1956; reprint: New York: Harper, 1961).
Bauer, *Orthodoxy and Heresy*
  Walter Bauer, *Orthodoxy and Heresy in Earliest Christianity* (Philadelphia: Fortress, 1971).
Betz, *Galatians*
  Hans Dieter Betz, *Galatians: A Commentary on Paul's Letter to the Churches in Galatia* (Hermeneia; Philadelphia: Fortress, 1979).
Bihlmeyer, *ApostVät*
  Karl Bihlmeyer, *Die apostolischen Väter: Neubearbeitung der Funkschen Ausgabe* (SQS; 2, 1, 1; 3d ed.; Tübingen: Mohr/Siebeck, 1970).
Black and Rowley, *Peake's Commentary*
  Matthew Black and H. H. Rowley (eds.), *Peake's Commentary on the Bible* (London: Nelson, 1962).
Bornkamm, *Experience*
  Günther Bornkamm, *Early Christian Experience* (London: SCM, New York: Harper, 1969).
Braun, *Studien*
  Herbert Braun, *Studien zum Neuen Testament und seiner Umwelt* (3d ed.; Tübingen: Mohr/Siebeck, 1971).
Bultmann, *Exegetica*
  Rudolf Bultmann, *Exegetica, Aufsätze zur Erforschung des Neuen Testaments* (ed. Erich Dinkler; Tübingen: Mohr/Siebeck, 1967).
Bultmann, *Existence and Faith*
  Rudolf Bultmann, *Existence and Faith* (ed. Schubert M. Ogden; New York: Meridian, 1960).
Bultmann, *Theology*
  Rudolf Bultmann, *Theology of the New Testament* (2 vols.; New York: Scribner's, 1951).
Burkert, *Homo Necans*
  Walter Burkert, *Homo Necans: The Anthropology of Ancient Greek Sacrificial Ritual and Myth* (Berkeley, CA: University of California Press, 1983).
Burkert, *Greek Religion*
  Walter Burkert, *Greek Religion* (Cambridge, MA: Harvard University Press, 1985)
Burkert, *Mystery Cults*
  Walter Burkert, *Ancient Mystery Cults* (Cambridge, MA: Harvard University Press, 1987).
Calder and Keil, *Anatolian Studies*
  W. M. Calder and Josef Keil (eds.), *Anatolian Studies Presented to William Hepburn Buckler* (Manchester: Manchester University Press, 1939).
CambAncHist 7–10
  S. A. Cook, F. E. Adcock, and M. P. Charlesworth, *The Cambridge Ancient History,* vol. 7: *The Hellenistic Monarchies and the Rise of Rome;* vol. 8: *Rome and the Mediterranean 218–133 B.C.;* vol. 9: *The Roman Republic 133–44 B.C.;* vol. 10: *The Augustan Empire 44 B.C.–A.D. 70* (New York: Macmillan, 1928–1934).
Cambridge History of the Bible 1
  P. R. Ackroyd and C. F. Evans (eds.), *Cambridge History of the Bible,* vol. 1: *From the Beginnings to Rome* (Cambridge: Cambridge University Press, 1970).

Cameron, *Other Gospels*
   Ron Cameron (ed.), *The Other Gospels: Non-Canonical Gospel Texts* (Philadelphia: Westminster, 1982).
von Campenhausen, *Tradition*
   Hans von Campenhausen, *Tradition and Life in the Church: Essays and Lectures in Church History* (Philadelphia: Fortress, 1968).
von Campenhausen, *Frühzeit*
   Hans von Campenhausen, *Aus der Frühzeit des Christentums* (Tübingen: Mohr/Siebeck, 1963).
Cartlidge and Dungan, *Documents*
   David R. Cartlidge and David L. Dungan (eds.), *Documents for the Study of the Gospels* (Philadelphia: Fortress, 1980).
Charles, *APOT*
   R. H. Charles (ed.), *Apocrypha and Pseudepigrapha of the Old Testament* (Oxford: Clarendon, 1913).
Charlesworth, *OTPseudepigrapha*
   James H. Charlesworth, *The Old Testament Pseudepigrapha* (2 vols.; Garden City, NY: Doubleday, 1983–1986).
Conzelmann, *Outline*
   Hans Conzelmann, *An Outline of the Theology of the New Testament* (New York: Harper, 1969).
Cullmann, *Vorträge 1925–1962*
   Oscar Cullmann, *Vorträge und Aufsätze 1925–1962* (Tübingen: Mohr/Siebeck; Zürich: Zwingli, 1966).
Dibelius, *Studies in Acts*
   Martin Dibelius, *Studies in the Acts of the Apostles* (London: SCM, 1956, and reprints).
Dibelius, *Botschaft und Geschichte*
   Martin Dibelius, *Botschaft und Geschichte* (2 vols.; Tübingen: Mohr/Siebeck, 1956).
Dihle, *Literatur der Kaiserzeit*
   Albrecht Dihle, *Die griechische und lateinische Literatur der Kaiserzeit: von Augustus bis Justinian* (München: Beck, 1989).
Easterling and Knox, *Greek Literature*
   Patricia E. Easterling and Bernard M. W. Knox (eds.), *The Cambridge History of Classical Literature*, vol. 1: *Greek Literature* (Cambridge: Cambridge University Press, 1985).
Elliott, *Apocryphal NT*
   J. K. Elliott, *The Apocryphal New Testament* (Oxford: Clarendon, 1993).
Finley, *Legacy*
   M. I. Finley (ed.), *The Legacy of Greece: A New Appraisal* (Oxford: Clarendon, 1981).
Fischer, *Die apostolischen Väter*
   Joseph A. Fischer, *Die apostolischen Väter* (Schriften des Urchristentums 1; Darmstadt: Wissenschaftliche Buchgesellschaft, 1956).
Foakes Jackson and Lake, *Beginnings*
   F. J. Foakes Jackson and Kirsopp Lake (eds.), *The Beginnings of Christianity* (5 vols.; London: Macmillan, 1920–1933, and reprints).
Foerster, *Gnosis*
   Werner Foerster, *Gnosis: A Selection of Gnostic Texts* (Engl. trans. and ed. R. McL. Wilson; 2 vols.; Oxford: Clarendon, 1972–1974).
Fraser, *Alexandria*
   P. M. Fraser, *Ptolemaic Alexandria* (3 vols.; Oxford: Clarendon, 1972; reprint 1984).
Goehring, *Gnosticism*
   James E. Goehring et al. (eds.), *Gnosticism and the Early Christian World: In Honor of James M. Robinson* (Sonoma, CA: Polebridge, 1990).
Grant, *Hellenistic Religions*
   Frederick C. Grant (ed.), *Hellenistic Religions: The Age of Syncretism* (The Library of Religion 2; New York: Liberal Arts, 1953).
Grant and Kitzinger, *Civilization*
   Michael Grant and Rachel Kitzinger (eds.), *Civilization of the Ancient Mediterranean: Greece and Rome* (3 vols.; New York: Scribner's, 1988).

Grant, *ApostFath*
Robert M. Grant, *The Apostolic Fathers: A New Translation and Commentary* (6 vols.; New York: Nelson, 1964–1968).
Haenchen, *Acts*
Ernst Haenchen, *The Acts of the Apostles: A Commentary* (Philadelphia: Westminster, 1971).
Haenchen, *Gott und Mensch*
Ernst Haenchen, *Gott und Mensch: Gesammelte Aufsätze* (Tübingen: Mohr/Siebeck, 1965).
Hedrick and Hodgson, *Nag Hammadi*
Charles W. Hedrick and Robert Hodgson, Jr. (eds.), *Nag Hammadi, Gnosticism, & Early Christianity* (Peabody, MA: Hendrickson, 1986).
Horsley, *New Documents*
G. H. R. Horsley, *New Documents Illustrating Early Christianity* (6 vols.; The Ancient History Document Centre; Sidney, Australia: Macquarie University, 1981–1991).
Käsemann, *Exegetische Versuche*
Ernst Käsemann, *Exegetische Versuche und Besinnungen* (2 vols.; Göttingen: Vandenhoeck & Ruprecht, 1960).
Käsemann, *New Testament Questions*
Ernst Käsemann, *New Testament Questions of Today* (Philadelphia: Fortress, 1969).
Kee, *Origins*
Howard Clark Kee, *The Origins of Christianity: Sources and Documents* (Englewood Cliffs, NJ: Prentice Hall, 1973).
Kenney, *Latin Literature*
E. J. Kenney (ed.), *The Cambridge History of Classical Latin Literature*, vol. 2: *Latin Literature* (Cambridge: Cambridge University Press, 1982).
Kirche: Festschrift Bornkamm
Dieter Lührmann und Georg Strecker (eds.), *Kirche: Festschrift für Günther Bornkamm zum 75. Geburtstag* (Tübingen: Mohr/Siebeck, 1980).
Koester, *Ancient Christian Gospels*
Helmut Koester, *Ancient Christian Gospels: Their History and Development* (Philadelphia: Trinity Press International, 1990).
Kraemer, *Maenads, Martyrs*
Ross 0. Kraemer, *Maenads, Martyrs, Matrons, Monastics: A Sourcebook on Women's Religions in the Greco-Roman World* (Philadelphia: Fortress, 1988).
Kuhrt and Sherwin-White, *Hellenism in the East*
Amélie Kuhrt and Susan Sherwin-White, *Hellenism in the East: The Interaction of Greek and Non-Greek Civilizations from Syria to Central Asia after Alexander* (London: Duckworth, 1987).
Lake, *ApostFath*
Kirsopp Lake, *The Apostolic Fathers* (LCL; 2 vols.; Cambridge, MA: Harvard University Press, 1912, and reprints).
Layton, *Nag Hammadi Codex II*
Bentley Layton (ed.), *Nag Hammadi Codex II, 2–7, Together with XIII, 2*, Brit. Lib. Or. 4926(1) and P. Oxy. 1, 654, 655* (NHS 20–21; Leiden: Brill, 1987).
Layton, *Rediscovery of Gnosticism*
Bentley Layton (ed.), *The Rediscovery of Gnosticism* (Proceedings of the International Conference at Yale, New Haven, 1978; NumenSup 16; 2 vols.; Leiden: Brill, 1981–1982).
Layton, *Gnostic Scriptures*
Bentley Layton, *The Gnostic Scriptures: A New Translation with Annotations and Introductions* (Garden City, NY: Doubleday, 1987).
Lightfoot, *Apostolic Fathers*
J. B. Lightfoot, *Apostolic Fathers: A Revised Text with Introduction, Notes, Dissertations, and Translations* (2 parts in 5 vols.; London: Macmillan, 1885–1890).
Lipsius-Bonnet, *ActApostApoc*
Richard Albert Lipsius and Maximilian Bonnet, *Acta Apostolorum Apocrypha* (2 vols; Leipzig: Mendelsohn, 1891–1903; reprint: Darmstadt: Wissenschaftliche Buchgesellschaft, 1959).

Meeks and Wilken, *Jews and Christians in Antioch*
  Wayne A. Meeks and L. Robert Wilken, *Jews and Christians in Antioch in the First Four Centuries of the Common Era* (SBLSBS 13; Chico, CA: Scholars Press, 1978).
Meyer and Sanders, *Self-Definition 3*
  Ben F. Meyer and E. P. Sanders (eds.), *Jewish and Christian Self-Definition,* vol. 3: *Self-Definition in the Greco-Roman World* (London: SCM, 1982).
Meyer, *Mystery Sourcebook*
  Marvin W. Meyer (ed.), *The Ancient Mysteries: A Sourcebook: Sacred Texts of the Mystery Religions of the Ancient Mediterranean World* (San Francisco: Harper & Row, 1987).
Miller, *Complete Gospels*
  Robert J. Miller (ed.), *The Complete Gospels: Annotated Scholars Version* (rev. ed.; Sonoma, CA: Polebridge Press, 1994).
Momigliano, *Pagans, Jews, and Christians*
  Arnoldo Momigliano, *On Pagans, Jews, and Christians* (Middletown, CT: Wesleyan University Press, 1987).
NagHamLibEngl
  James M. Robinson (ed.), *The Nag Hammadi Library in English* (3d ed.; San Francisco: HarperCollins, 1990).
Neusner, *Religions in Antiquity*
  Jacob Neusner (ed.), *Religions in Antiquity: Essays in Memory of Erwin Ramsdell Goodenough* (NumenSup 14; Leiden: Brill, 1968).
Nilsson, *Griechische Religion,* 2
  Martin P. Nilsson, *Geschichte der griechischen Religion,* vol. 2: *Die hellenistische Zeit* (HAW 5.2/2; 3d ed.; München: Beck, 1974).
Nock, *Essays*
  Arthur Darby Nock, *Essays on Religion and the Ancient World* (ed. Zeph Stewart; 2 vols.; Cambridge, MA: Harvard University Press, 1972).
Rice and Stambaugh, *Sources for Greek Religion*
  D. G. Rice and J. E. Stambaugh, *Sources for the Study of Greek Religion* (SBLSBS 14; Missoula, MT: Scholars Press, 1979).
Robinson and Koester, *Trajectories*
  James M. Robinson and Helmut Koester, *Trajectories through Early Christianity* (Philadelphia: Fortress, 1971).
Sanders, *Self-Definition 1*
  E. P. Sanders (ed.), *Jewish and Christian Self-Definition,* vol. 1: *The Shaping of Christianity in the Second and Third Centuries* (Philadelphia: Fortress, 1980).
Schmithals, *Paul and the Gnostics*
  Walter Schmithals, *Paul and the Gnostics* (Nashville: Abingdon, 1972).
Schmitt Pantel, *History of Women*
  Pauline Schmitt Pantel (ed.), *From Ancient Goddesses to Christian Saints* (A History of Women in the West 1; Cambridge, MA: Harvard University Press, 1992).
Schneemelcher, *NT Apoc.*
  Wilhelm Schneemelcher (ed.), *New Testament Apocrypha* (Revised edition of the collection initiated by Edgar Hennecke; 2 vols.; Cambridge: Clark, and Louisville, KY: Westminster/John Knox, 1991–1992).
Shelton, *As the Romans Did*
  Jo-Ann Shelton, *As the Romans Did: A Sourcebook in Roman Social History* (New York: Oxford University Press, 1988).
Smith, *Clement*
  Morton Smith, *Clement of Alexandria and a Secret Gospel of Mark* (Cambridge, MA: Harvard University Press, 1973).
Stone, *Jewish Writings*
  Michael Stone (ed.), *Jewish Writings of the Second Temple Period* (CRINT 2.2; Philadelphia: Fortress, 1984).

The Four Gospels 1992
F. Van Segbroeck, C. M. Yuckett, G. Van Belle, and J. Verheyden (eds.), *The Four Gospels: Festschrift Frans Neirynck* (3 vols.; BETL 100; Leuven: Peeters and Leuven University Press, 1992).

Völker, *Quellen*
Walther Völker, *Quellen zur Geschichte der christlichen Gnosis* (SQS 5; Tübingen: Mohr/Siebeck, 1932).

Veyne, *Private Life*
Philippè Ariès and Georges Duby (eds.), *A History of Private Life,* vol. 1, ed. Paul Veyne, *From Pagan Rome to Byzantium* (Cambridge, MA: Harvard University Press, 1987).

Vielhauer, *Geschichte*
Philipp Vielhauer, *Geschichte der urchristlichen Literatur* (GLB; Berlin: de Gruyter, 1975).

Wengst, *Didache, Barnabas, 2. Klemens*
Klaus Wengst (ed.), *Didache (Apostellehre), Barnabasbrief, Zweiter Klemensbrief, Schrift an Diognet* (Schriften des Urchristentums 2; München: Kösel, 1984).

HISTORY AND LITERATURE
OF EARLY CHRISTIANITY

The writings that are now included in the twenty-seven books of the New Testament are the product of the early Christian churches in the countries of the eastern Mediterranean world and, eventually, in Rome. They are, however, not the only Christian writings from the earliest period of Christian history. Numerous other writings from the same period have at least partially survived. They belong to the same historical developments. This book endeavors to introduce the student of the New Testament to all of these writings in the context of a reconstruction of the expansion and growth of the Christian communities from their beginnings to the middle of the second century CE.

The political, religious, cultural, and economic factors that constituted the setting for early Christian history have been discussed extensively in the first volume, including the history of Israel in the Hellenistic and Roman imperial periods. What has been said in that volume is essential for the understanding of the development of early Christianity; cross references in this second volume will point to the importance of understanding the historical environment.

The sources for early Christian history, which are almost exclusively Christian, present significant problems that have been the subject of specialized works of many scholars. Some acquaintance with the scholarly approaches to these ancient writings and with the present status of their learned investigation is prerequisite to the study of this literature in its historical context. The first chapter of this volume (§7) is therefore devoted to the various problems and methods of the investigation of the New Testament and other early Christian writings.

Although Christianity emerged from the ministry of Jesus and from the first communities in Palestine, soon spreading to other parts of Syria and Egypt, its most significant literature, which was to determine the future of this new religious movement, developed in the urban cultures of the eastern Mediterranean, principally in Antioch and the cities of the Aegean Sea. Thus the history of the Christian churches will be treated not only in chronological order, but also with respect to the different regions in which the establishment of the churches in the major centers of the Hellenistic world (Antioch, Ephesus, Corinth, and even Rome) marks the end of the formative period of early Christianity and thus concludes the production of most of the New Testament writings.

THE SOURCES FOR THE HISTORY OF EARLY CHRISTIANITY

1. SURVEY OF THE SOURCES AND THEIR TRADITIONS

(a) The Formation of the Earliest Christian Writings

Early Christian writings, including all the documents incorporated in the New Testament, are highly problematic literary sources for our understanding of the beginnings of Christianity. It is important to recognize why the surviving written materials from that period yield only very tenuous information. During the first two centuries, the only Holy Scripture that Christians accepted was the Bible of Israel, the "Law and the Prophets"; only much later was it called the Old Testament. It was mostly used in its Greek translation, the Septuagint, which had been produced by the Jews of Alexandria (§5.3b). This is what is meant when early Christians spoke generally of "Scripture" or when they used the quotation formula, "It is written."

Side by side with this "Scripture" stood from the beginning an oral tradition, which was transmitted under the authority of the "Lord." This second authority comprised the sayings of Jesus as well as short narratives about him. The words of

Bibliography to §7:   Text

Barbara and Kurt Aland, Johannes Karavidopoulos, Carlo M. Martini, and Bruce M. Metzger (eds.), *Nestle-Aland: Novum Testamentum Graece* (27th ed.; Stuttgart: Deutsche Bibelgesellschaft, 1994).

Wayne A. Meeks (ed.), *The HarperCollins Study Bible: New Revised Standard Version. With the Apocryphal/Deuterocanonical Books* (San Francisco: HarperCollins, 1993).

Bibliography to §7:   Tools

Walter Bauer, *Griechisch-deutsches Wörterbuch zu den Schriften des Neuen Testaments und der frühchristlichen Literatur* (6th ed. by Kurt and Barbara Aland; Berlin: de Gruyter, 1988).

Walter Bauer, *A Greek-English Lexicon of the New Testament and Other Early Christian Literature*, rev. by F. W. Gingrich and F. W. Danker (Chicago: University of Chicago Press, 1979).

Concordance to the Novum Testamentum Graece of Nestle-Aland, 26th Edition, and to the Greek New Testament, 3d Edition (Berlin: de Gruyter, 1987).

Bruce M. Metzger (ed.), *NRSV Exhaustive Concordance* (Nashville, TN: Nelson, 1991).

Paul J. Achtemeier (ed.), *Harper's Bible Dictionary* (rev. ed.; San Francisco: HarperCollins, 1996).

J. D. Allison, *The Bible Study Resource Guide* (Nashville, TN: Nelson, 1984).

Daniel H. Harrington, *The New Testament: A Bibliography* (Theological and Biblical Resources 2; Wilmington, DE: Glazier, 1985).

Joseph A. Fitzmyer, *An Introductory Bibliography to the Study of Scripture* (Subsidia Biblica 3; rev. ed.; Rome: Biblical Institute Press, 1981).

Otto Kaiser and Werner Georg Kümmel, *Exegetical Method: A Student's Handbook* (rev. ed; New York: Seabury, 1981).

the Lord were by no means restricted to the sayings of Jesus of Nazareth, but also contained words of the risen Lord (§7.4a–c). Some traditions under this authority may have been transmitted in written form at an early date—the earliest Christian missionaries and church leaders were by no means uneducated people who could neither read nor write. The culture of the Hellenistic and Roman period was to some extent a literary culture. This is certainly true for the people of Israel, especially for its Greek-speaking synagogue of the Jewish diaspora, which became the matrix for the formation of early Christianity. However, that which was written down still was part of the realm of oral communication in preaching, instruction, and common celebration. Whatever was written was designed to be read aloud and thus to return into the medium of oral communication—"oral literature." Therefore the earliest writings were collections of oral materials that were written down for ecclesiastical use, such as collections of Jesus' words in the form of catechisms and church orders, or series of parables and miracle stories. Some of these were later incorporated into larger writings, for example, the parables that were first written down in Aramaic and then translated into Greek and incorporated in the Gospel of Mark (chap. 4), or the early Eucharistic prayers and church orders used in the composition of the *Didache* (§10.1c).

The oldest written documents that are preserved, however, are not materials

Bibliography to §7: Surveys

Martin Dibelius, *A Fresh Approach to the New Testament and Early Christian Literature* (New York: Scribner's, 1936).
Philipp Vielhauer, *Geschichte der urchristlichen Literatur* (GLB; 2d ed.; Berlin: de Gruyter, 1978).
Werner Georg Kümmel, *Introduction to the New Testament* (Nashville, TN: Abingdon, 1975).

Bibliography to §7.1

Hans von Campenhausen, *The Formation of the Christian Bible* (Philadelphia: Fortress, 1972).
Paul Wendland, *Die urchristlichen Literaturformen* (HNT 1/3; 2d and 3d eds.; Tübingen: Mohr/ Siebeck, 1912).
Helmut Koester, "Apocryphal and Canonical Gospels," *HTR* 73 (1980) 105–30.
Idem, "Literature, Early Christian," *IDBSup* (1976) 551–56.

Bibliography to §7a

Kurt Aland, "The Problem of Anonymity and Pseudonymity in Christian Literature of the First Two Centuries," *JTS* NS 12 (1961) 39–49.
Horst R. Balz, "Anonymität und Pseudepigraphie im Urchristentum," *ZThK* 66 (1969) 403–36.
Norbert Brox, *Falsche Verfasserangaben: Zur Erklärung der frühchristlichen Pseudepigraphie* (Stuttgart: Katholisches Bibelwerk, 1975).
Wolfgang Speyer, *Die literarische Fälschung im heidnischen und christlichen Altertum* (HAW 1/2; München: Beck, 1971).
Pseudepigrapha I (Entretiens sur l'antiquité classique 18; Geneva: Vandoeuvres, 1972).
Adolf Deissmann, *Light from the Ancient East: The New Testament Illustrated by Recently Discovered Texts of the Greco-Roman World* (New York: Doran, 1927).
von Campenhausen, "Das Alte Testament als Bibel der Kirche," in idem, *Frühzeit,* 152–96.
Robert W. Funk, "The Apostolic Parousia: Form and Significance," in W. R. Farmer, C. F. D. Moule, and R. R. Niebuhr (eds.), *Christian History and Interpretation: Studies Presented to John Knox* (Cambridge: Cambridge University Press, 1967) 249–68.
Helmut Koester, "Writings and the Spirit: Authority and Politics in Ancient Christianity," *HTR* 84 (1991) 353–72.
Stanley K. Stowers, *Letter Writing in Greco-Roman Antiquity* (LEC; Philadelphia: Westminster, 1986).

about Jesus but the letters of Paul, all written in the fifties of the 1st century CE. These letters are our earliest and most direct source for the development of early Christian communities. They are neither just occasional writings nor are they composed in order to communicate religious truths. Rather, they are instruments of ecclesiastical policy, which functioned alongside the political and propagandistic medium of oral communication during the absence of the apostle, serving the continuing organization and maintenance of the Christian communities that had been founded by Paul. While these letters are composed according to Jewish and Greco-Roman prototypes, their rhetoric is informed by the demands of the specific Pauline situations and must be understood in the immediate context of the needs and problems of the communities he had founded.

Beginning with the last decades of the 1st century CE, that is, in the third generation of the Christian people, the use of the written medium for the communication and transmission of older traditions became more prominent. This, however, did not imply that the oral transmission had come to an end. As late as about 130 CE, Papias of Hierapolis still valued more highly than the written gospels the oral tradition from the apostles that had been passed down by their successors. On the other hand, the instrument of church policy that Paul had created had a strong impact on the following period, so that the use of the literary instrument of the letter for the purpose of propaganda and church organization became quite popular. Moreover, written forms of the traditions about Jesus, used as foundations of church order and as a device for the propagation of the Christian message, were in many instances better suited than oral materials—not, however, because of any beliefs in the greater reliability of written materials. Christian prophets still spoke words of the Lord with authority, while authors of books sometimes treated their traditional materials and sources with an amazing degree of freedom. The primary reason for the use of the written medium was cultural: writings and books were naturally expected by an educated audience in the culture of that time.

For such production of literature the Christians could make recourse to the letters of Paul as an available model. It was therefore the genre of the Pauline letter that was imitated by students of Paul in the so-called deutero-Pauline epistles: 2 Thessalonians, Colossians, Ephesians, the Pastoral Epistles (1 and 2 Timothy and Titus), *Laodiceans,* and *3 Corinthians.* Not only do all these writings imitate the model of the Pauline letter, but they also claim the authority of the apostle for their writings. Soon others also began to write under their own name or in the name of other apostles, but still employing the model of the original letters of Paul. *1 Clement,* written to Corinth from Rome at the end of the 1st century, is designed to achieve what Paul once had accomplished, namely, to motivate the Corinthians to patch up their internal quarrels. Bishop Ignatius of Antioch, traveling to his martyrdom in Rome at the very beginning of the 2d century, once more used this model in the series of letters that he wrote to communities in Asia Minor. The Pauline letter also influenced the authors of the two New Testament letters that were issued in the name of the apostle Peter and perhaps the three Johannine Epistles. The prophet John, writing the Book of Revelation in his exile on Patmos, included in his book seven letters to churches in Asia Minor, through which he tried to counsel these troubled communities. After the middle of the 2d century, Bishop Dionysios of

Corinth wrote letters to various communities in Asia Minor and on Crete in order to warn them about heretical forms of asceticism.

In all these instances, it is evident that the letter had become the primary political instrument with which leaders of Christian communities tried to shape the policies of Christian congregations and to forge, at least to some degree, a worldwide organization of the church. There is ample evidence that this continued into the 3d century. Most of the correspondence of Clement of Alexandria, bishop Irenaeus of Lyon, and bishop Dionysios of Alexandria has been lost or is preserved only in fragments. The letters of bishop Cyprian of Carthage (middle of the 3d century), however, have come down in a more complete collection. Seen as a whole, the letters from the period of early Christianity—whether they are "genuine" or "pseudepigraphic"—are the most important sources of early Christian history.

The next important corpus of literature includes collections or compilations of various materials that focus on the person of Jesus and began to be called "gospels" by the middle of the 2d century. They are extremely important sources but present considerable obstacles to the historian who wants to utilize them as information about Jesus of Nazareth and about the history of Christianity. It will be demonstrated in more detail later (§7.4a) that the tradition incorporated in these gospels does not commence with historical information but with proclamation, confession, legend, instruction, and prayer. The earliest written documents of this kind—which are not preserved but can be reconstructed through critical analysis of the later gospel writings—were simple written versions of traditions about Jesus in various forms that corresponded to the liturgical, catechetical, and theological interests of respective churches. Eventually these materials were incorporated in more extensive compositions, for which the literary models were drawn from various existing genres of Jewish and Hellenistic literature. Collections of miracle stories of Jesus are closely related to the genre of the aretalogy (§3.4d) and reveal a christology that understands Jesus as the prototype of the miracle healer and exorcist. Collections of Jesus' sayings are influenced by the genre of Jewish wisdom literature and correspond to a christological orientation, for which Jesus is a teacher of wisdom or the earthly appearance of heavenly Wisdom. An extant example of this literary genre is preserved in the *Gospel of Thomas,* which was discovered among the writings of the Nag Hammadi Library. Another sayings collection, the so-called Synoptic Sayings Gospel, can be reconstructed on the basis of the canonical Gospels of Matthew and Luke. The passion narrative was developed in the celebration of the Eucharist on the basis of Israel's prophetic books and Psalms, which speak about the suffering servant of God and the persecuted righteous. There is also an extensive literature, in which Jesus appears as the heavenly revealer; the oldest writing of this genre is the Revelation of John. Under the influence of Jewish apocalyptic literature, a number of Christian apocalypses were produced; the earliest of these is the small book known as the "Synoptic Apocalypse" that the Gospel of Mark incorporated (Mark 13; cf. Matthew 24–25). Somewhat later appeared the *Apocalypse of Peter,* the *Shepherd of Hermas,* and the additions to Jewish apocalyptic books known as *5 Ezra* and *6 Ezra.* The rich Gnostic revelation literature is closely related and is now fully accessible through the discovery and publication of the Nag Hammadi Library (§10.5b).

The Gospels of the New Testament are the product of those Christian communities that became the matrix for the later orthodox churches. They are compositions in which oral traditions and earlier written documents were incorporated into writings that took their point of departure from the kerygma of Jesus' cross and resurrection. While the passion narrative is constitutive for the rise of the gospel literature, the literary model of the biography (§3.4d) increasingly influenced its further development. In addition to the four canonical gospels, several fragments of apocryphal gospels are preserved (the *Gospel of Peter* and the Jewish-Christian Gospels), while a number of apocryphal writings that bear the designation "Gospel" (*Gospel of Truth, Gospel of Philipp*) do not belong here; they are theological meditations or treatises. The use of the gospels for historical information about Jesus is problematic; they are, however, important sources for the study of the early Christian communities, which produced and fashioned the materials and traditions that were used by the authors of the various gospels.

Equally problematic is the historical value of the Acts of the Apostles. Although the attempt to write history may have played a certain role in the canonical Book of Acts, theological interests and, in addition, aretalogical materials and elements of the Hellenistic romance (travel narrative and story of the shipwreck; §3.4c) predominate. The model of the Hellenistic romance is even more evident in the production of the numerous apocryphal acts of the apostles.

Writings that are essentially theological treatises emerged only gradually. Among the letters of Paul, the Epistle to the Romans has sometimes been assigned to this category, but its function as an instrument of church policy remains its primary characteristic, despite a clearly visible influence from Jewish apologetic literature. A real theological treatise appears for the first time several decades after Paul in the Epistle to the Hebrews; with its allegorical interpretation of passages from Scripture, it can be compared to the treatises of Philo of Alexandria (§5.3f). Among the noncanonical writings, the *Epistle of Barnabas* belongs in this category. The further production of theological treatises is closely related to the rise of Christian apologetic literature, which continues the tradition of Jewish apologetic writings (§5.3e) but also shows contacts with the Greek philosophical genre of protreptic literature. The Christian creed is a new element in this literature and provides its basic structure; scriptural proof is given for each individual statement of the creed. The treatment of one particular statement of the creed, for example, about the resurrection, could also be expanded to a treatise about that topic. Some examples for this apologetic and theological literature come from the 2d century, while the 3d-century writers such as Origen and Tertullian employed this literary genre more extensively. The apologists of the 2d century used this apologetic schema also in polemical writings (Justin Martyr's *Dialogue with Trypho the Jew* and Irenaeus' *Adversus haereses*).

Only very few writings document the life of the Christian churches and their worship services. Several writings seem to be publications of sermons. *2 Clement* could be such a writing, perhaps also the *Gospel of Truth* from the Nag Hammadi Library. The *Passover Homily* of bishop Melito of Sardes was composed toward the end of the 2d century. Accounts of martyrdoms that were written as circular letters were also designed to be read in worship services. Several of these accounts come from the 2d century: the *Martyrdom of Polycarp,* the martyrdom of *Justin and His Companions,* the account of the *Martyrs of Lyon and Vienne,* and the *Acts of the Scillitan Martyrs.* Finally, the church orders should be mentioned here. Of these, only the *Teaching of the Twelve Apostles* (*Didache*) can be dated with certainty into the early period of Christianity, while the (Syriac) *Didaskalia,* the *Church Order of Hippolytos,* and the *Apostolic Church Order* were all written after the year 200 CE.

(b) The Canon of the New Testament

(1) *The Lord and the Letters of Paul.* During the first decades after the death of Jesus, the apostles understood themselves as empowered by the spirit of God to proclaim the new message of the salvation of Israel to both Jews and Gentiles. Their proclamation was authorized by the prophecies of Israel and by the appearances of the risen Christ, the Lord. "The Lord" was therefore the primary authority that assured the validity of their preaching and the reliability of the tradition. In controversial questions, one would primarily rely on "what the Lord had said," or one would ask prophets what "the Lord" had revealed to them. Naturally, as Scripture "the Law and the Prophets" also could be referred to as authorities, but also authorization could simply be derived from the possession of the Holy Spirit, "Nature," general morality, or rational judgment as well. Not until the end of the first generation of apostles did one begin to appeal to the authority of specifically named apostles. The first evidence for this is the witness of the Pauline communities, who soon began to collect and distribute the letters of Paul and to produce new letters in the apostle's name, eventually incorporating them into a collection that became the Pauline corpus. It has been conjectured that the Epistle to the Ephesians was connected with the first collection of these letters and was written as a covering letter for this collection. However that may be, we possess clear evidence that the authority of a particular apostle, namely Paul, established a special authority for the writings that originated from the former realm of this apostle's activity.

(2) *Peter, Thomas, and John.* Unfortunately, sources are missing that could provide direct insights, similar to the case of Paul, into the ministry and sphere of activity of any of the other apostles. It is striking, however, that in several limited geographical areas surviving traditions and writings are preserved under the name of a specific apostle, whose authority they claim. A number of writings preserved

Bibliography to §7.1b

Lee M. McDonald, *The Formation of the Christian Biblical Canon* (rev. ed.; Peabody, MA: Hendrickson, 1995).

Wilhelm Schneemelcher, "On the History of the New Testament Canon," in idem, *NT Apoc* 1. 15–50.

Robert M. Grant, *The Formation of the New Testament* (New York: Harper, 1965).

Idem, "Literary Criticism and the New Testament Canon," *JSNT* 16 (1982) 24–44.

Ernst Käsemann (ed.), *Das Neue Testament als Kanon* (Göttingen: Vandenhoeck & Ruprecht, 1970).

Albert C. Sundberg, "Canon Muratori," *HTR* 66 (1973) 1–41.

Idem, "The Bible Canon and the Christian Doctrine of Inspiration," *Int* 29 (1975) 352–71.

Harry Y. Gamble, *The New Testament Canon: Its Making and Meaning* (GBSNTS; Philadelphia: Fortress, 1985).

G. M. Hahneman, *The Muratorian Fragment and the Development of the Canon* (Oxford Theological Monographs; Oxford: Clarendon, 1992).

from western Syria allege to have been written by Peter: the *Gospel of Peter,* the *Apocalypse of Peter,* and the *Kerygma of Peter* (and if not identical with this writing, the *Doctrina Petri*), as well as a source of the *Pseudo-Clementines,* which is known as the *Kerygmata Petrou.* After all, we do know that Peter stayed in the city of Antioch in Syria; this is confirmed by Paul's letter to the Galatians (Gal 2:11–14). It is therefore quite likely that the later writings under the authority of Peter derive from a Petrine tradition that arose from the actual missionary activity of the apostle in this geographical area. This is confirmed by the Gospel of Matthew, certainly a writing from western Syria, which contains the famous words of Jesus to Peter designating him as the rock on which Jesus will build his church (Matt 16:17–19).

The tradition of Thomas from eastern Syria resulted from a similar pattern, although it is impossible to prove that the legend of Thomas's missionary journey to the east, including even India, rests on historical foundation. All that is certain is the eastern Syrian provenance of the *Acts of Thomas,* which was written at the beginning of the 3d century. Most likely, two other writings belong here that appear under the authority of Thomas in the Nag Hammadi Library: the *Gospel of Thomas* and the *Book of Thomas.* The former was composed no later than the beginning of the 2d century, while the latter cannot be dated with any certainty. If all three writings come from eastern Syria (Edessa) they might rest on a tradition under the name of Thomas that had its origin in the actual mission of this apostle in this realm.

The relationship of the Johannine literature to the apostle John remains an enigma. It is evident that John was one of the three apostles of the Jerusalem church, who, together with Peter and Jesus' brother James were known as the "pillars," when Paul visited Jerusalem less than twenty years after the death of Jesus (Gal 2:9). At Paul's final visit to Jerusalem a few years later, however, James was the sole leader of the church; John is no longer mentioned (Acts 21:18). Jesus' answer to the question of John and James, the sons of Zebedee, in Mark 10:39 implies that both would suffer death as martyrs; yet only the death of James is reported in the tradition (Acts 12:2). Bishop Papias of Hierapolis (first half of the 2d century) knew of an oral tradition of Jesus' sayings connected with John, whom he calls the disciple of the Lord. Much later, at the end of the 2d century, it is told that John died a natural death in Ephesus (*Acts of John* 111–115). Also by that time the Johannine writings, the Gospel of John, as well as at least the first Johannine Epistle, are known in Ephesus. Yet it is more likely that the Gospel of John was written somewhere in Syria or Palestine. Moreover, this Gospel itself is anonymous and does not claim to be written by John; rather it appeals to the mysterious figure of the beloved disciple as its authority. It is therefore not possible to demonstrate that there was an actual historical link between the apostle John, son of Zebedee, and the Johannine literature. On the other hand, it is unquestionable that there was indeed a literary tradition that claimed the authority of this apostle. Not only do the four Johannine writings of the New Testament belong here, but also the *Acts of John* and the *Apocryphon of John.*

In the 2d and 3d centuries, names of specific apostles or disciples of Jesus were widely used in order to establish authority and legitimacy for numerous writings, especially in Gnostic sects and schools. John, Peter, Paul, Philipp, Thomas, and others appear frequently, but so also do Jesus' brother James and Mary (Magdalene). In general, the apostle is the recipient of a special revelation that is communicated in the book published under his or her name. In most instances, it is impossible to know whether the use of such names as literary authorities rests on the use of traditions that were previously connected with the apostle to which a particular writing appeals, though this may well sometimes have been the case. Since the formation of the concept of apostolicity, which became basic for the canon of the New Testament, took place in the ongoing controversy with Gnostic sects, it can be assumed that it was exactly the Gnostic appeal to apostolic authority that prompted the fathers of the church to emphasize on their part the apostolicity of the orthodox writings. It will be shown, however, that the concept of apostolicity played only a very minor role for the inclusion of writings in the New Testament canon.

(3) *The Twelve Apostles.* The general authority of the Twelve Apostles emerged fairly late in the 1st century. Paul knew only of the "Twelve," which he distinguished from "all the apostles" (1 Cor 15:5 and 7). At the time of Paul, the term "apostle" was not limited to the Twelve; it comprised a much larger group of all those to whom the Lord appeared. Not only does Paul include himself in that group, but also women are recognized as deserving this designation (cf. Junia in Rom 16:7). General appeals to the "Apostles" without giving a specific number appear in the Epistle to the Ephesians, in Ignatius of Antioch, in *1 Clement,* in Polycarp of Smyrna, and in 2 Peter. The limitation of the term "apostle" to the Twelve is a later fiction that appears first in the Gospels of the New Testament, is further elaborated in the Book of Acts, where they become the guarantors of the tradition and the prototype for an ecumenical presbytery. The "Twelve Apostles" are used as an authority for the composition of a church order in the *Teaching of the Twelve Apostles* (*Didache*), a document composed in its extant form in the 2d century. Many later church orders also used the authority of the (Twelve) Apostles (*Apostolic Constitutions, Apostolic Church Order,* etc.). But the concept of the Twelve Apostles would play no role in the formation of the canon of the New Testament.

(4) *Marcion.* The impelling force for the formation of the canon, that is, for the singling out of a limited number of traditional writings of Christian authors as authoritative Holy Scripture, came from a radical theologian of the first half of the 2d century, who came from the tradition of the Pauline churches: Marcion (for Marcion's life and teaching, see §12.3c). Up to this point, the unquestioned Holy Scripture of all Christians had been the Bible of Israel, the "Law and the Prophets," which the Christians shared in the Greek translation of the Septuagint with the Jewish diaspora. Although Christian churches and Jewish synagogues had by that time become separate organizations, they still claimed the same Scriptures as their authority. Marcion's endeavor was intrinsically bound to the question of this "Jewishness" of the Christian churches, epitomized in the very use of Israel's Scripture as ultimate authority. Marcion, however, had learned from the letters of Paul that Christ was the end of the law. How could that Jewish law still be authoritative Scripture? The Gnostics, to be sure, would interpret that law allegorically, but Marcion was a literalist and did not accept any allegorical interpretation. The entire Scripture of Israel was seen by him as testimonies of the activity of the just God

who ruled this world according to the principle of law and punishment; but salvation through Jesus had come from a very different, "foreign" God whose Son had brought mercy and love. There was only one possible solution: This "Jewish" Scripture had to go and a new Holy Scripture was needed for the Christians.

Marcion created this new Holy Scripture which became binding for his churches. It consisted of the Gospel of Luke and the corpus of the Pauline letters (except for the Pastoral Epistles). Marcion, however, had come to the conviction that these writings were not preserved in their original form. He therefore produced a new critical edition, purifying them of all those elements that he judged to be later additions, especially all references to the Scriptures of Israel. Although Marcion was later bitterly attacked for tampering with these writings, it should not be forgotten that his opponents also tried to correct the image of Paul transmitted in the genuine letters of the apostle, not least by the addition of the Pastoral Epistles to the Pauline corpus. Moreover, to make a new edition of a gospel conformed to a widespread procedure of the time: The Gospels of Luke and Matthew are, after all, new editions of the Gospel of Mark. Thus Marcion's editorial work in the production of his new scriptural canon did not differ fundamentally from the way in which these writings were handled by his contemporaries. The novel element in Marcion's work was the elevation of these newly edited Christian writings to the status of "Holy Scripture" and the simultaneous rejection of the Scriptures of Israel. Marcion himself was convinced that he was simply continuing a development that had been initiated by the great apostle Paul. The fateful implication of Marcion's work was the assertion that Christianity should not be understood as the rightful continuation of the religion and tradition of Israel.

Shortly after 140 CE Marcion was excommunicated by the Roman church, whereupon he founded his own church, which quickly spread and developed into a worldwide church that continued to exist as a separate organization for many centuries. Remnants of Marcion's church in the Balkans, known as the "Paulicians," were reorganized in the 10th century by a man known as "Bogomil" (="friend of God"). The movement of the Bogomils with its dualistic worldview became the most important sectarian movement of the Byzantine empire and a powerful resource for the medieval heretical movements in central and western Europe. Although persecuted by both Greek Orthodox and Roman Catholic ecclesiastical establishments, they were able to survive especially in Bosnia, where they finally accepted the protection of the Turkish conquerors (1463–1483), agreeing to convert to Islam—the Bosnian Muslims.

(5) *The Reaction to Marcion.* Only a part of the initial stage of the reaction to Marcion is known. Justin Martyr is the principal witness. He was active in Rome at that time and wrote the first known (but not preserved) book against Marcion. In his extensive preserved writings Justin never quotes the letters of Paul, which were the most significant part of Marcion's new canon. It seems that Justin deliberately avoided these letters. He knew, however, the Gospels of Matthew, Mark, and Luke, calling them "Memoirs of the Apostles," and produced a harmony of these three writings—without ever thinking that such an endeavor might violate their integrity. They were for him the only viable Christian authorities. Occasionally he quotes them with the formula "it is written," which until then had been used

only for quotations from the Scriptures of Israel. The fact that he thus elevates the gospels as written authorities to a status that is comparable to the dignity of the Holy Scriptures may be due to Marcion's influence. In a few instances, Justin calls these writings "gospels"—thus using a term for this literature that apparently only Marcion had used before him as a designation for such books.

Although Marcion's influence is visible in Justin's reevaluation of the writings from the Christian tradition—negative in his avoiding Paul's letters and positive in his appraisal of the status of the gospels—Justin does not attempt to create a new Christian canon. Rather, he makes a deliberate effort to reassert the status of Holy Scripture for the Law and the Prophets. Only these writings are truly inspired (Justin ascribes inspiration to the Greek translation of the Hebrew Bible). The importance of these Scriptures is underscored by his use of a new recension of the Septuagint that was designed to bring the Greek translation closer to the Babylonian version of the Hebrew text (§5.3b).

The question of a canon of Christian Scriptures, however, remained unresolved for a whole generation, until Irenaeus started on a path that would lead out of the perplexity caused by Marcion's challenge. Irenaeus was bishop of Lyon in southern Gaul during the last decades of the 2d century, but he came from the tradition of the Pauline churches of Asia Minor, where he had grown up. There, he had also become acquainted with the Gospel and Epistles of John, which he combined with the memory of another John, who had written the Book of Revelation. He boasts that he had sat at the feet of the famous bishop Polycarp of Smyrna (ca. 100–167 CE), even though he was still a child at the time. Though a bishop of a western church, he was in his (Greek) writings much more a representative of the tradition of Asia Minor than of Rome. In Asia Minor Paul's letters were still widely used (but see the warnings of 2 Peter 3:15–16) and continued to be an inviolable part of the Christian tradition, despite their high esteem in Marcionite and Gnostic circles. Although he rejected Marcion, Irenaeus had no hesitation in making the letters of Paul the basis for the new Christian Scripture, to which he added the four gospels.

The new Christian book of Holy Scriptures, which was thus created and which Irenaeus placed as the New Testament side by side with the Scriptures of Israel, now called the Old Testament, was much more broadly based than Marcion's canon. It included the letters of the Pauline corpus, to which the Pastoral Epistles were added, as well as some of the "catholic" epistles (that is, those which were directed to all churches). As for the gospels, Irenaeus accepted not just one gospel but the four "separate" gospels (that is, not in a harmonized form) of Matthew, Mark, Luke, and John. That there were four Gospels rather than only one he defended with the cosmological speculation that they corresponded to the four ends of the earth.

The evident inclusiveness of Irenaeus's conception of the Christian Scripture has extraordinary significance. Marcion, as well as the Gnostics and their Scriptures, many claiming apostolic authorship, were rejected; but Irenaeus did not use a narrow doctrinal concept as the criterion for his selection. All those writings that had a claim to have been in use in the Christian communities from the beginning were included; although Irenaeus knew quite well that some of these writings, like those of Mark and Luke, were not written by an apostle. On the other hand, if it was known that a writing had been composed only recently, it was banned from the canon even if it claimed apostolic authority and was used by some churches. The question of inspiration did not play any role whatsoever in this process of canonization, because the claim to possess the Holy Spirit was so common that this criterion would have caused nothing but confusion. The concept of apostolicity appears in a modified form. A strict application of the criterion of authorship by one of the Twelve Apostles would have resulted in the exclusion of the entire Pauline corpus. For Irenaeus, therefore, "apostolicity" includes those writings that had nourished and instructed the churches, had established their order, and had guided their worship from the beginning. This principle is evident in the fact that only gospels with a passion narrative were accepted in the canon because the passion narrative was and continued to be the story that was constitutive for the celebration of the central Christian ritual, the Eucharist. It is also visible in the preservation of the Pauline corpus with the Pastoral Epistles, because the latter presented Paul not so much as the great theologian but as the instructor of the church and the creator of its order.

The fact that the practices of the churches of Asia Minor and Greece conformed to Irenaeus's collection, and that Antioch, Carthage, probably also Alexandria, and later even Rome confirmed this usage, provided the church-political basis for the success of Irenaeus's creation. That this new canon of Christian writings, however, also excluded numerous writings and thus some Christian groups that used them should not be overlooked. The Marcionites, several Gnostic groups, and the Jewish Christians (not yet, however, the Montanists) were excluded, despite Irenaeus's principle of inclusivity and despite the claim that their writings were apostolic and inspired. Theological differences certainly played a role, and theological arguments sometimes figured prominently in controversies. Nevertheless, the underlying causes must be seen in the area of practice. The network of bishops, spanning the entire Roman world from Antioch to Africa, Rome, and Gaul and maintained by mutual visits, exchange of emissaries, and an extensive correspondence, had been able to establish common practices for baptism (including the instruction of catechumens) and the celebration of the Eucharist, moral and ritual codes, and a number of social institutions and avenues for mutual support. This commonalty is expressed in Irenaeus's creation of the canon. On the whole, this was an extraordinary achievement, considering the fact that a central authority did not exist. We do not know whether this included the majority of all Christians at the end of the 2d century. Marcionite churches could be found everywhere; Jewish Christians observing the ritual law of Moses were widespread in Asia Minor, Syria, and Egypt. A variety of Gnostic Christian groups, schools, and sects were present in Rome as well as in Asia Minor, Syria, and Egypt, and often members of the organized churches seem to have attended the meetings of such conventicles.

There was also a price to be paid. A consequence of the acceptance of the Pastoral Epistles into the corpus of the Pauline writings was the eventual exclusion of women from ecclesiastical office, while Marcionites and many Gnostic groups continued to accept women in leadership roles. Even today, many Christian churches have great difficulty liberating themselves from this fateful heritage. The exclusion of Jewish Christianity and, in general, the establishment of a Christian Holy Scripture, in addition to the Scriptures of Israel, claiming that the Old Testament could be read legitimately only from the perspective of the New Testament, cemented the establishment of Judaism and Christianity as separate religions. Episcopal leadership in the creation of a worldwide "catholic" church also introduced hierarchical structures into the local organizations of the churches, replacing the older more democratic structures of the churches of Paul and, for example, of the Gospel of Matthew. On the other hand, the creation of the canon of the New Testament preserved some of the most valuable documents from the earliest period of Christianity, although the early history of this religious movement can only be fully understood if the wealth of new discoveries of noncanonical materials is fully integrated into the historical quest.

(6) *The Muratorian Canon.* This list of canonical writings, written in Latin, has been accepted by many scholars as the oldest list of canonical books and has been dated to about the year 200 CE. There are very good reasons, however, for doubting this early date; a composition of this list in the 4th century is more likely. While the inclusion of the four Gospels, the Pauline corpus, and some catholic epistles into the New Testament is well accepted at the end of the 2d century—not only Irenaeus, but also Tertullian, Clement of Alexandria, Origen, and Cyprian agree with this concept—the discussion of the inclusion or exclusion of specific writings, that is, the exact delimitation of the canon, did not begin until the fourth century. The list of the *Canon Muratori* enumerates the four Gospels, thirteen letters of Paul (without the Epistle to the Hebrews), the Revelation of John and the *Revelation of Peter,* the Epistle of Jude, two Epistles of John, one of Peter, and the Wisdom of Solomon. Explicitly rejected are the letters of Paul to the *Laodiceans* and to the *Alexandrians,* and the writings of the heretics (Valentinus, Marcion, and others).

(c) Noncanonical Writings of Early Christianity

(1) *The Apostolic Fathers.* In addition to the writings of the canon of the New Testament, there are several other ancient and modern collections of early Christian writings. They include books that were recognized and used by the fathers of the church as well as those that were rejected as heretical. For many centuries, the most significant of these collections was considered to be that of the Apostolic Fathers, which was created in the 17th century. The title "Apostolic Fathers" (*Patres apostolici*) was chosen at that time because it was believed that all those writings

Bibliography to §7.1c (1):   Texts

Bihlmeyer, *ApostVät.*

Lightfoot, *Apostolic Fathers.*

J. B. Lightfoot and J. R. Harmer, *The Apostolic Fathers* (ed. and rev. Michael W. Holmes; Grand Rapids, MI: Baker, 1989).

Kirsopp Lake, *The Apostolic Fathers* (LCL; 2 vols.; Cambridge, MA: Harvard University Press, 1912 and reprints).

Bibliography to §7.1c (1):   Tools

Henricus Kraft, *Clavis Patrum Patrum Apostolicorum* (Darmstadt: Wissenschaftliche Buchgesellschaft, 1963).

were composed in the apostolic period by followers of the apostles. If, however, the "apostolic period" is more strictly understood as the time up to the end of the Judaic War, that is, from 30 to 70–73 CE, the claim of origin in the apostolic period cannot be upheld for any of these writings. In fact, even of the writings of the New Testament, only the genuine letters of Paul were composed in this period, while the gospels, the deutero-Pauline epistles, the catholic epistles, and the Book of Revelation were written during the last decades of the 1st century and the first decades of the 2d century CE. This latter period of the second and third generation of Christianity is indeed also the time, during which most of the writings of the Apostolic Fathers were composed. Of these writings, *1 Clement, the Epistle of Barnabas,* and the sources incorporated in the *Didache* (added to this collection after its discovery in 1883) were composed before the year 100 CE, the letters of Ignatius of Antioch and a part of the *Epistle of Polycarp* shortly after the turn of the century, while *2 Clement* and the *Martyrdom of Polycarp* were apparently not written until the middle of the 2d century. The *Shepherd of Hermas* has its rightful place in this collection, although it is difficult to determine its exact date. The *Epistle to Diognetus,* which is usually included in editions of the Apostolic Fathers, is an apologetic writing from a later period. In contrast to the writings of the New Testament, which are preserved in an immense number of manuscripts and translations, very few copies of the Apostolic Fathers have survived, in some cases only a single manuscript (the only known manuscript of the *Epistle to Diognetus* was burned in the municipal library of Strasbourg during the bombardment of the city in the war of 1870).

(2) *Gnostic and Manichean Collections.* Ancient Christian groups that did not recognize the canon of the Catholic church made collections of their own writings. The most important of these is the Nag Hammadi Library, which was discovered in 1945/46 in Upper Egypt and has now been fully published and translated. It consists of thirteen leather-bound codices containing more than fifty mostly Gnostic writings, all of which had been translated into Coptic from Greek originals. Some

Bibliography to §7.1c (2):   Texts

James M. Robinson (ed.), *The Nag Hammadi Library in English* (3d ed.; San Francisco: Harper-Collins, 1990).

Hans-Joachim Klimkeit, *Gnosis on the Silk Road: Gnostic Texts from Central Asia* (San Francisco: HarperCollins, 1993).

Layton, *Gnostic Scriptures.*

I. Gardner, *The Kephalaia of the Teacher: The Edited Coptic Manichaean Texts in Translation with Commentary* (NHMS 37; Leiden: Brill, 1995).

Bibliography to §7.1c (2):   Studies

Knut Schäferdiek, "The Manichean Collection of Apocryphal Acts ascribed to Leucius Charinus," in Schneemelcher, *NT Apoc* 2. 87–100.

Bibliography to §7.1c (2):   Tools

Craig A. Evans, R. L. Webb, and R. L. Wiebe (eds.), *Nag Hammadi Texts and the Bible: A Synopsis and Index* (NTTS 18; Leiden: Brill, 1993).

Bibliography to §7.1c (2):   Bibliography

David Scholer, *Nag Hammadi Bibliography 1970–1994* (NHMS 32; Leiden: Brill, 1997).

of these date as early as the period in which the Apostolic Fathers were written, such as the *Gospel of Thomas,* the *Dialogue of the Savior,* the *Apocryphon of James,* the *Apocalypse of Adam,* the *Hypostasis of the Archons,* the *First and Second Apocalypse of James,* and perhaps a few others. As a whole, the writings of this newly discovered Coptic-Gnostic Library are an important resource for a fresh understanding of the history of early Christianity and its literature.

The Manicheans were distinguished by their high literary culture. Although this movement originated only in the 3d century CE, its literary collections also included some earlier Christian writings, notably a set of five apocryphal acts of the apostles that was ascribed to a certain Leukios Charinos—although only some parts of the fragmentary remains of this literature (see §7.1.c[3]) may derive from this Manichean collection. Upper Egypt has yielded a Manichean library in Coptic, which is currently in the process of edition and translation. Numerous parts of Manichean writings were discovered between 1902 and 1914 by several German expeditions in Turfan at the northeastern edge of the Taklamakan Desert in Central Asia. A selection of these writings, translated into English from Parthian, Middle-Persian, and Old Turkish (Uighur), has recently been published by Hans-Joachim Klimkeit. Although all these texts were written after the period of early Christianity, they are important for a better understanding of early Christian Gnosticism.

(3) *The New Testament Apocrypha.* The corpus known as the New Testament Apocrypha is a modern collection of early Christian writings. Its intention has been to gather early Christian writings claiming apostolic authorship as well as otherwise anonymous gospels, acts of apostles, apocalypses, and letters that had not been included in the canon of the New Testament. These apocrypha include writings that may be dated as early as the 1st century and as late as the 4th, 5th, or even 6th centuries. None of these writings ever enjoyed canonical protection, often originating from Christian circles that were not part of the established catholic churches. They were therefore subject to repeated rewriting and to changes caused by continuing oral communication and deliberate adjustments to new ecclesiastical and political situations.

The apocrypha have come down to us in many different ways. Many of these books were still read in the Middle Ages and first published in the Renaissance period; others were known through quotations and excerpts in the church fathers.

Bibliography to §7.1c (3):   Texts

Schneemelcher, *NT Apoc.*

J. K. Elliott, *The Apocryphal New Testament: A Collection of Apocryphal Christian Literature in an English Translation* (Oxford: Clarendon, 1993).

Bibliography to §7.1c (3):   Studies

François Bovon and P. Geoltrain (eds.), *Écrits apocryphes chrétiens* (Bibliothéque de la Pléiade 442; Paris: Gallimard, 1997).

Bibliography to §7.1c (3):   Bibliography

J. H. Charlesworth with J. R. Mueller, *The New Testament Apocrypha and Pseudepigrapha: A Guide to Publications, with Excurses on Apocalypses* (ATLA Bibliography Series 17; Metuchen, NJ: Scarecrow, 1987).

Most of these materials, however, originate from discoveries of manuscripts, often fragmentary, during the last hundred years. The most recent publications of the apocrypha present more than twice as many writings as apocrypha included in editions published at the beginning of the 20th century. In many instances the text is preserved only in a single manuscript and often not in the original Greek language but only in translations or secondary translations into Latin, Coptic, Syriac, Armenian, Georgian, Ethiopic, or Arabic. Frequently, the original wording and composition of such a writing can be reconstructed only through painstaking comparison of various fragments, copies, and translations. Therefore, it is generally very difficult to decide with any degree of certainty questions of authorship, date, and original form of the text.

Whether or not any of these apocryphal writings can be dated early or originated at a later time, they are important witnesses for the history of early Christianity. Even in those instances in which a relatively late date must be assumed, traditions that can be traced back to the earliest period of Christianity are often incorporated. If their theological perspective deviates from that of the fathers of the church, it may well provide significant insights into popular religious perceptions and practices of early Christian people. Their colorful spectrum permits glances into the manifold diversity of early Christian piety and religious practice—a perspective that the polemical orientation of the canon of the New Testament obstructs or seeks to limit.

(d) Extra-Christian Testimonies

Non-Christian testimonies for the beginnings of Christianity are few and unfortunately not very informative. There is a report about Jesus in the *Antiquities* (18,63) of the late 1st century Jewish historian Josephus, but it is not preserved in its original form, since it was thoroughly redacted by a later Christian scribe. Reconstructions of the original text of Josephus's report have been attempted, yet remain uncertain. Josephus (*Ant.* 20.200) also tells of the death of James, "the brother of Jesus who was called the Christ," and says that he was accused by the high priest Ananos of having transgressed the law and delivered up to be stoned (probably in the year 62 CE)—a report that seems reliable, as it is much less legendary than the one by Hegesippos, which is preserved in Eusebius's *Ecclesiastical History* (2.23.11–18). Any other information about Jesus and early Christianity that comes from Jewish, that is, rabbinic, sources is of no historical value.

The earliest Roman testimonies appear in the writings of Suetonius, Tacitus, and Pliny the Younger—all three wrote at the beginning of the 2d century CE. Suetonius (*Vita Claudii* 25.4) gives a short report about the expulsion of Jews from Rome during the reign of Claudius (41–54 CE), because they constantly caused disturbances "incited by Chrestus" (*impulsore Chresto*). This is most likely

Bibliography to §7.1d

W. den Boer, *Scriptorum paganorum I–IV saec. de Christianis testimonia* (2d ed.; Leiden: Brill, 1965).

F. F. Bruce, *Jesus and Christian Origins Outside the New Testament* (rev. ed.; London: Hodder & Stoughton, 1984).

a reference to Jews in Rome who were followers of Christ ("Christus"). In his *Vita Neronis* (16.2) Suetonius says that the Christians, who were following a new and evil wrong belief (*maleficus superstitio*), were expelled from Rome by Nero. Tacitus reports in greater detail that the Christians, who derived their name from Christ, crucified under Pontius Pilate, were executed in a most cruel fashion by Nero after the great fire of Rome. He adds that they were not so much punished because of the suspicion of arson, but because of their hatred for humanity (*Ann.* 15.44.2–8). From the same period comes the first more extensive report about the Christians from the younger Pliny. In the year 112 CE he was governor of Bithynia in Asia Minor, and in this capacity he wrote a letter to the emperor Trajan asking for advice about the treatment of the Christians and the appropriate legal procedures against them (Epist. 10.96). From this letter we learn that the Christians met early in the morning, took oaths not to commit any crimes, and that they would gather together later for a common meal; it is also interesting that the only Christian ministers he mentions are two female slaves who were deacons. All this Roman information has little value as far as early Christian history is concerned. It is significant, however, because it reveals a considered official Roman attempt at the beginning of the 2d century to formulate an imperial policy concerning the treatment of this new religious movement. Pliny's correspondence with Trajan as well as Hadrian's rescript to Minutius Fundanus will be discussed in more detail later (§12.3d). Little can be learned from Dio Cassius's report (*Epitome* 67.14) about the execution of the consul Flavius Clemens and the banishment of his wife, who had been accused of atheism, and his comment that they perished together with others who were inclining toward Jewish beliefs. It is possible that this refers to the persecution of Christians by Domitian.

Information about Christians begins to flow more abundantly in the middle of the 2d century. Lucian of Samosata reports in great detail the death of the Cynic philosopher Peregrinus Proteus, who had once been a Christian. In his book about the pseudoprophet Alexander of Abunoteichos he places Christians, atheists, and Epicureans in the same category. The emperor Marcus Aurelius made some negative remarks about the Christians in his *Meditations*. His teacher, the Roman orator Fronto, published a speech against the Christians, which is now lost. The most detailed reports about the Christians are preserved in the writing of the Platonist Kelsos (Celsus), quoted in part by Origen in his refutation of Kelsos's writing. This material, however interesting, gives a vivid testimony to Christian diversity in the second half of the 2d century but contributes little to the history of Christian beginnings. It is more significant for the controversy between paganism and Christianity, which began in the 2d century CE.

2. THE TEXT OF THE NEW TESTAMENT

(a) Problems of the Transmission of New Testament Texts

Not a single autograph of any book of the New Testament has been preserved. The oldest surviving copies were made ca. 200 CE, except for a tiny fragment of the Gospel of John from a manuscript written in the first half of the 2d century CE ($\mathfrak{P}^{52}$). All of the earliest extant copies are papyri (for writing materials, see §2.6d) and all were found in Egypt, where the dry desert sand retards the decomposition of writing materials. They were "uncial" manuscripts, also called "majuscles," that is, they were written in capital letters without any separation of words. Later manuscripts are "minuscules"; they are written in small cursive letters, connecting several letters to groups or syllables. While the preferred format for a book in antiquity was the scroll, all New Testament manuscripts were codices (with the exception of a few that were written on the verso of older scrolls like $\mathfrak{P}^{13}$). The format of the codex made it possible to include more than just one gospel or one epistle in a single manuscript. In fact several manuscripts from the time before 300 CE were collections of a number of writings, such as $\mathfrak{P}^{45}$, which included all four gospels and the Book of Acts, or $\mathfrak{P}^{46}$, which included almost all letters of Paul. The oldest manuscripts containing the entire New Testament were written in the 4th century CE (Codex Sinaiticus and Codex Vaticanus). These are parchment codices and, like the earlier papyri, they are also "uncials." Although there are still numerous papyrus manuscripts of the New Testament from later centuries, the large parchment codex became the most frequently used format for manuscripts of the entire Christian Bible, comprising both the Old and the New Testament.

In some respects the problems of the textual transmission of the New Testament are the same as those found in the manuscript transmission of other ancient authors. The same mistakes are made in the copying of manuscripts in both instances: inversion of letters and omission of single letters, resulting in a different word; haplography (omission of identical letters or groups of letters); dittography (copying

Bibliography to §7.2:   Text

Barbara and Kurt Aland, Johannes Karavidopoulos, Carlo M. Martini, and Bruce M. Metzger (eds.), *Nestle-Aland: Novum Testamentum Graece* (27th ed.; Stuttgart: Deutsche Bibelgesellschaft, 1994).

Bibliography to §7.2:   Studies and Information

Frederick G. Kenyon, *The Text of the Greek Bible* (3d ed., rev. A. W. Adams; London: Duckworth, 1975).

Bruce M. Metzger, *The Text of the New Testament: Its Transmission, Corruption, and Restoration* (3d ed.; New York: Oxford University Press, 1992).

Kurt Aland and Barbara Aland, *The Text of the New Testament: An Introduction to the Critical Editions and to the Theory and Practice of Modern Textual Criticism* (2d ed.; Grand Rapids, MI: Eerdmans, 1989).

Hans Lietzmann, "Textgeschichte und Textkritik," in idem, *Kleine Schriften* (3 vols.; TU 67, 68, 74; Berlin: Akademie-Verlag, 1958–1962) 2. 15–250.

Kurt Aland, *Kurzgefaßte Liste der griechischen Handschriften des Neuen Testaments* (ANT 1; 2d ed.; Berlin: de Gruyter, 1994).

Idem (ed.), *Materialien zur neutestamentlichen Handschriftenkunde* (ANT 1; Berlin: de Gruyter, 1969).

Idem, *Text und Textwert der griechischen Handschriften des Neuen Testaments* (3 vols.; Berlin: de Gruyter, 1987–1993).

Bart Ehrman and Michael W. Holmes (eds.), *The Text of the New Testament in Contemporary Research: Essays on the Status Questionis: A Volume in Honor of Bruce M. Metzger* (SD 46; Grand Rapids, MI: Eerdmans, 1995).

a letter or a group of letters twice); confusing similar letters; and finally "homo-ioteleuton," that is, omission of an entire word or line because it ends with the same letters as a preceding word or line—a very frequent mistake. There are also delib-erate changes. Some of them are purely stylistic, such as the replacement of Koine (vernacular speech) expressions by a more literary Greek (Atticisms). Others re-sult from the comparison with different manuscripts of the same writing. Biblical quotations in New Testament writings are often corrected by comparing them with manuscripts of the Old Testament. Parallel texts of the gospels were assimilated to each other. Dogmatic motifs also caused corrections, for example, in 1 Thess 3:2, where Paul calls Timothy "fellow-worker (συνεργός) of God"; a scribe changed this to "servant (διάκονος) of God," another manuscript omits "of God," and a later combination of the variant readings results in a text that reads "servant of God and my fellow-worker." Even after the 2d century CE materials from the oral tradition were still added to the text of the gospels, such as the pericope of the laborer on the Sabbath in Luke 6:5 (Codex D) and the story of Jesus and the woman caught in adultery that is found in many later manuscripts after John 7:52, and in one man-uscript after Luke 21:38. The most blatant dogmatic addition is the insertion of the trinitarian formula into 1 John 5:6–7 in the Latin translation (the so-called *Comma Johanneum*).

In many other ways, however, the problems of New Testament textual criticism differ from those of its classical sister discipline. Classical authors are usually pre-served in only a few manuscripts, and often in just one, but there are thousands of manuscripts of the New Testament in Greek, numerous translations that derive from an early stage of the textual development, a large number of lectionaries, and finally, beginning in the 2d century CE, an uncounted number of quotations in the writings of the church fathers. Moreover, while the only surviving manuscripts of classical authors often come from the Middle Ages, the manuscript tradition of the New Testament begins as early as the end of the 2d century CE; it is therefore di-vided only by as much as a century from the time at which the autographs were written. Thus it would seem that New Testament textual criticism possesses a base that is far more advantageous than that for the textual tradition of classical authors.

Nevertheless, the advantages that this rich tradition appears to offer should not be overestimated. Problems in the reconstruction of an original text are, to a cer-tain degree, independent of the number of preserved manuscripts, because most of the corruptions of ancient texts have occurred during the first fifty to one hundred years, that is, before the oldest surviving manuscripts and a regular tradition of copy-ing. On the other hand, difficulties arise from the very richness of the manuscript tradition because of the complexity of the interrelationships of manuscripts, which makes the construction of a stemma (a family tree of manuscripts) impossible. The construction of a stemma is the fundamental method in the textual criticism of classical authors; as soon as the relationships and dependencies of the surviving manuscripts are clear, it is fairly easy to eliminate all secondary variants. For New Testament manuscripts, however, dependencies can be established only occasion-ally and for a limited number of manuscripts, or only for individual variants or groups of variant readings. In general, the various branches of the manuscript transmission crossed and became mixed at such an early date and to such a degree that a stemma becomes absurdly complex. This is also the case for the translations, of which some are preserved in large numbers of manuscripts, such as the Vulgate.

Instead of reconstructing a stemma, New Testament textual criticism tries to classify manuscript families. Such classifications have had a certain success and have helped to bring some order into the seemingly overwhelming diversity of the transmission. After some earlier attempts to establish families, the system of B. F. Westcott and F. H. Hort, the most influential British scholars of textual criticism (§7.2f), classified all manuscripts as either representatives or mixtures of four major families. The designations that Westcott and Hort used for these families are still useful as a device for a preliminary characterization of many manuscripts or groups of manuscripts. Further research, however, has questioned the validity of their "Neutral Text" (see below) and has added the "Caesarean Text" as a possible additional family.

1. *The Western Text.* This family is extant in Codex D of the Gospels and Acts, Codex D of the epistles, the Old Latin and Old Syriac translations, and in quotations in 2d- and 3d-century authors (Marcion, Justin, Irenaeus, Tertullian, Hippolytos, and Cyprian). Although there are only a few Greek manuscripts representing this text, it must have existed as early as the middle of the 2d century CE, and it was widely used, especially in the west. Yet, it is sometimes considered as a "wild," unrevised text with mostly unreliable readings

2. *The Alexandrian Text.* The primary criterion for this family is the occurrence of its special readings in the quotations of the Alexandrian church fathers from Clement and Origen to Cyril. Westcott and Hort assigned only a few uncial manuscripts to this family (such a C and L) as well as the minuscule 33 and the early Coptic translations. Today one would include in this family also codices ℵ and B as well as A and some other uncials and several papyri that were not known to Westcott and Hort. Whereas the later Alexandrian text was certainly an edited text, showing considerable philological erudition, it was preceded by an earlier text, closely related to it, which is in evidence in early papyri, in quotations in Clement and Origen, and perhaps also in ℵ and B.

3. *The Neutral Text.* According to Westcott and Hort, the two oldest extant Greek Bible codices ℵ and B (especially the latter) were witnesses of a text that was free of contaminations and deliberate revisions. Today, however, scholars classify these two manuscripts with the Alexandrian family.

4. *The Caesarean Text.* This family was not yet recognized by Westcott and Hort and appears to be the least well attested. It is assumed that this family derives from the text that Origen brought from Alexandria when he moved to Caesarea; but it was later contaminated, especially by Western readings. Its extant witnesses are the uncial Θ, several minuscules, and the older Armenian and Georgian translations.

5. *The Koine or Byzantine Text.* There is no question that this family of manuscripts is, on the whole, a mixture of all older families—a fact that does not exclude the survival of older readings. It seems to derive from a revision of the text of the New Testament that was prepared by Lucian of Antioch at the end of the 3d century CE. Although this family includes the vast majority of all extant manuscripts and translations, it is generally considered to be the latest and least trustworthy textual family. Indeed, the *textus receptus,* the "received text" of the Reformation

and post-Reformation period, based exclusively upon medieval Greek manuscripts, is more or less identical with this family.

Any attempt, however, to make text-critical decisions simply on the basis of the family relationships of variant readings is not satisfactory, because many manuscripts contain "mixed" texts, that is, some of their readings belong to one family, others to a different family. Furthermore, some families are so large and contain so many different texts that it is necessary to construct subfamilies, which adds more complexity. A further problem of the wealth of the transmission is sheer quantity. It is necessary to work through an immense amount of material in order to find witnesses for a possibly important ancient reading in some late manuscripts that are otherwise full of scribal errors and worthless variants. The evaluation of the quotations in the church fathers is also unusually difficult, although it would be of great importance for the geographical localization of manuscripts and their variant readings. The use of these witnesses, however, is complicated by the fact that often the writings of the church fathers are preserved only in medieval manuscripts, in which scribes may have corrected the wording of biblical quotations according to their own texts. Moreover, for the church fathers as well as for the ancient translations, which would also be valuable for the geographical location of the transmission of the Greek text, reliable modern editions are not always available. Thus, seen as a whole, the very richness of the tradition confronts the scholar with immense tasks and with many obstacles, which even the availability of computer research will not solve quickly and easily.

Granted, however, that a full and comprehensive recording and evaluation of all variant readings in manuscripts, translations, quotations, and lectionaries, would be at least theoretically possible, some fundamental problems of New Testament textual criticism cannot be fully solved in this way. Though the larger percentage by far of the text of the New Testament is fairly secure on the basis of the text-critical work that has been accomplished so far, numerous remaining problems call for solutions that cannot simply rely on the evaluation of extant readings, and of the text types and families in which they occur. The first of these problems derives from the fact that the manuscript transmission of the New Testament writings is very uneven. There are only a few dozen manuscripts that contain the entire New Testament, and only the smaller portion of these manuscripts are uncials from the 4th to the 10th centuries CE, the others are medieval minuscules, which usually represent the Byzantine text. The vast majority of the known manuscripts present only a fraction of the New Testament. Among these the majority are manuscripts of the gospels, while the Pauline Epistles are represented much less frequently, the Catholic Epistles appear only occasionally, and the Book of Revelation is rarely copied.

The second problem is the great divide of the early 4th century CE. The Great Persecution of Christianity from 303 to 311–313 CE meant the destruction of uncounted biblical manuscripts, especially of Greek manuscripts in the eastern part of the Roman empire, where the persecution was more severe and lasted longer. It seems that this destruction of Greek manuscripts had the result that some older text types survived only in translations based on earlier Greek texts, such as the Old Latin (*Vetus Latina* or *Itala*), Old Syriac, and Coptic Sahidic translations. The reconstruction of a Greek original from a translation, however, is notoriously difficult, because translations provide only a relative certainty with respect to the text of the Greek original. It is well-known that modern editors will rarely give serious consideration to a textual variant that is not preserved in any extant Greek manuscript but only in ancient translations, even if there is no question that such a variant must have existed in a Greek text of the 2d or 3d century.

The third problem arises from the fact that we have direct access to the Greek texts of the late 2d and 3d centuries through an increasing number of papyri—but all of them come from Egypt and do not tell anything about text types that were current at that time in Syria, Asia Minor, or Greece. Moreover, most of these papyri are fragmentary (§7.2b) and in some instances do not permit a satisfactory assessment of the text type that is represented. This is complicated by a surprising discovery in the study of these early papyri: one could expect that all the Egyptian papyri would confirm the text of just one of the families of manuscripts established by text-critical scholarship, namely the Alexandrian text; that, however, is not the case. Rather, in several instances 3d-century papyri present what, from the perspective of these families, has to be designated a "mixed text." That does not necessarily invalidate the hypothesis of these families; it simply means that these families derive from archetypes that were created in the early 4th century, while typical elements of all these families existed in earlier texts, though the families themselves did not yet exist.

Fourth, however valuable the information from the early papyri may be, they do not tell us anything about the history of the text before the end of the 2d century, that is, the time before the canonization of the New Testament (§7.1b). There can be no question that special care was given to the text of these writings only after they became "Holy Scripture" and only when the first great writers of New Testament commentaries such as Origen and Hippolytos appeared in the 3d century. How were texts treated in the 100 to 150 years that separate the autographs from the ascendancy of their written product to the status of Holy Scripture? It should also be noted that a much smaller number of copies was probably in circulation in the earliest decades of the transmission. If a scribe was confronted with a corrupt or illegible text and he had no access to another copy of the same text, he would have been forced to mend the text according to his own judgment. Another problem arose when a scribe found a marginal note in the manuscript that he was copying. Such marginalia are often words or sentences that an earlier scribe had accidentally forgotten. They could, however, also be later additions as, for example, the command that women should be silent in church, which someone wrote into the margin of 1 Cor 14, which was inserted by one scribe after 1 Cor 14:34 and by another after 1 Cor 14:40. Decisive textual corruptions, changes, and revisions of ancient texts usually occur during the first hundred years of their transmission, that is, during the period in which the lasting significance of a text or its author is either not yet recognized or still debated.

There are numerous examples of alterations and corruptions of the autographs of the New Testament writings during the earliest period of their transmission. These present the text-critical scholar with problems that cannot be solved with conventional text-critical methods that deal with extant manuscripts only. The edition of the Gospel of Mark, for example, that was used by Matthew and Luke must have been substantially different from the Gospel of Mark as it is transmitted in all ancient manuscripts (§10.2b). In the Gospel of John, a redactor of the early 2d century added several passages (the most important is John 6:52–59) and a final chapter (chap. 21) that cannot possibly have been part of John's original text (§10.3b), though they appear in all extant manuscripts. What all manuscripts transmit as Paul's Second Letter to the Corinthians is actually a compilation of a number of smaller letters that Paul had sent to Corinth (§9.3d); the same seems to be the case with respect to the letter of Paul to the Philippians (§9.3e [2]). How severely such new editions could alter the original text is demonstrated by Marcion's edition of the Pauline letters (§7.1b [4])—note that Marcion pursued no other purpose than to restore the original text of Paul's writings! Instructive is also the case of 2 Peter, which, written in the 2d century, incorporated the entire Epistle of Jude in a new edition (2 Peter 2; §12.2f). Textual criticism alone cannot solve, and in some instances cannot even recognize, these early corruptions of the original. The restoration of the original text requires in some instances the critical judgment and even conjecture of the interpreter of the New Testament writing in question and the application of other methods such as source and literary criticism.

(b) The Papyri

The papyri, especially those that were written in the period from the late 2d century to the 4th century CE, occupy an important place among the New Testament manuscripts. They are designated by a number preceded with a Gothic P ($\mathfrak{P}$). The first New Testament papyri were discovered at the end of the 19th and the beginning of the 20th century, though these were mostly small fragments, often measuring only a few square centimeters. An exception was Papyrus Oxyrhynchus 4, 657 ($\mathfrak{P}^{13}$) from the 3d or 4th century CE, containing major portions of Hebrews 2–5 and 10–12. A large number of more extensive papyri began to come to light with the discovery (in 1930) and publication (1933–34) of the Chester Beatty Papyri ($\mathfrak{P}^{45}$ and $\mathfrak{P}^{46}$) from the 3d century CE. A number of other more fully preserved papyri followed. These more recent discoveries are judged, on the basis of paleographical evidence, to have been written early in the 3d century and perhaps even at the end of the 2d century. As a consequence, papyri have played an increasing role in New Testament textual criticism during recent decades. In the following, I shall describe some of the more important papyri; the catalog of New Testament papyri now lists more than 100 (for full information about the present depositories of these papyri and their publication, see the bibliography).

$\mathfrak{P}^{13}$ (Papyrus Oxyrhynchus 657) contains Hebrews 2:14–5:5; 10:8–22; 10:29–

Bibliography to §7.2b

Kurt Aland, "Das Neue Testament auf Papyrus," in idem, *Studien zur Überlieferung des Neuen Testaments und seines Textes* (ANT 2; Berlin: de Gruyter, 1967) 91–136.

Frederic Kenyon, *Our Bible and the Ancient Manuscripts* (rev. A. W. Adams, New York: Harper, 1958).

Joseph van Haelst, *Catalogue des papyrus litteraires juifs et chrétiens* (Série Papyrologie 1; Paris: Publications de la Sorbonne, 1976).

11:13; 11:28–12:17). It was written no later than the beginning of the 4th century on the verso of a scroll, of which the recto contained an epitome of Livy, that is, this papyrus is an opistograph. Its text is closely related to Codex B (see below). Since the latter text ends with Heb 9:14, $\mathfrak{P}^{13}$ is an important witness for the text of Hebrews 10–12.

$\mathfrak{P}^{32}$ (Papyrus Rylands 5) contains only a few verses of the Letter to Titus (Tit 1:11–15; 2:3–8), but belongs to the very oldest of the New Testament papyri, written ca. 200 CE, and representing a text type that agrees with the famous Codex Sinaiticus (ℵ), which is dated to the 4th century (see below). It is thus an important witness for the early existence of this text.

$\mathfrak{P}^{45}$ (Papyrus Chester Beatty I) preserves 30 of originally 220 leaves of a papyrus book containing the four gospels and Acts, written in the 3d century. The leaves that have survived include major portions of Matthew 20; 21; 25; 26; Mark 4–9; 11–12; Luke 6–7; 9–14; John 10–11; and Acts 4–17. Only the fragments of Mark (this gospel appears here for the first time in an ancient manuscript), Luke, and Acts are fairly well preserved. The text is of special interest because it does not agree with the otherwise prevailing Alexandrian text type of Egypt. It presents also readings that belong to the Caesarean text family and, to a smaller extent, Western readings; it is thus a representative of an early "mixed" text.

$\mathfrak{P}^{46}$ (Papyrus Chester Beatty II) is a nearly complete codex of the Pauline letters, written about 200 CE. Eighty-six of originally 104 leaves are preserved in an only slightly damaged condition. Parts of the Epistle to the Romans are missing at the beginning, and parts of 1 Thessalonians, all of 2 Thessalonians, and Philemon are missing at the end. The text is related to the Alexandrian text family but is a century older than the oldest previously known witness of this text type. $\mathfrak{P}^{46}$ contains a number of peculiarities that are extremely significant for the early history of the Pauline corpus: Hebrews appears immediately after Romans, meaning that it was an uncontested Pauline writing and put into this position next to Romans because of its length; the Pastoral Epistles (1, 2 Timothy and Titus; §12.2g) are missing completely—since the exact number of the original pages of this numbered codex is known, it is not possible that they could have appeared at the end of this manuscript—which proves that the scribe of this copy of the Pauline corpus did not yet know the Pastoral Epistles; finally, $\mathfrak{P}^{46}$ places the concluding doxology of Romans not after chapter 16 but after chap. 15—this confirms that Romans 16 was originally an independent letter that Paul directed to another church, namely, to Ephesus (§9.4a).

$\mathfrak{P}^{47}$ (Papyrus Chester Beatty III) is the middle part (ten leaves) of a papyrus codex (originally containing thirty-two leaves) of the Revelation of John. The text of this book's chapters 9:10–17:2 is preserved with only a few lacunae. The readings agree frequently—though not always—with Codex Sinaiticus, thus testifying to the existence of its text in the end of the 3d century in Egypt.

$\mathfrak{P}^{48}$ (Florence) was written at the end of the 3d century and contains the text of Acts 23:11–17, 25–29. The significance of this fragmentary manuscript lies in the fact that it proves the existence of the Western text of Acts in Egypt at an early date.

$\mathfrak{P}^{52}$ (Papyrus Rylands 457) is a tiny piece with a few fragmentary verses from a codex of the Gospel of John (18:31–33, 37–38). Although it has no text-critical significance, it attracted much attention because the type of its letters has been dated with some certainty to the first half of the 2d century, making it the oldest preserved fragment of any New Testament writing, removed from its autograph by half a century or even less.

$\mathfrak{P}^{53}$ (Papyrus Michigan 6652). Two fragments from this 3d-century codex contain a "mixed" text of Matt 26:29–40 and Acts 9:33–10:1.

$\mathfrak{P}^{64}$ and $\mathfrak{P}^{67}$ (Oxford and Barcelona), written ca. 200 CE, are both parts of the same papyrus codex, which preserve the text of Matt 3:9–15; 5:20–22, 25–28, and verses from Matthew 26. It is possible that $\mathfrak{P}^4$, which presents fragments of the text of Matthew 1–6, was part of the same gospel codex.

$\mathfrak{P}^{65}$ (Florence), from the 3d century, contains 1 Thess 1:2–2:1 and 2:6–13 in the Alexandrian form of the text.

$\mathfrak{P}^{66}$ (Papyrus Bodmer II) is the first of the series of New Testament papyri from the collection of the Geneva philanthropist Martin Bodmer. These are the most significant finds of New Testament papyri that have come to light after the publication of the Chester Beatty papyri. $\mathfrak{P}^{66}$ was written ca. 200 CE or slightly later, consist of 104 of originally 156 pages, and contains the text of John 1:1–6:11 and 6:35–14:26, as well as numerous fragments from the remaining chapters of John. It is the most important early witness for the text of the Fourth Gospel. Its readings belong partly to the Alexandrian text family and partly to the Western text, but the scribe has corrected his Western readings in the margins and between the lines in order to bring his text closer to the Alexandrian text type. This demonstrates that both a "mixed" text and the Alexandrian text were known in Egypt at that time. In one instance, $\mathfrak{P}^{66}$ contains a reading that is not attested in any other manuscript, which many scholars had already conjectured as the original text: in John 7:52 it reads the definite article before the word "prophet."

$\mathfrak{P}^{67}$ belongs to $\mathfrak{P}^{64}$, see above.

$\mathfrak{P}^{70}$ (Papyrus Oxyrhynchus 2384) is another 3d-century witness for an early use of the Gospel of Matthew in Egypt (Matt 2:13–16; 2:22–3:1; 11:26–27; 12:4–5; 24:3–6, 12–15).

$\mathfrak{P}^{72}$ (Papyrus Bodmer VII and VIII) is a codex from the 3d or 4th century written by different hands, containing a number of noncanonical writings, including the *Protogospel of James,* the apocryphal correspondence of Paul with the Corinthians (*3 Corinthians*), the *11th Ode of Solomon,* the *Passover Homily* of bishop Melito of Sardes, and from the New Testament the letters of Jude and 1 and 2 Peter. It is the earliest witness for these texts.

$\mathfrak{P}^{75}$ (Papyrus Bodmer XIV–XV) has been dated by its editors to 175–225 CE. Of the original 144 pages of the book, 102 are preserved (some only in fragments) containing the text of Luke 3–24 and John 1–15 (with lacunae). It is the oldest witness for the text of Luke and rivals $\mathfrak{P}^{66}$ as the oldest source for the text of John. Its text closely resembles that of Codex Vaticanus.

(c) The Uncials

Almost all the papyri cited above were written before the middle of the 4th century. Papyrus was still used as a writing material for New Testament manuscripts in the following centuries, especially in Egypt. With the official recognition of

Christianity, however, parchment became the more highly valued writing material for biblical manuscripts. Parchment possesses many advantages over papyrus; it is more durable and it is more convenient for a codex, because both sides are equally well suited for writing. It is likely that the parchment codex found quick general acceptance in the 4th century for yet another reason: Eusebius reports that in 331 CE Constantine ordered fifty manuscripts of the Bible "on parchment" for use in the new churches of Constantinople. The oldest complete manuscripts of the New Testament, several of which are also manuscripts of the entire Bible, are such parchment codices from the 4th and later centuries, although none of the extant codices seem to belong to those ordered by the emperor. In addition, there are a number of ancient parchment uncial codices that contain only a portion of the New Testament, usually the Four Gospels. Their sigla were traditionally capital Latin letters—often the same letter is used more than once for different manuscripts, of which one presents the text of the Gospels, another the Book of Acts, and another the letters of Paul—and when all of them had been used, capital Greek letters were employed; Codex Sinaiticus is customarily designated by the first letter of the Hebrew alphabet (א, sometimes also "S"). The American-born German text-critical scholar Caspar René Gregory has proposed a different system that could bring an end to the rather arbitrary way in which letters are used as sigla: all uncials receive a number preceded by a "0," while the minuscules are designated by numbers without a "0." Nevertheless, the old system seems to endure; numbers preceded by a "0" are used only for those uncials that were discovered after all the letters of the Latin and Greek alphabet had already been used. There are now more than 250 known uncial manuscripts. The following list describes only those that occur more frequently in the text-critical apparatus of New Testament editions.

Codex Sinaiticus (א = 02 [=S]), discovered by Constantine Tischendorf in the years 1844 and 1853, is the most famous of all New Testament manuscripts (it also contains most of the Old Testament in Greek). It was found in the monastery of St. Catherine's on Mt. Sinai, and the story of its discovery, frequently told, need not be repeated here. The codex was first presented to the Russian Czar. After World War I it was bought from the Soviet Union and came to the British Museum in London. Out of 346 leaves, 147 contain the text of the New Testament, which is almost completely preserved. In addition, the codex presents the text of the *Epistle of Barnabas* and the *Shepherd of Hermas*. As Codex Sinaiticus and Codex Vaticanus (B; see below) are the two oldest complete manuscripts of the New Testament, they have greatly influenced the text-critical decisions of modern scholars, sometimes because they were seen as representatives of an unedited "neutral" text (Westcott and Hort), sometimes because they are closely related to the Alexandrian text family, which many scholars prefer over the readings of the Western and Byzantine families. Although there is no question that Codex Sinaiticus is one of the most valuable witnesses, there is agreement today that Tischendorf, who discovered this

Bibliography to §7.2c

E. G. Turner, *The Typology of the Early Codex* (Philadelphia: University of Pennsylvania Press, 1977).

codex, overestimated its value. Its text is mostly Alexandrian with strong Western influences. The corrections, which were made at a later date, show the influence of the text type that was then current in Caesarea.

Codex Alexandrinus (A = 02) also comes from Egypt. It was brought to the British Museum in the year 1628 via Constantinople. This manuscript was written in the 5th century and contains the entire Bible (with major lacunae) as well as *1* and *2 Clement.* In its gospel text it is one of the most important witnesses for the Alexandrian text type and often agrees with Sinaiticus and Vaticanus.

Codex Vaticanus (B = 03) rivals Sinaiticus for the title of the most valuable uncial of the Bible. Like Sinaiticus, it was written in the middle of the 4th century CE. For hundreds of years it was kept in the Vatican Library, where it was first cataloged in the year 1475; but it was never used in text-critical work before the middle of the 19th century, because Vatican officials did not want to surrender their text to the scholarly world. Tischendorf was allowed some brief access to the codex and was able to make some notes about its readings. The first facsimile edition was finally published at the end of the 19th century. Codex Vaticanus lacks Hebrews 9:14–13:25, the Pastoral Epistles, Philemon, and Revelation—a serious loss because of the great value of this manuscript. While Westcott and Hort saw in this codex the most important representative of their "neutral" text, it is, however, best classified as a relatively pure representative of the Alexandrian text family that had an excellent older textual basis and was written with few mistakes.

Codex Ephraemi rescriptus (C = 04) is a "palimpsest": in the 5th century its pages were inscribed with the text of the Greek Bible; but in the 13th century that text was imperfectly erased and the pages were filled with copies of the ascetic writings and sermons of the Syrian church father Ephrem, who lived in the 4th century. Approximately five-eighths of the pages that contained the text of the New Testament are preserved and include parts of all its writings except 2 Thessalonians and 2 John. With the use of chemical devices Tischendorf painstakingly succeeded in deciphering the erased text of the New Testament. The codex seems to have been written in Egypt; but it contains readings of various text types, including some readings belonging to the Byzantine textual family.

Codex Bezae Cantabrigiensis (D = 05) is one of the most interesting manuscripts among the ancient uncials. Written in the 5th or 6th century, it finally ended up, nobody knows how, in the possession of John Calvin's successor Theodore Beza, who donated it in the year 1591 to the University of Cambridge. Since then it has been published several times. Codex Bezae contains the four gospels and the Book of Acts as well as one leaf with the text of 3 John 11–13 (how this leaf ended up in this gospel codex has never been explained). The unusual feature of this manuscript is that it is the oldest presentation of both the Greek and Latin texts written on facing pages. Both texts are remarkable—although their readings often agree with each other, the Latin text of this codex is not a translation of its Greek text. The Latin text is that of the Old Latin translation that was made at the end of the 2d century, two hundred years before the Vulgate (§7.2e), while the Greek text is the primary witness of the so-called Western text type. It is characterized by numerous "additions" (as compared to most other texts) but also by some striking "omissions" in the text of the gospels. Its text of the Book of Acts is so remarkably different from all other Greek manuscripts that some scholars have suggested that it might derive from a second edition of the Book of Acts made by the author himself. Although the text of this manuscript has been known to editors of the New Testament since the 17th century, it has been the stepchild of textual critics, and it is still debated today whether this Western text is a secondary degeneration of the original text or possibly a source for valuable ancient readings. That this text is indeed ancient is evident from its many agreements with the Old Latin and Old Syriac translations; it also appears more than once in quotations of church fathers in the 2d and 3d centuries. Yet, rarely will a modern editor consider a Western reading as a witness to the original text. Only Westcott and Hort assigned great value to those instances in which the Western text is shorter than the text of most other manuscripts, which they called the "Western noninterpolations"; the most famous of these is the shorter text of the words of institutions in Luke 22:16–20: vv. 19b–20 are missing in Codex D and the Old Latin translation.

Codex Claromontanus (D = 06); this manuscript must be distinguished from the Gospel/Acts Codex D described above; this codex, also once in the possession of Theodore Beza, contains the text of the Pauline epistles. Like Codex Bezae, this 5th-century codex is a bilingual manuscript presenting the Greek and Latin texts side by side and also presenting the Western text; in the epistles of the New Testament, however, this text type is not as strikingly different as in the case of the Gospels and Acts.

Codex Laudianus (E = 08), another Greek-Latin bilingual from the 6th century with the text of Acts, contains many Western readings together with numerous Byzantine variants. The siglum E is also used for the 8th-century Codex Basiliensis with the text of the gospels (= 07) and for the 9th-century Codex Sangermanensis (=[06]) with the text of the epistles; the latter is a copy of Codex Claromontanus (D = 06) and has therefore no independent text-critical significance.

Codex Augiensis (F = 010) is a Greek-Latin bilingual of the Pauline letters. It was written in the 9th century in an Alemannic monastery and kept for a long time on the island of Reichenau in the Lake of Constance (= *Augia Dives*); today it is located in Trinity College of Cambridge. Another codex with siglum F (= 09) contains fragments of the text of the Gospels.

Codex Boernerianus (G = 012) is a Greek-Latin bilingual from the 9th century with the text of the Pauline epistles. It is closely related to Codex Augiensis. Many errors appear in both manuscripts and both represent the Western text. Boernerianus is either copied from Augiensis or both are copied from the same older manuscript. It is very peculiar that Boernerianus introduces on its last page "Paul's *Letter to the Laodiceans,*" without actually presenting its text. Another codex with the siglum G (= 011) is a very fragmentary gospel manuscript from the 9th century.

Codex Coislinianus (H = 015; in addition, the siglum H has been used for two less significant manuscripts, both from the 9th century: 013 with the text of the gospels and 014 with the text of Acts) is a very important witness for the text of the Pauline letters, unfortunately only preserved in fragments. It was written in the 6th century and brought to Mt. Athos at a later time, where its pages were used to strengthen the bindings of other books. A total of forty-three pages are preserved, but are now scattered through several of the world's libraries. On the whole, it represents the Alexandrian text type. At the end of the letter to Titus, the manuscript gives the information that it has been compared with a manuscript from the library of Pamphilus (early 4th century) at Caesarea—the very same library that was used by the church historian Eusebius.

Codex Regianus (L = 019), an almost completely preserved codex of the gospels from the 8th century, shows close connections with the gospel quotations of Origen and agrees frequently with the text of Codex Vaticanus. Before the secondary longer ending of the Gospel of Mark (16:9–20), which appears in many later manuscripts, Codex Regius has copied a shorter ending that otherwise occurs only in a few other witnesses in the margin.

Codex Purpureus Petropolitanus (N = 022) is a deluxe manuscript of the gospels, which was probably written in Constantinople in the 6th century in silver ink on purple parchment, with the names of God and Jesus in gold ink. Almost half of the original 462 leaves are preserved and are now in the possession of several libraries (St. Petersburg, Rome, London, Vienna, Athens, New York, Thessaloniki; a major portion of the manuscript is shown to visitors to the island of Patmos). This manuscript was apparently divided into several batches and brought to Europe by the crusaders. Closely related to the text of this codex are the uncials O (= 023) and Σ (= 042). The texts of these magnificent manuscripts are considered to be of lesser value because they present the Byzantine text type.

Codex Porphyrianus (P = 025) is one of the very few uncials that contain the text of the Book of Revelation in addition to the Pauline and Catholic epistles. Like codex Ephraemi rescriptus (C) it is a palimpsest: the text of the New Testament, written in the 9th century, was erased and replaced in the year 1301 by a commentary of Euthalios. The text of Revelation in this manuscript offers a number of significant ancient variants.

Codex Borgianus (T = 029) is a Greek-Coptic bilingual and the oldest representative of this genre. Unfortunately, only Luke 22–23 and John 6–8 are preserved. Written in the 5th or 6th century with the Coptic-Sahidic text in the left columns and the Greek text in the right columns, this codex attests readings that agree with Codex Vaticanus.

Codex Freerianus, also called *Codex Washingtonianus* (W = 032), comes from the monastery of Shenute in Atripe near Achmim in Upper Egypt and is one of the important discoveries of the 20th century. It is the most interesting uncial manuscript now kept in the United States (Freer Gallery of the Smithsonian Museum in Washington, D.C.). Written in the 4th or early 5th century, it presents the text of the gospels. Its readings are such a "mixture" of all known text types (Alexandrian, Western, and Byzantine) that it calls into question all theories about the value and antiquity of these families. Within the secondary "Longer Ending" of the Gospel of Mark (16:9–20) Freerianus presents a very interesting expansion after Mark 16:14, the so-called Freer Logion, in which the disciples respond to Jesus by saying that this age is under the dominion of Satan.

Codex Koridethi (Θ = 038) was written in the 9th century or earlier in a monastery of the Caucasus, apparently by a scribe who did not know Greek. This gospel codex attests the existence of different text types in the East (Armenia). Many

Page from *Codex Washingtonianus*
This page shows the text of Mark 16 with the unique interpolation of the "Freer-Logion" into the ending of the Gospel of Mark.

corrections appear in the manuscript. The Caesarean text prevails in the texts of Matthew, Luke, and John, while the Western text is present in the Gospel of Mark.

Codex Zacynthius (Ξ = 040) is another palimpsest with the text of Luke from the 8th century. It is the oldest known manuscript that also presents a commentary. Its text is closely related to Codex Vaticanus. The commentary is a catena of quotations from the church fathers and surrounds the single-column text of Luke on three sides.

Manuscript 0212 (Papyrus Dura 10) was found in the ruins of the Roman Fortress Dura Europos on the Euphrates, which was destroyed by the Persians in 256–57 CE; it was therefore written no later than the first half of the 3d century. It is apparently not a fragment of a codex but of a scroll, because it is inscribed only on one side. This important gospel manuscript, of which just a fragment of one page is preserved, is the only extant copy of the Greek translation of Tatian's *Diatessaron* (§7.2d) with the harmonized text of Matt 27:56–57; Mark 15:14–42; Luke 23:49–51, 54; John 19:38.

Almost all of the other uncials, now numbering over 300 manuscripts, date from the 6th to the 10th centuries, and many of them are representatives of the Byzantine text type.

(d) The Minuscules

There are several thousand minuscules (or "cursives" as they are also called) of the New Testament, that is, manuscripts written in a cursive hand. Most of them were produced in the late Middle Ages, and the text of the gospels is most abundantly represented; also the epistles appear in many manuscripts, while the Book of Revelation was rarely included. Parchment was still in use as writing material, but it was increasingly replaced by paper, which had been invented in China. Paper became known as early as the 10th century in Europe, where paper production began in the 12th century, and a century later it was the most widely used writing material. For biblical manuscripts, however, the more durable parchment was only slowly replaced by paper. Some manuscripts use parchment and paper side by side in the same codex.

All known minuscules are cataloged today with the use of Arabic numbers as sigla. The text of many minuscules, however, has not yet been critically evaluated. Although the vast majority present the less valuable Byzantine text, a careful scrutiny of the minuscules has demonstrated that even a very late manuscript can be a witness for some valuable ancient readings. The testimony of the minuscules should therefore not be disregarded. Because of their sheer number, only a few of the better known minuscules and their families can be listed here.

1 is a 12th-century minuscule that contains the text of the entire New Testament except for the Book of Revelation. It was already used by Erasmus for the first printed edition of the Greek New Testament. For Revelation, Erasmus relied on a paper manuscript (once lost, but now rediscovered), also designated by the siglum *1*, containing all of Revelation except for 22:16–21. Since Erasmus did not have access to any other Greek manuscript with the text of Revelation, he translated the missing verses from the Latin Vulgate into Greek in order to avoid a delay in the publication of the first ever printed edition of the Greek New Testament. According to the studies by Kirsopp Lake, Minuscule *1* forms a family together with *118, 131,* and *209,* with a number of other minuscules showing close affinities. The text of these minuscules contains elements that are otherwise only found in the Old Syriac and Old Latin translations.

13, written in the 12th century in southern Italy, is the leading witness of a family known as the Ferrar Group. Other members of this group are *69, 124, 346,* and half a dozen other minuscules. The text represented by this family is perhaps best preserved in the 15th-century manuscript *69,* and the archetype of this group was certainly written before the year 1000. Characteristic for this family is the position of the story of Jesus and the adulteress after Luke 21:39, rather than after John 7:52. The text type of this group shows remarkable connections with the Old Syriac translation and Tatian's gospel harmony, the *Diatessaron* (§§7.2e; 12.3e).

33, the oldest minuscule manuscript, written in the 9th century, has been called "the Queen of the Minuscules." It contains the whole Bible (except for the Book of Revelation) and presents a text that is closely related to Codex Vaticanus.

81, written in the year 1044, contains only the Acts of the Apostles and is one of the most important witnesses for this biblical book.

157, written in the 12th century, is a gospel codex. Its readings often agree with Codex Bezae, but also show affinities to Tatian's *Diatessaron,* and to Marcion's text of Luke. At the end of each Gospel appears a colophon that is also found in about a dozen other manuscripts, which says, "[copied] from the ancient manuscripts of Jerusalem."

565 comes from the area of the Black Sea and was written in the 9th or 10th century. It also presents the above-mentioned Jerusalem colophon. The text of this gospel codex is closely related to the Western type—evidence that this type of text was also known in the east.

700 is a peculiar gospel manuscript from the 12th century. It departs 2,724 times from the "Textus receptus," which is otherwise represented by most medieval minuscules (§7.2f), and contains 270 readings that are not found in any other manuscript. It seems that these peculiar readings derive from a very old archetype, because the miniscule's wording of the second petition of the Lord's prayer in Luke 11:2—"Your Holy Spirit come upon us and cleanse us"—is taken from Marcion's text of this gospel and is also attested by the 4th-century church father Gregory of Nyssa, but does not appear in any other manuscript.

1424 is the main witness of a family of minuscules identified by B. H. Streeter, which includes another two dozen manuscripts. This codex contains the entire New Testament (except for the Book of Revelation) and is provided with a commentary written into the margin.

1739, written in the 10th century, contains the text of the Book of Acts and the epistles. It is a very important manuscript because its text of the epistles agrees with that of Papyrus Chester Beatty II ($\mathfrak{P}^{46}$) from the early 3d century. Since this papyrus is often fragmentary, the minuscule *1739* can provide valuable information about its text.

2053 contains only the text of the Book of Revelation, and is provided with a commentary on that book by Oecumenicus (4th century CE). Although this manuscript was written as late as the 13th century in Messina, it is one of the best witnesses for the Book of Revelation, sometimes even superior to the Papyrus Chester Beatty III ($\mathfrak{P}^{47}$) from the third century and Codex Sinaiticus.

(e) The Ancient Translations

A few remarks about the ancient translations (or "versions") have already been made above (§7.2a). It is not easy to assess their value. Each of the three most important older translations—the Syriac, the Latin, and the Coptic—had a complex history, including several recensions, which show the continuing influence of the Greek text that was itself still in flux. The oldest stages of these translations belong into the late 2d century (no later than the early 3d century for the Coptic translation), and they presuppose a Greek text that is not always accessible through extant Greek manuscripts. Secondary translations are not without value, especially in those cases in which the primary translation that they used is no longer fully extant. Of course, the reconstruction of the original Greek text is more difficult than in the case of primary translations. The following will list and describe briefly the most important ancient translations, but the scope of this book does not permit a discussion of the problems involved in their text-critical evaluation.

(1) *The Syriac Translations.* In the second half of the 2d century (most likely between 165 and 180 CE), the Syrian Christian Tatian composed a harmony of the four gospels of the New Testament, which is called the *Diatessaron* (a name that seems to indicate the use of four sources but can also simply mean "harmony"). Its basis was a three-gospel (Matthew, Mark, and Luke) harmony in Greek, composed in Rome by Tatian's teacher Justin Martyr before the middle of the 2d century. It was this harmony that Tatian, probably after his return to the East, translated into Syriac (an Eastern Aramaic dialect spoken in northern Mesopotamia and the Osrhoëne), artfully weaving into his teacher's older harmony texts from the Gospel of John, which Tatian himself also translated into Syriac (it is unlikely that a Syriac translation of the Fourth Gospel existed at the time). It has been long debated whether Tatian employed, in addition to these sources, also an extracanonical gospel; a Jewish-Christian gospel and the *Gospel of Thomas* have been suggested, but the arguments are not convincing. It is more likely that some of the extracanonical materials were already part of Justin's harmony and that Tatian himself also had access to the still flourishing oral tradition. Tatian's *Diatessaron* was subsequently translated into Greek—the oldest extant fragment of the *Diatessaron* is a single page

Bibliography to §7.2e

Bruce M. Metzger, *The Early Versions of the New Testament: Their Origin, Transmission, and Limitations* (Oxford: Clarendon, 1977).

Idem, "The Early Versions of the New Testament," in Black and Rowley, *Peake's Commentary,* 671–75.

George A. Kiraz, *Comparative Edition of the Syriac Gospels: Aligning the Sinaiticus, Curetonianus, and Harklean Versions* (4 vols.; NTTS 21, 1–4; Leiden: Brill, 1996).

Barbara Aland and A. Juckel (eds.), *Das Neue Testament in syrischer Überlieferung,* II: *Die paulinischen Briefe* (ANT 23; Berlin: de Gruyter, 1995).

William L. Petersen, *Tatian's Diatessaron: Its Creation, Dissemination, Significance, and History in Scholarship* (VCChrSup 25; Leiden: Brill, 1994).

of its Greek translation (see §7.2c, manuscript *0212*). Since no single manuscript of the original Syriac version has been found, the primary source for its original text is the commentary on the *Diatessaron* by the 4th-century Syrian church father Ephrem (fully preserved in an Armenian translation; about two-thirds of the commentary in Syriac was recently discovered and published). Gospel harmonies in other languages (Arabic, Persian, Latin, Middle Dutch, Old Italian—among many others) were published in subsequent centuries. Not all of them are directly or indirectly dependent upon Tatian's work. The reconstruction of the Greek base of the original Syriac text is an extremely important task, because this would give access to an early text form of the gospels. The evident close relationship of the *Diatessaron* text to the Western text family and the Old Latin translation may well have its roots in the affinity of Justin Martyr's Greek Gospel text to that special early text type.

Probably as early as the end of the 2d century, a Syriac translation of the four separate gospels appeared: the Old Syriac. It is not known whether other New Testament writings also were translated at this time, because only the Old Syriac version of the Greek text of the gospels is preserved in two manuscripts, Codex Syrus Curetonianus (sy^c) and Codex Syrus Sinaiticus (sy^s) from the 5th and 4th centuries, respectively. The relationship of the two manuscripts is not entirely clear, though it seems best to assume that both are dependent upon the same archetype. The basis of this Old Syriac translation was certainly a Greek manuscript that belonged to the Western text family, because many of its special readings are also found in a number of witnesses to the Old Latin translation (see below) and the minuscules of the Ferrar group (§7.2d). The Old Syriac thus confirms that a Greek text of the Western family was widely distributed geographically and used in the 2d century. The Western text should therefore be considered seriously as a witness to a very early text type, rivaling in its importance the papyri and the great uncials of the 4th and 5th centuries. Another significant feature of the Old Syriac is the presence of numerous harmonized readings that derive from Tatian's *Diatessaron*, confirming that the latter was indeed the oldest Syriac version of the gospels.

A third Syriac version, which is known through several hundred manuscripts, some from the 4th and 5th centuries, is called the Peshitta (sy^p). It was developed gradually on the basis of the Old Syriac translation in successive recensions, which used Greek texts for comparison at each stage. The oldest tangible stage in its formation is the edition of bishop Rabbula of Edessa, who died in 435 CE. In the year 508, bishop Philoxenus of Mabbug on the Euphrates requested his suffragan bishop Polycarpus to make a "new translation," that is, a new edition, of the New Testament in Syriac, called the "Philoxenia." The older form of the Peshitta, which did not include 2 Peter, 2 and 3 John, Jude, and Revelation, contains readings that are related to Codex Vaticanus as well as to the Byzantine text type. The missing Catholic Epistles as well as the Book of Revelation were probably added in the Philoxenia. This revision is indirectly preserved in a later edition made by Thomas of Heraclea in 616, the so-called Harklensis (sy^h). The latter is actually a text-critical edition, which has preserved a number of valuable ancient, especially Western readings in its marginal notes (sy^{hmg}), especially in the Book of Acts. It is therefore the most valuable source for the Western text, next to Codex Bezae.

Independent of these Syriac versions are the translations into the Western Aramaic dialect of Palestine (sy^{pal}), which can be partially reconstructed from medieval lectionaries. Although this dialect is more closely related to the language of Jesus than the "Syriac" translations, this version from the 5th century has only minor text-critical significance.

(2) *The Latin Translations.* The *Acts of the Scilitan Martyrs* (ca. 200 CE) and the writings of Tertullian (ca. 150–225 CE) demonstrate that a Latin translation of the New Testament was known in North Africa at the end of the 2d century. This Latin translation was made in Africa, that is, the Roman province of Africa proconsularis (modern Tunisia), which was the center of Latin-speaking Christianity in the late 2d and early 3d centuries. It was later used in a revised form in Italy and other Latin-speaking countries in the west and is known as the *Vetus Latina* ("Old Latin," also called *Itala;* its text-critical siglum is "it"). About thirty-two manuscripts are preserved, none of them presenting the entire New Testament; small Latin letters are used as sigla for these manuscripts. The dates at which these manuscripts were written vary from the 5th to the 13th century. This shows that the Old Latin text was not completely replaced by Jerome's Vulgate until the late Middle Ages. An early witness for the African text of the *Vetus Latina* is Codex Palatinus 1185 (siglum "e") from the 5th century, a gospel codex with readings closely related to the quotations in Cyprian and Augustine. Even older, but very fragmentary is Codex Bobbiensis (siglum "k") from the 4th or early 5th century.

The European manuscripts of the *Vetus Latina* provide more complete evidence, but they represent a text type that slightly differs from the older African text. Codex Vercellensis (siglum "a"), dated to the 5th century, is the oldest gospel manuscript with the European text of the *Vetus Latina.* Codex Veronensis (siglum "b") represents the text that was used by Jerome for his revision that became the Vulgate. The Latin column of Codex Bezae (D; the Latin is quoted by the siglum "d")—not a translation of D's Greek text—is another 5th-century witness of the European text. The Old Latin text of Acts and Revelation is preserved in Codex Gigas (siglum "gig"), written in the 13th century. It is a manuscript of the entire Bible (with Vulgate text in the other New Testament books) and one of the largest manuscripts ever: its pages measure almost half a meter (over eighteen inches) wide and almost one meter (three feet) long. The Old Latin manuscripts are not uniform, but there is no question that they represent on the whole the Western text and are thus an important witness for this ancient text type. Some of the Old Latin manuscripts also seem to show influence from Tatian's *Diatessaron*—fewer in the African than in the European version. Most similarities, however, are simply due to the fact that both the *Diatessaron* and the Old Latin are dependent upon the Western text; true *Diatessaron* readings in these manuscripts are a secondary element. A comprehensive edition by the monastery of Beuron in Germany is in progress.

The lack of uniformity among the representatives of the Old Latin version that were circulating in the West was the primary reason that prompted bishop Damasus of Rome in the year 382 to entrust Jerome with the task of producing a new edition of the Latin Bible. Jerome began with the gospels, where a lack of uniformity was most obvious. In a letter written in 383 to bishop Damasus, Jerome gave an account of his work. The new edition was very carefully made for the gospels, but only superficially for the remainder of the New Testament. It was not a new translation, but a revision of the Old Latin on the basis of a comparison with Greek texts that were in circulation at the time. The result of this work became the basis of what is known as the Vulgate, that is the "common" translation. It was not, however, accepted everywhere immediately, and was revised several times over the following centuries ("vg" is the siglum for the Vulgate; "vg^s" designates the recension of the Sixtina in the year 1590, "vg^{cl}" the Clementina of 1592), while the influence of the *Vetus Latina* text still continued (textual variants that occur in both the Vulgate and the Old Latin are designated by the siglum "lat," those that are attested in *all* Latin manuscripts by the siglum "latt"). Today there are more than eight thousand known manuscripts of the Vulgate; many of them demonstrate that the lack of uniformity, which prompted Damasus to request a new edition, had by no means been overcome.

(3) *The Coptic Translation.* During the early Christian period, a number of Coptic dialects were spoken in Egypt, all of them derivatives of ancient Egyptian. The two most important of these dialects were Bohairic, spoken in Lower Egypt, and Sahidic, spoken in Upper Egypt. Little was known about the dialects of Middle Egypt (Memphitic, Fayyumic, Achmimic, and Subachmimic), though these dialects have gained new significance through the recent discovery of Christian texts written in them. The Sahidic translation (siglum "sa") is the oldest Coptic translation of the New Testament, dating to the early 3d century. A number of manuscripts are preserved, some of them quite old and probably deriving from more than one archetype. The Greek textual basis is closely related to the Alexandrian text type, but also contains a number of Western readings. The Bohairic translation (siglum "bo") was made later and is attested in a large number of manuscripts, because Bohairic became, and still is, the official language of the Coptic church. The oldest known manuscript, discovered only recently, dates from the 4th century; it contains the text of the Gospel of John. The Alexandrian text type predominates. Of the Fayyumic translation, which is closely related to the Sahidic, only a few fragments have survived.

(4) The oldest translation of the New Testament into a Germanic language is at the same time the oldest surviving document in any of the Germanic languages, namely, the *Gothic translation* (siglum "got"). It was made in the middle of the 4th century as part of a translation of the entire Bible by the Cappadocian Christian Wulfila (or Ulfilas), who had been deported by the Goths together with his family. He composed his translation for Gothic Christians who were then settled in Moesia on the lower Danube. An incomplete text of his Gothic version of the gospel is preserved in the famous Codex Argenteus, which was written in the 5th or 6th century in northern Italy on purple parchment with silver and gold ink and is now kept in Uppsala. Almost all other Gothic Bible manuscripts are palimpsests, and they preserve nearly every book of the New Testament. The Greek basis of the Gothic translation is the Byzantine text type. It is not certain whether its many Western readings were part of the original translation or were introduced later during the stay of the Goths in northern Italy.

(5) The *Armenian translation* (siglum "arm") was made ca. 400. More than a thousand manuscripts have been cataloged, the oldest from the year 887. A good critical edition does not exist. It is an open question whether the Armenian version

rests on a Greek text or was made on the basis of the Syriac translation, which was later compared with a Greek text and revised accordingly during the 8th century. The text type of the Armenian translations seems to be more closely related to the Caesarean than to the Byzantine Greek. Less well-known is the *Georgian translation* (siglum "geo"). Christianity was introduced to the Georgians, living at the foot of the Caucasus, in the 5th century. The oldest surviving manuscripts of this translation date to the 9th century. They probably represent a secondary translation, representing a text that, like the Armenian version, is related to the Caesarean family.

(6) The origin of the *Ethiopic translation* (siglum "aeth") is an enigma. It may have been made in the 6th or 7th century, or perhaps as early as the 4th century, but the oldest surviving manuscript dates from the 13th century. It is possible that it neither derives from a Greek original nor from a Coptic version, but rather rests on a Syriac translation of the Greek. On the whole, its text belongs to the Byzantine family, but in the epistles its text often agrees with $\mathfrak{P}^{47}$ and with Codex Vaticanus, especially in instances in which the readings of these two manuscripts are not supported by any other witnesses.

Other ancient translations have only little significance for New Testament textual criticism, or their use is burdened by too many difficulties. These include the Anglo-Saxon, the Nubian, and the Sogdian versions as well as translations into Arabic and Persian. Except for a small portion of the Arabic version, they were all made on the basis of other translations rather than from the original Greek.

(f) The Printed Editions of the Greek New Testament

The first complete book printed after the invention of the printing press was the Bible in the Latin text of the Vulgate—the Gutenberg Bible of 1456. It would take more than half a century, however, before the first Greek Bible appeared in print. In the year 1502 the Spanish cardinal Ximenes began with his preparations for a grand edition of the Bible in Hebrew, Aramaic, Greek, and Latin. The fifth volume of this polyglot with the text of the New Testament was printed in 1514, the other volumes within the following three years. Yet the approval of the Pope was not given until 1520, and the final publication was delayed for unknown reasons until 1522. Thus this "Complutensian Polyglot," as it was called from the Latin name of its place of publication, Alcala, was denied the honor of being the first ever printed edition of the Greek text of the New Testament.

This honor belongs to the famous humanist Erasmus of Rotterdam. In 1515 the Basel printer Froben suggested to Erasmus that he prepare an edition of the Greek New Testament. In July of that year Erasmus began with his preparations, typesetting was started on 2 October, and on 1 March 1516 the entire Greek text of the New Testament was published, together with Erasmus's Latin translation. Though the publication was at first received with somewhat mixed reactions, undeniably it was a success. In the first two editions, 3,300 copies were printed and sold. With only minor alterations this text persisted as the standard form of the Greek New Testament until the end of the 19th century. It was the basis of Luther's German translation, of the authoritative English translation known as the "King James

Version," and of all other Western translations that were based on the Greek text. Since Erasmus prepared this edition in great haste, it is no wonder that its text turned out to be inferior. Erasmus used only a very few late minuscules. The only superior manuscript to which he had access, Codex 1 from the 12th century, he dared not use at all, because the text differed so much from all the other manuscripts he knew! For the Book of Revelation he had only one single manuscript with a text that was unreadable in many passages and that lacked its last page. Erasmus repaired these defects by retranslating the missing passages into Greek from the Latin Vulgate, creating in this process a number of Greek words that had never before existed. Later editions, to be sure, corrected hundreds of misprints of the overly hasty first edition. On the other hand, Erasmus also introduced the *Comma Johanneum* (the mention of the Trinity in John 5:7–8) into his later editions, although it was missing in all Greek manuscripts: a Greek manuscript with the *Comma Johanneum* (translated from the Vulgate) was forged in order to deceive Erasmus— and it succeeded!

During the 16th century, several scholars began to add a text-critical apparatus to their printed editions, listing variant readings, first taken from other Greek manuscripts, but soon also from quotations in the church fathers and from other translations of the New Testament. The Parisian publisher Robert Etienne (= Stephanus) printed several editions of this kind, and after him Beza, Calvin's successor in Geneva, who had two ancient uncial manuscripts in his possession—Codex Bezae and Codex Claromontanus (D = 05 and 06)—but he made very little use of them for his edition. Both editors printed a text that mixed readings from Erasmus's edition and from the Complutensian Polyglot. In the year 1624 the Dutch printing firm of Elzevir issued a handy and convenient edition of the New Testament, which again produced the text of Erasmus that had been compared with the Complutensian Polyglot. This edition was advertised as "the text that is now received by all." The designation "Textus Receptus" is derived from this advertisement. Critique and confutation of this Textus Receptus has been the primary task of New Testament textual criticism ever since, well into the 20th century.

Until the 18th century many scholars were engaged in the task of enriching the material for text-critical work by collating known and newly discovered manuscripts. Remarkable is the edition of John Mill (1707), the first major critical edition, listing thirty thousand variants from a hundred manuscripts, ancient versions, and quotations by the church fathers. It is characteristic, however, that Mills did not touch the Textus Receptus itself but reprinted it without any change. Shortly thereafter Edward Wells published a new edition that departed from the Textus Receptus in 210 cases (1709–1719). A similar critical edition of Daniel Mace followed in 1729. Wells's edition, however, was ignored, Mace's fiercely attacked and soon forgotten; the belief in the Textus Receptus as the inspired, original Greek text was too strong. A major step forward in method came in the edition of Johann Albrecht Bengel, which was published in 1734. To be sure, Bengel's text departs from the Textus Receptus only in those instances in which such readings had already occurred in previous editions. He had gained new insights, however, from his elaboration of families of manuscripts, and he signaled in his text-critical apparatus all readings that he judged superior to the Textus Receptus. Nor was Bengel spared from hostile attacks by ecclesiastical authorities and theologians. A few years later (1751–1752), Johann Jacob Wettstein in his monumental edition again produced the Textus Receptus, banishing all readings that he deemed superior to the apparatus. Wettstein left an important legacy, as he was the first to designate all uncial manuscripts by capital letters and all minuscules by Roman numbers.

A new period was initiated, when Johann Jacob Griesbach, a student of the famous Enlightenment scholar Johann Salomo Semler, defined his task as producing a better Greek text. Griesbach used Bengel's and Semler's insights—classification of manuscripts into families and rational application of the known principles of textual criticism—producing a pioneering edition of a new Greek text, which was published in the years 1774 and 1775. This text was the first that tried to improve upon the Textus Receptus in many sections of the New Testament by recourse to the manuscripts and versions that represented the two "African" texts, the Western and the Alexandrian families. Griesbach, however, did not yet dare to question the basic validity of the hallowed Textus Receptus, which insured its survival, albeit in a revised form, in the several reprints of his text (the primary editions appeared in 1796 and 1806 in Halle and London) and the numerous editions of other scholars who followed him throughout the 19th century.

The decisive break with the Textus Receptus came with the edition of the philologian Carl Lachmann in 1831 and 1842–1850. Lachmann had developed more objective methods in his work on editions of Classical and Middle-High German texts, which enabled him to construct his text quite independently of the Textus Receptus. This was a momentous achievement, though Lachmann's belief in the most ancient text of the New Testament used in the East was based on a too narrow foundation of manuscripts and his methodological schema was too rigid. In England, it was Samuel Prideaux Tregelles, who established the principle that the most original text of the New Testament must be found independently of the Textus Receptus by a careful comparison and evaluation of the best available manuscript evidence. For his edition, which was published in three parts from 1857 to 1872, Tregelles was not only able to incorporate his own meticulous collations of almost all the important manuscripts that were known at the time, but he also scrutinized the church fathers and included variants from the ancient versions.

It became clear at this point that a larger number of ancient manuscripts had to be discovered in order to challenge the Textus Receptus. This was accomplished by Constantin von Tischendorf, who continued Lachmann's work. Beginning in 1841, Tischendorf published a whole series of new editions of the Greek New Testament, repeatedly attempting to improve upon the text of previous editions in numerous passages. The manuscripts that Tischendorf himself discovered and/or collated, especially his beloved Codex Sinaiticus ($\aleph$ = 01), as well as Codex Vaticanus (B = 03), had a decisive influence on the Greek text of these new editions. That he could claim that his text rested on manuscripts that were many hundreds of years older than those used for the Textus Receptus, together with his indefatigable efforts to collect and to collate new manuscripts, were his chief merits. His *Editio octava critica maior* of 1869–1872 is unsurpassed even today in its abundance of information and still indispensable critical apparatus.

In rank and scholarly substance equal to Tischendorf's edition was the text-critical work and edition of the Greek New Testament by B. F. Westcott and F. J. Hort, published in 1881 as the fruit of many years of collaboration. Unlike Tischendorf, Westcott and Hort were not collectors, but were mainly interested in the creation of the best possible text on the basis of careful and well-balanced reconstruction of its history. Their extensive labors in the determination of the family trees of manuscripts and translations led to the assumption of four manuscript families, which they called "Syrian" (="Byzantine"), "Western," "Alexandrian," and "Neutral." The variants of these families were carefully weighed in each single instance, but in the final judgment, Westcott and Hort almost always preferred the readings of the "Neutral" text and of its main representatives, primarily Codex Vaticanus and to a lesser degree Codex Sinaiticus.

A certain significance must be ascribed to two further editions, which appeared just before and after the turn of the 19th century. The first was published by Bernhard Weiss 1894–1900. In his text-critical decisions, Weiss did not give primary attention to the history of the texts and manuscripts, but based his judgment in each textual problem upon consideration of subject matter and exegetical perspective. This procedure led Weiss to agree with Westcott and Hort—though starting from very different principles—that Codex Vaticanus must be the manuscript that is closest to the original text. After Weiss, Hermann von Soden once more embarked upon a large-scale text-critical experiment. In 1902 he began with the publication of his preliminary studies; his text with critical apparatus followed in 1913. It is still the major text-critical edition of the 20th century, with elaborate collection of witnesses and a new reconstruction of the histories of the manuscript families. His willful and not always reliable work—in fact his collations are riddled with mistakes—prevented this new edition from having the desired success. Von Soden also followed the principle that normally readings must be preferred if they appear in two of his three text families; this gave too much weight to the Byzantine family; as a result, his text resembles the Textus Receptus more than the text of his predecessors. Von Soden's work is further burdened by an entirely new system of sigla for the textual witnesses and their families, a system that is consistent but so complex that it is nearly inaccessible.

A number of scholars endeavored to publish new editions during the first half of the 20th century, though not one of these editions could match the erudition and comprehensive scholarly knowledge and judgment of either Tischendorf or Westcott and Hort. The greatest success and broadest influence fell to the edition of Eberhard Nestle, which was published for the first time in the year 1898 and has been republished since that time in twenty-five editions. Better and more useful than the other competing editions (Merk, Bover, Souter) and equipped with a marvelously rich text-critical apparatus printed in the smallest possible space, it is nevertheless not an independent work of critical scholarship, but a school edition that was originally produced according to a purely mechanical principle. Initially, Nestle used the following principle: the majority judgment of the three editions of Tischendorf, of Westcott and Hort, and of Weiss established the text to be printed. Since all three editors, however, prefer the readings of Codex Vaticanus or its closely related ally Codex Sinaiticus, the text printed in Nestle's edition primarily reflects the preferences of the great text-critical scholars of the second half of the

19th century. Thus it became the extension of the achievements of that period of scholarship and in some way a kind of new "Textus Receptus" for the 20th century. There is no doubt, however, that this text was vastly superior to the old Textus Receptus.

In subsequent editions of Nestle's text, the purely mechanical principle of the majority judgment of the three editors of the late 19th century was no longer used, as the discovery of more early papyri and further work of more recent scholarship strongly argued for a revision. Yet such improvements of the Nestle text were made ad hoc and unsystematically. A fresh systematic effort began with the work of the Institut für neutestamentliche Textforschung in Münster, Germany, under the direction of Kurt Aland and now Barbara Aland. This institute assembled and cataloged all available materials, that is, manuscripts of the Greek text and of all ancient versions, lectionaries, church father quotations, and also casual pieces of evidence such as ostraca and amulets. It also encouraged and directed investigations of particular aspects and needs of text-critical scholarship. The sheer quantity of the available evidence implies that such work could not be accomplished in just a few years. Kurt Aland had already participated in the supervision of the 23d edition of the Nestle text, published in 1957. On the basis of preliminary results of the Münster institute's work, however, subsequent editions tried to reflect more strongly the results and achievements of recent scholarship in the reconstruction of the most original text. In the most recent 26th edition, published in 1979, and in a revised form as the 27th edition of 1993 (still published before the death of Kurt Aland), Eberhard and Erwin Nestle are still mentioned, but the responsible editors are Barbara and Kurt Aland, Johannes Karavidopoulos, Carlo M. Martini, and Bruce M. Metzger. This is now a new text, no longer the text of the majority judgment of the scholars of the late 19th century, and it has to be judged on its own merits. The same efforts have also determined the edition that has been published and distributed by the United Bible Societies. Yet that edition, though presenting the same text, lists so few variants (although these few are supplied with the full manuscript evidence) that it is entirely useless for the serious student of the text of the New Testament.

Is this new, end-of-the-20th-century edition our future "Textus Receptus"? This is not the place to present an extensive critical evaluation of the principles that have guided the establishment of this new text. A few remarks, however, are in order. It is perhaps a minor concern that some of the textual decisions are simply not good and that the use of brackets, for cases where no definite decision has been made, is a bit excessive. Surprisingly the text presented here is not much different from the text of the manuscripts preferred by Tischendorf and Westcott and Hort. Its base is strengthened by the witness of the early papyri. It is, however, essentially still nothing else but the earliest attainable text of the Egyptian tradition, reflecting an archetype that was current in Egypt in the 3d century, occasionally corrected by evidence from the papyri and other text families. It is thus an eclectic text, that is, it is certainly a text that never actually existed in ancient times. The witness of the Byzantine majority text is rarely, perhaps too rarely, seriously considered—but nobody wants to reconstitute the old Textus Receptus. The major problem is the question of the Western family, the text that was the basis for Tatian's *Diatessaron,* for the Old Latin and the Old Syriac translation, and the text that has strongly influenced even many of the older Egyptian papyri. The witness of this text has been banned completely from the new Nestle-Aland edition, even in those instances in which Westcott and Hort had allowed its witness as valid in the "western noninterpolations." There is, however, plenty of evidence that this text existed in the 2d century, that is, prior to the establishment of the Egyptian text type, and indeed influenced the earlier Egyptian papyri. If the Nestle-Aland edition has been successful it is in the reconstruction of the best Egyptian archetype. It has indeed improved this Egyptian text by numerous suggestions of better readings. The contribution of the Western text, however, remains a problem. There is evidence that it existed earlier than the Egyptian text, but it was not permitted access to the court of justice in this new edition. Unless the problem of the Western text is solved, the original text of the New Testament, especially for the gospels, still remains elusive.

(g) Principles of New Testament Textual Criticism

In its historical development, the method of New Testament textual criticism has been in each instance a combination of various factors, such as the availability of manuscripts, scholars' dogmatic judgments, step-by-step development of basic canons of criticism (here biblical and classical textual criticisms influenced each other), statistical and mechanical procedures, reconstruction of families of manuscripts, and criticism of subject matter, which occasionally resulted in conjectural emendations. At the present state of scholarship there is an attempt to consider all these factors in a comprehensive way. Technical criteria, of course, are

Bibliography to §7.2g

Bruce M. Metzger, *A Textual Commentary on the Greek New Testament* (2d ed.; New York: United Bible Societies, 1994).

Ernest C. Colwell, *Studies in Methodology in Textual Criticism of the New Testament* (NTTS 9; Leiden: Brill, 1969).

Günther Zuntz, *The Text of the Epistles: A Disquisition upon the Corpus Paulinum* (London: Oxford University Press, 1953).

J. H. Greenlee, *Introduction to New Testament Textual Criticism* (rev. ed.; Peabody, MA: Hendrickson, 1995).

Kurt Aland, "Glosse, Interpolation, Redaktion und Komposition in der Sicht der neutestamentlichen Textkritik," in *Apophoreta,* 7–31.

Eldon J. Epp, "The Eclectic Method in New Testament Textual Criticism: Solution or Symptom?" *HTR* 69 (1976) 211–57.

Idem, "Textual Criticism in the Exegesis of the New Testament, with an Excursus on Canon," in Stanley E. Porter (ed.), *Handbook to Exegesis of the New Testament* (NTTS 25; Leiden: Brill, 1997) 45–97.

Idem, "The Multivalence of the Term 'Original Text' in New Testament Textual Criticism," *HTR* 92 (1999) 245–81.

Idem and Gordon D. Fee, *Studies in the Theory and Method of New Testament Textual Criticism* (SD 45; Grand Rapids, MI: Eerdmans, 1993).

John Strugnell, "A Plea for Conjectural Emendation in the New Testament," *CBQ* 36 (1974) 543–58.

Bart D. Ehrman, *The Orthodox Corruption of Scripture: The Effect of Early Christological Controversies on the Text of the New Testament* (New York: Oxford University Press, 1993).

Edward Hobbs, "Prologue: An Introduction to Methods of Textual Criticism," in Wendy Doniger O'Flaherty (ed.), *The Critical Study of Sacred Texts* (Berkeley Religious Studies Series, 1979) 1–27.

universally accepted. Mistakes that have been introduced in the process of copying manuscripts can be easily recognized (§7.2a). The ancient versions contain a number of mistakes that are detected without difficulty, such as misreading Greek words, mistaking one Greek word for another, or simple mistranslations. Deliberate corrections of scribes have also been frequently observed. In all these instances, the principle that the more difficult reading is to be preferred (*lectio difficilior placet*) has found common acceptance. Such decisions are not always purely mechanical, but involve matters relating to the interpretation of the meaning of the text. This is especially the case with respect to such scribal corrections as additions of complementary expressions, historical and geographical rectification, and dogmatic alterations.

It is necessary to base decisions upon insights into the history of the textual development; in the practice of textual criticism they play a considerable role. The value of such considerations, however, is limited, because of both the large number of manuscripts and the complexity of their transmission. The establishment of manuscript families has not resulted in a clean and consistent stemma, since the tracks of the manuscript transmission cross each other frequently. Westcott and Hort had still believed that clearly distinguishable text types could be identified. Indeed, such identifications are valuable for the time of the 4th century onward. The trouble is that the earlier papyri often present what from the perspective of the later families must appear as a "mixed" text. This observation leads to the conclusion that the archetypes of the later manuscript families were not created until the 4th century and that they are the result of "editions," all of which were only made after the Great Persecution at the beginning of the 4th century, when a large number of manuscripts was systematically confiscated by the authorities of the Roman state and burned. This limited the textual basis for the production of new manuscripts, which were greatly in demand at the time of Constantine and his successors in the later decades of the 4th century. All that is known to us about the Greek text of the period before the 4th century comes from the papyri, all of which have come from Egypt, that is, from one single geographical area. What survived in the West, where the persecution was less severe, is mostly preserved in Latin translations—and their text reflects the Western text, not the Alexandrian text that is presented by the great Greek uncials of the 4th century.

Classical textual criticism of Greek and Latin authors has long since recognized that the establishment of families or of a stemma leads back to the earliest edition(s), but not to the autograph itself. In the case of more than one archetype, each of the archetypes/editions may have preserved some elements of earlier texts extant in unedited copies of manuscripts, which ultimately depended upon the autographs or, in the case of the Pauline letters, upon the publication of these letters by the churches that had received them. Thus the ultimate and most difficult task of New Testament textual criticism is the description of the history of the text in the 1st, 2d, and 3d centuries. For the latter, the Egyptian papyri provide some valuable evidence, but only for that particular geographical area. For the 2d century, however, there are only indirect witnesses, such as quotations in Justin Martyr, Irenaeus, and Clement of Alexandria, the Old Latin and the Old Syriac translations, and the evidence for Marcion's edition of the New Testament and Tatian's *Diatessaron* (and the reconstruction of Tatian's and Marcion's texts are the most complex tasks of textual criticism!). Textual criticism must therefore establish criteria that help to understand this early, uncontrolled, and precanonical period of the transmission. Here are some of the principles of this most significant step in the search for the earliest text of the New Testament:

1. It must always be kept in mind that even the best possible decision on the basis of the available manuscript evidence and the most sound identification of the oldest archetype of a manuscript family does not give us information about the textual transmission during the first fifty to one hundred years of the transmission of a text.

2. The best attainable manuscript reading may still be a scribe's reconstruction of a corrupt text, that is, of corruptions that are most likely to have happened during the earliest period of the transmission of the text, especially at a time when a writing did not yet enjoy the protection of canonical status.

3. Archetypes of the textual families are represented by extant ancient manuscripts only for a limited geographical area, namely, Egypt, while the reconstruction of the archetypes of geographically more distant witnesses, such as ancient translations, is burdened with numerous factors of uncertainty.

4. One must be prepared to recognize a potentially valuable ancient reading in manuscripts and translations that come from the marginal areas of the textual transmission. The agreements, for example, of the Old Latin and the Old Syriac translations must be recognized as a witness of readings that existed as early as the 2d century.

5. A comparatively late manuscript may have preserved valuable ancient readings, while even the oldest manuscripts may contain readings that have little value in the reconstruction of the earliest text. A good example for this is the minuscule 1739 from the 10th century, with a text that is almost identical to that of the oldest Papyrus of the Pauline epistles from ca. 200 CE ($\mathfrak{P}^{46}$). Even the judgment about the general character of a later manuscript does not necessarily determine the value of all of its variants.

6. Quotations by the church fathers are an important guide to the date and location of the texts that were actually in use during the early centuries.

7. Major uncertainties and a wide spread of variants in the extant witnesses can point to an ancient corruption of a text from a time before any of the extant manuscripts were written. It is quite possible in such instances that all variant readings are different attempts of correcting a corrupt text and that no single manuscript has preserved the original text.

8. If it is impossible to reconstruct a sensible text with the help of all available witnesses, hypothetical reconstruction of the earliest text (conjecture) cannot be excluded. Such a reconstruction, however, requires not only a skillful handling of the methods of textual criticism, but also an exact knowledge of the language, terminology, and theology of the author in question. Textual criticism and criticism of subject matter are inseparable parts of scholarship.

9. The notion of an "original" text is problematic in itself. Paul may have issued his Epistle to the Romans in several forms, one designated to be sent to Rome, a second form as a missive to Ephesus, and a third version for more general distribution.

2 Corinthians is a compilation of four or five letters of Paul. The earliest text of the Gospel of Mark used by Matthew and Luke was not identical with the text later appearing in the earliest manuscripts as Mark's Gospel.

If all that has been said suggests that the problems of the reconstruction of an "original" text of the New Testament writings is a daunting and possibly impossible task, it must be added that only a very small portion of the New Testament text is subject to doubt. There is, on the whole, a high degree of certainty with respect to the earliest texts. As an important discipline of biblical scholarship, however, textual criticism has to be reapplied constantly, even in those instances in which a solution seems to have been reached. Every printed edition of the Greek New Testament is a hypothetical reconstruction. Moreover, variant readings demonstrate in many instances how certain passages have been interpreted in the earliest period of the church and often point to difficulties and problems in the understanding of a text. Thus textual criticism is often the first step in discovering and solving issues in the interpretation of the New Testament writings.

3. SOURCE CRITICISM

(a) General Remarks

Only a small portion of the writings of the New Testament and other early Christian literature can be viewed as the creative product of an individual author. Rather, the use of written sources was widespread and determined the content and form of such writings to a large degree. Furthermore, many books are not preserved in their original form, but are in their extant form the product of secondary redaction, editions, and compilations. This confronts the student of the New Testament with multiple problems of source criticism. The following discussion will sketch several fundamental and characteristic problems of this kind. Fuller treatments can be found in the books dealing with the history of early Christian literature, which are listed in the bibliography to this chapter.

(b) The "Synoptic Problem" and the Sources of the Gospels

"Synoptic gospels" is the designation for the first three gospels of the New Testament, Matthew, Mark, and Luke. It has long been noticed that these three gospels present parallel materials in a similar framework and often in the same sequence of individual pericopes. Moreover, the wording of the respective parallel passages in any two or three of these gospels is often nearly the same or so closely related that some kind of literary relationship must be assumed. On the other hand, if one compares the Gospel of John with these three gospels, there are, to be sure, certain similarities but, with the exception of the passion narrative, the wording and sequence of the materials are quite different, and large portions of the materials of the Fourth gospel, especially Jesus' long discourses, have no parallels in the Synoptic Gospels. It is rather easy to print the three first gospels side by side to demonstrate their sequences of parallel pericopes, while the Fourth Gospel can be incorporated into such a "synopsis" only with difficulty.

This close relationship of the Synoptic Gospels has engendered a series of hypotheses about their literary relationship. The oldest hypothesis, which at the same time agrees with a venerable ecclesiastical tradition, argued for the priority of Matthew. In this case, Mark is seen as a condensation of Matthew, and Luke as a later composition on the basis of both Matthew and Mark. The assumption of Matthean priority was presented in a modified form at the end of the 18th century by Johann Jacob Griesbach. According to Griesbach, Matthew was first used by Luke, while Mark is seen as an abbreviation of both Matthew and Luke. This "Griesbach hypothesis" is of interest only insofar as it has been revived recently

Bibliography to §7.3b: Texts

Albert Huck, *Synopsis of the First Three Gospels with the Addition of the Johannine Parallels* (rev. ed. by Heinrich Greeven; Tübingen: Mohr/Siebeck, 1981).

Kurt Aland (ed.), *Synopsis Quattuor Evangeliorum* (10th ed.; Stuttgart: Württembergische Bibelanstalt, 1978).

Idem (ed.), *Synopsis of the Four Gospels: Greek-English Edition of the Synopsis Quattuor Evangeliorum with the Text of the Revised Standard Version* (United Bible Societies, 1972 and later editions).

M.-É. Boismard and A. Lamouille, *Synopsis Graeca Quattuor Evangeliorum* (Leuven: Peeters, 1986).

Burton H. Throckmorton (ed.), *Gospel Parallels: A Comparison of the Synoptic Gospels: With Alternative Readings from the Manuscripts and Non-Canonical Parallels* (5th ed.; Nashville, TN: Nelson, 1992).

John S. Kloppenborg, *Q Parallels: Synopsis, Critical Notes & Concordance* (F&F; Sonoma, CA: Polebridge, 1988).

Robert W. Funk (ed.), *New Gospel Parallels* (2 vols.; Philadelphia: Fortress, 1985).

James M. Robinson, Paul Hoffmann, and John S. Kloppenborg (eds.), *The Critical Edition of Q: A Synopsis* (Leuven: Peeters, and Minneapolis: Fortress, 2000).

Bibliography to §7.3b: Studies

Heinrich-Julius Holtzmann, *Die synoptischen Evangelien: Ihr Ursprung und ihr geschichtlicher Charakter* (Leipzig: Engelmann, 1863). The classic presentation of the two-source hypothesis.

Julius Wellhausen, *Einleitung in die drei ersten Evangelien* (2d ed.; Berlin: Reimer, 1911; reprinted in idem, *Evangelienkommentare*; Berlin: de Gruyter, 1987).

B. H. Streeter, *The Four Gospels: A Study of Origins* (London: Macmillan, 1924 and reprints). The most detailed reconstruction of the sources for the Synoptic Gospels.

William R. Farmer, *The Synoptic Problem* (Dillsboro, NC: Western North Carolina Press, 1976). Farmer questions the two-source hypothesis.

James M. Robinson, "LOGOI SOPHON: On the Gattung of Q," in idem and Koester, *Trajectories*, 71–113.

James M. Robinson, Paul Hoffmann, and John S. Kloppenborg (eds.), *Documenta Q: Reconstruction of Q through Two Centuries of Gospel Research Excerpted, Sorted and Evaluated* (Leuven: Peeters, 1996–).

John S. Kloppenborg, *The Formation of Q: Trajectories in Ancient Wisdom Collections* (Studies in Antiquity and Christianity; Philadelphia: Fortress, 1987).

Koester, *Ancient Christian Gospels*, 128–72 (on Q) and 216–39 (on the passion narrative).

Bibliography to §7.3b: Bibliography and History of Scholarship

T. R. W. Longstaff and P. A. Thomas, *The Synoptic Problem: A Bibliography, 1716–1988* (New Gospel Studies 4; Macon, GA: Mercer University Press, 1988).

Arthur J. Bellinzoni with J. B. Tyson and W. O. Walker (eds.), *The Two-Source Hypothesis: A Critical Appraisal* (Macon, GA: Mercer University Press, 1985).

by the American scholar William R. Farmer and his associates, albeit without wider acceptance. A second solution is the "primitive gospel hypothesis," proposing that there was originally one single all-inclusive gospel writing, once available to all the authors of our gospels but now lost, from which the extant gospels, including the Gospel of John (!), made excerpts according to the needs of their communities. The third attempt at an explanation of the synoptic problem, known as the "fragment hypothesis," was first proposed by Friedrich Schleiermacher. He argued that it is sufficient to think that the oldest form of gospel writings consisted of several fragmentary collections of the materials about Jesus. These fragments must have been different, depending upon the interest of the collector, one person being interested only in Jesus' sayings, another only in Jesus' miracle stories. It is evident that Schleiermacher's hypothesis is in fact a kind of two-source hypothesis—one source for sayings, another for the stories about Jesus—though he does not discuss the possible dependence of any of the synoptic Gospels upon another.

The studies of Christian Gottlob Wilke and Christian Hermann Weisse, both published in the year 1838, argued persuasively that the Gospel of Mark must have been the oldest gospel and that it was used by both Matthew and Luke. It was shortly thereafter that Heinrich Julius Holtzmann further developed this proposal by demonstrating that Matthew and Luke must have used a second common source, the so-called *Synoptic Sayings Source* (its siglum is "Q" from the German word *Quelle;* see §10.1a [1]). While the later two gospels drew their framework as well as most of the materials about Jesus' life and activities from the Gospel of Mark, the *Sayings Source* provided them with Jesus' sayings, which were then composed into speeches of Jesus in different ways. This solution of the synoptic problem, known as the "two-source-hypothesis," is now widely accepted, though some objections are still being raised, especially with respect to the actual existence of the *Sayings Source (Q).*

The arguments in favor of the two-source hypothesis have shifted somewhat since its inception. The strongest argument was proposed at the very beginning of the discovery of Markan priority, namely, that Matthew and Luke agree in the sequence of their pericopes only in those instances in which Mark presents the same sequence. This argument is still valid. However, it was originally connected with the assumption that this sequence corresponded to the actual course of events in the ministry of Jesus, thus making the Gospel of Mark the oldest witness for the life of the historical Jesus. This confidence was shattered when, shortly after the beginning of the 20th century, William Wrede demonstrated that Mark's sequence of events in the ministry of Jesus has little relationship with the historical ministry of Jesus but is, in fact, a theological construct by the author of the oldest gospel. This strengthened the arguments for the priority of Mark. Whatever knowledge, if any, Matthew and Luke may have had of the ministry of the historical Jesus, they followed in their compositions the artificial construction of the sequence of events in Mark's Gospel; this reinforces the arguments for their literary dependence upon Mark.

More difficult than the demonstration of Markan priority is the reconstruction of the second common source of Matthew and Luke, the *Sayings Gospel Q.* In some instances the sayings common to both of these gospels not only occur in a similar sequence, but they also exhibit close detailed resemblances in composition and wording. This is especially evident in the parallel portions of the Sermon on the Mount (Matthew 5–7) and the Sermon on the Plain (Luke 6). In other portions of the common sayings, however, one can observe striking differences in both wording and sequence. One has to assume therefore that "Q" was indeed the written source, but that either Matthew or Luke or both also used considerable freedom in their use of this source—or that they each had access to different stages of its development. However, the International Project on Q, guided by the American scholar James M. Robinson, recently successfully completed the reconstruction of the Greek text of this second source used by Matthew and Luke. The work of this international group of scholars provides ample evidence for the existence of this second source of Matthew and Luke as a Greek text—even if some of its materials were originally translated from Aramaic.

The recognition that Matthew and Luke employed the same two written sources, the Gospel of Mark and the *Sayings Gospel Q,* does not solve all the problems of the sources of Matthew and Luke. Apart from their common materials drawn from these two sources, Matthew and Luke both present other discrete materials. Among these are the infancy narratives of Matthew 1–2 and of Luke 1–2, a number of parables in Matthew 13 and special apocalyptic materials in Matthew 24–25, and in Luke especially much of the material incorporated into the travel narrative of Luke 9:51–18:15. This has prompted the suggestion of two additional sources, one for the special materials of Matthew (designated as "M"), the other for the special materials of Luke (designated as "L"). As far as the latter is concerned, there seems to be widespread agreement, although determining the extent of this source is more difficult (did it contain only the special Lukan materials or also pericopes that parallel sections of the Gospel of Mark?). In any case, refining source theories in terms of more and more complex detail reveals the limits of their usefulness. Neither in the formative stage of the gospels nor in their later development is it possible to explain all features exclusively with the assumption of written sources. Rather, the free and mostly oral tradition, which stood at the very beginning of the process of transmission, continued well into the 2d century and beyond, and was thus a constant resource for the growth of the written gospels.

Important for the establishment of the hypothesis of the *Sayings Gospel Q* is not only the judgment that Matthew and Luke must have used some written materials, but also the determination of its genre and its literary character. This has been done successfully by James M. Robinson, who recognized that the genre of this writing corresponds to a type of Jewish literature that he has called *Logoi Sophon,* "Words of the Wise." John S. Kloppenborg has further elaborated Robinson's suggestion in his comparison of Q with other ancient wisdom literature. Another representative of this genre in early Christian literature is the *Gospel of Thomas* (§10.1b [1]). The source for Luke's special materials can perhaps also be classified as a book of this genre.

The literary genre of another early written source for the extant gospels of the New Testament can also be recognized: one or several collections of miracle stories of Jesus, which were used by the Gospel of Mark and also by the Gospel of John. This type of literature enumerates the great deeds of a god, hero, or famous person; it must be properly designated as an "aretalogy" (§3.4d). The content and

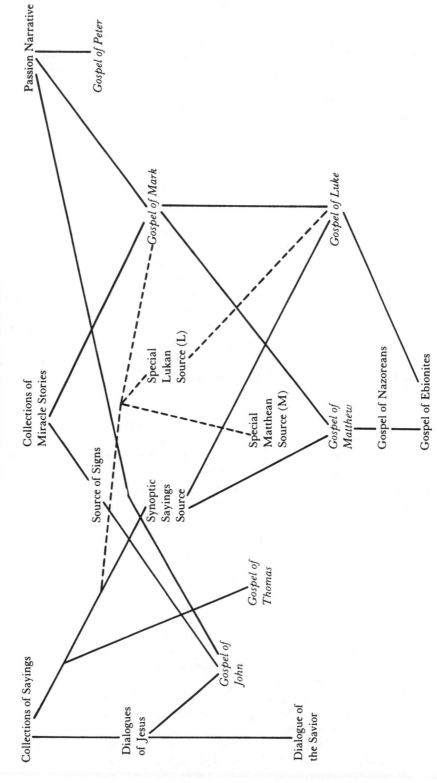

THE SOURCES OF THE GOSPELS

sequence of several miracle stories in Mark and John share enough in common to allow the conclusion that they used different versions of the same literary collection. This source, which in the Gospel of John is called the *Semeia Source* ("Source of Signs"; §10.3a [5]), presents Jesus as a healer endowed with miraculous powers, who can control even the forces of nature (see the narratives about the Stilling of the Tempest, the Walking on the Sea, and the Feeding of the Multitudes).

A third written source shared by the gospels of the New Testament is the passion narrative. Different versions of this source were used by the Gospel of Mark, the Gospel of John, and the *Gospel of Peter* (§10.2a [2]); Matthew's and Luke's passion narratives are on the whole dependent on the Gospel of Mark. The literary genre of the passion is the story of the suffering righteous, which occurs repeatedly in the literature of Israel in the period of the Second Temple and is ultimately based upon the "suffering servant" of Deutero-Isaiah.

The Gospels of the New Testament are thus based upon three different older Christian compositions, each of which belongs to a special literary genre. It is quite possible that other gospel materials also derive from written sources; however, those sources are not "literature," but casual compositions of oral materials in written form, such as collections of parables (Mark 4), apocalyptic materials (Mark 13; another collection of such apocalyptic sayings is preserved in *Didache* 16), and strings of catechetical instructions. In all instances, it is necessary to recognize written sources in order to assess the redactional contributions of the authors of the gospels. Ultimately, however, all materials preserved in the gospels of the New Testament derive from oral traditions (see below on Form Criticism, §7.4a).

(c) The Acts of the Apostles

Luke, the author of the third gospel of the New Testament and of the Acts of the Apostles, belongs to the third generation of Christianity (§12.3a). He was hardly an eyewitness of the events he describes and certainly not a travel companion and fellow-worker of the apostle Paul. There is no question that he was dependent upon written sources—primarily Mark and Q—for his composition of the Gospel; but

Bibliography to §7.3c (see also under §12.3a.3)

Henry J. Cadbury, *The Making of Luke-Acts* (2d ed.; London: SPCK, 1958).

Idem et al., "The Composition and Purpose of Acts," in Foakes Jackson and Lake, *Beginnings,* 2. 3–204.

Ernst Haenchen, "Das 'Wir' in der Apostelgeschichte und das Itinerar," in idem, *Gott und Mensch,* 227–64.

Idem, "Tradition und Komposition in der Apostelgeschichte," in idem, *Gott und Mensch,* 202–26.

Idem, "The Book of Acts as Source Material for the History of Early Christianity," in Leander Keck and J. Louis Martyn (eds.), *Studies in Luke-Acts: Essays Presented in Honor of Paul Schubert* (Nashville, TN: Abingdon, 1966) 258–78.

Peter M. Head, "Acts and the Problem of Its Texts," in B. W. Winter and A. D. Clark (eds.), *The Book of Acts in Its Ancient Literary Setting,* vol. 1: *The Book of Acts in Its First Century Setting* (Grand Rapids, MI: Eerdmans, 1993) 415-44.

J. Wehnert, *Die Wir-Passagen der Apostelgeschichte: Ein lukanisches Stilmittel aus jüdischer Tradition* (Göttinger Theologische Arbeiten 40; Göttingen: Vandenhoeck & Ruprecht, 1998).

also for the second part of his work, the Acts of the Apostles, Luke had to rely on sources. While the sources used for the composition of Luke's Gospel are fairly clear, the sources used in the Book of Acts remain a conundrum. Scholars have tried to identify two different written sources, an "Antiochian Source" for the materials in the first part of the book (Acts 6–12 and 15), and a travel narrative, called the "We Source," for the second part (Acts 16–28). Both theories, however, are burdened with considerable difficulties. A convincing explanation of the literary genre of an assumed Antiochian Source has never been found. It would have included miracle stories as well as archival information, a martyrdom report (the martyrdom of Stephen), and even some speeches of apostles. The combination of all these elements can better be explained as the result of the literary efforts of Luke, who connected partly legendary traditions with some authentic documents, adding speeches at appropriate occasions and thus creating a coherent narrative. The search for an Antiochian source appears therefore as a futile effort, though no one denies that the Book of Acts preserves some historical information. Such information would include, for example, the list of the Hellenistic "deacons" (Acts 6), the martyrdom of Stephen (Acts 7), the founding of the Antiochian church (Acts 11), and the list of the prophets and teachers at Antioch (Acts 13). Also the We Source is problematic because the "we-style" of the narrative appears in passages that are evidently the composition of the author of the Book of Acts; this style alone can therefore not be used as a criterion of distinction between source and redaction. On the other hand, the often unexpected appearance of the first person plural ("we") in reports about Paul's travels allows the conclusion that the author of Acts indeed used an itinerary or travel report, which a travel companion of Paul may have written. At the same time it appears that the author of Acts also employed "we" as a stylistic device in sections for which he certainly did not use any sources whatsoever; this is most evident in his narrative of the sea travel and shipwreck (Acts 27–28).

Acts presents still another literary problem insofar as it is transmitted in two versions that frequently differ from each other. The text that is usually printed in critical editions of the New Testament is that of the Egyptian uncials from the 4th century (‪א‬, B, etc.), whose readings are largely identical with those of the Alexandrian church fathers. Another version is found in the representatives of the Western Text (Codex D and the Old Latin translation) with readings that are supported by the Latin church fathers. This version contains numerous special readings and passages that appear to be "additions." Among these is the famous addition of the Golden Rule to the Apostolic Decree in Acts 15:29. Whether or not one considers the Western text of Acts as secondary, there is no question that it existed already in the 2d century. An interesting suggestion sees this version as either the original text of Acts or as the author's second edition of the book. This could explain the fact that the Western text presents some valuable information that is missing in the Alexandrian version, such as information about places (Acts 12:10; 20:15) and times (Acts 19:9; 27:5). At the same time, other Western readings must be secondary, especially the attempts to adjust contradictions and to enhance the anti-Judaic tendencies of the book. It is therefore more likely that the Western text of Acts is a second edition (by Luke himself?), but not a degeneration of the original text.

The problem of the sources of the Book of Acts is closely related to the question of its literary genre. Many scholars assume that Luke intended to produce a historical work and that his use of sources can be compared with analogous procedures in ancient writers of history. Typical for such Greek and Latin historical works is, for example, the composition of speeches, which authors inserted into their sources in order to highlight particular situations and to underline their significance. In this respect, Acts can be judged to employ a literary device of the historian. Also the conception of the whole book, which describes a historical development that begins in Jerusalem and ends in Rome could be classified as typical for an ancient history (§3.4c). On the other hand, the use of numerous legendary materials and miraculous stories, often even enhanced by the author, would lead to the conclusion that Luke was a very uncritical historian, even measured by the standards of antiquity. Only such information as the report about the beginnings of the church of Antioch (Acts 11) is intrinsically suitable to the intention of historiography. The rich historical information about Paul's travels is also suitable, but a description of Paul's organizational work in the founding of churches is lacking and the presentation of the missionary's activity consists mainly of miraculous stories.

These observations have resulted in the suggestion that Luke's literary model was not the writing of history but the ancient romance (§3.4e). This hypothesis has been reinforced by the lengthy narrative of the shipwreck (Acts 27–28). The Acts of the Apostles would thus be closely related to the apocryphal acts, of which the older examples were written not long after Luke's own work (see, for example, the *Acts of Peter,* the *Acts of Paul* [§12.3b], and the *Acts of John* [§10.3d]). These apocryphal acts also employ the travel motif, make uncritical use of a rich tradition of stories of miraculous deeds and events, insert frequent speeches by the apostles (which reflect the practice of missionary preaching of the times of the composition of these books), and are almost completely devoid of historically valuable information. As appealing as this hypothesis is, it neglects the fact that the Book of Acts is but one half of a major work that comprises the Gospel of Luke as well as the Acts of the Apostles.

A solution may have been found in the recent Harvard dissertation of Marianne Bonz, who argues convincingly that the literary model for Luke's work was the ancient Greek epic that had been recreated in the Latin work of Virgil's *Aeneid.* The epic is a political and highly charged endeavor to provide a foundation story for a community. As Virgil's *Aeneid* is connected to the legendary events of ancient Troy, from where its hero, Aeneas, originates, so is the hero of Luke-Acts, Jesus of Nazareth, presented as the heir of Israel's ancient prophecies. Divine providence guides the course of his activity and the activity of the apostles in a story that, similar to the story of Aeneas, begins in an ancient country of the East and ends gloriously in Rome. The course of events demonstrates divine legitimation for a new nation that, in spite of adversity, is destined to set the stage for a new era of history that is seen as the eschatological fulfillment of ancient prophecy. In the composition of an epic, the inclusion of legendary materials is legitimate because it highlights the divine sanction of the course of events. If epic is indeed the literary model for Luke, it is possible to assess the entirety of Luke's work as a self-contained unit, for which the author was able to employ his sources and materials regardless of their specific value as possibly reliable historical information. (For further discussion of Luke's work, see §12.3a.)

(d) Composition and Literary Character of the Letters of Paul

Only the certainly genuine letters of Paul will be discussed here, namely, Romans, 1 and 2 Corinthians, Galatians, Philippians, 1 Thessalonians, and Philemon (on the individual deutero-Pauline epistles, see §§12.1a; 12.2a, b, g). Their literary unity has been questioned with more or less convincing arguments. In the cases of 1 Corinthians, Galatians, and 1 Thessalonians, division hypotheses have not been persuasive, but for Romans, 2 Corinthians, and Philippians it can be assumed with a high degree of probability that these three letters in their extant form are the result of the combination of several shorter letters.

Chapter 16 of the Epistle to the Romans was probably not a part of the letter that Paul sent to Rome from Corinth. In this chapter Paul sends greetings to Priska and Aquila (Rom 16:4), his associates from Corinth who had gone to Ephesus according to 1 Cor 16:19 and Acts 18:18; a greeting follows to Epainetos, whom Paul calls the first-born of Asia (Rom 16:5). Moreover, Romans 16:6–15 contains greetings to as many as twenty-three fellow workers and personal acquaintances of Paul, who must be located in Ephesus rather than in Rome, unless one wants to assume that there was a mass immigration of Ephesian Christians to Rome within less than a year after Paul's departure from that city. Romans 16 therefore is most likely a part of a letter that was originally written to Ephesus and not part of the letter to the Romans. It was written primarily in order to recommend Phoebe, a minister and patron or president of the church of Kenchreae, to the Ephesian community, a community that Paul knew very well—not to the Roman church, with which Paul was not acquainted personally. That Romans 16 was not yet a part of some early edition of the letters of Paul is confirmed by some interesting manuscript evidence: The (secondary!) final doxology of the Epistle to the Romans, Rom 16:25–27, appears after Rom 15:33 in the oldest preserved manuscript of the letters of Paul, $\mathfrak{P}^{46}$, that is, there was an early edition of these letters, in which Romans 16 was not

---

Bibliography to §7.3d

Dieter Georgi, *The Opponents of Paul in Second Corinthians: A Study in Religious Propaganda in Late Antiquity* (Philadelphia: Fortress, 1986).

Joseph A. Fitzmyer, "Qumran and the Interpolated Paragraph in 2 Cor 6:14–7:1," *CBQ* 23 (1961) 271–80.

Hans Dieter Betz, "2 Cor 6:14–7:1: An Anti-Pauline Fragment?" *JBL* 92 (1973) 88–108.

Günther Bornkamm, "Der Philipperbrief als paulinische Briefsammlung," in idem, *Geschichte und Glaube 2* (München: Kaiser, 1971) 195–205.

B. D. Rathjen, "The Three Letters of Paul to the Philippians," *NTS* 6 (1959/1960) 167–73.

Johannes Müller-Bardorff, "Zur Frage der literarischen Einheit des Philipperbriefes," *WZ(J)* 7 (1957/58) GS 4. 591–604.

Philip Sellew, "*Laodiceans* and the Philippians Fragments Hypothesis," *HTR* 87 (1994) 17–28.

Lukas Bormann, *Philippi: Stadt und Christengemeinde zur Zeit des Paulus* (NovTSup 78; Leiden: Brill 1995).

Walther Schmithals, "Die Korintherbriefe als Briefsammlung," *ZNW* 64 (1973) 263–88.

Idem, "Erwägungen zur Literarkritik der Paulusbriefe," *ZNW* 87 (1996) 51–82.

attached to the Epistle to the Romans. That the majority tradition of the Pauline letters includes the 16th chapter should not come as a surprise if the edition of Paul's letters was not produced in Rome but in the East, most likely in Ephesus; the Ephesian editor used the manuscript available to him, which was the copy of the Letter to the Romans that Paul had sent to Ephesus together with an additional letter to Ephesus, namely Romans 16. Naturally, the Ephesian editor would include that letter in his edition.

2 Corinthians is the most heterogeneous of all letters of Paul. Although its individual parts are thematically related, several breaks in continuity cannot be explained as leaps in Paul's thought. The initial report about the situation in which Paul found himself after he had left Ephesus (2 Corinthians 1:1–2:13) is suddenly interrupted in 2 Cor 2:13 and not continued until 2 Cor 7:5. Chapters 8 and 9 both have a new beginning, and though they treat a similar topic, they are addressed to different communities. Altogether surprising is the last part, 2 Corinthians 10–13 with its harsh polemics—after all, Paul had already stated in chapter 7 that he was reconciled! The most probable solution is the thesis that 2 Corinthians as it is now preserved in the manuscript tradition of the New Testament is a composition of five letters that Paul had sent to Corinth and that it was published by the Corinthian church only after the first corpus of the Pauline letters had been circulated—quotations from 2 Corinthians are missing in *1 Clement* (§12.2e) and in the letters of Ignatius of Antioch (§12.2d), the earliest witnesses to the Pauline corpus. When the church of Corinth published several smaller letters in the form of the extant letter called 2 Corinthians, it preserved only the body of these five letters and dropped almost all of the prescripts and final greetings, except for those which now provide the framework of the composite letter. The first of these five letters is preserved in 2 Corinthians 2:14–6:13 and 7:2–4. It is Paul's first reaction, written in Ephesus, to the information received from Corinth that foreign apostles had come to Corinth and had questioned the legitimacy of his ministry. The second letter, 2 Corinthians 10–13, presupposes that Paul had meanwhile made a personal but ineffectual visit to Corinth that did not solve the conflict. He then sent his fellow worker Titus to Corinth, who intervened on his behalf. Only then did it become possible to reestablish good terms with the Corinthian church. Paul, having left Ephesus and already on his way to Corinth, wrote 2 Corinthians 1:1–2:13 and 7:5–16 from Macedonia as soon as Titus had brought him the good news of the reconciliation. Together with this third letter, he sent two additional letters concerning the collection for Jerusalem; one of these was addressed to the Corinthians and is now preserved as 2 Corinthians 8; the second, addressed to the churches of Achaea, appears in 2 Corinthians 9.

Philippians also appears to be a compilation of several smaller letters of Paul. The first of these letters is now preserved in Philippians 4:10–20; it is a note of acknowledgment that Paul had sent to Philippi when he had received a gift from that church, delivered to him through Epaphroditus. The second letter, Philippians 1:1–3:1, must have been written somewhat later because it presupposes a different situation: Paul was still imprisoned in Ephesus, but Epaphroditus had meanwhile been seriously ill; now recovered, he would serve as the messenger of the second letter (Phil 2:25–30). Moreover, Paul indicates that he intends to send Timothy to

Philippi (Phil 2:19–24). A third letter, Philippians 3:2–4:1, belongs to Paul's controversies with Jewish-Christian missionaries. What is preserved is only a fragment, but the abrupt transition from Phil 3:1 to 3:2 indicates that these verses belong to a letter that Paul sent to Philippi at some other time. It remains uncertain, to which letter the remaining pieces Phil 4:2–3, 4–7, and 8–9 should be assigned. All three letters were apparently sent from Ephesus (on the Ephesian imprisonment of Paul, see §9.3e).

If the letters of Paul are thus not preserved as direct copies of the autographs, but as later editions, it is not surprising that they also contain a number of editorial additions, which characteristically occur at the seams of composite letters. Such an addition is clearly recognizable both by its topic and by its non-Pauline terminology in 2 Cor 6:14–7:1. Another addition is the doxology at the end of the Epistle to the Romans (Rom 16:25–27; after Rom 15:33 in $\mathfrak{P}^{46}$); its vocabulary is closely related to that of the Pastoral Epistles. Also closely related to the Pastoral Epistles is the interpolation 1 Cor 14:33b–35, which forbids women to speak in the assembly of the congregations (cf. 1 Tim 2:9–15)—contrary to the clearly established leadership of women in the churches at the time of Paul. Some other sections of the Pauline letters have also been considered as spurious, such as Rom 13:1–7, which reflects the spirit of the political parenesis of Hellenistic diaspora Judaism, and—much more likely—the anti-Judaic polemic of 1 Thess 2:13–16. Smaller interpolations cannot always be determined with certainty, but cannot be excluded a priori. It seems likely, for example, that Rom 2:16, which shares the phrase "according to my gospel" with Rom 16:25 and 2 Tim 2:8 (both certainly not Pauline), was added by a later editor.

The observation that some Pauline letters are the result of the compilation of several smaller letters shows that only two of the original fourteen letters of Paul are at all extensive: Romans (chaps. 1–15) and 1 Corinthians. All other letters do not belong to the category of more voluminous didactic writings; they are occasional writings, composed for specific situations. Numerous letters of this kind have been preserved from antiquity, such as those among the Oxyrhynchus Papyri or in the published correspondence of the younger Pliny. The church-political interest is the primary concern of Paul's letters: they are written in order to advance the organization of the congregations and their preservation, designed to resolve problems that threaten the existence of these communities, and composed to promote the collection of money for the church of Jerusalem. Such interests are clear in the letter of recommendation for Phoebe (Romans 16) and for Onesimus (Philemon), in letters of credence (2 Corinthians 8 and 9), notes of acknowledgment (Philippians 4:10–20), but also in the polemical letters (Galatians, Philippians 3; 2 Corinthians 2:14–6:13). Because the person of the apostle plays a significant role in questions of church policy and in polemical situations, two elements are of primary significance in the letters: the personal apology (see especially Galatians 1–2; 2 Corinthians 10–13; Philippians 3) and the travel plans of the apostle (1 Corinthians 16; 2 Corinthians 1:1–2:13 and 7:5–16). The same elements also determine the more extensive letters of Paul. The foremost motive of Romans 1–15 is Paul's intention to travel to the West. Paul was therefore obliged to direct an explanation, or apology, of his message to the church of Rome, which grew into a major presentation of his theology. In 1 Corinthians, the main motif throughout is the organization of the community and the regulation of Christian life; thus the letter became a church order, in which the various questions that had been addressed to Paul were treated point by point. Whatever the letter presents in terms of theological arguments is part of the rhetoric through which Paul tries to convince his readers.

The formal schema of the Pauline letter corresponds to the Jewish letter formula, but also contains elements of the Greek letter—indeed even of the official letter form of the Greco-Roman world. The development of the Pauline letter also reveals some experimentation in the process of creating a new form that would be appropriate for the apostolic letter as a tool of community organization—and it was indeed copied by later Christian letter writers, in the deutero-Pauline letters as well as in 1 Peter, *1 Clement*, and the letters of Ignatius of Antioch. The prescript carries the name of the sender, the addressee, and the greeting as a separate sentence according to the Jewish form. The wish of peace also reflects the Jewish letter formula; thus the greeting is "grace and peace" (χάρις καὶ εἰρήνη) rather than the Greek "greetings" (χαίρειν). The proem follows instantly upon this prescript and usually features an extensive thanksgiving, speaking about the status of the church, its relationship to the apostle, but also about the personal experiences of the apostle and his present situation; but it could also take the form of an eruption of angry surprise (Gal 1:6–9). The body of the letter may be primarily parenesis (1 Thess 4:1–12; Romans 12–14; 1 Corinthians 5–14), but it could also be—as in Galatians and 1 Thessalonians (here the interpolation of 2:13–16 gives the false impression that the thanksgiving proem is still continuing)—an apology of the apostle's past or present behavior and plans (1 Thessalonians 2:1–3:13; Galatians 1:10–2:21). The final part of the body is often an eschatological section (1 Thess 4:13–5:11; 1 Corinthians 15). The conclusion is formed by the greetings, in which individual persons are specially named. The frequent and striking peculiarities in the form of the Pauline letter can be explained as modifications of this basic schema. In Romans, the theological reflections that precede the parenesis (Romans 1:18–11:36) are elaborations of the thesis that Paul had proposed in the proem. The discussion of the travel plans can also be resumed in the context of the final greetings (Rom 15:14–23; 1 Corinthians 16). Only a portion of some of the letters is preserved, of course. Of the letter of recommendation for Phoebe (Romans 16) only the body, that is, the actual recommendation (Rom 16:1–2) and the greetings (Rom 16:3–23), are extant. Of the letter of the acknowledgment, Phil 4:10–20, only the body proper has survived. This is also the case with the two letters of credence concerning the collection for Jerusalem in 2 Corinthians 8 and 9.

The form of the Christian letter that had been developed by Paul was subsequently employed in the composition of the deutero-Pauline letters. In Colossians, the prescript (Col 1:1–2) is followed by an extensive proem (Col 1:3–2:5), which presents comments about the mission and the fate of the apostle. The next section—the body of the letter—is a polemic interspersed with parenesis (Colossians 2:6–4:6), and greetings form the letter's conclusion (Col 4:7–18). In Colossians as well as in Ephesians, material is employed in the parenesis that has the character of church order (Colossians 3:18–4:1; Ephesians 5:22–6:9). In the later Pastoral Epistles as well as in 1 Peter and *1 Clement*, church order materials have become the primary content of the writings. This reinforces the concept that the primary purpose of the Pauline letter was indeed understood to be political and concerned with organization of the Christian community.

(e) The Second Letter of Peter and the Epistle of Jude

The most striking case of literary dependence within the letters of the New Testament appears in the relationship of 2 Peter to Jude. In its second chapter, 2 Peter reproduces almost the whole letter of Jude, albeit with many alterations. The Epistle of Jude was probably written toward the end of the 1st century and is strongly, even explicitly, dependent upon Jewish apocalyptic materials (see Jude 14). From this apocalyptic perspective, Jude argues against (Gnostic) heretics who claim to be the truly spiritual people (Jude 19) and are thus seen as a danger to the churches to which they belong and in which they participate in the common *agape* meals (Jude 12).

From the perspective of 2 Peter, probably written about half a century later, the situation has changed fundamentally. The heretics who had been attacked by Jude are now excluded from the churches, and relationships with them exist only on the private level (compare 2 Pet 2:13 with Jude 12). Moreover, the citations of apocalyptic materials from noncanonical books appeared questionable to the author of 2 Peter; they are therefore eliminated. Otherwise, however, the whole design of the Epistle of Jude as well as many details are clearly reproduced in 2 Pet 2:1–3:2. In addition, there are borrowings from Jude in other chapters of 2 Peter (cf., e.g., 2 Pet 1:5 with Jude 3; see §§12.1b; 12.2f).

(f) The Letters of Ignatius of Antioch

The story of the transmission and revision of the letters of Ignatius of Antioch is a striking example of the possible fate of ancient documents that are not protected by canonical status. It is known from a letter of bishop Polycarp of Smyrna to the church of Philippi, written some time in the first half of the 2d century, that he sent copies of a collection of the letters of Ignatius to Philippi (Polycarp, *Phil.* 13; see §12.2h). Eusebius of Caesarea reports in his *Church History* (3.36.2–11) that Ignatius, the bishop of Antioch, was transported to Rome for martyrdom, that he visited churches in Asia, and that he wrote letters to the churches of Ephesus, Magnesia on the Maeander, Tralles, Rome, Philadelphia, Smyrna, and to Polycarp—a total of seven letters.

The extant manuscripts and translations of Ignatius's letters, however, which circulated in the Middle Ages, contained thirteen letters in their Greek version and twelve letters in their Latin version. In addition to the letters mentioned by Eusebius

Bibliography to §7.3e: see under §12.1b

Bibliography to §7.3f (see also under §12.2d)

Theodor Zahn, *Ignatius von Antiochien* (Gotha: Perthes, 1873). The classic treatment of the question.
Milton Perry Brown, *The Authentic Letters of Ignatius: A Study of Linguistic Criteria* (Durham, NC: Duke University Press, 1963).

STEMMA OF THE TRANSMISSION OF IGNATIUS' LETTERS

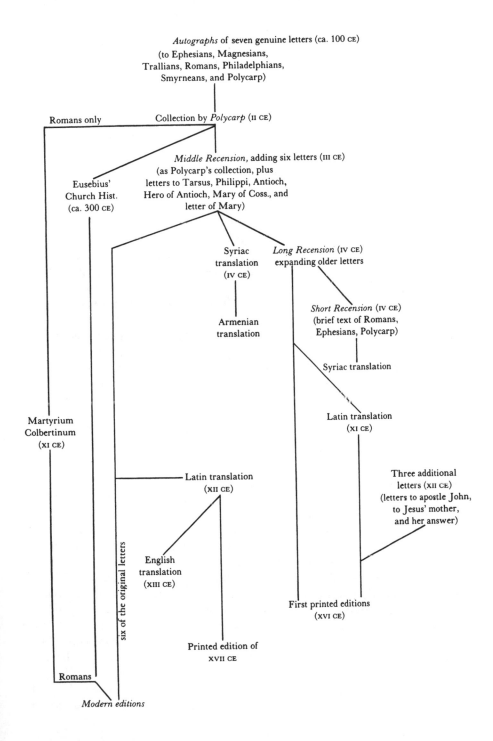

Autographs of seven genuine letters (ca. 100 CE)

(to Ephesians, Magnesians, Trallians, Romans, Philadelphians, Smyrneans, and Polycarp)

Romans only

Collection by *Polycarp* (II CE)

Middle Recension, adding six letters (III CE)
(as Polycarp's collection, plus letters to Tarsus, Philippi, Antioch, Hero of Antioch, Mary of Coss., and letter of Mary)

Eusebius' Church Hist. (ca. 300 CE)

Syriac translation (IV CE)

Long Recension (IV CE) expanding older letters

Armenian translation

Short Recension (IV CE) (brief text of Romans, Ephesians, Polycarp)

Syriac translation

Martyrium Colbertinum (XI CE)

Latin translation (XI CE)

Latin translation (XII CE)

Three additional letters (XII CE) (letters to apostle John, to Jesus' mother, and her answer)

six of the original letters

English translation (XIII CE)

First printed editions (XVI CE)

Romans

Printed edition of XVII CE

Modern editions

they present a letter to Ignatius from a certain Maria of Cassobola (missing in the Latin version), a letter of Ignatius to her, letters to the churches of Tarsus, Philippi, and Antioch, and a letter to the deacon Hero of Antioch. This collection of the Ignatian epistles, known as the "Longer Recension," was first printed in the 16th century, but its authenticity had already been questioned in the Renaissance period. A later version of this recension appears in some Latin medieval manuscripts that contain additional letters of Ignatius to the apostle John, to Mary mother of Jesus, and a letter of Mary to Ignatius. A different edition of Ignatius's letters, was also known in the Middle Ages, when it was translated into Latin, English, and Armenian. In Greek, however, this edition is preserved only in one single manuscript, the *Codex Mediceo Laurentianus* of Florence, written in the 11th century. It also presents the letters of the "Longer Recension" but it differs from it insofar as six of the seven letters mentioned by Eusebius (the letter to the Romans is missing) appear in a shorter form; it has therefore been called the "Middle Recension." Also the letter to the Romans is preserved in a shorter form in a Greek manuscript of the martyrdom of Ignatius, called the *Martyrium Colbertinum* (of which also Latin and Syriac versions exist). This "Middle Recension" of the Ignatian letters was rediscovered in the 17th century, was reprinted several times, and in the course of time, it generally became accepted that the letters of this recension that had been mentioned by Eusebius were the original letters of Ignatius. In the year 1845, however, the English scholar Cureton published still another recension, preserved in a Syriac translation and containing only three letters in a still shorter form, namely, letters to the Ephesians, to the Romans, and to Polycarp. Some scholars subsequently accepted only these three letters in their short form as authentic Ignatian letters.

The various collections and recensions of Ignatius's letters thus present a total of fourteen letters of Ignatius and two letters to Ignatius. The seven letters mentioned by Eusebius are transmitted in a shorter and a longer version, and three of them in an even shorter recension. The studies of Theodor Zahn and J. B. Lightfoot at the end of the 19th century were able to argue convincingly that the six letters of the Middle Recension and the letter to the Romans in the form in which it appears in the *Martyrium Colbertinum*—that is, the seven letters mentioned by Eusebius— were the original letters of Ignatius. This view has been successfully defended against several more recent critics in the commentary of William Schoedel. The Long Recension resulted from theological controversies in the divided church of Antioch in the 4th century, in which both sides appealed to Ignatius's authority. At that time, the original letters of Ignatius were expanded and other pseudepigraphical letters were added to the collection. The original letters survived in only two textual traditions, one, the letter to the Romans, in the *Martyrium Colbertinum,* the other six in the *Codex Mediceo Laurentianus.* That the letter to the Romans did not appear in the latter may have been due to the fact that the Middle Recension is dependent upon the collection made by Polycarp, to whom the letter that was sent to Rome was not obtainable, or it might otherwise have been removed from the collection; Eusebius knew of its existence. The Middle Recension, surviving in *Codex Mediceo Laurentianus,* incorporated also the pseudepigraphical letters of the Longer Recension. It is therefore dependent upon the Longer Recension, though preserving, at the same time, six of the letters in their original form. The shortest Syriac version of three of these letters is a secondary abbreviation, not of the original letters but of the form of these letters that appears in the Longer Recension; they are thus worthless for the reconstruction of the original text, which must rely primarily upon the Greek text of one single early medieval manuscript, aided by several translations and by a Greek papyrus that presents parts of the text for *Smyrneans* 3.1–12.1.

The history of the transmission and expansion of the Ignatian letters clearly demonstrates the possible fate of a collection of early Christian literature that was not protected by canonical status. As canonical protection for the letters of the New Testament did not begin until the end of the 2d century, it must be remembered that also the letters of the New Testament might have been subject to major revision and additions before the canon of the New Testament was created. Such revision and addition indeed occurred in the Pauline corpus with the addition of the Pastoral Epistles and in the new edition of Paul's letters by Marcion (§12.3c).

4. PROBLEMS OF FORM, TRADITION, NARRATIVE, AND RHETORICAL CRITICISM

(a) The Synoptic Tradition

The father of form criticism (*Formgeschichte*) was Johann Gottfried Herder (1744–1803). He recognized that the forms of language, through which the past becomes present, are not a matter of free individual choice, inasmuch as language is not something that an individual invents spontaneously in every new situation. On the contrary, language is already given as a social reality; it belongs to a people or community. This does not only refer to the conventional forms of vocabulary and syntax but also to the genres by which words and sentences are fixed into certain

Bibliography to §7.4

Gerhard Lohfink, *The Bible: Now I Get It! A Form-Criticism Handbook* (Garden City, NY: Doubleday, 1979).

Erich Dinkler, "Form Criticism of the New Testament," in Black and Rowley, *Peake's Commentary*, 683–85.

Vielhauer, *Geschichte*, 9–57.

J. L. Bailey and L. D. Vander Broek, *Literary Forms in the New Testament: A Handbook* (Louisville, KY: Westminster John Knox, 1992).

Klaus Berger, *Formgeschichte des Neuen Testaments* (Heidelberg: Quelle & Meyer, 1984).

Georg Strecker, *Literaturgeschichte des Neuen Testaments* (Uni-Taschenbücher, no. 1682; Göttingen: Vandenhoeck & Ruprecht, 1992).

Bibliography to §7.4:   Seminal classic studies

André Jolles, *Einfache Formen* (2d ed. A. Schossig; Halle [Saale]: Niemeyer, 1956; reprint ed.: Darmstadt: Wissenschaftliche Buchgesellschaft, 1964).

Eduard Norden, *Agnostos Theos: Untersuchungen zur Formengeschichte religiöser Rede* (2d ed.; Leipzig: Teubner, 1923; reprint: Darmstadt: Wissenschaftliche Buchgesellschaft, 1956).

Alfred Seeberg, *Die Didache des Judentums und der Urchristenheit* (Leipzig: Deichert, 1908).

Idem, *Der Katechismus der Urchristenheit* (Leipzig: Deichert, 1903; reprint: ThBü 26; München: Kaiser, 1966).

forms, like song, joke, proverb, legend, epic, and myth. All of these forms, however fluid in themselves, are sociologically bound to institutionalized patterns of communication and conventions, through which a society regulates the relationships of its members. All these forms are by definition oral because orality is the life situation of communication among members of the same society. Orality must be understood in the widest sense as everything that is not controlled by the critical standards of publication in written from.

Herder's insights came to fruition only after the establishment of the two-source hypothesis. One of the first consequences of this hypothesis was the conviction that the Gospel of Mark reflected the original course of Jesus' life and ministry. The publication of William Wrede's book *The Messianic Secret in the Gospels* in 1901 destroyed that confidence. According to Wrede, the entire framework of the Gospel of Mark is the result of a theological reflection of the author and has no relationship to the actual course of events in the ministry of Jesus. In the following years, Julius Wellhausen in his commentaries on Matthew, Mark, and Luke, published in 1903 and 1904, tried to show how the authors had used and shaped materials that were originally transmitted in oral form. This opened up both the question of the history of the oral tradition as well as the question of redaction criticism.

In the year of the publication of Wrede's work, 1901, Hermann Gunkel demonstrated in his commentary on the Book of Genesis that this book was essentially a collection of stories that originally had been circulating in oral form. Further support came from the side of classical philologists. In his work *Forms of Early Christian Literature* (3d ed. 1912), Paul Wendland argued "that insight into the earlier stage of oral tradition and its special features is an essential presupposition for the understanding of the literary productions." In 1913, another classics scholar, Eduard Norden, published his still famous work ΑΓΝΟΣΤΟΣ ΘΕΟΣ, with the subtitle "Investigations into the History of the Forms of Religious Speech." The thesis of this book is that the Areopagus Speech of Paul in Acts 17 reflects the forms of the oral style of religious propaganda speeches.

This set the stage for the decisive form-critical works of Rudolf Bultmann and Martin Dibelius on the synoptic tradition. In his dissertation of 1911, "The Style of Paul's Preaching and the Cynic-Stoic Diatribe," Bultmann had already shown that

Bibliography to §7.4a

Rudolf Bultmann, *The History of the Synoptic Tradition* (2d ed.; New York: Harper, 1968).
Idem and Karl Kundsin, *Form Criticism* (New York: Harper, 1962).
Martin Dibelius, *From Tradition to Gospel* (2d ed.; New York: Scribner's, 1934).
Karl Ludwig Schmidt, *Der Rahmen der Geschichte Jesu* (Darmstadt: Wissenschaftliche Buchgesellschaft, 1964). The works of Bultmann, Dibelius, and Schmidt, first published from 1919 to 1921, are the foundations of the form-critical method.
Vincent Taylor, *The Formation of the Gospel Tradition* (New York: St. Martin's, 1953).
Edgar V. McKnight, *What Is Form Criticism?* (GBSNTS; Philadelphia: Fortress, 1969).
Norman Perrin, *What Is Redaction Criticism?* (GBSNTS; Philadelphia: Fortress, 1969).
Helmut Koester, "Formgeschichte/Formenkritik II. Neues Testament," *TRE* 11 (1983) 286–99.
Ferdinand Hahn (ed.), *Zur Formgeschichte des Evangeliums* (WdF 81; Darmstadt: Wissenschaftliche Buchgesellschaft, 1985).
Klaus Berger et al., *Studien und Texte zur Formgeschichte* (TANZ 7; Tübingen: Francke, 1992).

the style and rhetoric of Paul's letters were indebted to the popular preaching of religious and philosophical missionaries of antiquity. Martin Dibelius had published a book in 1913, demonstrating that the stories about John the Baptist were composed on the basis of oral traditions about this famous forerunner of Jesus. The works of 1919 and 1921 by Dibelius and Bultmann now endeavored to analyze all of the materials in the first three Gospels of the New Testament and to explain how they relied on a period of oral tradition. In this process they identified certain "forms" of oral usage and transmission that were still recognizable in the way in which they were written down. At the same time, gospel materials for which forms of oral antecedents could not be identified were classified as "redactional." The method that three decades later became known as "redaction criticism" did not contribute anything new but simply further refined the analysis of the redactional materials in the Gospels and thus resulted in a more detailed recognition of the literary strategies of the Gospel writers.

That the materials about Jesus were at first transmitted orally was not due to any lack of ability by the earliest Christians to produce written records—Paul's letters show that early Christian missionaries were quite able to communicate by writing—or by any dogmatic preference for the oral medium (as in the case of rabbinic Judaism); rather, the interests and needs of the early Christian communities made an oral transmission necessary. The tradition from and about Jesus was alive in missionary propaganda and preaching, praxis and liturgy, and in the teaching and polemic of the early Christian communities. It was in these contexts that the sayings of Jesus were formed and taught, and the stories about him received their contours so that they could be told and remembered. The form and content of the tradition was thus shaped by the sociological and religious demands of the preaching of the gospel and of the forming of Christian communities. Whatever Jesus himself did, taught, and preached, its memory and transmission were inscribed by the needs and situation of the Christian communities. Not Jesus himself, but the communities created the forms of the tradition that preserved the memory of Jesus. To be sure, some of the earliest Christian communities still belonged to the cultural and religious milieu of the Jewish people of Palestine, of which Jesus himself was a part. Very soon, however, Christianity moved beyond the horizons of that milieu into the Hellenistic-Roman world. Its sociological, cultural, and religious situation changed; that is, the life situation (*Sitz im Leben*) was no longer the same as that of the historical Jesus. A non-Palestinian life situation became thus determinative for the forming of the tradition.

For form criticism, the determination of the life situation is crucial. The Lord's prayer, transmitted in the Gospels of the New Testament in two different forms, was shaped by the situation of Matthew in a Jewish-Christian community outside Palestine, and differently by the situation of Luke in the Hellenistic community— in neither case is its form dependent upon the situation of Jesus' life in Galilee. Example stories and parables are told according to their function as part of the Christian sermon in edification and community building. In these situations, parables—whether or not they were originally told by Jesus—underwent many changes, such as allegorical interpretations. Collections of sayings have their life situation in parenesis and baptismal instruction, miracle stories in the missionary propaganda of the church. In each case, the term "life situation" refers first of all to the Christian community. To be sure, a particular tradition may not have its origins there, but it still owes this community its very existence and form. It is therefore not possible to draw a direct line from a tradition of the community to Jesus himself, nor can one simply peel away secondary accretions in order to gain access to the historical Jesus. Whatever Jesus said and did has been refracted in various ways like through a prism in the process of being formed into a tradition of the community. The original life situation of a saying or story in the life of Jesus is no longer accessible, because the formation of all traditions is deeply embedded in communal life situations. The incorporation into coherent accounts, as in the written gospels, is again another step, in which these stories and sayings are incorporated in a secondary redactional framework.

In order to define in more detail the specific forms of the tradition, it is necessary to distinguish between sayings and narrative materials. The authors of the gospels, of course, derived both types of materials from traditions that were formed in the life of the early Christian communities. All of the narrative materials, however, are formed by these communities, while some materials in the sayings tradition may indeed mirror what Jesus said. It is unlikely, however, that they preserve the exact form in which they were pronounced by Jesus, because the very forms of the sayings are the result of refraction that took place in the life situation of the community. Among the sayings materials, wisdom and prophetic sayings predominate. Their forms have analogies primarily in the prophetic and wisdom books of the Scriptures of Israel, which points to the life situation of the early Jewish-Christian communities for their formation.

The parables, parabolic narratives, and example stories in their nonallegorical forms may indeed derive from Jesus; the communities' interpretations are all too obvious in their secondary allegorization. The original parable invites the listeners to make the story their own and thus to become "story" themselves. The parable of the "Father who had two sons" (generally known as "The prodigal son," Luke 15:11–32), for example, appeals to the listener to become a loving human being like the father of the story; Luke's placement of this parable suggests an allegorization that understands the father as a figure of God, who forgives the sinner who repents. The parable of the "Laborers in the vineyard," better called the story of "The man who owned a vineyard" (Matt 20:1–15), gives an example of someone who is determined in his effort to let all others share equally in his goodness; Matthew allegorizes this into a story that demonstrates that the last shall be first (Matt 20:16). The parable of the man who invites guests to his dinner party ("Parable of the Great Supper," Luke 14:16–24) is the story of a person who breaks all social conventions in order to achieve his goal; in its allegorized form ("Parable of the Marriage Feast," Matt 20:1–14) it becomes a narrative about God, who punishes Israel for the killing of the prophets and then invites the Gentiles to the feast. While the original parables have analogies in the prophetic tradition of Israel, allegorizing was typical for the culture of the time. It is therefore most likely that the original parables reflect the prophetic preaching of Jesus more directly than any other parts of the sayings tradition.

Rules of the community and legal sayings that are concerned with the ordering of the Christian life are creations of the community in their entirety. A portion of the legal sayings is probably derived directly from the Jewish environment of early Christian communities or is formulated in the controversies with the Pharisees and other Jewish groups. Such life situations are especially evident in the formation of the apophthegmas (Bultmann's term; Dibelius calls them "paradigms"). Apophthegmas are short scenes, in which a question is asked or a problem is presented, to which a traditional saying provides the answer (see, e.g., the question about fasting, the plucking of corn on the Sabbath, and the healing of the man with the withered hand, Mark 2:18–3:6). Questions can be asked by the disciples, by opponents, by Jesus, or by any other individual. In several instances questions by either the disciples or the opponents are provoked by some action of Jesus, like the exorcism of a demon (Luke 11:14–20). The majority of these apophthegmas are controversy stories, while others can be classified as scholastic or instructional dialogues. The occasion for the formation of all types of apophthegmas was the interest of the community, which needed materials for polemical purposes or for the instruction of their members. The gospels also contain biographical apophthegmas that owe their origin to the communities' interest in the life and ministry of Jesus, which is thus represented in short paradigmatic scenes. One has to distinguish here between those apophthegmas that provide a secondary framework for a traditional saying and others in which the scene and the saying were composed as a unified piece (to the latter belongs the story of Mary and Martha, Luke 10:38–42). Only in the first case is it possible that a traditional, and possibly original, saying of Jesus has been preserved. Characteristic for the tradition of the apophthegmas is the attachment or inclusion of additional free sayings or of secondary analogous formulations (cf., e.g., Mark 2:23–28 with Matt 12:1–8) so that it is not rare to find in one apophthegma competing answers to the question that originally gave rise to its formation.

Most of the traditional narratives are miracle stories. A characteristic type of such stories is the exorcism, which is usually told according to a fixed schema: encounter of the possessed person with Jesus; the demon's recognition of the exorcist's power; Jesus threatens and drives out the demon, often with demonstration; presentation of the success; acknowledgment by the witnesses (e.g., Mark 1:21–28; 5:1–20). In the healing miracles the encounter of the sick person with Jesus is usually followed by a remark about the severity of the disease. The healing is either accomplished through a word of Jesus (magical terms from Aramaic are sometimes preserved; cf. Mark 5:41; 7:34), through some manipulation (Mark 8:23), or a combination of both; the conclusion tells of the success of the healing and the applause of the bystanders. All these features correspond to the standard forms of the telling of exorcisms and healing narratives in antiquity, although it is remarkable that complex and lengthy adjurations of demons and elaborate manipulations— otherwise very common in such stories—do not appear in the narrative materials of the gospels. Nature miracles (e.g., the Stilling of the Tempest, Mark 5:35–41) are comparatively rare in the Synoptic tradition. As in the exorcisms and the healing miracles, the brevity of such accounts is a striking feature of such miracle stories in the Synoptic tradition. Their basic form and narrative schema, however, closely correspond to those of analogous stories from the Greco-Roman world, including those that can be found in the apocryphal acts of the apostles.

A number of legends have also been incorporated in the Synoptic tradition. A "legend" is a story that relates a particular event by using amazing or wondrous details. Only one cult legend is found in the Synoptic tradition, namely the legend of the institution of the Lord's Supper. All other legends are biographical (the birth and infancy narratives, the stories about John the Baptist, the temptation of Jesus, his entry into Jerusalem). Most of these legends are shaped in analogy to narratives from the Bible of Israel. This is particularly evident in the passion narrative, which uses throughout the biblical motifs of the story of the suffering righteous from Deutero-Isaiah and several psalms. It is typical for these legends that they use descriptive embellishments sparingly and that they highlight only one single event. Novelistic features are rare (but see the Emmaus story in Luke 24:13–35).

The stories of Jesus' baptism, the transfiguration, and the appearances of the risen Lord are all epiphany stories. They should not be classified with legends or miracle stories. Their primary purpose is to speak of divine authorization for the commissioning of a human person, and their form therefore corresponds to the stories of the commissioning of a prophet in Israel. These epiphany stories begin with the introduction of the person who will be the recipient of the divine appearance and the designation of a special place (desert, mountain, river), give a description of the situation, and continue with the report of an extraordinary experience (a dove, bright light, the risen Lord), the voice of God, or the risen Jesus as the self-revelation of the authorizing deity, a description of the impression that the bystanders receive, and finally a command, a commission, or a designation. The stories of the appearance of the risen Lord in the gospels were originally analogous to the story of the call of the apostle Paul in Acts 9, which emphasizes the sending of Paul as an apostle to the Gentiles. Only at a secondary stage have the stories of the resurrection of Jesus been interpreted as proofs for the physical resurrection. Their original purpose—as in the stories of the calling of a prophet—is the designation and commissioning of a person for a divinely authorized mission. That is also the case in the oldest extant version of the story of Jesus' baptism (Mark 1:9–11), where the divine voice, "You are my son," designates Jesus as the messenger of God; the later redaction has transformed the story into a presentation of Jesus to the crowds ("This is my son," Matt 3:17). The names of the apostles are an important element of the resurrection stories; the community that transmits and tells such a story thereby establishes its own claim of legitimate succession. In the older stories, these names may well be historical, and the stories may have been told first by the apostle, who had "seen the Lord." A first-hand report is indeed preserved in Paul's own account in Gal 1:12–17. The difference between such an early report and the later development of such stories is strikingly visible in the comparison of Paul's account with the epiphany story of his calling in Acts 9. While both reports are cast in a proper traditional form, Paul's report echoes the call of Jeremiah, but Luke's later version follows the form of the calling of Ezekiel.

All of the narrative materials of the gospels are not straight reports of events observed or experienced, but are stories cast into the popular forms of communication. The quest for a historical kernel is therefore doomed to miss the point of these narratives. All of them were told in the interests of mission, edification, cult, apology, or theology (especially christology) and they do not provide answers to the quest for reliable historical information. While epiphany (resurrection) stories may still preserve the original name of the person who was the recipient of the epiphany, exact details of names and places are otherwise always secondary and are often introduced for the first time in the literary stage of the tradition. Precisely those elements and features of narratives that lead to the climax of the story are not derived from historically trustworthy information, but belong to the style of the genres of the several narrative types. Unexpected features may sometimes reflect some historical memory, such as that Jesus was baptized by John, the leader of a rival sect that was competing with the disciples of Jesus (§8.1). It is possible, however, to draw some historical conclusions from the totality of the narratives of a particular genre. The prominence of exorcism stories of Jesus, for example, allows the conclusion that Jesus' ministry was indeed characterized by his activity as an exorcist. On the other hand, it is highly problematic to propose that the many healing and nature miracles reported in the synoptic tradition suggest that Jesus must be classified as a typical Hellenistic magician. Religious (and political!) propaganda in antiquity always present great personalities—be they gods or human beings—as powerful healers. In a society that lacked public health services sickness and disease were so common that no message of salvation could be successful without the claim that the savior was a "divine man" capable of providing miraculous healing.

(b) Early Traditions in the Letters of the New Testament

Materials appearing in the letters of the New Testament that were not created by the authors but were derived from the traditions of the church are preserved in great richness and variety. Only rarely are such traditional materials explicitly quoted or identified as traditional. Moreover, any passages that rely on traditional material may not reproduce them in their original form. Their exact delimitation and wording from the context in which they appear therefore remains a notorious problem. Since external indications for the employment of traditional materials are usually absent, their identification within a given passage has to rely on other criteria, such as terminology that differs from the normal vocabulary of the author, metrical or poetic language within a section of the normal prose style of the letter, stereotyped formulaic sentences and phrases, and finally the occurrence of parallels in other writing where literary dependence cannot be established. Sometimes

Bibliography to §7.4b

Rudolf Bultmann, *Der Stil der paulinischen Predigt und die kynisch-stoische Diatribe* (FRLANT 13; Göttingen: Vandenhoeck & Ruprecht, 1910; reprint: 1984).

Martin Dibelius,"Zur Formgeschichte des Neuen Testaments (außerhalb der Evangelien)," *ThR* NF 3 (1931) 207–42.

Walter Bauer, "Der Wortgottesdienst der ältesten Christen," in idem, *Aufsätze und kleine Schriften* (Tübingen: Mohr/Siebeck, 1967), 155–209.

James M. Robinson, "Die Hodajot-Formel in Gebet und Hymnus des Frühchristentums," in *Apophoreta*, 194–235.

Ernst Käsemann, "Sentences of Holy Law in the New Testament," in idem, *New Testament Questions*, 66–81.

it is also possible to discover that there are contradictions between quoted materials and the opinion of the author.

Kerygmatic formulas about the suffering, death or cross, and raising or resurrection of Jesus are frequently used; the earliest quotation of such a formula is found in 1 Cor 15:3–5. The basic schema of these formulas was expanded at an early date by such characteristic items as the reference to Jesus' death as an expiation (see Rom 4:25 and the typical addition of "for us": Rom 3:25–26; Gal 1:4–5; 1 Pet 2:21–25). The expectation of the coming again of Jesus in glory for judgment was soon combined with such kerygmatic formulas (1 Thess 1:10). A somewhat different theological expectation appears in formulaic expressions that speak of Jesus' suffering and death and of his exultation and enthronement (Heb 1:2b–3; 1 Pet 3:18–19 and 4:1). Later Christian confessional formulas combine the statement of the resurrection with that of the exaltation. It is remarkable, however, that very rarely is such a formula repeated verbatim in the extant literature. The basic schema remains the same, but the exact wording allows great freedom of innovation in the formulation of detail. There is a tradition, but it is not yet subject to canonical control.

Christological hymns are quoted frequently. They have an easily recognizable form with strings of relative and participial clauses, for which Christ is always the subject. The content of these hymns is informed by the mythic story of the descent of a heavenly figure, his or her work and experiences among human beings, and final ascent and enthronement. The oldest of these hymns is preserved in Phil 2:6–11. It is modeled on Israel's myth of heavenly Wisdom. In particular, the presentation of Christ as the mediator of creation, which introduces many of these hymns, is derived from this Wisdom myth (Col 1:15–20; John 1:1–5, 9–12, 14, 16). In many instances, only fragments of such hymns are quoted (Eph 2:14ff.; 1 Tim 3:16; 2 Cor 9:9; cf. 2 Cor 5:19).

Like these hymns, the doxologies are also derived from the liturgical tradition. They sometimes appear in the conclusion of epistles, where they may have been added secondarily (this is certainly the case in Rom 16:25–27), but are also found in the body of letters (Rom 11:36; 1 Cor 8:6). Blessings at the end of a letter may also reflect liturgical materials, like 2 Cor 13:13, which is still used in Christian liturgies today. From the liturgy of the Eucharist Paul quotes the words of institution of the Lord's supper (1 Cor 11:23–27) and the call "Our Lord come!" (1 Cor 16:22; cf. Rev. 22:20). Differences in the wording of various quotations of the words of institution (compare 1 Cor 11:23–25 with Mark 14:22–25) reflect differences in liturgical practice. It is likely that various passages of the letters have preserved liturgical materials from the rite of baptism; it has been difficult, however, to identify such passages with certainty. The short confession "Jesus is Lord" (1 Cor 12:3) and the call "Awake, o sleeper!" (Eph 5:14) seem to come from baptismal liturgies.

Even parenetic sections of the letters have been assigned to the liturgy of baptism; but parenetic traditions did not have their exclusive life situation in the instruction of catechumens. There are two basic forms in which parenetic materials were transmitted, namely, as catalogs of vices and virtues and as compositions of groups of sayings. Catalogs of vices and virtues had already been formed in Jewish circles under the influence of Hellenistic philosophy and are frequently used and interpreted in early Christian writings. They occur in parenetic contexts as simple lists (1 Cor 6:9–10; Gal 5:19–24; Col 3:5–8, 12) or as the underlying structure of more elaborate admonitions (1 Thess 4:3–7; Eph 4:17–5:6; and frequently in the Pastoral Epistles). Parenesis in the form of sayings was typical for the Jewish tradition in the Hellenistic period. One letter of the New Testament, the Epistle of James, is nothing but a collection of traditional sayings (of which some have parallels in Matthew 5–7). Groups of traditional sayings often appear in the concluding parts of the letters (Rom 12:9–21; Gal 6:1–10; 1 Thess 5:14–22). Such groups may be arranged in the "two-way" schema, the way of life and the way of death. In other instances, they follow the schema of household duties, a form that is derived from the Stoic diatribe of the Hellenistic world. Such a table of household duties speaks of the mutual obligations of the members of a household (man and wife, parents and children, masters and slaves), and about one's duties toward friends, governments, and foreigners. They appear in Christian parenesis for the first time in the deutero-Pauline letters (Col 3:18–4:1; Eph 5:22–6:9; 1 Pet 2:13–3:7). The Pastoral Epistles use this traditional schema for the development of church order; thus not only are the duties of old and young people mentioned but also the qualifications and obligations of holders of church office, namely, bishops, presbyters, deacons, and widows (1 Tim 2:1–3:13; 5:1–21; 6:1–2; Tit 1:7–9; 2:1–10).

Sayings of Jesus are also used in parenesis, sometimes explicitly quoted (1 Cor 7:10–11; 9:14), in many instances, however, without a special acknowledgment of Jesus' authority (Rom 12:14, 17; 14:13–14; 1 Thess 5:15; Eph 4:29; a saying of Jesus that is not found in our gospels is quoted in Acts 20:35). The absence of a reference to Jesus in the use of some sayings in parenesis is striking, especially in 1 Peter (2:19–20; 3:9, 14, 16; 4:14) and in the Epistle of James (e.g., 4:9, 10; 5:12). Are some of these traditional sayings that were only later ascribed to Jesus? Apocalyptic materials are sometimes quoted as words of the Lord. These are probably pronouncements of Christian prophets, who made predictions about the future in the name of the Lord. Paul cites such a "word of the Lord" in 1 Thess 4:15–17; another time he refers to the same tradition as a "mystery" (1 Cor 15:51). References to such mysteries, that is, revelations about the future, which are accessible only to the initiated, are not rare. In Paul's letters, the term μυστήριον ("mystery" in the singular) always designates a specific saying or tradition (Rom 11:25–26a; see also 2 Thess 2:7), while in the plural the term refers to a number of such revelation sayings (1 Cor 13:2; 14:2). Even in 1 Cor 2:7, the term seems to refer to a specific saying about the coming of the Lord (cf. Matt 13:35), and the close connection between such traditions of sayings is now evident in the following quotation of a saying in 1 Cor 2:9 that has been found as a saying of Jesus in the *Gospel of Thomas* (#17). It is only at a later time that the term "mystery" becomes identical with the term "gospel" (Eph 3:3–8; Col 1:26–28; and the secondary ending of Roman in 16:25–27). There is also another activity of Christian prophets that manifested itself in sentences that became traditional: the formulation of sentences of sacred law; these are pronouncements that state the *ius talionis* (the law of retribution) formulated for the sacral and religious realm of the life of the community. Paul quotes such sentences several times (e.g., "If someone destroys the temple of God, God will destroy that person," 1 Cor 3:17; see also 1 Cor 14:38; 16:22; Rom

10:11, 13). It is evident that such pronouncements of prophets added to the store of sayings of Jesus (cf. 1 Tim 2:11–13 with Mark 8:30).

The use of traditional materials is evident last but not least in the quotations and interpretation of passages from Scripture. A number of such quotations were drawn from traditional collections of testimonia for specific topics (e.g., Rom 10:18–21; Heb 1:5–13). In general, however, it must be assumed that New Testament authors, and especially Paul, were familiar with the entire context of scriptural passages, even if only one or a few verses are actually quoted. Moreover, comments on such passages of Scripture often reveal acquaintance with traditions of scriptural inter-pretation, which may have come from pre-Christian exegetical conventions (e.g., 1 Cor 10:1–10) or from scriptural interpretations created by opponents that are critically annotated by Paul (this is the case in 2 Cor 3:7–18).

As gospels are not free creations of their authors but compilations of sources and oral traditions, also the epistles must not be envisioned as products of the free-ranging minds of creative theological thinkers but as elaboration of various and diverse traditional materials that were current in Israel, the Hellenistic-Roman world, and specifically in early Christian communities.

(c) Traditional Materials Preserved in the Apostolic Fathers, the Apocrypha, and the Apologists

What has been said above also applies to the noncanonical early Christian writ-ings. These writings, however, have all received much less attention than the New Testament itself, and therefore much of the wealth of often very valuable and very early traditional materials in these writings remains largely unexplored. Many of these materials have not been clearly recognized. In the following I shall refer only to a few typical examples from this rich literature.

Words of Jesus and traditions about Jesus that are comparable to the canonical gospels are found in writings belonging to the genre of the gospels as well as in other literatures. For many of these writings, literary dependence upon the canon-ical gospels cannot be assumed. Rather, the sources of such Jesus traditions are either the free oral transmission or independent written materials. *1 Clement* quotes two small collections of sayings of Jesus from the oral tradition (*1 Clem.* 13.2; 46.8). A similar collection of sayings has been inserted into the first chapter of the *Didache,* while *2 Clement* apparently used a collection of Jesus' sayings that was partially based upon the canonical gospels and partially upon noncanonical oral traditions. An independent transmission of Jesus' sayings has recently come to light in the newly discovered (Coptic) *Gospel of Thomas* that presents mostly prophetic sayings, wisdom sayings, and parables of Jesus with parallels in the canonical gospels, but has been enriched by numerous Gnosticizing sayings in the course of its literary history. A fragment of an *Unknown Gospel (Pap. Oxy.* 840) and the gospel fragment *Papyrus Egerton 2* present sayings of Jesus that have been set into scenes resembling the Synoptic apophthegmas, but are somewhat more elaborate. Bishop Papias of Hierapolis (early 2d century) collected sayings of Jesus from the oral tradition, including legends and revelations—unfortunately, only a few frag-ments of his writings are preserved. Finally, from the 2d to later centuries one still finds large numbers of so-called *Agrapha*—sayings of Jesus that are not otherwise found in written gospels—quoted in the writings of the Church Fathers. Even if most of these *Agrapha* cannot be claimed as genuine words of Jesus, they are still important witnesses for the early development of the tradition of Jesus' sayings in the early Christian communities. While new sayings of Jesus were still created and allowed to circulate freely, new miracle stories of Jesus are rarely found in the extracanonical tradition; on the other hand, miracle stories of the apostles became increasingly popular. Legends, however, dealing with the birth and childhood of Jesus were formed at an early time. Collections and editions of such stories resulted in the publication of the *Protevangelium of James* and the *Infancy Gospel of Thomas*. At the same time, epiphany stories about Jesus' appearance to his disciples seemed to circulate orally and make a secondary reappearance in the literary genre of Jesus' discussions with his disciples after the resurrection (though the latter scarcely preserve older traditions). The fragment of the *Gospel of Peter* preserves an older version of the story of the empty tomb in the form of an epiphany story. Fragments of the same story may indeed appear in Mark 9:2–9 and Matt 27:51–53, 62–66; 28:2–4. Ignatius of Antioch (*Smyrn.* 3.2–3) quotes an independent variant of Luke 24:36–43. The so-called *Gospel According to the Hebrews* contained a story about Jesus' appearance to his brother James; there is no reason to doubt that this is an old traditional story.

Kerygmatic and confessional or credal formulas are frequently quoted in the extracanonical literature. The variety of the citations demonstrates that second-century Christianity did not yet have a universally accepted formulation of the Christian faith and that traditional formulations could be freely modified, though the beginnings of the later ecclesiastical creeds can be recognized. Rich materials are presented by Ignatius of Antioch. His fight against the so-called docetists, who denied the true humanity of Jesus, led to the inclusion into the creed of a statement about the birth of Jesus by Mary—in order to emphasize the true humanity of Jesus (*Eph.* 18.2 and often elsewhere)! He also quotes formulations that juxtapose Jesus' divinity and humanity in antithetical sentences, which assume hymnic character through their frequent repetitions (*Eph.* 7.2). Other creeds enumerate in chronological order the events of salvation from the birth of Jesus to the resurrection (*Smyrn.* 1.1–2). Even if some of these passages are compositions by Ignatius, they still reveal that such credal formulations were used in the liturgy of the churches. Similar formulations are quoted by Justin Martyr (*1 Apol.* 31.7; *Dial.* 85.2; 132.1). In Justin's citations, statements about the ascension and the second coming for judgment have been added and are now fixed parts of the confessional tradition. That such confessions had their life situation in the liturgy of baptism is shown by Justin *1 Apol.* 61; once the older baptismal formula "in the name of Jesus" was replaced by the trinitarian formula (Matt 28:19; *Did.* 7.1), credal formulations were expanded accordingly, eventually resulting in the tripartite baptismal creed of belief in God the Creator, Jesus the Savior, and the Holy Spirit.

Hymns were especially transmitted in the writings from Gnostic circles. The *Acts of John* (94–96) preserves a long hymn of the community as the "Song of Christ," together with the responses of the participants. The *Acts of Thomas* (6–7) quotes a "wedding hymn" that speaks allegorically of the sacred marriage of the church with her celestial bridegroom. The same book also recites the famous "Hymn of the Pearl" (*Act. Thom.* 108–113), a Gnostic proclamation in the form of a mythological poem. Both hymns are certainly older than the *Acts of Thomas,* a third-century writing. An originally pagan hymn about God and the soul, which was used in superficially revised Christian form by the Gnostic sect of the Naassenes, is quoted by Hippolytos. In the *Odes of Solomon* a whole early-Christian hymnbook has been preserved. The Gnosticizing tendencies of these hymns—a total of forty-two— demonstrate how deeply Gnostic imagery and mythology has influenced the piety and liturgy of early Christian communities even in the 1st century CE.

Other liturgical materials are quoted in abundance. The *Didache* (7.1–4) preserves an instruction for the baptismal liturgy together with the trinitarian baptismal formula (perhaps the first appearance of this formula), cites the Lord's Prayer (*Did.* 8.2) in a form that is closely related to but not dependent upon Matthew 6:9–13, and also quotes eucharistic prayers and a part of the eucharistic liturgy (*Did.* 9–10). In his report about the baptismal praxis of the Christians, Justin Martyr (*1 Apol.* 61.3) quotes an expanded baptismal formula together with a saying of Jesus in its original liturgical form (John 3:3, 5 cites the same saying in a secondary version). In Justin's description of the Eucharist (*1 Apol.* 66) one finds the words of institution in a formulation that is shorter than any of the forms preserved in the New Testament. Numerous doxologies and invocations are preserved in the apocryphal acts of the apostles, especially in the *Acts of Thomas,* but also in many of the Gnostic writings. All this is evidence for a very rich and diversified development of liturgies in the early Christian communities.

Quotations of parenetic traditions are so frequent that a full account is impossible here. Tables of household duties and catalogs of vices form an important part of extracanonical literature (see *Did.* 4.9–11; 5.1–2; *1 Clem.* 1.3; *Barnabas* 20). The predominance of the Jewish teaching of the Two Ways is striking . While the description of the way of death is usually nothing more than a catalog of vices, traditional sayings materials, customarily connected with admonitions and prohibitions related to the Decalogue, are the essential ingredients of the description of the way of life (see *Didache* 1–4; *Barnabas* 19; and especially the *Mandata* of the *Shepherd of Hermas*).

(d) Narrative and Rhetorical Criticism

Narrative criticism pays attention to how a story or other writing is constructed: its elements of plot, characterization, structure, dominant themes, and point of view. Rhetorical criticism explains how writers used the tools of Greco-Roman oratory to organize and deploy persuasive speech. Both methods focus on communication models and can be understood as extensions or supplements to redaction and composition criticism, since they focus on locating the goals and strategies of the authors of the biblical books. These and other approaches inspired by scholarship on general or secular literature (such as reader-response criticism) are rich and complex and have many possible applications, which can lead to historical as well as more purely literary observations and conclusions.

Recent years have seen fruitful applications of narrative criticism to the

Gospels, Acts, Pauline epistles, and even the Book of Revelation. The Gospels and Acts present the more obviously developed narratives, whose plot lines, major and minor characters, thematics, and narrational perspectives can be analyzed with profit. But Paul's letters also carry embedded stories, especially the narrative of his career as an apostle with its successes, struggles, and setbacks. That narrative is not always expressed explicitly, but nonetheless it provides a structure within which Paul's particular letters can be read, compared, and classified. This in turn can lead to literary and historical observations on the persuasive intent of Paul's brief letter to Philemon about Onesimus, for example, when his words are read in the context of the larger story of Paul's relations with the Christians of Colossae and Laodicea. Narrative (and rhetorical) analysis can sharpen our awareness of the integrity or secondary composition of other letters such as 2 Corinthians or Philippians, by noting how the story line either develops or is abruptly broken.

The plot and narrative themes of the Gospel of Mark may serve as another example. Form and redaction criticism have combined to identify Mark's secondary or

Bibliography to §7.4d

Amos N. Wilder, *The Language of the Gospel: Early Christian Rhetoric* (New York: Harper & Row, 1964).

Robert C. Tannehill, "The Disciples in Mark: The Function of a Narrative Role," *JR* 57 (1977) 386–405.

Idem, *The Narrative Unity of Luke-Acts: A Literary Study* (2 vols.; Philadelphia and Minneapolis: Fortress, 1986, 1990).

Norman R. Petersen, *Literary Criticism for New Testament Critics* (GBS; Philadelphia: Fortress, 1978).

Idem, *Rediscovering Paul: Philemon and the Sociology of Paul's Narrative World* (Philadelphia: Fortress, 1985).

F. Forrester Church, "Rhetorical Structure and Design in Paul's Letter to Philemon," *HTR* 71 (1978) 17–33.

Betz, *Galatians.*

Stanley K. Stowers, *The Diatribe and Paul's Letter to the Romans* (SBLDS 57; Chico, CA: Scholars Press, 1981).

R. Alan Culpepper, *Anatomy of the Fourth Gospel: A Study in Literary Design* (Philadelphia: Fortress, 1983).

George A. Kennedy, *New Testament Interpretation through Rhetorical Criticism* (Chapel Hill, NC: University of North Carolina Press, 1984).

John R. Donahue, *The Gospel in Parable: Metaphor, Narrative, and Theology in the Synoptic Gospels* (Minneapolis: Fortress, 1988).

Mary Ann Tolbert, *Sowing the Gospel: Mark's World in Literary-Historical Perspective* (Minneapolis: Fortress, 1989).

Burton L. Mack, *Rhetoric and the New Testament* (GBS; Minneapolis: Fortress, 1990).

Bernard Brandon Scott, *Hear Then the Parable: A Commentary on the Parables of Jesus* (Minneapolis: Fortress, 1990).

Janice Capel Anderson and Stephen D. Moore, *Mark and Method: New Approaches in Biblical Studies* (Minneapolis: Fortress, 1992).

Edgar V. McKnight and Elizabeth Struthers Malbon (eds.), *The New Literary Criticism and the New Testament* (Valley Forge, PA: Trinity Press International, 1994).

Stanley E. Porter and David Tombs (eds.), *Approaches to New Testament Study* (JSNTSup 120; Sheffield: Sheffield Academic Press, 1995).

David L. Barr, *Tales of the End: A Narrative Commentary on the Book of Revelation* (Santa Rosa, CA: Polebridge, 1998).

artificial arrangement of isolated episodes about Jesus performing miracles, exorcising demons, calling some to "follow" him, and frequently confronting opposition. Building on these insights with narrative analysis, we can appreciate how the author deployed those disparate elements to compose a far-reaching and ironic story line with a fascinating use of characters running contrary to the reader's expectations. The narrator informs the reader from the start of Jesus' identity as the Son of God (1:1; also 1:11; 9:7; cf. 15:39); yet this presumably important fact is left hidden from most of the other participants in the story. The narrator insists on Jesus' identity as a teacher, and his followers' role as pupils (disciples), and yet the story builds much of its dramatic momentum precisely from the continuing failure of these "students" to understand and learn Jesus' central message. Exorcisms and healings (signs of Jesus' divine mission) are often presented as the content of his "teaching," which astounds the crowds, enrages the demons, and mystifies the disciples. At first the reader identifies with Jesus and his close followers; but then this commitment is called severely into question as Jesus' fate becomes ever more certain and the disciples' doubt and alarm throw their status into question. The final lesson brought home is Jesus' agony of obedience to God's will in the face of abandonment and desolation: a bleak ending that points to a future only partly resolved.

Attention to the directional flow of Mark's plotted narrative helps resolve some problems left unresolved by genre or grammatical analysis. The oddly truncated ending of Mark is a classic case: ἐφοβοῦντο γάρ. A reader who has three times seen Jesus predict the arrest, trial, and execution of "the Son of Man"—followed each time by the insistence that he will "rise after three days" (Mark 8:31; 9:31; 10:33–34)—is not left as devastated as Mary and her friends when they found the empty tomb and ran away "and said nothing to anyone—since they were afraid" (16:8). The reader, who is presumably already a member of a Christian congregation, knows that Jesus' predictions will (and indeed already have) become true outside the story as told on the page: the reader is able, indeed compelled, to fill in the rest of the story. Nonetheless, the message is also made abundantly clear that deprivation and suffering are sure to accompany any persistent follower of Jesus—they will receive their reward "one hundredfold in this age—with persecutions!—and in the world to come, eternal life" (Mark 10:30).

The parables ascribed to Jesus in the gospels are especially amenable to literary study. These short stories (especially those told or retold by Luke) can often display an unusual sophistication in twists of plot, sharpness of characterization, use of symbol and hyperbole, and vivid detail. The "Prodigal Son," the "Good Samaritan," and the "Sower and the Seed" are deeply imprinted into Western literary consciousness. Scholars note how Jesus' parables and similitudes capture the audience's attention with striking immediacy and then challenge their assumptions boldly with surprising and sometimes shocking reversals of fortune. Though most is lost, some of the scattered seed will end in productive fruit and abundant harvest (Mark 4:3–8 par.); the one whom God sends in aid of the desperate turns out to be just the sort of person that the victim (and the audience within the narrative) most despises (Luke 10:30–35); the dissolute and impatient son who shows little respect and no regard for his aged father is the one welcomed home with the fatted calf (Luke 15:11–32).

Literary analysis of the Book of Revelation has emphasized the construction of the work as a dramatized liturgical experience, enveloped within an epistolary framework (see §12.1c). The point of view adopted within the cycles of auditory and visual revelations is that of a transported seer who experiences the high drama of the angelic worship offered God around the heavenly throne. The repetitions, abrupt transitions, and apparent contradictions are not signs of an inadequate combination of disparate sources but instead a literary attempt to imagine and recreate the effects of a disorienting visionary event. Once again, however, literary analysis cannot be divorced from sociohistorical understanding. Despite its complicated theatrical interventions, the book is clearly directed toward impressing an audience of contemporary believers within late-first-century Roman imperial Asia of their need to remain faithful to Christ despite the threat of political and even criminal sanctions.

Rhetorical analysis at its best also blends the literary sensibilities of narratology with the historical concerns of redaction and social-scientific criticism. Current study of rhetoric in New Testament literature is based on research into the varieties and purposes of public oratory in particular settings of the Hellenistic world: forensic or judicial (used in law courts); deliberative (used in political assemblies); and epideictic (designed to praise or blame, typically used in funerary or encomiastic speeches). Removed from those immediate sociopolitical settings, authors could arrange their compositions using a mixture of styles to achieve particular effects. Scholars have shown, for example, how Paul deployed both apologetic (forensic) and deliberative rhetoric in writing to the Galatians in defense of his apostolate (as also in 1 Cor 9), while in turn the gospel writers exercised varieties of deliberative and epideictic oratory to develop and elaborate *chreiai* (instructive anecdotes) about Jesus.

Though early Christian writers would only rarely follow the ideal patterns developed by the rhetorical schools with any exactitude or rigidity, they (and thus by extension their ancient readers) do seem to have been at home with rhetorical conventions of composition and argument, which would ordinarily follow a more or less set structure of introduction, historical narration, and various types of proofs and appeals. When Peter and Paul deliver missionary speeches in the story line of Acts, for example, they refer consistently to their miraculous deeds (narrated alongside the speeches) as part of the proofs for their divine authority. When Jesus is charged with exorcising demons with the power of Beelzebul, the author(s) of the Sayings Gospel Q compose an elaborated version of Jesus' answer to the charge (Luke 11:14–23 par.), combining several originally separate elements to characterize and defend Jesus through forensic and epideictic argument and example. In the Synoptic tradition more generally, Jesus is shown debating through use of analogy, example, and symbolic anecdote (parable), but his practice is exceptional in its infrequent appeal to any authority other than his own.

Since Paul's letters were not private communications but instead were meant for public reading aloud in the assembled congregations (cf. §9), he naturally drew as needed on established techniques of persuasion in deliberative settings. Understanding these and similar techniques of ancient rhetoric improves the modern reader's appreciation of his style of argument. Paul's use of the Cynic-Stoic diatribe style (§4.2a), especially in Romans, is an adaptation of rhetorical techniques used in the philosophical schools to draw out and rebut the potential objections of one's opponents or students (cf. Epictetus). Far from being an artificial or merely literary exercise, Paul's use of persuasive rhetoric like the diatribe must reflect his practices as a missionary preacher and teacher. A good example of the apostle's use of deliberative oratory is his defense of the future hope of bodily resurrection in 1 Corinthians 15, offered against spiritual believers who hesitated to accept this rather un-Hellenic notion (cf. Acts 17:32). Paul's argument begins with a brief introductory transition (exordium, 1 Cor 15:1–2), followed by a historical narration of both the credal summary of Christ's resurrection (vv. 3–7) and Paul's own experience of the risen Lord (vv. 8–11), then offers a set of alternating proofs by way of refutation of his opponents' views (vv. 12–19, 35–44) and confirmation of his own position with examples and analogies (vv. 20–34, 44–57). The whole argument is concluded with a summarizing exhortation (peroration) in v. 58: "Therefore know that your work in the Lord is not in vain!"

FROM JOHN THE BAPTIST
TO THE EARLY CHURCH

It is not possible to give a succinct historical account of the life and ministry of either John the Baptist or Jesus of Nazareth. Except for a brief report about John the Baptist by the Jewish historian Josephus (*Ant.* 18.116–118), all information about both John and Jesus must be extrapolated from Christian sources, primarily from the canonical gospels of the New Testament. This implies that all traditions about both men are in their present form creations of the Christian community. The character of such traditions, created in the interests of this community, does not permit ascribing any of these materials directly to John or Jesus. Their actual life and ministry, the "historical John the Baptist" and the "historical Jesus," are therefore not directly available for the inquiry of the historian. All that historical investigation will yield are a few external data, such as the execution of John by the tetrarch Herod Antipas and the condemnation of Jesus to death on the cross by the governor Pontius Pilate, and a few erratic blocks in these traditions that do not fit the tendencies and purposes of those who fashioned these traditions. Their ministries and messages can be assessed only in the form of a trajectory that can be drawn from the eschatological expectations of 1st-century CE Israel to John's activity, to Jesus himself, and, finally, to the proclamation of the followers of Jesus. The inclusion of both figures in the Christian traditions affirms that the Christians saw themselves in continuity with the purpose and aim of Jesus' ministry, and they saw John the Baptist as a precursor of Jesus. Their history has become a memory of the community, a memory that has not come to us as a recording of facts but as a dialogue, in which that which was and had been said once has become story and words of meaning for the present. It is in this dialogue, in which the memory is alive, that the historian can discover the fundamental elements of those creative events and words that made the ministries of John and Jesus the wellspring of a new vision for the community of Israel.

i. John the Baptist

(a) Life and Message

The birth narrative of John (Luke 1:5–25, 57–80) is most likely a Christian, if not even Lukan, composition, or perhaps a pious legend inherited from the followers of John. It is impossible to say whether the information that John came from a priestly family is trustworthy. The gospels' presentation of John's ministry (Mark 1:2–8; Matt 3:1–12; Luke 3:1–18; John 1:19–34) is entirely dominated by Christian features, such as the description of John as Elijah, his activity in the desert, and John's "social teaching" (Luke 3:10–14). That John was active, however, not only in Judea but also in other regions of Palestine is evident, since he was executed by Herod Antipas, who was the ruler of Galilee and Peraea. While the information that John announced the appearance of Jesus is certainly a Christian product, there should be no doubt about the eschatological character of his message. Even Christian redaction was not completely successful in deleting all traces of John's original message, namely, that he announced the coming of God's judgment; God is originally the "stronger one" who is coming after him. The saying about the ax that is already set at the root of the tree (Matt 3:10 = Luke 3:9) is a metaphor referring to God's impending judgment. Also the announcement of the one who would "baptize with spirit and fire" (Matt 3:11 = Luke 3:16) refers to the eschatological divine judgment from which no one will escape (Matt 3:12 = Luke 3:16). The baptism of John must therefore be understood as an eschatological seal that reconstituted the elect of Israel, who would be spared in God's judgment. Finally, that Jesus was once a follower of John and was baptized by him is hardly a Christian invention. The gospels and Josephus give different reasons for John's execution by Antipas. Mark 6:17–29, a legend that dates the death of John into the time of Jesus' ministry, says that Herod imprisoned John because he had criticized his marriage with Herodias. Josephus (*Ant.* 18.116–118), who suppresses the information about the eschatological character of John's message, says that the reason for the execution was Antipas's fear of a popular insurrection, which indirectly confirms that John was an eschatological prophet and that his message had political consequences.

(b) The History-of-Religions Background

John the Baptist must be seen as an exponent of the rising eschatological or messianic temper that permeated large circles of the Jewish population of Palestine. The foundations of this eschatological temper had been laid in a history of many centuries by what has been called Jewish apocalypticism (§5.2b; §5.3e). The 1st century CE, however, is characterized by a decisive shift. While earlier apocalyptic movements and literatures, including the Dead Sea Scrolls of the Essenes

Bibliography to §8.1

C. H. Kraeling, *John the Baptist* (New York: Scribner's, 1951).

Charles H. H. Scobie, *John the Baptist* (Philadelphia: Fortress, 1964).

Ronald Schütz, *Johannes der Täufer* (AThANT 50; Zürich: Zwingli, 1967). Comprehensive listing of older literature.

Walter Wink, *John the Baptist in the Gospel Tradition* (SNTSMS 7; Cambridge: Cambridge University Press, 1968).

Josef Ernst, *Johannes der Täufer: Interpretation—Geschichte—Wirkungsgeschichte* (BZNW 53; Berlin: de Gruyter, 1989).

Robert L. Webb, *John the Baptizer and Prophet: A Socio-Historical Study* (JSNTSup 62; Sheffield: Sheffield Academic Press, 1991).

Bibliography to §8.1b

W. H. Brownlee, "John the Baptist in the Light of the Ancient Scrolls," in Krister Stendahl (ed.), *The Scrolls and the New Testament* (New York: Harper, 1956) 33–53.

John A. T. Robinson, "The Baptism of John and the Qumran Community," and "Elijah, John, and Jesus," in idem, *Twelve New Testament Studies* (SBT 34; London: SCM, 1962) 11–27 and 28–52.

(§5.2c) as well as the Pharisees (§5.3d), were concerned with the prediction and expectation of one or several messianic figures, the prophets who were rising now seem to have been leaders whose message announced the imminent coming of God himself, the liberation of Israel, and the final divine judgment. Josephus mentions several such prophets: Judas the Galilean (*Ant.* 18.23–24), whom he considers to have been the founder of the group of the Zealots, who "are convinced that God alone is their leader and master"; Theudas (*Ant.* 18.20.97–98); the Egyptian Prophet (*Ant.* 20.169–170); and others. Judas the Galilean and Theudas are also mentioned in the speech of Gamaliel in Acts 5:36–37. It is questionable, however, whether John the Baptist should simply be identified as one of these prophets of liberation. Most of the suggested parallels do not stand the test, neither for John the Baptist nor for Jesus of Nazareth. While these prophets were evidently revolutionary leaders, who wanted to initiate a divinely authorized war of liberation against Rome, John the Baptist does not seem to have had any such intentions. John's preaching of baptism also stands without a parallel. Jewish proselyte baptism (which is attested much later anyway) lacked the eschatological component. The ritual washings of the Essenes at Qumran are rites of a very different sort; they were priestly ceremonies that could be repeated and were designed to guarantee ritual purity, albeit that the concept of ritual purity at Qumran is closely related to an eschatological perspective.

What connects John the Baptist and Jesus to other eschatological prophets of the time is the absence of the proclamation of any intermediate messianic figure who would appear on earth at the end of the times as the anointed king of Israel. Both announce the imminent coming of God and God's kingdom. Different, however, from other messianic prophets of the time, they do not assign any revolutionary messianic role to the people of the elect. It is therefore not possible to understand John as a representative of the political messianism that eventually resulted in the Jewish War. John speaks solely about the coming of God in order to judge Israel— as Jesus speaks solely about the coming of the rule of God (§8.2c). The only precedent for such a message can be found in the preexilic prophecy of Israel, which knew neither a messianic figure nor a messianic role for the elect of Israel. If the theme of the renewal of the people in the wilderness also played a role in John's prophecy, the baptism that John offered should be understood in the context of the Exodus typology (passage through the Red Sea). John the Baptist must therefore be distinguished from those prophets who saw the fulfillment of God's promise for Israel in the uprising against Rome. His preaching of the coming judgment of God calls Israel to repentance and offers baptism as a guarantee for entrance into God's promise.

(c) The Effects of John's Ministry

John the Baptist created a movement that lasted beyond his death. Mark 2:18–19, formulated from the perspective of the followers of Jesus, contrasts the fasting of the disciples of John and of the Pharisees with the celebration of Jesus' disciples. The episode of the disciples of John the Baptist in Ephesus reported in Acts 18:1–7 may indicate that the movement spread even beyond Palestine. Nothing more, however, is known about the Baptist's sect, although it is not impossible that the Mandaeans, a religious group still in existence today in Mesopotamia (Iraq), which may have had its origin in the country of the Jordan, derives from John the Baptist. But most momentous was the influence that John exercised upon Jesus and his disciples. That Jesus was John's disciple is evident from the fact that he was baptized by him. There are also some pieces of information in the tradition that some of Jesus' first disciples came from the circles of John the Baptist (cf. John 1:35–40). We do not know why Jesus parted from John and his movement; it is not necessary to assume that there was any hostility involved. If the information in John 3:22–23 is reliable (see also John 4:1), Jesus and John would have been active at the same time (John 4:2 seeks to correct that somewhat). Indeed, Jesus' message may well have repeated John's call for repentance and the proclamation of the coming of God. An important testimony of Jesus about John is preserved in Matt 11:7–11, where Jesus says about John that he was "greater than a prophet" and "the greatest among all born by woman" (that is, "among all human beings"). These sayings, whether said by Jesus or formulated in the early tradition of sayings, preserve the memory that Jesus continued to hold John in very high regard, a memory that later editors of this tradition try to correct by the addition of Matt 11:10 and 11b ("the smallest in the kingdom is greater than he").

2. JESUS OF NAZARETH

(a) The External Data of His Life

No direct and first-hand information about Jesus survives. Information from outside Christian sources is not available. One must therefore rely exclusively on Christian sources. The semibiographical framework of the gospel stories, however, is the result of the editorial work of the gospel writers (see especially §10.2b) and can therefore not be used for the reconstruction of the ministry of Jesus. All traditional materials about Jesus preserved within the framework of the canonical and

Bibliography to §8.2:　　Studies

Günther Bornkamm, *Jesus of Nazareth* (Minneapolis: Fortress, 1995; first published in German 1956).

Amos N. Wilder, *Jesus' Parables and the War of Myths: Essays on Imagination in the Scripture*, ed. James Breech (Philadelphia: Fortress, 1982).

John Dominic Crossan, *The Historical Jesus: The Life of a Mediterranean Jewish Peasant* (San Francisco: HarperCollins, 1991).

Marcus J. Borg, *Meeting Jesus Again for the First Time: The Historical Jesus & the Heart of Contemporary Faith* (San Francisco: HarperCollins, 1994).

Bruce D. Chilton and Craig A. Evans (eds.), *Studying the Historical Jesus: Evaluation of the State of Current Research* (NTTS 19; Leiden: Brill, 1994).

Robert W. Funk, *Honest to Jesus: Jesus for a New Millenium* (San Francisco: HarperCollins, 1996).

Stephen J. Patterson, *The God of Jesus: The Historical Jesus and the Search for Meaning* (Harrisburg, PA: Trinity Press International, 1998).

Gerd Theissen and Annette Merk, *The Historical Jesus: A Comprehensive Guide* (Minneapolis: Fortress, 1998).

some noncanonical gospels have been formed ("inscribed") by the needs of the communities of Jesus' followers after his death. Moreover, all traditions—sayings as well as stories—were formed in the milieu of Greek-speaking communities. Even if underlying formations of such materials in an Aramaic-language milieu can be found, it must remain questionable whether they are the direct recording of what Jesus actually said and did. From the very beginning, the only interest in the process of the formation of the traditions in the communities of Jesus' followers was to apply what was remembered to the needs of their own situation. The attempts to identify the possibly oldest layer of the tradition, especially of the sayings, and assign these to the "historical Jesus," which characterize so many of the more recent efforts to recover the original voice of Jesus, are therefore fundamentally misguided. This becomes especially evident, if such attempts try to isolate those parts of the tradition in which Jesus appears to be different from both his Jewish environment and from the voices of his later followers. Whatever Jesus was and whatever he said and did must have been a congenial part of the trajectory that begins with the Jewish environment of Jesus' milieu and John the Baptist, continues in the formation of the tradition of the early communities of his followers, and finally results in the images of Jesus that are presented in the extant gospel literature. In other words, Jesus' message, deeds, and ministry belong within the context of a continuum that originates with the eschatological preaching of John and ends with the eschatological speech of Matthew 24–25. It cannot be recovered by isolating materials that seem not to belong to this continuum. On the other hand, whatever seems to have a special flavor or emphasis within this trajectory may well point to the earthly Jesus himself and his ministry.

A few external data of Jesus' life are visible as erratic blocks of the tradition. He must have come from the Galilean town of Nazareth in the north of Palestine, where he was born and grew up (his birth in Bethlehem is a later theological fiction that tried to connect Jesus to the town of David). The year of Jesus' birth is not known. Matthew dates the birth in the reign of Herod the Great, who died in the year 4 BCE. Luke, on the other hand, connects the birth of Jesus with the census, which was held when Judea and Samaria became a Roman province in the year 6 CE. Jesus' family was Jewish, which is clear from the names of his parents (Joseph and Mary) and his brothers (James, Joses, Judas, and Simon). Jesus' father was a

Bibliography to §8.2:   History of Scholarship

Albert Schweitzer, *The Quest of the Historical Jesus: A Critical Study of Its Progress from Reimarus to Wrede* (reprint ed.: Albert Schweitzer Library; Baltimore/London: Johns Hopkins University Press, 1998).

James M. Robinson, *A New Quest of the Historical Jesus and Other Essays* (Philadelphia: Fortress, 1983).

Marcus Borg, *Jesus in Contemporary Scholarship* (Valley Forge, PA: Trinity Press International, 1994).

Werner Georg Kümmel, *Dreissig Jahre Jesusforschung (1950–1980)* (ed. H. Merklein; BBB 60; Königstein/Ts: Hanstein, 1985).

Bibliography to §8.2:   Bibliography

Craig A. Evans, *Jesus* (IBR Bibliographies 5; Grand Rapids, MI: Baker, 1992).

building artisan or a carpenter (Matt 13:55), as was perhaps Jesus himself (Mark 6:3; according to Justin *Dial.* 88 he made yokes and plows). Jesus' mother tongue was Galilean Aramaic. It is possible that he also knew some Greek, but it is unlikely that such knowledge is reflected in early sayings of the tradition. No reliable information about his education survives. It is not probable, however, that he was an uneducated peasant. The earliest traditions of his disciples about him—*pace* the legend about the uneducated fishermen from Galilee—demonstrate a good knowledge of the Scriptures of Israel, which suggests that Jesus himself was able to read and write.

At some point after Jesus had joined the movement of John the Baptist and had been baptized by John, he parted from the circle of John's disciples and began his own ministry. It is fair to assume that the eschatological message of John had attracted him to that movement and that a different understanding of such a message prompted Jesus to part company with John. The tradition suggests that Jesus began his ministry in Galilee, but the places where he was active remain uncertain, because places named in the tradition may be cities and towns where the followers of Jesus were successful. It is remarkable, however, that the most important Hellenistic cities (Caesarea, Sepphoris, and Tiberias) are missing in the tradition, although the non-Jewish areas in the north (Caesarea Philippi) and west (Gadara east of the Sea of Galilee) are occasionally mentioned. It can therefore not be concluded from the outset that Jesus never visited pagan country. How often Jesus traveled to Jerusalem must remain uncertain—only once according to the Synoptic Gospels and at least three times according to the Gospel of John. Whether he also included areas of Judea and Samaria (see the episode of Jesus and the Samaritan woman in John 4) in his activities is uncertain. Nothing can be said about the duration of his ministry. Calculating the years according to the different reports of the gospels from at least one year to as many as three years is not helpful because all these calculations are based exclusively upon later, redactional data. Early traditions do not exist. It is certain, however, that Jesus was arrested when he visited Jerusalem for the Passover, probably in the year 30 CE, and that he was executed there. Except for Pilate's sentencing Jesus to death on the cross and perhaps the inscription on the cross, it is debatable, whether any historical data about the last days of Jesus' life are preserved in the passion narrative.

Our earliest witness, the apostle Paul, refers to the last meal "in the night in which Jesus was handed over" (1 Cor 11:23) but lacks any reference to the Passover. According to the Johannine passion narrative, Jesus' last meal with his disciples was not a Passover meal but took place on the day before Passover; John 18:28 refers explicitly to the fact that the Passover meal would be held in the evening after Jesus' crucifixion and death. The dating of the Synoptic Gospels is ambiguous. According to Mark 14:1–2 ("not on the festival, or there may be a riot among the people"), one would expect the execution to take place before the festival, and the report about the meal does not, in itself, contain any reference to the Passover (Mark 14:17–25). The impression that this was, nevertheless, a Passover meal was created by the later insertion of the legend about the finding of the room for the Passover meal (Mark 14:12–16) and then by Luke's redaction of the Markan account of the meal (Luke 22:15). Thus all the references to the Passover in the Synoptic

Aureus of Augustus
This gold coin shows the wreathed head of Augustus with the inscription AUGUSTUS DIVI F[ILIUS] = Augustus Son of the Divinized (Caesar). A coin like this might have been shown to Jesus when he was asked whether one should pay taxes to Caesar.

Gospels are secondary. The Johannine dating of the meal is preferable. After all, even someone as ruthless as Pontius Pilate would hesitate to execute a Jew on a festival day as important as Passover.

The tendentious development of the tradition is transparent with respect to the identification of those who were primarily responsible for the execution of Jesus. The major responsibility is further and further shifted toward the Jerusalem authorities. In Matthew, Pilate washes his hands in innocence (Matt 27:24), and a later tradition (the apocryphal *Letter of Pilate*) even claims that Pilate had already come to believe in Jesus in his heart, but that the Jews had forced him to go ahead with the execution. The responsibility of the Roman authorities for the condemnation and execution of Jesus is clear for two reasons. First, the Jerusalem authorities did not have the right of capital punishment; that was the exclusive reserve of the Roman prefect. The only two cases that might suggest that the Jewish court could pass the death sentence are the stoning of Stephen and the murder of Jesus' brother James. But the former was a case of mob lynching (§8.3b), while the latter occurred during a vacancy in the Roman governor's office (§6.6e). That the Jewish authorities were not permitted to put anyone to death is also reflected in the statement of John 18:31. Under no circumstances would they be able to do so in the presence of the Roman prefect, who regularly came to Jerusalem from Caesarea on the high holidays in order to forestall any possible unrest.

Second, the reason for Jesus' condemnation was certainly not the blasphemy that is reported in the Synoptic Gospels (Mark 14:64). All gospels agree in reporting the inscription that Pilate put on the cross: "Jesus of Nazareth, king of the Jews" (Mark 15:26; John 19:19). This inscription says only too clearly that the Roman prefect had a substantive political reason for Jesus' condemnation. Whatever Jesus' own claims might have been, in the eyes of Pilate he was an actual or potential political criminal—and, to be sure, not the first made short shrift of by Pilate (§6.6.c). One can, of course, assume that the leading circles in Jerusalem were usually interested in cooperating with the Roman governor. But in the case of Jesus, the tendency of the tradition to shift the blame to the Jewish court does not permit us to be certain about its complicity. Pilate would have exercised his legal authority in any case, however grateful he might have been for the cooperation of the Jerusalem authorities. Executed by the horribly cruel method of crucifixion, Jesus died a painful death.

(b) Jesus as Prophet, Wisdom Teacher, and Exorcist

The character of the extant materials does not permit the writing of a biography of Jesus. What Jesus' consciousness was and what he might have thought about his own mission lies beyond the reach of historical inquiry. Messianic or christological titles cannot be used for the reconstruction of Jesus' self-consciousness because not one of these titles (Messiah/Christ, Son of David, Son of Man, Son of God, Lord) is fixed firmly enough in the oldest tradition to be a reliable witness. Of the nonmessianic religious offices, the office of priest can be excluded right away. The title "priest" or "high priest" is applied to Jesus fairly late and only in very limited circles of early Christianity, which do not even attempt to construct a Levitic origin for Jesus (Hebrews 7), although the expectation of the anointed priest from Levi played a considerable role among the Essenes (§5.2c). Three other religious offices, however, have exercised a certain influence upon the way in which Jesus is presented in the gospel literature, namely those of the philosopher, the apocalyptic visionary, and the magician. (1) Philosophical influences were present in Palestine as early as the Hellenistic period, and they helped to shape rabbinic Judaism. Philo of Alexandria demonstrates how the ideal of the philosopher could be combined with that of the Jewish teacher of wisdom. But Jesus was not the head of a philosophical school, and it remains questionable whether he can be seen as a wandering philosopher. Nowhere before the 2d-century writings of Christian apologists were Jesus' teachings presented as philosophical insights. (2) Nothing indicates that Jesus was an apocalyptic visionary. With respect to Jesus as an apocalyptic visionary, the gospels present speeches of Jesus about the future (e.g., Mark 13; Matthew 24–25), but these are later compositions of disparate traditional materials. There are no elaborate visions of the future or celestial journeys reported about him (the Book of Revelation and the Gnostic revelations stepped into this breach). And, in any case, there is no evidence that Jesus used the written medium of communication that is characteristic for the production of an apocalypse. (3) As far as "magician" as a description of Jesus' office is concerned, it is evident that the gospels contain reports of Jesus performing miracles. But such reports lack the typical elements of the professional magician, such as performance for payment and instruction of apprentices, only rarely do they report elaborate manipulations (Mark 8:22–26 is the only exception), and the use of magical formulas is rare (only Mark 5:41; 7:34).

Philosophers and apocalyptic visionaries and magicians were religious professionals who were then "modern" and fully in keeping with their time. There is indeed a desire of the gospel tradition and of the authors of the gospels themselves to present Jesus as memorable and extraordinary according to these categories, his deeds as miraculous, his teaching as remarkable and his knowledge and wisdom as discerning, and his performance of miracles as powerful. Any reading of the gospel literature reveals the resulting depiction of Jesus as a divine human being, who was a teacher of esoteric wisdom, a miracle worker, and an apocalyptic prophet. No wonder that eclectic recent works about the historical Jesus have tried to follow more or less exclusively one of these tendencies, presenting Jesus as apocalyptic visionary, or as magician, or as philosopher, or as wise man with esoteric insights, sometimes taking such a Jesus completely out of the context of the tradition of Israel and the Jewish milieu of his time. Such attempts, however, disregard those materials in the gospels that are deeply rooted in the tradition of Israel and its Scripture.

There remain considerable materials in the gospel tradition that do not fit any of these—at that time "modern"—professional categories. Rather, such materials correspond instead to outmoded and archaic genres of prophetic speech and wisdom teaching. Prophetic sayings preserved in the gospel tradition lack any speculations about the timetable of future events but address the present situation in view of the coming of the rule of God. Interpretations of the law know neither casuistry nor a spiritualizing leap over the literal meaning. On the contrary, they are unequivocal and indisputable proclamations of the will of God and correspond as such to the prophetic Torah of the Scriptures of Israel. Among the wisdom sayings, proverbs and short metaphors prevail that are similar to the venerable proverbial wisdom of Israel. The wisdom speculations of the sapiential literature of Judaism have few parallels in the older stages of the Synoptic tradition. As in the case of John the Baptist (§8.1a), these phenomena are best understood as a conscious recourse to the prophetic tradition of Israel. It is also remarkable that such recourse does not have the appearance of artificiality; no archaizing features can be discovered. Rather what is present in these materials exhibits the features of a genuine and immediate renewal.

At the same time, some of the typical signs of a prophetic mission are missing. There is not a single tradition that reports Jesus' call (unless one wants to find such a tradition in the baptism of Jesus as it is reported in Mark 1:9–11). There are no visions, auditions, or stories of receiving a commission. Jesus' words are not introduced with the formula "Thus says the Lord." Nothing is said about Jesus attempting to express his prophetic mission in his external behavior or in his dress (as is indeed reported about John the Baptist, see Mark 1:6). Similarly, there is no sign in the tradition of Jesus' wisdom teaching of an appeal to the antiquity and reliable transmission of the sayings or, at least in the oldest layer of the tradition, of a special wisdom instruction for the disciples—not to mention the founding of a school. The absence of these features shows that parallels to the office of the rabbi and the rabbinic school house are totally lacking. The visible documentation of Jesus' authority thus remains an enigma. Whoever wants to understand Jesus' authority is referred absolutely to his words and to that which they announce.

Are there any narrative materials that point to the way in which Jesus himself understood his authority? Attempts have been made to claim historicity for such stories as the entry to Jerusalem (Mark 11:1–11), the cleansing of the temple (Mark 11:15–17), and at least some of the miracle stories. The two former stories are part of the passion narrative and have their roots in the development of that narrative on the basis of the interpretation of Israel's Scripture; this will be discussed later (§8.2e; 10.2a–b). With respect to the miracle stories, all attempts to claim their historicity are burdened with the danger of a rationalist interpretation (Jesus' suggestive power as a healer, etc.) or with supernaturalist claims. It is not improbable, however, that the numerous exorcisms reported in the tradition have their ultimate root in Jesus' activity as an exorcist. This should not mislead us to speculate about Jesus' extraordinary psychological powers, lest we fall once again into the trap of a rationalist explanation. The significance and function of these exorcisms of demons as they were remembered becomes clear when they are seen in the context of some traditional sayings of Jesus (Mark 3:23–25, 26, 27; especially Matt 12:28; see also Luke 10:18). These sayings, whether genuine sayings of Jesus or not, demonstrate that Jesus' exorcisms were remembered as visible signs of victory over Satan and the beginning of the realization of the rule of God in the present.

(c) The Proclamation of the Rule of God

This and the following chapter should not be understood as an attempt to reconstruct the original words of the historical Jesus of Nazareth. Such attempts are doomed to failure as they either uncritically construct an image of Jesus that is indiscriminately composed of possibly genuine sayings and secondary accretions, or—worse—use the criterion of dissimilarity and isolate as genuine Jesus sayings whatever seems to differ both from Jesus' Jewish environment on the one hand and from the traditions of the church on the other hand, thus creating a "historical" Jesus who has no relationship whatsoever to the history to which he belongs. There is no possibility of direct access to any of the words actually spoken by Jesus in his native Aramaic language. All that is available for the historian's inquiry are reflections or mirrors of Jesus' preaching and teaching in the tradition that was formulated for the purposes of the early (Greek-speaking) communities. Such reflections may reveal success as well as failure in the understanding of what has been remembered, genuine translation as well as mistranslation, and congenial representation as well as inadequate attempts to make Jesus' voice heard in a new context and for purposes and situations not anticipated or intended by Jesus himself. Jesus and his proclamation, however, are part of a trajectory that encompasses Jesus' Jewish milieu and John the Baptist, Jesus' ministry itself, and the interpretations of the tradition in the early Christian communities. It is a historical process in which Jesus' own contribution is crucial, and it is the very place and role of Jesus in this trajectory that can be assessed in our inquiry.

If Jesus was indeed a disciple of John the Baptist (§8.1c), it is most likely that he began his ministry by continuing the eschatological message of his teacher. In the oldest traditions of Jesus' announcements of the coming of the rule of God there are indeed, as in the preaching of John, no predictions of another messianic figure (the predictions of the coming of the Son of Man belong to a later stage of the tradition); God's coming and rule on earth are the object of the eschatological message. But in contradistinction to his teacher John, Jesus did not primarily emphasize the coming of God for the final judgment. Rather, he proclaimed the coming of God's "rule" (or "kingship," which translates the Greek term βασιλεία more accurately than "kingdom"). This rule of God, however, is not seen as an event of the distant future but as a process that is initiated with Jesus' words, as those who are able to hear are drawn into that rule here and now. The conduct of the disciples is therefore not motivated by the threat of the coming judgment but by the invitation to participate. It is characteristic of the difference between the disciples of John and the disciples of Jesus that the former are fasting while the latter are celebrating (Mark 2:18–19). This does not imply that the rule of God is fully realized in this celebration. It is typical for the prophetic announcement of a realized eschatology that the present is seen as an anticipation of an eschatological promise, in which the celebration in the present time envisages a future fulfillment.

This blending of present and future is especially visible in the parables of Jesus. Although they are preserved only in their Greek reformulations, they seem to be a

Bibliography to §8.1c

C. H. Dodd, *The Parables of the Kingdom* (first published 1935; rev ed.: London: Collins, 1961).
Joachim Jeremias, *The Parables of the Kingdom* (2d rev. ed.; New York: Scribner's, 1972).
James Breech, *The Silence of Jesus: The Authentic Voice of the Historical Man* (Philadelphia: Fortress, 1983).

distinct feature of Jesus' proclamation of the rule of God. The parables were originally free of any allegorical interpretations (such interpretations as, e.g., Mark
4:13–20 and Matt 13:36–43 are certainly secondary additions), and they did not
serve the purpose of illustrating Jesus' proclamation. Rather, they are themselves
invitations that challenge the hearer to enter into the new possibility of the rule of
God. They unlock for the hearer a realm of a new understanding of existence under an eschatological perspective, not serving as explanations but calling for a decision to enter. Those who enter into this realm will understand that the coming of
God's rule is God's sovereign act (Mark 4:26–29). Human care and activity will
not have any influence with respect to its miraculous harvest (Mark 4:3–8). God's
acting contradicts human criteria of both moral (Luke 16:1–8) and religious values
(Luke 18:9–14). It is also beyond the categories of just reward (Matt 20:1–16), because love cannot be measured by human criteria: the love of the father in the so-
called parable of the "Prodigal Son" (better: "About the Father Who Had Two Sons")
transcends all that can be expected as a normal human response. All these parables
contain an element of surprise, which appears especially in those features that do
not correspond to the normal criteria of necessity, fairness, and equity. Where is
the employer who would pay the same wages to everybody, no matter whether they
had worked all the day or just for one hour (Matt 20:1–16)? What sort of farmer
does nothing during the entire growing season, or simply allows the weeds to grow
with the wheat? Or what kind of dignified father would run down the street joy-
fully in order to meet his misfit son and, moreover, slaughter the fatted calf for
him? Or whenever did a rich man invite the hoodlums from the street corner when
his distinguished guests had declined the invitation? The miracle, mystery, and in-
calculability of the coming of God's rule—these are the topics of the parables.

The communities of Jesus' disciples, who formulated the earliest traditions that
are preserved, understood that Jesus had called them into the unfathomable eschatological tension between the blessings for the present and the fulfillment of
God's rule in the future. The blessings are pronounced in the present to the poor,
to those who weep, and to those who are hungry (see the beatitudes in Matt 5:3–12
and Luke 6:20–23—but note that, in their extant forms, they are all typical formulations of the Greek-speaking communities!). The fulfillment of the will of God on
earth in the petitions of the Lord's prayer is directly related to the petition for the
daily bread (Matt 6:10–11). Social injustice is certainly addressed here as also in
stories of the feeding of the multitudes (Mark 6:30–34 and parallels; Mark 8:1–10;
John 6:5–13). What Isaiah had prophesied (Isa 35:5–6; 61:1) is already here (Luke
11:20). It would be utterly futile for the disciples to look for any signs of the rule
of God and its coming in the future, or even to calculate the times, because the
rule of God is already present in their midst (Luke 17:20–21).

It is impossible to ignore the claim that is expressed in the earliest traditions
about Jesus' proclamation: if one wants to get involved in the rule of God and its
coming, there is no way to avoid the person of Jesus. If those who see what he is
doing are called blessed (Luke 10:23–24), the condition for accepting is that one
not take offense at his person (Luke 7:23). The tradition about Jesus indicates why
people might take offense: Jesus is just a human being, the son of Joseph and Mary
(see Mark 6:3; John 6:42). To accept Jesus as the one who makes God's rule present

in his words, however, does therefore not imply ascribing a particular dignity to him, such as a messianic title; rather, acceptance means new conduct in accordance with the coming rule of God (Luke 6:46), as this rule becomes present in Jesus' words.

This coming of the rule of God to human beings is not just a matter of personal conversion and moral renewal; rather, it concerns the creation of a new people, a new Israel. The message of John the Baptist was directed to Israel, and so Jesus' proclamation must be understood as addressed to Israel. A visible documentation of the creation of a new community must have been the celebration of meals, in which the coming of the messianic banquet was anticipated. Unfortunately, all materials in the extant gospel literature about Jesus' meals with his disciples and with many others must be judged as redactional. No direct historical information is available. There are, however, numerous indications that the celebration of such meals was an essential part of Jesus' ministry: the central rite of the post-Easter Christian community, the Eucharist, is anchored in the last meal of Jesus; the petition of the Lord's Prayer for the daily bread is closely related to the petitions for the coming of the rule of God and the realization of God's will on earth (Matt 6:10–11). An early Christian tradition that compares Jesus and John the Baptist speaks of Jesus as eating and drinking wine with tax collectors and sinners (Luke 7:34; see also Mark 2:15–16), which indicates that Jesus' meals were inclusive. This is stated also in the saying about those who will come from east, west, north, and south to sit at table in the kingdom of God (Luke 13:28–29). In any case, such meals are not events of individual edification; they are the nucleus of the formation of a ritual for the eschatological community.

(d) The New Human Situation

The ethical proclamation of Jesus has been interpreted in various ways. It was understood as eschatological ethics, that is, as a special morality valid only for the brief interval before the coming of God (or the Messiah); or as a formulation of a high morality that is obtainable only in theory; or as a moral standard that is designed to highlight human sinfulness; or finally as "evangelical" advice for the higher morality of a select group. Moreover, almost always this ethical proclamation is seen as addressed to individuals, their moral problems, or their sinfulness. Closely connected with this individualistic interpretation is the assumption that the validity of Jesus' commands is limited. In the way, however, in which Jesus' ethical teachings are preserved in the gospels, especially in the Sermon on the Mount (Matthew 5–7), it is evident that they are addressed to a community and designed to regulate the community's moral and religious conduct. Indeed, whatever is remembered from Jesus' teaching is preserved only because it was deemed to be useful for the life of the community that understood itself to be the eschatological people of Israel. Although it is unlikely that Jesus understood himself as an organizer of a new community—and certainly not as the founder of the church—it is

Bibliography to §8.2d

Amos N. Wilder, *Eschatology and Ethics in the Teachings of Jesus* (Cambridge, MA: Harvard University Press, 1958).

equally unlikely that he would have had any interest in the formation of moral individuals. If he understood his mission in terms of the prophets of Israel, his moral teaching must have been addressed to the people of Israel as a whole. Within the horizon of the coming of God's rule his ethical teaching is then the blueprint for the moral perimeters of the eschatological people of God, that is, eschatological ethics, but not in the sense of ethics for an interim period. The situation of the people under the coming of the rule of God is not a provisional one. On the contrary, it is the new abiding reality, which brings an end to everything that is provisional. The morality under the coming of God's rule involved a reevaluation of time-honored values. This is still remembered in Matthew's formulations, "You have heard what has been said to the people of old. . . , but I say to you" (Matt 5:21–48). Some of the old commandments of loving God and loving one's neighbor are, to be sure, repeated (Mark 12:29–31), but the command to love also one's enemies calls for a move into a new realm that lies beyond the boundaries of Israel's traditional ethics. Behavior designed to protect the integrity of Israel ("Love your neighbor and hate your enemy") becomes obsolete.

The conduct of many characters in the parables of Jesus transcends the framework of conventional behavior and moral criteria. Thus the signposts for conduct in the face of the coming rule of God cannot be united organically with traditional ethical rules, but can only be presented in contrasts, in radical intensification, in hyperbolic and paradoxical formulations, and finally—and it seems that here Jesus' words are most faithfully preserved—in parables and example stories. The example story of the Good Samaritan (Luke 10:29–37) is characteristic. The characters are carefully chosen: the priest, the Levite, and precisely a hated Samaritan. The first two pass by and take no notice. Why they do so is not told; a moral judgment is deliberately avoided. But the listener is expected to be irritated. What is also missing is any attempt to expound the moral superiority of the Samaritan. He does nothing more than what is necessary in the situation, and he does it with all his heart and with circumspection. To do well what is right, without regard for religious affiliation or political usefulness, is all that is demanded.

This is not, however, situational ethics without fundamental principles and criteria. Yet these principles are not based in general moral presuppositions, like assumptions of natural law; rather they are criteria deriving from the human situation in the face of the coming of God's rule—not the human situation in general! It is the situation in which human beings, as created and as children of God, recognize God as their creator and call upon him as their father, and in which they become sisters and brothers. The address of God in the Lord's Prayer (Matt 9:9–13) as "Our Father" reflects the substitution of more general categories for the definition of social relationships (such as master, slave, friend, patron, client) by family language. This also is present in the saying, "Whoever does the will of God is my brother and my sister and my mother" (Mark 3:35). A typical element of this eschatological ethics is the recourse to "what was from the beginning" and thus corresponds to the will of the creator, which is contrasted to the legislation of Moses, which was given solely because of the hardness of the human heart (Mark 10:5–6). It is noteworthy that in this case the recourse to the beginning of creation points to a matriarchal structure of the society, in which the man would leave the house of his parents to be joined to his wife (Mark 10:7 = Gen 2:24). Eschatological ethics takes away the pretense of the security of the law; the law can no longer be used as a veil behind which human beings can hide when they are confronted with the will of God. The woes against the Pharisees, though mostly creations of the community, especially in their Matthean form (Matthew 23), also argue that justice and mercy are shortchanged when righteousness according to the law permits the establishment of walls between human beings (see especially Matt 23:13, 16–19, 23, 25, 29).

The command to love one's neighbor, which already occupied a central position in Judaism (Lev 19:18), is also emphasized in the tradition of Jesus sayings, but it is rejected if it becomes the sole rule of social conduct (Matt 5:46–47) and replaced by the love of one's enemies (Matt 5:44). Respect for the dignity of human beings cannot be limited to membership in a particular religious group or by political goals such as liberation from the hated Roman rule (see Matt 5:41—Roman law demanded that a peasant be obligated to carry a soldier's luggage for one mile).

As for the consequence of such behavior, the Christian community remembered well that Jesus did not raise utopian hopes. His call to discipleship is not said to promise paradise on earth as a result of fulfilling the commandment of love. Whoever wants to follow Jesus must be prepared to suffer, and the disciples must expect that they have to risk their lives (Mark 8:34–35). Discipleship means to give up one's security (Luke 9:62; 14:26), which does not exclude intelligent and circumspect behavior. The numerous wisdom sayings in the oldest layers of the Synoptic tradition, whether they derive from Jesus' teaching or are formulations of the community, leave no doubt that prudence without falsehood is part of the discipleship of Jesus. Here, the early Christian community shares with the Pharisaic-rabbinic tradition the recourse to rules of behavior that are indebted to vernacular and common everyday wisdom. The use of power and force, however, is excluded because the rule of God becomes a reality exactly in the exercise of love and mercy. The recourse to Jesus' teaching here is paradoxically expressed in the recommendation to follow popular wisdom in the exercise of love and mercy rather than in demands to take Jesus as the exemplar of an especially virtuous behavior. But even such wise conduct is understood as a possible cause of hatred and rejection on account of "righteousness." While thus the recourse to a special august ethics for the building of a moral character of the individual is missing, the view of the new human situation is, on the one hand, unique insofar as it calls human beings into a special eschatological obedience according to the will of God as it is revealed in the beginning of creation. But on the other hand, it identifies this new human behavior with the popular rules of wise conduct—assuring the disciples that they will encounter hatred and enmity even then.

(e) The Resurrection

The preaching of Jesus, though certainly directed to Israel, did not, it seems, envisage the creation of a distinct entity that was later called "the church," nor is there any indication that its purpose was to identify and establish an entity of the elect of Israel, as distinct from Israel as a whole. There is no indication that Jesus intended to design any constitution for the organization of a group of disciples. All this is in accord with the proclamation of the ancient prophets of Israel, whose message was directed to Israel as a whole without any attempt to organize a special sect of the elect of Israel (that is a later development, which is evident in the Book of Daniel). Whatever Jesus had said could be all but disregarded in the development of the constitutional ideology of churches such as the congregations of the missionary work of Paul. Whenever words of Jesus were used, be it in Paul's communities or elsewhere, they did not provide the foundation for the definition of a group's identity but served as instructions and catechisms.

Easter changed everything. The one who had announced the presence of the rule of God in his invitation to enter into its realization in a new dimension of conduct was dead, cruelly executed by the Roman authorities as a political criminal. Yet, he was mysteriously alive. At this point several different developments must have started at the same time, although no direct records are available. One can judge only on the basis of records that were composed about twenty years later. The most important records are (1) the formation of the written collection of sayings of Jesus that appears to have resulted in the first composition of the Synoptic Sayings Gospel (Q; see §10.1a); (2) the letters of Paul; and (3) a report about the pouring out of the Holy Spirit (Pentecost) that was used by the author of Acts (chap. 2). The testimonies in the letters of Paul are more directly related to what can be called the Easter experience, because the traditions extant in Paul's letters can be dated to the time before Paul's calling, that is, no later than within five years after Jesus' death. It is much more difficult to decide how and on what basis or event the communities were formed for which the sayings of Jesus became the source of encouragement and inspiration.

All these sources have one common element: the conviction that the Jesus who had died on the cross was alive. Some of his followers had returned to Galilee and remembered in the breaking of the bread that Jesus' words had given them hope for an eschatological renewal that would eventually be realized in the banquet of the kingdom of God, at which people from the east and the west, the north and the south, would be fed and be gathered at the table of the kingdom. Was Jesus alive? Certainly his words were alive as the words of the living Jesus, and they gave strength and inspiration for the life of communities awaiting God's coming. The memory of Jesus' words and a new understanding of these words became the foundation of these communities.

Others had gathered again in Jerusalem. As they broke the bread and shared the cup, as they had done with Jesus before his death, they would have read the Scriptures and sung the psalms. "He was despised and rejected" (Isa 53:3); "He was wounded for our transgressions" (Isa 53:5); "My God, my God, why have you forsaken me?" (Ps 22:1); and "When you make his life an offering for sin, he shall see his offspring, and prolong his days. . . . The righteous one, my servant, shall make

Bibliography to §8.2e

Heinz-Wolfgang Kuhn. "Die Kreuzesstrafe während der frühen Kaiserzeit: Ihre Wirklichkeit und Wertung in der Umwelt des Urchristentums," *ANRW* 2.25.1 (1982) 648–793.

Hans Werner Bartsch, "Inhalt und Funktion des urchristlichen Osterglaubens," *ANRW* 2.25.1 (1982) 794–890.

many righteous" (Isa 53:10–11). Thus the arrival of God's rule was not initiated by one coming in glory but by the suffering of Jesus, the righteous one, who was now alive as God had promised in the Scriptures. In this context, the experience of the presence of the risen Jesus is intimately connected with the celebration of the common meal and with knowledge that the death of the suffering servant of God and his vindication is the beginning of a new age. The birth of the church and its mission is here authorized by the appearances of the one who died on the cross, who died "according to the Scriptures" and was raised "according to the Scriptures" (1 Cor 15:3–4).

Paul preserves a tradition of appearances of Jesus after his death in 1 Cor 15:5–7 to a number of people: first Peter and then the Twelve, then more than 500 brothers and sisters, then James, and then all the apostles. Elsewhere, a number of additional individuals to whom Jesus appeared are remembered: Mary of Magdala (John 20:11–18); Thomas (John 20:24–29); Peter, Nathaniel, the sons of Zebedee (James and John), and two others (John 21:2); Jesus' brother James (*Gospel According to the Hebrews*). It does not matter whether such appearances can be explained psychologically or otherwise, or whether they were "subjective" or "objective" appearances. The fact remains that they were remembered as events of calling and appointment for a mission. It is evident that, from the very beginning, the office of an apostle was firmly tied to the authorization for apostleship through an appearance of the risen Jesus ("Am I not an apostle? Have I not 'seen' Jesus, our Lord?" 1 Cor 9:1; cf. 15:5–11). The effect of these appearances of the risen Jesus were decisive. The appearances proclaimed that this Jesus of Nazareth, who had been executed by the Roman authorities, was alive. That, however, is not a statement of a fact about Jesus' fate after his death but a declaration that a new period in the story of humankind had begun. If one human being had been raised from the dead, a new age of the world had been initiated. It was for this reason that the appearances of the risen Jesus resulted in the proclamation of his resurrection as the turning point of the ages.

The missionary activities resulting from these appearances demonstrate that they did not stand alone. It is evident that the authorization of such missionary activity presupposed the creation of a community with its rituals and documentation of its identity as the new people of Israel. The oldest tradition about the establishment of a central communal ritual, namely, a common meal, is preserved in 1 Cor 11:23–26, where the words of institution for this meal appear as a tradition that Paul had received, that is, the tradition must have been formulated very soon after the death of Jesus. It is difficult to say whether this ritual had its origin just in the last meal that Jesus celebrated with his disciples "in the night in which he was handed over," as Paul says in 1 Cor 11:23, or whether it was just a continuation of meals that Jesus had celebrated with others regularly and often during his ministry. The latter is more likely for two reasons: (1) For all believing Jews, in fact, for all people in antiquity, a common meal is unthinkable without the proper thanksgiving to the deity who had provided the food. That thanksgiving was the religious element of such meals is preserved in the abiding name for the Christian celebration of the Lord's Supper, namely Eucharist (εὐχαριστία), the Greek term for "thanksgiving." (2) It can be conjectured that Jesus' meals were celebrated under an eschatological

Jesus Christ

From the Apse Mosaic of Osios David in Thessaloniki. One of the oldest Christian mosics (perhaps V c.e.), it presents Christ standing in the sun and leaning against the rainbow (Genesis 9), surrounded by the four "creatures" of the divine throne (Revelation 4; the one with the face of a man is visible in the upper left corner).

perspective ("messianic banquet" would be the appropriate term, but it is unlikely that Jesus expected the future coming of a messiah), that is, in the anticipation of a future meal in the rule of God (see also Mark 14:25). The most tangible continuity of this community with the historical Jesus therefore may have been the ritual of the Eucharist. In the words of institution, as they are quoted by Paul (and later also in Mark 14:22–24 and parallels), the ritual is intimately connected with the death of Jesus. But there are early-Christian meal traditions that lack this connection (see the eucharistic prayers of the *Didache*).

The documentation of the new community's identity is formulated in the report of the pouring out of the Holy Spirit, preserved in a revised and heavily edited form in Acts 2:1–13, where the significance of the event is appropriately highlighted with the reference to Joel 3:1–5: "In the last days, says God, I shall pour out my spirit upon all flesh." The pouring out of the Holy Spirit signifies that the self-definition of this new community appeared in its claim to be the new eschatological Israel. Very soon after Jesus' death, a second ritual must have been established: baptism of all new members with the transfer of the gift of the Holy Spirit to the new initiate. Although this baptism was done "in the name of Jesus," there is no obvious reference to such a practice in any of the traditions about Jesus. John 4:1–2 indicates that Jesus himself had not resumed the practice of John the Baptist. The establishment of baptism as the rite of initiation into the new community of Israel is therefore a return to the practice of John the Baptist under an eschatological perspective. The emphasis, however, is now no longer on the protection from the coming judgment of God, who would come "to baptize with fire and the spirit" (Matt 3:11), but on the receiving of the eschatological spirit of God. Like the Eucharist, also baptism could be understood in relation to the death of Jesus ("All those who have been baptized into Christ Jesus have been baptized into his death," Rom 6:3).

What has been characterized here is the development of a tradition about the death and resurrection of Jesus that probably began in the Jerusalem community of followers of Jesus, found its decisive formulation in the earliest Greek-speaking community of Antioch, became the catalyst for the missionary activities that must have begun immediately after the death of Jesus, and is most clearly visible in the letters of Paul. It was not, however, the only continuation of traditions about Jesus and of the formation of communities in Jesus' memory. The multiplicity of christological titles applied to Jesus (Messiah/Christ, Son of God, Son of Man, Lord) proves the opposite. The diversity of Christian beginnings is evident in the sources, and it must have had its origin in diverse responses to the event of the death of Jesus and to documentation that this crucified Jesus was now alive again. In all cases, however, the result was the crystallization of traditions about Jesus and his ministry. Whatever the specific form of the formation of the various traditions was, all were unanimous in the belief that Jesus was alive and that therefore sorrow and grief, or even hate and rejection, were changed into joy, creativity, and faith. Although the resurrection revealed nothing new, it nonetheless made everything new for those who had followed him and for all those who cared to listen to the message of Jesus' resurrection.

3. THE EARLIEST CHRISTIAN COMMUNITIES

(a) The Earliest Gatherings of Jesus' Followers

The reports in the first chapters of the Book of Acts cannot be used as a reliable source for the beginnings of the earliest Christian community. These chapters are dominated by legendary and idealizing tendencies (§7.3.c). But from some information in the letters of Paul and from indirect evidence provided by the gospels of the New Testament it is possible to draw some conclusions about the earliest formation of traditions and rituals among the followers of Jesus. It is much more difficult to arrive at any assumption about the earliest formation of community structures, because it is improbable that these followers of Jesus renounced their membership in the religious community of Israel. On the contrary, those who remained in Jerusalem—some traditions show that many went back to Galilee (cf. Mark 16:7)—participated in the worship of the Temple (Acts 2:46), while those who settled elsewhere in Palestine continued to attend the services in their synagogue. Later controversies regarding the admission of Gentiles demonstrate that these followers of Jesus kept up the practice of circumcision and observed the dietary laws. That they remained within the boundaries of Jewish synagogues in

Bibliography to §8.3

Maurice Goguel, *The Birth of Christianity* (London: Allen and Unwin, 1953).

Hans Conzelmann, *History of Primitive Christianity* (Nashville, TN: Abingdon, 1973), 29–77.

Martin Hengel, *Acts and the History of Earliest Christianity* (London: SCM, and Philadelphia: Fortress, 1980).

Robin Scroggs, "The Earliest Hellenistic Christianity," in Neusner, *Religions in Antiquity,* 176–206.

Nock, "Early Christianity and its Hellenistic Background," in idem, *Essays,* 1. 49–133.

John Dominic Crossan, *The Birth of Christianity: Discovering What Happened in the Years Immediately after the Execution of Jesus* (San Francisco: HarperCollins, 1998).

Helmut Koester, "The Memory of Jesus' Death and the Worship of the Risen Lord," *HTR* 91 (1998) 335–50.

Bibliography to §8.3:   On the Theology of the Earliest Churches

Bultmann, *Theology,* 1. 33–183.

Conzelmann, *Outline,* 29–93.

Oscar Cullmann, *The Earliest Christian Confessions* (London: Butterworth, 1949).

C. H. Dodd, *The Apostolic Preaching and Its Development* (New York: Harper & Row, 1951).

Werner Kramer, *Christ, Lord, Son of God* (SBT 50; London: SCM, 1966).

Philipp Vielhauer, "Jesus und der Menschensohn," and "Ein Weg zur neutestamentlichen Christologie," in idem, *Aufsätze zum Neuen Testament* (ThBü 31; München: Kaiser, 1965) 92–140 and 141–98.

Ernst Käsemann, "The Beginnings of Christian Theology," and "On the Subject of Primitive Christian Apocalyptic," in idem, *New Testament Questions,* 82–107 and 108–137.

Erich Grässer, *Das Problem der Parousieverzögerung in den synoptischen Evangelien und in der Apostelgeschichte* (BZNW 22; 3d ed.; Berlin: de Gruyter, 1977).

Bibliography to §8.3a

Foakes Jackson and Lake, *Beginnings,* 1. 265–418.

Haenchen, *Acts,* 166–75, 190–96.

Robinson and Koester, *Trajectories,* 119–26, 211–16.

other places of Palestine, and soon also elsewhere, is evident from the fact that Paul, before his calling, persecuted those members of synagogue communities who confessed their belief in Jesus' resurrection.

These believers in Jesus were radically different, however, from their fellow-Jews because of their enthusiastic consciousness of the spirit; this was the spirit of God to be poured out at the end of times, which brought the gift of tongues and prophecy, worked miracles, and granted the assurance that they belonged to God's elect people. In its original form, the story of Pentecost (Acts 2:1–13) did not tell of the speaking in many languages—that is Luke's secondary interpretation—but of glossolalia, that is, the speaking in tongues. The story was probably composed in Jerusalem in order to document, in the form of a narrative, the arrival of the spirit. That the arrival of the spirit was understood as the creation of the eschatological Israel is demonstrated in the establishment of the "Twelve." These Twelve were neither apostles nor community leaders but the symbolic representation of the twelve tribes of Israel. Closely related to these expressions of the claim that the eschatological new creation of Israel had now begun is the practice of eschatological baptism, known from John the Baptist—Jesus himself apparently did not baptize his followers. Through baptism "in the name of Jesus" more and more people were given the seal of their belonging to the new Israel and received the spirit as a pledge. Thus baptism became one of the rituals that anticipated the creation of community structures that would eventually distinguish these groups of followers of Jesus from the boundaries of Israel's Temple and synagogue communities.

The most important ritual, however, was the common meal, which also constituted the most important link to Jesus of Nazareth. It is most likely that Jesus had celebrated table fellowship with his friends and followers and that these meals were accompanied by prayers expressing the hope for the coming of God's kingdom, that is, such meals were understood as anticipation of the "messianic banquet." Parallels to such understanding of the common meal can be found in the Qumran community (§5.2c) and in traditional prayers for the regular meal in Judaism. The oldest tradition about this common meal is quoted in Paul's First Letter to the Corinthians (1 Cor 11:23–26)—a tradition that explicitly connects this meal with the story of his suffering and death: "In the night in which he was handed over." The tradition about the institution of this meal in Jesus' last meal is also found in the Synoptic Gospels (Mark 14:22–25 and parallels) and, independently, in John 13. A different tradition, though equally old and perhaps reflecting the meal practice of Jesus and his followers more directly, has survived in the eucharistic prayers of the *Didache* (9–10). All three, Paul's tradition, the Synoptic accounts, and the prayers of the *Didache,* share three elements: (1) The bread is understood as the symbol of the community. In Paul's words, all those who eat the same bread are therefore "one body" (1 Cor 10:16–17); in the *Didache* the bread that has been scattered on the mountains and has been brought together into one bread symbolizes the eschatological gathering of Israel from the four corners of the world. (2) The cup represents the fulfillment of the promise of Scripture; in Paul's words of institution, it is the cup of "the new covenant," in the Didache it is the "holy vine of David" (see also Mark 14:24). (3) The meal is understood as an anticipation of the banquet in the kingdom of God. "As often as you eat this bread and drink from this cup you shall proclaim the death of the Lord until he comes" (1 Cor 11:25). "I shall not drink from this fruit of the vine until I drink it anew in the kingdom of God" (Mark 14:25). The meal prayers of the *Didache* 10 conclude with the words, "May grace come and this world pass away, . . . Maranatha!" (="Our Lord come!" *Did.* 10.6; cf. 1 Cor. 16:22; Rev 22.20). Although distinct liturgical practices were developing in different circles of the followers of Jesus, it is likely that these three common elements have their roots in the meal practices instituted by Jesus himself during his ministry. The Eucharist therefore constitutes the most important link to the historical Jesus.

In other respects, very early different developments are evident in the way in which various circles of Jesus' followers expressed their relationship to the memory of Jesus of Nazareth. The circles that apparently gathered in Galilee made no recourse to Jesus' suffering and death. The community that preserved the earliest collection of sayings of Jesus, which eventually resulted in the composition of the Synoptic Sayings Gospel ("Q," see §10.1a–c), did not value the recollection of Jesus' suffering and death but, although celebrating an eschatological meal (see Luke 13:28–29), emphasized the presence of the saving message of Jesus in his words as they were remembered and as Jesus spoke again through his prophets (see also the *Didache,* the Epistle of James [§10.1c] and eventually the *Gospel of Thomas* [§10.1b]). Christological titles for Jesus are strikingly absent here; only at a later stage did prophets of these communities announce Jesus' return in the near future as the "Son of Man" (see §10.1a).

On the other hand, there is good evidence that the circles of Jesus' followers who settled at Antioch in Syria told a story of Jesus' suffering and death, which was most likely developed in the context of the Eucharist, and that they also ascribed christological titles to Jesus, with which they expressed his divine dignity. It is most probable that both had their origin among the disciples of Jesus who had gathered in Jerusalem. To be sure, although Paul derived his tradition from the Greek-speaking community of Jesus' followers at Antioch, the relationship of that community with Jerusalem remained very intimate for several decades; this is also evident in Paul's several visits to Jerusalem. Antioch's traditions should therefore be understood as the transformation of Jerusalem's traditions into the Greek milieu. As the memory of Jesus' last meal was anchored in the story of his last days, his trial, and his death (§10.2a–b), he was worshiped in Jerusalem as the "Lord" and as the "Messiah/ Christ." With these titles, Jesus is honored as the coming redeemer of Israel. In its Aramaic form *Maran,* the title "Lord" is firmly established in the liturgy of the common meal and assigned there to Jesus' return in the near future. "Messiah" must have been used very early in the Aramaic-speaking community—in its Greek translation "Christos" it became quickly a proper name without any specific messianic connotations, but it is still found in some early credal formulas (e.g., 1 Cor 15:3; cf. 1 Cor 5:7 and elsewhere). The title "Son of David" also derives from the early Jerusalem period (see the old formulas in Rom 1:3–4; 2 Tim 2:8; and also "the holy vine of your servant David" and "Hosanna to the God of David" in the eucharistic prayers of the *Didache*). While these messianic titles can be understood in continuity with Jesus' eschatological preaching of the kingdom of God, the most difficult problem was the explanation of Jesus' death. In this context, several Jewish conceptions of cultic sacrifice were operative, including the concept of Jesus' death as a sacrifice for the expiation of sins. This concept lies at the root of the frequently used formula "for us," which was later also connected with the Eucharist. Side by side with this concept one finds the understanding of Jesus' death as a sacrifice that seals the new covenant (1 Cor 11:25; Heb 13:20). Jesus' death was also interpreted as a Passover sacrifice (1 Cor 5:7). These christological developments, as well as the proclamation of Jesus' death and resurrection, clearly present in the early community at Antioch, must have had their origin in Jerusalem. When Paul, Barnabas, and Titus visited Jerusalem for the Apostolic Council (§9.1d), they found that they were in full agreement with the apostles in Jerusalem about the "gospel" that they preached.

At the time of Paul's missionary activities in Arabia and Antioch, Syria, and Cilicia (ca. 33–35 to 48–50 CE; see §9.1c) the leaders of the believers in Jerusalem, known as the "pillars" (Gal 2:9), were Peter (whom Paul usually calls "Cephas"), John, and James (not the disciple but Jesus' brother). Peter, however, must have left Jerusalem soon after the Apostolic Council and moved to Antioch (Gal 2:11), while John seems to have taken up missionary work elsewhere, because the churches that later claimed the name of John as their authority had no direct relationship with Jerusalem (§10.3a). When Paul visited Jerusalem in the middle or late 50s CE, Jesus' brother James was alone, the uncontested leader of the believers in Jerusalem, where he suffered martyrdom in the year 62 CE. Shortly thereafter, before the beginning of the Jewish War (§6.6c), the Jerusalem community emigrated, probably to Pella on the Jordan. But by this time, Jerusalem had long since lost its significance as a center of missionary activities. Greek-speaking Jewish and Gentile communities had moved into prominence in such new centers as Antioch, Ephesus, Corinth, and Rome. This development, however, also had its beginnings in Jerusalem within a few years after Jesus' death.

(b) The Hellenists and Stephen

Jerusalem was a metropolis of worldwide significance, largely because of the Jewish dispersion, for which that city was still the true center of the cult and the symbol of the religion of Israel during the early Roman imperial period. But the vast majority of all adherents to this religion lived in the diaspora and had long since adopted the language and culture of their various places of residence outside Palestine, where most of them had lived for centuries, that is, they had become Hellenized (§5.1e). This Hellenization had also affected Jerusalem itself to some degree, where the Greek language was as much at home among Jews as Aramaic. "Hellenists," that is, Greek-speaking Jews, were not an unusual phenomenon in Jerusalem. The

Bibliography to §8.3b

Haenchen, *Acts*, 259–308.

Henry J. Cadbury, "The Hellenists," in Foakes Jackson and Lake, *Beginnings*, 5. 59–74.

Marcel Simon, *St. Stephen and the Hellenists in the Primitive Church* (the Haskell Lectures; London: Longmans, Green, 1958).

Martin Hengel, "Zwischen Jesus und Paulus: Die 'Hellenisten,' die 'Sieben' und Stephanus," *ZThK* 72 (1975) 151–206.

first known conflict in Jerusalem concerning the Christians resulted from differences between those adherents of Jesus who had come mostly from Galilee and "Hellenists" who had become Christians. Luke has preserved older traditions about this conflict in Acts 6:1–8:3. Contradictions between these older traditions and Luke's harmonizing tendencies can still be detected. For Luke, the "Twelve" appear as the representatives of the entire Christian community, though they were actually the symbolic representatives of the Aramaic-speaking members. Other community leaders had emerged, who spoke Greek and claimed for themselves the title *diakonos*—a title used elsewhere for preachers and missionaries (2 Cor 3:6; 11:23). Luke never uses the title *diakonos* and instead characterizes them as people who were chosen for the daily service (*diakonia*) at table—clearly a secondary construction; why should exactly the Hellenists, the Greek-speaking Jews, be chosen for table service? Acts 6:5 preserves a list of these inspired Hellenist missionaries who were active among the Greek-speaking Jews of Jerusalem. Indeed, such activity by one of the Hellenists, namely Stephen, is reported immediately afterward.

The speech of Stephen in Acts 7:2–53 is a Lukan composition and cannot be used for the reconstruction of Stephen's views or those of his Hellenist associates. But there is a chance that the tradition used by Luke gave the reason for the eruption of the persecution that led to Stephen's martyrdom. Acts 6:11 has preserved the information: Stephen is accused of criticizing Moses, that is, the law, and of blaspheming (in contrast, the Lukan verses in Acts 6:13–14 and Stephen's speech give criticism of the Temple as the reason for the accusation). Relying on the information of Acts 6:11 it appears that the controversy centered on the question of the continuing validity of the law of Moses for the Christians—a question that reappeared as the central issue in Paul's debates with the leaders in Jerusalem. This understanding of the traditional material underlying Luke's story in Acts 6–7 is confirmed by the events after the persecution of the Hellenists. The beginnings of a Christianity that is free from the obligations of the law thus belong in the Jerusalem community itself. It is not surprising that this type of Christianity was unable to make much headway in that city. According to Luke's description, Stephen was brought before the Jewish court for regular proceedings against him, and he is even given the opportunity to preach a long missionary sermon before that court. What is still preserved from Luke's source, however, gives the impression that Stephen was lynched, not stoned in a regular legal fashion (Acts 7:54, 57, 58a, 59). The Jewish authorities did not possess the right of capital punishment anyway. The Lukan report that Saul/Paul participated in this persecution (Acts 7:58b) must be disputed on good grounds because Paul freely admits that he persecuted the Christians, but states that he was unknown to the Christian community in Judea before his call and even for some years thereafter (Gal 1:22). On the other hand, since Luke's chronological sequence seems to be correct, the event of Stephen's martyrdom must be dated before the founding of communities of adherents of Jesus in Antioch, Damascus, and elsewhere and before the call of Paul. These communities were founded only after the dispersion of the Hellenists after the death of Stephen and most likely through their missionary activities. Paul persecuted the followers of Jesus in these Greek-speaking communities and his call cannot be dated later than the year 35 CE, possibly earlier (§9.1b, c). Thus the dispute about the validity of the law and Stephen's martyrdom took place within a year or two after the death of Jesus.

Nothing is said in Luke's report about the role of Peter, John, and James, or of the Twelve in the persecution of the Hellenists. Thus they were not affected by the persecution. Only the Hellenists were expelled from Jerusalem, while the law-abiding followers of Jesus were not harmed. The expulsion of the Hellenists, however, resulted in the founding of communities outside Jerusalem and Judea. Philipp went to Samaria (Acts 8:1ff.), others to Antioch, where they were later joined by Barnabas (Acts 11:19ff.), a Jew from the diaspora of Cyprus, who had earlier been a member of the Jerusalem church (Acts 4:36).

(c) The Christian Church of Antioch

Freedom from the law had already been demanded by the Hellenistic Jewish followers of Jesus in Jerusalem. But a city that was not under the control of the Temple and its authorities would become a more opportune place for the building of a community that was no longer subject to the law of Moses. The founding of such a community in Antioch, major metropolis of the East and capital of the province of Syria, was therefore a crucial step in the direction of a major missionary effort in the Jewish diaspora and in the Gentile world of the Roman realm. Antioch thus became the home base and headquarters for the spread of the gospel to Gentile communities founded by Barnabas, Paul, and others. Older traditions about Antioch are preserved in Acts 11:19ff. and 13:1ff., where Luke reports a list of prophets and teachers that includes Paul. Paul indeed notes in Gal 1:21 that he had worked as a missionary from Antioch in the areas of Syria and Cilicia for more than a decade. The question is whether that activity can be dated, which depends upon the analysis of Paul's report in Galatians 1 (see §9.1c) and the dating of the Apostles' Council (§9.1d). The latter cannot have taken place any later than the year 49 CE. Thus Paul must have come to Antioch eleven years (perhaps even fourteen years) earlier, that is, no later than in 38 CE, with his call to have happened three years earlier, which implies that these Hellenistic communities of followers of Jesus in Syria were active missionary communities as early as the year 35 CE. Thus only a very few years lie between the death of Jesus and the beginning of the Gentile mission that was free from the law of Moses. The movement must have spread with an explosive power.

For the reconstruction of the teachings and practice of the Antiochean community the Pauline letters are eminently significant. Whatever traditions are quoted and used by Paul are certainly derived from this congregation, in which he had worked for so many years. If we are speaking about the proclamation of the Hellenistic church before Paul, we are talking about the formation of traditions and

Bibliography to §8.3c

Haenchen, *Acts*, 364–72.

Eduard Schweizer, *Lordship and Discipleship* (SBT 28; London: SCM, 1960).

Robinson and Koester, *Trajectories*, 219–29.

Meeks and Wilken, *Jews and Christians in Antioch*.

the development of ecclesiastical structures in the thirties of the 1st century CE. The center of this proclamation was the kerygma of the crucified Jesus whom God had raised from the dead, the story of his trial and suffering, and the report about his epiphanies as the turning point of the ages. Luke's report (Acts 11:26) that the disciples in Antioch called themselves "Christians" for the first time, however, is anachronistic because Paul does not yet know this term. But the designation of the message as "gospel" (*euangelion*) and the self-designation of the community as "church" (*ekklesia*) must have originated in Antioch, not in Jerusalem or in other Aramaic-speaking communities, because both terms belong to the Greek world, where the general meaning of *euangelion* is "news," especially the news announcing the beginning of a new age through the benefactions of the Roman emperor, and where "church" (*ekklesia*) designates the assembly of the free citizens. At the same time, there is a connection to the Scriptures of Israel in their Greek translation, where *ekklesia* is the term for the assembly of Israel. Very soon the designation of the proclamation as *euangelion* was also connected to the Greek Bible, where the corresponding verb *euangelizesthai* ("to proclaim") describes the message of the liberation of Israel (see the quotation of Isa 52:7 in Rom 10:15).

The development of the gospel formulas (Paul cites one such formula as "gospel" in 1 Cor 15:1ff.) falls into the earliest years of the church of Antioch; Paul received this gospel as a tradition. These gospel formulas do not speak about the coming of Jesus in the future but proclaim the past events of cross and resurrection as the turning point of the ages. Accordingly the Lord's supper is also understood as a commemoration of the same eschatological event. The participation in the "one bread" not only directs one's view to the future assembly of all believers in God's kingdom, it also becomes the participation in the one body of Christ, namely the church, in the present. Similarly, the cup is the sign of one's present sharing in the new covenant, which has been founded through the shedding of Jesus' blood. This is expressed in the words of institution of the Eucharist, which were formulated in the church of Antioch and which Paul quotes as a tradition in 1 Cor 11:23–25. Further reflections about the death of Jesus and its significance also most likely derive from Antioch. Such traditions are reflected in Rom 3:25ff.; 4:25; Gal 1:4, and elsewhere.

As for the organization of the Antiochian church, Acts 13:1–2 tells that there were prophets and teachers. No doubt the office of apostle was also known; in the Syrian church order of *Didache* 11–13 apostles, prophets, and teachers occur side by side. As early as his Antiochian activity Paul understood his own office as that of an apostle. Acts 15 and Galatians 2 make clear that the church of Antioch did not understand itself as subject to the jurisdiction of Jerusalem. It took more than a decade before Paul, Barnabas, and the Gentile Christian Titus went from Antioch to Jerusalem to work out an agreement on the controversial question of the validity of the law (§9.1d). By that time the primary activity of this church, namely the Gentile mission, had been carried out successfully not only in Antioch itself, but also in other cities of Syria and Cilicia. Although Acts 13–14 is an idealized presentation of a missionary journey by Barnabas and Paul, it still demonstrates the character of the missionary efforts of Antioch. It is also typical that the missionary work was organized in such a fashion that it used a major political and economic metropolitan center as administrative headquarters— a pattern that Paul would later adopt for his mission in Asia Minor and Greece.

(d) Other Christian Communities in East and West

At the time of the founding of the Christian community in Antioch, a number of other churches must have come into existence elsewhere in the area of Syria-Palestine. Some of this missionary activity was probably due to the efforts of the Hellenists, who had been driven out of Jerusalem after the martyrdom of Stephen. Acts 8 speaks of a successful mission of Philipp in Samaria. If the report in Acts 9:32–43 rests on older tradition, it demonstrates that Peter worked as a missionary among Jews of other Palestinian cities, in this particular case in Joppa (today a part of Tel Aviv). But the story of the beginning of the Gentile mission by Peter in Caesarea (Acts 10) is entirely legendary. Mark 16:7 could be understood as an indication that there were congregations in Galilee that claimed to be founded by appearances of the risen Jesus. Luke 6:17 speaks of people who came from the *Paralios,* that is, from the seacoast with its cities of Tyre and Sidon: does this provide evidence for the existence of congregations in that area that derived the tradition of their founding from Jesus' own ministry? A church in Damascus must have existed before the calling of Paul (Acts 9:1ff.; 2 Cor 11:32), and Paul began his missionary work in Arabia (the area east of the Jordan river, probably using Damascus as the basis for his activity (Gal 1:17).

The expansion of the proclamation beyond the areas of Syria and Palestine in these early years can be determined with certainty only for the Pauline mission and its competitors in Asia Minor, Macedonia, and Greece. The leader of this missionary effort was certainly Paul, though others followed soon, and Paul apparently found that there was already a community in Ephesus when he arrived there in the last years of his missionary career. Although nothing is known about the beginnings of a community in Rome, it must have existed before Paul, as he wrote a letter to introduce himself to that community, probably in the year 55 CE. The Roman community of followers of Jesus may have been founded by diaspora Jews who had been converted elsewhere and then settled in Rome. Diaspora Judaism had worldwide connections, which would serve well also for the founding of Christian communities in the Cyrenaica, on Cyprus (Acts 11:20 mentions preachers who had come from there), and in Alexandria, although our only reliable information comes from a later period. It is curious, however, that the Alexandrian church later chose the otherwise obscure Mark as its founder: was Mark indeed the first missionary who went to Alexandria?

In all these missionary efforts originating in Antioch the proclamation of the death and resurrection of Jesus as the turning point of the ages was the basis for the spread of the gospel and the founding of communities. A very different message,

Bibliography to §8.3d

Charles H. H. Scobie, "The Origins and Development of Samaritan Christianity," *NTS* 19 (1972/73) 390–414.

however, of the followers of Jesus is evident in other areas of Palestine and especially eastern Syria. Evidence has appeared only more recently in the investigation
of the early stages of the Synoptic Sayings Gospel (Q; see §10, 1a [1]) and the tradition that forms the core of the *Gospel of Thomas* (§10, 1b [1]) as well as one of
the sources of the Gospel of John (§10, 3a [1]). In these sources the understanding of Jesus' sayings is the center of the new message, while references to Jesus'
death and resurrection are absent. Rather, Jesus' sayings are seen as saving words
of divine wisdom that call the disciple into a life of radical rejection of this world
and its institutions. The eschatological expectation of God's coming kingdom is
here internalized into a knowledge of the disciple's divine origin and destiny. In
areas of Palestine (Galilee and the areas east of the Jordan) and (eastern) Syria, this
understanding of Jesus' sayings resulted in the formation of groups of wandering
ascetics, who despised the human body and rejected home and family. Similar
Gnosticizing beliefs, however, also appeared elsewhere in established communities;
they were not restricted to the social conditions of the Syrian hinterland. Paul had
to discuss such a wisdom theology in 1 Corinthians 1–4 (§9.3c), and a considerable
portion of the theological debates in the Johannine communities are dominated by
a concern with the understanding of Jesus' sayings as revelations about the divine
self of the human individual (§10.3a [1]). This understanding of Jesus' message can
therefore not be explained as a result of the social disenfranchisement of certain
marginal groups at the eastern fringes of the Roman world. Rather, it is a theological phenomenon that is best characterized as realized and individualized eschatology—a 1st-century precursor of the Gnostic movements of the 2d century
(§§10, 5 and 11, 2), which was embraced not only by the monastics of the Syrian
and Egyptian deserts but also by the educated elites of Edessa and Alexandria.

However fragmentary the total picture may be, it is nevertheless obvious that
the earliest mission and expansion of the new message during the first years and
decades after Jesus' death was a phenomenon that utterly lacked unity. On the contrary, great variety was the result of these quickly expanding groups of followers
of Jesus. The Pauline mission is the only one about which we possess any direct
information; but the formation of other and often very different groups cannot be
doubted, even if it can only be reconstructed through the critical analysis of later
materials and often fragmentary information. Although Paul's missionary effort
constituted but a small segment of the beginnings of Christianity, it became very
important and had momentous consequences. It is therefore advisable first to describe the Pauline mission and then attempt to trace the development of those
churches and groups that were initially independent of it.

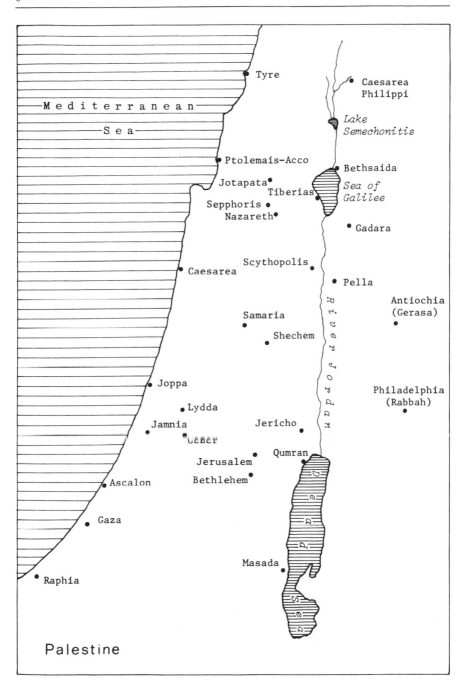

Tyre

Caesarea
Philippi

Mediterranean

Sea

*Lake
Semechonitis*

Ptolemais–Acco

Bethsaida

Jotapata

*Sea of
Galilee*

Tiberias

Sepphoris

Nazareth

Gadara

Scythopolis

Caesarea

Pella

Antiochia
(Gerasa)

Samaria

River Jordan

Shechem

Joppa

Philadelphia
(Rabbah)

Lydda

Jamnia

Jericho

Gezer

Qumran

Jerusalem

Dead Sea

Bethlehem

Ascalon

Gaza

Masada

Raphia

Palestine

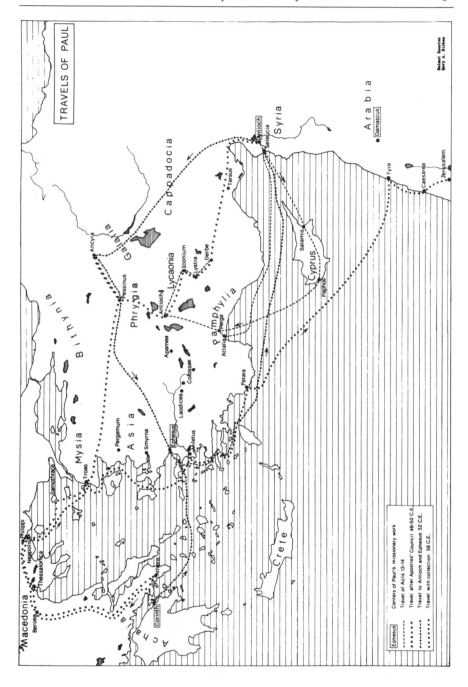

PAUL

1. Life and Ministry to the Apostolic Council

(a) Origin and Education

In several of his letters, each time provoked by opponents, Paul refers to his origin and life before his call as an apostle, most extensively in Phil 3:5–6 (see also 2 Cor 11:22; Gal 1:14; 2:15). According to these pieces of information, Paul came from an Israelite family from the tribe of Benjamin, was circumcised on the eighth day, received a strict Jewish education, and became a member of the sect of the Pharisees. All this must have included a formal education in the interpretation of the law and of Israel's Scriptures in general. It is also evident, however, that Paul grew up in the diaspora in an environment in which Greek was the everyday language. His letters furthermore reveal such a mastery of Greek as well as a knowledge of popular philosophical views and rhetorical skills that it must be assumed that he had received formal education in Greek schools beyond the elementary level, specifically in the tradition of the Cynic-Stoic diatribe (§4.2a).

Bibliography to §9:   General studies

Ferdinand Christian Baur, *Paul the Apostle of Jesus Christ* (2 vols.; Theological Translation Fund; London: Williams and Norgate, 1873). First published in 1866–1867, this book set the pattern for the debate in modern scholarship.

Günther Bornkamm, *Paul* (reprint: Minneapolis: Fortress, 1995). The best comprehensive account of Paul's career and thought.

Wayne A. Meeks, *The Writings of St. Paul* (New York: Norton, 1972). An excellent introduction to the reading of Paul's letters.

Rudolf Bultmann, "Paul," in idem, *Existence and Faith*, 111–46 (first published in *RGG* 4, 2d ed., 1019–45).

Arthur Darby Nock, *St. Paul* (first published 1938; New York: Harper, 1963).

A. Descamps, *Littérature et théologie pauliniennes* (RechBib 5; Bruges: Desclée de Brower, 1960).

Beda Rigaux, *The Letters of St. Paul* (Chicago: Franciscan Herald, 1968).

Samuel Sandmel, *The Genius of Paul: A Study in History* (2d ed.; New York: Schocken, 1970).

J. Christiaan Beker, *Paul the Apostle* (Philadelphia: Fortress, 1980).

Idem, *Paul's Apocalyptic Gospel* (Philadelphia: Fortress, 1982).

Jürgen Becker, *Paulus: Der Apostel der Völker* (2d ed.; Tübingen: Mohr/Siebeck, 1992).

Joachim Gnilka, *Paulus von Tarsus: Apostel und Zeuge* (HThKSup 6; Freiburg: Herder, 1996).

Eduard Lohse, *Paulus: Eine Biographie* (München: Beck, 1996).

Troels Engberg-Pedersen (ed.), *Paul in His Hellenistic Context* (Minneapolis: Fortress, 1995).

Abraham J. Malherbe, *Paul and the Popular Philosophers* (Minneapolis: Fortress, 1989).

Dale B. Martin, *Slavery as Salvation: The Metaphor of Slavery in Pauline Christianity* (New Haven: Yale University Press, 1990).

Calvin J. Roetzel, *Paul: The Man and the Myth* (Columbia, SC: University of South Carolina Press, 1998).

Although this information drawn from Paul's letters is valuable, it is still limited. It is therefore tempting to utilize also the Book of Acts in order to paint a fuller portrait of the apostle. That Paul's name was originally "Saul" as reported in Acts 7:58; 8:1 and elsewhere is not improbable since diaspora Jews often chose a Greek or Roman name that sounded similar to their Hebrew name. But in his letters Paul always uses his Roman name "Paulus." If his Hebrew name was indeed Saul, the change of his name should not be connected with his call as an apostle but with the custom of Israelites in the diaspora to use a Greek or Roman name that had some similarity with their given Hebrew name. Acts (9:11; 21:39; 22:3) also claims that Paul came from the Cilician city of Tarsus, an important trade center on the thoroughfare from Syria to Anatolia, which was known for a relatively high level of cultural life. On the other hand, it must be remembered that Paul was a craftsman who would have settled somewhere to pursue his trade: If he really came from Tarsus, why was

Bibliography to §9:   Tools

Fred O. Francis and J. Paul Sampley (eds.), *Pauline Parallels* (F&F; 2d ed.; Philadelphia: Fortress, 1984).

Bibliography to §9:   Bibliography and History of Scholarship

Ulrich Luck and Karl Heinrich Rengstorf (eds.), *Das Paulusbild in der neueren Forschung* (WdF 24; 2d ed.; Darmstadt: Wissenschaftliche Buchgesellschaft, 1969).

Hans Hübner, "Paulusforschung seit 1945: Ein kritischer Literaturbericht," *ANRW* 2.25.4 (1987) 2649–2840.

Watson E. Mills, *An Index to Periodical Literature on the Apostle Paul* (NTTS 16; Leiden: Brill, 1993).

Duane F. Watson, "Rhetorical Criticism of the Pauline Epistles since 1975," *CRBS* 3 (1995) 219–48.

Bibliography to §9:   Theology of Paul

Bultmann, *Theology,* 1. 185–352. The most significant interpretation of Paul's theology.

Conzelmann, *Outline,* 155–286.

Johannes Munck, *Paul and the Salvation of Mankind* (London: SCM, 1959).

Ernst Käsemann, *Perspectives on Paul* (London: SCM, and Philadelphia: Fortress, 1974).

Dieter Georgi, *Theocracy in Paul's Praxis and Theology* (Minneapolis: Fortress, 1991).

Bibliography to §9:   The History-of-Religions Question

Albert Schweitzer, *The Mysticism of Paul the Apostle* (New York: Macmillan, 1931). A classic in the history-of-religions approach to Paul.

Erwin R. Goodenough with A. Thomas Kraabel, "Paul and the Hellenization of Christianity," in Neusner, *Religions in Antiquity,* 23–70.

Egon Brandenburger, *Fleisch und Geist: Paulus und die dualistische Weisheit* (WMANT 29: Neukirchen-Vluyn: Neukirchener Verlag, 1968).

Hans-Joachim Schoeps, *Paul: The Theology of the Apostle in the Light of Jewish Religious History* (Philadelphia: Westminster, 1961; reprint 1979).

E. P. Sanders, *Paul and Palestinian Judaism: A Comparison of Patterns of Religion* (Philadelphia: Fortress, 1977).

W. D. Davies, *Paul and Rabbinic Judaism: Some Rabbinic Elements in Paul's Theology* (4th ed.; Philadelphia: Fortress, 1980).

Bibliography to §9.1

John Knox, *Chapters in the Life of Paul* (Nashville, TN: Abingdon, n.d.).

Martin Hengel and Anna Marie Schwemer, *Paul Between Damascus and Antioch: The Unknown Years* (Louisville: Westminster John Knox, 1997).

he in Damascus at the time of his call? And why did he remain there afterward for several years? Many typical features of his theology, such as his pronounced apocalyptic expectations, are certainly part of his Jewish heritage and would fit much better into a milieu that was not as strongly Greek as that of Tarsus.

It is scarcely credible that Paul had inherited Roman citizenship from his father (Acts 22:25–29). As a Roman citizen Paul would have had no difficulty escaping from the various punishments that he received according to his own statements (2 Cor 11:24f.); it is only in the Book of Acts that Paul's reference to his Roman citizenship saves him from corporeal punishment. Paul's appeal to the emperor in his trial before Festus does not prove his Roman citizenship since every free subject of the empire had the right to such an appeal. Moreover, in the first decades of the 1st century Roman citizenship was much less frequently granted than in later centuries. Finally, Acts 22:3 indicates that Paul grew up in Jerusalem and studied there with the famous rabbi Gamaliel I. Since the first part of this information is not trustworthy, the second is pure invention. Paul was a Pharisee, to be sure, but he came from the diaspora and his fanatic defense of the law before his call has little relationship with Gamaliel's attested liberal halakhic wisdom. Thus the Book of Acts contributes very little to our knowledge of Paul's origin and education; in fact, it only confounds the effort to achieve some clarity with respect to this question. It is better to rely exclusively upon the information that can be gleaned from the letters, in which Paul presents himself as a Hebrew from the diaspora with a good Greek education and a Pharisee inspired by a deep religious fervor, which made it a matter of course that he would fight for the preservation and defense of the traditions of the fathers.

(b) Paul's Call

Paul's zeal for the law made him a persecutor of the followers of Jesus (Gal 1:13, 23; 1 Cor 15:9; Phil 3:6). We can only speculate, however, about the manner of such persecutions. The account of the Book of Acts says more than is credible. Paul's presence at the death of Stephen (Acts 7:58) is excluded through Gal 1:22. Acts 8:3 is unhistorical for the same reason, and consequently also Acts 26:10–11. It is unthinkable that Paul, equipped with letters from the high priest, could have taken Christians from outside Palestine to Jerusalem for punishment. Neither the high priest nor the Jewish Sanhedrin in Jerusalem ever had such powers of jurisdiction. Paul's activities must be located outside Palestine, wherever he actually lived. The persecution would have taken the regular process in the local synagogue: members of the synagogue who had confessed Jesus, and perhaps spread the message within the synagogue community, were subjected to normal synagogue punishments and excluded from its religious community. Such excommunication had serious social and economic consequences; followers of Jesus could also be maligned before the local court or the Roman authorities.

Bibliography to §9.1b

Haenchen, *Acts,* 318–36.

Ulrich Wilckens, "Die Bekehrung des Pauls als religionsgeschichtliches Problem," in idem, *Rechtfertigung als Freiheit* (Neukirchen-Vluyn: Neukirchener Verlag, 1974).

Paul experienced the vision of his call near Damascus (Acts 9:3ff., confirmed by Gal 1:17; 2 Cor 11:32–33). Since it is hard to imagine that Paul's primary profession was that of an itinerant persecutor, he must have been a resident of Damascus, where he became acquainted with the Christian message, especially with the Hellenists' version of a new faith that was free from the obligations of the law (§8.3b, d). Only such propaganda would have caused a law-abiding Jew to persecute the bearers of this message. The question of the validity of the law was also intimately connected with the essential content of Paul's call.

The use of the term "conversion" for Paul's experience obscures what was in fact essential to him in this event. Paul never understood his experience as a conversion but always as a call. This understanding is even evident in the version presented in Acts 9:3ff.; 22:3ff.; and 26:9ff., which is written in the style of a legend of a prophetic call, although here the commission is not directly given to Paul but mediated through Ananias (Acts 9:15). Luke introduced the disciple Ananias in order to present Paul's commissioning as an apostle as a legitimate act of the Christian church; Paul had to become first of all a baptized Christian (Acts 9:18). That Paul was indeed baptized is likely because he always includes himself in the community of baptized believers. Even baptism, however, did not connote for Paul a personal experience of conversion but meant inclusion into the community of the elect who had received the spirit and whose life was determined by the death and resurrection of Christ (1 Cor 12:12–13; Rom 6:1ff.). The decisive element in Paul's experience, as he saw it, was his divine appointment as apostle to the Gentiles through the appearance of the risen Christ (1 Cor 9:1). He counts this appearance as one of the resurrection epiphanies of Christ, which began with the epiphany to Peter (1 Cor 15:5–8), and characterized it as a revelation (Gal 1:15–16), that is, as part of the eschatological event of Christ's death and resurrection.

The content of this eschatological event, of which Paul's call as an apostle was a part, as he was called to proclaim the gospel to the Gentiles, also determined his position toward the law. If the time of the salvation began with the resurrection of Christ—and Christ's appearance to Paul convinced him that the Christian claim was not a lie—and if he was called by the risen Lord to bring this message to all nations, then the period of the validity of the law must have come to an end. From now on, the work of fulfilling a law that God had once enjoined upon his people could only become resistance to God's will. It did not imply that his own past zealous pursuit of fulfilling the law was bad or sinful; rather, it was now anachronistic; the times had changed. God, through Jesus' death, had declared the sinners righteous, Jews and Gentiles alike. It made no longer sense to pursue one's own righteousness through fulfillment of the law. It is significant that Paul never states that the fulfillment of the law was impossible; on the contrary, he could say that he himself had been blameless in that respect (see Phil 3:5ff.). But existence in this pursuit to fulfill the law—by all means a law that can be fulfilled!—had lost its meaning because a new divine demand had taken its place, a demand that lays claim on the whole human being and on all human beings, no matter whether they are Jews or Gentiles: "to be in Christ." This "being in Christ" cannot be reconciled with life under the law because the law separates the Jew from the Gentile. This is therefore not a purely theological question but a fundamental moral, social, cultural, and political question. The baptismal formula that Paul quotes in his controversy with the circumcision apostles accordingly defines the "being in Christ" in social and cultural terms: "There is neither Jew nor Gentile, neither slave nor free, not male and female" (Gal 3:28). What the call to become the apostle to the Gentiles had meant for Paul personally therefore results in an ecclesiological vision of the community of the new ages established by the actions of God in Christ, for which freedom from the law is an indispensable ingredient.

(c) The First Period of Paul's Mission; Chronology of Paul's Ministry

There are no direct attestations for the first period of Paul's missionary activity. Not one of his letters can be dated with any probability to his missionary work in the fourteen (or even seventeen) years before the Apostolic Council. Some scholars assumed that the Galatian mission belonged to the journey of Barnabas and Paul to regions in southeastern Anatolia (described in Acts 13–14) and that therefore the Letter to the Galatians could have been written at an early date—provided that also the Apostolic Council could be dated early. This hypothesis, however, is burdened with too many difficulties (see below on the south-Galatian hypothesis, §9.3b). The report of the Book of Acts about this missionary journey is legendary anyway; the only reliable information for this early period is the scanty narrative given by Paul in Gal 1:17–2:1.

According to this report, Paul was first active as a missionary in "Arabia," that is, Damascus, its environs, and the area to the south. After three years, he traveled to Jerusalem in order to visit Peter, stayed there for two weeks, and also had a chance to see Jesus' brother James. That was his only visit to Jerusalem before the Apostolic Council. The Jerusalem visit mentioned in Acts 9:26–30 refers to this same event; on the other hand, another visit of Paul and Barnabas to "the brothers in Judea" during the famine under Claudius (Acts 11:27–30) is a Lukan invention; it is not mentioned in Paul's own account. The second stage of Paul's mission was his activity in Syria and Cilicia (Gal 1:21). It is most likely that the headquarters for this activity was the community of Antioch and that this missionary effort was primarily aimed at the conversion of Gentiles. At the end of this rather long period, Paul went to Jerusalem, together with Barnabas and Titus (an uncircumcised Gentile; Gal 2:1, 3). According to Gal 2:11, he was back in Antioch for the incident with Peter and Barnabas. Barnabas may indeed have been the senior apostle during Paul's long Antiochian period; both Barnabas and Paul are mentioned in the list of Acts 13:1 as prophets and teachers of Antioch, and Barnabas is always mentioned first in the report of the missionary journey of Acts 13–14. It may have been

Bibliography to §9.1c

Kirsopp Lake, "The Chronology of Acts," in Foakes Jackson and Lake, *Beginnings,* 5. 445–74.
Haenchen, *Acts,* 60–71.
Robert Jewett, *A Chronology of Paul's Life* (Philadelphia: Fortress, 1979).
Gerd Lüdemann, *Paulus, der Heidenapostel,* vol. 1: *Studien zur Chronologie* (FRLANT 123; Göttingen: Vandenhoeck & Ruprecht, 1980).
John C. Hurd, "Pauline Chronology and Pauline Theology," in William R. Farmer (ed.), *Christian History and Interpretation* (Cambridge: Cambridge University Press, 1967) 225–48.

indeed Barnabas who invited Paul to come to Antioch (Acts 11:25–26). Paul gives the length of this period as "fourteen years" (Gal 2:1), but it is problematic whether this period should be calculated from the time of Paul's call (including the three years in Arabia) or from his first visit to Jerusalem three years after his call. Additional uncertainty arises from the custom of the time of counting the first and last of years as full years, even if only a portion of a year was included in the period in question. "Three years" may be only a little more than one year, and "fourteen years" could have been as little as twelve years and a few months. We are thus confronted with a total period of at least twelve years and not more than seventeen years. The Apostolic Council concludes this period, after which a new phase of Paul's mission began. All of Paul's extant letters belong to the time after the Apostolic Council.

A discussion of Paul's chronology is indispensable here, although some questions can be treated in more detail only in the following sections. The Book of Acts describing Paul's activities in a succession of rather restless missionary journeys misrepresents Paul's patterns of missionary work. Contrary to the image created by Acts, Paul stayed for quite some time in a particular urban missionary center from which he organized his work in cooperation with his associates. Nevertheless, the dates that Acts provides in the context of the description of these journeys may contain some reliable information—as long as they do not contradict the information obtained from the letters of Paul. If at least some dates of Acts deriving from the "We Source" (§7.3c) can be trusted, the following reconstruction can claim some degree of probability.

The dating of Paul's stay in Corinth is decisive for Pauline chronology. According to Acts 18:12–18, Paul was forced by the proconsul Gallio to leave the city after he had stayed there for a year and a half. Fortunately, an inscription found at Delphi permits the dating of Gallio's proconsulship to the period from the spring of 51 to the spring of 52 CE (proconsuls were appointed for just one year of service; see §6.2a). Thus the earliest date for the expulsion from Corinth is the spring or early summer of 51, the latest the early spring of 52. For reasons to be discussed later, the latter date is to be preferred. A second point of reference may be Acts 24:1ff.: Paul was imprisoned in Jerusalem during the procuratorship of Felix; but when Felix was recalled to Rome and replaced by Festus (Acts 24:27 speaks about a period of two years) and Paul appealed to the emperor, Felix's successor Festus sent him to Rome as prisoner for further trial. This information is problematic because it is not possible to date the change in the procuratorship from Felix to Festus with any degree of certainty. It has been argued that it must have occurred before the downfall of Felix's brother Pallas and the murder of Britannicus, that is, in December 55 CE. Yet, neither the information from the Book of Acts nor Paul's own statements in his letters can be reconciled with such an early date for the transfer of the collection to Jerusalem and Paul's subsequent arrest. In any case, there is no compelling reason for such an early dating of the change from Felix to Festus (§6.6e)—the "two years" of Acts 24:27 must refer to the duration of Paul's imprisonment, not to the length of Felix's tenure as proconsul. It is therefore advisable to reconstruct Paul's chronology in both directions from the Gallio date. Assuming that Paul's activities from his departure from Antioch to his expulsion from Corinth (mission in Galatia, Macedonia, and Corinth) must have taken at least three years, the Apostolic Council in Jerusalem (§9.1d) should be dated in the year 48—a much earlier date creates difficulties with respect to Paul's own statement that between his call and the Apostolic Council lie at least fourteen and perhaps as many as seventeen years (in the latter case, the first dates below have to be moved back two to three years):

35: Call of Paul as an apostle to the Gentiles
35–38: Missionary activity in Arabia (Gal 1:17)
38: Visit with Peter in Jerusalem (Gal 1:18; Acts 9:26–30)
38–48: Missionary activity in Cilicia and Syria (Gal 1:21; Acts 13–14)
48: Apostles Council in Jerusalem (Gal 2:1–10; Acts 15)
48/49: Incident in Antioch (Gal 2:11ff.)
49: Mission in Galatia (Acts 16:6)
50: Mission in Philippi, Thessalonica, and Beroea (Acts 16:11–17:14)
Autumn, 50: Travel to Corinth via Athens (Acts 17:15; 18:1); writing of 1 Thessalonians
Autumn, 50 to spring, 52: Mission in Corinth (Acts 18:11)
Summer, 52: Travel to Antioch, then to Ephesus via Asia Minor; second visit to Galatia on the way (Acts 18:18–23; Gal 4:13)
Autumn, 52 to spring, 55: Mission in Ephesus (Acts 19:1, 8–10, 22); writing of Galatians, 1 Corinthians, and the letter preserved in 2 Cor 2:14–6:13; 7:2–4
54: Interim visit to Corinth (presupposed in 2 Cor 13:1)
Winter, 54–55: Ephesian imprisonment, writing of correspondence with Philippians, Philemon, and the letter preserved in 2 Cor 10–13
Summer, 55: Travel from Ephesus via Troas through Macedonia to Corinth; writing of the letter preserved in 2 Cor 1:1–2:13; 7:5–16 and the collection letters, that is, 2 Corinthians 8 and 9
Winter, 55–56: Stay in Corinth; writing of the letter to the Romans
56: Travel to Jerusalem (Acts 20); preparation for the transfer of the collection (Acts 21:15ff.); arrest of Paul in the Temple
56–58: Imprisonment in Caesarea
58: Replacement of Felix by Festus; Paul is sent to Rome
58–?: Roman imprisonment

The circumstances of Paul's martyrdom are not known.

(d) The Apostolic Council

The only reliable source for the Apostolic Council of the year 48 is Gal 2:1–10. The tradition used by Luke in Acts 15 was so thoroughly revised that little more can be learned. The report in Acts 11:27–30 of the visit of Barnabas and Paul in Jerusalem must rest upon a tradition about the delivery of the collection that Luke inserted in the wrong place; it is useless as a source for the Council.

The Council became necessary because of the expansion of the new communities during the preceding fifteen years. There were now two centers, Jerusalem and

Antioch, each taking a very different position with respect to the Gentile mission. After the expulsion of the Hellenists (§8.3b), the church in Jerusalem was composed of law-abiding, Aramaic-speaking members. It did not apparently engage in any missionary activities among Gentiles (if Acts 10 rests on a reliable tradition, it must belong to a later period); it expected the coming of the Lord in the place designated by God (Jerusalem/Zion), and expressed its eschatological consciousness in its self-designation as the "poor" (§8.3a). The church of Antioch, on the other hand, had a number of Jewish members but consisted for the most part of uncircumcised Gentiles and did not consider the law as binding for all its members. Greek was the language of this church and of its missionary activities, which went far beyond the boundaries of Antioch itself. Although Antioch shared the eschatological outlook with Jerusalem, this did not imply that it accepted the eschatological ideal of poverty (§8.3c).

The contrast between Jerusalem and Antioch in the question of the validity of the law was the reason for the convening of the Apostolic Council. But it cannot be assumed that the authorities in Jerusalem convened the conference; they never had such powers of jurisdiction. Moreover, Gal 2:1–2 clearly states that the initiative came from the community of Antioch, which needed a clarification because of the people called the "false brothers" in Gal 2:4, namely, Jewish believers (not simply Jews) who were raising a stir against the Gentile converts' freedom from the law and thus caused serious difficulties for the Antiochian mission (Paul had to face similar Judaizing propaganda later in Galatia, which jeopardized his missionary work in that area; see §9.3).

Paul, Barnabas, and Titus, as emissaries of the Antiochian church, wanted to establish unanimity with the authorities in Jerusalem lest the "false brothers" should claim that Jerusalem was on their side. Paul's goal was to assure ecclesiastical unity through which the Jewish and Gentile believers were bound together despite the differences with respect to the observation of the law. The touchstone of the agreement was the question whether the uncircumcised Gentile convert Titus, with whom Paul and Barnabas had gone to Jerusalem, would be accepted as a brother in Christ without first being circumcised. Despite the opposition of the "false brothers," the leaders of the Jerusalem church, Jesus' brother James, Cephas (Peter), and John, recognized the independence of the Gentile mission, its freedom from the law, and its ecclesiastical integrity. On the other hand, the Antiochian emissaries assured the leaders of the Jerusalem church that they would remember the special eschatological role of the "poor" in Jerusalem, which included the obligation to make intercession for them in prayer and to collect money for their benefit. The agreement is very significant because it provides a model for the establishment of church unity on the basis of prayer and charity in spite of differences in doctrine and

Bibliography to §9.1d

Haenchen, *Acts,* 440–72.

Betz, *Galatians,* 81–103.

Martin Dibelius, "The Apostolic Council," in idem, *Studies in Acts,* 93–101.

Günter Klein, *Galater 2:8–9 und die Geschichte der Jerusalemer Gemeinde: Rekonstruktion und Interpretation* (BEvTh 50; München: Kaiser, 1969) 99–128.

praxis. The careful formulations of Gal 2:1–10 demonstrate that the agreement was a contract between two equal partners. Nothing is said about the recognition of the Jerusalem authorities as a kind of church government. Peter's right to be active as a missionary was explicitly recognized, though that work should remain restricted to the Jews as Paul's work should be directed toward the conversion of the Gentiles (Gal 2:7–8). Whoever was concerned with the creation of law-abiding communities—and Paul does not deny their legitimacy—should stay away from missionary activity among the Gentiles. Nonetheless, this agreement opened the way for further conflicts, as became clear very soon in Antioch (§9.2a). The obligation to make a collection for Jerusalem became a significant ingredient of Paul's mission among the Gentiles (§9.3f.).

2. From Antioch to Ephesus

(a) The Conflict in Antioch

Soon after the Apostolic Council, Paul parted company with Barnabas, left Antioch, and began his independent missionary work. Acts 15:37–39 says that the cause for this separation was a quarrel between Paul and Barnabas about the usefulness of John Mark on their next missionary journey. Acts does not mention the conflict reported by Paul in Gal 2:11–15, which was apparently the cause for Paul's departure from Antioch. Peter, in principle favorably disposed toward the Gentile mission, had visited Antioch shortly after the Apostolic Council, perhaps in the context of beginning his own mission in Syria (§10.2a). During his stay, he had first participated in the common meals with Gentile believers (Gal 2:12)—a gesture revealing his liberal attitude with respect to the ritual law. When messengers from James arrived, however, Peter withdrew from the table fellowship. Peter did not want to embarrass these guests, who must have insisted upon the observation of Jewish dietary laws. Other Jewish members of the community, and even Barnabas himself, also withdrew from the table fellowship with the Gentiles. But for Paul, this was a dishonest display of legal observance, which denied fellowship to the Gentile members unless they also made themselves subject to Jewish dietary laws. Those who compelled them to do so were not consistent in their own obedience (Gal 2:14), and Paul took Peter to task for this action. What others might consider a liberal gesture was for Paul hypocrisy dictated by fear (Gal 2:12).

Paul does not report the outcome of the confrontation, but he evidently lost out in this conflict. Thus he parted with Barnabas and left Antioch to begin his own missionary work elsewhere. The conflict also prompted Paul to reformulate the

Bibliography to §9.2a

Betz, *Galatians,* 103–12.

Anton Dauer, *Paulus und die christliche Gemeinde im syrischen Antiochia: Kritische Bestandsaufnahme der modernen Forschung mit einigen weiterführenden Überlegungen* (BBB 106; Weinheim: Beltz Athenäum, 1996).

Meeks and Wilken, *Jews and Christians in Antioch,* 13–18.

question of the fulfillment of the law more radically. The Jerusalem agreement had still granted Jewish members the privilege to take the fulfillment of the law seriously. Now, however, Paul concludes that it is especially the Jew who must recognize that nobody can be justified by the works of the law (Gal 2:15–21). The conflict with Peter had made it clear that liberal tolerance of a religious convention like the Jewish ritual law endangered the unity of the church. Henceforth Paul insisted that the constitution of the church "in Christ" abolished all traditional religious, social, and cultural particularities and every claim based upon such privileges (Gal 3:26–28). It is exactly because of the abolition of such traditional identities that the church becomes the eschatological community. As a consequence of this insight, Paul no longer conceded a position of eschatological preeminence to Jerusalem and its law-abiding community (Gal 4:24–25).

(b) Mission in Anatolia and Macedonia

After Paul's departure from Antioch (48 or 49 CE), the next reliable information concerns the Macedonian churches (1 Thessalonians). Acts 16:1–8 reports a journey through Lystra and Derbe and travel through Phrygia and Galatia (in this order!) to Mysia, all of which is quite credible. But according to 1 Thess 1:1, it is certain that Paul must have been accompanied on this journey by his coworkers Silvanus (Silas) and Timothy; however, that Paul circumcised Timothy "for fear of the Jews" (Acts 16:3) is scarcely believable.

The debated question is the time of the founding of the churches in Galatia. Although Acts mentions Galatia only in passing, it is best to assume that Paul stayed for at least some months in Galatia during this journey. "Galatia" designated the central highlands of Anatolia with the cities of Ankyra, Pessinus, and Gordium. Following the "North Galatian hypothesis" the Galatian churches must be located here and not in the south of the Roman province Galatia, that is, in the cities of Lystra, Derbe, and Iconium (the "South Galatian hypothesis"), which Paul had visited earlier when he was still stationed at Antioch (Acts 14:6ff.; see also the place names given in the *Acts of Paul*). Though a part of the Roman province of Galatia, these cities were not considered to belong to Galatia but rather to Lykaonia (so correctly Acts 14:6). Gal 4:13–14 suggests a passage of time and alludes to Paul being ill while he was there. Furthermore, Gal 1:2 speaks of a number of Galatian communities that Paul must have founded during his stay. If Paul arrived in Galatia in the summer of the year 49, he may well have stayed into the spring of the year 50. It must also be remembered that winter travel was difficult in central Anatolia.

When Paul came to Troas he had a vision: a man from Macedonia appeared to him and invited him to preach the gospel in Macedonia (Acts 16:9). The report of this vision marks a turning point in the sources available to Luke for his narrative of Paul's missionary activities. Immediately after this vision begins the first part of the "we passages" (Acts 16:10). Whether or not these reports told in the first person derive from a particular source (diary or itinerary; see §7.3c), there is no

Bibliography to §9.2b

Betz, *Galatians*, 1–5.

question that some of these sections contain much more trustworthy information than other parts of the Book of Acts. Troas, more precisely Alexandria in the region of Troas (not far from the ancient Troy), an important trading center in the Roman period, was the natural point of departure for travel by boat to Macedonia— much faster than the long land route via Byzantium. Paul took this shortcut again a few years later (2 Cor 2:12–13) and in the opposite direction on his last journey (Acts 20:6). The connecting point in Macedonia was Neapolis (today Kavala), from where the Via Egnatia, the important Roman road from Byzantium to Dyrrhachium on the Adriatic Sea, led a few miles inland to Philippi (Acts 16:11–12). Individual features of Paul's stay in Philippi remain in the realm of legend (Acts 16:13–40), though Lydia (Acts 16:14–15) may indeed have been the first person converted. That Paul suffered persecution in that city is confirmed by 1 Thess 2:2. Nevertheless, his missionary work was successful, and the church in Philippi maintained a close and cordial relationship with Paul during the following years (§9.3e).

Thessalonica, where Paul went next, again traveling on the Via Egnatia, was the largest and most important city of Macedonia, a port and commercial center, where the trade routes from the interior of the Balkan met the Via Egnatia and the Aegean Sea. It is characteristic for his mission that Paul established churches first in the most important urban centers of commerce and industry. Like Corinth and Ephesus, where Paul went afterward, Thessalonica was a provincial capital and seat of the Roman proconsul. Again, Luke's description of the stay in this city is legendary (Acts 17:1–10). Although Acts leaves the impression that Paul was mostly on the road and never stayed very long in any one place, the duration of Paul's stay should not be calculated as too short a period; Paul had to get settled, find a place to pursue his trade (1 Thess 2:9), establish close personal relationships (1 Thess 2:7–12), and build a church organization that was able to carry on the proclamation of the gospel (1 Thess 1:7–9). Since 1 Thess 2:13–16 is probably a later interpolation, the letter does not confirm the report of Acts 17:5ff. that the Jews of Thessalonica stirred up a riot against Paul. Such reports belong to the standard literary design of Acts and are as unhistorical as the Lukan report that Paul always went first to the local synagogue to preach. Acts 17:10–14 reports a mission of Paul in Beroea after his expulsion from Thessalonica; the Pauline letters do not confirm this.

(c) From Thessalonica to Corinth

When Paul arrived in Athens, he sent Timothy to Thessalonica to complete the work of consolidating the church there, having ended his work prematurely due to adverse circumstances (1 Thess 3:1–4). Paul probably did not stay long in Athens, since it must be assumed that he arrived in Corinth no later than the autumn of the year 50. Luke reports the famous speech of Paul to the Council of the Areopagites, while in Athens (Acts 17:22–31). Like the other speeches of Acts, it is a Lukan composition. Among the converts in Athens, two names probably came from the

Bibliography to §9.2c

Gerd Theissen, *The Social Setting of Pauline Christianity: Essays on Corinth* (Philadelphia: Fortress, 1982).

source used by Luke: Dionysius the Areopagite and a woman named Damaris (Acts 17:34). These names show that Paul must have stayed long enough to establish a community in that city.

Corinth, completely destroyed by the Romans in 146 BCE and refounded by Caesar a hundred years later as a Roman colony, had become at that time the largest city in Greece. By virtue of its position between the Saronic Gulf in the east and the Corinthian Gulf in the west it was the leading port of Greece as well as one of the largest industrial centers of the ancient world (pottery, metal industries, and carpet weaving). Fundamentally different from other cities of Greece, Corinth was a Roman city with Latin as its official language, little connection to its once glorious past, and a heterogeneous population. Its inhabitants, who were mostly descendants of immigrants, had introduced a large number of foreign religions. Pausanias reports that he found four temples of the Egyptian cult alone in Corinth. There must have been also a Jewish synagogue, although the archaeological evidence comes from a much later period. The immorality of Corinth was proverbial in antiquity but was probably no worse than that of any other major port and commercial center.

Some of the information in the Book of Acts (18:1ff.) is confirmed by Paul's letters. Aquila, originally from Pontus, and his wife Priscilla took Paul into their house. They were Jewish Christians who had been driven out of Rome by the edict of Claudius. Since Paul does not mention them among the first converts of Corinth, they must have become believers while they were still in Rome—important evidence for the existence of a church in Rome as early as the 40s of the 1st century. According to 1 Cor 16:19 (and probably also Rom 16:3), Aquila and Priscilla were later in Ephesus. As guest of Aquila, who was a tent-maker like Paul, the apostle could pursue his trade and thus earn a living. Later he also received support from Macedonia so that he could devote himself fully to his missionary work (2 Cor 11:9). Crispus, converted by Paul, is also mentioned in 1 Cor 1:14; Luke claims that he was the leader of the synagogue (Acts 18:8). According to 1 Cor 16:15 (see also 1:16), Stephanas was the first convert of Achaea. The successful missionary activity also reached members of the upper class: Erastus the city treasurer, mentioned in Rom 16:23, appears in an inscription that was found in the floor of a plaza below the theater of Corinth—the very first time that a member of an early Christian church is attested in a public inscription!

Paul's missionary activity in Corinth lasted eighteen months (Acts 18:11), from the autumn of the year 50 to the spring of 52 (§9.1c). His associates were Timothy and Silvanus, named also as coauthors of 1 Thessalonians. Other associates soon joined Paul's staff (see Stephanas in 1 Cor 16:15). Apollos, a Jewish Christian from Alexandria (Acts 18:24), must also have been active in Corinth (1 Cor 3:4–6; later he is with Paul in Ephesus; 1 Cor 16:12 should be preferred against Acts 18:25–28). The missionary work of Paul and his associates was not limited to the city of Corinth but must have included other cities, which is clearly shown by the repeated mention of Achaea in Paul's letters (1 Thess 1:7–8; 1 Cor 16:15; 2 Cor 1:1; 9:2; 11:10; Rom 15:26. 2 Corinthians 9 is a circular letter to the churches in Achaea; see §9.3d, f). Another piece of evidence for the establishment of viable congregations in the area comes from Rom 16:1–2: a letter of recommendation for Phoebe, a woman who was the president of the church at Cenchreae, the eastern port city of Corinth.

View of Corinth
In the foreground, the North Market; behind it the remaining monolithic columns of the Temple of Apollo (built in VI B.C.E.); in the background the fortress Acro-Corinth, rising more than 1500 feet above the ancient city.

The picture that emerges is characteristic for Paul's missionary method. Together with a few tested associates he settled in the capital of a province, gathered any Christians already living there, expanded his staff, and with the help of these co-workers established congregations in other cities of the province. During his absence, Paul maintained contacts with these congregations through messengers and letters in order to direct the further development of these churches. These were not humble efforts of a lonely missionary. On the contrary, Paul's letters reveal an ambitious, well-planned, large-scale organization that included the use of letters as an instrument of ecclesiastical policy. Otherwise, Paul could not have claimed in Rom 15:19 that, in just a few years, he had completed the preaching of the gospel from Jerusalem to as far as Illyricum, encompassing Syria, Asia Minor, Macedonia, and Greece.

The report about Paul's expulsion from Corinth in Acts 18:12–18 was thoroughly edited by Luke, who wanted to emphasize the correct attitude of the Roman authorities toward the Christian movement and present this as a paradigm. But the report preserves the reliable information that Paul was forced by the proconsul Gallio to leave the city in the spring of the year 52 (§9.1c). The problems of the Corinthian church, however, continued to occupy Paul for several years and required further visits and the writing of several letters (§§9.3c, d, f).

(d) The First Letter to the Thessalonians

This letter was written a few months after Paul's visit to Thessalonica. Timothy, whom Paul had sent to Thessalonica from Athens (1 Thess 3:1f.), returned to Paul, who had meanwhile moved to Corinth (Acts 18:5). Since Timothy is named as a

Bibliography to §9.2d: Commentaries

B. Rigaux, O.F.M., *Saint Paul: Les épitres aux Thessaloniciens* (EtBib; Paris: Gabalda, 1956).

Traugott Holtz, *Der erste Brief an die Thessalonicher* (EKKNT 13; Neukirchen-Vluyn: Neukirchener Verlag, 1986).

Willi Marxsen, *Der erste Thessalonicherbrief* (Zürcher Bibelkommentare NT 11, 1; Zürich: Theologischer Verlag, 1979).

Bibliography to §9.2d: Studies

Hendrikus Boers, "The Form Critical Study of Paul's Letters: 1 Thessalonians as a Case Study," *NTS* 22 (1975/76) 140–58.

Helmut Koester, "Apostel und Gemeinde in den Briefen an die Thessalonicher," in *Kirche: Festschrift Bornkamm,* 287–98.

Idem, "I Thessalonians—An Experiment in Christian Writing," in F. Forrester Church and Timothy George (eds.), *Continuity and Discontinuity in Church History: Essays Presented to George Huntston Williams* (SHCT 19; Leiden: Brill, 1979) 33–44.

Walter Schmithals, "The Historical Situation of the Thessalonian Epistles," in idem, *Paul and the Gnostics,* 123–218.

R. F. Collins, *Studies on the First Letter to the Thessalonians* (BETL 66; Leuven: Peeters, 1984).

R. F. Collins (ed.), *The Thessalonian Correspondence* (BETL 87; Leuven: Peeters, 1990).

Abraham J. Malherbe, *Paul and the Thessalonians: The Philosophic Tradition of Pastoral Care* (Philadelphia: Fortress, 1987).

Birger A. Pearson, "1 Thessalonians 2:13–16: A Deutero-Pauline Interpolation," in idem, *The Emergence of the Christian Religion: Essays on Early Christianity* (Harrisburg, PA: Trinity Press International, 1997) 58–74.

coauthor, the letter must have been written from Corinth, probably still in the year 50 CE. It is therefore the oldest preserved Pauline letter and thus the oldest extant Christian document. Paul may have written letters earlier in his career, but it is possibly the beginning of a large-scale missionary effort that forced him to make use of the letter as an additional instrument of church organization. 1 Thessalonians mirrors throughout the problems that would result in a young congregation that was firm in its convictions but, within a matter of a few weeks or months, confronted by difficulties in the exposition and defense of its new faith. Such questions concerned the integrity of the apostle, hostilities from outsiders, consequences regarding moral conduct, and the significance of life and the problem of death in view of the expectation of the coming of the day of the Lord. The way in which Paul discusses these questions in detail gives testimony to his pastoral insights and care. It also attests the capability of his associate Timothy, who had been in Thessalonica as Paul's envoy and had given a comprehensive report to Paul after his return.

The formal structure of 1 Thessalonians presents some problems. The prescript (1:1) is simple; the senders, Paul, Silvanus, and Timothy, are named at the beginning (without titles!), addressee (the church of the Thessalonians) and greeting follow. The proem begins at 1:2 with the characteristic thanksgiving and seems to end at 1:10. A new section, containing the description of Paul's ministry and his relationship to the church, begins at 2:1. This is interrupted, however, by a resumption of the thanksgiving in 2:13; thus the proem appears to continue until 3:13. Yet, this is misleading because 2:13–16 interrupts the close connection between 2:11–12 ("like a father with his children") and 2:18 ("now we were made orphans"). There are other indications that 2:13–16 is an interpolation, especially its blatant anti-Judaic attitude, which takes up a Jewish tradition about the leaders of the people as the murderers of the prophets and sets the death of Jesus as well as the experiences of a later church into that context. The proem and thanksgiving thus indeed end in 1:10. The first section of the body of the letter—2:1–3:13 (without 2:13–16)—discusses questions of the presence and absence of the apostle. The second section of the body (4:1–12) is a parenesis consisting of an interpretation of traditional catalogs of vices and virtues. An eschatological section follows (4:13–18; 5:1–11). The letter concludes with final admonitions and greetings (5:12–28).

Since the validity of the gospel cannot be separated from the question of the credibility of the apostle—especially in view of Paul's relatively short stay in Thessalonica—Paul had to draw a clear line between himself and the itinerant Cynic preacher. Neither did Paul preach the gospel for personal gain, nor was the purpose of his proclamation the moral or psychological improvement of individuals. The relationship of the preacher to the audience and of the audience to the subject matter is therefore fundamentally different from the philosophical and religious propaganda of the time (2:1–12). The gospel wants to establish a community that is

Bibliography to §9.2d: Bibliography and History of Scholarship

Wolfgang Trilling, "Die beiden Briefe des Paulus an die Thessalonicher: Ein Forschungsbericht," *ANRW* 2.25.4 (1987) 3365–3403.

Jeffrey A. D. Weima, *An Annotated Bibliography of 1 and 2 Thessalonians Letters* (NTTS 26; Leiden: Brill, 1998).

bound together by mutual love (3:11–13), and the apostle is but a link in this common bond of love and care. Paul thus uses images of family relationships (wet-nurse, father, children; 2:9–12)—note that in 2:17 Paul applies the image of orphan to himself as he is absent from the church! The church is not an isolated club of religious individuals but has a share in the eschatological office of the apostle and the eschatological destiny of other churches, through the suffering of persecution as well as in the propagation of the gospel (1:6–9). The concluding eschatological admonitions are concerned with the life of the community in the expectation of the coming of the Lord. They are based on traditional materials, namely on apocalyptic predictions, of which the first is introduced as a saying of Jesus about the sequence of the events at the time of the parousia: because the dead will be raised first, they will not be disadvantaged but will join the living in welcoming the Lord (4:13–18). The second prediction is a saying about the day of the Lord that comes like a thief in the night (5:1–11; cf. Rev 3:3). Here, Paul radicalizes the eschatological perspective. Those who preach "peace and security"—a slogan of Roman imperial propaganda—will be surprised by the sudden appearance of the "day" while the believers are already now children of the day and children of light. It therefore does not matter at all for their future being "with the Lord" whether they "wake or sleep" (5:10). It is remarkable that church order materials (5:12–22) are given only minimal space in this letter to a church that had been founded only quite recently; this is also the case in other genuine Pauline letters (in contrast to the deutero-Pauline Pastoral Epistles). This does not imply, however, that there was no ecclesiastical organization. Rather, references to ecclesiastical offices, which occur occasionally elsewhere (Phil 1:2; 1 Corinthians 12; Rom 16:1–2), demonstrate that there were church offices with clearly defined functions. Yet such authorities were not fixed in any hierarchical structure. 1 Thess 5:12–22 shows that Paul is confident that the spirit will effect democratic teamwork, which requires both mutual respect and recognition as well as critical judgment.

3. Paul's Stay in Ephesus

(a) Missionary Activity in Ephesus

After his departure from Corinth early in the year 52, Paul was active in Ephesus for some time. Acts 18:18–23 states that Paul went first to Ephesus, where he left his companions Priscilla and Aquila, and went on to Antioch (also to Jerusalem?) in order to return to Ephesus later in the same year via Galatia and Phrygia. If Paul

Bibliography to §9.3

Helmut Koester (ed.), *Ephesos: Metropolis of Asia: An Interdisciplinary Approach* (HTS 41; Valley Forge, PA: Trinity Press International, 1995).

W. Theissen, *Christen in Ephesus: Die historische und theologische Situation in vorpaulinischer und paulinischer Zeit und zur Zeit der Apostelgeschichte und der Pastoralbriefe* (TANTZ 12; Tübingen: Francke, 1995).

Rick Strelan, *Paul, Artemis, and the Jews in Ephesus* (BZNW 80; Berlin: de Gruyter, 1996).

Market Gate in Miletus
(Reconstruction in the Pergamum Museum, Berlin GDR)
The Romans constructed large and elaborate entrance
gates for the main markets (*agora* or *forum*) of major
cities. These served not only decorative purposes, but
also allowed better control of crowds in case of riots.

indeed went to Antioch at that time, his relationship with the leaders of that community must have improved; or else he went there in order to establish good relations. His later remarks about Barnabas and Peter (1 Cor 9:6; 1:12; 3:22; 9:5) are not hostile. A second visit to Galatia (Gal 4:13f.) is also best placed in the context of his return journey from Antioch to Ephesus. In any case, Paul must have come to Ephesus in the fall of the year 52 for an extended stay.

Acts 19:1–20:1 gives only scanty information about this stay. Nearly everything here is legendary. The unmasking of the Jewish exorcists and the burning of the magical books (Acts 19:13–20) rest on an older Jewish or pagan tale. The riot of the people, instigated by the silversmiths, who produced small images of Artemis for sale (Acts 19:23–40), fits Luke's time much better than Paul's, because it is known that the growth of Christianity in the postapostolic period severely hurt attendance at the temples and thus certainly also the sale of souvenirs (see Pliny's correspondence with the emperor Trajan, *Epist.* 10.96). On the other hand, Luke also used and edited some reliable traditions about the Ephesian church. His source presented two problems: First, it told that Apollos was teaching in Ephesus; thus there was already a Christian presence in Ephesus before Paul's arrival. Luke adds the unlikely remark that Apollos "knew only the baptism of John," introduces Priscilla and Aquila, who explain "the way of God to him more accurately" and dispatch him quickly to Achaea (Acts 18:24–28). Second, the source spoke of the presence in Ephesus of a group of disciples of John the Baptist—a surprising but not unlikely piece of information! Luke takes care of this problem with the story that Paul, as soon as he arrived, lay his hands on them, whereupon the Holy Spirit immediately descended upon them (Acts 19:1–7). The only other pieces of possibly historical information from Luke's source are the statements about the duration of Paul's stay in Ephesus (three months and two years; Acts 19:8, 10) and about the place of Paul's activity (the lecture hall of Tyrannus). The Book of Acts, however, is silent with respect to the most important aspects of Paul's ministry in this city. It certainly involved the organization of a missionary center as a headquarters for the founding of churches in other cities in the province of Asia. Acts also is silent about Paul's extensive correspondence during this period (most of the extant letters were written from Ephesus) and about Paul's imprisonment toward the end of his stay. The analysis of Paul's letters with their numerous statements about travel plans, projects, and adverse circumstances provides a rather detailed picture of this crucially important period of Paul's mission.

Fixed points for a reconstruction of the chronology for this period and its letters can be found, first, in Paul's statements about the progress of the collection for Jerusalem and, second, in various statements related to the controversy with the Corinthian church and the changes in his travel plans. The letter to the Galatians mentions the collection but does not promote it actively (Gal 2:10); this letter is therefore best placed at the beginning of the Ephesian stay. 1 Corinthians belongs to a somewhat later time because here Paul has resumed his plans for the collection in earnest (1 Cor 16:1–4). The next letter, 2 Cor 2:14–7:4, faces a new problem in Corinth: the arrival of foreign missionaries. Paul must have traveled to Corinth for a brief visit after the writing of this letter, because such visit is presupposed in the next letter, 2 Cor 10:1–13:14 (see especially 13:1). The other fragments preserved in 2 Corinthians were written after Paul's departure from Ephesus. They indicate, however, that Paul had been in serious danger of death during the last months of his stay in that city (2 Cor 1:8–9). This is best understood as a reference to an Ephesian imprisonment; this makes it possible to date the letters written from prison (Philippians and Philemon) to the last period of Paul's sojourn in Ephesus.

(b) Judaizing Propaganda and the Letter to the Galatians

The controversy of Paul with his opponents in Galatia raises a fundamental problem as to the character and origin of the various opponents whom Paul had to combat there and elsewhere (Corinth, Philippi). Closely related is the question of opponents at the root of controversies that are visible in documents from the next generation (Ephesians, Colossians, the letters of Ignatius of Antioch, the Revelation of John). Information about such opponents is available only indirectly, by drawing conclusions from the letters written against them—a difficult task! But it seems even more hazardous to use information from the much richer materials of the following centuries. In any case, without a reconstruction of the thoughts and purposes of the opponents, many sections of the Pauline letters would remain incomprehensible. In order to discuss whether these opponents were a diverse phenomenon or a unified group (Judaizers or Gnostics), it must be understood first of all that we can neither presuppose a set of firmly formulated doctrines nor a unified organization for the earliest missionary movements as a whole. A fixed body of doctrines (creed and canon) and a generally recognized ecclesiastical organization (episcopate) were developed much later and over several generations. A similar diversity existed in fact also in Israel at that time; firm structures were created by rabbinic Judaism during the centuries after the destruction of Jerusalem. Moreover, a clear line separating "Judaism" and "Christianity" did not exist (strictly speaking, both terms should actually be used in quotation marks for the time of

Bibliography to §9.3b: Commentaries

J. B. Lightfoot, *Galatians: A Commentary on Paul's Letter to the Galatians* (19th ed.; London: Macmillan, 1896). A classic, still very instructive.

Betz, *Galatians*.

Dieter Lührmann, *Galatians: A Continental Commentary* (Minneapolis: Fortress, 1992).

Bibliography to §9.3b: Studies

James Hardy Ropes, *The Singular Problem of Galatians* (HTS 14; Cambridge, MA: Harvard University Press, 1929).

Wilhelm Lütgert, *Gesetz und Geist: Eine Untersuchung zur Vorgeschichte des Galaterbriefes* (BFChTh 22, 6; Gütersloh: Bertelsmann, 1919).

Hans Dieter Betz, "The Literary Composition and Function of Paul's Letter to the Galatians," *NTS* 21 (1974/75) 353–79.

Idem, "Spirit, Freedom, and Law: Paul's Message to the Galatian Churches," *SEÅ* 39 (1974) 145–60.

Philipp Vielhauer, "Gesetzesdienst und Stoicheiadienst im Galaterbrief," in *Rechtfertigung: Festschrift für Ernst Käsemann zum 70. Geburtstag* (Göttingen: Vandenhoeck & Ruprecht, 1976) 543–55.

C. K. Barrett, *Freedom and Obligation: A Study of the Epistle to the Galatians* (Philadelphia: Westminster, 1985).

Alfred Suhl, "Der Galaterbrief—Situation und Argumentation," *ANRW* 2.25.4 (1987) 3067–3134.

Paul and his successors). Neither Paul nor his opponents knew that they were "Christians," although both were in agreement that they belonged to Israel and its traditions and Scriptures. All these missionaries and apostles were at the same time part of the religious marketplace that encouraged free competition and assigned victory to the most successful contestant. The means employed in such propaganda varied widely and were subject to the condition and mood of the market. Mastery of rhetorical tricks was as important as the demonstration of one's supernatural power through miracles and magic or the recourse to a dignified ancient tradition such as the holy Scriptures of Israel.

All missionaries of the first generation belonged to the people of Israel. They were seen in the Greco-Roman world as "Jews," although their "Judaism" should not be confused with the type of Judaism that grew out of the rabbinic consolidation after the destruction of the Temple. The most aggressive missionaries, in fact, all came from the diaspora and spoke Greek as their mother tongue, like Stephanus, Philipp, Paul, Barnabas, and Apollos—and, alas, also Paul's opponents. Only slowly did Gentile converts like Titus assume leadership roles in the missionary effort. For all of them, including Gentile converts, the Scriptures of Israel in their Greek translation (the Septuagint) were decisive for their understanding of the new message and played a significant role in their propaganda. Controversies were not about the use of these Scriptures themselves (Marcion was the first to pose this question in the middle of the 2d century CE) but about their interpretation. Where the Scriptures were understood as "the Law," that is, a book of ritual prescriptions (circumcision, dietary requirements, Sabbath observances, religious festivals), their observance would assure the true people of God of protection from the powers of the universe; this was the position of the opponents in Galatia, normally known as "Judaizers." Or the Bible could be understood as a guide to a life of perfection, which would guarantee full possession of the transcendent salvation already in the present life; Paul attacks such perfectionists in Philippians 3. Or the Scriptures could be commended as a book of deep truths: its interpretation through spiritual exegesis could reveal to the hearer the presence of spiritual powers. The opponents of 2 Corinthians used such arguments for their propaganda. For Paul, the Bible was a book of ancient promises that had became a reality through the coming of Christ, his death and resurrection, the preaching of the gospel, and the faith of the churches. Paul's concerted missionary efforts may have been the first to preach the gospel and organize communities of believers beyond the realm of Palestine and Syria in other areas of the Roman empire. But others would soon follow. Evidence mostly comes from Paul's controversies with rival apostles and is restricted to the areas of Asia Minor, Macedonia, and Greece. Most likely, the gospel was also carried to the east of Syria and to Egypt at this time. Testimonies from a somewhat later period demonstrate once more the amazing variety that was characteristic for the beginnings in these areas.

The Galatian opponents are the first known wandering apostles who invaded a Pauline church. Their message recommended that the new Gentile converts be circumcised and observe the ritual law in order to enjoy the full benefits of their newly acquired status as members of the people of God. These apostles were not simply representatives of traditional Jewish observance of ritual. Although Paul cannot admit this, they were men filled with the spirit and convinced of the spiritual power and cosmic significance of the law. If they were not identical with the "false brothers" of Gal 2:4, who schemed against Paul in Jerusalem (§9.1d), they may have had connections with them or appealed to them as the true guardians of the Jerusalem agreement. That Paul gave such a careful exposition of his relationship to Jerusalem in Galatians 1 and 2, and that he emphasized the independence of the Gentile mission, recognized by the authorities of Jerusalem, indicates that his opponents in Galatia had accused him of violating the Jerusalem agreement.

The letter that Paul wrote to the Galatian churches in defense of his gospel is saturated with biting invectives. Its prescript and proem already predict the polemical style of what will follow. The apostle's title, here appearing in a Pauline letter for the first time, is expanded by the words "not by human beings and not through human beings" (Gal 1:1). The thanksgiving, usually opening the proem ("I give thanks to God on your part . . ."), is replaced by "I am astonished that you are so quickly deserting the one who called you . . ." (1:6). Hyperbolic polemical formulations appear repeatedly in the letter (such as 3:1 and 5:12). Other proems always recount the apostle's experiences and talk about their relationship to the situation of the church addressed (cf. 1 Thess 1:2–10; 2 Cor 1:3–11). In Galatians, the proem is a description of his call, of his relationship to Jerusalem, and of the conflict in Antioch (Gal 1:10–2:14). The addressees should learn that the opponents have no right to appeal to Jerusalem. Later in the letter, the daring allegory of 4:21–26 includes the note that Jerusalem/Zion has no right to consider itself as the symbolic center of the true Israel.

Answering the claim of the opponents that the old covenant had been renewed through Christ, Paul responds that the old covenant has come to an end, that its curse had run the course, and that therefore the promises given to Abraham before the law arrived had now become valid (3.6–18). The law is by no means the guarantor of membership in the elect people of the covenant. Rather, it is limited to a specific historical period that ended with Christ's death. During that period the law played the role of jail-keeper and slave-master until the arrival of the freedom for God's children, which includes all people, Jews and Greeks, slaves and free, men and women (3:19–29). The assertion that the law as cosmic power can reconcile people with the elements and powers of the universe is rejected by Paul with the statement that this would only enslave people once more to these elements. Paul mocks the Galatians, converts from pagan worship: obedience to the law would be nothing but a return to the old idols (4:8–11). The parenetic section of the letter (5:1–6:10), once more interspersed with polemical remarks and introduced by the challenging statement, "For freedom Christ has set us free" (5:1), presents a fundamental juxtaposition of conduct in the spirit (freedom and love) to the works of the "flesh," which are identical with the works of the law. The final greetings (6:11–18) are a last appeal to turn away from the opponents, who are once more accused of dishonesty and self-interest.

It appears that the controversy with the opponents in Galatia, who threatened to destroy his entire missionary work there, forced Paul to rethink the contrast of gospel and law more radically. From this time on, he insisted that the law had run its course and had come to the end of its validity. It was terminated through Christ's death on the cross and could be fulfilled only through the commandment of love, which presupposed the freedom and equality of all members of the community of Israel of the new age. It appears that Paul was successful. A year later, he was able to tell the Corinthians that the collection had made good progress in the Galatian churches (1 Cor 16:1). Since nothing is said about the collection in the letter to the Galatians, Paul must have had some contacts meanwhile with the Galatian churches through letters or messengers and was confident that his endeavor to make a collection for the "poor" in Jerusalem would not be misinterpreted.

(c) The Spiritual People in Corinth and the First Letter to the Corinthians

Before Paul wrote the letter that is preserved as 1 Corinthians he had already written another letter to the church in Corinth, now lost but mentioned in 1 Cor 5:9 (some have claimed that it is partially preserved in 2 Cor 6:14–7:1; but those verses were not written by Paul— they are a Jewish-Christian piece that somehow got incorporated in the collection of Paul's letters). The occasion of the writing of 1 Corinthians was a report from Chloe's people about the situation in Corinth (1 Cor 1:11) and a letter from Corinth (7:1). At the time of the writing, Paul must have been in Ephesus for some time; he is already making plans to leave (16:5–7), but wants to stay in that city until Pentecost because of more opportunities for missionary work as well as hostilities and controversies (16:8–9). If Paul had arrived in the fall of 52, the letter must have been written in the winter of 53–54. Paul could

Bibliography to §9.3c: Commentaries

Hans Conzelmann, *1 Corinthians: A Commentary on the First Epistle to the Corinthians* (Hermeneia; Philadelphia: Fortress, 1975).

Wolfgang Schrage, *Der erste Brief an die Korinther,* vol. 1: *1Kor 1, 1–6, 11,* vol. 2: *1Kor 6, 12–11, 16* (EKKNT 7/1–2; Neukirchen-Vluyn, Neukirchener Verlag, 1991–1995).

Bibliography to §9.3c: Studies

John C. Hurd, *The Origin of I Corinthians* (London: SPCK, and New York: Seabury, 1965).

Birger A. Pearson, *The Pneumatikos-Psychikos Terminology in 1 Corinthians: A Study in the Theology of the Corinthian Opponents of Paul and Its Relation to Gnosticism* (SBLDS 12; Missoula, MT: Scholars Press, 1973).

Karl-Gustav Sandelin, *Die Auseinandersetzung mit der Weisheit in 1 Korinther 15* (Meddlander från Stiftelsens för Åbo Akademi Forskninginstitut 12; Åbo: Åbo Akademi, 1976).

Gerd Theissen, *The Social Setting of Pauline Christianity: Essays on Corinth* (Philadelphia: Fortress, 1982).

Wayne Meeks, *The First Urban Christians: The Social World of the Apostle Paul* (New Haven: Yale University Press, 1983).

Margaret M. Mitchell, *Paul and the Rhetoric of Reconciliation: An Exegetical Investigation of the Language and Composition of 1 Corinthians* (Hermeneutische Untersuchungen zur Theologie 28; Tübingen: Mohr/Siebeck, 1991).

Günther Bornkamm, "Lord's Supper and Church in Paul," in idem, *Experience,* 123–60.

Hans-Josef Klauck, *Herrenmahl und hellenistischer Kult: Eine religionsgeschichtliche Untersuchung zum ersten Korintherbrief* (NTA.NF 15; Münster: Aschendorff, 1982).

Dale B. Martin, *The Corinthian Body* (New Haven: Yale University Press, 1995).

Bibliography to §9.3c: Bibliography and History of Scholarship

Gerhard Sellin, "Hauptprobleme des Ersten Korintherbriefes," *ANRW* 2.25.4 (1987) 2940–3044.

not have foreseen at that time that further developments would oblige him to stay in Ephesus much longer, forcing him to change his travel plans several times— the Corinthians later accused him of that (2 Cor 1:15ff.).

In 1 Corinthians Paul is not dealing with opposing apostles who had come to his church from outside. Apollos, to be sure, had meanwhile gone to Corinth. But Paul accuses neither Apollos nor other missionaries; his charges are directed to the Corinthians themselves. The problems must have resulted from the consequences that some Corinthians had drawn from Paul's own preaching or, and this is more likely, from the teachings of Apollos. Two charges are obvious: the formation of parties in Corinth (1 Cor 1:11ff.) and the behavior of the "strong people." 1 Cor 6:12 and 10:23 quote their slogan, "I am free to do anything" (the translation, "All things are lawful for me," is misleading because their slogan had nothing to do with the "law"). What are these parties, in which believers claim that they belong to Paul, Apollos, Cephas (Peter), or Christ (1:12), and how are they related to the boasting of the "strong people"? Moreover, why does Paul discuss in this context baptism (1:13–17), words of wisdom (1:19–2:13), knowledge (1:21; 2:8–16), and mystery (2:1, 7)—topics that recur several times later in the letter, especially in the debate with the strong people (see, e.g., 8:1–12; 13:2, 8)? And why are such topics repeatedly juxtaposed to the word of the cross (1:18; 2:1–4) and to the commandment of love (13:8–13)?

Since Paul does not attack any particular party but the phenomenon as such, it is not possible to assume that each of these parties stood for a different theological program. The close connection of the four names with baptism and with the possession of wisdom suggests that the names of Paul, Apollos, Cephas, and Christ are the names of mystagogues, either functioning as baptizers—baptism is thus understood as a mystery rite—or as authorities for words of saving wisdom. Some people in Corinth were convinced of their possession of divine saving wisdom mediated through certain apostles, through whom they had been initiated by baptism, or received under the authority of Christ. It is remarkable that words of Jesus are quoted in 1 Corinthians more frequently than in any other letter of Paul (see 7:10–11; 9:14; 11:23–24). There is also an allusion to Luke 10:21 in 1 Cor 1:21. Most remarkable is the quotation (as Scripture) in 1 Cor 2:9 of a passage that appears in the *Gospel of Thomas* (#17) as a saying of Jesus, and 1 Cor 4:8 ridicules the saying about "becoming kings" that stands at the beginning of the *Gospel of Thomas* (#2).

After the prescript and proem (1 Cor 1:1–3 and 1:4–9), Paul responds to this wisdom theology first in a fundamental polemic (1:10–4:21), continues with a discussion of the negative repercussions of such beliefs for the life and order of the community (5:1–14:40), and concludes with a rejection of the resulting realized eschatology that denies the expectation of the resurrection at the time of Christ's return (15:1–58). The letter closes with instructions for the collection, statements about his travel plans, and final greetings (16:1–24). Crucial for the fundamental polemic is Paul's assertion that insights drawn from any sort of wisdom are valid only if they are directed to the event of salvation itself (2:12; cf. 2:8–9). This event of salvation is proclaimed in the word of the cross (1:18), which has nothing whatsoever in common with words of wisdom (2:1–4); the Crucified One can only appear to be foolishness and a stumbling block (1:19–31). Neither the proclaimer nor the baptizer can add to its authority—Paul emphasizes that he did not come to baptize (1:14–17), because both he and Apollos are nothing but servants for the sake of faith (3:5). Indeed, the apostles are not superhuman beings, but ridiculous, persecuted, despised, and overworked fools. The Corinthians are ridiculed: in their spiritual achievements, they are already full and rich participants in the rule of God (4:6–13).

In the discussion of the resulting behavior of the Corinthians, the letter's outline uses traditional patterns of parenesis (interpretation of a catalog of vices: fornication, adultery, idolatry, 5:1–11:1) and church order (women in the service, Eucharist, baptism, spiritual gifts, church offices, order of worship, 11:2–14:40). The first part (5:1–6:11) deals with grievances that are not necessarily related to the wisdom teaching. Paul recommends that the Corinthians should excommunicate a member who lives in concubinage with his father's wife, and he instructs them not to bring disputes between members of the congregation before secular courts. With the quotation of the slogan of the strong ones in 6:12, however, Paul now turns to address the problems in the Corinthian church that are caused by people who hold the demonstration of their own spiritual freedom against the welfare of the community. The consequences that they drew from their self-consciousness for their sexual and marital life were apparently sexual license (intercourse with prostitutes, 6:12–20) as well as ascetic practices, such as refusal of sex in marriage, rejection of marriage, or remarriage of divorced and widowed people (7:1–16). What kind of behavior is discussed in 7:25–40 is debated among scholars. The most plausible explanation is that some people in Corinth were living together as virgins in spiritual marriages (*subintroductae*). Since "realized eschatology" (cf. Luke 20:34–36: those who are worthy of the coming age neither marry nor are given into marriage) appears repeatedly in the following discussions (see below) one must assume that they wanted to be released already from all earthly and social bonds, even in matters of sex and marriage. Paul counters that abstinence is advisable for practical reasons because the end has *not* yet come (1 Cor 7:29–35). Here as well as in this entire chapter, Paul's parenesis is distinguished by sober and rational advice and the rejection of enthusiastic and religious motivations for moral decision-making. In this respect, his judgment is quite different from his Jewish (Philo) and pagan (Musonius) philosophical contemporaries, especially since he argues without compromise for equal rights of women (e.g., 7:3–4). To this equal status of men and women corresponds the relativising of the status of circumcised and uncircumcised people and of masters and slaves (cf. Gal 3:28), though slaves who could become free should use their newly acquired freedom even more for the service of the Lord (1 Cor 7:17–24; the interpretation that Paul advises those slaves rather to remain in slavery cannot be maintained).

The arguments concerning participation in the worship of idols (8:1–11:1) are addressed even more directly to the strong people. Their behavior raises the question whether spiritual achievement allows the indiscriminate exercise of personal freedom; later Paul asks whether such conduct actually builds up the community (10:23). Freedom and privilege resulting from knowledge (*gnosis*) are fully granted but are not necessarily compatible with love (8:1–8). This is exemplified with respect to the rights of an apostle: such privileges should not be exercised if they conflict

Cultic Dining Room in the Demeter Sanctuary at Corinth
A whole series of dining rooms was excavated in this sanctuary, each large enough to serve seven, nine, or eleven persons. The picture shows the substructures for the dining
couches along the walls of the room, the offcenter door in the
left, with other dining rooms in the background.

with demands of apostolic integrity in the service of the gospel (9:1ff., especially 9:19–27) or if they violate the weak conscience of other members of the community (8:9–13)—or even the conscience of a pagan observer (10:28–29). Not one's own conscience but the conscience of the other should be the criterion of one's action. The analogy of the Eucharist with the "sacrament of Israel" with a typological interpretation of scriptural passages about the exodus is designed to demonstrate that the community as a whole must understand itself as the body of Christ, whereas the experimentation with religious privileges by the individual may well destroy both the individual and the community (10:1–22). Paul does not make recourse to any law that forbids participation in pagan sacrificial meals. The freedom of the Christian is not questioned as such, but it is subordinated to the required respect for the weak conscience and to the necessity to build up the community. Throughout the entire discussion of church order that follows, Paul never castigates immoral or unlawful behavior as destructive for the church. Rather, he demonstrates that free exercise of religious privilege and the demonstration of advanced spiritual insight and knowledge violate the building up of the community. Whether women should preach and pray in the church without a veil is not a question of emancipation but a question of the generally acceptable custom of the church (11:2–16). The Lord's Supper is not a mystery meal for the perfect, but an eschatological meal of the entire community, which should demonstrate respect for all members of the "body of Christ," particularly for the poor (11:17–34). That is the meaning of "discerning the body" (11:29), namely, discerning that the body of Christ is the entire community. With regard to spiritual gifts, there is no rank or order; all members of the community—not only those who want to prove their special possession of the spirit in the speaking in tongues, prophecy, the working of miracles, or the display of "knowledge" (*gnosis*)—have received the spirit in baptism through which they confess that Jesus is Lord. Paul exemplifies the equality of all gifts of the spirit, even the most humble ones, with the use of the metaphor of the "body," in which all members must work together—an example that is not taken from the religious but from the secular political tradition (12:1–31). No single charisma can prove the presence of God in the midst of the community except one, namely love, as Paul explains in a didactic poem. Prophecy, tongues, and knowledge will come to an end, only love is the real presence of eternity (13:1–13). The instructions for the community's worship services are once more directed against the demonstration of special religious possessions. Speaking in tongues neither edifies nor can it be understood by the layperson or the unbeliever (14:1–33a and 37–40). The verses 33b–36 contradict the Pauline practice, attested many times, of the full participation of women in all offices, activities, and worship of the church. Moreover, they interrupt the context and must be viewed as a later interpolation.

The identity of the people who deny the resurrection of the body, whom Paul attacks in 1 Corinthians 15, is one of the most debated problems of New Testament scholarship. Certainly there were no such members of the church whose faith was so weak that they could not believe in the future resurrection. It is more plausible that Paul's arguments were directed against the same religious enthusiasts whose advanced religious knowledge is discussed throughout the letter. Certainly, these people did not argue that death would put an end to everything; why would they have practiced vicarious baptism for those who had died before baptism (15:29)? The self-consciousness of these Corinthians rather led them to believe that they had already obtained full participation in Christ's salvation and that their spiritual self had become immortal so that death would not touch them. 1 Cor 15:44–49 shows that they were convinced that they had already returned to the first spiritual Adam and left the earthly Adam behind. Paul contrasts this belief with a historical perspective of salvation that reckons with the fact that we are still living in the image of a first Adam who was earthly, taken from the dust of the earth, and that the future has not been fulfilled. The resurrection of Christ, which the gospel proclaims (15:1ff.), is an event of past history, attested by historical witnesses. Thus resurrection is not a timeless truth but another historical event that is tied to the future event of Christ's coming, which would signal the resurrection of all believers. Paul makes recourse here to an apocalyptic mystery saying (15:51–52) and to a traditional apocalyptic schema (15:23ff.). Earthly human existence is still a reality and will not end until the coming of Christ, which will bring the final unification with the heavenly human being, the true spiritual second Adam, through the resurrection of the dead and the transformation of the living into a new spiritual "body," that is, a new existence of human beings that cannot be attained prematurely in the present life in this world.

In the final chapter (16), Paul discusses the collection and his travel plans. In 1 Thessalonians the collection is not mentioned at all, and even in Galatians Paul does not promote the matter of the collection (although he must meanwhile have written instructions also to Galatia). In 1 Cor 16:1–4 Paul gives specific instructions for the collection for the "saints," which he intends to send to Jerusalem through delegates from various churches, equipped with letters of commendation, adding that he might personally go to Jerusalem together with this delegation (16:4). He then announces his travel plans. At this point, he intends to stay in Ephesus until Pentecost, then travel via Macedonia to Corinth, where he plans to remain for a longer period (16:5–9). Paul had already sent his associate Timothy to Corinth (4:17; 16:10), whose return he now expects together with a Corinthian delegation (16:11). In any case, he anticipates being in Corinth very soon (cf. also 4:19). One learns from 2 Corinthians, however, that Paul had to change his travel plans several times—to the great displeasure of the Corinthians (see below). The final verses of the letter (16:10–20) speak about Paul's concern that others working in behalf of the gospel should be recognized and supported (16:10–11, 15–16; cf. also 4:17); the last verses confirm that the exchange between Paul and the church in Corinth must have been very lively (16:17–18).

(d) New Opposition in Corinth: The Second Letter to the Corinthians

While 1 Corinthians gives the impression that Paul's association with the Corinthian church was cordial, the fragments of various letters now preserved in 2 Corinthians (§7.3d) clearly show an almost disastrous deterioration of this relationship. New opposition against Paul had been instigated by foreign missionaries who had invaded the Corinthian church. Missionaries agitating against Paul are now explicitly mentioned and the central questions of the debate have changed. What was discussed in 1 Corinthians is mentioned only marginally; indeed Paul seems to take a more conciliatory position with respect to the previous issues (compare, e.g., 2 Cor 5:1–10 with 1 Corinthians 15), which seem to fade in view of the new controversy. The opponents of 2 Corinthians cannot be identified with those of the first letter; the activities of these foreign apostles constituted a much more serious threat to the success of Paul's Corinthian mission.

They were Jewish-Christian missionaries who boasted that they were "Hebrews, Israelites, seed of Abraham" (2 Cor 11:22). But since the law and circumcision are never mentioned, they must be distinguished from the missionaries who had disturbed the churches in Galatia (§9.3b). On the other hand, the Scriptures and the covenant of Israel played a significant role in their propaganda (2 Corinthians 3). Their message was the renewal of the true religion of Israel through Christ, whose mighty works they repeated in their own actions. Theirs were the true works of the spirit, documented through powerful deeds and miracles (12:11–12), reports of mystical experiences and fulfillment of their prayers (12:1–9), and spiritual exegesis of the Scriptures (3:4–18). As divine power had been present in Moses and in Jesus, they themselves were now "divine men" documenting the presence of this power in the midst of the churches. It is probable that their preaching also included narratives of the powerful deeds of Christ as they appear in the sources of the Gospel of Mark and the *Semeia Source* of the Gospel of John (§7.3b). The letters of recommendations that these apostles produced (3:1–3) were records of their own powerful performances and their missionary successes.

The Corinthians were impressed. Why had Paul not done similar powerful deeds among them? Why had he not at least reported some of his own religious experiences? Had Paul simply withheld from them an essential and important element of

---

Bibliography to §9.3d: Commentaries

Rudolf Bultmann, *The Second Letter to the Corinthians,* ed. Erich Dinkler (Minneapolis: Augsburg 1985).

Victor Paul Furnish, *II Corinthians: Translated with Introduction, Notes and Commentary* (AB 32A; Garden City, NY: Doubleday, 1984).

Christian Wolff, *Der zweite Brief des Paulus an die Korinther* (ThHK 8; Berlin: Evangelische Verlagsanstalt, 1989).

Hans Dieter Betz, *2 Corinthians 8 and 9: A Commentary on Two Administrative Letters of the Apostle Paul* (Hermeneia; Philadelphia: Fortress, 1985).

Bibliography to §9.3d: Studies

Dieter Georgi, *The Opponents of Paul in Second Corinthians: A Study in Religious Propaganda in Late Antiquity* (Philadelphia: Fortress, 1986).

Günther Bornkamm, "Die Vorgeschichte des sogenannten Zweiten Korintherbriefes," in idem, *Geschichte und Glaube* (2 vols.; München: Kaiser, 1971) 2. 162–94.

C. K. Barrett, "Paul's Opponents in II Corinthians," *NTS* 17 (1970/71) 233–54.

Gerhard Dautzenberg, "Der Zweite Korintherbrief als Briefsammlung: Zur Frage der literarischen Einheitlichkeit und des theologischen Gefüges von 2 Kor 1–8," *ANRW* 2.25.4 (1987) 3045–66.

Rudolf Bultmann, "Exegetische Probleme des zweiten Korintherbriefes," in idem, *Exegetica,* 298–322.

Ernst Käsemann, "Die Legitimität des Apostels," *ZNW* 41 (1942) 33–71.

Hans Dieter Betz, *Der Apostel Paulus und die sokratische Tradition: Eine exegetische Untersuchung zu seiner "Apologie" 2. Kor. 10–13* (BHTh 45; Tübingen: Mohr/Siebeck, 1972).

religious life? Paul had not even used his apostolic right to receive payment for his missionary work (12:11ff.; cf. 11:7ff.). When such questions implying profound doubts about his apostolic legitimacy were first brought to him, Paul responded with a letter that must have been written in the summer of 54, which is essentially preserved in 2 Cor 2:14–6:13 and 7:2–4. Paul here argues that the splendor on the face of Moses did actually fade away (3:13), that this kind of Christ was a "Christ according to the flesh" (5:16), and that these apostles were just preaching themselves (4:5). Paul describes his own role as an apostle as part of an eschatological event that the community shares. Tangible presentation of the divine power in the person of the missionary is irreconcilable with the eschatological action of God. The use of impressive instruments through which one tries to "peddle" the gospel as successfully as possible in the religious market (2:17; cf. 4:2) is as inappropriate for this eschatological event as are letters of recommendation for the successful missionary (3:1–4). What the gospel proclaims is no less than the beginning of the new creation (5:17). In the proem of this letter, the thanksgiving, Paul describes this in a daring image: as a prisoner in the triumphal procession of God, Paul delivers his life- and death-bringing message (2:14ff.); but his own life means nothing in terms of his personal achievements. Letters of recommendation for him would say nothing about his person. This is argued in another striking image: the church is a heavenly letter administered by the apostle. The juxtaposition of this letter, written on tablets of the heart by the spirit of God, and that which had once been written on tablets of stone (3:3), leads to a criticism of the opponents' theology of the covenant. Even a spiritual interpretation of the written records of the old covenant cannot help to visualize the glory of God, which remains hidden until today. Paul expounds this in a critical commentary on his opponents' exegesis of Exodus (3:4–18).

The claim of the opponents that the divine power of Christ can unambiguously be present and tangible forces Paul into a seemingly Gnostic speech about the presence of the eschatological event. To be sure, nothing less is at stake than the resplendent rise of the light of creation through the apostle's work (4:5); but it comes forth from the "heart" of the apostle as a treasure in earthen vessels (4:7). Not the powerful deeds of the apostle but paradoxically his tribulations make that light visible and tangible as his fate represents the dying of Jesus in order that life might become real in the congregation (4:8–15). Only the inner human being is renewed, while the outward one perishes as does everything that is visible (4:16–18). Only the conscience of the hearer, not any outward documentation, can prove the truth of the proclamation and the legitimacy of the apostle (4:2; 5:11–12; 6:12; 7:3). Paul, entrusted with the office of the eschatological reconciliation, can point the Corinthians only to a rather paradoxical documentation of this event in his own experiences and activities: "in tribulations, beatings, prisons . . . as dying, and behold, living" (6:3–10).

All this was apparently not a very impressive defense of the legitimacy of Paul's apostolic ministry. It must be assumed that this letter did not do anything to help his cause and apparently only provoked his opponents' mockery. Informed of his letter's failure, Paul decided to go to Corinth himself for a quick visit (the "interim visit"), which proved to be a catastrophe. The Corinthians gave no indication that they were willing to accept such a miserable proof of apostolic power and, what was even more damaging to the relationship, someone must have personally offended Paul so severely (7:12) that his personal relationship to the church was seriously called into question. Back in Ephesus without having achieved his purpose, Paul wrote to the Corinthians once more. This letter is at least partially preserved in 2 Corinthians 10–13. This is most likely the letter "written with many tears" mentioned later in 2 Cor 2:4. It is an apology for Paul's apostolic ministry that goes to the very limits of good taste in the choice of literary and rhetorical methods. Satire and irony go hand in hand with scorn and open threats. Evidently Paul was at the end of his wits and, in this situation, resorted to using the most powerful tools of rhetoric, including invective and irony.

It is clear in this letter that Paul had an opportunity to meet his opponents in person and that he did not cut a very good figure in comparison to these super-apostles. He could under no circumstances do the Corinthians the favor of comparing himself with these apostles on their own grounds because "measuring," "estimating," and "comparing" would involve him in accepting their criteria of apostolic legitimacy. He therefore requests that the Corinthians should judge his letters as well as his personal appearance on the basis of the only appropriate criterion in question, namely, the proclamation of the gospel (10:1–18). The charge, however, that Paul had not used his right as a messenger of the gospel to receive his livelihood from the church was grave, especially since the suspicion had been raised that his collection of money for Jerusalem sprang from ignoble motives (12:11–18). If this renunciation of his apostolic right, through which he wanted to express his love for the Corinthians (11:7–10), could be misconstrued in such a way, Paul had to conclude that his whole work had been in vain. As an honest matchmaker, he wanted to procure the church for Christ as a pure bride; but if the church now dallied with these superapostles, who were nothing but disguised messengers of Satan, then his church was indeed in danger of being lost (11:1–6; cf. 12:19–21).

Since so much was at stake, Paul accepted after all the challenge to compare himself with his opponents—but he does this in a "fool's speech" (11:16–12:10). This section, carefully drafted in every detail, is a mockery of the religious achievements of which his opponents boasted, a satire of an aretalogy. As far as titles of apostolic dignity are concerned, he can match the claims of the opponents (11:22–23), but instead of an enumeration of his successful deeds as a missionary one finds a catalog of crises and disasters (*peristaseis*), in which he enumerates all the adverse circumstances, dangers, insults, and misfortunes he had experienced in his work as an apostle (11:23–33), mentioning even that he is often suffering from insomnia (11:27) and concluding with an ironic account of his undignified escape from Damascus (11:32–33). The second part of this fool's speech (12:1–10) concerns his accomplishments of personal piety, which indicates that his opponents also boasted of their visions and successful prayers. With respect to visions, Paul is not quite certain about the identity of his own person when he was taken up in a rapture to the third heaven, and nothing that could be communicated emerged from the whole affair anyway. With regard to his prayers, he received only a negative answer from the Lord. Thus the Corinthians cannot learn anything by comparing the apostle with his opponents. Rather, they have to judge themselves: if they stand firm in the faith, Paul is their rightful apostle; if not, the apostle must use his authority to dissolve the church (13:1–10).

This letter was certainly written much earlier than the last piece of the Corinthian correspondence, 2 Cor 1:1–2:13; 7:5–16, a letter that Paul wrote from Macedonia after his departure from Ephesus, when Titus had brought him the good message that the Corinthian church had been reconciled with him. The whole tenor of 2 Cor 10–13, the violence of the attack, and the exhaustive use of all rhetorical tricks make it necessary to accept the hypothesis and to date this "letter of tears" to the early and most bitter stage of the conflict. We do not know how the letter was received in Corinth, though Paul decided that it was necessary to send Titus to Corinth in the hope that his faithful associate might accomplish a reconciliation. This mission as well as some other unforeseen events in Ephesus delayed Paul's anticipated visit to Corinth and forced him once more to change his travel plans.

(e) Ephesian Imprisonment; Letters to the Philippians and to Philemon

(1) *The Ephesian Imprisonment.* Statements such as 2 Cor 6:5 and 11:23 show that Paul had been in prison more than once. Written shortly after Paul's departure from Ephesus, 2 Cor 1:8–11, reports an affliction in which Paul was already prepared to receive the death sentence. This report implies that he was imprisoned in Ephesus for some time. The information from Phil 1:12–26 and the Letter to Philemon fit this situation very well and favor the thesis that these letters were written during an Ephesian imprisonment in the winter of 54–55. This eliminates many problems that burden the traditional assumption of the composition of these letters during a later Roman imprisonment. Most of all, travel to Rome from Philippi was a long, expensive, and time-consuming affair, while travel between Philippi and Ephesus was not a big problem. While in prison, Paul received a gift of money from Philippi, for which he sent a brief receipt to that church (Phil 4:10–20). Epaphroditus came to Paul from Philippi as the bearer of this gift (Phil 2:25, 4:18). Before Paul wrote the next letter, the Philippians had already heard that Epaphroditus became sick while he was with Paul (2:26). Paul now wanted to send Timothy to Philippi as soon as possible (2:19) and, in case he received a favorable sentence, he wanted to come to Philippi in person in the near future (1:26; 2:24). It is hard to imagine that Paul intended to go to Philippi after he arrived in Rome; according to Rom 15:24–28, he expected to be sent on to Spain by the Roman church. But after his Ephesian imprisonment he indeed went to Macedonia and certainly

Bibliography to §9.3e (1)

Wilhelm Michaelis, *Die Gefangenschaft des Paulus in Ephesus und das Itinerar des Timotheus* (Gütersloh: Bertelsmann, 1925).

G. S. Duncan, *Paul's Ephesian Ministry: A Reconstruction with Special Reference to the Ephesian Origin of the Imprisonment Epistles* (New York: Scribner's, 1929).

Idem, "Paul's Ministry in Asia—The Last Phase," *NTS* 3 (1956/57) 211–18.

Idem, "Chronological Table to Illustrate Paul's Ministry in Asia," *NTS* 5 (1958/59) 43–45.

T. W. Manson, "St. Paul in Ephesus: The Date of the Epistle to the Philippians," *BJRL* 23 (1939).

visited Philippi. Moreover, the slave Onesimus, who had run away from the house of Philemon in Colossae, would likely have come to Ephesus, the next major port city, and it would have been easy for Paul to send him back to Colossae from there together with a letter, in which he states that he might possibly visit Colossae soon (Phlm 22). There should be no doubt that the letters to the Philippians and to Philemon were written during Paul's Ephesian imprisonment.

(2) *The Letters to the Philippians.* It is necessary to accept the hypothesis that the preserved Letter to the Philippians is composed of fragments of three smaller letters (§7.3d) because various parts of the extant letter reflect very different situations. The first of these letters, Phil 4:10–20, is a formal receipt (4:18 uses the regular formula for a receipt) that acknowledges the gift of money sent to Paul from Philippi. In this brief letter Paul emphasizes his self-sufficiency (*autarkeia*) and independence (4:11–13), and he never says "Thank you," which must strike the modern reader as very strange. But Paul wants to make clear that this gift is not a fulfillment of an obligation and that he is not the client of any patrons, namely, the Philippians. The gift is an offering of thanks to God (4:18), which makes God the patron of the Philippians. This includes the congregation not only in a relationship of mutual give and take with the apostle, it also rejects any patron-client relationship between the church and the apostle and makes both the congregation and Paul clients of their patron God, who is responsible for their care and welfare (4:19).

The second letter, Phil 1:1–3:1 (perhaps also 4:4–7), throughout reflects the situation of Paul's imprisonment. After the prescript (1:1–2; "bishops" and "deacons"

Bibliography to §9.3e (2): Commentaries

J.-F. Collange, *The Epistle of St. Paul to the Philippians* (London: Epworth, 1979).

Wolfgang Schenk, *Die Philipperbriefe des Paulus: Kommentar* (Stuttgart: Kohlhammer, 1984).

U. N. Müller, *Der Brief des Paulus an die Philipper* (ThHK 11/1; Leipzig: Evangelische Verlagsanstalt, 1993).

Markus Bockmuehl, *The Epistle to the Philippians* (Peabody, MA: Hendrickson, 1998).

Bibliography to §9.3e (2): Studies

Lukas Bormann, *Philippi: Stadt und Christengemeinde zur Zeit des Paulus* (NovTSup 78; Leiden: Brill 1995).

Ernst Käsemann, "Kritische Analyse von Phil. 2, 5–11," in idem, *Exegetische Versuche,* 1. 51–95.

Günther Bornkamm, "On Understanding the Christ-Hymn (Philippians 2:6–11)," in idem, *Experience,* 112–22.

Dieter Georgi, "Der vorpaulinische Hymnus Phil. 2, 6–11," in *Zeit und Geschichte: Dankesgabe und Rudolf Bultmann zum 80. Geburtstag* (Tübingen: Mohr/Siebeck, 1964) 262–93.

Ralph P. Martin, *A Hymn of Christ: Philippians 2:5–11 in Recent Interpretation & in the Setting of Early Christian Worship* (Downers Grove: Inter-Varsity, 1997).

Walter Schmithals, "The False Teachers of the Epistle to the Philippians," in idem, *Paul and the Gnostics,* 65–122.

Helmut Koester, "The Purpose of the Polemic of a Pauline Fragment (Phil III)," *NTS* 8 (1961/62) 317–32.

Bibliography to §9.3e (2): History of Scholarship

Wolfgang Schenk, "Der Philipperbrief in der neueren Forschung (1945–1985)," *ANRW* 2.25.4 (1987) 3280–3313.

must be understood as titles of missionaries), the proem (1:3–26) treats comprehensively the imprisonment and the possibility of Paul's death with respect to their significance for the church, for the proclamation of the gospel, and for Paul himself. Great emphasis is placed on the fellowship (κοινωνία) of the church with himself, insofar as they already share in the proclamation of the gospel. The bond of love that unites them with the apostle will guarantee their continuing growth in knowledge and discernment (1:3–11). As for the gospel, Paul knows that his imprisonment has even encouraged its proclamation, although some proclaim it out of envy and rivalry, and in any case both the church and the gospel do not depend upon Paul's fate (1:12–18). What finally happens to Paul is irrelevant because Christ will be glorified whether through life or through death. Although it would be gain for Paul to die and to be with Christ, he would still choose life and service on behalf of the church (1:19–26). Since Paul in this letter speaks of a direct entrance into the "being with Christ" through death, without expressing an expectation of the future coming of Christ, it has been argued that Paul has here further developed his eschatological expectations after the writing of 1 Cor 15:51–52. But this is unwarranted; as early as 1 Thessalonians Paul was able to say that it is irrelevant for the "being with Christ" whether one is alive or dies (1 Thess 5:10).

Also the parenesis of this letter, Phil 1:27–2:18, is closely related to the theme of the suffering of the apostle (esp. 1:29–30; 2:17). But the church is not dependent upon the fate of the apostle. On the contrary, the apostle is nothing more than a sacrifice poured out in behalf of the faith of the church, while the church's salvation is directly dependent upon God and Christ. The central concept of the parenesis is therefore not the example of Paul but Christ as the foundation of the new existence. This is stated in the hymn about Christ (2:6–11). This hymn is an important piece of evidence for the early appropriation and modification of traditions from mythical wisdom theology. As the hymn is quoted by Paul, however, it is no longer an offer of salvation for those individuals who are willing to follow the call and the path of heavenly Wisdom. Rather, it announces the cosmic rule of the crucified Christ and demands from the entire congregation a fundamental disposition (φρονεῖν) that corresponds to Christ's way of humiliation, namely, unanimity, mutual respect, and renunciation of one's own importance, summarized in the term ταπεινοφροσύνη (2:3), which appears here as a Christian virtue for the first time (it is only poorly translated by the English word "humility"). "Considering others better than oneself" (2:3) is the obedience that the believers owe to God (not to Paul! 2:12).

The conclusion of this letter, 2:19–3:1, begins with recommendations for Paul's associate Timothy, who had once spent himself selflessly for the proclamation in behalf of the church and whom Paul intends to send to Philippi soon, hoping that he himself would also be able to visit the Philippians in due time. Paul then discusses the question of Epaphroditus, who had been sent from Philippi. The Philippians probably protested his long absence. Paul explains that Epaphroditus was not able to return immediately because he had fallen sick and had also become very useful in the service of Paul. It is surprising that exactly this letter, so concerned with Paul's imprisonment and possible sentence of death, is dominated by repeated invitations to joy (1:4, 18, 25; 2:2, 18–19, 3:1; 4:4). In the face of death the eschatological joy as the festive attire of the church must demonstrate more than ever all that faith is worth.

A completely different tone predominates in Phil 3:2–4:3. The exact date of this letter, of which only this fragment is preserved, is difficult to determine; it may even have been written before the two letters from prison. Paul had learned about a dangerous threat to the church when foreign missionaries had invaded the community in Philippi. What is preserved in Phil 3:2–21 (perhaps also 4:1–3 and 8–9) corresponds to the literary form of a "testament." According to Jewish prototypes (see the *Testaments of the Twelve Patriarchs,* §5.3c), this genre consists of a biographical history, an ethical admonition, and an eschatological instruction, including curses and blessings (in the case of Phil 3 these are represented by the warning about false teachers). The literary genre of the testament is used elsewhere in early Christian literature, most obviously in the deutero-Pauline letter 2 Timothy (§12.2g). The identity of the opponents of Philippians 3 is debated. They certainly differ from those of 2 Corinthians, but as they preach circumcision and the observance of the law one is reminded of the "Judaizers" of Galatians. In Philippians 3, the central message of their preaching is an emphasis upon a perfection that can be obtained in the present life by means of obedience to the law, and the claim that such perfection would guarantee the full possession of the heavenly blessings (3:12, 15, 19). It is not possible to understand the invectives of 3:2 and 18–19 as attacks upon libertines; they are polemical reversals of the perfectionist slogans of the opponents.

The biographical introduction (3:5–11) is an important testimony to Paul's understanding of his "conversion" (§9.1b). The perfection extolled by the opponents parallels Paul's former possession of blameless righteousness under the law, which he surrendered in order to obtain the righteousness through faith in Christ. This new existence is therefore fundamentally different from perfection through fulfillment of the law, because it is determined by the suffering and death of Christ, while fulfillment and resurrection from the dead belong strictly to the future. The ethical admonition (3:12–16) can therefore not be an encouragement to obtain a status of fulfillment. Rather, it must take into account that Christian existence is an open movement, a stretching out to an eschatological fulfillment that cannot be obtained through one's own efforts in the present. Those attempting to reach perfection through such efforts are threatened by the curse (3:18–19). The goal toward which those who, together with Paul, imitate Christ are moving transcends earthly existence and presupposes its transformation (3:20–21). Paul's arguments against the apostles of perfection in Philippi are thus similar to those he used against the enthusiasts in Corinth. In both instances, Paul fears Gnosticizing beliefs that deny the paradox of an eschatological existence that remains still bound to the realities and challenges of life in this world.

(3) *The Letter to Philemon* must have been written at about the same time, when Paul was imprisoned in Ephesus. It is the sole extant letter of Paul to an individual. Paul therefore omits his title in the prescript but calls himself instead "a prisoner of Jesus Christ" (Phlm 1). Directing his petition to Philemon, he does not dress himself in the garment of his authority as an apostle who can demand obedience,

but presents himself as "an old man and a prisoner" (v. 9). The addressee, Philemon, was apparently living in Colossae (cf. Col 4:9, 17). Since Philemon is also called a fellow worker, and greetings are directed to the church in his house, one can assume that he was the founder or the first convert of the Colossian church. The letter presupposes that Philemon's slave Onesimus had run away (because of a theft? see v. 18) to Ephesus and had taken refuge with Paul, who was then in prison. Onesimus had rendered useful services to Paul, who had grown fond of him. But Paul could not keep him, probably for reasons both practical and legal. Thus he was now sending him back, together with this letter, to his master Philemon.

It has been debated whether this letter demands that Philemon release Onesimus from slavery. Traditional exegesis, both in antiquity and in 19th-century America among white exegetes (not among black preachers!) answered this question negatively. Although Paul does not employ his apostolic authority and leaves the decision in the hands of Philemon, Paul's advice to accept the runaway slave "as a brother . . . both in the flesh and in the Lord" can hardly be understood in any other way than as a recommendation to give Onesimus his freedom. "Brother in the Lord" is a status that the slave Onesimus would have anyway; "brother in the flesh" must therefore refer to his worldly status (v. 16). Instead of demanding something as an apostle, Paul gives a personal guarantee in writing, which would have been legally binding: if necessary, Paul will defray all expenses (vv. 18–19). This clearly shows that the letter was written to Philemon in order to achieve Onesimus's manumission. Paul's letter is strikingly different from a letter written by Pliny the

Bibliography to §9.3e (3):   Commentaries

Eduard Lohse, *Colossians and Philemon: A Commentary on the Epistles to the Colossians and to Philemon* (Hermeneia; Philadelphia: Fortress, 1971).

Peter Stuhlmacher, *Der Brief an Philemon* (EKKNT; Neukirchen-Vluyn: Neukirchener Verlag, 1975).

Richard Lehmann, *Epître á Philémon: Le Christianisme primitif et l'esclavage* (Commentaires Bibliques; Geneva: Labor et Fides, 1978).

Joachim Gnilka, *Der Philemonbrief* (HThK 10/4; Freiburg: Herder, 1982).

Hermann Binder, *Der Brief des Paulus an Philemon* (ThHK 11/2; Berlin: Evangelische Verlagsanstalt, 1990).

Allen D. Callahan, *Embassy to Onesimus: The Letter of Paul to Philemon* (New Testament in Context; Valley Forge, PA: Trinity Press International, 1997).

Bibliography to §9.3e (3):   Studies

John Knox, *Philemon among the Letters of Paul: A New View of Its Place and Importance* (2d ed.; Nashville, TN: Abingdon, 1959).

Theo Preiss, "Life in Christ and Social Ethics in the Epistle to Philemon," in idem, *Life in Christ* (SBT 13; London: SCM, 1954) 32–42.

F. Forrester Church, "Rhetorical Structure and Design in Paul's Letter to Philemon," *HTR* 71 (1978) 17–33.

Norman R. Petersen, *Rediscovering Paul: Philemon and the Sociology of Paul's Narrative World* (Philadelphia: Fortress, 1985).

Bibliography to §9.3e (3):   History of Scholarship

Wolfgang Schenk, "Der Brief des Paulus an Philemon in der neueren Forschung (1945–1987)," *ANRW* 2.25.4 (1987) 3439–95.

Younger in an analogous situation (*Epist.* 9.21). In this letter, Pliny appeals to his friend's magnanimity, which should enable him to forgive a runaway servant, so that the servant would henceforth be bound to Pliny's friend by lasting gratefulness. In contrast, Paul's letter to Philemon does not even so much as mention forgiveness and is meticulously concerned not to put Onesimus into a situation that would henceforth bind him in thankfulness to his master's magnanimity. Manumission should not make the slave a client of his former owner. On the contrary, for Paul the commandment of love requires that freedom be granted without any personal obligations, and if Philemon is owed anything Paul writes a businesslike guarantee that he himself will pay (v. 18).

(f) The Collection; Paul's Last Visit to Corinth

In the agreement at the Apostolic Council, Paul had promised to remember the "poor" in Jerusalem (Gal 2:10; see §9.1d). But in the letters to the Thessalonians and the Galatians, Paul did not make an attempt to follow up on this promise by organizing a collection of money. The tense situation in Galatia at that time might not have been the most opportune occasion for such an attempt. However, 1 Cor 16:1–4, demonstrates that he had seriously resumed his plan of making such a collection and reveals that he had in the meantime also written once more to the Galatians giving detailed instructions for the procedures to be followed in the collection of this money. He furthermore states his intention to send accredited envoys to Jerusalem for the delivery of the money, adding that he might even decide to go himself. In the interval between the writing of 1 Corinthians and the letter of 2 Corinthians 10–13, Paul had sent Titus and another brother to Corinth to expedite the collection in Greece (2 Cor 12:18). The controversy with the superapostles interrupted the progress and, what was worse, in the course of this controversy accusations had surfaced that questioned Paul's integrity with regard to the money he wanted to collect (2 Cor 12:13–18). Paul's imprisonment in Ephesus and the fears that he might receive the death sentence must have ended the plans for the collection at least temporarily.

As soon as Paul had been released from prison at the beginning of the year 55, his first care had to be the reconciliation with the Corinthian church. For this reason he changed his travel plans: he would go directly to Corinth from Ephesus and visit the churches of Macedonia afterward (2 Cor 1:15–16). But since he did not want to repeat the catastrophe of his last visit (the "interim" visit; see §9.3d), he would wait in Ephesus and first send Titus to Corinth. Titus was well known to the Corinthians, who had acknowledged his integrity (2 Cor 12:18). Paul himself would leave only after he had received the news of the reconciliation from Titus. We do not know why Paul then changed his travel plans once more, left Ephesus, and went to Troas with Timothy; perhaps Ephesus was no longer a safe place for him (Acts 20:15–16 reports that Paul also avoided Ephesus later on his journey from Macedonia to Jeru-

---

Bibliography to §9.3f

Dieter Georgi, *Remembering the Poor: The History of Paul's Collection for Jerusalem* (Nashville, TN: Abingdon, 1992).

salem). But when Titus did not show up in Troas as expected, Paul and Timothy continued to Macedonia, even though Troas had opened some promising possibilities for missionary work (2 Cor 2:12). In Macedonia he finally met Titus, who brought the most welcome news that the Corinthians were willing to be reconciled.

In this situation Paul wrote another letter to Corinth, of which the major part is preserved in 2 Corinthians 1:1–2:13 and 7:5–16. Timothy is named in the prescript as coauthor. Thus he accompanied Paul on this journey (see also Rom 16:21). In the proem Paul speaks in general of the afflictions that he had to endure and of the experience of God's comfort (2 Cor 1:3–7). Both topics are further elucidated in the body of the letter. The afflictions are characteristically not understood as isolated events concerning the personal fate of the apostle—in view of the threat of a death sentence in Ephesus Paul would have sufficient reason to speak only about himself (1:8–10)—but as experiences that involve the church in many ways. The petitions of the church have also contributed to his rescue (1:11). The Corinthians must also recognize that the repeated changes in Paul's travel plans did not arise from any irresoluteness on his part. His entire behavior was rooted in his unwavering commitment to the gospel that he had preached in Corinth (1:12–22). With reference to the "interim" visit in Corinth and to the letter written after that visit (=2 Corinthians 10–13; see §9.3d), Paul explains that even the offense he had received in Corinth—the topic "affliction" is here continued—concerned everyone, not only Paul himself. Therefore the congregation should help to reconcile the person who had caused the offense, since Paul had to change his travel plans to prevent future distress (1:23–2:11). The apostle's afflictions did not end when he had been rescued from almost certain death, nor were they ended through new missionary opportunities (2:12–13; 7:5). They ended only when he received the news about the reconciliation with the Corinthian church (7:6–16). Titus had not only earned the gratefulness of the apostle, but the church also owed him thanks. He had accomplished what Paul himself had been unable to do, namely, to change affliction into comfort, joy, and revival for all involved. All this gives insight into the most important constituent factor in Paul's missionary work, namely the role of his extremely able associates, especially Timothy and Titus, but also many others, whose names occasionally appear in the letters of Paul. The founding and building of these churches, which were able to survive and to grow in the following centuries in spite of many adversities, was not the result of the superhuman efforts of one single apostle but of a successful collaboration of a number of Jewish and Gentile missionaries who worked together in a well-planned organization.

The two letters about the collection (2 Cor 8 and 9), sent at this time to Corinth and to Achaea, respectively, show that the reconciliation with the Corinthians opened the way for a successful completion of the great design of a collection for Jerusalem. These two short letters do more than encourage generous giving, they also measure the eschatological horizon for this work of the Gentile communities. With their gift for Jerusalem they are doing more than giving support for the poor; their giving is in itself a participation in the glorification of God on behalf of his grace, which is fully experienced in the act of giving. Because they share this experience now, the

Gentile believers rank first as the recipients of the eschatological revelation of the righteousness of God.

4. CORINTH—JERUSALEM—ROME

(a) The Last Stay in Corinth; Letters to the Romans and to the "Ephesians"

According to the information available from the genuine letters of Paul and from the Book of Acts, Paul's stay in Corinth in the winter of 55–56 marks the conclusion of his missionary work in the countries of the Aegean Sea. Further strengthening of the newly founded churches, preparation for his travel to the West, and organization of the delivery of the collection occupied the apostle during this period.

Bibliography to §9.4a: Commentaries

Ernst Käsemann, *Commentary on Romans* (Grand Rapids, MI: Eerdmans, 1980).
C. E. B. Cranfield, *A Critical and Exegetical Commentary on the Epistle to the Romans* (ICC; 2 vols.; Edinburgh: Clark, 1975–1979).
Ulrich Wilckens, *Der Brief an die Römer* (3 vols.; EKKNT 6; Neukirchen-Vluyn: Neukirchener Verlag, 1978–1982).
Peter Stuhlmacher, *Paul's Letter to the Romans: A Commentary* (Louisville: Westminster John Knox, 1994).
James D. G. Dunn, *Romans 1–8* (WBC 38A; Dallas: Word, 1988).

Bibliography to §9.4a: General Studies

Ferdinand Christian Baur, "Über Zweck und Veranlassung des Römerbriefes und der damit zusammenhängenden Verhältnisse der römischen Gemeinde," *Tübinger Zeitschrift für Theologie* (1836) 59–113.
Dom Jacques Dupont, "Le problème de la structure littéraire de l'Epître aux Romain," *RB* 62 (1955) 365–97.
Albert Descamps, "La structure de Rom 1–11," in *Studiorum Paulinorum Congressus* (AnBib 17; Rome: Pontificio Istituto Biblico, 1963) 1. 3–14.
Ulrich Luz, "Zum Aufbau von Römer 1–8," *ThZ* 25 (1969) 161–81.
Walter Schmithals, *Der Römerbrief als historisches Problem* (Gütersloh: Mohn, 1975).
James D. G. Dunn, "Paul's Epistle to the Romans: An Analysis of Structure and Argument," *ANRW* 2.25.4 (1987) 2842–90.
Stanislas Lyonnet, *Études sur l'épître aux Romains* (AnBib 120; Rome: Pontificio Istituto Biblico, 1989).
Karl P. Donfried (ed.), *The Romans Debate* (rev. ed.; Peabody, MA; Hendrickson, 1991).
Stanley K. Stowers, *A Rereading of Romans: Justice, Jews, and Gentiles* (New Haven: Yale University Press, 1994).

Bibliography to §9.4a: Studies of specific chapters

Günther Bornkamm, "The Revelation of God's Wrath (Romans 1–3)," in idem, *Experience,* 47–70.
Egon Brandenburger, *Adam und Christus: Exegetisch-religionsgeschichtliche Untersuchung zu Römer 5, 12–21 (1 Kor. 15)* (WMANT 7; Neukirchen-Vluyn: Neukirchener Verlag, 1962).
Günther Bornkamm, "Baptism and New Life in Paul (Romans 6)," in idem, *Experience,* 71–86.
Idem, "Sin, Law, and Death (Romans 7)," in idem, *Experience,* 87–104.
Rudolf Bultmann, "Romans 7 and the Anthropology of Paul," in idem, *Existence and Faith,* 147–65.
Ernst Käsemann, "Principles of the Interpretation of Romans 13," in idem, *New Testament Questions,* 169–216.
Robert J. Karris, "Rom 14:1–15:13 and the Occasion of Romans," *CBQ* 35 (1973) 155–78.

Romans 16:1–23 is a testimony for the first of these activities. It is a letter that was sent to Ephesus together with a copy of the letter to the Romans (Romans 1–15). This explains why this short letter "To the Ephesians" ended up in the later collection of Pauline letters as part of the letter to the Romans. The first collection of the letters of Paul was most likely made in the East, perhaps even in Ephesus, certainly not in Rome. Thus the editor of the collection was relying upon the copy of the letter to the Romans that he found in Ephesus, together with the letter "To the Ephesians" (=Romans 16); he combined the two letters and added a doxology (Rom 16:25–27) that certainly is not Pauline. A number of manuscripts place this doxology at the end of Romans 14 or 15, clear evidence that Romans at some time circulated in different versions (the one used by Marcion apparently ended with Romans 14!). Most important for the hypothesis of Romans 16 as originally a separate "Letter to the Ephesians" is the long list of greetings in this letter, containing the names of many people who were well known to Paul (unlikely for Rome) and who are known to have been in Ephesus, especially Prisca and Aquila (Rom 16:3; for their residence in Ephesus, see 1 Cor 16:19). It is unlikely that they had all migrated to Rome in the meantime (see also §7.3d).

This short letter "To the Ephesians" permits an interesting glance into Paul's activities as an ecclesiastical politician. He did not devise church orders but settled individual questions in the context of fortifying personal relationships. The first few verses (Rom 16:1–2) constitute the oldest extant letter of recommendation for a Christian minister, namely, for the woman Phoebe, who was the "missionary" and "congregational president" of the church of Cenchreae; the traditional translations of her titles as "deaconess" and "helper" cannot be justified on linguistic grounds. In the long list of greetings, a number of women are mentioned who were not personal friends of Paul in the Ephesian church but associates and coworkers, which is shown by the repeated references to their functions. The appearance of such a large number of women is undeniable evidence for the unrestricted participation of women in the various offices of Paul's churches. Striking is the reference to Junia, who is named as prominent among the apostles (16:7). Attempts have been made to read here instead the male name "Junias," in order to avoid the conclusion that Paul's churches also knew female apostles; this male name, however, is not attested anywhere else in antiquity. The mention of house churches and individual groups (16:5, 15) points to the existence of several "congregations" within the church of Ephesus. The conclusion of the letter brings a short warning of false teachers, which echoes that of Philippians 3—also very unlikely to have been directed to the Roman church, whose situation and problems Paul did not know.

Bibliography to §9.4a: The Question of Romans 16

T. W. Manson, "St. Paul's Letters to the Romans—and Others," *BJRL* 31 (1948) 224–40.

J. J. MacDonald, "Was Romans xvi a Separate Letter?" *NTS* 16 (1969/70) 369–72.

Wolf-Henning Ollrog, "Die Abfassungsverhältnisse von Röm 16," in *Kirche: Festschrift Bornkamm*, 221–44.

Helmut Koester, "Ephesos in Early Christian Literature," in *Ephesos: Metropolis of Asia* (HTS 41; Valley Forge, PA; Trinity Press International, 1995) 119–40.

Walter Schmithals, "The False Teachers of Romans 16:17–20," in idem, *Paul and the Gnostics*, 219–38.

The writing of the letter to the church of Rome (Romans 1–15), as well as Paul's decision to deliver the collection for Jerusalem in person, reveals that much more was at stake here than just opening up a new missionary field after the completion of the work in the East. Both the letter to the Romans and the collection are part of the effort to establish a new relationship between Gentile and Jewish believers. The letter to the Romans as well as the collection for Jerusalem deny the validity of the law and the eschatological preeminence of Jerusalem. Instead, Paul insists upon the equal standing of all people who are united not through law, tradition, and organization, but through mutual care for each other and through the divine promise. The first of these concerns is expressed in the collection of the Gentile believers for Jerusalem; it is a service and thanksgiving to God. As far as the divine promise is concerned, Paul insists that it is universal and inclusive because it extends to all the nations of the earth, remaining nevertheless valid for Israel.

The Letter to the Romans (chaps. 1–15) does not contain polemical controversies as do so many other letters of Paul. Yet, it is not a theoretical theological treatise either. The letter is best understood as a letter of recommendation, written by Paul on his own behalf. In the prescript, Paul does not emphasize his own apostolic authority (compare Rom 1:1 with Gal 1:1!). Only insofar as his gospel can claim universal validity is he himself important as bearer of this message to the entire inhabited world. The topic of the letter is therefore the gospel, and not the person of the apostle. This gospel, however, is universalistic, aimed at including also the Gentiles into the ancient promises of Israel. A dialogue with Judaism and the validity of the law is therefore unavoidable. The possible presence of many Jews in the community of the Roman believers explains this interest only superficially. Reasons germane to the subject itself required that the exposition of the gospel for the Gentiles could not avoid the question of freedom from the law. The law is the only alternative to the freedom of the gospel, not only for the Jew but also for the Gentile. Resuming the tradition of Jewish apologetics (§5.3e), Paul assigns to the law a universal significance but must at the same time limit that significance under an eschatological perspective. The promise to Abraham, given before the law, overrides the law's validity for the Gentiles, to whom the gospel proclaims salvation. But do these promises also extend to a law-abiding Israel that rejects the gospel?

The letter to the Romans throughout reflects and updates insights gained from former controversies. For the promise given to Abraham (Romans 4) compare Gal 3:16–18; for the topic of Adam and Christ (Rom 5:12ff.) compare 1 Cor 15:45–49; on the gifts of the spirit (Rom 12:1ff.) compare 1 Cor 12:1ff.; for the relation of the strong and the week (Romans 14:1–15:6) compare 1 Corinthians 6:12–11:1. The justification by faith alone without the law had been the primary topic of Philippians 3 and Galatians. But the literary genre of Romans has little in common with the other letters of Paul; its general outline is borrowed from the tradition of Jewish apologetics. This schema is especially evident in Romans 1:18–3:31, though it has been decisively modified. According to the traditional schema, the Gentiles would have been characterized as possessing only a partial knowledge of God and the law; apologetic arguments are formulated in order to invite them into the full knowledge of God through the acceptance of the law as it is given in the biblical revelation. Paul seems to accept this schema, when he speaks about the revelation of the wrath of God about all people who knew God but worshiped creatures rather than the creator (Rom 1:18–32; vv. 26–27 are not designed specifically to condemn lesbians and homosexuals, but serve as examples that the entire human race is subject to the wrath of God and therefore deserves death). Then, however, Paul continues to argue that those who know the law and judge others but do the same things fall under the same condemnation (2:1–13). Indeed, also the Gentiles have full knowledge of the law, because the law of nature was given into their hearts (2:14–16). Therefore all people, Jews and Gentiles alike, fall under the same verdict. The section concludes with the statement that no person can be justified on the basis of the works of the law (3:9–20). According to the protreptic interests of traditional apologetics, Paul should now have continued with expositions about right conduct and with an explanation about the path on which those who aspire to follow his message can reach the goal of a righteous life. But the possibility of works as instruments for attaining that goal had already been denied by the preceding arguments. Righteousness can no longer be defined as a human capability; it belongs exclusively to God, who has revealed his righteousness through Jesus, who trusted God alone. God thus revealed his righteousness through the faithfulness of Jesus Christ. Faith is the realization of this righteous act of God, which is now offered as a gift to be given to all people, Jews and Gentiles alike (3:18 31).

The example of Abraham (4:1–24) wants to show that his faith was established before the law so that Abraham becomes the father of those from the circumcision as well as those from the uncircumcision. Beginning with chapter 5, a basic shift is indicated in the introduction of the first person plural ("we")—the last verses of chapter 4 already signaled this shift. Whereas in the preceding discussion one might think that Paul spoke about the justification by faith for the individual believer, it is now clear that Paul speaks about the creation of a new people. The typology of Adam and Christ (5:12–21) brings this into a global perspective; as sin and death ruled through the transgression of Adam, henceforth those who have received the gift of righteousness shall rule through Jesus Christ. The law is now nothing more than a temporary episode (5:20). The freedom gained, however, is qualified by the "eschatological reservation," that is, the life of the resurrection cannot be enjoyed fully in the present life; instead, the life of the believer now stands under the commandment of a new conduct (6:1–23). The "I" that appears in 7:7–25 has been the subject of much debate. It is best understood as the voice of the human existence that wants to obtain the good by its own efforts, namely, by the fulfillment of the law, but only results in death because life can only be received as a divine gift. Romans 8 reflects most profoundly the paradox of the divine presence through the spirit among those who are still in the flesh and of their experience that they participate in the suffering of Christ in the midst of an unredeemed creation (8:18–25). The chapter culminates in the assurance that nothing can separate us from the love of God, which sustains us in the midst of tribulation (8:31–39).

The unresolved question is the validity of the promises for "Israel according to the flesh," which has not accepted the gospel (Romans 9–11). Paul treats this question not in the manner of later Christian apologetics, which argue that the promises of Israel of old have now passed to the Christians. Rather, Paul here speaks as one who fully belongs to Israel, although he would never dream of abandoning the preaching of faith through the revelation of the righteousness of God in order to oblige Israel: that would destroy God's act of salvation in Christ, reestablish the vicious cycle of human righteousness under the law, and confirm once more the separation of the Jews from the Gentiles. But he does not recommend increased missionary efforts. On the contrary, the Gentile believers are warned that they may well be rejected if they boast of their superior status (11:11–24). Paul simply insists that God's promises to Israel cannot be revoked. It remains hidden in a mystery that in the end also all of Israel will be restored (11:25–36).

The final part of the letter (12:1–15:13) is not ethical instruction in the manner of a protreptic admonition. It is written as a definition of the fundamental principle of a new existence in faith that requires the sacrifice of all personal interest in an ethical conduct that wants to build up an individual's moral or spiritual character. New existence implies giving up all of one's own interests of moral fulfillment of the self in order to promote the welfare of the neighbor and to build up the community. What is required is a rational discernment of one's own abilities for this service. Remarkably, gifts of the spirit are no longer mentioned, although the subject matter is the same as that treated in 1 Corinthians 12. The debated advice that one should be subject to political authorities (Rom 13:1–7) rejects political engagement (if this indeed Pauline and not a piece of Hellenistic-Jewish parenesis interpolated here at a later date). The main concern in these chapters is that the commandment of love, which fulfills the entire law (13:8–10), defines under the perspective of the eschatological expectation (13:11–14) that the building up of the community takes precedence over every ideal of personal perfection.

(b) The Journey to Jerusalem and the Fate of the Collection

At the end of the letter to the Romans, Paul had announced his impending arrival in Rome (15:22–24), but he interrupted this announcement with the information that he had to go to Jerusalem first because of the collection for the saints. Only from there would he travel to Rome and then on to Spain (15:25–28). In 1 Cor 16:3–4, Paul had indicated that he would send the collection to Jerusalem through delegates elected by the churches and accredited with letters, while he himself would go only if absolutely necessary. Now he deems that his participation is demanded because of the hostility of the nonbelievers in Judea. A welcome reception of the collection in Jerusalem appeared to be imperiled because of this hostility (Rom 15:31).

This is the last piece of information that is preserved about the life and ministry of Paul from his own letters. For the course of events after the writing of Romans, the only source is the Book of Acts. Occasionally it uses reliable sources, but Luke shapes the narrative according to his own purposes and, most remarkably, treats the collection for Jerusalem only in an aside (Acts 24:17). No doubt, the journey described in Acts 21–22 is indeed the journey of Paul and of the delegates from the Gentile churches for the delivery of the collection. Paul did not take the direct

Bibliography to §9.4b

J. Paul Sampley, *Pauline Partnership in Christ* (Philadelphia: Fortress, 1980).

sea route from Corinth to the eastern Mediterranean, because Jews traveling in the boat on which Paul had booked passage were planning an attempt on his life. Thus Paul first took the land route to Macedonia (Acts 20:3), accompanied by the delegates from the churches that had participated in the collection (Acts 20:4 preserves a partial list of the names of these delegates). The delivery of the collection by such a sizable delegation, whose travel expenses had to be paid, indicates not only the significance of the collection, but also proves that the sum of money brought to Jerusalem was by no means negligible. The ports of call during the trip by boat from Macedonia are given according to one of the easily accessible ancient itineraries but may indeed correspond to the actual stations of Paul's journey: Philippi, Troas (Acts 20:6), Assus, Mytilene, Chios, Samos, Miletus (bypassing Ephesus! Acts 20:14–15), Cos, Rhodes, Patara, and (bypassing Cyprus) Tyre in Syria (Acts 21:1–3), Ptolemais, and finally Caesarea Maritima (Acts 21:7–8).

While the narratives inserted into this itinerary are legendary, beginning with Acts 21:15 Luke is returning to his source. When Paul arrives in Jerusalem, the responsible leader of the Jerusalem church is Jesus' brother James; Peter had long since left Jerusalem, and John is no longer mentioned. The Jerusalem community of believers is depicted as strictly law-abiding, while Paul had acquired the reputation of having seduced Jews in the diaspora away from circumcision and observance of the law. Because of these widespread rumors, James persuaded Paul to demonstrate his faithfulness to the law: he should redeem people who had taken a Nazirite vow and use the collection to pay for the expenses of this redemption, including the necessary sacrifices (Acts 21:17–26). Paul's demonstration of a law-abiding act might end all malicious rumors about him. It has been rightly assumed that this is a direct reflection of the difficulties that resulted for the law-abiding Jewish believers in Jerusalem from the delivery of a collection of money from Gentiles. Paul was smart enough to expect such difficulties, as Rom 15:31 demonstrates. He surely knew that the offer of a considerable amount of financial aid from the Gentiles for the Jerusalem church might constitute an overexacting encumbrance on the relationship of the believers in Jerusalem to other Jews in the city. Despite this worry Paul had insisted on organizing the collection in faithful compliance with the agreement of the Apostolic Council, devoted a lot of time on this enterprise during his missionary activities, and finally decided that he himself had to make the journey to Jerusalem in order to insure a smooth conveyance of the money, although his primary concern had been to go to the West as soon as possible.

All this shows how highly Paul valued this kind of demonstration of the unity of all churches, whether they were Jewish or Gentile communities, and how much he rejected the attempt to establish unity on the basis of common beliefs, doctrines, or observances. Unity could only be established through mutual loving care and charity. It was exactly Paul's desire to document this concept of ecclesiastical unity—ecumenicity would be the modern term—that caused difficulties for the Jewish believers in Jerusalem and finally sealed Paul's own personal fate as well. James, the brother of Jesus, and the believers in Jerusalem insisted that Paul visit the Temple, which was necessary for the redemption of the Nazirites. Only on this condition would they accept the collection from the Gentiles. While in the Temple, Paul was recognized and accused of having brought a Gentile into the Temple (was this a false accusation?). The ensuing turmoil was broken up by Roman soldiers who arrested Paul. Thus the consistent pursuit of one of the most important goals of Paul's missionary work, namely, the documentation of the unity of the church of Jews and Gentiles, resulted in the apostle's arrest.

In Rom 15:14–32, Paul had returned to the occasion for this writing, namely, his intention to come to Rome in order to be dispatched from there to Spain. As a whole, the letter was written in order to explain to the Roman church that this was not a matter of the fulfillment of his personal wish; in that case, a letter of recommendation would not have been necessary. Rather, the letter had to be written in order to incorporate the Roman church in the universal event of the progress of the gospel, which included the delivery of the collection to Jerusalem as well as the proclamation of the gospel in the far west of the Roman world. Both concerns are explicitly mentioned and joined together as a unity.

(c) Paul's Trial and His Journey to Rome

Although the Book of Acts devoted a total of seven chapters (Acts 22–28) to the narrative of Paul's trial and his journey to Rome, historically reliable data about these last years of Paul's life are very few. Paul's speech before the people after his arrest (Acts 22:1–21), his appearance before the Sanhedrin (22:30–23:11), the trial before Felix, Agrippa II, and Festus with several long speeches (24–26), and all the details of the journey to Rome with a full account of a shipwreck (27:1–28:16) are products of the novelistic literary ingenuity of Luke. The "we" that is used in Acts 27 and 28 cannot be understood as the "we" of an eyewitness; it fits the typical literary style of such legendary narratives perfectly well. The most reliable pieces of information are Paul's transfer to Caesarea (23:31–35), his two-year imprisonment in Caesarea until the replacement of the procurator (24:27), and perhaps his appeal to the emperor and the decision that he be transferred to Rome (25:11–12; cf. 26:32). Paul was thus arraigned before the Roman court in Caesarea under the ill-reputed procurator Felix (see Josephus, *Ant.* 20.137–181; *Bell.* 2.247–270), who delayed his decision. When Felix was replaced by the more energetic Festus (Josephus, *Ant.* 20.182; *Bell.* 2.271–272), the new procurator granted the appeal or otherwise decided to refer the entire affair to Rome. The change in the procurator's office cannot be dated with certainty; the most likely date is the year 58.

Acts is silent about the end of Paul's life. The purpose of Luke's epic work is to end the story that began in Bethlehem and Jerusalem with the victorious arrival of the gospel in the capital of the empire (§12.3a). Thus the conclusion of the work describes the successful preaching of Paul—then under house arrest—in Rome (Acts 28:30–31). The next piece of information comes from *1 Clement,* written in Rome ca. 96 CE (§12.2e):

Bibliography to §9.4c

Henry J. Cadbury, "Roman Law and the Trial of Paul," in Foakes Jackson and Lake, *Beginnings,* 297–338.

Haenchen, *Acts,* 599–732.

Paul showed the way to the prize of endurance; seven times he was in bonds, he was exiled, he was stoned, he was a herald in both east and west, he gained noble fame for his faith, he taught righteousness to all the world, and when he had reached the limits of the west, he gave testimony before the rulers, and thus passed from the world and was taken up in the holy place—the greatest example of endurance. (*1 Clem.* 5.5–7)

The martyrdom of Paul is presupposed here, but neither the time nor the place of his death is indicated in this eulogy. It is doubtful, whether the mention of the martyrdom of Peter just before the eulogy of Paul (*1 Clem.* 5.4) allows the conclusion that Paul was indeed martyred in Rome under Nero, as the later legends assume, none of which is attested before the end of the 2d century! The Pastoral Epistles, especially 2 Timothy (§12.2g), rely on a tradition that Paul returned to the East and that Philippi was perhaps the place of Paul's martyrdom. This claim seems to be confirmed by recent excavations in Philippi. That Paul was able to fulfill his wish to go from Rome to Spain (Rom 15:28) must remain doubtful; it is not necessarily implied in *1 Clement*'s statement that "he had reached the limits of the west." There are no traces of Paul's missionary activity in Spain. The Christian churches that claimed to be Pauline foundations in the following decades and centuries are all located in the East, in Asia Minor, Macedonia, and Greece.

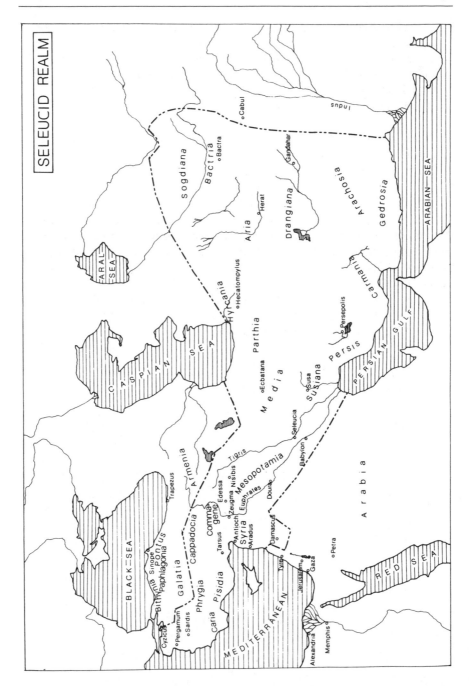

PALESTINE AND SYRIA

1. The Tradition of the Message of Jesus

(a) Eschatological Interpretation

The eschatological orientation of the earliest communities of followers of Jesus has already been discussed (§8.3a–d). In the tradition and development of the sayings of Jesus it is visible in two ways. First, the sayings of Jesus, who had not announced his own return but proclaimed the coming of God's rule, were transformed so that they spoke more clearly about Jesus as the future bringer of salvation. Second, the prophetic proclamation of Jesus was continued in the activity of prophets, who pronounced sayings of revelation about the present and the future in Jesus' name and in his authority. In both instances, the development of the tradition of Jesus' sayings was aimed at the organization of communities or groups of disciples. The tradition of Jesus' sayings becomes therefore increasingly enriched by rules for the community. Attestations for this development are abundantly present in the Synoptic tradition, that is, in units of sayings that eventually were gathered together in the oral and written sources used by the Synoptic Gospels. It is difficult to locate the communities who shaped and transmitted these sayings. There seems to be an Aramaic substratum because some of these materials show traces of having been translated from Aramaic into Greek. That in itself is not surprising because Jesus' language was Aramaic. But it is possible that some of the earliest collections were made in an Aramaic-speaking or bilingual milieu. Moreover, these sayings have been shaped in direct controversy with Jewish circles, especially with regard to Jewish observances. It is therefore most likely that the sayings tradition received its earliest formation in the context of Aramaic-speaking Judaism somewhere in Palestine, perhaps in Galilee. On the other hand, translation into Greek must have taken place quite soon. When the sayings were for the first

Bibliography to §§10–12

Johannes Weiss, *Earliest Christianity: A History of the Period A.D. 30–130* (New York: Harper, 1959). A classic of which the German original was published 1914–1917.

Hans Lietzmann, *The Beginnings of the Christian Church* (New York: Scribner's, 1937).

Walter Bauer, *Orthodoxy and Heresy in Earliest Christianity* (Philadelphia: Fortress, 1971). This work, first published in German in 1934, revolutionized modern scholarship.

Rudolf Bultmann, *Primitive Christianity in Its Contemporary Setting* (New York: Meridian, 1956).

Hans Conzelmann, *History of Primitive Christianity* (Nashville, TN: Abingdon, 1973).

Arnold Ehrhardt, "Christianity Before the Apostles' Creed," in idem, *The Framework of the New Testament Stories* (Cambridge, MA: Harvard University Press, 1965) 151–99.

Robinson and Koester, *Trajectories*.

James D. G. Dunn, *Unity and Diversity in the New Testament* (Philadelphia: Westminster, 1977).

time collected into a writing, they had long since been translated into the vernacular Greek language. In fact, some of these sayings must have reached Corinth at the time of Paul's mission in that city (§9.3c). It is therefore safe to say that this tradition had become part of the Greek-speaking communities within less than two decades.

(1) *The Synoptic Sayings Gospel.* The most important witness for the eschatological theology of the communities who transmitted the sayings of Jesus is the Synoptic Sayings Source ("Q"; see §7.3b), also designated as the "Sayings Gospel Q"—quoted in the following according to chapter and verse of the Gospel of Luke. It is a sayings gospel that may have been composed as early as around the year 50 CE on the basis of existing casual collections of sayings that had been put together for catechetical, polemical, and homiletic purposes. It is dominated by the consciousness of an eschatological community committed to a new conduct as demanded by Jesus in the light of the rule of God, whose coming Jesus had announced. The key to the understanding of the theology of the earliest form of Q is the "Inaugural Sermon" of Jesus that is largely preserved in Luke 6:20–49. The promise of the blessings for the poor, the hungry, and those who are in sorrow determines the status of these believers and commits them to Jesus' command to love even their enemies, that is, to relinquish all worldly power. Discipleship of Jesus implies renunciation of the world and of its social bonds (Q/Luke 14:26–27). The portions of the speeches about the sending of the disciples that derive from Q

Bibliography to §10.1a (1): Text

John S. Kloppenborg, *Q Parallels: Synopsis, Critical Notes & Concordance* (F&F; Sonoma, CA: Polebridge, 1988).

Robert L. Miller (ed.), *The Complete Gospels: Annotated Scholars Version* (rev. ed.; Sonoma, CA: Polebridge, 1994).

Frans Neirynck, *Q-Synopsis: The Double Tradition Passages in Greek* (SNTA 13; Leuven: Peeters, 1995).

James M. Robinson, Paul Hoffmann, and John S. Kloppenborg (eds.), *The Critical Edition of Q: A Synopsis* (Leuven: Peeters, and Minneapolis: Fortress, 2000).

Bibliography to §10.1a (1): Studies

Dieter Lührmann, *Die Redaktion der Logienquelle* (WMANT 33; Neukirchen-Vluyn: Neukirchener Verlag, 1969).

James M. Robinson, "LOGOI SOPHON: On the Gattung of Q," in idem and Koester, *Trajectories*, 71–113.

John S. Kloppenborg, *The Formation of Q: Trajectories in Ancient Wisdom Collections* (SAC; Philadelphia: Fortress, 1987).

Idem, "Tradition and Redaction in the Synoptic Sayings Source," *CBQ* 46 (1984) 34–62.

Idem (ed.), *The Shape of Q: Signal Essays on the Sayings Gospel* (Minneapolis: Fortress, 1994).

Idem (ed.), *Conflict and Invention: Literary, Rhetorical, and Social Studies on the Sayings Gospel Q* (Valley Forge, PA: Trinity Press International, 1995).

Koester, *Ancient Christian Gospels,* 128–72.

Arland D. Jacobson, *The First Gospel: An Introduction to Q* (Sonoma, CA: Polebridge, 1992).

Paul Hoffmann, *Tradition und Situation: Studien zur Jesusüberlieferung in der Logienquelle und den synoptischen Evangelien* (NTA, NF 28; Münster: Aschendorff, 1995).

Ronald A. Piper (ed.), *The Gospel Behind the Gospels: Current Studies on Q* (NovTSup 75; Leiden: Brill, 1995).

Christopher M. Tuckett, *Q and the History of Early Christianity* (Edinburgh: T&T Clark, 1996).

demand homelessness and renunciation of all possessions (Q/Luke 10:2–12, 16). Discipleship requires the adoption of an itinerant lifestyle (Q/Luke 9:57–60). Jesus is the example for this separation from the established structures of society. But christological titles for Jesus are strikingly absent, nor is Jesus proclaimed as the one who rose from the dead and who will return in the future. It is likely, however, that Jesus' fellowship meals were continued in the community of the Sayings Gospel; the meal prayers of this community may have been preserved in *Didache* 9–10 (§10.1c [2]). In these Eucharistic prayers, the eschatological perspective is evident, but a reference to the death of Jesus is missing.

The Sayings Gospel Q was revised later, probably in the time of the outbreak of the Jewish War in 66 CE (§6.6e). These groups of Jesus' followers in Palestine had to decide where they stood in the face of an increasing fervor that sought the fulfillment of messianic hopes in a violent insurrection against Roman rule, primarily instigated by the Zealots. Other Jewish groups such as the Essenes, the Sadducees, and even some of the Pharisees were not able to escape from its appeal. At that time prophets among the Jesus disciples in Judea and Galilee announced the unexpected and sudden coming of the Son of Man on the clouds of heaven, rejecting a violent messianic uprising. This seems to be the origin of the Son of Man sayings and the sayings of judgment about "this generation," which were incorporated into a new edition of the Sayings Gospel Q (e.g., Q/Luke 12:39–40; 17:22–37; 11:29–32). Similar prophetic pronouncements were collected in the "Synoptic Apocalypse" (see below). The disciples are therefore called to constant watchfulness (Q/Luke 12:35–46). The communities of the Sayings Gospel thus made a political decision that was significant for the separation of this community from those committed to the war within the realm of Jewish culture in Palestine. The acceptance of the ancient prophetic polemic against the leaders of the people as the murderers of the prophets (Q/Luke 11:49–51) and against Jerusalem (Q/Luke 13:34–35) is characteristic for the position of the later Q community toward Judaism (see also the beatitude about those who are hated because of the Son of Man, Q/Luke 6:22–23). With such polemics, however, Q has not cut all its ties with the tradition of Israel, although the question of the law does not seem to have played a role. References to the Bible of Israel appear in the final edition of Q (e.g., Q/Luke 17:26–30; see also the quotations in the temptation story, 4:1–13). The understanding of Jesus as the coming Son of Man, ultimately derived from Jewish apocalyptic concepts (Dan 7:13–14), became the key christological concept in the second edition of the Sayings Gospel Q, to which also the materials about John the Baptist (Q/Luke 3:3–4, 7–9, 16–17; see also 7:18–35) and the story about the temptation of Jesus (Q/Luke 4:1–13) were added, thus resulting in the form of this gospel, in which it was used by Matthew and Luke.

(2) *The Synoptic Apocalypse.* Another important witness for the later development of words of Jesus among his followers in Palestine is the so-called Synoptic Apocalypse of Mark 13, a written document, perhaps a pamphlet written for a wider distribution, which seems to be even more closely connected with the beginning of the Jewish War than the sayings of the second edition of the Sayings Gospel Q. The sayings announcing the coming of Jesus as the Son of Man at a time that nobody knows predominate this collection of prophetic sayings (Mark 13:26),

specifically in words that clearly mirror Dan 7:13–14 (see also allusions to Dan 9:27 and 12:11 in Mark 13:14). These prophecies seek to distinguish the eschatological expectation of the Jesus community explicitly from current events, such as news of war, that could be interpreted as signs of the coming of the Messiah (13:7–8), which was apparently done by those who were rejected as false prophets (13:21–23). Again, the coming destruction of Jerusalem is announced (13:1–3). That the disciples distanced themselves from the preparation for the war resulted in persecution by Jewish authorities (13:9).

(3) *The Collection of Parables.* The Sayings Gospel Q and the Synoptic Apocalypse are not the only testimonies for the development of a Jesus tradition that had no relationship to the proclamation of the cross and resurrection of Jesus. Also the parables of Jesus were collected as words that reveal saving wisdom. The parable collection that Mark has incorporated into his Gospel (Mark 4) is explicitly characterized as a store of "mystery of the kingdom" narratives that are accessible only to the disciples (Mark 4:11–12). Similarly, *Gos. Thom.* 62 introduces a collection of three parables with the words, "I tell my mysteries to those who are worthy of my mysteries." Yet these mysteries are not related to the person of Jesus. Rather, they speak about the kingdom of God that is hidden from those outside but that can be recognized by the wise, who patiently guard its secret presence until it will be revealed in the future by God's eschatological actions. In a more radical form, such mysteries can also be understood as already now fully revealed in the hearts of the wise and understanding. Such interpretation of the parables of Jesus point to a sectarian self-consciousness of those who are the bearers of this tradition. Isolated from the rest of humanity and the world, they wait for the divine disclosure of the mystery or boast of the possession of ultimate truth in themselves. Allegorical interpretation of the parables is a natural consequence. The allegorical interpretation that was added by these circles to the parable of the sower (Mark 4:13–20) emphasizes that only the right condition of the human heart, not any external events, will determine the fruits born for the kingdom of God.

(b) Jesus as the Teacher of Wisdom

(1) *The Gospel of Thomas.* The understanding of the sayings of Jesus that appears in the *Gospel of Thomas* is closely related to the earliest version of the Sayings Gospel Q and its itinerant radicalism as well to the mystery understanding of

Bibliography to §10.1a (2)

Lars Hartmann, *Prophecy Interpreted: The Formation of Some Jewish Apocalyptic Texts and the Eschatological Discourse Mark 13 Par* (ConB NT Series 1; Lund: Gleerup, 1966).
Egon Brandenburger, *Markus 13 und die Apokalyptik* (FRLANT 134; Göttingen: Vandenhoeck & Ruprecht, 1984).
Adela Yarbro Collins, "The Eschatological Discourse of Mark 13," in *The Four Gospels 1992*, 2. 1125–40.

Bibliography to §10.1a (3)

Willi Marxsen, *Mark the Evangelist: Studies on the Redaction History of the Gospel* (Nashville, TN: Abingdon, 1969).
Philip Sellew, "Oral and Written Sources in Mark 4.1–34," *NTS* 36 (1990) 234–67.

Oxyrhynchus Papyrus 655:
Fragment of the *Gospel of Thomas*

This papyrus was found at Oxyrhynchus in Egypt in 1903 and was first labeled "Fragment of a Lost Gospel." After the discovery of the Coptic text of the *Gospel of Thomas* it was recognized that it contained the Greek text of Sayings 36–41 of that Gospel.

the parables. Also in this gospel there are no references to the death and resurrection of Jesus. Furthermore, the prophetic eschatology that appears in the later edition of the Sayings Gospel Q with its Son of Man and judgment sayings has left no trace in the *Gospel of Thomas*. This gospel is therefore not dependent upon the Synoptic Gospels nor upon the Sayings Gospel Q. Instead, the sayings preserved in this gospel that have parallels in the Synoptic tradition (about 50 percent) must be assigned to an earlier stage of the formation of the sayings tradition as it is also evident in the first edition of Q, although the *Gospel of Thomas* does not seem to be directly dependent upon that edition of Q. An early circulation of the Thomas

Bibliography to §10.1b (1): Text

A. Guillaumont et al. (eds.), *The Gospel According to Thomas: Coptic Text Established and Translated* (San Francisco: Harper & Row, 1984). Reduced reprint of the editio princeps of 1959 with English translation.

Harold W. Attridge, Helmut Koester, and Thomas O. Lambdin, "The Gospel of Thomas (Introduction, Text, Translation, Greek Fragments, and Testimonia)," in Layton, *Nag Hammadi Codex II*, 37–128.

Hans-Gebhard Bethge, Stephen J. Patterson, and James M. Robinson, *The Fifth Gospel: The Gospel of Thomas Comes of Age* (Harrisburg, PA: Trinity Press International, 1998). The best English translation, with introduction and essays.

Helmut Koester and Thomas O. Lambdin, "The Gospel of Thomas (II, 2)," in Robinson, *NagHamLibEngl*, 124–38.

Layton, *Gnostic Scriptures*, 376–99.

Cameron, *Other Gospels*, 23–37.

Beate Blatz, "The Coptic Gospel of Thomas," in Schneemelcher, *NT Apoc.*, 1. 110–33.

Miller, *Complete Gospels*, 301–329.

Joannes Karavidopoulos, *ΤΟ ΓΝΩΣΤΙΚΟΝ ΚΑΤΑ ΘΩΜΑΝ ΕΥΑΓΓΕΛΙΟΝ* (Thessaloniki, 1967). Translation of the Coptic Text into Greek.

Bibliography to §10.1b (1): Studies

R. McL. Wilson, *Studies in the Gospel of Thomas* (London: Mowbray, 1960).

Oscar Cullmann, "Das Thomasevangelium und die Frage nach dem Alter der in ihm enthaltenen Traditionen," in idem, *Vorträge 1925–1962*, 566–88.

Philipp Vielhauer, "ΑΝΑΠΑΥΣΙΣ: Zum gnostischen Hintergrund des Thomasevangeliums," in idem, *Aufsätze zum Neuen Testament* (ThBü 31; München: Kaiser, 1965) 215–34.

Helmut Koester, "One Jesus and Four Primitive Gospels," in Robinson and Koester, *Trajectories*, 158–204.

Idem, *Ancient Christian Gospels*, 75–124.

Stephen J. Patterson, *The Gospel of Thomas and Jesus* (F&F, Reference Series; Sonoma, CA: Polebridge, 1993).

James M. Robinson, "On Bridging the Gap from Q to the Gospel of Thomas (or Vice Versa)," in Hedrick and Hodgson, *Nag Hammadi*, 127–75.

William E. Arnal, "The Rhetoric of Marginality: Apocalypticism, Gnosticism, and Sayings Gospels," *HTR* 88 (1995) 471–95.

Risto Uro (ed.), *Thomas at the Crossroads: Essays on the Gospel of Thomas* (Edinburgh: T&T Clark, 1998).

Bibliography to §10.1b (1): History of Scholarship

Francis T. Fallon and Ron Cameron, "The Gospel of Thomas: A Forschungsbericht and Analysis," *ANRW* 2.25.6 (1988) 4195–4251.

Stephen J. Patterson, "The Gospel of Thomas and the Synoptic Tradition: A Forschungsbericht and Critique," *F&F Forum* 8 (1992) 45–97.

Gregory J. Riley, "The *Gospel of Thomas* in Recent Scholarship," *CRBS* 2 (1994) 227–52.

sayings is also confirmed by the appearance of such sayings in Corinth (1 Corinthians 1–4; §9.3c) and in the sayings tradition used by the author of the Gospel of John (§10.3a). It is therefore quite likely that an early version of the *Gospel of Thomas* was composed as a sayings gospel around the year 50 CE, probably also in the area of Syria/Palestine.

It is important to note that the full text of the *Gospel of Thomas* is available only in a Coptic translation from the 3d century, preserved in one of the 4th-century codices of the Nag Hammadi Library (NHC II, 2). A few Greek fragments of this gospel, found in Oxyrhynchus in Egypt and dated to the late 2d or early 3d century, demonstrate that it was originally written in Greek. They also show that the text of this gospel was by no means stable. Like the Sayings Gospel Q, the *Gospel of Thomas* was subject to later revisions with additions of materials that were not contained in its earliest form. On the other hand, its sayings with parallels in the Synoptic Gospels show no signs of the redactional activities of the authors of these gospels and in several instances appear in a form that is doubtless more original than those preserved by the gospels of the New Testament canon. Also the name of the apostle under whose authority these sayings were written down, Judas Didymus Thomas (*Gos. Thom.* #1), points to an early Aramaic-speaking milieu. Judas was no doubt the original name of this apostle; "Thomas" is the Greek transcription of the Aramaic word for "Twin," of which "Didymus" is the Greek translation. This formation of this apostle's name has no parallels in the canonical tradition. It is at home, however, in the Syrian church, where it appears in the *Acts of Thomas* and in the Syriac version of the Gospel of John (14:22). The contrast between Thomas and Jesus' brother James (*Gos. Thom.* ##12 and 13) allows the conjecture that the author of this gospel belongs to circles of disciples who sought to strengthen and defend the right of their tradition in the name of Thomas against the authority of James of Jerusalem, without denying the latter's claim to leadership in ecclesiastical matters. This reflects a church-political situation in Palestine in the middle of the 1st century rather than a controversy from a later period.

While the itinerant radicalism of the earliest version of the Sayings Gospel Q is enforced by an eschatological perspective of the coming of God's rule in the near future, the *Gospel of Thomas* has fully spiritualized the eschatological expectation. Jesus is no longer a prophet but the teacher of wisdom, who speaks with the authority of the heavenly figure of Wisdom. With such words Jesus grants salvation to those who are able and prepared to understand them. Similar sayings of Jesus are also preserved in the Sayings Gospel Q (Q/Luke 10:21–24; see also 11:49–51), but they appear in Q as occasional intrusions, while the *Gospel of Thomas* has made them the dominant theme of its message. Wisdom sayings, formulated as general truths, lack any eschatological perspective (##31–35; 47; 67; 49). Admonitions to recognize oneself appear repeatedly (##2; 19; 49; 50; 111). Knowledge of one's own divine essence and destiny is the demand laid upon the disciple who is able to find the meaning of Jesus' sayings and will thus not taste death (#1). Parables, of which many have parallels in the Synoptic Gospels, express the significance of the discovery of one's own divine identity (cf., e.g., *Gos. Thom.* 8 with Matt 13:47–50). The prophetic sayings and future-oriented eschatological sayings no longer speak about the coming of the rule of God but announce the presence of the rule of the Father in the person of Jesus as well as in the believer (*Gos. Thom.* ##5–6; 18; 22; 51; 91; 111) and in one's recognition of self (##3; 113). Wisdom sayings that once described the general human experience and exhorted people to appropriate behavior have become conveyors of the same internalized truth (##6a; 26; 32–35; 39b; 45; 47; 62b; 82; 86; 93; 95; 103). Sayings of Jesus formulated in the first person singular (I-sayings) never speak about his future role as the redeemer but always document saving knowledge both in Jesus and his words; thus Jesus speaks to his disciples in the voice of heavenly Wisdom (##23; 28; 90).

The identification with heavenly Wisdom or with one's divine origin and destiny is the message of these sayings. This message of the *Gospel of Thomas* is fundamentally esoteric—indeed the term "Gnostic" is quite appropriate here—and is directed to a limited group of the elect people. A typical sign of this esoteric interpretation of the meaning of Jesus' sayings is the clause, "Whoever has ears to hear let him hear," which is frequently attached to parables (##8; 21; 63; 65; 96; see Mark 4:9!). Renunciation of the world is preached, just as in the Sayings Gospel Q (*Gos. Thom.* ##21c; 56), but this renunciation now implies the liberation of the soul from the body (##29; 87; 112). Here the Gnostic message appears most clearly. The author often attaches such phrases as "and the two will become one," "they will not taste death," and "they will find rest" to traditional sayings (##4; 18; 19; 90; cf. 22; 30; 106). In such mystical and spiritualizing interpretations, the author goes beyond the traditional admonitions of wisdom theology to recognize oneself into Gnostic concepts. This move from wisdom theology into Gnosticism appears as a natural progression. It is therefore often difficult to decide whether such sayings belong to the original composition of the gospel or are later additions. The elect and the "single ones" know their origin and are conscious of their destiny: they come from the kingdom of the Father, and they will return to it and find rest (##49; 50). This is further radicalized in the ascetic sayings, which reject the world as well as the human body (##37; 42; 56; 60; 70; 111). To be a "single one" implies participation in the unity of all those who are one with their divine origin (##16; 23); only this "single one" will enter into the bridal chamber (#75). His prototype is Jesus himself, "who is the one who comes from the one who is always the same" (#61), in whose experience as a redeemer the existence in this world as a stranger is represented (#28) and in whom the rest and the new world are already realized (#51). Sometimes traditional sayings fit well into this message, especially the parables, but also sayings of Jesus that reject traditional Jewish piety (##6; 14; 27; 104) and criticize the Pharisees as the guardians of this piety (##39; 102). But later additions are also evident as, for example, in speculations about the biblical creation story (redemption as the discovery of the heavenly prototypes, which are superior to the earthly Adam; ##83–85) or the saying about the blessedness of the lion that a person will eat (#7), which is a metaphor borrowed from later Egyptian asceticism. The *Gospel of Thomas* is thus in its development a witness for the trajectory that leads from the earliest spiritualizing interpretation of the sayings of Jesus to the full recognition of the Gnostic potential of such understanding of Jesus as teacher of divine wisdom.

(2) *The Dialogue of the Savior.* A Gnostic interpretation of the sayings of Jesus that explores the depth of his words to find divine wisdom, to recognize the divine

self, and to gain immortality, appears in at least one other document of the Nag Hammadi Library: the *Dialogue of the Savior* (NHC III, 5). In its original form, or in its major source, it must also be dated to the 1st century. Because of its close relationships with the *Gospel of Thomas* and the Gospel of John, a Syrian origin is likely. In its extant form, however, the *Dialogue of the Savior* exhibits the signs of a secondary compilation. The introductory Gnostic sermon, prayer, and instruction (##1–3; 120, 2–124, 22) contain allusions to the Deutero-Pauline Letters, the Catholic Epistles, and the Epistle to the Hebrews. Also some other sections, not necessarily of Christian origin, have been interpolated into the original dialogue. The composition of this writing, distinguishing the original parts of the dialogue and the secondary intrusions, are best presented in the following table of contents, which shows that about two-thirds of the extant writing belongs to the original dialogue (titles of secondary parts in Italics; page and line numbers are given in parenthesis):

Scribal *Incipit* (120:1)	*Title "The Dialogue of the Savior"*
##1–3 (120, 2–124, 22)	*Introduction*
##4–14 (124, 23–127, 19)	Dialogue, part I
##15–18 (127, 19–128, 23)	*Creation myth*
##19–20 (128, 23–129:16)	Dialogue, part II
##21–24; (129, 16–131, 18)	*Creation myth, continued*
##25–34a (131, 19–133, 21)	Dialogue, part III
##34b–35; (133, 21–134, 24)	*Wisdom list*
##36–40 (134, 24–137, 3)	*Apocalyptic vision*
##41–104a (137, 3–146, 20)	Dialogue, part IV
#104b (146, 20–147, 22)	*Concluding instructions*
Scribal *Explicit* (147:23)	*Title*

The original writing is a dialogue between Jesus, Judas (=Thomas?), Matthew, and Mariam (=Mary of Magdala) and is thus different from the introductory and interpolated discourses. The dialogue is not composed as an explication of a coherent topic, like a philosophical dialogue. It is indeed not related to known genres

Bibliography to §10.1b (2):   Text

Stephen Emmel, Helmut Koester, Elaine Pagels, *Nag Hammadi Codex III, 5: The Dialogue of the Savior* (NHS 26; Leiden: Brill, 1984).

Stephen Emmel, Helmut Koester, and Elaine H. Pagels, "The Dialogue of the Savior (III, 5)," in *NagHamLibEngl*, 244–55.

Cameron, *Other Gospels,* 38–48.

Beate Blatz, "The Dialogue of the Savior," in Schneemelcher, *NT Apoc,* 1. 300–312.

Miller, *Complete Gospels,* 343–56.

Bibliography to §10.1b (2):   Studies

Stephen Emmel, "A Fragment of Nag Hammadi Codex III in the Beinecke Library: Yale Inv. 1784," *Bulletin of the American Society of Papyrologists* 17 (1980) 53–60.

Elaine Pagels and Helmut Koester, "Report on the Dialogue of the Savior (CG III, 5)," in R. McL. Wilson (ed.), *Nag Hammadi and Gnosis: Papers Read at the First International Congress of Coptology (Cairo, December 1976)* (NHS 14; Leiden: Brill, 1978) 66–74.

of Hellenistic dialogue literature. Rather, it is composed of smaller units, of which each quotes or alludes to a traditional saying. Questions and answers are usually fairly brief, sometimes consisting of just one question from one of the disciples and an answer from the Lord. These units resemble many "sayings" of the *Gospel of Thomas,* which are often introduced by a question from one of the disciples. Thus this dialogue is an expanded collection of traditional sayings with added interpretations, which may lead to more questions resulting in the addition of further sayings in many instances. Sometimes the question of a disciple quotes a saying while the answer given by the Lord is actually a commentary. The sayings used here have parallels in the Gospels of Matthew and John and, more frequently, in the *Gospel of Thomas.* The intention of the dialogue as a whole corresponds to the first saying of the *Gospel of Thomas,* namely, to find the interpretation of the words of Jesus and, thus, to overcome death.

If there is an overall compositional principle, it may be found in the topics of the second saying of that gospel (in its original form in which it is preserved in the Greek Oxyrhynchus fragment): seeking, finding, marveling, ruling, resting. The concentration of sayings about seeking and finding is evident at the beginning (##4–9; the topic occurs once more in #20). Significant are also ##25–30, which, in their discussion of arriving at the place of light and giving the Gnostic answer that one must find it in oneself, present a striking parallel to John 14:2–12. The topic of "ruling" appears in ##49–50. The disciples are asked to recognize that they have not yet achieved rule and rest but must carry the burden of earthly labor, which Jesus himself also shares (##52–53). Here it is Mary who gives the final answer by quoting sayings that have parallels in Matt 6:34b; 10:10, 24, to which the comment is added, "She uttered this as a woman who had understood completely." Questions about dying and living (##56–59; parallels in *Gos. Thom.* ##11; 17; 90; and John 11:25) lead to the discussion of the "rest" (*Dial. Sav.* ##65–68), the "path" (##73–74), and the "garments" (##84–85; parallels in *Gos. Thom.* ##37; 51; John 14:5–6), with the repeated answer that one must find these things in oneself and strip away whatever belongs to the earthly existence. A question about prayer (*Dial. Sav.* ##90–95; cf. *Gos. Thom.* #6) receives the answer, "Pray in the place where there is no woman," with the added comment, "Destroy the works of womanhood" (cf. *Gos. Thom.* #114), prompting Mary to ask whether they will ever be obliterated. Unfortunately, the remainder of *Dial. Sav.* #95b and ##96–104 is very poorly preserved. At the very end, however, the topic that those who have understood will live forever (#104b; cf. *Gos. Thom.* #1; John 6:53; 8:51) appears once more.

With respect to the history of early Christian literary genres, this dialogue is a significant document because it shows the further development of the sayings tradition into a new genre, which makes its appearance as the "revelation dialogue" or "revelation discourse" in the Gospel of John and later in Gnostic revelation writings. In the latter, however, the interpretation of Jesus' sayings is no longer the formative literary principle, while the relationship of the *Dialogue of the Savior* to the sayings tradition is still very close; this is also the case in the Gospel of John (§10.3a) and perhaps also in parts of the *Apocryphon of James* (§11.1b). With respect to its theological theme, namely, the treatment of the problem of realized eschatology and its Gnostic consequences, the *Dialogue of the Savior* is an important witness for a discussion that the Gospel of John continues in its dialogues and discourses. In this entire tradition of interpretation, Jesus is remembered as the teacher of wisdom, who remains alive in his words and challenges his disciples to discover in themselves how the truth has become a reality in their own existence. Only in the recognition of the self does the revelation become effective, because here the believers become equals of Jesus insofar as they have come to know their origin and their destiny. Here lie the roots of Gnostic theology. Paul recognized this in his discussion in 1 Corinthians, and the author of the Gospel of John had to come to terms with this Gnostic proclivity of the interpretation of Jesus' sayings.

(c) Order of Life and Organization of the Church

It is very difficult to obtain any information about the communities of Jesus' followers who were the bearers of the interpretation of Jesus' words of wisdom. What were their community rules and moral principles? The answer is problematic, because it is questionable whether they indeed advocated organized communities as they are found in the circle of the Pauline churches. The term "church" (*ekklesia*) never appears in these documents (it is also absent in the Synoptic tradition!). The bearers of this message of Jesus' sayings were most likely wandering apostles, pledged to the ideal of poverty and frugality, who went from place to place, preaching, healing the sick—and then moving on. This is evident from the relevant sections of the Sayings Gospel Q (see especially Q/Luke 10:2–12). The ideal of the homeless disciple became the epitome of the new existence. In *Gos. Thom.* #42, Jesus says, "Become passers-by." These wandering ascetics rejected marriage, accepted women into their groups (*Gos. Thom.* ##61; 114) and even assigned a special place to them (*Dial. Sav.* #53), denied the world, and scorned normal practices of piety such as fasting and almsgiving.

Real church organizations developed first in Jerusalem and Antioch. The leadership in Jerusalem consisted of the "pillar apostles," Jesus' brother James, Peter, and John (later James alone). The tradition of the later Jewish-Christian churches anchors its legitimacy in this brother of the Lord, James the Just, whose authority is also somehow recognized by the *Gospel of Thomas* (#12). This probably implies that the jurisdiction of Jesus' brother extended beyond the Jerusalem church and included several organized communities. This circle of churches was kept together through the dispatching of messengers at certain occasions (Paul reports the arrival of "the people of James" in Antioch in Gal 2:12). It demonstrates that James also tried to extend his influence into the Greek-speaking churches outside Palestine. In addition, these Jewish Christians later followed the Pauline model of sending letters, in which the order of life for these congregations and the moral conduct of their members was set forth.

(1) *The Epistle of James.* One such writing under the authority of James is preserved in the canon of the New Testament, the so-called Epistle of James. The authority claimed for this writing is no doubt James, the brother of the Lord, who bears the weighty honorary title "Servant of God" in Jas 1:1 and in a 2d-century fragment by the author Hegesippus that is preserved in Eusebius (*Hist. eccl.* 2.23.7). No other known person of this name ever had a comparable authority. Of course, this letter is not a product of the Aramaic-speaking brother of Jesus. The

fluent Greek style of the letter as well as the polemic against Paul's doctrine of justification by faith (Jas 2:14–26) make this impossible and assign this letter to the generation after Paul and after the death of James in Jerusalem in 62 CE. Nevertheless, this letter is an important witness for the continuation of the law-abiding tradition of the Jerusalem church in the Greek-speaking world. This group had much in common with the believers of Jerusalem: emphasis upon the validity of the law (Jas 2:8–13)—although the law is now described in categories that had been developed in Hellenistic Judaism ("the perfect law of freedom," Jas 2:8–13)— the ideal of poverty (2:1–7; see the polemic against the wealthy landowners, 5:1–6), and the eschatological orientation (5:7–11). The address "To the Twelve Tribes in the Diaspora" points to a Jewish Christianity that had taken shape in the Hellenistic world. At this point, Jewish Christianity, like the gospel preached by Paul, had left the confines of the Aramaic-speaking world of Palestine and had become a thoroughly Hellenistic phenomenon.

The Epistle of James is not a true letter but a general circular in the form of parenesis. It is essentially a compilation of traditional sayings, admonitions, instructions, and proverbial rules of conduct that are loosely woven together. Thematic arrangements combine a number of sayings in each case. The materials are derived from the parenesis of Hellenistic Judaism; specifically Christian features are not easily detected, although the phrase "the honorable name by which you are called" (2:7) probably refers to the name of Christ and "the parousia of the Lord" (5:7) refers to his coming. There are also some echoes of sayings that occur in the Sayings Gospel Q, for example, the blessing of the poor (Jas 2:5; cf. Q/Luke 6:20) and the saying about humiliation and exaltation (Jas 4:10; cf. Q/Luke 14:11). Especially striking is the appearance of the prohibition of oath taking in Jas 5:12 in a form that is older than the formulation of Matt 5:35–37. The author of James clearly did not know any of the canonical gospels, but was familiar with some early Synoptic materials, although he never quotes them as sayings of Jesus, which might imply that such sayings had not yet been assigned to Jesus as their author. The

Bibliography to §10.1c (1):   Commentaries

Martin Dibelius, *James: A Commentary on the Epistle of James* (rev. Heinrich Greeven; Hermeneia; Philadelphia: Fortress, 1976).
François Vouga, *L'épitre de saint Jacques* (CNT, 2d ser., 13a; Geneva: Labor et Fides, 1984).
Luke Timothy Johnson, *The Letter of James: A New Translation with Introduction and Commentary* (AB 37A; New York: Doubleday, 1995).

Bibliography to §10.1c (1):   Studies

Roy B. Ward, "The Works of Abraham: James 2:14–26," *HTR* 61 (1968) 283–90.
Idem, "Partiality in the Assembly: James 2:2–4," *HTR* 62 (1969) 87–97.
Dan O. Via, "The Right Strawy Epistle Reconsidered: A Study in Biblical Ethics and Hermeneutic," *JR* 49 (1969).
Christoph Burchard, "Gemeinde in der strohernen Epistel: Mutmaßungen über Jakobus," in *Kirche: Festschrift Bornkamm*, 315–28.
Patrick J. Hartin, *James and the Q Sayings of Jesus* (JSNTSup 47; Sheffield: JSOT Press, 1991).

Bibliography to §10.1c (1):   History of Scholarship

Peter H. Davids, "The Epistle of James in Modern Discussion," *ANRW* 2.25.5 (1988) 3621–45.

conclusion of the writing is a short church order (Jas 5:13–20), which shows that the addressees were organized groups of Christians led by presbyters (5:14). The Jerusalem authority of Jesus' brother James is invoked in order to reject certain conclusions that could be drawn from Paul's proclamation of Christ as the end of the law and justification by faith alone without works (2:14–26). The author wants to defend faithful adherence to the law and the Jewish parenetic tradition in a developing worldwide church. But as James understands fulfillment of the law as an enlightened conduct, never even mentioning circumcision and the ritual laws, he shares this position with the Gospel of Matthew's insistence upon the fulfillment of the law (Matt 5:17–20; see §10.2c). At the same time, James also attacks those who claim to possess heavenly wisdom: the peculiar rejection of false wisdom in 3:13–18 is best understood as a criticism of Gnostic circles. The Epistle of James contrasts such claims to the validity of the inheritance of a Jewish diaspora morality, which should be of great value in fostering a Christian life that is pious, intelligent, and responsible.

(2) *The Teaching of the Twelve Apostles (Didache).* Clear evidence for the attempt to erect a barrier against the further spread of religious enthusiasm by means of traditional Jewish moral teachings can be found in the adoption of the Jewish doctrine of the Two Ways. This Jewish document became a constitutive part of the *Teaching of the Twelve Apostles,* commonly known as the *Didache,* the oldest extant Christian church order, composed some time in the 2d century, but incorporating precious materials from the 1st century, most likely from early churches in Syria. Although known by name and frequently used in later Christian church orders, it was only discovered in the 10th-century Codex Hierosolymitanus and published in 1883 (some Greek and Coptic fragments have been published more recently). It is a compilation of various older materials; the Two Ways document is used in the first section (*Did.* 1–6), but it is also preserved independently in a Latin translation and was used in the *Epistle of Barnabas* (*Barn.* 18–20; see §12.2c). What appears as a description of the way of life is a parenesis based on the Decalogue

Bibliography to §10.1c (2):   Text

Bihlmeyer, *ApostVät,* xii–xx and 1–9.
Lake, *ApostFath,* 1. 303–33.
Wengst, *Didache, Barnabas, 2. Klemens,* 3–100.

Bibliography to §10.1c (2):   Commentaries

Kurt Niederwimmer, *The Didache: A Commentary* (Hermeneia; Minneapolis: Fortress, 1998).
Jean-Paul Audet, *La Didaché: Instructions des apôtres* (EtBib; Paris: Gabalda, 1958).
Robert A. Kraft, *Barnabas and the Didache,* in Grant, *ApostFath* vol. 3.

Bibliography to §10.1c (2):   Studies

J. M. Creed, "The Didache," *JTS* 39 (1938) 370–87.
Bentley Layton, "The Sources, Date, and Transmission of Didache 1.3b–2.1," *HTR* 61 (1968) 343–83.
Martin Dibelius, "Die Mahlgebete der Didache," in idem, *Botschaft und Geschichte,* 2. 117–27.
Clayton N. Jefford (ed.), *The Didache in Context: Essays on Its Text, History, and Transmission* (NovTSup 77; Leiden: Brill, 1995).
Jonathan A. Draper (ed.), *The Didache in Modern Research* (Arbeiten zur Geschichte des Altjudentums und des Urchristentums 37; Leiden: Brill, 1996).

(*Did.* 2), admonitions based on catalogs of virtues and vices (3.1–10), rules for the community (4.1–4, 12–14), rules about giving and receiving (4.5–8; 1.5–6), and a table of household duties (4.9–11). The way of death is simply described in the form of an extensive catalog of vices (5.1–2). All materials presented here have numerous parallels in Jewish literature and are also adopted by other early Christian authors: Paul is quite familiar with some of these traditions, and the Epistle of James and the *Shepherd of Hermas* (§12.1d) drew numerous admonitions from the Two Ways doctrine.

The author of the *Didache* has placed the Two Ways document into a larger context by introducing it with a quotation of the double commandment of love and the golden rule (*Did.* 1.2) and attaching quotations of sayings of Jesus (1.3–4). The understanding of the sayings of Jesus is thus tied to the developing Christian catechism and denies ascetic and Gnostic enthusiasts the right to use this tradition. Moreover, the conclusion of the Two Ways (6.2) is altered so as to ensure that the document cannot be misunderstood as a special instruction for the perfect and instead is seen as general teaching of morality, which everybody should follow as best as possible. The Two Ways has thus become part of a church order, which is continued with instructions for baptism (7; the trinitarian formula appears here for the first time in Christian literature), prayer (8.2–3, including a full quotation of the Lord's prayer in a form closely resembling, but not dependent upon, Matt 6:9–13), and instructions and prayers for the Eucharist (*Did.* 9–10).

The Eucharist prayers also have their origin in Hellenistic Judaism. Even in their pre-Christian form they may have included some spiritualized interpretations (bread and wine as symbols of the knowledge of life). In their Christian form they relate the cup to the covenant of David and understand the bread as the symbol of the oneness of the congregation. There is no attempt to connect wine and bread (in this order!) to the death of Jesus. This does not imply, however, that these prayers were used only for a common meal that preceded the formal Lord's Supper, for which some interpreters have suggested *Did.* 10.4–6 as the introduction. But there is no reason to assume that the communities of Syria, for whom the *Didache* was written, followed the same eucharistic practice and formulae that are attested in 1 Cor 11:23–26. Rather, these prayers may well belong to a direct continuation of the fellowship meal that Jesus celebrated with his disciples and friends. A similar meal was probably celebrated by the community of the Sayings Gospel Q, which also lacks a connection of its message to the death and resurrection of Jesus. Although different from Paul's Eucharist, these prayers share with Paul three fundamental elements, namely, the understanding of the cup as the symbol of the covenant, of the bread as the symbol of the unity of the community, and the eschatological outlook.

The second part of the church order deals with the church offices (*Did.* 10.7–15.4). This is essentially a compilation of older rules about apostles, prophets, and teachers. Rules about the rights of wandering charismatic apostles and prophets are accepted on the whole but their validity is limited. Not only are abuses by wandering charismatics criticized, the communities are also advised to free themselves from their dependence upon such people and elect from among their own members bishops and deacons, who could take over the functions of these itinerant prophets and teachers.

The last chapter of the *Didache* (16) is a small apocalypse that has many materials in common with the Synoptic Apocalypse (§10.1a), demonstrating that the author of the *Didache* draws on the same materials but does not share the expectation of the coming of the Son of Man. Most statements are more closely related to Jewish apocalyptic views. There is no expectation of the coming of the Lord in the immediate future: other events must still take place before that event. The entire tone of the *Didache* seeks to discourage uncontrolled enthusiasm and to institute the ideal of regulated Christian conduct in firmly organized communities. Although most of the materials incorporated in this writing are derived from the traditions of diaspora Judaism, the author does not try to advance any one particular cause. He also avoids appealing to a particular apostolic authority like Thomas or James but acknowledges in general the authority of the Twelve Apostles, who thus become the regular authority for later Christian church orders (*Didascalia, Apostolic Constitutions*). This *Teaching of the Twelve Apostles,* however, is still a document that reflects the organization of a limited circle of churches, probably closely related to the Sayings Gospel Q and not affected by the proclamation of the cross and resurrection of Jesus that was first fully developed in Antioch and had become the basis of the Pauline mission. There is also no evidence for further developments of Christianity in western Syria, where this kerygma was closely connected with the authority of Peter.

2. FROM THE KERYGMA OF THE RESURRECTION TO THE GOSPELS OF THE CHURCH

(a) Traditions under the Authority of Peter

(1) *Peter.* The point of departure for the preaching of Jesus' resurrection as the turning point of the ages was Antioch, the capital of the Roman province of Syria (§8.3c). Converted Hellenistic Jews had founded its congregation, which was the first to admit uncircumcised Gentiles to its table fellowship. This did not rule out conflicts (§9.2a). Jesus' brother James and his associates in Jerusalem maintained a somewhat reserved attitude about these developments. Among the leaders in Jerusalem, Peter must have been more open and supportive. When Paul first visited Jerusalem three years after his call, his primary purpose was to visit Peter and open up some conversation with him (James is mentioned only in a marginal reference in Gal 1:18–19). Years later, at the Apostolic Council, Peter was still one of the "pillars" in Jerusalem, but he might have been active before that time as a missionary outside Jerusalem (§8.3d). In any case, after the council Peter came to Antioch and stayed as a member of its church, which was composed of both Jews and Gentiles. It is possible that during the conflict in Antioch (§9.2a) Peter's position

Bibliography to §10.2a (1)

Raymond Brown, Karl P. Donfried, John Reumann (eds.), *Peter in the New Testament* (Minneapolis: Augsburg, New York: Paulist, 1973).

prevailed over that of Paul. During Paul's last visit to Jerusalem, Peter was no longer present; only James is named as the undisputed leader of that church. No record exists that could provide reliable information about Peter's ministry and life beyond the information that he had gone to Antioch. The "party of Peter" in Corinth (see "Cephas" in 1 Cor 1:12) indicates that his influence extended beyond Syria. The tradition about his arrival in Rome and martyrdom under Nero is legendary.

On the other hand, one of the most reliable pieces of information of the early Christian tradition is the firm establishment of Peter as a prominent witness of the appearance of Jesus after his death; even Paul's tradition names Cephas as the first witness (1 Cor 15:5). He also plays a prominent role in the Gospels of the New Testament, especially here again as the first resurrection witness (cf. Luke 24:34; also Ignatius, *Smyrn.* 3, where Jesus appears "to Peter and to those with him"). Furthermore, he is singled out as the one who first confesses that Jesus is the Messiah (Mark 8:29; cf. John 6:68). The story of the transfiguration (Mark 9:2–8) may also have been originally a story about the epiphany of Jesus to Peter (John and James were added by the later redaction). Moreover, traditions in Peter's name were kept alive in Syria. This tradition under Peter's authority is attested in Matt 16:17–19, where Peter is addressed as the "rock of the church" and is given the keys of the kingdom of heaven. The Aramaic address here, "Simon bar Jona," combined with the Greek term *ekklesia* show that this tradition originated in a bilingual community in Syria. It establishes the validity of traditions under his name (not his or his successor's personal claim to universal leadership!). The same tradition is used in the supplement to the Gospel of John, where the address "Simon son of John" appears once more (John 21:15–23), although Peter's authority is here superseded by the "disciple whom Jesus loved," in the same way in which the authority of James is superseded by Thomas in the *Gospel of Thomas* (§10.1b). These passages, of course, do not reflect a personal rivalry of these apostles. They attest that some time after the death of these apostles various Christian traditions were competing with each other under the authority of apostolic names. Oral or written traditions under the authority of different apostles may even have been in competition with each other in a larger Christian community in such major cities as Antioch.

(2) *The Gospel of Peter.* It cannot be doubted that Peter was a personal disciple of Jesus. But the transmission of Jesus' sayings is never connected with his name. Beginning with bishop Papias of Hierapolis, however, the ecclesiastical tradition about the Gospel of Mark considered this gospel to be a transcript of Peter's lectures—and this gospel may indeed have been written in western Syria (§10.2b).

Bibliography to §10.2a (2): Text

Erich Klostermann, *Apocrypha I: Reste des Petrusevangeliums, der Petrusapokalypse und des Kerygma Petri* (KlT 3; 2d ed.; Berlin: de Gruyter, 1933).
Cartlidge and Dungan, *Documents,* 83–86.
Cameron, *Other Gospels,* 76–82.
Miller, *Complete Gospels,* 399–407.
Christian Maurer and Wilhelm Schneemelcher, "The Gospel of Peter," in Schneemelcher, *NT Apoc.,* 1. 216–27.

The oldest writing under the authority of Peter himself is the *Gospel of Peter.* Its attestation once more points to western Syria. According to Eusebius (*Hist. eccl.* 6.12.2–6), bishop Serapion of Antioch (ca. 200 CE) had been told about a *Gospel of Peter* that was used by the Christians at Rhossus, a city in northwestern Syria. Eusebius reports that Serapion at first had no objections to its use, but then studied it more closely and determined that while most of it agreed with the teachings of the Savior, it also contained some accretions that revealed a docetic theology. Neither Serapion nor any of the church fathers who knew about the *Gospel of Peter* ever quoted any of its content. In 1886, however, a fragment was discovered in Akhmim in upper Egypt. It is a manuscript from the 8th century, and it is generally assumed to be a copy of the gospel that Serapion once read. More recently a few lines belonging to the *Gospel of Peter* were identified in a Papyrus from Oxyrhynchus (#2949), which do not add anything to our knowledge of the content but show that this gospel was known in Egypt as early as ca. 200 CE. The Akhmim fragment contains the major part of the passion narrative as well as the story of the empty tomb; it breaks off with the introduction to the post-Easter story of the disciples' catch of fishes (cf. John 21:1–14).

The *Gospel of Peter* is a remarkable witness for the early development of the passion narrative. Although it parallels on the whole the passion narrative as it is preserved in the canonical gospels, it contains a number of features that can be traced back to a stage that predates the form of the narrative in the Synoptic Gospels and in John. Features of the passion narrative that are developed from passages of the Old Testament reveal their scriptural origin still more clearly. For example, *Gos. Pet.* 16 says, "Give him gall to drink with vinegar"; this feature is developed from Ps 68:22. But Matthew divided this verse from the Psalms into two episodes, the first in Matt 27:34 (gall) and the second in Matt 27:48 (vinegar). In several other instances, the narrative of the *Gospel of Peter* demonstrates how the narrative was developed in the oral tradition in the process of the interpretation of passages from the Psalms and from Deutero-Isaiah. The day of Jesus' crucifixion is given in the *Gospel of Peter* as the day before the festival as in the Gospel of John, certainly the correct historical date. In the legend of the finding of the empty tomb, only Mary of Magdala is named—most likely the person connected with this story in its most original version (Matthew, Mark, and Luke add the names of other women, and John introduces Mary in competition with Peter and the beloved disciple). The epiphany story of Jesus' resurrection in the *Gospel of*

Bibliography to §10.2a (2):   Studies

John Dominic Crossan, *The Cross That Spoke: The Origins of the Passion Narrative* (San Francisco: Harper & Row, 1988).

Idem, "The Gospel of Peter and the Canonical Gospels," *F&F Forum* NS 1 (1998) 7–51.

Léon Vaganay, *L'évangile de Pierre* (2d ed.; EtBib; Paris: Gabalda, 1930).

Jürgen Denker, *Die theologiegeschichtliche Stellung des Petrusevangeliums: Ein Beitrag zur Frühgeschichte des Doketismus* (EHS.T 36; Bern and Frankfurt: Lang, 1975).

Karl Ludwig Schmidt, *Kanonische und apokryphe Evangelien und Apostelgeschichten* (AThANT 5; Basel: Majer, 1944).

Martin Dibelius, "Die alttestamentlichen Motive in der Leidensgeschichte des Petrus- und Johannesevangeliums," in idem, *Botschaft und Geschichte,* 1. 221–47.

Peter is, to be sure, replete with secondary legendary features, but it is not a secondary patchwork of pieces drawn from the canonical gospels. Features that were secondarily added by Matthew to his presentation of the empty tomb story (Matt 28:2–4) and used for his apologetic legend of the guard at the tomb (Matt 27:62–66; 28:11–15) appear in the *Gospel of Peter* as constitutive elements of an older story of an epiphany of Jesus from the tomb, for which the soldiers of the guard are the witnesses. Even if a number of features of this gospel may be due to the later legendary growth of a writing not protected by canonical status, its basis must be an older text under the authority of Peter that was not dependent upon the canonical gospels. If Peter was known as the first and most important witness in the oldest tradition of the Syrian churches—Paul attests this because the tradition he quotes in 1 Cor 15:3–7 must have come from Syria—it is not surprising that an old story about the passion, death, and resurrection of Jesus was first written down under Peter's authority. This is confirmed by the passion narratives of the canonical gospels, where Peter is the only disciple whose name appears in this context (see the story of Peter's denial).

(3) *The Kerygma of Peter.* Another document under the authority of Peter, the *Kerygma of Peter* (to be distinguished from the *Kerygmata Petrou,* one of the sources of the *Pseudo-Clementines;* see §10.4c), was probably written ca. 100 CE. This writing is preserved in a few fragments quoted by Clement of Alexandria (*Strom.* 6.5.39–41, 43, 48; 6.5.128). Its theme is once more the passion of Jesus, but it is introduced as an apologetic discourse, beginning with the confession of the invisible God and a polemic against pagan idol worship and Jewish worship of angels. The Christians are distinguished from Greeks and Jews as people of the new covenant (with reference to Jer 31:31–34) and as the third race. As elected apostles, the disciples are first sent to Israel, then to the nations. The apologetic principle of the interpretation of Jesus' death is fully developed. The disciples have recognized that Jesus is mentioned in the books of the prophets, partly in parables, partly literally: "his death, the cross, and all the other torments which the Jews inflicted upon him, his resurrection and assumption into the heavens, before Jerusalem was judged." The writing continues: "For we know that God really commanded these things, and we say nothing without [the testimony of] scripture." This principle of the scriptural testimony is visible in the development of the passion narrative, for which the *Gospel of Peter* is the earliest witness. At the same time, the apologetic introduction of *Kerygma of Peter* testifies that the authority of Peter was made fully serviceable to the purposes of the Gentile mission.

(4) *Other Writings under Peter's Authority.* Among later writings under the authority of Peter only the *Apocalypse of Peter* was probably written in Syria.

Bibliography to §10.2a (3): Text

Erich Klostermann, *Apocrypha I: Reste des Petrusevangeliums, der Petrusapokalypse und des Kerygma Petri* (KlT 3; 2d ed.; Berlin: de Gruyter, 1933).
Wilhelm Schneemelcher, "The Kerygma Petri," in idem, *NT Apoc.,* 2. 34–41.

Bibliography to §10.2a (3): Studies

Henning Paulsen, "Das Kerygma Petri und die urchistliche Apologetik," *ZKG* 88 (1977) 1–37.

Other writings that claim Peter as their authority belong to the major ecclesiastical developments that lead to the establishment of what has been called "early catholicism." The First Epistle of Peter is dependent upon the Pauline corpus and the second epistle under Peter's name raises some concerns with respect to Paul's letters (§12.2f); both do not originate from Syria, nor can Syrian origin be assumed for the *Acts of Peter* (§12.3b). Thus one part of the Syrian tradition of Peter merged with the larger movement of Gentile Christianity, which is also apparent in Rome's claiming Peter's authority for itself. The *Letter of Peter to Philipp* (NHC VII, 2) is a Gnostic document from the end of the 2d century that contests the claim of Peter's authority by the catholic church. At the same time, Jewish-Christian sects of the subsequent centuries contend that they had preserved Peter's true teachings (§10.4c). There Peter is closely allied with James and, together with him, he upholds the cause for the faithful observance of the law, while Paul becomes the archenemy of the true faith. Direct connections may have existed between the early Petrine traditions of Syria and later anti-Pauline Jewish Christianity. In that case, Petrine literature influenced by Paul could be understood as a polemical answer to these Jewish-Christian claims upon the authority of Peter.

(b) The Oldest Gospel of the Church: The Gospel of Mark

In the apostolic and early postapostolic period, various and independent developments in Syria resulted in the establishment of written traditions of considerable variety. They mirrored the various types of piety, theology, and practice of individual churches or circles of churches. The written passion narrative stems from churches in which the proclamation of the cross and resurrection of Jesus was the focus of the religious experience and where passages from Scripture about the

Bibliography to §10.2b: Text of the Secret Gospel of Mark

Smith, *Clement*, 445–54 (Greek text with translation).
Otto Stählin (ed.), *Clemens Alexandrinus*, vol. 4: *Register* (GCS; 2d ed. by Ursula Früchtel, Berlin: Akademie-Verlag, 1980) xvii–xviii (Greek text).
Cameron, *Other Gospels*, 67–71.
Miller, *Complete Gospels*, 408–10.
H. Merkel, "Appendix: The 'Secret Gospel' of Mark," in Schneemelcher, *NT Apoc.*, 1. 106–9.

Bibliography to §10.2b: Text of the Papias Fragments

Bihlmeyer, *ApostVät*, xliv–xlvii, 133–40.
Ulrich H. J. Körtner, *Papiasfragmente* (Schriften des Urchristentums 3; Darmstadt: Wissenschaftliche Buchgesellschaft, 1998) 58–59 (Greek text and German translation).

Bibliography to §10.2b: Commentaries on the Gospel of Mark

Julius Wellhausen, *Evangelienkommentare* (Berlin: de Gruyter, 1987; first published 1904–1911).
C. E. B. Cranfield, *The Gospel According to Saint Mark* (CGTC; Cambridge: Cambridge University Press, 1959).
Vincent Taylor, *The Gospel According to Saint Mark* (2d ed.; London: Macmillan, New York: St. Martin's, 1966).
Ernst Haenchen, *Der Weg Jesu: Eine Erklärung des Markusevangeliums und der kanonischen Parallelen* (Berlin: Töpelmann, 1966).
D. E. Nineham, *The Gospel of Mark* (rev. ed.; Baltimore: Penguin, 1969).
Eduard Schweizer, *The Good News According to Mark* (Richmond: Knox, 1970).

suffering righteous had provided the language for the story that belonged to the ritual practice of the Eucharist. A very different religious orientation appears in the communities in which the sayings of Jesus were understood as the invitation of heavenly wisdom. Another orientation is visible in the reference to the sayings of Jesus as apocalyptic prophecy, where the expectation of the coming of the Son of Man in the near future was proclaimed, which resulted in the production of apocalyptic pamphlets that called for preparedness and endurance. Further developments of each of the different traditions and their writings could eventually result in a narrowing of perspective and in sectarian isolation. On the other hand, the reception of Hellenistic-Jewish moral teachings and the development of church order were important instruments of ecumenical unification of ecclesiastical practice, which proved to be more significant than the resolution of theological conflicts.

Yet another and quite distinct propagation of the new message must have originated in Syria at a very early period: the propaganda of Jewish-Christian missionaries, who proclaimed a new covenant and reinforced their preaching through powerful deeds and miracles. As they cultivated their own type of Jesus traditions, they must have been responsible for the earliest collections of Jesus' miracles sto-

---

Bibliography to §10.2b: Studies

William Wrede, *The Messianic Secret* (Library of Theological Translation; Cambridge: Clark, 1971). First published in German 1901, it set the stage for research on Mark until today.

Willi Marxsen, *Mark the Evangelist: Studies on the Redaction History of the Gospel* (Nashville, TN: Abingdon, 1969).

Étienne Trocmé, *The Formation of the Gospel According to Mark* (Philadelphia: Westminster, 1975).

James M. Robinson, *The Problem of History in Mark and Other Marcan Studies* (Philadelphia: Fortress, 1982).

Burton L. Mack, *A Myth of Innocence: Mark and Christian Origins* (Philadelphia: Fortress, 1988).

Heikki Räisänen, *The 'Messianic Secret' in Mark* (Studies of the New Testament and Its World; Edinburgh: T&T Clark, 1990).

Heinz-Wolfgang Kuhn, *Ältere Sammlungen im Markusevangelium* (SUNT 8: Göttingen: Vandenhoeck & Ruprecht, 1971).

Paul J. Achtemeier, "Toward the Isolation of Pre-Markan Miracle Catenae," *JBL* 89 (1970) 265–91.

George W. Nickelsburg, "The Genre and Function of the Markan Passion Narrative," *HTR* 73 (1980) 153–84.

Egon Brandenburger, *Markus 13 und die Apokalyptic* (FRLANT 134; Göttingen: Vandenhoeck & Ruprecht, 1984).

Demetrios Trakatellis, *Authority and Passion: Christological Aspects of the Gospel According to Mark* (Brookline, MA: Holy Cross Orthodox Press, 1987).

Howard C. Kee, *Community of the New Age: Studies in Mark* (Philadelphia: Westminster, 1977).

Mary Ann Tolbert, *Sowing the Gospel: Mark's World in Literary-Historical Perspective* (Minneapolis: Fortress, 1989).

Adela Yarbro Collins, *The Beginning of the Gospel: Probings of Mark in Context* (Minneapolis: Fortress, 1992).

Bibliography to §10.2b: Mark and Secret Mark

Helmut Koester, "History and Development of Mark's Gospel: From Mark to Secret Mark and 'Canonical' Mark," in Bruce C. Corley (ed.), *Colloquy on New Testament Studies: A Time for Reappraisal and Fresh Approaches* (Macon, GA: Mercer University Press, 1983) 35–58.

Philip Sellew, "*Secret Mark* and the History of Canonical Mark," in *The Future of Early Christianity: Essays in Honor of Helmut Koester* (ed. Birger A. Pearson; Minneapolis: Fortress, 1991) 242–57.

ries as manuals for their activities. Jesus here plainly appears as the divine man, and the demonstration of divine power, in which "the Christ" is present, assumes the character of a binding message. A controversy with these missionaries and their message surfaced in Paul's letters now collected in 2 Corinthians (§9.3d). For Paul, as we have seen, this is nothing more than a "Christ according to the flesh" (2 Cor 5:16), whom he confronts with his thesis that Jesus was not the most powerful of all human beings but the one who failed on the cross, and whose resurrection has now become power for the weak and freedom for the despised. Paul had countered the letters of recommendation, of which the opponents had boasted, with his paradoxical apology of weakness in his missionary activity. But the debate of the aretalogical tradition about Jesus with the proclamation of Jesus as crucified, which was meanwhile fixed in written passion narratives, remained a task that early post-Pauline Christianity had still to solve.

The author of the Gospel of Mark took on this task. That Mark was written in Rome, which has been assumed in the tradition because of its several Latinisms and its relationship to Peter, is very unlikely. At this early period, Peter's authority was probably more dominant in Syria than in Rome, and Latinisms could occur at any place where a Roman garrison was stationed and Roman administration of a province was established. Moreover, the convergence of various Jesus traditions suggest a major metropolis of the east like Antioch as the place where Mark was written. If the catastrophe of the Jewish War was a catalyst for the composition of Mark, the Syro-Palestinian realm would then be preferred anyway.

The earliest attestation for Mark comes from the two gospels that used his gospel, namely, Matthew and Luke; the likely places of writing of these two gospels are again in the eastern part of the Roman empire, and since at least Matthew was composed well before the end of the 1st century (§10.2c) Mark must have been written no later than in the years immediately following the Jewish War, that is, between 70 and 80 CE. The next external attestation for the Gospel of Mark, including for the first time information about the author's relationship to Peter, comes from the writings of the Phrygian bishop Papias of Hierapolis (ca. 100–150). He writes that his informant, whom he calls a "presbyter," had told him that Mark was the amanuensis of Peter and that he recorded the words and the deeds of the Lord

Bibliography to §10.2b: Bibliography and History of Scholarship

William R. Telford, *The Interpretation of Mark* (SNTI; 2d ed.; Edinburgh: T&T Clark, 1995).

Idem, "The Pre-Markan Tradition in Recent Research," in *The Four Gospels 1992*, 2. 693–723.

Petr Pokorny, "Das Markus-Evangelium: Literarische und theologische Einleitung mit Forschungsbericht," *ANRW* 2.25.3 (1985) 1969–2035.

Frans Neirynck et al., *The Gospel of Mark: A Cumulative Bibliography, 1950–1990* (BETL 10; Leuven: Peeters, 1992).

Rudolf Pesch (ed.), *Das Markusevangelium* (WdF 411; Darmstadt: Wissenschaftliche Buchgesellschaft, 1979).

Watson E. Mills, *The Gospel of Mark* (BBR.NTS 2; Lewiston, NY: Mellon, 1994).

Günter Wagner, *An Exegetical Bibliography of the New Testament: Matthew and Mark* (Macon, GA: Mercer University Press, 1983).

Hugh M. Humphrey, *A Bibliography for the Gospel of Mark, 1954–1980* (Studies in the Bible and Early Christianity 1; New York: Mellon, 1981).

accurately as far as he could remember them from Peter's preaching, but not in the correct sequence. Papias adds that Mark could not be blamed for proceeding in this way since he had never heard the Lord himself (Eusebius *Hist. eccl.* 3.39.15). The reliability of these "presbyter traditions" is questionable, especially as Papias values more highly than written gospels whatever he was able to learn from the memory of these presbyters (people who had supposedly still known the disciples of the apostles) about the words of Jesus. He then applies this artificial schema to the written gospels. But even for Mark, the oldest gospel writing, this view is not appropriate because Mark wrote primarily on the basis of written materials, while oral traditions incorporated into his gospel have been formed in the life of the community and are not informed by the memory of an eyewitness like Peter. On the other hand, Peter's dominant role in the Gospel of Mark reflects Peter's continuing authority for the traditions of the Syrian churches.

The most important source of the Gospel of Mark is a written passion narrative, which presented in a continuous narrative the events from Jesus' entry into Jerusalem (Mark 11:1–10) to the finding of the empty tomb (16:1–8). The passion narrative of the Gospel of John derives from the same or a similar source. Closely related to the "signs source" of the Gospel of John (§10.3a) are two catenae of miracle stories used in the first part of Mark's composition. Parallels include the feeding of the multitudes (Mark 6:32–44; also 8:1–10; John 6:1–13), the walking on the sea (Mark 4:35–41; also 6:45–52; John 6:15–21), and the healing of a blind man (Mark 8:22–26; John 9:1–7). Mark probably also found his exorcism stories in a written collection (Mark 1:21–28; 5:1–20; 9:14–29). The sayings of Jesus play only a secondary role in Mark's work. Some of the sayings have parallels in the Sayings Gospel Q (compare Mark 8:34–38 with Q/Luke 14:26–27; 17:33; 12:8–9) but it is not likely that Mark used Q as a source. Such sayings, as also the apophthegms of Jesus (Mark 2:23–28; 3:1–6, 22–30; 11:27–33; 12:13–37), could have come to Mark through the oral tradition, probably already organized into smaller collections. Only in two cases is it possible to be certain about the use of written sources for sayings materials: in the parable collection in Mark 4 and in the Synoptic Apocalypse in Mark 13 (§10.1a).

It is justified to ask whether the text of Mark that is preserved in the manuscripts of the New Testament is identical with the original text of this gospel. In a number of instances Matthew and Luke agree in the presentation of passages that have been drawn from Mark, while Mark's extant text differs. It is likely that they have preserved an earlier text of Mark whenever this is the case. Moreover, a major section of Mark (6:45–8:26) is not reproduced at all by Luke. But precisely this section contains a number of doublets, especially the story of the feeding of the multitudes that had already been told in Mark 6:30–44, but appears once more in a slightly different version in Mark 8:1–10. Did an older version of Mark not yet contain this entire section? The question of the original text of Mark is further complicated through the discovery of a previously unknown, but probably genuine letter of Clement of Alexandria, which quotes sections from a *Secret Gospel of Mark*. This gospel, which was used by some of the Christians in Alexandria, on the whole agrees with canonical Mark. But it contained some additional materials, especially the story of the raising of a young man that was inserted after the third prediction of the passion (Mark 10:32–34). The story continues by telling that this young man then came to Jesus, dressed only with a linen cloth, in order to be initiated into the mystery of the kingdom. This may be a later expansion of the original story, which is evidently a variant of the story of the raising of Lazarus in John 11, however in a more original form that is free of all typical Johannine elements. Whatever the source of this story, it is certainly an insertion into the original Markan text. While this insertion occurs only in the *Secret Gospel,* it raises the question, whether similar additions or alterations survive even in the canonical text. This may be the case in two instances. The first appears in Mark 9:14–29, a very long and complex healing story that ends with the possessed boy falling down as if dead and Jesus taking his hand and raising him. Matthew and Luke, however, agree in presenting instead a short and simple story of an exorcism—most likely the version of the story that they found here in Mark's Gospel. The second instance occurs in the account of Jesus' arrest, where only Mark reports that there was a young man with Jesus, dressed in but a linen cloth, whom they wanted to apprehend, but the young man let go of the linen cloth and fled naked (Mark 14:51–52). Again, Matthew and Luke show no traces of this incident in their reproductions of Mark. Both instances may come from the same redactor, who inserted the story of the raising of the young man. This would mean that the canonical text of Mark, which is not attested in manuscripts until the middle of the 3d century, is actually derived from the *Secret Gospel of Mark,* from which only the problematic story of the raising of the young man and his secret initiation had been deleted. If that was the case, also other minor agreements of Matthew and Luke in their reproduction of Markan passages may have preserved Mark's original text, while the text extant in all manuscripts shows the hand of the redactor who had produced the *Secret Gospel of Mark.* Even that does not mean that the text of Mark then remained stable. While Mark's original text ended with the story of the empty tomb and the remark that the women fled from the tomb "because they were afraid," a number of later manuscripts have tried to eliminate this awkward ending and added a story of Jesus' appearance before the disciples—an ending to which later scribes affixed further improvements (see Codex Washingtonianus, §7.2c). The text of the gospels, especially the text of Mark, remained unstable for a long time—particularly in the first decades, which is shown most clearly by Matthew and Luke, who did not hesitate to replace Mark with their own improved versions.

Unlike the first edition of the Sayings Gospel Q, Mark's work is not simply a continuation of the oral tradition in written form. Mark has subjected all available written and oral materials to a new concept, namely, the writing of the story of Jesus' from the beginning of his ministry to his death. In this way, he has produced a special type of "biography," although the biographical outline has nothing in common with the actual career of the historical Jesus (which is no longer accessible for us). The guiding principle in the writing of this story is the passion narrative, so that Mark's Gospel could be characterized as a passion narrative with a biographical introduction. The traditional passion narrative is, of course, closely related to the kerygma of Jesus' suffering, death, and resurrection, which Paul calls "gospel" in 1 Cor 15:1. Yet, Mark was not aware that he was now writing a "gospel," nor do Matthew, Luke, and John designate their works as gospels. "Gospel" still remained the word for the oral proclamation (even in Mark 1:1!). Only in the middle of the 2d century are such writings more commonly called "gospels." The genius of Mark's literary design is visible in the way in which he uses the passion narrative. Death and resurrection become the climax of a dramatic development, in which the one who is called by a heavenly voice to a prophetic ministry (Mark 1:10–11; note that the heavenly voice here addresses Jesus and not the crowd!) must experience in the conduct of his office the vicissitudes of earthly life even to suffering and death. In this design, Mark follows in the footsteps of a venerable literary genre of Scripture, namely, the biography of the prophet as it is extant in Jeremiah and especially in the story of the suffering servant of Isaiah 40–56. This type of biography differs fundamentally from the Greco-Roman philosophical biography, which is primarily interested in the psychology, development of moral character, and achievement of victory over passions and emotions. The prophetic biography is exclusively interested in the conduct of office and the adversities and obstacles that face the divinely authorized servant in this world; enmity and suffering are therefore always part of the prophetic biography.

Mark has divided his writing into two different parts: the first part is building up to the confession of Peter at Caesarea Pilippi (8:27–30); the second begins with the first prediction of the passion (8:31) and ends with the burial of Jesus (15:42–47). In the first part, Jesus' ministry is characterized by powerful preaching, masterful defeats of his opponents in debates, driving out demons, healing the sick, and even demonstrating his powers over nature. Jesus is here constantly on the move, one event follows upon the other "immediately" (this word is used in Mark 1–8 more than thirty times!). Early on, however, there are hints of his eventual suffering and death. After a healing on a Sabbath, the Herodians and Pharisees are plotting Jesus' death (3:6). Mark then brings the scribes from Jerusalem to Galilee to give them the opportunity to accuse Jesus of being possessed by Beelzebul (3:22, 30). There is also a strange sense of mystery in which the activity of Jesus is clothed. It has been called the "messianic secret," which is expressed in three ways: in the commands to the demons not to reveal Jesus' identity publicly (1:34; 3:12; etc.), in the lack of understanding among the disciples (6:52; 8:16–21), and in the view that his parables should not be understood by those outside (4:10–12; 33–34). These features warn the reader that there will be no simple answer to the question of who this Jesus is and what all his powerful preaching and miracle working reveals about his identity. The climax is reached when Jesus discusses with his disciples what people say about him. It is evident that the answers (he is John the Baptist, or Elijah, or one of the prophets) are inadequate (8:27–28). But then Peter's confession that he is the Christ (that is, the Messiah; 8:29) is strangely followed by a command, with which he has heretofore only threatened the demons, namely, that they should not tell anyone about him (8:30).

Mark now introduces a fundamental shift in the description of Jesus' ministry with the first prediction of the passion that the "Son of Man" has to suffer and to die (8:31), which is repeated in 9:30–32 and 10:32–34. The mystery of Jesus' identity is thus enhanced. That the title Messiah/Christ is the correct response to Jesus' powerful teaching and miracle working is not questioned. But the title Son of Man is set over against this title, and when Peter tells Jesus that suffering and death are inappropriate experiences for the Messiah, Jesus refutes him, even calling him Satan (8:32–33). From here on the reader will look in vain for another use of the title Messiah for Jesus, until the high priest asks him in his trial, whether he is the Messiah (14:61), to which Jesus responds that he will see the "Son of Man" enthroned at the right hand of the Power and coming on the clouds of heaven (14:62), and in the remainder of the gospel, the title "Christ" is used only by those who mock Jesus (15:32). Mark sets forth a new vision of discipleship: those who want to follow Jesus have to take up their cross (8:34–9:1). When the disciples try to emulate Christ by the performance of a miracle, they fail badly (9:14–29). The section of the gospel, from the confession of Peter to the entry into Jerusalem, is dominated by the perspective of Jesus' suffering, death, and resurrection. Most of the teaching in the first part of the gospel was directed to the crowds; now it is dominated by the instruction of the disciples, for which Mark uses many traditional church order materials: about rank in the community (9:34–37), about offenses and excommunication (to cut off the member of the body that is offending, 9:42–48), about divorce (10:1–12), acceptance of children (10:13–16), about the dangers of wealth (10:17–31), about the obligation of leaders to serve (10:35–45). "Son of Man" (not "Messiah") is the title that Jesus claims for himself, as he has come to serve and to give his life as a ransom for many (10:45; Mark has here introduced this title into the traditional saying). Jesus' Jerusalem ministry, from the cleansing of the Temple (11:15–19)—hardly a historical event—to his successful debates with the leaders of the people (11:27–12:40), demonstrates his mastery in the interpretation of Israel's Scriptures and the superiority of his teaching over the scribes and Pharisees; and probably reflects debates with Judaism at the time of the writing of Mark's Gospel. Mark's narration of the trial and passion of Jesus, however, does not blame "the Jews" for the death of Jesus, but in true prophetic fashion, only the leaders of Jerusalem. It is still clear that the Roman governor was ultimately responsible for this miscarriage of justice.

Various competing christological concepts, especially Messiah/Christ for the miracle-working Savior, Son of Man for the one who comes on the clouds of heaven, are combined by Mark in such a way that one cannot doubt the messianic power of the earthly Jesus nor his coming in power as the Son of Man, but must accept that as the Son of Man Jesus is first of all the one who must suffer in the fulfillment of his ministry. The presentation of the ministry of Jesus in the genre of the prophetic biography makes it possible that the church can define discipleship in terms of Jesus' way to his death in Jerusalem. The church should not understand itself as the power that works miracles, nor should the church listen to a radicalized apocalyptic propaganda; not even the Son of Man knows the time of the parousia (13:31–32). Neither should the disciples listen to miracle-working apostles nor to a radicalized apocalyptic prophecy. Rather, they should stand with the Gentile centurion, who confesses at the cross when Jesus dies, that this one was truly the Son of God (15:39). The Gospel of Mark ends with the story of the empty tomb (16:1–8), which is not told in order to demonstrate the reality of the resurrection—this is the case only when Matthew elaborates this story as an apologetic legend. Rather, the story of the finding of the empty tomb rejects the worship at the tomb of a hero—such hero worship was widespread in Israel at that time (cf. Matt 23:29)—and points the community to the future, "He is going ahead of you to Galilee; there you will see him" (Mark 16:7).

(c) Jesus' Teaching and Ministry as the Canon
of the Church: The Gospel of Matthew

The Gospel of Mark was designed to unify various churches and their traditions, a legacy that Matthew further developed. Mark, in creating the genre of the
gospel, endeavored to unify conflicting traditions of a divided Syrian Christianity.
Matthew's design is even more ecumenical and fully exploits the potential for ecclesiastical unification provided by the genre of the gospel: Jesus' life, teaching,
ministry, and suffering should become the canon of a universal church. Tradition
identifies the author of this gospel with the Matthew mentioned as a tax collector
in Matt 9:9; but it is not certain that the author wanted to present himself in this
pericope. Papias of Hierapolis (see above §10.2b) says about Matthew that "he
collected the sayings in the Hebrew language, and each translated them as best he

Bibliography to §10.2c: Text of the Papias Fragment

Bihlmeyer, *ApostVät,* xliv–xlvii, 133–40.

Ulrich H. J. Körtner, *Papiasfragmente* (Schriften des Urchristentums 3; Darmstadt: Wissenschaftliche Buchgesellschaft, 1998) 58–59 (Greek text and German translation).

Bibliography to §10.2c: Commentaries

Julius Wellhausen, *Evangelienkommentare* (Berlin: De Gruyter, 1987; first published 1904–1911).

A. H. McNeile, *The Gospel According to St. Matthew* (London: Macmillan, 1915).

Eduard Schweizer, *The Good News According to Matthew* (Atlanta: Knox, 1975).

Francis W. Beare, *The Gospel According to Matthew: Translation, Introduction, and Commentary*
(San Francisco: Harper & Row, 1981).

Ulrich Luz, *Matthew 1–7: A Commentary* (Minneapolis: Augsburg, 1989).

Idem, *A Commentary on the Gospel of Matthew,* vol. 2: *Matthew 8–19* (Hermeneia; Minneapolis, Fortress, 2000).

Idem, *Das Evangelium nach Matthäus* (4 vols.; EKKNT 1/1–4; Neukirchen-Vluyn: Neukirchener
Verlag, 1985–1997).

W. D. Davies and Dale C. Allison, *A Critical and Exegetical Commentary on the Gospel According
to Saint Matthew*[1] (3 vols.; ICC; T&T Clark, 1988–1997).

Hans Dieter Betz, *The Sermon on the Mount: A Commentary on the Sermon on the Mount, Including
the Sermon on the Plain (Matthew 5:3–7:27 and Luke 6:20–49* (Hermeneia: Minneapolis: Fortress,
1995).

Joachim Gnilka, *Das Matthäusevangelium* (HThK; 2 vols.; Freiburg: Herder, 1986–1988).

Bibliography to §10.2c: Studies

Günther Bornkamm, Gerhard Barth, and Hans-Joachim Held, *Tradition and Interpretation in Matthew*
(2d ed.; London: SCM, 1982).

Krister Stendahl, *The School of St. Matthew and Its Use of the Old Testament* (2d ed.; Philadelphia:
Fortress, 1968).

Georg Strecker, *Der Weg der Gerechtigkeit: Untersuchung zur Theologie des Matthäusevangeliums*
(FRLANT 82; Göttingen: Vandenhoeck & Ruprecht, 1962).

Reinhart Hummel, *Die Auseinandersetzung zwischen Judentum und Kirche im Matthäusevangelium*
(BEvTh 33; München: Kaiser, 1963).

Jack Dean Kingsbury, *Matthew as Story* (2d ed.; Philadelphia: Fortress, 1988).

Graham N. Stanton, *A Gospel for a New People: Studies in Matthew* (Edinburgh: T&T Clark, 1992).

Idem, "Matthew: βίβλος, εὐαγγέλιον, or βίος?" in *The Four Gospels 1992,* 2. 1187–1201.

Idem (ed.), *The Interpretation of Matthew* (SNTI; Edinburgh: T&T Clark, 1995).

Idem, *The Theology of the Gospel of Matthew* (Cambridge: Cambridge University Press, 1995).

Ulrich Luz, *Matthew in History, Interpretation, and Effects* (Minneapolis: Fortress, 1994).

could" (Eusebius *Hist. eccl.* 3.39.16). This remark has been the beginning of a long ecclesiastical tradition assuming that Matthew was originally written in Hebrew (or Aramaic) and later translated into Greek, an entirely mistaken assumption that has been repeated from the time of Jerome until today. Whatever fictitious and erroneous apologetic notions about the Hebrew original of Matthew have been or may yet be proposed, there should not be the slightest doubt that the Gospel of Matthew was originally written in Greek on the basis of two Greek sources, namely, the Greek Gospel of Mark and the Greek Sayings Gospel Q. If Papias knew anything about a Hebrew or Aramaic Matthew, this cannot refer to a Hebrew original of the extant first gospel of the New Testament, but must refer to another document under the authority of Matthew.

It is tempting to understand Papias's remarks as a reference to an Aramaic original of the Sayings Gospel Q, especially since Papias speaks about the collection of "sayings." That is, however, problematic because the Sayings Gospel was originally composed in Greek, although some of its materials were most likely translated from Aramaic writings or traditions. If one can infer that such earlier materials were transmitted under the authority of Matthew and that the Sayings Gospel Q preserved this traditional authority, Papias's remarks about "Matthew" might rest on reliable historical information, namely, that the Sayings Gospel Q was circulating under the authority of Matthew. In this case, the author of the Gospel of Matthew, when he incorporated the Sayings Gospel into the framework of Mark's prophetic biography of Jesus, might have continued its apostolic authority for his own writing. Matthew and Thomas would then have been the two earliest apostolic authorities for the transmission of the sayings of Jesus. It is perhaps no accident that these two apostles appear side by side in several lists of the disciples of Jesus (Mark 3:18; Matt 10:3; Luke 6:15). In any case, the use of the Sayings Gospel, as well as the fact that the authority of Peter is even enhanced, locate the author of the Gospel of Matthew in western Syria. Evidence for a controversy with early rabbinic Judaism as it began to be constituted after the catastrophe of the Jewish War requires a location not too far away from Palestine as well as a date before the end of the 1st century.

Although Matthew used the framework of the Gospel of Mark, the composition and outline of his gospel differ fundamentally. The passion narrative no longer dominates, and the ministry of Jesus is more than a prelude to the passion. As Matthew begins his gospel with the narrative of Jesus' birth, the stories of Jesus'

Bibliography to §10.2c: Bibliography and History of Scholarship

Graham Stanton, "The Origin and Purpose of Matthew's Gospel: Matthean Scholarship from 1945 to 1980," *ANRW* 2.25.3 (1985) 1889–1951.

Joachim Lange (ed.), *Das Matthäus-Evangelium* (WdF 525; Darmstadt: Wissenschaftliche Buchgesellschaft, 1980).

Alexander Sand, *Das Matthäusevangelium* (EdF 275; Darmstadt: Wissenschaftliche Buchgesellschaft, 1991).

Günter Wagner, *An Exegetical Bibliography of the New Testament: Matthew and Mark* (Macon, GA: Mercer University Press, 1983).

Janice Capel Anderson, "Life on the Mississippi: New Currents in Matthaean Scholarship," *CRBS* 3 (1995) 169–210.

birth and death become the external framework for his ministry. The ministry itself is highlighted as a teaching ministry, which thus becomes the foundation of the church. There is less emphasis on Jesus' miracle-working activity in favor of his teaching, which Matthew presents essentially, but not exclusively, in five major discourses. In composing these discourses, he fully utilizes the materials drawn from the Sayings Gospel Q, in addition to sayings drawn from Mark and from a special source: the Sermon on the Mount (chaps. 5–7), the discourse on the sending of the Twelve (9:35–11:1), the parable discourse (13:1–53), the discourse on the order of the community (18:1–19:1), and the eschatological discourse (24:1–26:1). Each of these discourses concludes with the sentence, "and it happened when Jesus had finished these words. . . ." The last speech, however, is concluded with the sentence, "and it happened when Jesus had finished *all* these words." This is immediately followed by the hierarchs' council of death (26:1–2).

All five discourses are compositions of Matthew, for which he used traditional materials that were often already collected as smaller units of sayings. About 30 percent of the Sermon on the Mount already formed a unit in Q, which is essentially preserved in Luke's "Sermon on the Plain" (Luke 6:20–49). The discourse on the sending of the disciples (Matt 9:35–11:1) connects the small corresponding speech from Mark 6:7–11 with several units from Q (=Luke 10:1–12; 12:2–9, 51–53; 14:26–27) and special materials (Matt 10:17–25). Most of the material for the parable discourse is derived from Mark 4, though Matthew adds several parables. The order for the community (Matthew 18) is based upon materials from Mark 9:33–48 but is mostly a Matthean composition. The eschatological discourse reproduces Mark 13 in its first part; in the second part Matthew adds more material, especially eschatological parables. In addition to these five major discourses, there are a number of smaller units of sayings, which Matthew reproduces from his sources without major changes: the speech about John the Baptist from Q (Matt 11:2–19 = Q/Luke 7:18–35), the sayings about clean and unclean from Mark (Matt 15:1–20 = Mark 7:1–23), the sayings about suffering and discipleship, also from Mark (Matt 16:21–24 = Mark 8:43–9:1), and the speech against the Pharisees from Q (Matt 23:1–36 = Q/Luke 11:37–52).

In addition to the materials drawn from Mark and Q, Matthew has appended the following special materials at various points of his writing:

1:18–25	The birth of Jesus
2:1–23	The visit of the magi, flight to Egypt, and murder of the innocent
11:28–30	The comfort for the heavy-laden
13:24–30, 36–43	Parable of the tares and its interpretation
13:44	Parable of the hidden treasure
13:46	Parable of the pearl
13:47–50	Parable of the fishnet
13:52	Parable of the learned scribe of the kingdom
16:17–19	The keys of the kingdom for Peter
17:24–27	The Temple tax
18:23–35	The parable of the unmerciful servant

21:28–32	Parable of the two sons
23:2–3, 5, 8–10, 15–21, 28	Many materials in the speech against the Pharisees
25:1–13	Parable of the ten virgins
25:31–46	Parable of the last judgment
27:3–10	The death of Judas
27:24–25	Pilate washing his hands
27:51b–53	The signs at the death of Jesus
27:62–66; 28:2–4	The guard at the tomb
28:11–15	The bribing of the soldiers
28:16–20	Appearance in Galilee and command to baptize

In the description of the course of Jesus' ministry, Matthew usually follows Mark, and most of the redactional connections that Mark had introduced are reproduced by Matthew, including information about times and places. Nevertheless, the resulting portrait of Jesus' ministry is quite different. This is mostly due to the fact that Matthew has removed most of the miracle stories from their original location in Mark and has gathered them in one particular section, Matthew 8–9, together with one miracle story from Q (Matt 8:5–18). Only a few miracles stories remained in their original Markan context: the healing of the withered hand, a Markan apophthegm (Mark 3:1–6) that Matthew has transformed into a school discussion (Matt 12:9–14), the Canaanite woman (Mark 7:24–30 = Matt 15:21–28) and the epileptic boy (Mark 9:14–29 = Matt 17:14–21)—both stories have become in Matthew example stories for true faith—and the healing of the blind man before the entry into Jerusalem (Mark 10:46–52 = Matt 20:29–34). The result is obvious: Jesus is no longer a wandering miracle worker who demonstrates his divine power by his deeds. Rather, he is the Lord and redeemer, in whose ministry the mercy of God is made present, so that the prophecy of Isaiah is fulfilled: "He took our infirmities and bore our diseases" (Isa 53:4 = Matt 8:17). Matthew has also edited the miracles stories thoroughly, usually by shortening them drastically and concentrating on the central features; the healing of the Gerasene demoniac (Mark 5:1–20), for example, has been cut from its original twenty verses to just seven (Matt 8:28–34). Only the descriptions of the encounters of sick people with Jesus have occasionally been amplified: they worship Jesus and address him with honorific titles, such as "Son of David" and "Lord."

Mark had used the passion narrative as the hermeneutic principle for the understanding of Jesus' mission, demonstrating in this way that the criteria of Hellenistic propaganda were not capable of defining Jesus' identity. Jesus' actions as a "divine man" and Messiah became a paradox in the perspective of his suffering and death as the Son of Man. Matthew, however, removes Jesus' entire life, teaching, and actions from the categories of the divine man, as he raises Jesus' biography consistently above the level of human and even superhuman existence. Already in his earthly ministry Jesus is always the "Lord," so that such criteria as divine charisma, inspiration, and power are no longer applicable. The miracles are ascribed to the unique and unrepeatable mission of Jesus, while miracle-working disciples of Jesus, if they do not do what Jesus has commanded, will be subject to the verdict that they are "workers of lawlessness" (Matt 7:21–23). In this way, the story of Jesus and his disciples mirrors the story of the Lord and his church. The story of the stilling of the tempest (Mark 4:35–41) becomes in Matthew's Gospel the story of the Lord who rescues his church from the eschatological tribulations (Matt 8:23–27).

At the same time, Matthew maintains the biographical framework and even enlarges it, beginning his gospel with the genealogy of Jesus, which makes him a true son of Abraham (Jesus is truly from Israel), and with the birth narrative, which Matthew binds closely into the Scriptures of Israel. The hermeneutic principle that Matthew uses here is drawn from an apologetic scheme, which argues that the divinity of an event can be demonstrated by its agreement with ancient predictions in divine oracles. Matthew not only occasionally inserts scriptural references into traditional materials or enhances sayings of Jesus by adding sentences from Scripture (e.g., 9:13; 12:5–7, 40; 21:16), he repeatedly points explicitly to the fact that reported events fulfill divine prophecy by introducing such sentences with the words, "This happened in order to fulfill what had been said [by the prophet]." These so-called formula quotations highlight particularly the birth narrative, in which four references to the fulfillment of prophecy have been inserted (1:11; 2:15, 17, 22), and the passion narrative, which includes three more of them (21:4; 26:56; 27:9). In the narrative of Jesus' ministry, they are used more sparingly as they highlight important moments: at the beginning of Jesus' preaching (4:14), for Jesus' healing activity (8:17), at the healing of the multitudes, ending with the sentence, "And in his name the Gentiles will hope" (12:17), and underlining the rejection of those from whom the parables are hidden (13:14). The scriptural texts quoted with this formula are not drawn from the Septuagint, but are the result of the learned scribal activity of people who knew both Hebrew and Greek, the "School of St. Matthew." Such scholarly endeavors may have played some role in the controversy with learned rabbis, but they are primarily addressed to the pagan world in order to show that Jesus' birth, ministry, and death belong to a comprehensive eschatological plan of God that is documented in Israel's Scriptures and is now fulfilled and has become a message that concerns all nations.

As the gospel is thus bound to the Scriptures, Matthew also insists that the heart of the revelation to Israel, namely the law, remains fully valid. The Sermon on the Mount leaves no doubt that Jesus has not come to dissolve the law but to fulfill it, and it binds the disciples to its fulfillment—although their righteousness must be better than that of the Pharisees (5:17–19). In order to explain this "better righteousness" Matthew formulated the antitheses of the Sermon on the Mount (5:21–48), which contrast "what has been said to those of ancient times" with Jesus' own "but I say to you." What is at stake in each case is a radicalization of the demands of the law. Not only is murder forbidden, even hatred and evil words are prohibited; not only is the act of adultery sin, the design is already sinful; the commandment to love one's neighbor is radicalized to the request to love also one's enemy. Matthew establishes these radicalizations of the law as a new righteousness that can be the catechism of the church. These are not ethics for an elite, nor eschatological ethics that are impossible to fulfill. These ethical teachings take into account the realities of the world; for instance, divorce is permitted in the case of adultery (5:23). Praying, fasting, and almsgiving are required exercises of piety (note their rejection in the *Gospel of Thomas*), but their observance must differ from the "Hypocrites." In fulfilling the ethics of the new community, all its members become "perfect" (only Matthew employs this term, which is missing in the other Synoptic Gospels). Like the other discourses of Matthew's Gospel, the Sermon of the Mount is church order (*didache;* parallels to the *Teaching of the Twelve Apostles* are obvious), not a prescription for the perfection of individuals. Twice Matthew refers to commandments with the remark that they comprise the whole law and the prophets: the first time to the "golden rule" (7:12), the second time to the double commandment of love of God and of one's neighbor (22:37–40). Both of these commandments stand at the beginning of the way of life in the *Teaching of the Twelve Apostles* (*Did.* 1.2). The "better righteousness" is conduct fitting for all members of a new world religion that fulfills whatever the law of Israel demanded. That circumcision and the ritual observances of the law are not even mentioned certainly distinguishes this better righteousness according to the law of Israel from the program of the heirs of the Pharisees, Matthew's neighbors, who were at that same time trying to reorganize Israel at Yavneh, whom Matthew bitterly attacks in Jesus' speech against the Pharisees (Matt 23).

Also in the other discourses Matthew is primarily concerned with establishing education for the entire community. The instruction for the apostles is supplemented by general advice for all members in the case of persecution (10:17–42). The church order regulations (18:1–19:1) emphasize the election of the weak and the duty of forgiving those who have failed, underlined by the parable of the unmerciful servant (18:23–35). Striving for individualistic perfection is excluded (note the addition to the discussion of rank in the community, 18:4). Excommunication is requested when someone scandalizes the "little ones" in the church (18:6–9). Democratic principles of procedure are clearly recommended: the assembly of all members has the final authority (18:17). The speech against the Pharisees (23:1–36) is not simply a polemic against their assumption of piety in the observation of the law; it is directed against any and every pretense of individualistic fulfillment of the law. It is not a speech against the "Jews" or against Israel, because Matthew writes his gospel from the perspective of a law-abiding Israelite. Unlike Luke, Matthew does not yet distinguish between "Jews" and "Christians." Matt 23:2–3 and 8–10 are addressed to people who claim the privilege of office in the congregations for which Matthew is writing. The criticism of such church officers reveals one decisive difference with the *Didache:* Matthew does not promote any particular office but sees the disciples always as representatives of all members. Although Matthew elevates the authority of Peter (16:17–19), there is no concept of a succession. The tradition in the name of Peter is valid, but the responsibility for the fulfillment of the law of the better righteousness is assigned to the whole community without any limitations.

That Matthew highlights five speeches of Jesus may indeed recall the five books of Moses, but Jesus is not designated as the new Moses. Rather, Jesus is an interpreter, who radicalizes the law of Moses and demands a more perfect obedience, even though such demand should not be seen as a difficult obligation. Jesus is also "Wisdom," who invites people to take his easy burden (11:28–30). The community that accepts the obligation of the better righteousness is not obedient to a legislator but to a revealer (11:25–27), who himself, as a wise and righteous man, has taken upon himself the fate of the suffering righteous. Among the materials that Matthew has added to Mark's passion narrative, the scene of Pilate's washing his hands in innocence (Matt 27:24–25) has been singled out as a hateful anti-Jewish polemic. It is certainly a step in the effort of shifting the blame for the death of Jesus away from the Roman authorities, not to the "Jews" but to the leaders in Jerusalem and the people led astray by them (see 27:20!). Matthew here continues the polemic against the leaders of the people that began in the prophetic tradition of Israel and was particularly developed in the Jewish wisdom movement. From this same tradition Matthew also drew the polemic against the murderers of the prophets (23:34–36), clearly a piece of Israel's wisdom tradition (cf. Luke 11:49). Just as in the sect of the Essenes, "Jerusalem" is the symbol for the murderers of the messengers of God (Matt 23:37–39). This was all written in retrospect, after the destruction of Jerusalem in the Jewish War. Matthew was not alone (see *4 Ezra*) in seeing the fall of Jerusalem as divine retribution for the acts of the official leaders of Israel (see the allegorical interpretation of the parable of the wedding feast, 22:6–7).

The enigma and, at the same time, the eventual success of the Gospel of Matthew is visible in the way in which the author indicates that the relationship of Jesus and the new community to Israel is a vexing problem. Jesus is certainly the son of David (1:1, 20) and the king of the Jews (2:2)—but Gentiles come to worship the child. He is still hailed as "king" and "son of David" when he enters Jerusalem (21:5, 9; both titles are missing in the Markan version of the story!); but the last debate with the Pharisees (22:41–46; the Pharisees are not mentioned here in Mark!) questions the adequacy of the designation "son of David," and when Pilate asks Jesus whether he is the king of the Jews, Jesus answers, "You say so" (27:11). This title finally is used in contempt, when the soldiers mock him (27:29) and when Pilate puts it into the inscription on the cross (27:37). Who this Jesus really is, who suffered the same fate as many prophets and righteous people in Israel before him, is stated by the Gentile centurion and the soldiers with him when Jesus dies, "Truly, this man was God's Son" (27:54). In the proclamation of Matthew's law-abiding community, Jesus has broken the boundaries of the tradition of Israel and ended the vicious cycle of the killing of God's messengers—the dead saints rise from their tombs when Jesus dies (27:51–53). Women are the recipients of an epiphany when they come to Jesus' tomb (28:2–4; this is another addition of Matthew to the text of Mark's Gospel). Galilee, not Jerusalem, is the place where the disciples are commissioned to preach to all nations (28:10, 16). But for him the new community of Jesus' disciples knows that Jesus is the Lord over all, who will be with them until the end of the world (28:16–20). The disciples are instructed to teach the nations everything that he has taught them, that is, that they must abide by the better righteousness that fulfills the law. How Jesus will be present when he returns is explained in the parable of the last judgment (25:31–46), which shatters once more all established criteria of piety and morality according to the law: whatever anyone did (whether Christian, Jew, or Gentile) to the least of Jesus' brothers and sisters (the hungry, the thirsty, the naked, those in prison), was done to Jesus himself.

3. THE JOHANNINE CIRCLE

(a) The Development of the Johannine Tradition

The Gospel of John is the product of a special tradition that should be located in Syria, but it presupposes a development of communities independent of other

Syrian churches, at least in its beginnings. In the course of its evolution, contacts with other (Petrine) circles of Syria become evident, especially in the appropriation of the miracle stories and the passion narrative. A dependence upon the Synoptic Gospels is only possible in the very last stage of the redaction of the Gospel of John. Characteristic for the Johannine tradition is the material that resulted in the formation of the dialogues and discourses, which reflect the particular Johannine christology and soteriology. The large discourses of the Gospel of Matthew are compositions of older units of sayings ultimately formed in the oral tradition; their history and development can be reconstructed with great accuracy through form-critical analysis; but a different process of growth must have taken place in the formation of the discourses of the Gospel of John. Rudolf Bultmann proposed the hypothesis that John used a (non-Christian) Gnostic discourse source for their composition. Although this hypothesis has been widely criticized—and the assumption of the use of a non-Christian source is highly problematic—Bultmann may well have been correct with his notion that the Johannine discourses are indebted to a debate with Gnostic materials and were formulated in the context of that debate. The discovery of the Nag Hammadi Library has made a number of writings accessible that assist in the reconstruction of the evolution of such discourses.

(1) *Dialogues of Jesus.* The dialogue gospel that is preserved in the *Dialogue of the Savior* (§10.1b) demonstrates how dialogues of Jesus with his disciples have been developed in the process of the interpretation of sayings of Jesus. The composition of longer discourses, only occasionally or not at all interrupted by questions of the disciples, may have proceeded along the same lines. If the Johannine discourses and dialogues belong to the trajectory of the development of Jesus' sayings, they emerge as genuine gospel materials. That older sayings are embedded in these discourses has become more evident as hitherto unknown sayings were

---

Bibliography to §10.3a

Raymond E. Brown, *The Community of the Beloved Disciple* (New York: Paulist, 1979).

Oscar Cullmann, *The Johannine Circle* (Philadelphia: Westminster, 1976).

James M. Robinson, "The Johannine Trajectory," in idem and Koester, *Trajectories,* 232–68.

J. D. Kaestli, J.-M. Poffet, and J. Zumstein (eds.), *La communauté johannique et son histoire: La trajectoire de l'évangile de Jean au deux premier siècles* (Monde de la Bible; Geneva: Labor et Fides, 1990).

Rudolf Bultmann, "Der religionsgeschichtliche Hintergrund des Prologs zum Johannesevangelium," and "Die Bedeutung der neuerschlossenen mandäischen und manichäischen Quellen für das Verständnis des Johannesevangeliums," in idem, *Exegetica,* 10–35 and 55–104.

Oscar Cullmann, "Das Rätsel des Johannesevangeliums im Lichte der neuen Handschriftenfunde," in idem, *Vorträge 1925–1962,* 260–91.

George MacRae, "The Fourth Gospel and *Religionsgeschichte,*" *CBQ* 32 (1970) 13–24.

Haenchen, "Johanneische Probleme," in idem, *Gott und Mensch,* 78–113.

Bibliography to §10.3a (1)

Helmut Koester, "Gnostic Sayings and Controversy Traditions in John 8:12–59," in Hedrick and Hodgson, *Nag Hammadi,* 97–110.

Idem, "Gnostic Writings as Witnesses for the Development of the Sayings Tradition," in Layton, *Rediscovery of Gnosticism,* 238–61.

Heinz Becker, *Die Reden des Johannesevangeliums und der Stil der gnostichen Offenbarungsrede* (FRLANT 68; Göttingen: Vandenhoeck & Ruprecht, 1958).

discovered in the Nag Hammadi Library, especially in the *Gospel of Thomas.* In addition to sayings, also proverbs, kerygmatic formulae, scriptural interpretations, and theological traditions have been used in their formation. The author of the Gospel of John did not compose these discourses *de novo,* but utilized and expanded older existing discourses.

The discourse in John 3 (the Nicodemus dialogue) can serve as an example. It begins in John 3:3 with the quotation of a saying about rebirth that appears in a more original form in Justin Martyr in the context of his discussion of the liturgy of baptism (*1 Apol.* 61.4–5). The author of the Nicodemus dialogue appropriated this saying from the baptismal liturgy, but changed the traditional "to be reborn" into "to be born anew" (="to be born from above") and he replaced the traditional "enter into the kingdom of God" (which is still preserved in the repetition of the saying in 3:5) with "see the kingdom of God." The sentence juxtaposing spirit and flesh (3:6) is a theological maxim also known to Ignatius of Antioch (*Phld.* 7.1), perhaps derived from the same liturgical context. This is further illustrated by a traditional wisdom saying about the wind ("spirit"), which one can hear, but whose origin one does not know (3:8). Nicodemus's repetition of the question (3:9) is answered by a communal confessional statement, quite unexpectedly given by Jesus in the first-person plural ("We speak what we know . . . "; 3:11). Traditional materials are also employed in what follows. John 3:13 is a reference to the descent and ascent of the revealer. Then an exegesis of Nu 21:8–9 (Moses raising the snake in the wilderness, John 3:14a) is interpreted as an oblique reference to the crucifixion ("the Son of Man must be raised up," i.e., on the cross; 3:14b), and a theological statement about God giving his son is added and interpreted.

Similar analyses of other discourses of the Gospel of John show how many sayings and other traditional materials are embedded in them. The *Gospel of Thomas* is especially important in the effort of discovering the core sayings of the Johannine dialogues and discourses. Numerous passages in them have parallels in the *Gospel of Thomas,* and in all instances the latter undoubtedly preserves the more original form of such sayings. Only a few examples can be cited here. Jesus' statement about himself, that one may seek him but cannot find him (John 7:33–34), appears as a saying in *Gos. Thom.* 38. A parallel from *Baruch,* an unknown wisdom book that is quoted in Cyprian's *Testimonia* (3.29), demonstrates that this saying was originally a statement of heavenly Wisdom about herself, saying that she would be among human beings only for a short time and then return to her heavenly abode (cf. also John 16:16ff.). The words about the light in John 11:9–10 and 12:35–36 are paralleled in *Gos. Thom.* 24b. John 8:52, "Whoever keeps my word will not taste death," is a variant of *Gos. Thom.* 1 and is quoted as a saying of Jesus in *Dial. Sav.* #104 (147, 18–20). The *Dialogue of the Savior* also provides independent information about sayings used in John; John 16:24 (to ask—to find—to rejoice) is attested as a word of Jesus in *Dial. Sav.* #20 (129, 14–16). Occasionally another dialogue gospel from the Nag Hammadi Library, the *Apocryphon of James,* provides a parallel to a saying in the Gospel of John; the blessing of those who have not seen and yet believe (John 20:29) appears in *Apoc. Jas.* 12, 31–13, 3. The disciples' statement that Jesus is now speaking openly and no longer in parables (John 16:29) appears as a saying of Jesus in *Apoc. Jas.* 17, 1–6.

The *Gospel of Thomas,* moreover, presents several sayings of Jesus in the I-style, which are rare in the Synoptic Gospels but occur frequently in John. They belong to a branch of the sayings tradition that developed in a direction different from that of the Sayings Gospel Q. *Gos. Thom.* 77a ("I am the light that is above them all)" has a parallel in John 8:12 ("I am the light of the world"). *Gos. Thom.* 108 ("Whoever drinks from my mouth") is used in a dialogue in John 7:38 ("Let anyone who is thirsty come to me"). The style of the revelation speech of *Gos. Thom.* 28, in which the savior speaks about his coming and his mission in the world in terms that are analogous to the speech of Wisdom in Jewish wisdom literature, is paralleled in several speeches of Jesus in the Gospel of John. In a typical pattern of this speech of Wisdom, she introduces herself, which is followed by an invitation, a call to conversion or a request for faith, and a promise. To this one can compare John 6:35, "I am the bread of life, whoever comes to me shall not hunger, and whoever believes in me shall never thirst." As we shall see, however, the typical "I am" sayings of the Gospel of John have few parallels elsewhere, especially not in Gnosticizing sayings of Jesus, where the emphasis is placed on the finding of light and life in oneself. John's "I am" sayings, on the other hand, signal that life, light, and resurrection can only be found in Jesus and therefore require faith in Jesus and his divinity rather than recognition of one's own divine self.

The dialogues and discourses of the Gospel of John presuppose more than just sayings, as they can be found in such writings as the *Gospel of Thomas.* They are developed in a controversy with Gnostic interpretations of Jesus' sayings in the form of dialogues. The most striking example for this is the dialogue in John 14:2–12, which has a close parallel in *Dial. Sav.* ##27–30 (132, 3–9). There the question about seeing the place of life is answered by Jesus' statement that seeing is knowing oneself and that everyone who knows himself will do works out of his own goodness. In John 14, however, the question about the way to the heavenly abode is answered by Jesus saying, "I am the way," and by the statement that seeing the father is knowing and believing Jesus and then doing the works that Jesus is doing. Countering the Gnostic interpretation of Jesus' call to self knowledge, the Gospel of John calls for faith in Jesus. It is out of this perspective that John has developed the "I am" sayings of Jesus.

(2) *Traditions of the Johannine Church.* It appears from this close relationship of the Johannine dialogues to the Gnostic interpretation of Jesus' sayings that a significant part of the traditions of his gospel consisted of debates about the understanding of the heritage of Jesus' words. Also for the Gospel of John, the word of the earthly Jesus is the voice of the heavenly revealer, who calls human beings into a new existence determined by the spirit. Baptism is rebirth into this new spiritual life, not an act of incorporation into an eschatological community. If the words about the bread of life and the true vine (John 6:26ff.; 15:1ff.) are interpretations

Bibliography to §10.3a (2)

C. H. Dodd, *Historical Tradition in the Fourth Gospel* (Cambridge: Cambridge University Press, 1963).
George W. MacRae, "Gnosticism and the Church of John's Gospel," in Hedrick and Hodgson, *Nag Hammadi,* 89–96.

of the Eucharist, bread and wine are understood as symbols of the participation in Jesus' heavenly message, representing his words that give life; they are not symbols of the messianic banquet, for which Jesus will return in the future, nor are they directly related to his fate of suffering and death, as is the case in the Pauline understanding.

The Gospel of John is therefore an important witness for the early development of a Gnostic understanding of the tradition of Jesus' sayings and a spiritualized interpretation of the sacraments. Can the Gospel of John also provide some information about the location of such developments? To be sure, most of John's statements about the places of Jesus' ministry appear in redactional materials of the gospel, but there are some interesting pieces of information coming from the dialogues themselves. Jesus is known as a Galilean, and one of the objections raised in the dialogues is that a prophet does not come from Galilee (7:52). Even if this reflects nothing more than the knowledge of his actual origin, the accusation "You are a Samaritan" is striking (8:48). In the narrative and dialogue of Jesus and the Samaritan woman, the location in Samaria must have been part of this tradition from the very beginning (John 4:4ff.). The land "on the other side of the Jordan" is referred to several times as the setting of John the Baptist's and Jesus' sojourn (1:28; 3:26; 10:40–41). Whether or not such information rests on older tradition, it may indicate that the Johannine communities were at home in Palestine, but outside the jurisdiction of the Jerusalem sanhedrin. It is impossible to know, however, whether John the son of Zebedee, who was once one of the "pillars" in Jerusalem and who must have left Jerusalem like Peter before Paul's final visit, is in any way related to the formation of the early "Johannine" churches because there is no attestation for the name "John" in this tradition.

(3) *Papyrus Egerton 2.* Controversies about the interpretation of Scripture, dealing particularly with the question of the authority of Abraham and Moses, played a

Bibliography to §10.3a (3): Text

H. Idris Bell and T. C. Skeat, *Fragments of an Unknown Gospel* and *The New Gospel Fragments* (London: British Museum, 1935).

Michael Gronewald, "Unbekanntes Evangelium oder Evangelienharmonie (Fragment aus dem Evangelium Egerton)," *Kölner Papyri (P. Köln),* vol. 6 (Abh.RWA, Sonderreihe Papyrologica Colonensia 7; Köln, 1987).

Joachim Jeremias and Wilhelm Schneemelcher, "Papyrus Egerton 2," in Schneemelcher, *NT Apoc.,* 1. 96–99.

Cameron, *Other Gospels,* 73–75.

Miller, *Complete Gospels,* 412–18.

Bibliography to §10.3a (3): Studies

Goro Mayeda, *Das Leben-Jesu-Fragment Papyrus Egerton 2 und seine Stellung in der urchristlichen Literaturgeschichte* (Bern: Haupt, 1946).

Jon B. Daniels, "The Egerton Gospel: Its Place in Early Christianity" (Dissertation Claremont Graduate School, Claremont, CA, 1990).

Dieter Lührmann, "Das neue Fragment des P. Egerton 2 (PKöln 255)," in *The Four Gospels,* 3. 22–2255.

Helmut Koester, "Apocryphal and Canonical Gospels," *HTR* 73 (1980) 105–130.

Idem, *Ancient Christian Gospels,* 205–16.

major role in the formation of the Johannine tradition. There is a piece of evidence for such controversies that has not received enough attention, namely, *Papyrus Egerton 2,* which was published first in 1935 under the title *Fragments of an Unknown Gospel.* It consists of two damaged pages from a codex, a fragment of a third page, and scrap of a fourth page with only one readable letter. More recently *Papyrus Köln Nr. 255,* containing five lines, has been identified as belonging to the same gospel fragment. The style of the handwriting leads to a date not later than ca. 200 CE. In addition to the story of the healing of a leper, a controversy about paying taxes, and the beginning of a miracle on the Jordan, the manuscript contains two units that are very closely related to the Gospel of John. The first is a controversy of Jesus with "the rulers of the people," which presents sentences agreeing almost verbatim with John 5:39 ("Search the Scriptures . . . "), 5:45 ("there is one who accuses you, Moses . . . "), 9:29 ("We know that God has spoken to Moses . . . "), and 5:46 ("Because if you had believed Moses . . . "). Although one might call the language "Johannine," typical Johannine terms are missing (e.g., *Pap. Eg. 2* says "life" where John has "eternal life") and phrases are used that are never found in the Gospel of John, for example, "rulers of the people" (John's enemies are always "the Jews"), "unbelief," "Jesus answered and said." Moreover, the dialogue in *Papyrus Egerton 2* is more compact and shows no signs of the more elaborate Johannine parallels. The second unit that is relevant here is the report that the rulers tried to arrest Jesus but were not able to lay hands on him. It appears that John knew this report and used parts of it on three different occasions (John 7:30; 10:31, 39) in order to create the impression of repeated attempts upon Jesus' life.

It is hard to imagine that *Papyrus Egerton 2* could have patched its text together from half a dozen passages of the Gospel of John—and, in addition, from several Synoptic Gospels. With its language, which contains Johannine elements but reveals a greater affinity with the language of the Synoptic Gospels, this document must belong to a stage of the tradition that preceded the canonical gospels. It thus reflects early controversies of the followers of Jesus with other influential groups within Palestinian Judaism at a time when the opponents were not yet stereotyped as "the Jews," as is the case in John's Gospel. This raises the probability that other dialogues of the Gospel of John dealing with the authority of Abraham and Moses (7:19, 22–23; 8:33ff.; cf. 3:14) are also elaborations of a source similar to, or identical with, *The Unknown Gospel of Papyrus Egerton 2,* of which we possess unfortunately only a small fragment.

(4) *The Passion Narrative.* In the course of their history, the Johannine communities had to come to terms with other churches of Syria and their traditions. The most striking piece of evidence for this encounter is the acceptance of the passion narrative. As it was accepted by the Johannine communities, it agrees in its essential outline and in many details with the passion narrative used by the Gospel

Bibliography to §10.3a (4)

D. Moody Smith, "The Sources of the Gospel of John: An Assessment of the Present State of the Problem," *NTS* 10 (1963/64) 336–51.

of Mark. The following table will show the similarities and differences and thus also highlight the secondary elements in the two versions of the narrative:

The passion narratives of Mark and John	Mark 11:1–16:8	John 12, 13, 18–20
Entry into Jerusalem	11:1–10	12:12–19
Cursing of the Fig Tree	11:12–14, 20	———
Cleansing of the Temple	11:15–19	(2:13–17)
Discourses and Debates in Jerusalem	11:22–12:44	———
Apocalyptic Discourse	13:1–37	———
Conspiracy of the high priests	14:1–2	11:47–53
Anointing in Bethany	14:3–9	12:1–8
Betrayal of Jude	14:10–11, 18–21	6:70–71; 13:21–30
Finding of the Room for the Passover	14:12–16	———
Lord's Supper	14:22–25	13:1–20
Peter's Denial Predicted	14:27–31	13:36–38
Fare-well discourses	———	14:1–17:20
Walk to the Mount of Olives	14:26	18:1
Jesus in Gethsemane	14:32–42	———
Arrest of Jesus	14:43–52	18:2–11
Jesus before the Sanhedrin/ Peter's Denial	14:53–79	18:12–27
Mocking by the servant's	14:65	———
Jesus delivered to Pilate	15:1	18:28
Trial before Pilate	15:2–5	18:29–38
Jesus or Barabbas	15:6–14	18:39–40
Flagellation of Jesus	15:15	18:1
Mocking by the Soldiers	15:16–20a	19:2–3
Discourse of Jesus and Pilate	———	19:4–15
The Way to Golgotha	15:20b–21	19:16–17a
The Crucifixion	15:22–24a	19:17b
Dividing Jesus' Garments	15:24b	19:23–24
Inscription on the Cross	15:26	19:19
Debate about the Inscription	———	19:20–22
Crucifixion with two Criminals	15:27	19:18
Mocking of Jesus Crucified	15:28–32	———
Jesus' Call of Despair	15:33–35	———
Jesus is Given a Drink of Vinegar	15:36	19:28–29
Jesus dies	15:37	19:30
Prodigies at the Death of Jesus	15:38	———
The Centurio's Confession	15:39	———
Women at the Cross	15:40–41	19:25–27
Jesus' Side Pierced	———	19:31–37
Burial of Jesus	15:42–47	19:38–42
The Empty Tomb	16:1–8	20:1–13

In both cases the story begins with Jesus' entry into Jerusalem, or with the anointing in Bethany (John, or perhaps Mark, may have reversed the sequence) and ends with the discovery of the empty tomb. The name of Peter is fixed even more firmly in the Johannine version; in Mark's story of the discovery of the empty tomb, Peter appears (Mark 16:7) only as an afterthought. We are certainly dealing with the same basic narrative of the passion, which was perhaps circulated under the authority of Peter and which was also used in the *Gospel of Peter.* Some of the features in John's version are more original, especially the dating of Jesus' death on the day before Passover (John 18:28). The story of the finding of the room for the Passover in Mark 14:12–16 is secondary. Neither Mark's source nor John presents Jesus' last meal as a Passover meal. Rather, Jesus' last meal must have been an ordinary meal with bread and wine, and that Jesus was crucified before the beginning of Passover is most probably historical. In the story of the discovery of the empty tomb, the name of Mary of Magdala is the original name connected with this story—Peter and the "other disciple" are secondary intrusions—and her appearance as the first one to whom the risen Jesus appears could rest on a very old tradition. Other features, however, have been added by the Johannine redaction: an unnamed second disciple appears in John's account ("the other disciple"; John 18:15–16; cf. 20:2; "the disciple whom Jesus loved"; 19:26–27). Secondary is also a stronger martyrological coloring of the story and the tendency to put the blame for the death of Jesus on the Jews and to exonerate Pilate. The reason for this tendency is possibly found in the experience of persecution by "the Jews," not to mention the excommunication from the synagogue on the basis of the confession of Christ (9:22; 16:2).

(5) *The Source of Signs.* Another complex of materials used by the author of the Gospel of John is a tradition of miracle stories, which is closely related to sources of the Gospel of Mark. It has been designated as the Source of Signs (*Semeia Source*) because of the term "sign" (*semeion*) used for miracles in John's Gospel (2:11; 4:45; etc.). The following stories are drawn from this source: John 2:1–11; 4:46–54; 5:1–9; 6:1–21; 9:1–7; 11:1–44. Its conclusion is preserved in 20:30–31. This source is a collection of stories from the Hellenistic propaganda in which Jesus is proclaimed as the divine man. But since the language points to an Aramaic milieu, the stories must have been developed in the missionary activities among Aramaic-speaking Jews and Gentiles; they were written down in Greek in a bilingual community. It is characteristic of religious syncretism in the areas of Syria and Palestine that one of these miracle narratives, the wine miracle at Cana (2:1–11), derived its main features from the cult of Dionysus. In all stories, the miraculous power of Jesus is even more enhanced than in the Markan parallels. Jesus here becomes the god walking on earth, endowed with a divine power that can even call

Bibliography to §10.3a (5):　Text
Miller, *Complete Gospels,* 175–93.

Bibliography to §10.3a (5):　Studies
James M. Robinson, "The Johannine Trajectory," in idem and Koester, *Trajectories,* 232–68.
Robert T. Fortna, *The Fourth Gospel and Its Predecessor: From Narrative to Present Gospel* (Philadelphia: Fortress, 1988).

the dead from their tombs (John 11). Perhaps, also other traditions used by John were already connected with this source, especially the story of Jesus' encounter with the Samaritan women (John 4), in which Jesus appears as a prophet possessing supernatural powers (4:16–19). Although the language of these stories is in general "Johannine," the author of the Gospel of John exhibits a very critical attitude with respect to such miracles as a basis of faith.

(6) *Eschatological Traditions.* The eschatological expectation of Jesus' return as the Son of Man or Messiah was not unknown to the Gospel of John but was critically received and appropriated by the author. Both titles are used—Son of Man is even enhanced (John 1:51)—but unequivocal predictions of the future parousia and the accompanying apocalyptic events are missing (John 5:28–29 and 6:39b, 40b, 44b are later interpolations). The farewell discourses (John 14–17) interpret Jesus' return as the coming of the spirit. Baptism is not an act of sealing for the eschatological time, but rebirth through the spirit (3:3–8). Passages that allude to the Eucharist (6:26–51; 15:1–10) do not contain any eschatological components (John 13:1–38 also lacks any words of institution). Eschatological terms like "judgment" and "eternity" are current, but are always understood as gifts or events of salvation that are taking place in the present. Thus while eschatological terminology and concepts are well-known, they are always interpreted in accordance with a piety and theology that is based on altogether different christological and soteriological presuppositions. The author of the Gospel of John rejected the Gnostic understanding of Jesus' words by binding their interpretation to the passion narrative without resorting to an apocalyptic eschatology. The result of this effort is a new and quite independent theological concept.

(b) Exaltation on the Cross as Gospel: The Gospel of John

The author of the Gospel of John is deeply rooted in the special traditions of the Johannine communities, which he tries to reconcile with the more dominating Syrian traditions present in Mark's and Matthew's Gospels. This attempt must have been accomplished before the end of the 1st century since the writing can no longer be dated as late as the middle of the 2d century, as was often assumed in earlier discussions. The discovery of *Papyrus Rylands 457* (=𝔓⁵²), a small fragment with some verses from John 18 that was found in Egypt, has been dated to ca. 125 CE. Thus

Bibliography to §10.3b: Commentaries

Julius Wellhausen, *Evangelienkommentare* (Berlin: de Gruyter, 1987; first published 1904–1911).

Rudolf Bultmann, *The Gospel of John: A Commentary* (Philadelphia: Westminster, 1971). This Work and C. H. Dodd's *Interpretation of the Fourth Gospel* (see below) are the two most formidable and stimulating works on the Gospel of John in the 20th century.

Raymond E. Brown, *The Gospel According to John* (2 vols.; AB 29; Garden City, NY: Doubleday, 1966–1970).

C. K. Barrett, *The Gospel According to Saint John* (2d ed.; Philadelphia: Westminster, 1978).

Ernst Haenchen, *John: A Commentary on the Gospel of John* (Hermeneia; Philadelphia: Fortress, 1984).

Rudolf Schnackenburg, *The Gospel According to Saint John* (3 vols.; New York: Crossroad, 1980–1982).

the Gospel of John must have been brought from Syria to Egypt at the beginning of the 2d century, where it remained popular. Among the Egyptian papyri it is better attested than any other gospel, although all of these papyri are fragmentary: $\mathfrak{P}^{90}$ (2d century), $\mathfrak{P}^{66}$ (ca. 200), $\mathfrak{P}^{75}$ (early 3d century). On the other hand, the tradition that the Gospel of John belongs to Ephesus is attested relatively late. Polycarp of Smyrna (first half of the 2d century; see §12.2h) knows nothing of the Gospel of John, although he may have been familiar with the prophet John who wrote the Book of Revelation. Also Papias of Hierapolis is silent about John's Gospel. But by the end of the 2d century, the two "Johns"—the author of the gospel and the prophet of Revelation—were united into the one "John of Ephesus" (Irenaeus; *Acts*

Bibliography to §10.3b: Studies

C. H. Dodd, *The Interpretation of the Fourth Gospel* (Cambridge: Cambridge University Press, 1953 and reprints).

Rudolf Bultmann, "Untersuchungen zum Johannesevangelium," in idem, *Exegetica,* 124–97.

Ernest Cadman Colwell, *The Greek of the Fourth Gospel* (Chicago: University of Chicago Press, 1931).

Erwin Goodenough, "John a Primitive Gospel," *JBL* 54 (1945) 145–83.

F. L. Cross (ed.), *Studies in the Fourth Gospel* (London: Mowbray, 1957).

Ernst Käsemann, "Structure and Purpose of the Prologue to John's Gospel," in idem, *New Testament Questions,* 138–67.

Idem, *The Testament of Jesus: A Study of the Gospel of John in the Light of Chapter 17* (Philadelphia: Fortress, 1966).

Wayne A. Meeks, "The Man from Heaven in Johannine Sectarianism," *JBL* 91 (1972) 44–72.

J. Louis Martyn, *History and Theology in the Fourth Gospel* (2d ed.; Nashville, TN: Abingdon, 1979).

Peder Borgen, *Logos Was the True Light and Other Essays on the Gospel of John* (Trondheim: Tapir Publishers, 1983).

R. Alan Culpepper, *Anatomy of the Fourth Gospel: A Study in Literary Design* (Philadelphia: Fortress, 1983).

Udo Schnelle, *Antidoketische Christologie im Johannesevangelium: Eine Untersuchung zur Stellung des vierten Evangelisten in der johanneischen Schule* (FRLANT 144; Göttingen: Vandenhoeck & Ruprecht, 1987).

Martin Hengel, *The Johannine Question* (Philadelphia: Trinity Press International, 1989).

Daniel J. Harrington, *John's Thought and Theology: An Introduction* (Good News Studies 33; Wilmington, DE: Glazier, 1990).

D. M. Smith, "John and the Synoptics and the Question of Gospel Genre," in *The Four Gospels 1992,* 3. 1783–97.

Bibliography to §10.3b: Bibliography and History of Scholarship

Robert Kysar, *The Fourth Evangelist and His Gospel: An Examination of Contemporary Scholarship* (Minneapolis: Augsburg, 1975).

Idem, "The Fourth Gospel: A Report on Recent Research," *ANRW* 2.25.3 (1985) 2389–2480.

Karl Heinrich Rengstorf (ed.), *Johannes und sein Evangelium* (WdF 82; Darmstadt: Wissenschaftliche Buchgesellschaft, 1973).

D. Moody Smith, *John Among the Gospels: The Relationship in Twentieth-Century Research* (Minneapolis: Fortress, 1992).

Gilbert van Belle, *Johannine Bibliography 1966–1985: A Cumulative Bibliography on the Fourth Gospel* (BETL 82; Leuven: Peeters, 1988).

Watson E. Mills, *The Gospel of John* (BBR.NTS 4; Lewiston, NY: Mellen, 1995).

Günter Wagner (ed.), *An Exegetical Bibliography of the New Testament,* vol. 3: *John and 1, 2, 3 John* (Macon, GA: Mercer University Press, 1987).

of John). Even less historical is the modern legend that John moved to Ephesus with Jesus' mother Mary; the entire ancient tradition is unanimous in the assertion that Mary died in Jerusalem.

It is questionable, however, whether the extant manuscripts preserve the original text of the Gospel of John. The narrative about Jesus and the woman taken in adultery (7:53–8:11) is certainly a late interpolation; it is not only missing in the older papyri but also in the uncial manuscripts of the 4th century (the Ferrar group of manuscripts place this story after Luke 21:38). John 21:1–35, though present in all extant manuscripts, is also widely recognized as a later addition; John 20:30–31 is the original ending of the gospel, which is repeated in an exaggerated version in John 21:25. The original gospel had reached the climax of its story with the Jesus' appearance before Thomas (20:24–29), and Thomas's confession "My Lord and my God" and the blessedness of those who believe though they have not seen. John 21:1–14 with its story of the miraculous catch of fishes (cf. Luke 5:1–11) is unmotivated, and the following discussion of Peter's rank in comparison with that of the "beloved disciple" (21:15–23) belongs to a later discussion of competing claims of apostolic authorities. The authority of the tradition of Peter is here confirmed in the leadership of the ecclesiastical organization ("Tend my sheep!" John 21:15, 16, 17). In contrast, the authority of the disciple whom Jesus loved, described with the mysterious words, "It is my will that he remain until I come," underlines the authority of the special tradition of this gospel as the report of an eyewitness (21:24).

The redactor who added chapter 21 apparently added some other materials to the original text of John's Gospel. The comment about the reliability of the eyewitness in 19:35 closely resembles the statement in 21:24. A number of obviously interpolated remarks about the future resurrection of the dead (5:28–29; 6:39b, 40b, 44b) and the future judgment (12:48b) contradict the Johannine proclamation of the presence of judgment and resurrection in Jesus himself and in his words (5:24–26; 11:25–26); they may have been interpolated by the same redactor. Finally, the verses speaking about the physical eating of Jesus' flesh and drinking of his blood (6:51b–59)—an interpretation of the Eucharist as magic food and drink— are certainly a later interpolation into the discourse about Jesus as the bread from heaven. It interrupts the context of Jesus' statement that he is the bread that has come down from heaven (6:51a), which the disciples interpret as a harsh word (6:60) to which Jesus responds with the question, "[What will you say] when you see the Son of Man ascending to where he has been before?" (6:62). What the disciples should understand is that the bread from heaven is present in Jesus' words, which are spirit and life (6:63). The magical understanding of the Eucharist belongs in the early 2d century, where it is attested by Ignatius of Antioch (§12.2d). Some scholars have suggested that also some other verses showing an almost verbatim agreement with passages in the Synoptic Gospels (John 1:27; 12:8) do not belong to the original text of John; but such agreements may result simply from the use of closely related sources.

Peculiar and still unresolved problems of the Johannine text relate to the sequences of several units of passages as they are presented in all manuscripts. John 3:31–36 is not appropriate as a continuation of the words spoken by John the Baptist (3:22–30); this passage belongs to the discourse of Jesus that ends in 3:21. In

John 6:1, Jesus is quite unexpectedly found in Galilee although he was still in Jerusalem at the end of chapter 5. Should 6:1–71 and 7:1–13 be placed after 4:43–54? There the Galilean locale is still presupposed. Most puzzling is the conclusion of the first section of the farewell discourses with the words, "Rise, let us go hence" in 14:31, which leads directly into the scene of the arrest of Jesus in 18:1ff. With 15:1–17:26, however, the farewell discourse continues. In this case there should be no doubt: 15:1–17:26 must be placed elsewhere, probably after 13:38 and before 14:1. This misplacement as well as that of 6:1–71 could be explained as an accidental exchange of leaves in an early copy of the gospel. Such explanation, however, cannot be used as an argument for the rearrangement of smaller units (this had been proposed by Rudolf Bultmann). A better solution is the suggestion that some parts of the Gospel of John were never completed in its intended final form but remained drafts and collections of materials designed for further elaboration. In 4:43–54 a miracle story is told setting the stage for a major discourse about the problem of miracles and faith (4:48!)—but no such discourse follows. Moreover, the many fragments of discourses and dialogues in John 7 and 8 suggests that the gospel contains various materials that the author never composed into coherent discourses. Also John 17, the so-called high-priestly prayer of Jesus, is a Gnostic discourse that has not been subject to the critical interpretation of the author of the Fourth Gospel.

These, however are minor disorders. On the whole, the outline of the Gospel of John is clear and well designed. The first part (chaps. 2–11) was composed on the basis of the Signs Source. Larger discourses and dialogues follow upon each of the miracle stories (except 4:43–54), or they are inserted into the story itself as in John 11. The framework of the second part is provided by the passion narrative (chaps. 12–20), beginning with the anointing at Bethany and the entry into Jerusalem (12:1ff.) and ending with the death and burial of Jesus and the finding of the empty tomb (18:1–20:10). Into the passion narrative, the author has inserted the farewell discourses (13:31–17:26). The external frame of the entire gospel is a tripartite introduction consisting of the prologue, the testimony of John the Baptist, the calling of the disciples (1:1–51), and a tripartite conclusion consisting of the appearances of Jesus to Mary, to all disciples, and to Thomas (20:11–29). Thus the following schema of the composition emerges:

1:1–51 INTRODUCTION
    1:1–18 Prologue
    1:19–34 John the Baptist
    1:35–51 First disciples

    2:1–11:54 THE REVELATION TO THE WORLD (source: miracle stories)
        2:1–12 First Epiphany (Marriage Feast at Cana)
            2:13–25 First Jerusalem appearance (Cleansing of the Temple)
                3:1–21 Jesus and Nikodemus—**discourse**
                    3:22–4:3 Materials about the Baptist
                4:1–42 The Samaritan Women—**discourse**
                    4:43–54 Healing of the son of a royal officer
                6:1–7:13 Feeding of 5000 and Tempest—**discourse**
            5:1 + 7:14–52 Second Jerusalem appearance

5:2–47 Healing at the pool of Bethzatha—**discourse**
8:12–58 Materials consisting of short discourses
9:1–41 Healing of the blind man—**discourse**
10:1–39 **discourse** of the Good Shepherd
10:40–54 Second Epiphany (Raising of Lazarus)

11:55–19:42 THE REVELATION TO THE DISCIPLES (source: passion narrative)
    11:55–12:50 Anointing at Bethany and Entry into Jerusalem—**discourse**
    13:1–14:31 Last meal and original farewell **discourse**
    15:1–16:33 Second draft of farewell **discourse**
       17:1–26 Unedited Gnostic revelation speech (High-priestly prayer)
    18:1–19:42 Arrest, trial, death, and burial —(**discourse** with Pilate)

20:1–31 EPILOGUE
    20:1–18 Empty tomb and appearance to Mary of Magdala
    20:19–23 Appearance to the disciples
    20:24–29 Appearance to Thomas

The language of the Gospel of John is strikingly different from that of the other gospels. Terms missing or rare in the Synoptic Gospels are dominant in this gospel, while other terms that are overwhelmingly present in the former rarely occur in John's Gospel. The following comparison of some important terminology makes this quite clear:

John's special terminology

	Matt	Mark	Luke	John
love, to love (ἀγάπη, ἀγαπᾶν)	9	6	14	44
truth, true (ἀλήθεια, ἀληθής, ἀληθινός)	2	4	4	46
to know (γινώσκειν)	20	13	28	57
life (ζωή)	7	4	5	35
world (κόσμος)	8	2	3	67
witness (μαρτυρεῖν, μαρτυρία, μαρτύριον)	4	6	5	47
light (φῶς)	7	1	7	23
to believe (πιστεύειν)	11	10	9	102
kingdom (βασιλεία)	57	20	46	5
repentance, to repent (μετάνοια, μετανοεῖν)	7	3	14	0
prayer, to pray (προσευχή, προσεύχεσθαι)	19	13	22	0
gospel, to proclaim (εὐαγγέλιον, εὐαγγελίζεσθαι, κηρύσσειν)	14	19	19	0

The Gospel of John has its origin in a very different linguistic environment. This is already signaled in the prologue of the gospel (1:1–18), which speaks about the "Logos" as creator and savior in a hymn, which must have been at home in the Johannine churches. The author of the Gospel has added several comments to this hymn in order to make it more compatible with the message of his writing (1:8–6, 15; cf. 1:19–34; also 1:17; see 5:39–47; 9:28–29; 19:7). In the form in which this hymn was appropriated by the author of the gospel, it was certainly a hymn of John's community. But it is altogether dependent upon Jewish wisdom theology (§5.3e) although the term "wisdom" (*sophia*) has been replaced by the Greek term "word" (*logos*), which has also happened in the writings of the Jewish philosopher Philo of Alexandria under Greek influence. Like Wisdom, the Logos is preexistent with God, who creates the world through him. He appears in the world as the revealing light, is not understood, but gives to those who accept him the right to be called God's children. Up to this point nothing has been said that goes beyond the scope of wisdom theology. A typical Christian confession does not appear until 1:14 in the sentence about the Logos becoming flesh, and then in the praise of the glory of God that has appeared in the form of a human being, now formulated in the credal style of the first-person plural (1:14b, 16). These latter statements are undoubtedly Christian, although they also belong to the hymn that the author of the gospel is quoting here. The Johannine community has here appropriated concepts from Jewish wisdom theology, but it also confessed the incarnation of the heavenly Logos, thus repudiating a Gnostic understanding of the event of revelation, for which the radical rejection of the earthly and human sphere would have been the criterion of salvation. The anti-Gnostic stance, which appears in the hymn, is programmatic for the entire gospel, although the author frequently uses mythical language that is closely akin to the language of Gnosticism.

It is debated whether the description of the activity of John the Baptist (1:19–34) in the second part of the introduction of the gospel implies a polemic against still-existing circles of John's disciples. John 1:6–8, interpolated by the author into the hymn of the Logos, patently rejects the claim that John the Baptist is the savior; also 3:22–30 belongs to the polemic against Baptist circles. In any case, the tradition used in John's Gospel knew about conflicts between the two groups, Jesus' followers and the Baptist's followers, and also remembered that some of Jesus' disciples had come from among the disciples of the Baptist (1:35–42). Note also that the Gospel of John does not report Jesus' baptism! On the other hand, the primary interest of the entire section, including the report of the calling of the disciples, lies in a discussion of traditional titles of dignity for Jesus (Prophet, Messiah/Christ, Son of God, King of Israel; see 1:20–25, 34, 41, 49), in order to introduce the title that, provisionally, in addition to the title "Son," describes Jesus' divinity most adequately: the Son of Man (1:51).

The first major part of the gospel (chaps. 2–11) is composed in order to discuss traditional criteria for the recognition of the revelation. This discussion is introduced by the description of the peoples' reaction to the miracles of Jesus and in the criticism of Jesus by the "Jews." Criticism of the miracles and polemic against the Jews are, to be sure, topics already provided by the tradition. John, however, uses this tradition for the discussion of a more fundamental problem, namely, the dilemma of the visible documentation of divine presence that is easily accepted, because it confirms already existing religious desires and prejudices; or that is rejected, because it does not agree with preconceived theological criteria. Not only the rejection of the presence of revelation, but also its cheerful acceptance is seen by John as the judgment of the "world," which cannot listen to the word of the revealer. The "world" cannot understand that true revelation comes by words of the revealer and in an appearance of the revealer that does not agree with established and traditional religious criteria. This concept of revelation is derived from the Gnostic understanding that John has inherited from the sayings and dialogues of his tradition (§10.1b; 10.3a). According to this Gnostic concept, the word of the revealer can only be understood by those who are not "from the world" but "from God" (8:47) or "from the truth" (18:37). This Gnostic determinism, however, has been modified and, at the same time, radicalized in John's interpretation. First of all, not just the word of the revealer but also his very presence is an answer to a really existing human need, namely, to the question of true life that is at the basis of all quests of humanity. To this quest Jesus responds with the frequently repeated "I am" statements. These statements of the Johannine Jesus are not traditional but most likely designed by the author of the gospel, since they differ fundamentally from the "I am" statements in which divine figures introduce themselves with their name, their dignity, or their accomplishments. In contrast, in the Johannine formula Jesus states that here, in his presence, has come all that human beings ultimately want, hope for, and most deeply desire. This formula has therefore rightly been called a "recognition formula" because in the acceptance of Jesus' word and person the hearer recognizes the fulfillment of genuine human hope. The word of the revealer thus does not, as it would in Gnosticism, appeal to the ultimate—though still not yet realized—knowledge of divine identity of the hearer; rather it engages the yearnings and expectations that derive from human experience in the world.

The Gnostic concept is radicalized yet in another respect, namely, in the emphasis upon the fact that all this fulfillment is now present in the human person Jesus of Nazareth, and especially insofar as the full divine presence in the human Jesus comes to its consummation only in his suffering and death on the cross. At this point, the Gnostic schema of revelation has been altogether discredited. John has accomplished this by recourse to the church's proclamation of Jesus' suffering and death as the event of salvation and has applied it as the bracket to bind the two major parts of his work together. As early as John 2:18–22 the author refers to Jesus' death and resurrection as the key for the understanding of Jesus' ministry. The exaltation no longer designates, as it would in Gnosticism, the return of the revealer to his heavenly abode, untouched, as it were, by the sphere of earthly humanity; rather, his exaltation is identical with his death, the glorification on the cross (3:14; 8:28; 12:32–34). As this Johannine theology radically breaks with Gnosticism, it also contradicts the theology of the divine miracle worker. It is exactly the last and greatest miracle of Jesus, the raising of Lazarus, that is the immediate cause for the decision of the sanhedrin to put Jesus to death (11:46–52). The paradox of John's Gospel is evident at this very point. Jesus is drawn radically into the sphere of humanity but, at the same time, the hearer is challenged to recognize that exactly the word of this human Jesus is already the presence of judgment and life for those who are willing to risk to believe in Jesus. John's reinterpretation of the traditional future-oriented eschatology into a realized eschatology—passing through the final judgment and entering into eternal life can be obtained now by believing in Jesus' words—makes the claim of the presence of the revelation in the human Jesus even more paradoxical. This is further explored in the farewell discourses that John has inserted into the passion narrative.

John has thus split the passion narrative into two parts. The anointing in Bethany and the entry into Jerusalem (in this order! 12:1–8 and 12:9–19) precede the fare-well discourses (chaps. 13–17), which are set into the scene of the last supper—containing the unique foot-washing scene but not reporting any words of institution. This should not lead to the conclusion that John did not know, or that his commu-nity did not observe, the celebration of the Lord's supper. The terminology used in the discourses about the bread of life (6:26–65, without the vv. 51b–59) and about the vine (15:1–8) reveal a terminology that resembles the eucharistic prayers of the *Didache* (§10.1c). It is also probable that John deliberately avoided a materialistic understanding of the Eucharist as it appears in his younger contemporary, Ignatius of Antioch (§12.2d). He is concerned with "the bread that remains for eternal life, which the Son of Man gives" (6:27), namely, the words of Jesus (6:63).

The farewell discourses provide the basis for the understanding of the exaltation on the cross as the consummation of Jesus' work of revelation. As he goes back to the Father, so will his return as the Paraclete (NRSV: "Advocate") guarantee the lasting presence of the revelation in the community. John composed the farewell discourses, like the other discourses of his gospel, on the basis of older Gnostic interpretations of sayings and units of dialogue, which he recast into critical dis-cussions of Gnostic understandings of Jesus' words and, at the same time, of the futuristic understanding of the eschatology of the church. Gnostic theological con cepts appear frequently but especially in the last of these discourses in chapter 17, such as the emphasis that the disciples are "not from the world" (17:14) and the definition of eternal life as "recognition of the true God and his messenger" (17:3). Elsewhere, the criticism of the Gnostic concept of obtaining the kingdom of God by recognizing one's divine origin is more pronounced. In 14:1–14, this is rather plain by comparison with the parallel dialogue in *Dial. Sav.* 27–30 (§10.1b). John makes clear that "knowing the way" is not knowledge of oneself but believing in Jesus who says "I am the way, the truth, and the life," that "seeing the Father" is not a beatific vision but knowing Jesus, and that the works the disciples do are not the result of their own goodness but of believing and loving Jesus and thus doing the works that he does. Although Jesus came from the Father and is returning to him as he leaves the world (16:38, etc.), the disciples are not asked to follow him on this way (13:33) but they will remain in the world and he will return to them as the Paraclete or the "Spirit of Truth" to guide them in their sorrow, suffering, fear, and experience of the hostility of the world (13:36–38; 15:18–25; 16:20–24, 32–33). All the disciples are asked to do is to keep the "new commandment" to love each other, which will distinguish them from the world (13:34–35; 14:12, 15; 15:9–10).

The radicalization of the eschatological expectation is not only presented as an alternative to Gnosticism, it attacks also the apocalyptic concept of a future event of salvation. John insists upon demythologizing traditional eschatology. The parousia of Jesus after his exaltation is not an apocalyptic but an ecclesiological event as Jesus returns to the disciples as the spirit that is given to the church (14:15–17, 25–26; 15:26; 16:7–15). The Paraclete as the "Counselor," "Defender," also called the "Spirit of Truth," is originally an angelic figure, as shown by the texts of Qumran. In John, this angelic figure is identified with the parousia of Jesus as he becomes present again among the disciples. This parousia is not described in mythological terms as the apocalyptic conquest of the powers of evil, but as the response to the prayers of the community, which is continuing the earthly ministry of Jesus in its own work (14:12–14). Jesus has already conquered the world (16:33) and his ascension is nothing other than the assurance of peace for the community, not the beginning of the apocalyptic labor pains (14:27–31). If the disciples have sorrow as Jesus is leaving them, this only points forward to the clarity of understanding that they will achieve after Jesus has gone (16:16–24). Jesus will appear to the world as the exalted Lord, but only insofar as the obedience of the church to his commandments demonstrates to the world who Jesus really is (14:21–24). Through the fulfillment of the commandment of love the disciples are the witnesses for Jesus in the world as the Paraclete, through whom Jesus has returned, guides them in all they do and say (15:9–26). In this way the farewell discourses discuss all important topics of traditional eschatology. All that is conventionally expected to come to pass at some future time now defines the community in its present existence.

As is visible in the comparative chart above (§10.3a.4), in the Johannine version of the passion narrative, all elements that are clearly secondary in the Synoptic account are missing: the finding of the donkey in the preparation for the entry into Jerusalem (Mark 11:1b–6), the finding of the room for the Passover (Mark 14:12–16), the elaborate preparation of the betrayal of Judas (Mark 14:10–11; see also Matt 27:3–10), Jesus in Gethsemane (Mark 14:32–42; it is doubtful whether John 12:27 shows a knowledge of this story), Jesus before Herod (Luke 23:6–12), the two criminals (Luke 23:39–43), and the guard at the tomb (Matt 27:62–66). This confirms that John relies on a more original version of the passion narrative, which has also preserved the correct designation of the day of Jesus' crucifixion as the day before Passover (John 18:28) and the historically correct information that Jesus' last meal was not a Passover meal but a regular meal with bread and wine. The most important Johannine additions to the passion narrative appear in the trial of Jesus before Pilate (18:29–19:15). Only a few verses in this section derive from John's source (18:33, 39–40; 19:1–3, 13–14). Everything else has been composed by the author of the gospel. The scene does more than to absolve Pilate from all guilt in the death of Jesus. The tendency to shift responsibility from the Roman authority to the Jewish sanhedrin was most likely already present in John's source. The discourse of Pilate and Jesus contrasts for the last time Jesus as the revelation of divine truth with the "world," which is here represented by the world's governing authority, and demonstrates that a government is guilty when it wants to retreat to a neutral position in the confrontation with the "truth."

The three appearances of Jesus after his resurrection, to Mary, the disciples, and Thomas, form the conclusion of the gospel (20:11–29). They do not point forward to a future understood in terms of an apocalyptic expectation, nor to the parousia. Their message is instead that Jesus can no longer be grasped in human terms, that his presence and authority is now given to the disciples in the gift of the spirit, and that true faith is independent of "seeing." Easter, Pentecost, and parousia are thus one and the same event. It was left to the further development of the Johannine tradition to test whether this radical and ingenious new interpretation of traditional Christian concepts with the help of categories derived from Gnostic language could succeed or even survive.

(c) The Ecclesiastical Reception of the Johannine Tradition

The further developments show that the writing of the Gospel of John marked an important turning point in the history of the separated Johannine communities. The gospel itself, soon after its appearance, was subjected to a revision that moved it more closely to the theology of the majority of Syrian Christianity. This was done specifically through the recognition of the authority of the tradition in the name of Peter (John 21), and through the interpolation of a doctrine of the sacrament and eschatological views that were more in keeping with concepts of the Syrian churches.

(1) *The First Epistle of John* is an important witness for this development. Its author's theological position is still closely related to that of the author of the gospel. It may even be assumed that the author of this epistle was identical with the redactor of the gospel. In any case, the author belongs to what may be called the "school of St. John." The epistle is perhaps attested even earlier than the gospel (in Papias of Hierapolis; Eusebius *Hist. eccl.* 3.39.17). Its text is well preserved; the trinitarian section in 1 John 5:7–8, however, is an interpolation. It appears for the first time in late editions of the Vulgate and in a few very late Greek minuscules;

Bibliography to §10.3c.   Commentaries

C. H. Dodd, *The Johannine Epistles* (The Moffat New Testament Commentary; New York: Harper, 1946).

Rudolf Bultmann, *The Johannine Epistles: A Commentary on the Johannine Epistles* (Hermeneia; Philadelphia: Fortress, 1973).

Raymond E. Brown, *The Epistles of John: Translated with Introduction, Notes, and Commentary* (AB 30; Garden City, NY: Doubleday, 1982).

Georg Strecker, *The Johannine Letters: A Commentary on 1, 2, and 3 John* (Hermeneia; Minneapolis: Fortress, 1996).

François Vouga, *Die Johannesbriefe* (HNT 15/3; Tübingen: Mohr/Siebeck, 1990).

Rudolf Schnackenburg, *The Johannine Epistles: Introduction and Commentary* (New York: Crossroad, 1992).

Werner Vogler, *Die Briefe des Johannes* (ThHK 17; Leipzig: Evangelische Verlagsanstalt, 1993).

Bibliography to §10.3c: Bibliography and History of Scholarship

Johannes Beutler, "Die Johannesbriefe in der neuesten Literatur," *ANRW* 2.25.5 (1988) 3773–90.

Klaus Wengst, "Probleme der Johannesbriefe," *ANRW* 2.25.5 (1988) 3753–72.

Hans-Josef Klauck (ed.), *Die Johannesbriefe* (EdF 276; Darmstadt: Wissenschaftliche Buchgesellschaft, 1991).

Günter Wagner (ed.), *An Exegetical Bibliography of the New Testament,* vol. 3: *John and 1, 2, 3 John* (Macon, GA: Mercer University Press, 1987).

Bibliography to §10.3c (1):   Commentaries

Hans-Josef Klauck, *Der erste Johannesbrief* (EKKNT 23/1; Neukirchen-Vluyn: Neukirchener Verlag, 1991).

through the third edition of Erasmus's Greek New Testament (the first editions did not include the section) it made its way into many modern translations. The final section, 1 John 5:14–21, gives the impression of an appendix that was added later, after the conclusion in 5:13, though its language and content would still argue for the same author.

1 John is not a true letter—prescript and postscript are lacking—but a polemical treatise that seeks to intervene in the controversy about the interpretation of the Johannine tradition and the Gospel of John. Even if the author of that gospel had clearly distanced himself from Gnosticism, there is evidence (see below and §10.5b.3) that Gnostic theologians were quite comfortable in citing the gospel as a witness for their position. 1 John tries to draw a sharp line between those people and his own position and defines this line also in terms of ecclesiastical policy. He identifies the opponents as people who deny the validity of the creed of the community (1 John 4:2–3) and enters into a controversy with them. According to his characterization of the opponents, they must have been members of the Johannine circle (it is of no use to try to identify them with any one particular heretic known to later church fathers, such as Cerinthus), since they read the Gospel of John and appealed to it, claiming that the Jesus of that gospel fully supported their Gnostic theology. They boasted of their knowledge of God (2:4; 4:8), their love of God (4:20), their sinlessness (1:8–10), and their walking in the light (2:9). Like Jesus himself, they claimed to have come "from God" and to speak in the voice of the spirit (4:2–6). But they denied that Jesus had come in the flesh (4:2), and denied the identity of the heavenly Christ and the earthly Jesus (2:22).

The author of 1 John refutes this Gnostic foreshortening of the Johannine Gospel, to which he himself also appeals with good reason. He belongs to the same tradition, speaks the same language as the author of the gospel, and he states explicitly in the prologue of his writing (1 John 1:1–4), which paraphrases portions of the prologue of the gospel (John 1:1–18), that he has the gospel on his side. In agreement with the gospel, he argues that love of God without the love of brothers and sisters is impossible (1 John 4:16–17, 20); the special reference to almsgiving (3:17) reveals a pastoral motivation. It is exactly in the mutual love of the members of the community that victory over death and the entrance into a new life become a present reality (3:14). But if the presence of divine salvation can be documented

Bibliography to §10.3c (1):　Studies

C. H. Dodd, "The First Epistle of John and the Fourth Gospel," *BJRL* 21 (1937) 129–56.

Rudolf Bultmann, "Analyse des ersten Johannesbriefes," and "Die kirchliche Redaktion des ersten Johannesbriefes," in idem, *Exegetica,* 105–23 and 381–93.

Wolfgang Nauck, *Die Tradition und der Charakter des 1. Johannesbriefes* (WUNT 3; Tübingen: Mohr/Siebeck, 1957).

Herbert Braun, "Literatur-Analyse und theologische Schichtung im ersten Johannesbrief," in idem, *Studien,* 210–42.

Hans-Martin Schenke, "Determination und Ethik im 1. Johannesbrief," *ZThK* 60 (1963) 203–15.

Hans Conzelmann, "Was von Anfang an war," in *Neutestamentliche Studien für Rudolf Bultmann* (BZNW 21; Berlin: Töpelmann, 1954) 194–201.

Judith Lieu, *The Theology of the Johannine Epistles* (Cambridge: Cambridge University Press, 1991).

in the life of the community, it is also necessary to insist upon the identity of the Son of God with the earthly Jesus who came in "water" and "blood" (5:5–8; it is in this passage that the reference to the Trinity was later interpolated), which means that Jesus shared human experience from his baptism to his death. With his credal formula that Jesus came "in the flesh," however, the author does not quite recapture the meaning of the sentence in the gospel's prologue that "the Logos became flesh" (compare 1 John 4:2 with John 1:14).

1 John goes beyond a simple defense of the Gospel of John against a Gnostic interpretation; he expands Johannine theology by appropriating other concepts that were current in Syrian Christianity and also in the communities of the Pauline mission. Among these are the expectation of the parousia and the last judgment as future events (1 John 4:17; 3:2), as well as the coming of the "anti-Christ," which is turned against the Gnostic opponents (2:18, 22; 4:3). While the radical realized eschatology of the Gospel of John is here softened, the understanding of Jesus' death as a sacrifice for the expiation of sin (2:2; 4:10) and the concept of the purification through his blood (1:7) have no foundation in the Fourth Gospel, but correspond to a widespread understanding in the developing early catholic theology. 1 John not only emphasizes the necessity to forgive sins repeatedly (1:8–10), but also gives instructions in the form of a church order for such forgiveness (5:16–17) and warns of the seduction of the world (2:15–17). Clearly, the writer of this epistle is a church politician from the Johannine circles, who argues in his writing for the practical aspects of a continuation of the Johannine heritage. Through his efforts the Johannine tradition, and especially the Gospel of John, would eventually become acceptable to the church at large.

(2) *The Third Epistle of John.* The writings transmitted in the New Testament as 2 John and 3 John also belong to the Johannine circle, as is clearly shown by their language and theology. Both letters claim to be written by the "Presbyter" or "Elder," but only 3 John is a true letter. Various attempts have been made to reconstruct the situation to which this letter belongs, but the circumstances that prompted the writing of this letter are enigmatic. We do not know who the Elder was, nor the Gaius to whom he writes, nor Diotrephes whom the author accuses, nor the places where the Elder and Diotrephes resided. Since the Elder charges Diotrephes with love of power and lack of willingness to cooperate, but does not accuse him for any theological reasons (3 John 9–10), one must assume that the conflict was about matters of church organization or missionary activities. The

Bibliography to §10.3c (2 and 3):   Commentaries

Hans-Josef Klauck, *Der zweite und dritte Johannesbrief* (EKKNT 23/2; Neukirchen-Vluyn: Neukirchener Verlag, 1992).

Bibliography to §10.3c (2):   Studies

Ernst Käsemann, "Ketzer und Zeuge (zum johanneischen Verfasserproblem)," in idem, *Exegetische Versuche,* 1. 168–87.

Rudolf Schnackenburg, "Der Streit zwischen dem Verfasser des 3. Joh. und Diotrephes," *MThZ* 4 (1953) 18–26.

Abraham J. Malherbe, "Hospitality and Inhospitality in the Church," in idem, *Social Aspects of Early Christianity* (2d ed.; Philadelphia: Fortress, 1983) 92–112.

Elder seems to commission and supervise wandering missionaries, while Diotrephes (a bishop?) wants to maintain control over his own church and apparently
expels everyone who does not obey him. Was Diotrephes suspicious because the
Johannine tradition was too closely associated with wandering Gnostic apostles?
Perhaps the letter was written at a time when the Johannine communities had not
yet separated themselves clearly from their Gnostic friends.

(3) *The Second Epistle of John* was written later than 1 John and 3 John, because
it borrows from both writings. It is not a true letter, but a rather superficial compilation of Johannine sentences in the form of a catholic epistle; the "elect lady"
of 2 John 1 is the church in general. From the Third Epistle of John the author
of 2 John draws the title of the "Elder," and from the First Epistle he copies the
confession that Jesus Christ has come in the flesh (2 John 7), which he propagates
as right teaching (*didache*, 2 John 9–10). 2 John is important because it demonstrates how Johannine Christianity, following in the footsteps of 1 John, becomes
an advocate of anti-Gnostic theology.

(d) The Gnostic Inheritance of John

There are indeed attestations for a Gnostic continuation of the Johannine tradition, against which 1 John and 2 John struggled at the beginning of the 2d century.
Such writings, however, which were rejected by the church, have been preserved
only in fragmentary form or in later editions. The most important document is the
Acts of John, a history of the apostle John in the form of a romance. A number of
Greek manuscripts and translations have preserved various parts so that the reconstruction of anything like an original text, which might have been written some
time during the 2d century, is burdened with immense difficulties. Several pieces
may be assigned with some degree of certainty to this original *Acts of John,* or
identified as portions of sources used by the later author. The most significant
pieces are the so-called *Gospel Preaching of John* (chaps. 87–105) and a long hymn
(chaps. 94–96), which is the oldest tradition preserved in that section. This hymn

Bibliography to §10.3d: Text

Lipsius-Bonnet, *ActApostApoc,* 2.1. 151–216.

Eric Junod and Jean-Daniel Kaestli (eds.), *Acta Iohannis. 1. Praefatio-Textus; 2. Textus alii–
    commentarius–indices* (CChr.SA 1–2; Turnhout: Brepols, 1983).

Knut Schäferdiek and Ruairi ó hUiginn, "The Acts of John," in Schneemelcher, *NT Apoc.,* 2. 152–
    212.

Cameron, *Other Gospels,* 87–96.

Bibliography to §10.3d: Studies

Eric Junod and Jean-Daniel Kaestli, *L'histoire des actes apocryphes des apôtres du IIIe au IXe siècle:
    le cas des Actes de Jean* (Cahiers de la Revue de Théologie et de Philosophie 7; Geneva: Revue
    de Théologie et de Philosophie, 1982).

Karlmann Beyschlag, *Die verborgene Überlieferung von Christus* (München and Hamburg: Sieben-
    stern, 1969) 88–116.

Walther von Löwenich, *Das Johannesverständnis im zweiten Jahrhundert* (BZNW 13; Giessen:
    Töpelmann, 1932).

Richard I. Pervo, "Johaninne Trajectories in the *Acts of John,*" *Apocrypha* 3 (1992) 47–68.

Jan N. Bremmer (ed.), *The Apocryphal Acts of John* (Kampen: Pharos, 1995).

must once have been used in the Johannine community as a liturgical song with responses. Its terminology is closely related to the language of the prologue of the Gospel of John. In both instances the terms Father, Logos, grace, and spirit occur (94.1–2; note the trinitarian formula Father-Logos-Spirit at the end of the hymn, 96.51), as well as the contrast light/darkness (94.3) and a number of themes that are important elements in the Johannine discourses: house, place, way (95.21–22, 27; cf. John 14:2–6), door (95.26; cf. John 10:9). The sentence, "Who I am, you will recognize when I leave," is a fitting summary of the theme of the farewell discourses of John's Gospel. It is not certain that this hymn depends upon the text of the Fourth Gospel; references to the gospel's special interpretations are not evident, and it is not impossible that the hymn comes from Johannine circles whose materials the author of the gospel used. The basic Gnostic message of the hymn is evident, although an elaborate Gnostic mythology is missing. The revealer is not the one who he seems to be (96.39), but the believer recognizes himself in the person of the revealer: "If you follow my dance you will see yourself in me who is speaking" (96.28–29). This hymn is the prototype of the "Hymn of the Dance" that has become popular in American spirituality.

The docetism that appears in the hymn is further elaborated in the *Gospel Preaching of John*. It is a gospel that the author ("John") tells in the I-style (note the I-style in the *Gospel of Peter,* §10.2a). This section is clearly dependent upon the Gospel of John. In addition to such titles of Jesus as Logos, door, and way, which may be pre-Johannine, also "Resurrection," "Life," and "Truth" appear as well as a clear reference to the passion narrative of John (97; 101; cf. John 19:34). At the same time, other canonical gospels are used: Mark 1:16–20 for the calling of John, James, Peter, and Andrew; Mark 9:2–8 for the story of the transfiguration; and Luke 7:36 for the narrative of a meal. Like 1 John, this author also utilizes materials that were current in the circles of the early catholic church in Syria and Asia Minor. Moreover, the author identifies "John" with the son of Zebedee, the brother of James, and he accepts the transfer of the locale of John's activities to western Asia Minor. At the time this was written, probably late in the 2d century, both the ecclesiastical as well as the Gnostic traditions of John had moved well beyond the confines of its original Syrian home base.

The primary purpose of the gospel section of the *Acts of John* is the validation of docetism against ecclesiastical attacks upon Gnostic docetic christology. This is cast into a narrative of the earthly semblance of Jesus, who appears in constantly changing shapes, sometimes as a small boy, sometimes as a beautiful man, then again as bald-headed man with a long beard, while James perceives him as a youth with a pubescent beard; sometimes Jesus' body is soft or immaterial, in other instances it is as hard as a rock—and when he walks he leaves no footprints. While all this is extremely docetic but not necessarily "Gnostic," in the passion narrative the author emphasizes the difference between the heavenly Lord, who speaks with the voice of the revealer from the cross of light separating this world and the transcendent realms, and the earthly phantom that the people hung on the wooden cross. This extreme and certainly Gnostic docetism, which separates radically the divine Logos from the earthly shell Jesus in which he appears, still struggles with the bold statement of the Johannine prologue that the Logos became flesh. This struggle appears at the end of the passion narrative in the quotation of a formulated tradition: "recognize me as . . . the piercing of the Logos, the blood of the Logos, the wounding of the Logos, the hanging of the Logos, the death of the Logos. . . . First therefore recognize the Logos, then you will recognize the Lord, and third you will recognize the human being and its sufferings" (*Acts of John* 101).

By the end of the 2d century, John, the son of Zebedee, had received a new home in Ephesus, where also his tomb was placed, assimilating the traditions from the Synoptic Gospels and becoming identified with the John of Revelation. In the West, however, especially in Rome, John's letters and gospel were still debated at that time. On the other hand, Egyptian Christianity accepted John very early, and it must be assumed that Gnostic Christians were responsible for the introduction of John to Egypt, where the Gospel was fully at home in the second half of the 2d century. The first commentary on the Gospel of John—probably the first commentary ever written on any book of the New Testament—was written on the gospel's prologue (a fragment is quoted in Irenaeus *Adv. haer.* 1.8.5–6). It is a Gnostic document as is also the commentary on this gospel by the Valentinian Heracleon, of which fragments are quoted in Origen's *Commentary on John.* That the tradition of John lived on in Egypt is also evident in the *Apocryphon of John,* an Egyptian document preserved in the Nag Hammadi Library (see §10.5b.3).

4. Jewish Christianity

(a) The Fate of the Jerusalem Church

The term "Jewish Christianity" is problematic. All early apostles and missionaries of the new message of Jesus came from Israel, although not necessarily from those Palestinian circles that emerged as "rabbinic Judaism" after the destruction of the Temple; indeed, many like Barnabas and Paul and others came from the Greek-speaking diaspora. For all of them, the Scriptures of Israel, the law, and the prophets (only much later called the "Old Testament") were Holy Scripture, and

Bibliography to §10.4:   Text

A. F. J. Klijn and G. F. Reinink, *Patristic Evidence for Jewish-Christian Sects* (NovTSup 36; Leiden: Brill, 1973).

Bibliography to §10.4:   Studies

Jean Daniélou, *The Theology of Jewish Christianity* (Philadelphia: Westminster, 1965; reprint 1977).

Marcel Simon, *Verus Israel: Étude sur la relations entre chrétiens et juifs dans l'empire romain (133–425)* (Bibliothèque des écoles françaises d'Athènes et de Rome 166; Paris: Boccard, 1948).

Idem, *Recherches d'histoire Judó-Chrétienne* (EtJ 6; Paris: Mouton, 1962).

Hans-Joachim Schoeps, *Theologie und Geschichte des Judenchristentums* (Tübingen: Mohr/Siebeck, 1949).

Georg Strecker, "On the Problem of Jewish Christianity," in Bauer, *Orthodoxy and Heresy,* 241–85.

Gerd Luedemann, "The Successors of Pre-70 Jerusalem Christianity: A Critical Evaluation of the Pella Tradition," in Sanders, *Self-Definition 1,* 161–73.

Richard Bauckham, *Jude and the Relatives of Jesus in the Early Church* (Edinburgh: T&T Clark, 1990).

this Scripture as well as the tradition of its interpretation—both in its Palestinian form (attested in part in the early rabbinic Jewish materials) and in the diaspora version (present in Philo of Alexandria) provided the matrix, the categories, and the reference points for the understanding of the message from and about Jesus. The categories for the formation of theology and christology as well as the codes of moral conduct were formed here (see the Two Ways, §10.1c) and became binding also for the development of community structures. Moreover, the Scriptures of Israel would continue to determine later Christian theology and ethics for centuries to come, well into the present time. With very few exceptions, Christianity has never severed these roots and it will remain a religion with the legitimate claim to be a continuation of the religion of Israel. When one speaks of the phenomenon of Jewish Christianity in the narrower sense, one is dealing with a very special development within the formation of congregations of followers of Jesus, who interpreted the law of Moses in a fashion that was not shared by the majority of Gentile Christians.

Typical for what we shall call Jewish Christianity is the commitment to the ritual observance of the law of Moses, including circumcision and the purity and dietary laws. Such observance was characteristic of the Jerusalem community, and it first appears in the world of Gentile converts among the missionaries of Galatia, who are usually called today "Judaizers" (§9.1d, 3b). Specifically "Jewish-Christian" here referred to the acceptance of circumcision as well as the observance of other portions of the Mosaic law. Missionaries insisting upon such practice were found outside Jerusalem, which is demonstrated not only by Paul's letter to the Galatians (note also Philippians 3). It is difficult, however, to obtain any information about the formation of such Jewish-Christian communities for the early period other than the Pauline polemic against such propaganda. For a description of the beginnings of Jewish Christianity it is therefore advisable to begin with the community in Jerusalem.

Some information about this community is instructive because, at least at the time of Paul, it was committed to the observance of the ritual law of Israel, especially the law of circumcision. When Paul came to Jerusalem for his last visit, bringing the collection from the Gentile churches, the Jerusalem church was continuing its observance of the law and participated in the ritual of the Temple. Difficulties in the collection's delivery were related to this attitude of the Jerusalem church (§9.4b), which was then under the leadership of Jesus' brother James, who was the stalwart advocate for a continuing observance of the law. For a further development of such law-abiding Jewish Christianity, Jerusalem would without any doubt have played a leading role. Several events, however, prevented such a development. During a vacancy in the Roman procuratorship, James was murdered in Jerusalem in the year 62 CE, and the Jerusalem community left the city shortly before the beginning

Bibliography to §10.4a

Roy Bown Ward, "James of Jerusalem," *Restoration Quarterly* 16 (1973/74) 174–90.
Hans von Campenhausen, "Die Nachfolge des Jakobus," in idem, *Frühzeit*, 135–51.
Marcel Simon, "La Migration á Pella: Légende ou réalité?" in *Judéo-Christianisme: volume offert au Cardinal Jean Daniélou, = RechSR* 60 (1972) 37–54.

of the Jewish War (§8.3a). Eusebius says that a prophecy had prompted their emigration to Pella on the east side of the Jordan (*Hist. eccl.* 3.5.3). This recalls the prophetic sayings about the future coming of Jesus as the Son of Man, which have been incorporated into the final edition of the Sayings Gospel Q (§10.1a. 2 and 3), through which the followers of Jesus in Palestine distanced themselves from the propaganda that resulted in the Jewish War.

There are a few scattered pieces of information indicating that the Jerusalem community, now in exile east of the Jordan, continued to exist, but they do not permit a coherent picture to be drawn. It is said that Simeon, son of Clopas, a cousin of James and Jesus, was elected as James's successor (Eusebius *Hist. eccl.* 3.11.1). The community apparently wanted to stay with leaders who were descendants of David, as were Jesus and James (see "descended from David according to the flesh," Rom 1:3; also the genealogies of Matt 1:1–17; Luke 3:23–38). There is more information about relatives of Jesus in connection with the Jewish-Christian community. Eusebius reports Vespasian's search for descendants of the house of David (*Hist. eccl.* 3.21.1), and he produces a report from Hegesippus that says that Domitian arrested two grandnephews of Jesus, grandsons of his brother Judas, because they were from the house of David, and then released them when it appeared that, though Christian, they were nothing other than simple farmers (*Hist. eccl.* 3.19 and 3.20.1–7). Thus even in the later history of the church that had once been based in Jerusalem, members of Jesus' family may have played a part after the death of James and his cousin Simeon. But it is questionable whether there is any connection between the remnants of this community and the later history of Jewish Christianity. One would look therefore with some suspicion on Eusebius's report that Simeon's successor as bishop of Jerusalem was a convert named Justus and on the list of another fifteen names of Jerusalem bishops down to the time of Hadrian (*Hist. eccl.* 4.5).

The only possible relationship of later Jewish Christianity to the Jerusalem early church appears in the name *Ebionites* = "the poor," which some of these groups later used as a self-designation. One or several sects with this name were known in the 2d century CE. The church fathers were unable to understand this name. Paul, however, knows that the Jerusalem church of his time called itself "the poor" (Gal 2:10), and it is possible that they used this self-designation because they identified themselves with the elected poor, the people of God who were the recipients of the promises of the messianic time. It is therefore likely that the later Jewish-Christian Ebionites preserved a memory of their ultimate derivation from the Jerusalem community. On the other hand, there is no indication that these sects possessed traditions that were independent of, or older than, the writings and traditions of other Christian churches.

(b) Jewish Christianity as a Branch of the Development of the Catholic Church

(1) *The Jewish-Christian Gospels.* Among the important witnesses for Jewish Christianity are the so-called Jewish-Christian gospels, of which fragments are quoted by a number of church fathers. Sorting out these fragments and assigning

them to one or several pieces of literature has been bedeviled by the assumption that Jewish-Christian communities still preserved and used copies of the Aramaic original of the Gospel of Matthew. One source of this assumption was the report of Papias that Matthew had composed the sayings in Hebrew (Eusebius *Hist. eccl.* 3.29.16; see §10.2c). On the bases of this and other pieces of information Jerome produced the claim of only one Jewish-Christian gospel, assigned all known quotations of Jewish-Christian gospels to this one document, the "Gospel According to the Hebrews," identified it with the original Hebrew or Aramaic Matthew, and finally claimed that he himself had still found this gospel in use among some Christians in Syria. This hypothesis has survived into the modern period; but several critical studies have shown that it is untenable. First of all, the Gospel of Matthew is not a translation from Aramaic but was written in Greek on the basis of two Greek documents (Mark and the Sayings Gospel Q). Moreover, Jerome's claim that he himself saw a gospel in Aramaic that contained all the fragments that he assigned to it is not credible, nor is it believable that he translated the respective passages from Aramaic into Greek (and Latin), as he claims several times. Rather, Jerome found a number of these quotations in the writings of other church fathers (e.g., Origen and Eusebius) and arbitrarily assigned them to his "Gospel According to the Hebrews." It can be demonstrated that some of these quotations could never have existed in a Semitic language. Furthermore, it is impossible to assign all these quotations to one and the same writing. It is more likely that there were at least two, probably even three different Jewish-Christian gospels, of which only one existed in a Semitic language.

(2) *The Gospel of the Nazoreans.* A gospel in Aramaic or Syriac was in use among Jewish Christians in Syria as early as the 2d century in a group that called itself "Nazoreans." It is therefore best designated as the *Gospel of the Nazoreans*, since we do not know its actual name. Hegesippus, a 2d-century Palestinian

Bibliography to §10.4b (1)

Alfred Schmidtke, *Neue Fragmente und Untersuchungen zu den judenchristlichen Evangelien* (TU 37.1; Leipzig: Hinrichs, 1911).

Hans Waitz, "Judenchristliche Evangelien," in Edgar Hennecke (ed.), *Neutestamentliche Apocryphen* (2d ed.; Tübingen: Mohr/Siebeck, 1924) 17–55.

Idem, "Neue Untersuchungen über die sogenannten judenchristlichen Evangelien," *ZNW* 36 (1937) 60–81.

Philipp Vielhauer and Georg Strecker, "Jewish-Christian Gospels," in Schneemelcher, *NT Apoc.*, 1. 134–78.

R. McL. Wilson, "Jewish Christianity and Gnosticism," in *Judéo-Christianisme: volume offert au Cardinal Jean Daniélou,* = *RechSR* 60 (1972) 261–72.

A. F. J. Klijn, *Jewish-Christian Gospel Tradition* (VigChrSup 17; Leiden: Brill, 1992).

Bibliography to §10.4b (2):   Text

Erich Klostermann (ed.), *Apocrypha II: Evangelien* (KIT 8; 3d ed.; Berlin: de Gruyter, 1929) 5–15.
Schneemelcher, *NT Apoc.,* 1. 160–64.
Cameron, *Other Gospels,* 79–102.
Miller, *Complete Gospels,* 441–46.

Bibliography to §10.4b (2):   Studies

A. F. J. Klijn, "Das Hebräer- und das Nazoräerevangelium," *ANRW* 2.25.5 (1988) 3997–4033.

(probably of Jewish origin), from whose work Eusebius has preserved some fragments, is the first to report about that gospel (Eusebius, *Hist. eccl.* 4.22.8). It is
also independently attested by Eusebius and Epiphanius, and was probably the
only Jewish-Christian gospel that Jerome ever saw. Furthermore, textual readings
from this gospel have been preserved in marginal notes of a number of medieval
manuscripts of Matthew, all of which derive from a gospel edition made in
Jerusalem before 500 CE. An additional number of medieval quotations may also
be assigned to this *Gospel of the Nazoreans.* An investigation of the roughly thirty-
six passages and readings belonging to this gospel demonstrates that it was an
Aramaic translation of the Greek Gospel of Matthew. In the process of this translation, Matthew's text was repeatedly expanded, annotated, and illustrated, and new
materials were occasionally inserted. In each instance, however, the Greek text of
Matthew holds the priority. No heretical alterations can be identified in the *Gospel
of the Nazoreans,* which seems to have produced the entire text of Matthew, including the birth narrative. These Jewish Christians evidently did not deny the
divine birth of Jesus from the virgin Mary. On the contrary, they must have been
quite in agreement with the general development of early catholic theology—in
fact, they were dependent upon it. It is not known whether they used any other
New Testament writings in addition to their Aramaic translation of Matthew. But
nothing indicates that they maintained any special Jewish-Christian doctrines or
practices.

(3) *The Gospel of the Ebionites.* This Jewish-Christian gospel, from which quotations are preserved by Epiphanius, was a writing of a different character. Irenaeus
is the first to refer to this writing as the *Gospel of the Ebionites,* so named since it
was used by the sect of the Ebionites. Its actual name is not known, though it was
possibly called "Gospel of the Twelve." The Ebionites were Greek-speaking Jewish Christians, and their Gospel was written in Greek. It was composed on the
basis of both Matthew and Luke, and possibly also drew materials from Mark. In
some instances, the extant quotations show similarities to the gospel harmony of
the 2d-century apologist Justin Martyr (§12.3e). Insofar as the few preserved quotations permit a conclusion, there are no traces of extracanonical materials. This is
striking since the Ebionites were considered as a heretical Jewish-Christian group.
They are reported to have rejected the virgin birth, and their gospel therefore
omitted the birth narratives. They assumed that the spirit came down upon Jesus
and entered into him at his baptism—a concept that has parallels in Gnostic texts.
They rejected the sacrificial cult; in one of their sayings, Jesus said, "I have come
to do away with sacrifices, and if you do not cease to sacrifice the wrath of God

Bibliography to §10.4b (3):   Text

Erich Klostermann (ed.), *Apocrypha II: Evangelien* (KlT 8; 3d ed.; Berlin: de Gruyter, 1929) 5–15.
Schneemelcher, *NT Apoc.,* 1. 169–70.
Cameron, *Other Gospels,* 103–106.
Miller, *Complete Gospels,* 435–40.

Bibliography to §10.4b (3):   Studies

Georg Strecker, "Ebioniten," *RAC* 4. 487–500.
George Howard, "The Gospel of the Ebionites," *ANRW* 2.25.5 (1988) 4034–53.

shall not cease from you." They also practiced vegetarianism. Apart from the name "Ebionites," the position they assigned to the twelve apostles is also Jewish-Christian: they were elected as the representatives of the twelve tribes of Israel. Not much more can be learned from the extant fragments, nor do we know whether the Ebionites had any connections to other Jewish-Christian groups.

While these two Jewish-Christian gospels were at home in the area of Syria and Palestine, the third of these gospels, the so-called *Gospel of the Hebrews,* belongs to Egypt. Since there is no relationship between this and the other two Jewish-Christian gospels, it will be discussed below in the treatment of early Egyptian Christianity (§11.1c).

(c) The Fight against Paul

The preceding discussion of the Jewish-Christian gospels has shown the difficulties of finding signs of an independent Jewish-Christian tradition. Indeed, it seems to be the case that the formation of later Jewish Christianity did not have its roots in the continuing tradition of the Jerusalem church but was formed in a constant controversy with Gentile Christianity and its claims of freedom from law and circumcision—a controversy that began as early as the founding of the Pauline communities. Whatever survived of the Jerusalem community and of other independent Jewish communities of followers of Jesus was apparently absorbed by mainstream Gentile Christianity (see the story of the Sayings Gospel Q) or by the Gnostic movement (as the *Gospel of Thomas*) or by the later anti-Pauline, but Greek-speaking Jewish Christian groups.

(1) *The Judaizers.* The effort to defend the law, especially its ritual observances and circumcision, was triggered by Paul's proclamation of freedom from the law. The challenge was that it was necessary to compete with Paul in the mission to the Gentiles. The agreement that Paul had reached with the Jerusalem authorities at the Apostolic Council may have seemed satisfactory at the time. If the Lord was expected to come soon, Peter could proclaim the gospel to the Jews, while Paul would go to the Gentiles, and there should be no reason that they would get into each other's way—which, however, happened soon thereafter in Antioch (§9.2a). Moreover, there were the people in Jerusalem, whom Paul calls "the false brothers" (Gal 2:4), who apparently insisted that all of Israel, including all converted Gentiles, should be circumcised so that they could enjoy fully the benefits that the observance of the law would bring to its adherents. Whether this Jerusalem group, who disagreed with both James and Paul, was identical with those who began to preach circumcision in the Pauline churches, or whether they only referred to them as their authority, the Jewish-Christian mission in Galatia and in Philippi was an anti-Pauline movement. It was, however, a missionary movement, directed to the conversion of the Gentiles, and it fully belongs in the Greek-speaking world of Rome.

Bibliography to §10.4c

Gerd Lüdemann, *Paulus der Heidenapostel.* Band II: *Antipaulinismus im frühen Christentum* (FRLANT 130; Göttingen: Vandenhoeck & Ruprecht, 1983).

Paul's refutation of the so-called Judaizers did not do away with this movement. In the Letter to the Colossians, a student of Paul issued a general warning regarding dangers of Jewish practices. He pictures a Jewish-Christian propaganda with thoroughly syncretistic features, namely, observation of the Jewish festivals and dietary regulations as instruments of initiation into the cosmic realities (§12.2a). Somewhat later Ignatius of Antioch, writing to churches in western Asia Minor, attacks "Judaizers" as well as Gnostics (or docetists) in such a way that it is not clear whether he addresses two separate groups or just one single group (§12.2d). Ignatius refers to the fact that his opponents appeal to the "Archives" (= the Scriptures) as authorities (*Phld.* 8) and acknowledges that their arguments might impress many Christians much more than his own Paulinism, which stands at a considerable distance from the Scriptures of Israel and their interpretation. Around the year 100, a teacher with the name of Cerinthus was active in Asia Minor; he advocated a Gnostic-type teaching, but seems to have been a Jewish Christian who insisted upon circumcision. However uncertain the scanty available information about Cerinthus may be, the Jewish Christianity that appears in all these witnesses must have been a syncretistic phenomenon, in which speculative interpretation of the law went hand in hand with insistence upon the ritual law. It is not unlikely that the opponents of the Book of Revelation also belong here; see especially such references as "those of the synagogue of Satan who say that they are Jews and are not" (Rev 3:9; see further §12.1c).

(2) *The Book of Elkasai.* All these scattered references belong to Asia Minor and show that a syncretistic Judaizing missionary movement was here competing with the heirs of the message of Paul. But Syria remained the home of Jewish Christianity. Jewish Christians could still be found here in the early Byzantine period. One of the important witnesses for the formation of Jewish Christian groups in Syria is the *Book of Elkasai*. This book, whose author called himself Elkasai (="Power of God") and appeared in the year 101 CE (according to his own statement in the third year of Trajan), is preserved in fragments by Hippolytus and Epiphanius. The sect founded by Elkasai is attested several times during the following centuries, but received little attention until the recent publication of an autobiography of Mani, the founder of the Gnostic world religion of Manichaeism. This writing reveals that Mani's parents were Elkasaites and that he himself received his first religious impressions as a member of this sect. This assigns a special significance to Syrian Jewish Christianity in general and to Elkasai in particular.

The extant fragments of the book testify to a renewal of apocalyptic prophecy. The eruption of a battle of godless angelic powers of the north is predicted for the third year after Trajan's Persian campaign. Elkasai, as did the *Shepherd of Hermas* (§12.1d), connects with his message the announcement of a second repentance, but also the granting of a second baptism for the forgiveness of sins. The book's primary

Bibliography to §10.4c (2):   Text

Johannes Irmscher, "The Book of Elchasai," in Schneemelcher, *NT Apoc.*, 2. 685–90.

Bibliography to §10.4c (2):   Studies

Hans Waitz, "Das Buch Elchasai," in *Festgabe von Fachgenossen und Freunden Adolf von Harnack zum siebzigsten Geburtstag dargebracht* (Tübingen: Mohr/Siebeck, 1921) 87–104.

concern was the preservation of cultic purity through precepts that rely on scriptural law and emphasize the necessity of repeated baths for purification. Syncretistic elements are evident in such rites as the invocation of the "seven witnesses" (heaven, water, holy spirits, angels of prayer, oil, salt, and earth) and the warnings of evil stars and of the moon, which reveal cosmic speculations. The command to turn one's face toward Jerusalem in prayer shows Jewish influence. Elkasai is connected with the Ebionites in his rejection of sacrificial rites. Typical for the development of heretical Jewish Christianity is also the distinction between true and false pericopes of Scripture, use of the canonical gospels, and rejection of the letters of Paul (attested for the Elkasaites by Origen in Eusebius *Hist. eccl.* 6.38). The same characteristics are found again in the most important testimony for Jewish Christianity in Syria, the Jewish-Christian sources of the *Pseudo-Clementines.*

(3) *The Pseudo-Clementines and the Kerygmata Petrou.* The *Pseudo-Clementines* is a romance centering around Clement of Rome. The story tells of his religious development, especially his experiences as a disciple of Peter, whom he accompanied on his missionary journeys. The romance is preserved in two recensions, the Greek *Homilies* and the Latin *Recognitions,* which were both written in the 4th century CE. Their common source, which is lost, must have been composed early in the 3d century. Unquestionably this source in turn used extensive earlier written materials, but there is no agreement in scholarship about their character and extent. Nevertheless, some probability can be assigned to the identification of one of these sources, the *Kerygmata Petrou,* which can be dated to the 2d century. This hypothesis is the most plausible explanation for the appearance of large sections in the *Pseudo-Clementines,* of which the Jewish-Christian character is totally obvious. These *Kerygmata Petrou* consist of Peter's letter to James of Jerusalem, a "Contestatio" (James's testimony about the recipients of the letter), and lectures and debates of Peter. Though distinguished by their Jewish-Christian commitment, the *Kerygmata Petrou* depend upon the general tradition of the Syrian church, especially in their appeal to the authority of Peter and their use of the Gospel of Matthew (some quotations seem to come from a gospel harmony related to that of Justin Martyr).

Laying claim on the authority of Peter for a law-abiding Christianity is a most important phenomenon. In several ways, this claim is prefigured by the Gospel of

Bibliography to §10.4c (3):   Text

Bernhard Rehm (Georg Strecker) (ed.), *Die Pseudoklementinen,* vol. 1: *Homilien* (GCS; 3d ed.; Berlin: Akademie-Verlag, 1992).

Johannes Irmscher and Georg Strecker, "The Pseudo-Clementines," in Schneemelcher, *NT Apoc.,* 2. 483–541.

Betz, *Galatians,* 331–33 (English translation of the Epistle of Peter to James and of parts of *Ps. Clem. Hom.* 11 and 13).

Bibliography to §10.4c (3):   Studies

Georg Strecker, *Das Judentum in den Pseudoklementinen* (TU 70; Berlin: Akademie-Verlag, 1958).

A. Salles, "La diatribe antipaulinienne dans le 'Roman pseudoclémentin' et l'origin des 'Kerygmes de Pierre,'" *RB* 64 (1957) 516.

Oscar Cullmann, "Die neuentdeckten Qumrantexte und das Judenchristentum der Pseudoklementinen," in idem, *Vorträge 1926–1962,* 241–59.

Matthew, where it is also Peter who is the rock on whose tradition a law-abiding church is built, and where Gentile missionaries who do not obey the law are rejected. The *Kerygmata Petrou* go a step beyond Matthew in denying the right of an appeal to Peter for those who assert that Peter was Paul's successor in the Gentile mission free from the law (§12.2f). Although it is recognized that Peter indeed followed Paul in the Gentile mission, the theory that the second in any pair of two is always the superior one (see below on the teaching of the syzygies) establishes Peter's precedence. Peter is always presented as the champion of a law-abiding mission to the Gentiles, which is thus superior to Paul's mission. The *Kerygmata Petrou* explicitly rejects the idea that Peter could ever have taught the abolishment of the law. Peter's true teaching, which is recorded in his lectures, is thus submitted to James of Jerusalem in Peter's letter, and in the "Contestatio" it is formally approved by James. James is the undoubted authority for a law-abiding Christianity. The appeal to James is described as an act of legal ecclesiastical sanction (this is not a novelistic motif). In the lectures and debates of Peter, it is Paul who is actually attacked whenever Peter refutes Simon Magus. The doctrine of the law that is held against Paul is thoroughly Jewish, especially in its emphasis upon ritual rules of purification—an element that is missing in Matthew's teaching about the continuing validity of the law—and while Matthew never explicitly names Moses or connects Jesus with Moses, the *Kerygmata Petrou* conjoin Moses and Christ in such a way that they both appear as revelations of the true prophet. The "gnosis" that is mediated through Jesus is presented as identical with the law of Moses. There are, however, false pericopes that have been interpolated into the Scriptures of Israel, since Moses did not write the law himself, and the Jews did not always prove reliable in their transmission. But from the true prophet as he appeared in Jesus one can learn to identify the true pericopes.

This concept of the repeated incarnation of the true prophet shows some relationship to Gnostic teaching, which becomes even more obvious in the *Kerygmata's* teaching of the syzygies. In the creation of the world and of human beings in pairs, the first member of the pair is always the stronger one (heaven and earth, man and woman). But in the history of humankind, which also proceeds in syzygies, the inferior members always come first. This is demonstrated in the pairs from Cain and Abel to Paul and Peter. In this explanation of the world and of history, the universalistic claims of the *Kerygmata's* Jewish Christianity appear in their clearest form. The law is not just a prescription of certain rituals and observances; rather, it is the critical principle through which the revelation and the universe can be better understood than through the preaching of Paul, who has foolishly thrown away the right to appeal to either the law or the teachings of Jesus.

5. Syria, the Country of Origin of Christian Gnosticism

(a) Summary of Previous Observations

In the course of the discussion of the development of early Christianity in Syria, it was necessary to refer repeatedly to Gnosticism. Gnostic concepts, terms, hymns, and sayings traditions have been mentioned frequently. Not to do so would make the history of early Christianity in Syria an impenetrable puzzle. To portray the history of Syrian Gnosticism in its own right, however, is burdened with difficulties. The definition of "Gnosticism" is debated anyway. The term has been used here for a particular phenomenon that is characterized by the discovery of the divine self in the individual and, at the same time, a radical rejection not only of the "world" in all its physical realities, but also of the body, the social fabric of the society, and of all its institutions—regardless of the presence or absence of any elaborate Gnostic mythology (see also §6.5f). Such Gnostic tendencies do not appear as independent movements; rather they are part of a process of interpretation of biblical materials, traditions, and sayings. As such they are visible in the spiritualizing of realized eschatology, denial of the earthly and physical reality of the appearance of the revelation, and the lack of interest in building viable community structures.

The history of Gnosticism in its early stages during the period of early Christianity cannot be written as the history of a tangible sociological phenomenon. "Gnostic churches" with a membership that was clearly distinguished from the early catholic churches or from Jewish-Christian churches never existed. Where communities with incipient organizational structures began to be developed, they were repeatedly disturbed or altered by wandering charismatics. Such wandering charismatics would not necessarily identify themselves as followers of Jesus. Among them the most famous and most notorious was Simon Magus, a Samaritan and contemporary of the apostles, who worked in Syria and Palestine and came to Rome at the time of the emperor Claudius (41–54 CE). Although most of the information about him is problematic because it comes from Christian authors (see especially Acts 8:9–25; Justin *1 Apol.* 26.1–3; Irenaeus, *Adv. haer.* 1.23.1–4) who presented him as the father of all heretics, often relying on data drawn from Simon's students and followers, it is still evident that Simon was a representative of an early pre-Christian Gnosticism of the Syrian type. Worshiped as the first god or as the supreme power by his followers, he called himself "he who stands," thus describing the unshakable presence of the divine world in his own person. As a charismatic preacher, he traveled together with a woman called Helena, whom he allegedly bought from a brothel in Tyre and in whom he found the persecuted "first

Bibliography for §10.5a: Text

Völker, *Quellen,* 1–11 (Latin and Greek Texts about Simon Magus).
"Simon and Menander," in Foerster, *Gnosis,* 1. 27–33 (Texts about Simon Magus in English translation with Introduction).
John D. Turner, "The Book of Thomas the Contender (II,7)," *NagHamLibEngl,* 188–94.
Idem, "The Book of Thomas the Contender," in Layton, *Nag Hammadi Codex II,* vol. 2.
Idem, *The Book of Thomas the Contender* (Missoula MT: Scholars Press, 1975).

Bibliography for §10.5a: Studies

Karlmann Beyschlag, *Simon Magus und die christliche Gnosis* (WUNT 16; Tübingen: Mohr/ Siebeck, 1974).
Gerd Lüdemann, *Untersuchungen zur simonianischen Gnosis* (Göttingen: Vandenhoeck & Ruprecht, 1975).
Kurt Rudolph, "Simon – Magus oder Gnosticus? Zum Stand der Debatte," *ThR* NF 42 (1977) 279–359.

thought" (*ennoia*), who had to be liberated from her captivity in ever-changing bodies, beginning with Helen of Troy. The Simonian Gnosticism that was developed by Simon's students incorporated many Christian elements—a typical example of the syncretistic milieu in which Gnosticism developed.

The names of various apostles guaranteed the authority of particular traditions, but the challenge was their interpretation and reformulation. Continuity in a theological position was by no means a matter of course. This was most clearly visible in the history of the traditions under the name of the apostle "John" (§10.3a–d). The history of Gnosticism was part of such developments and can therefore be described only as the history of particular tendencies and aims that appear in the interpretation of traditional materials. Gnosticism is a hermeneutic principle in the process of interpretation.

In the tradition of the sayings of Jesus, Gnosticism appears in the emphasis upon wisdom sayings and the spiritualizing of eschatological sayings. The *Gospel of Thomas* offers such interpretation under the authority of the apostle Thomas, a tradition that continued under the name of this apostle in communities of Syria. In the early 2d century this is evident in the *Book of Thomas* (NHC II, 7; falsely often called the *Book of Thomas the Contender*). A hundred years later the same tradition reappears in the *Acts of Thomas,* which continues this same Syrian Thomas tradition but also draws the aretalogical tradition of the apostles' miraculous deeds into the process of Gnostic interpretation: individual miracle stories become descriptions of the encounter of the heavenly world and its messenger with the lower world of demons and transitoriness. Within the circle of the Johannine churches, Gnostic interpretation was again tied to the sayings of Jesus, which were used for the development of dialogues in which Jesus speaks about the presence of eschatological salvation, mediated through himself as he has come from the Father who resides in the home to which all shall return if they can hear his voice. The hymn, used by the author of the Gospel of John for the prologue, demonstrates the intimate connection between the myth of Wisdom and the Gnostic understanding of revelation. A fully developed Gnostic christology, however, does not appear until later among the opponents of 1 John and in the *Acts of John,* where it took shape in an explicit controversy with the Gospel's attempt to bind the concept of the heavenly revealer to the kerygma of the suffering and death of the earthly Jesus.

The history of Jewish Christianity again indicates how viable Gnosticism was as a possibility of interpretation within the tradition of Christian (or Jewish) communities. To be sure, that the opponents in Galatia were "Gnostics" can be doubted with good reason. Nevertheless, they ascribed a cosmic dimension to the power of the law, and the perfection preached by the Judaizing opponents of Philippians 3 has obvious Gnostic overtones. It was especially in their christology that Jewish Christians used mythological constructs that are unequivocally Gnostic. This is the case when the *Gospel of the Ebionites* speaks of the descent of the "person" of the spirit and of his unification with Jesus in baptism. The *Kerygmata Petrou,* in order to defend the lasting validity of the law, used the Gnostic concepts of the repeated manifestations of the heavenly figure of the true prophet and distinguished between true and false pericopes in the law, a distinction that later appears in the Gnostic *Letter to Flora* by Valentinus's student Ptolemy. The appearance of Gnostic ideas

Page from Codex II of the Nag Hammadi Library

Page 97 of Codex II shows the beginning of the *Hypostasis of the Archons* (note the colophon in the lower middle of the page) and the ending of the *Gospel of Philip*. The last line of the text of the *Gospel of Philip* is filled up with a decoration.

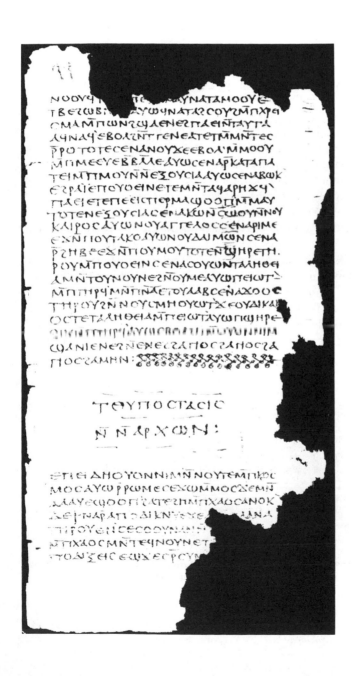

in Jewish Christianity in Syria is one factor among others that has led to the suggestion that roots of Gnostic thought might be found in heretical Judaism. A suitable milieu for the development of Jewish Gnosticism was the area of Palestine and Syria. Investigation of the texts from the Nag Hammadi Library tends to support this assumption. Some of these texts, though found in Egypt, originated in Syria, and they show that Gnosticism owed much to Jewish influence.

(b) The Texts from Nag Hammadi and Syrian Gnosticism.

The first chapters of the biblical Book of Genesis played a decisive role in the development of Gnostic cosmogonies. Allusions to the biblical story of creation are found even in the pagan Gnosis of the tractate *Poimandres* of the *Corpus Hermeticum* (§6.5f). Alongside this interest in the biblical creation story, these texts are preoccupied with the primeval figures of Genesis. This once more moves the origins of Gnosticism into the close neighborhood of Jewish apocalypticism that flourished in Palestine up to the end of the 1st century CE (§§5.3c and 6.6f), especially with respect to the topic of chaos and creation. It is quite apparent that several of the writings from Nag Hammadi drew much of their inspiration and some of their materials from Jewish sources in Palestine, which includes some writings that occasionally exhibit Christian features.

(1) Christian features are completely lacking in the *Apocalypse of Adam* (NHC V, 5). Its basis is an apocalyptic interpretation of the stories of Adam, Seth, and Noah. Just before Adam's death, Seth receives the knowledge of the future from his father in the form of a testament. This Jewish apocalypse has then been revised by a Gnostic interpreter so that it speaks, in its extant form, about the repeated acts of salvation for the children of the true transcendent God, or of the coming of the "illuminator of knowledge" (76, 9–10), who is recognized solely by the generation without a king (82, 19–20). This illuminator is a typical Gnostic

Bibliography for §10.5b: Texts

James M. Robinson (ed.), *The Nag Hammadi Library in English* (3d ed.; San Francisco: Harper & Row, 1988).

Bibliography for §10.5b: Studies

Layton, *Rediscovery of Gnosticism,* vol. 2: *Sethian Gnosticism.*

Birger A. Pearson, "The Problem of 'Jewish Gnostic' Literature," in Hedrick and Hodgson, *Nag Hammadi,* 15–35.

John D. Turner, "Sethian Gnosticism: A Literary History," ibid., 55–86.

Stephen Gero, "With Walter Bauer on the Tigris: Encratite Orthodoxy and Libertine Heresy in Syro-Mesopotamian Christianity," ibid., 287–307.

Gedaliahu Stroumsa, *Another Seed: Studies in Gnostic Mythology* (NHS 24; Leiden: Brill, 1984).

Alexander Böhlig, *Mysterium und Wahrheit* (Leiden: Brill, 1968) 80–111, 149–61.

Carsten Colpe, "Heidnische, jüdische und christliche Überlieferung in den Schriften von Nag Hammadi," *JAC* 15 (1972) 5–18; 16 (1973) 106–26; and in subsequent volumes.

Bibliography for §10.5b: Survey and Bibliography

George MacRae, "Nag Hammadi," *IDBSup* (1976) 613–19.

David M. Scholer, *The Nag Hammadi Bibliography 1948–1968* (NHS 1; Leiden: Brill, 1971); idem, *The Nag Hammadi Bibliography 1970–1994* (Leiden: Brill, 1997).

redeemer figure. Through him those who are redeemed receive "the words of im-perishability and truth" (83, 13–14). The community from which this writing orig-inated apparently practiced baptism with water, which was understood as rebirth through the word (84, 24ff.). Since this book contains no reference to specific Christian names, themes, or traditions, it should be assigned to a Gnostic baptismal sect with Jewish roots. Seth is the recipient of the revelation, which classifies this writing as a representative of "Sethian Gnosticism" and argues strongly for the Jewish roots of this type of Gnostic religion. It is likely that other Gnostic tractates of the Sethian type derive from Syria or Palestine, especially those which show no Christian influence, such as *Zostrianus* (NHC VIII, 1) and *The Three Steles of Seth* (NHC VII, 5).

(2) *The Hypostasis of the Archons,* better designated as *The Reality of the Rulers* (NHC II, 4) belongs in this context, since it also contains references to Sethian

Bibliography for §10.5b (1):   Text

George MacRae, "NHC V,5: The Apocalypse of Adam," in Douglas M. Parrott (ed.), *Nag Hammadi Codex V,2–5 and VI with Papyrus Berolinensis 8502, 1–4* (NHS 11, Leiden: Brill, 1979) 151–95.

Françoise Morard, *L'Apocalypse d'Adam (NH V,5): Texte etabli et présenté* (BCNH.ST 15; Quebec: Laval University Press, 1985).

Alexander Böhlig, *Koptisch-gnostische Apokalypsen aus Kodex V von Nag Hammadi* (Wissenschaft-liche Zeitschrift der Martin-Luther-Universität, Sonderband; Halle-Wittenberg, 1963).

George W. MacRae and Douglas M. Parrott, "The Apocalypse of Adam (V,5)," in *NagHamLibEngl,* 277–286.

Layton, *Gnostic Scriptures,* 52–64 *(The Elevation of Adam).*

"The Apocalypse of Adam," in Foerster, *Gnosis,* 2. 13–23.

Bibliography for §10.5b (1):   Studies

George MacRae, "The Coptic Gnostic Apocalypse of Adam" *HeyJ* 6 (1965) 27–35.

Charles W. Hedrick, *The Apocalypse of Adam: A Literary and Source Analysis* (SBLDS 46; Chico, CA: Scholars Press, 1980).

Andrew J. Welburn, "Iranian Prophetology and the Birth of the Messiah: The Apocalypse of Adam," *ANRW* 2.25.6 (1988) 4752–94.

Luther H. Martin, "Genealogy and Sociology in the Apocalypse of Adam," in Goehring, *Gnosticism,* 25–36.

Bibliography for §10.5b (2):   Text

Bentley Layton and Roger A. Bullard, "The Hypostasis of the Archons," in Layton, *Nag Hammadi Codex II,* 220–59.

Bentley Layton, "The Hypostasis of the Archons or the Reality of the Rulers . . . edited . . . with a Preface, English Translation, Notes, Indices," *HTR* 67 (1974) 351–425; 69 (1976) 31–101.

Peter Nagel, *Das Wesen der Archonten aus Codex II der gnostischen Bibliothek von Nag Hammadi* (Wissenschaftliche Beiträge 1970/6; Halle: Martin-Luther Universität, 1970).

Bernard Barc, *L'Hypostase des Archontes (NH II,4)* (BCNH.ST 5; Quebec: Laval University Press, 1980) 1–147.

Roger A. Bullard and Bentley Layton, "The Hypostasis of the Archons (II,4)," in *NagHamLibEngl,* 161–169.

Layton, *Gnostic Scriptures,* 65–76 *(The Reality of the Rulers).*

"The Hypostasis of the Archons," in Foerster, *Gnosis,* 2. 40–52.

Bibliography for §10.5b (2):   Studies

Karen L. King, "Ridicule and Rape, Rule and Rebellion: The Hypostasis of the Archons," in Goehring, *Gnosticism,* 3–24.

speculations. In its extant form, it has received a secondary Christian framework, possibly at a later date, once it had been brought to Egypt in the 2d or 3d century CE. This later introduction quotes "the great apostle" (=Paul; Col 1:13; Eph 6:12; cf., *Hyp. Arch.* 86, 21–25), and the conclusion (97, 17ff.) alludes to Christian concepts of salvation. Apart from this secondary framework, the writing altogether lacks Christian elements. The first part (87, 11–93, 2) presents a Gnostic exegesis of Genesis 1–6, which often quotes biblical texts verbatim. Its purpose is to show that Adam and Eve actually belong to the heavenly world, while only their forms of earthly semblance are under the power of the evil rulers. These earthly semblances are driven out of paradise by the rulers and tortured by the flood. But Seth and his sister Norea, "the man through God" and "the virgin whom the forces did not defile," arise as the incorporation of the heavenly true "human being" (*anthropos*) and the prototypes of salvation (91, 30–92, 3). The second part of the book is a discourse of the heavenly angel Eleleth with Norea—a later addition to the Genesis interpretation of the first part (92, 3–96, 17). It is a narrative of the Gnostic myth of the fall of Sophia. Even if this second part were of Christian origin, it reflects the milieu of a Semitic language. The names of the evil creator Samael ("god of the blind"), Sakla ("fool"), and Yaldabaoth ("the one born from chaos") are all Semitic, and Sabaoth certainly has its origin in the Bible. A direct connection to Jewish exegesis is evident in the name "Norea"; it is an artificial fabrication from the first letter of the Hebrew name *Na'ama* (Gen 4:22) and the Greek equivalent in the Septuagint *oreia* (=beautiful).

(3) *The Apocryphon of John.* In some cases Gnostic writings are transmitted under an apostolic name, which may indicate the conscious resumption of a particular apostolic tradition. This is apparently the case with the *Apocryphon of John,* a work that also belongs to Sethian Gnosticism. Since it was known to Irenaeus, it was composed no later than the middle of the 2d century CE. The work is preserved in two shorter (NHC III, 1; BG 8502, 2) and two longer versions (NHC II, 1; IV, 1). The introduction reports the appearance of Jesus to John, in which Jesus first looks like a youth, then again like an old man, which is reminiscent of the *Acts of John* (§10.3d), and is in any case not unique in Gnostic literature. The content of the work is a coherent narrative of the fall of Sophia, the creation of the lower world by Yaldabaoth, including the creation of the human race, and the final salvation through Christ, which is accomplished through his descent to the lower world, even to Hades, and through his call. The writing draws on an abundance of materials from Jewish apocalypticism and angelology, a number of mythological names (often no longer understood and hence distorted), and mythological and astrological

Bibliography for §10.5b (3): Texts

Martin Krause and Pahor Labib, *Die drei Versionen des Apokryphon des Johannes im Koptischen Museum zu Alt-Kairo* (ADAI.K 1; Wiesbaden: Harrassowitz, 1962).

Michael Waldstein and Frederik Wisse, *The Apocryphon of John: Synopsis of Nag Hammadi Codices II,1; III,1; and IV,1 with BG 8502,2* (NHMS 33; Leiden: Brill, 1995).

Frederick Wisse, "The Apocryphon of John (II,1, III,1, IV,1" BG 8502,2) in *NagHamLibEngl,* 104–123.

Layton, *Gnostic Scriptures,* 23–51 *(The Secret Book According to John).*

lists, which must have found their way into this Gnostic document and its mythology via Judaism. Citation and exegesis of the first chapters of Genesis again play an important role. But despite the name "John," nothing points to a continuation of the tradition of the Johannine communities. The popularity, however, of the Gospel of John among later Gnostic writers may indicate the path by which Syrian Gnostics once took these materials under apostolic authority, together with the Gospel of John itself to Egypt at an early date in the 2d century. (see also §11.1b).

(4) *The First and Second Apocalypse of James.* These two writings from the Nag Hammadi Library continue the tradition of Jewish-Christian Gnosticism from Syria. The appearance of the name of Jesus' brother James as an authority for Gnostic writings is intriguing. Even more indicative of the close relationship of Jewish Christianity and Gnosticism is the connection of the names of James and Peter in another Gnostic writing from Nag Hammadi, the *Apocryphon of James* (also called the *Epistula Jacobi,* NHC I, 2). The *First Apocalypse of James* (NHC V, 3) introduces James the brother of Jesus as the recipient of a revelation of the "Lord" (addressed by James as "Rabbi"). It discusses primarily questions of suffering and the ascent of the soul. A number of features point to a Jewish-Christian origin: the name of God, "He Who Is," is derived from Exod 3:14 (see also the play on the same passage in *Gos. Thom.* #61); the discussion of the weaker female principle presupposes the same doctrine of syzygies that also appears in the *Kerygmata Petrou* of the *Pseudo-Clementines* (§10.4c.[3]), to which is also related the statement that the Bible contains only partial truths and requires Jesus' revelation in order to be fully understood. The designation of Sophia as "Achamoth" is Aramaic. A Syrian origin is finally indicated by the mention of Addai, known later as the apostle of Edessa, to whom James is instructed to transfer these teachings. The theology of the writing is Gnostic, including the traditions used in the writing of the hymn to the revealer (28, 7–20) and a catechism of answers to the questions of the cosmic guardians (33, 11–34: cf. *Gos. Thom.* #50). The *Second Apocalypse of James* (NHC V, 4) is based upon a report of the martyrdom of James that is essentially identical with the report of Hegesippus preserved by Eusebius (*Hist. eccl.*

Bibliography for §10.5b (4):   Texts

William Schoedel, "NHC V,3: The (First) Apocalypse of James," in Douglas M. Parrot (ed.), *Nag Hammadi Codices V,3–5 and VI with Papyrus Berolinensis 8502,1 and 4* (NHS 11; Leiden: Brill, 1979) 65–103.

Charles W. Hedrick, "NHC V,4: The (Second) Apocalypse of Adam," ibid., 105–49.

Wolf-Peter Funk (ed.), *Die zweite Apokalypse des Jakobus aus Nag-Hammadi-Codex V: Neu herausgegeben, übersetzt und erklärt* (TU 119; Berlin: Akademie-Verlag, 1976).

William R. Schoedel and Douglas M. Parrott, "The (First) Apocalypse of James (V,3)," in *NagHamLibEngl,* 260–268.

Charles W. Hedrick and Douglas M. Parrott, "The (Second) Apocalypse of James (V,4)," in *NagHamLibEngl,* 269–276.

Wolf-Peter Funk, "The First Apocalypse of James," and idem, "The Second Apocalypse of James," in Schneemelcher, *NT Apoc.,* 1. 313–41.

Bibliography for §10.5b (4):   Studies

William R. Schoedel, "Scripture and the Seventy-two Heavens of the First Apocalypse of James," *NovT* 12 (1970) 18–29.

2.23.4ff.)—a report that also comes from a Palestinian tradition. A number of Gnostic hymns have been inserted into this report. The conclusion contains a prayer of petition of James, in the face of death, which is in keeping with the biblical psalms of lamentation. These two writings have preserved in their hymns and songs a genre that Syrian Gnosticism cultivated as a biblical inheritance.

(c) Gnostic Hymns and Songs

(1) *Prologue of John's Gospel and Hymn of the Dance.* A large number of hymns and songs have been preserved from Syria, or through the tradition of Syria, that are either of Gnostic origin or reveal the influence of Gnostic terms and imagery. It is difficult to determine the dates for the composition of such poetry, but it is reasonable to assume that many of these pieces were created between 40 and 150 CE. All these hymns and songs belong to the genre of Semitic poetry; their prototypes are the psalms of Scripture, the *Psalms of Solomon,* and the *Thanksgiving Hymns (Hodayot)* from Qumran. The oldest preserved Christian hymn is quoted by Paul in Phil 2:6–11 and shows that the prototype was a hymn to Wisdom that came from the Jewish wisdom movement. Complex mythological speculations are absent from these hymns, but myths are told and mythical metaphors appear, not as pieces of theological doctrines but as expressions of the piety and devotion of the believer. Christological statements are central and religious concepts can be identified, though they are translated into the metaphorical language of poetry. Many hymns are dominated by the first-person singular, representing either the voice of the revealer or the voice of the believer—in fact, sometimes they flow together into the voice of the redeemed redeemer. But the savior can also be addressed in the second person, or his coming and deeds are told in the third person. Occasionally the "we" of the confessing community appears.

Some of these hymns have already been mentioned. The hymn that is used in the prologue of the Gospel of John describes the action and the coming of the Logos in the third person, but concludes with a confession of the community in the first-person plural. Theological terms are used abundantly: light, darkness, life,

Bibliography for §10.5c

Joseph Kroll, *Die christliche Hymnodik bis zu Klemens von Alexandrien* (Verzeichnis der Vorlesungen der Akademie zu Braunsberg, 1921–22; reprint Darmstadt: Wissenschaftliche Buchgesellschaft, 1968).

Michael Lattke, *Hymnus: Materialien zu einer Geschichte der antiken Hymnologie* (NTOA19: Freiburg/Schweiz: Universitätsverlag, and Göttingen: Vandenhoeck & Ruprecht, 1991).

Jack T. Sanders, "Nag Hammadi, Odes of Solomon, and NT Christological Hymns," in Goehring, *Gnosticism,* 51–66.

Bibliography for §10.5c (1):   Text

Lipsius-Bonnet, *ActApostApoc.* 2.1. 197–99.
Knut Schäferdiek, "The Acts of John," in Schneemelcher, *NT Apoc.,* 2. 181–84.

Bibliography for §10.5c (1):   Studies

P. G. Schneider, *The Mystery of the Acts of John: An Interpretation of the Hymn of the Dance in the Light of the Acts' Theology* (Distinguished Dissertations 10; San Francisco: Mellen Research University Press, 1991).

father, only-born son, glory, grace, and truth. The *Hymn of the Dance* in the *Acts of John* (94–96) begins with the "we" of the congregation ("We praise you, Father"), but then the revealer speaks about himself in the first-person singular. Everything he says, however, expresses the believer's hope of salvation ("I want to be saved"). Cosmological concepts are used: "The Ogdoad sings praises . . . the Twelve (=the Zodiac) are dancing up on high." Metaphors that are characteristic of Gnosticism dominate the language (the revealer is light, mirror, door, way). The believer is once more included in the description of suffering. In the summons to recognize the revealer, which is identical with the summons to recognize oneself, the person of the revealer and the believer flow together into one.

(2) *Hymns in the Apocalypses of James.* In the hymn of the *First Apocalypse of James* (28, 7–27), the poet speaks to the revealer in the second person: "You have come with knowledge, that you might rebuke their ignorance." In the conclusion, the believer speaks about himself in the first person, clearly distinguished from the revealer: "There is in me a forgetfulness, yet I remember." In the hymns of the *Second Apocalypse of James* (55, 15–56, 14; 58, 2–24), doxological predications of the revealer are used that only rarely contain Gnostic terminology. In the first hymn, the revealer is called illuminator and savior, is admired for his powerful deeds, blessed by the heavens, and called the Lord. In the second part, however, the poet speaks in Gnostic language about those who are to be saved: they will receive the call, find the rest, rule, be kings. The second hymn is a doxology, speaking about God in the third person: he is life, light "the one who will come to be . . . an end for what has begun and a beginning for what is about to be ended. . . . Holy Spirit and the Invisible One . . . virgin." The conclusion is a typical Gnostic addition: "I saw that he was naked, for there was no garment clothing him."

(3) *Hymns in the Acts of Thomas.* A Gnostic orientation is evident in the hymns of the *Acts of Thomas.* The book itself, to be sure, cannot be dated earlier than the beginning of the 3d century. But its hymns and songs are older. *Acts Thom.* 6–7 is a bridal song modeled upon popular prototypes. The beauty of the bride is described, but the description is soon interrupted by allegorical sentences ("truth rests upon her head"), although later on the "thirty-two who praise her" are nothing more than her perfect teeth. The second stanza, however, speaks about the queen of heaven. The seven best men are the planets, the twelve servants the signs of the

Bibliography for §10.5c (2):   Texts

see the texts under §10.5b (4)

Bibliography for §10.5c (3):   Texts

Lipsius-Bonnet, *ActApostApoc,* 2.2. 109–10, 219–24.
Han J. W. Drijvers, "The Acts of Thomas," in Schneemelcher, *NT Apoc,* 2. 341–42, 380–85.
"The Acts of Thomas," in Foerster, *Gnosis,* 1. 345–46, 355–58.
Layton, *Gnostic Scriptures,* 366–75.

Bibliography for §10.5c (3):   Studies

Paul-Hubert Poirier, *L'Hymne de la perle des Actes de Thomas: Introduction, texte, traduction, commentaire* (Homo Religiosus 8; Louvain-la-Neuve: Centre de l'Histoire des Religions, 1981).
Alfred Adam, *Die Psalmen des Thomas und das Perlenlied als Zeugnisse vorchristlicher Gnosis* (FRLANT NF 33; Göttingen: Vandenhoeck & Ruprecht, 1954).

zodiac. The bridegroom thus becomes the corporate image of the redeemed, who are attending the heavenly wedding feast. The second song of the *Acts of Thomas,* the *Hymn of the Pearl* (108–113), is even less related to congregational hymns than the bridal song. It is instead an allegorical poem, based upon a fairy tale about a prince who went into far lands in order to snatch a precious pearl from a dragon, expecting to become coregent as a reward. This fairy tale was used by the author to describe the journey of the soul from its heavenly home into foreign terrestrial realms and its subsequent salvation through the celestial call. Features alien to the original fairy tale can be easily detected: the prince leaves his shining garment behind in the Persian homeland, dresses in the dirty garments of Egypt, and falls into sleep and forgetfulness (in the original fairy tale, it was probably told that he served the king of Egypt). A letter—the Gnostic motif of the heavenly letter—awakens him, and he recognizes in this letter what is written in his heart; the radiant garment sent to meet him is the mirror of his own true self.

(4) *The Odes of Solomon.* A whole collection of community hymns has been preserved in the *Odes of Solomon.* Until the beginning of this century nothing was known about them except their name, which occurred in an ancient canon list and in a quotation in Lactantius. This hymnbook, originally written in Greek, was discovered in 1909 and 1912 in two Syriac manuscripts, containing *Odes* 3–42 and *Odes* 17.7–42, respectively. *Odes* 1, 5, 6, 22, and 25 were subsequently identified in a Coptic translation in the Gnostic writing *Pistis Sophia,* and *Ode* 11 was discovered

Bibliography for §10.5c (4): Text

Michael Lattke, *Die Oden Salomos in ihrer Bedeutung für Neues Testament und Gnosis* (3 vols.; OBO 25,1–4; Freiburg/Schweiz: Universitätsverlag, and Göttingen: Vandenhoeck & Ruprecht, 1979–1998). This is the definitive edition, containing the Syriac and Coptic texts (with the Greek Pap. Bodmer XI) and a German translation in vols. 1 and 1a, a concordance in vol. 2, an extensive scholarly bibliography in vol. 3, and a selection of essays in vol. 4.
Idem, *Oden Salomos: Übersetzt und eingeleitet* (FC 19; Freiburg: Herder, 1995).
Walter Bauer (ed.), *Die Oden Salomos* (KIT 64; Berlin: de Gruyter, 1933).
James H. Charlesworth, *The Odes of Solomon: The Syriac Texts, Edited with Translation and Notes* (SBLTT 13, Pseudepigrapha 7; Missoula, MT: Scholars Press, 1977).
J. A. Emerton, "The Odes of Solomon," in H. F. D. Sparks (ed.), *The Apocryphal Old Testament* (Oxford: Clarendon, 1984) 683–731. A good English translation.

Bibliography for §10.5c (4): Commentaries

Michael Lattke. *Die Oden Salomos: Text, Übersetzung, Kommentar,* part 1: *Oden 1 und 3–14* (NTOA; Freiburg/Schweiz: Universitätsverlag, and Göttingen: Vandenhoeck & Ruprecht, 1999).

Bibliography for §§10.5c (4): Studies

Gerhard Kittel, *Die Oden Salomos, einheitlich oder überarbeitet?* (BWANT 16; Leipzig: Hinrichs, 1914).
Robert M. Grant, "The Odes of Solomon and the Church of Antioch," *JBL* 63 (1944) 363–77.
Michael Lattke, "Zur Bildersprache der Oden Salomos," *Symbolon* NF 6 (1982) 85–110.
Idem, "Dating the *Odes of Solomon,*" *Antichthon* 27 (1993) 45–58.
Gerald R. Blaszczak, *A Formcritical Study of Selected Odes of Solomon* (HSM 36; Atlanta: Scholars Press, 1985).
M. Franzmann, *The Odes of Solomon: An Analysis of the Poetical Structure and Form* (NTOA 20; Fribourg: Editions Universitaires, 1991).
M.-J. Pierre, *Les Odes de Salomon* (Apocryphes 4; Turnhout: Brepols, 1994).

in its Greek text in *Pap. Bodmer XI*. A search for one particular author of these *Odes of Solomon* is just as futile as a determination of a specific date for their composition. Some of them may have been written as early as the hymn of the prologue of the Gospel of John; but a date in the 2d century is just as likely. There is no reason to assume that they were all written at the same time and by the same author. Many of the songs are closely modeled upon psalms from Scripture and are direct continuations of Jewish psalm poetry. *Ode* 5 is a thanksgiving psalm for the protection from persecutors. *Ode* 14 is a psalm of confidence. *Odes* 22 and 25 are hymns praising God for his victory over his enemies, especially over death and hell. *Ode* 29 praises Christ for the gift of his word, through which the believers are victorious.

The language of the *Odes of Solomon* is rich with images and metaphors, including many that are familiar from Gnostic texts. Such statements as "the Lord is the crown of truth on the head of the believer" (*Ode* 1), however, do not necessarily imply a Gnostic meaning. Nor does the image of the community as the planting in paradise (*Ode* 11, 18ff.), or the comparison of the gift of God with the milk from the breasts of the Father who is milked by the Holy Spirit, even though the continuation (the virgin conceived in her womb from this milk) might not quite agree with our sense of good taste (*Ode* 19). Clearly Gnostic, however, are the images of the Lord as the mirror (*Ode* 13) and of *gnosis* as a mighty stream of water (*Ode* 6; cf. 11.6–7; 30). The christological statements contain many sentences that formulate generally accepted Christian beliefs. The praise of the appearance of the Lord in human form (*Ode* 7) is by no means typical for Gnosticism, nor are the hymns of the praise for the eschatological victory of Christ over the lower world (*Ode* 24), the enumeration of the deeds of the Lord with the request to listen to them and to hold to them (*Ode* 8; cf. 9), and the Hellenistic missionary sermon (*Ode* 24). It is noteworthy, however, that in those *Odes* that are formulated in the I-style, the person of the revealer often flows together with the person of the believer. The possession of immortality and the activity in the world can therefore be described as referring to both redeemer and believer at the same time (*Ode* 10), and sometimes it is impossible to distinguish between the one who works the salvation and the one who receives it (*Ode* 17). Through rebirths, the redeemed becomes identical with the redeemer (*Ode* 36), is one and the same with the suffering Christ in his own suffering (*Ode* 28; cf. 31), and even becomes the redeemer as he descends with Christ into hell (*Ode* 42).

Finally, there are a number of verses and portions of these psalms that are direct reflections of Gnostic piety. Sometimes individual sentences in a context otherwise not informed by Gnostic thought betray a Gnostic understanding of the whole song, such as in the hymn of praise in *Ode* 26: "It is enough to have *gnosis* and to find rest" (26.12). Putting off the earthly garment and putting on the heavenly garment of light (*Ode* 11.10–11; cf. 15.8) is as Gnostic as the description of the heavenly journey of the soul (*Ode* 35), the description of the lower world as an empty illusion (*Ode* 34), the praise of the truth as the pathfinder in the ascension (*Ode* 38), and of Christ as the guide over the abyss of the hostile waters (*Ode* 39). The *Odes of Solomon* may indeed not deserve the title of a "Gnostic Hymnbook," but the Gnostic origin and character of a considerable portion of its imagery and metaphorical language cannot be doubted. Yet, this probably means nothing more than that Gnostic images and terms were very welcome in order to express the individual's religious aspirations and hopes for resurrection and anticipation of a future life in communities that were by no means committed to a Gnostic theology. This early Christian hymnal may simply be a witness for the way in which Gnosticism very deeply affected the piety and spirituality of Christianity in general.

EGYPT

1. THE BEGINNINGS OF CHRISTIANITY IN EGYPT

(a) The Problem of Sources and Evidence

Egypt was a country with unusual political, social, and economic structures that were fundamentally different from all other regions of the Greco-Roman world. Its one major city, Alexandria, was the second-largest city of the Roman empire and one of its most significant cultural and economic centers. The rest of the country was mostly rural, with a few major settlements like Oxyrhynchus, Arsinoë, and Hermoupolis. These towns, although they were not organized as Greek "cities," had some share in civic culture and offered some of the amenities of civic life, but could not be compared with other major cultural and economic centers elsewhere in the Roman world. The contrast between Alexandria and the Egyptian hinterland was sharpened by differences in language and education. Alexandria boasted a thoroughly Hellenized Greek-speaking population, including a large Jewish community, while the native population of the rural areas continued to speak several vernacular Egyptian dialects and was mostly illiterate. The Christian mission apparently began to reach the Egyptian countryside only as late as the end of the 2d century. The beginnings of Christianity were thus more or less limited to Alexandria and a few settlements that had some Greek-speaking inhabitants, but would have been unlikely to develop a church life independent of the history of Alexandrian Christianity—not until a new writing system for the Egyptian dialects was developed on the basis of the Greek alphabet, which took place upon the initiative of Christian missionaries during the 3d century (this is the Egyptian language that is known today as Coptic). Discoveries of Greek papyri in places like Oxyrhynchus can therefore be considered representative of Alexandrian Christianity. Alexandria, on the other hand, because of its large Greek-speaking population of various ethnic origins, would offer ample opportunity for the simultaneous development of several competing Christian groups.

Unfortunately, there is no direct evidence for the beginnings of Christianity in Egypt, although there should be little doubt that the Christian mission reached

Bibliography to §11

Bauer, *Orthodoxy and Heresy,* 44–60.

Colin H. Roberts, *Manuscript, Society and Belief in Early Christian Egypt* (The Schweich Lectures 1977; London: Oxford University Press, 1979).

Bibliography to §11.1a

Birger A. Pearson and J. E. Goehring (eds.), *The Roots of Egyptian Christianity* (SAC 1; Philadelphia: Fortress, 1986).

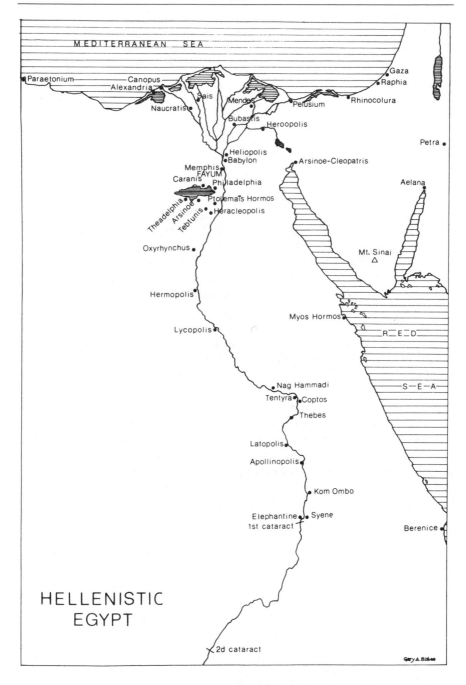

MEDITERRANEAN SEA

Paraetonium

Canopus
Alexandria
Sais
Naucratis
Mendes
Bubastis
Heroopolis
Pelusium
Rhinocolura
Gaza
Raphia

Petra

Heliopolis
Babylon
Memphis
FAYUM
Caranis
Philadelphia
Theadelphia
Arsinoe
Tebtunis
Ptolemaïs Hormos
Heracleopolis
Arsinoe-Cleopatris

Aelana

Oxyrhynchus

Mt. Sinai
△

Hermopolis

Myos Hormos

Lycopolis

R E D

Nag Hammadi
Tentyra
Coptos
Thebes

S E A

Latopolis
Apollinopolis

Kom Ombo

Elephantine
1st cataract
Syene

Berenice

HELLENISTIC
EGYPT

2d cataract

Gary A. Bisbee

Alexandria during the 1st century CE. One must therefore attempt to draw conclusions from various pieces of later information. This can be hazardous, as is already evident in the case of the ancient church historian Eusebius of Caesarea, who wrote in the early decades of the 4th century CE. In agreement with other ecclesiastical traditions, Eusebius names Mark as the first Christian preacher in Egypt, founder of the church of Alexandria and its first bishop and martyr. In order to give more life to the picture of the earliest Alexandrian community, Eusebius borrows the description of the Therapeutai from the Jewish philosopher Philo of Alexandria (*De vita contemplativa;* §5.3f) and concludes, quite consistently with Philo's report, that the first Christians of Egypt were a group of ascetic philosophers (Eusebius *Hist. eccl.* 2.16.2). This information, of course, has no value whatsoever; neither has Eusebius's list of bishops of Alexandria, who followed upon Mark, nor the information about their years in office: Annianus, twenty-two years; Abilius, thirteen years; Cerdo, eleven years (?); Primus, twelve years—and at this point the reader has already arrived at the third year of the emperor Hadrian (120 CE). The continuing list of bishops for the following seventy years is surprisingly fragmentary (Justus, Aggripinus, Julian), until the first tangible historical figure appears with Demetrius, who became bishop of Alexandria in the year 189 CE.

It is indeed unthinkable that the Christian mission should have bypassed Alexandria for decades. One or several communities must have existed there as early as the second half of the 1st century. That Mark appeared as the patron saint of Alexandria may well have some roots in history; the *Acts of Mark* make their first appearance in the 4th century but certainly used much older stories. Why did a famous episcopal see like Alexandria not choose a more famous apostle as its founder? It is also not unlikely that the Christian message was brought to Rome from Alexandria no later than the forties of the 1st century. Acts 18:24 reports, after all, that Apollos, the fellow worker of Paul, was an Alexandrian Jew. Among the writings of the Apostolic Fathers, there are two for which an Alexandrian origin has been claimed: the *Epistle of Barnabas,* because of its "Alexandrian" exegesis of Scripture (§12.2b), and *2 Clement,* because of the relationship of one of its gospel quotations to the *Gospel of the Egyptians* (§11.2b). Although such judgments are not completely misguided, and in the latter case even persuasive (§11.3a), they do not explain why the information about the earliest period of Christianity in Egypt is so scanty, while the Christian traditions from Syria, Asia Minor, Macedonia, and Greece, though incomplete, are still rich and diversified enough to allow at least a hypothetical reconstruction of their history and development.

In his book *Orthodoxy and Heresy in Earliest Christianity,* first published in 1934, Walter Bauer provided an answer to the astounding absence of reliable sources for the Christian beginnings in Egypt. Seen from the perspective of the later catholic church, Bauer argues, the beginnings of Christianity in Egypt were "heretical," and therefore Christian writings composed in Egypt in the early period were not preserved, while other pieces of information were suppressed or not admitted to the treasure of ecclesiastical tradition. What Eusebius is able to report indicates that the traditions available to him were either silent about early Christian history in Egypt or, more likely, conflicted with his historical construct of orthodox beginnings everywhere. Here the modern historian has some advantage over Eusebius. On the one hand, several church fathers, especially Clement of Alexandria and Origen, have preserved more than Eusebius was willing to include into his historical work; on the other hand, manuscript discoveries in Egypt have brought to light a great deal of valuable information, among them many writings that Eusebius would have refused to admit. In addition to a large number of Greek and Coptic papyri from Egypt (§6.2b), the most significant discovery is the Coptic Gnostic Nag Hammadi Library (§§10.1b; 10.5b). It is especially the writings from this library that lead directly to the question of a very early Syrian origin of Egyptian Christianity.

(b) Syrian Traditions in Egypt

Missionaries from Palestine or Syria must have brought Christianity to Egypt. We do not know their names, but it is possible to form some impressions of their preaching and teaching. The two oldest manuscript discoveries of Christian books from Egypt point to the Gospel of John. The fragment of the Gospel of John in $\mathfrak{P}^{52}$ and the *Unknown Gospel of Papyrus Egerton 2* (§10.3a.3) were both written in the 2d century, the former possibly at the beginning of that century. Thus both the Gospel of John and a gospel that probably served as one of its sources were known in Egypt at an early date. Later witnesses prove that John was a favorite book among Egyptian Gnostics. Christians who were later called Gnostics may well have been the first Christians in the country of the Nile. There are further testimonies to confirm this hypothesis. Three fragments of different copies of the Greek original of the *Gospel of Thomas* have been found in Egypt (*Pap. Oxyrh. 1, 654, 655;* see §10.1b); at least one of these manuscripts was written before the year 200, the others not much later. Although the accidental nature of such manuscript discoveries must be kept in mind, it is difficult to avoid the conclusion that these two gospels, those of John and of Thomas, were well known in Egypt during the 2d century, while there is no manuscript attestation of the Gospels of Matthew, Mark, and Luke before the year 200, although we know from Clement of Alexandria that they were known and read in Alexandria during his stay in that city (180–200 CE). However, they were by no means the only gospels known to Clement and Origen (see below).

The evidence of a *Secret Gospel of Mark* from a recently published letter of Clement of Alexandria is very intriguing (§10.2b). At the time of Clement this gospel was used among the "perfect" Christians in Alexandria, but Clement also reveals that the Gnostic sect of the Carpocratians used a version of this *Secret Gospel of Mark,* which may have arrived in Egypt even before its abbreviated version was produced, which was then admitted into the canon of the New Testament. The *Secret Gospel* gives evidence of a secret initiation rite: Jesus spends a night with the young man he had raised from the dead; he comes to Jesus dressed only in a linen cloth, and Jesus teaches him the mystery of the kingdom of God. This fits well with what is otherwise known about secret rites of initiation among Gnostic circles of Egypt. Some of these writings preserved in the Nag Hammadi Library

Bibliography to §11.1b: Text

Smith, *Clement,* 445–54. For other editions and translations of the *Secret Gospel of Mark,* see §10.2b.

Bibliography to §11.1b: Studies

See the literature for §10.3a and 10.5b.

apparently originated in Syria and were then brought to Egypt as secret books; formulae designed to guarantee the secrecy occasionally occur (cf. the conclusion of the *Apocryphon of John*).

(c) Egyptian Jewish Christianity

(1) *The Gospel of the Hebrews.* A number of fragments of the Jewish-Christian gospels (§10.4b) should be assigned to a gospel that was used in Alexandria and was known under the name *Gospel of the Hebrews.* The two Jewish-Christian gospels discussed above were dependent upon the Synoptic Gospels of the New Testament, the *Gospel of the Nazoreans* being a version of the Gospel of Matthew and the *Gospel of the Ebionites* a harmony of the Synoptic Gospels. The *Gospel of the Hebrews,* judging from the few extant fragments, had a different character. Although it was composed in Greek, the Spirit is called "the mother of Jesus," which would fit a Semitic language, where the word "spirit" is a feminine noun. Mary is introduced as the earthly appearance of a heavenly power (Michael). In baptism the "whole fount of the Holy Spirit" descends upon Jesus and rests upon him, saying, "My Son, in all the prophets I was waiting for you that you should come and I might rest in you. For you are my rest; you are my first-begotten Son who reigns forever." This concept is derived from the Jewish wisdom myth; the Spirit in this gospel speaks like personified Wisdom, who comes into the world repeatedly, appearing in prophets and divine messengers, seeking her rest (Wis 7:27; Sir 24:7). The *Gospel of the Hebrews* uses here a motif from Jewish theology, but no special relationship to the *Kerygmata Petrou* is discernible.

The authority of James, however, is emphasized in this gospel. In its story of the resurrection, Jesus appears to his brother James and breaks bread with him. Paul records a tradition that names James explicitly as one of the witnesses to whom Jesus appeared (1 Cor 15:7) but no such story has made its way into the canonical gospels. As the *Gospel of the Hebrews* reports the story of such an appearance, it should be considered as an independent parallel of the canonical gospels. Contrary to the canonical accounts, where only the Twelve are present at the last meal of Jesus, the *Gospel of the Hebrews* implies that his brother James participated in Jesus' last supper, because "James had sworn that he would not eat bread from that day at which he had drunk the cup of the Lord, until he should see him risen from among them that sleep." This story can also be understood as a reflection of a community's fasting ritual before the celebration of Easter. Very little is unfortunately known about most of the content of this gospel, which, according to the stichometry of Nicephorus, was only a little shorter than the Gospel of Matthew! The saying, "And never shall you be joyful, save when you behold your brother with love," which belongs to the *Gospel of the Hebrews,* suggests that its sayings were of the same character as those of the Synoptic Gospels (or the Gospel of John). But Clement

Bibliography to §11.1c (1):   Text

Philipp Vielhauer and Georg Strecker, "The Gospel of the Hebrews," in Schneemelcher, *NT Apoc.,*
    1. 172–78.
Cameron, *Other Gospels,* 83–86.
Miller, *Complete Gospels,* 427–34.
See also the literature to §10.4b

of Alexandria also assigns to this gospel a saying that we know now as the second saying of the *Gospel of Thomas* (*Strom.* 2.9.45 and 5.14.96). This Gnostic saying about the sequence of seeking, finding, marveling, ruling, and resting could have circulated in the free tradition of Jesus' sayings. But if the *Gospel of Thomas* was brought to Egypt at an early date, the *Gospel of the Hebrews* may have drawn it from that source. In any case, this Jewish Christianity of Egypt shows a close affinity to a Gnostic tradition of Syrian origin.

(2) *The Apocryphon of James.* Like the Jewish Christians in Syria, those of Alexandria may have used a number of other writings under the authority of James. The *First* and the *Second Apocalypse of James* should be considered here since both originate with the traditions of James from Syria, although they are Gnostic writings (§10.5b). That the distinctive Jewish-Christian authority of James is invoked in Gnostic writings is not as surprising as it may seem; also the Jewish-Christian *Gospel of the Hebrews,* in which James is the witness of the risen Jesus, exhibits some affinities to Gnosticism. The *Apocryphon of James,* also known as the *Epistula Jacobi* (NHC I, 2) from Nag Hammadi, is of a somewhat different character, although in its external frame it appeals to the typically Jewish-Christian authorities; the introduction presents it as a secret book revealed by the Lord to James and Peter, and written down by the former in the Hebrew language (*Apoc. Jas.* 1, 8–18). Its content is a farewell discourse of Jesus, based upon sayings that have parallels in the Gospel of John, the Synoptic Gospels, and the *Gospel of Thomas,* though literary dependence is not evident. On the contrary, the blessing of those "who have not seen and yet believe" (*Apoc. Jas.* 12, 41–13, 1) appears in a more original setting of a sequence of sayings of Jesus, while John 20:29 has added this saying secondarily to the story of Jesus' appearance before Thomas. Especially intriguing are a number of parables in this writing, of which some do not have parallels in the Synoptic Gospels. With respect to its genre, the *Apocryphon of James* closely resembles the *Dialogue of the Savior* (§§10.1b; 10.3a). An interpretation of traditional sayings in dialogue and discourse form present Gnostic teaching as the legitimate (Jewish-Christian?) continuation of the teaching of Jesus. All this argues for a date of composition around the year 100 CE.

Bibliography to §11.1c (2):   Text

Francis E. Williams, "The Apocryphon of James," in Harold W. Attridge (ed.), *Nag Hammadi Codex I (The Jung Codex)* (2 vols.; NHS 22–23; Leiden: Brill, 1985) 1. 5–53; 2. 7–37.

Idem, "The Apocryphon of James (I,2)," *NagHamLibEngl,* 29–37.

Dankwart Kirchner, "The Apocryphon of James," in Schneemelcher, *NT Apoc.,* 1. 285–99.

Cameron, *Other Gospels,* 55–66.

Miller, *Complete Gospels,* 332–42.

Hans-Martin Schenke, "Der Jakobusbrief aus dem Codex Jung," *OLZ* 66 (1971) 117–30. German translation of the *Apocryphon of James.*

Bibliography to §11.1c (2):   Studies

Ron Cameron, *Sayings Traditions in the "Apocryphon of James"* (HTS 34; Philadelphia: Fortress, 1984).

B. Dehandschutter, "L'Epistula Jacobi apocrypha de Nag Hammadi (CG I,2) comme apocryphe néotestamentaire," *ANRW* 2.25.6 (1988) 4529–50.

Dankwart Kirchner, *Epistula Jacobi Apocrypha: Die zweite Schrift des Nag Hammadi Codex I* (TU 136: Berlin: Akademie-Verlag, 1998).

2. EGYPTIAN GNOSTICISM

(a) The Testimony of the Writings from Nag Hammadi

The codices of the Nag Hammadi Library (NHC) were composed in Egypt in the Coptic language shortly after the middle of the 4th century. Since this library is a collection of some fifty-two writings that had been translated from Greek into Coptic, this date is of little help in determining the place where the Greek originals were written. Moreover, assigning dates of composition for each of these books presents considerable difficulties. Through the efforts of the Institute of Antiquity and Christianity in Claremont, California, under the leadership of James M. Robinson and with the cooperation of numerous scholars from the United States and abroad, all writings from this library have now been published in critical editions, and some consensus has been reached with respect to the dating of the Greek originals as well as their geographical origin. The following is an attempt to discuss some of those writings that may be significant for the understanding of early Christian Gnosticism in Egypt in the first two centuries.

Among those writings of the Nag Hammadi Library that originated in Syria, the *Gospel of Thomas* must have been brought to Egypt before the middle of the 2d century, together with the *Hypostasis of the Archons* and the *Apocryphon of John* (§10.5b.2–3), both of which show so many parallels to the Sophia myth of the Valentinian school (§11.2c.4) that they should be counted among its sources. The Sethian type of Gnosticism from Syria was further developed in Egypt; the predecessor of this development may have been the Syrian *Apocalypse of Adam* (§10.5b.1). In any case, if it can be assumed that certain types of Gnosticism originated in Syria, it necessarily followed that Syrian writings were brought to Egypt at early at the beginning of the 2d century.

(1) *Pre-Christian Gnosticism in Egypt.* In addition to this Syrian influence upon the development of Egyptian Gnosticism, there were independent Egyptian formations of Gnostic theology that reveal no specifically Christian influence. As Jewish Gnostic speculations were the predecessors of Christian Gnosis in Syria, pagan Gnostic mythology and philosophy preceded its Christian offspring in Egypt and even developed further without direct borrowings from Christianity. The writings of the *Corpus Hermeticum,* certainly from Egypt, have already been discussed (§6.5f). Even the Nag Hammadi Library included two Hermetic tractates, Gnostic to be sure, but without Christian influence: *The Discourse of the Eighth and the Ninth* (NHC VI, 6) and *Asclepius 21–29* (NHC VI, 8). Another pre-Christian Gnostic tractate is the *Paraphrase of Shem* (NHC VII, 1). It is a very complex and elaborate creation myth, revealed by Derdekeas to Shem, "who comes from the unmixed power" and is "the first being on earth" (*Paraph. Shem* 1, 18–21). The myth differs from those of the Syrian-Christian type, since it knows three principles: light, darkness, and the spirit standing between them. In order that "nature" can come into existence, Derdekeas, the son of infinite light, has to intervene repeatedly. Although

Bibliography to §11.2a

Alexander Böhlig and Frederik Wisse, *Zum Hellenismus in den Schriften von Nag Hammadi* (Göttinger Orientforschungen 6.2; Wiesbaden: Harrassowitz, 1975).

there are faint allusions to the creation story of Genesis, one does not find any extensive biblical exegesis, and Genesis 2–3 is not used; though there are complex discussions of the evil power of the flood, an allusion to the building of the tower, and a mention of Sodom. The last part of the writing is an apocalypse predicting the final cosmic catastrophe, in which the light will be separated from the darkness. Some want to see in the polemic against baptismal rites (37, 14–29) and in the prediction of an evil demon, who will come forth from the power of the serpent and will do many wonders (44, 31–45, 8), a polemic against John the Baptist and thus against the baptism practiced by the church. That, however, is not convincing because it could also be a polemic against other Gnostic sects that practiced baptism. Nor is it believable that the prediction that Nature wants to "fix Soldas who is a dark flame" (39, 28–33) is a reference to the crucifixion of Jesus' earthly body. It is another matter that the *Paraphrase of Shem* was later rewritten by Christians to produce a book with many similarities, namely, the *Paraphrase of Seth* (known to Hippolytus).

(2) *Eugnostos the Blessed and the Sophia of Jesus Christ.* There is one very revealing instance in which the Nag Hammadi Library has preserved both an original treatise of pre-Christian Gnostic philosophy, the book *Eugnostos the Blessed* (NHC III, 3; V, 1), and its secondary Christian adaptation, the *Sophia of Jesus Christ* (NHC III, 4; BG 8502, 3). The former describes in the form of a letter from "Eugnostos the Blessed to those who are his" the origin and structure of the transcendent divine world. Insight into the view presented by Eugnostos, which is a confession of the God of Truth and gives immortality, is explicitly contrasted to the three erroneous philosophical views, which claim that the world has come into existence "by itself," "through providence," or "by fate." In his presentation of the three primary figures of the divine sphere, derived from each other through emanation, Eugnostos uses theological concepts that became significant in the following

Bibliography to §11.2a (1):   Text

Frederik Wisse, "The Paraphrase of Shem," in Birger A. Pearson (ed.), *Nag Hammadi Codex VII* (NHS 30; Leiden: Brill, 1996), 15–127.

Martin Krause, *Die Paraphrase des Sêem* (Christentum am Roten Meer 2: Berlin: de Gruyter, 1973) 2–105. Coptic Text with German translation.

Frederik Wisse, "The Paraphrase of Shem (VII,1)," *NagHamLibEngl*, 339–61.

Bibliography to §11.2a (1):   Studies

Frederik Wisse, "The Redeemer Figure in the Paraphrase of Shem," *NovT* 12 (1970) 118–29.

Bibliography to §11.2a (2):   Text

Douglas M. Parrott (ed.), *Nag Hammadi Codices III,3–4 and V,1 with Papyrus Berolinensis 8502,3 and Papyrus 1081: Eugnostos and the Sophia of Jesus Christ* (NHS 27; Leiden: Brill, 1991).

Idem, "Eugnostos the Blessed (III,3 and V,1) and the Sophia of Jesus Christ (III,4 and BG 8502,3)," in *NagHamLibEngl*, 220–243.

Bibliography to §11.2a (2):   Studies

Martin Krause, "Das literarische Verhältnis des Eugnostosbriefes zur Sophia Jesu Christi," in *Mullus: Festschrift für Theodor Klauser* (JAC.E 1; Münster: Aschendorff, 1964) 15–23.

Demetrius Trakatellis, *The Transcendent God of Eugnostos* (Brookline, MA: Holy Cross Orthodox Press, 1991). Contains also Coptic text, Greek retroversion, and English translation.

Site of the Discovery of the Nag Hammadi Library

Twelve codices were found accidentally in a jar that was buried at the foot of the fallen boulders on the right. The site lies at the edge of the Nile Valley, not far from the oldest known Christian monastery (of Pachomius), near the ancient Chenoboskion in Upper Egypt.

centuries for the definition of God who was Father, Son, and Holy Spirit. The Christian adaptation *Sophia of Jesus Christ,* according to its narrative framework, is a revelation discourse of the resurrected redeemer with the twelve disciples and seven women. But the revelation discourse itself, including Jesus' answers to various questions of the disciples and the women, is nothing but an often verbatim reproduction of the book of *Eugnostos the Blessed.* Exegetical comments are occasionally added in order to explain the thoughts presented by the source, and additional material has been interpolated at the end, including the myth of the fall of Sophia and the imprisonment of the particles of light under the powerful archon Yaldabaoth, as well as a discourse about the role of the redeemer as their liberator. Thus the Gnostic philosophical writing of *Eugnostos the Blessed* has been put to the service of constructing a Christian dialogue, in which its philosophy has become the basis of Gnostic mythology.

(3) *The Gospel of the Egyptians (Sethian).* The mythological counterpart of *Eugnostos the Blessed* is the *Holy Book of the Great Invisible Spirit,* also called the *Gospel of the Egyptians,* which is preserved in two independent translations from the Greek original (NHC III, 2 and IV, 2; this work should not be confused with the completely different apocryphal *Gospel of the Egyptians* to be discussed in §11.2b). This book is one of the most important writings of Sethian Gnosticism. It was probably composed in Syria and received the title "Gospel of the Egyptians" only after it had been brought to Egypt. The first part of the work treats in detail the complex evolution of the divine world through emanation from the primordial Father, whose name cannot be pronounced. In contrast to *Eugnostos the Blessed,* numerous mythological names are used here (Barbelo, Ainon, Esephech, etc.), and one finds multiple ogdoads, triads, and other groupings of divine powers. The entire process of divine evolution is characterized by an almost feverish activity rather than calm contemplation. The final outcome is the birth of the Great Seth, son of Adamas and father and savior of the incorruptible seed. At this point in the mythological narrative one finds the first allusions to Genesis in the mention of Sodom and Gomorra.

The second section begins with the installation of the ruler of the chaos, Saclas, along with a description of his arrogance and the creation of his own aeons and demons. It continues with the sowing of the seed of the Great Seth in the world and the institution of guardian angels, who are charged with the protection of this seed until the time of salvation. This section concludes with the appearance of Seth in the person of Jesus, who brings rebirth through baptism. This identification of Seth

Bibliography to §11.2a (3):   Text

Alexander Böhlig and Frederik Wisse with Pahor Labib (eds.), *Nag Hammadi Codices III,2 and IV,2: The Gospel of the Egyptians (The Holy Book of the Great Invisible Spirit)* (NHS 4; Leiden: Brill, 1975).

Alexander Böhlig and Frederik Wisse, "The Gospel of the Egyptians (III,2 and IV,2)," *NagHamLibEngl,* 208–219.

Layton, *Gnostic Scriptures,* 101–20.

Bibliography to §11.2a (3):   Studies

Hans-Martin Schenke, "Das Ägypterevangelium aus Nag-Hammadi-Codex III," *NTS* 16 (1969/70) 196–208.

with Jesus shows how Sethian mythology and soteriology was secondarily Christianized. The work ends with a hymn and an elaborate self-characterization of a
secret book written by Seth himself. The lack of explicit references to Christian
traditions and the scanty appearance of Christian elements in these materials drawn
from Syrian Gnostic mythology are striking (some of the mythological names of
the *Apocryphon of John* reappear in the *Holy Book of the Great Invisible Spirit*).
It was only later, probably toward the end of the 2d century, that Sethian Gnosticism began to defend and modify its doctrine and message in a critical controversy
with Catholic theology (see *The Second Treatise of the Great Seth,* NHC VII, 2) or
to accommodate it to the doctrines of emerging Neoplatonism (see *The Three
Steles of Seth,* NHC VII, 5).

On the whole, early Egyptian Gnosticism is either dependent upon pagan and
philosophical Gnostic speculations, originates from imported Syrian Sethian Gnosticism, or continues Jewish-Christian Gnosticizing traditions under the authority
of James, which probably also have their origin in Syria/Palestine. The emerging
picture of Christian beginnings in Egypt, however, is even more complex. In addition to these various Gnostic groups, which probably competed with each other,
there was also an indigenous Egyptian Christianity that was more closely related
to the tradition of the words of Jesus as they are represented by the *Gospel of
Thomas*—not to speak of the great and influential schools of Christian Gnostics
that began no later than in the middle of the 2d century.

(b) Vernacular Gnostic Christianity: The Gospel of the Egyptians

Most of the Gnostic writings mentioned so far are esoteric books that must have
had their home in Christian mystery associations rather than in congregations comparable to those in Antioch and in the area of the Pauline mission. Whether organized congregations of Gnostic believers existed in Egypt during the same period remains an open question that is very difficult to prove or to disprove. No
material survives and no conjectures are possible, for example, with respect to the
question of ecclesiastical offices. Was baptism the regular entrance rite? Wherever
it is mentioned, it is either seen as a mystery rite (e.g., in the *Holy Book of the
Great Invisible Spirit,* NHC III, 2, 66, 24–25) or is utterly rejected (*Paraphrase of
Shem* 37, 14–29). Whenever institutional structures appear, they resemble those
of a philosophical school or of a private mystery association. Congregations may
have existed on the periphery of Gnosticism, where such writings as the gospel of
the *Papyrus Egerton 2* and the Gospel of John were used. This may be confirmed
by another writing that represents a more vernacular Gnostic Christianity, the
Gospel of the Egyptians (to be distinguished from the writing of the same name
in NHC III and IV mentioned above). Only a few fragments are preserved, and
Clement of Alexandria is the only reliable witness. To judge from its name, this

Bibliography to §11.2b: Text

Erich Klostermann (ed.), *Apocrypha II: Evangelien* (KlT 8; 3d ed.; Berlin: de Gruyter, 1929) 15–16.
Wilhelm Schneemelcher, "The Gospel of the Egyptians," in idem, *NT Apoc.,* 1. 209–15.
Cameron, *Other Gospels,* 49–52.

writing may have once claimed to be the true gospel of communities of the "Egyptians," that is, Gentile Greek-speaking Christians, as distinct from the Jewish Christians of Alexandria, whose gospel was the *Gospel of the Hebrews* (this suggestion was made by Walter Bauer).

Quotations from this gospel are found in two closely related passages. In the first passage, Jesus responds to Salome's question, "Until when shall people die?" with the word, "So long as women bear children." Salome's further question, whether she did well not to bear children, receives the answer, "Eat every plant, but that which has bitterness do not eat." In the second passage, Salome once again is the one who asks a question, namely, when she would know what she had inquired about; and she receives the answer, "When you have trampled upon the garment of shame, and when the two become one, and the male with the female [is] neither male nor female." Both sayings are clearly encratite; they demand sexual abstinence so as to disrupt the cycle of birth and to eliminate the sexual differences between male and female. The second of these sayings appears also in the *Gospel of Thomas* (#22); it should also be noted that *Gos. Thom.* #61 introduces Salome as one who asks questions of Jesus. Since the very few fragments of the *Gospel of the Egyptians* exhibit as many as two links to the *Gospel of Thomas,* it is not unreasonable to assume that the former was dependent upon the latter. Little more can be said about this writing; the assignment of other materials to this gospel is problematic. But the character of the few certain quotations points to a vernacular Gnostic Christianity of Egypt that was not nourished by complex mythological speculations about cosmology and soteriology, but by transmitted sayings of Jesus and their interpretation. It is tempting to ask whether "neither male nor female" was a formula related to baptism. In that case baptism was the entrance rite into an encratite community, while the apostle Paul had understood this baptismal formula as defining the social dimensions of the new community, which is expressed in the addition of "neither Jew nor Greek, neither slave nor free" (Gal 3:28; see §9.3b).

(c) The Formation of Gnostic Schools

(1) *The Naassenes.* While the *Gospel of the Egyptians* could be a witness to a vernacular version of "Gnostic community" in Egypt, other writings mentioned above could be assigned to Gnostic groups that may be designated as representatives of "Sethian Gnosticism" or philosophically oriented circles like those who produced the writings of the *Corpus Hermeticum* (§6.5f) and *Eugnostos the Blessed.* The question of the institutional definition of the people who produced such writings remains a conundrum. At this moment of the discussion, the suggestion to assume the existence of "schools" on the model of a philosophical school seems to be the most useful, especially when particular names designating their enterprise or names of heads of such schools are preserved in the tradition. The Naassenes or Ophites, about whom Irenaeus and later church fathers have preserved information, may be classed as such a school. Nothing is known about the time of their origin because no direct evidence is extant until the last third of the 2d century. The Naassenes drew their name from the serpent of Genesis 3 (Hebrew *nahas,* Greek *ophis*) as the first revealer of divine knowledge. Like the early representatives of

Syrian Gnosticism, they drew their message from the interpretation of the first chapters of the Bible but not from the complex creation myths related to Genesis 1. According to Hippolytus's report about the Naassenes, their syncretistic attitude permitted them to borrow materials from Hellenistic religions. Thus one finds a pagan speech of religious propaganda (known as the "Naassene Sermon") based on a hymn to Attis, which surprisingly also contains some Jewish elements, but was only superficially Christianized. Hippolytus quotes another Naassene hymn that might have been used liturgically; it is actually a pagan Gnostic psalm about the spirit that redeems the soul from chaos, composed in the customary anapestic foot of the Roman imperial period; the name "Jesus" was added only later. Thus these Naassenes may have been a group that developed out of pagan philosophical circles and who drew their inspirations from the interpretations of Genesis 2–3.

(2) *The Carpocrations* are one of the first known Gnostic schools named after its founder Carpocrates. How "Gnostic" they were is difficult to judge. A writing in the name of Carpocrates' son Epiphanes, *About Righteousness,* is preserved in some fragments. It proclaims communistic ideals like the community of goods and the sharing of women, which reflects earlier utopian ideals of the Hellenistic world. The writer apparently knew the letters of Paul; his work should therefore be dated to a time in the 2d century after the arrival of the Pauline corpus in Egypt. As was mentioned above (§11.1b), according to Clement of Alexandria, the Carpocratians used a version of the *Secret Gospel of Mark* that contained the sentence "naked man with naked man." According to such information, the Carpocratians may have been some kind of sect practicing egalitarian rites rather than a "philosophical" school.

(3) *Basilides,* who was active in Alexandria before 150 CE, is considered to be the first founder of a Gnostic school. Reports about his teaching and preserved fragments are few and sometimes contradictory. The most reliable witnesses are Clement of Alexandria and Irenaeus (apparently dependent upon a lost writing of Justin Martyr), while Hippolytus ascribes an altogether different teaching to Basilides, which probably relies on the writing of one of Basilides' students. Basilides' teaching can be classified as philosophical, Christian, or Gnostic. Neopythagorean speculations may have affected him as much as Stoic ethics. His cosmology and soteriology is Gnostic, and his *Commentaries* perhaps show the influence of Christian writings. Most striking is his cosmogonic theory. The universe

Bibliography to §11.2c (1):   Texts

Völker, *Quellen,* 11–33.

"Ophites and Ophians" and "Systems Involving Three Principles: The Naassenes," in Foerster, *Gnosis,* 1. 84–99 and 261–82.

Bibliography to §11.2c (2):   Texts

Völker, *Quellen,* 33–38.

Extensive Collection of Greek and Latin sources for Carpocrates and the Carpocratians in Smith, *Clement,* 295–350.

Bibliography to §11.2c (3):   Texts

Völker, *Quellen,* 38–57.

Layton, *Gnostic Scriptures,* 417–44.

"Basilides," in Foerster, *Gnosis,* 1. 59–83.

developed through 365 stages of emanation from one principle until it reached the lowest circle, the visible heaven. The ruler of the universe is called "Abraxas" (the sum of these seven letters in the Greek numerical system is 365). The angels of the visible heaven fashion the things of the world. But their archon, the god of the Jews, who gave the law, wants to subject all nations to his people. The soteriology is Gnostic: the savior descends under the secret name Kaulakau (drawn from Isa 28:10), appears as a man, but the Jews mistakenly crucify Simon of Cyrene while Jesus is standing by mocking them. The savior ascends without ever dying and being raised from the dead. Salvation comes to those who know these things, but those who confess Jesus as crucified are still under the power of the world. Only the soul is saved. Therefore such things as eating meat sacrificed to the idols do not matter. A few fragments of Basilides' *Commentaries* discuss the problem of suffering and providence: suffering is ultimately bound up with the fundamental condition of being in the world and is not necessarily the consequence of sin, but does not deny the goodness of God—and those who have "gnosis" cannot suffer anyway. It is thought that Basilides is here writing a commentary on 1 Peter 4:12–19. That, however, is doubtful; it is anachronistic to suppose that this work was in fact a series of commentaries on books of the New Testament. Basilides' teaching influenced Valentinus, and his followers were still known in the 3d and 4th century.

(4) *Valentinus.* Speculative Gnostic mythologies continued to be cultivated in esoteric circles, but had little impact upon the life of the church. Basilides created a school and had some followers. His somewhat younger contemporary Valentinus (ca. 100–175 CE), however, made a difference. Born in a city of the Nile delta, he was educated in the Christian church of Alexandria, studied with Gnostic teachers, and learned the philosophy of Plato and probably also the allegorical method of the Jewish philosopher Philo of Alexandria. Poet, mystic visionary, teacher, exegete, and church politician, Valentinus founded his school in Alexandria, then moved to Rome just before the year 140 CE, where he even tried to be elected as bishop, and left gifted students in the East (Theodotus and Ambrose) and the West (Ptolemy and Heracleon), who refined his system and propagated his message for generations

Bibliography to §11.2c (3):   Studies

H. A. Wolfson, "Negative Attributes in the Church Fathers and the Gnostic Basilides," *HTR* 50 (1957) 145–56.

Werner Foerster, "Das System des Basilides," *NTS* 9 (1962/63) 233–55.

Ekkehard Mühlenberg, "Wirklichkeitserfahrung und Theologie bei dem Gnostiker Basilides," *Kerygma und Dogma* 18 (1972) 161–75.

Robert M. Grant, "Place de Basilide dans la théologie chrétienne ancienne," *Revue des études Augustinennes* 25 (1979) 201–16.

Bibliography to §11.2c (4):   Texts

Völker, *Quellen,* 57–141.

Harold W. Attridge and George W. MacRae, "The Gospel of Truth," in Harold W. Attridge (ed.), *Nag Hammadi Codex I (The Jung Codex)* (2 vols.; NHS 22–23; Leiden: Brill, 1985) 1. 55–122; 2. 7–135.

George W. MacRae, "The Gospel of Truth (I,3 and XII,2)," *NagHamLibEngl,* 38–51.

Layton, *Gnostic Scriptures,* 217–353.

"The Gospel of Truth," in Foerster, *Gnosis,* 2. 53–70.

to come; Valentinian communities (as distinct from schools) were eventually formed that were still in existence in the 5th and 6th centuries.

Only a very few fragments of his own work have been preserved by quotations of the church fathers who opposed him. A full reconstruction of his work requires recourse to the better attested works of his students. But even the few fragments that are extant show that Valentinus was the most creative Christian theologian of the 2d century. The style of Valentinus's Greek composition is at the height of literary art of those days. The one poem that is preserved is composed in Greek metric verse. Fortunately, the discovery of the Nag Hammadi Library provided the full text of a sermon that was almost certainly written by Valentinus himself, *The Gospel of Truth* (NHC I, 3 and a few fragments in a different translation from the Greek original in NHC XII, 2), the most sublime and most beautiful writing of the entire Nag Hammadi corpus. It is not a "gospel" but a meditation about the gospel, written by a preacher and gifted theologian with a deep sense of true piety. Although there are no explicit quotations in the writing, the author not only knew the Scriptures of Israel but also some gospels, especially the Gospel of John, and some of the letters of Paul very well. No one should miss the opportunity of reading this book, or be deterred by the fact that it is most likely the work of one of the archheretics of the later Christian church. It is a breath of fresh air after the laborious study of the cosmological speculations of the documents of mythological Gnosticism.

Gnostic mythology must be presupposed for Valentinus. The brief report of Valentinian cosmogony that is preserved by Irenaeus, and for which more information can be derived from Irenaeus's report of Ptolemy's system, shows a typically Gnostic system of emanations from a duality that is called the "Ineffable" and "Silence." From these two come three more pairs that, together with the original pair, form the "Ogdoad" out of which other aeons evolve to a total of twenty-four. But the pleroma is disturbed through the revolt of one of its last members, the Mother (Sophia), whose son Christ heads back up into the pleroma—it is Christ who then

Bibliography to §11.2c (4):   Studies

Eugène de Faye, *Gnostique et Gnosticisme: Étude critique des documents du gnosticisme chrétien aux IIe et IIIe siècles* (2d ed.; Bibliothèque de l'Ecole des Hautes Études, Sciences Religieuses 27; Paris: Leroux, 1925).

Werner Foerster, *Von Valentin zu Herakleon* (BZNW 7; Giessen: Töpelmann, 1928).

F. L. M. M. Sagnard, *La Gnose Valentienne et le témoignage de Saint Irénée* (EPhM 36; Paris: Vrin, 1947).

Gilles Quispel, "La conception de l'homme dans la gnose Valentienne," *ErJb* 15 (1948) 249–86.

G. C. Stead, "The Valentinian Myth of Sophia," *JTS* 20 (1969) 75–104.

Idem, "In Search of Valentinus," in Layton, *Rediscovery of Gnosticism,* 1. 75–102.

R. McL. Wilson, "Valentinianism and the *Gospel of Truth,*" ibid., 133–45.

Harold W. Attridge, "The Gospel of Truth as an Exoteric Text," in Hedrick and Hodgson, *Nag Hammadi,* 239–55.

J. A. Williams, *Biblical Interpretation in the Gnostic Gospel of Truth from Nag Hammadi* (SBLDS 79; Atlanta: Scholars Press, 1988).

Bibliography to §11.2c (4):   History of Scholarship

J. Helderman, "Das Evangelium Veritatis in der neueren Forschung," *ANRW* 2.25.5 (1988) 4054–4106.

sends Jesus. The Mother then issues another child, the "demiourge" who fashions the visible world. What is remarkable here is the replacement of the mythical names by abstract philosophical concepts; and the designer of the visible world is no longer an evil archon named Yaldabaoth but the "craftsman," the demiourge of Plato's *Timaeus*. Thus the mythical actors of the Gnostic myth are philosophically dignified; evidence for the cosmogony as well as for the process of salvation are found in biblical texts by interpreting them through the time-honored method of allegory. Valentinus and his students develop their teaching inside the Christian communities as the learned guides into the deeper meaning of Scripture. For Valentinus himself, this is a pastoral invitation to mystical contemplation and vision of the true identity of self. Among his students, his teachings are systematized, expounded in biblical commentaries—especially in the exegesis of the Gospel of John—and, indicating the beginning controversy with the ecclesiastical establishment, lines are drawn between those who have "knowledge" and the average church Christians. Thus there are three classes of human beings, the spiritual people (*pneumatikoi* = the true Gnostics), who are saved by nature; those who merely possess a soul (*psychikoi* = the ecclesiastical Christians), who are saved by works; and those who are solely made up of matter (*hylikoi*), who are lost forever. This may not have been Valentinus's own agenda, but the elitism of his schools' teachings set the stage for the battle between them and the defenders of the ordinary members of the fast-growing Christian churches.

3. The Beginnings of Catholicism

(a) Vernacular Catholic Christianity: The Second Letter of Clement

The beginnings of non-Gnostic Christian communities in Egypt are obscure. Indeed, they may have been obscured, not so much by the existence of Gnostic sects and schools in general, but by the towering figure and inspired Christian church leader Valentinus and his students, whose mission was not the creation of an esoteric Gnostic circle but the inspiration of the church by the deep wisdom and pastoral care that Christian Gnosticism was able to disclose to troubled souls in an age of spiritual uncertainty. It can be assumed that the beginnings of vernacular Christianity in Egypt were related to developments in other provinces. Some of the writings that would later form the canon of the New Testament came to Egypt in the first half of the 2d century; Valentinus and his students were acquainted with such books and used them extensively. One of the writings comprising the collection of the Apostolic Fathers, the *Second Letter of Clement*, may have been written in Egypt in the middle of the 2d century. The Egyptian origin of *2 Clement* is by no means certain and is suggested by only a few scholars. Nonetheless, there are

Bibliography to §11.3a: Texts

Bihlmeyer, *ApostVät*, xxix–xxxi, 71–81.
Wengst, *Didache, Barnabas, 2. Klemens*, 103–202.
Lake, *ApostFath*, 123–63.

important reasons to support this hypothesis. In the later tradition of the church, *2 Clement* was linked to *1 Clement* (§12.a2e); in extant manuscripts they were copied together. Thus *1 Clement* and *2 Clement* occur side by side in two manuscripts of the New Testament Codex Alexandrinus (5th century) and Codex Hierosolymitanus (1056 CE, the complete text of the *Didache* was found in this codex; only in the Hierosolymitanus is the text of *2 Clement* fully preserved). The Syriac translations of the New Testament also transmitted both writings together.

Since *1 Clement* was written from Rome to Corinth it was assumed that *2 Clement* was composed either in Rome or in Corinth. It is difficult, however, to find in either of these two churches or in their relationship with each other any situation that would explain *2 Clement*'s purpose. Adolf von Harnack's hypothesis that the Roman bishop Soter (165–174) was the author of this writing is farfetched and assumes a date of authorship that is probably too late. Moreover, it is unlikely that the later connection of the two writings has its roots in ancient tradition. Eusebius states explicitly that he knew of no recognition of *2 Clement* by older writers (*Hist. eccl.* 3.28.4), while he found *1 Clement* well attested (*Hist. eccl.* 4.23.11; 5.6.3). Thus they were not transmitted together in the time before Eusebius. Furthermore, *2 Clement* says nothing about its author, nor does it ever refer to *1 Clement*. The title "Second Epistle of Clement" appears only in the colophons of the manuscripts. The writing itself contains no prescript with author and address, and no final greetings. In fact, it is not a letter at all but a homily or, better, a programmatic theological writing with homiletic features. Origin and purpose must be decided by internal evidence alone.

The assumption of Egyptian origin would solve a number of problems arising from special features of *2 Clement*. It is striking, on the one hand, that the writing presents a very simple and practical piety. Hans Windisch's characterization has been frequently repeated: "The theological basis of *2 Clement* is, stated briefly, a Synoptic-Gospels Christianity understood in terms of contemporary Judaism." Its central feature is the call for repentance and the demand for good works in the face of the coming judgment. Jesus is primarily a teacher; nothing points to a developed christology. Still, on the other hand, there is evidence that *2 Clement* cannot

Bibliography to §11.3a: Commentaries

Lightfoot, *Apostolic Fathers*, part 1, vols. 1–2.

Robert M. Grant and Holt H. Graham, *First and Second Clement* (Grant, *ApostFath 2*).

Rudolf Knopf, *Die Lehre der zwölf Apostel, die zwei Clemensbriefe* (HNT.E. 1; Tübingen: Mohr/Siebeck, 1920) 151–84.

Adolf Lindemann, *Die Clemensbriefe* (HNT 17, Die Apostolischen Väter 1; Tübingen: Mohr/Siebeck, 1992).

Bibliography to §11.3a: Studies

Karl Paul Donfried, *The Setting of Second Clement in Early Christianity* (NovTSup 38; Leiden: Brill, 1974).

Hans Windisch, "Das Christentum des 2. Clemensbriefes," in *Festgabe von Fachgenossen und Freunden Adolf von Harnack zum siebzigsten Geburtstag dargebracht* (Tübingen: Mohr/Siebeck, 1921) 122–34.

Helmut Koester, *Synoptische Überlieferung bei den Apostolischen Vätern* (TU 65; Berlin: Akademie-Verlag, 1957) 62–111.

have been written in the earliest period of Christianity. The sayings of Jesus that are quoted in the writing presuppose the New Testament Gospels of Matthew and Luke; they were probably drawn from a harmonizing collection of sayings that had been composed on the basis of these two gospels. *2 Clem.* 8.5 refers to the written "gospel" as a well-established entity (though it is not necessary to understand the reference to the "apostles," *2 Clem.* 14.2, as a reference to writings under apostolic authority). It is also difficult to reconcile the otherwise quite simple christological statements of the writing with *2 Clem.* 14.2, where the sentence from Gen 1:27, "God created the human being as male and female," is interpreted as a statement about Christ and the church, which in turn is understood as the body of Christ. This presupposes either the deutero-Pauline Letter to the Ephesians or analogous speculations about the heavenly beings "Church" and "Christ." The latter seems more likely, especially since *2 Clement* elsewhere rarely, if ever, attests any knowledge of the Pauline corpus.

Silence with respect to Paul's letters would be strange if the book were composed in Corinth, where those letters were well known. But if *2 Clement* was written in Egypt at just before the middle of the 2d century, such silence is less surprising, and an occasional reference to a Gnostic mythological concept can be easily explained. What looks like an early "Synoptic-Gospels Christianity understood in terms of Judaism" is actually the Christianity of a later period, which insisted upon the basic principles of active and practicing piety in order to strengthen its position over against a more dominant Gnostic faith. This explains the anti-Gnostic statement that *gnosis* is the confession of the one who has saved us: "But how do we confess him? By doing what he says, and by not disregarding his commandments" (3.2–4). Also the Gnostic goal of salvation, "to find rest," is critically interpreted: one finds rest by doing the will of Christ (6.7). The view that our flesh is the temple of God is especially emphasized, and *2 Clement* explicitly rejects the statement that "this flesh is not judged and does not rise again" (9.1–3). In the context of this anti-Gnostic posture, he also proposes a new interpretation of the Gnostic speculation about Gen 1:27 concerning the heavenly aeons Christ and the Church: Christ made the church manifest by appearing in the flesh in order to demonstrate "that those of us who guard her [the church] in the flesh without corruption shall receive her back again in the Holy Spirit" (14.2–3). In the same context, additional statements leave no doubt that the author is arguing against Gnosticism: "the flesh is the copy of the spirit," and "guard the flesh that you may receive the spirit" (14.3). Elsewhere *2 Clement* presents an interpretation of a saying of Jesus that was used in Gnostic gospels: "When the two shall be one, and the outside as the inside, and the male with the female neither male nor female" (12.2). This saying also appears in the *Gospel of Thomas* (#22) and in the *Gospel of the Egyptians* (§11.2b). *2 Clement* directs his interpretation against a Gnostic understanding; he explains the first of these sentences as "speaking with one another in truth, so there is but one soul in two bodies," the second as meaning that the soul (the inside) should become visible in good works just as the body (the outside) is visible, and the third sentence as pointing to a new relationship between brothers and sisters in the faith, in which they learn to think about each other in terms other than sexual relationship (12.3–5).

All these observations place *2 Clement* squarely into the context of an Egyptian Christian community that tries to establish its own piety in obedience to Jesus' words against a predominant Gnostic Christianity in that country. This writing is then the first tangible evidence for the existence of vernacular catholicism in Egypt before the middle of the 2d century. Although the beginnings of these Christian communities are obscure, *2 Clement* demonstrates that traditions of the early catholic church were being established at that time. This also laid the ground for the development of an ecclesiastical organization, eventually directed by a bishop, which first appeared in Alexandria during the last two decades of the 2d century.

(b) The Controversy with Gnosticism: The Epistula Apostolorum

The *Epistula Apostolorum* was not known until the discovery of major portions of the work in a Coptic translation in the year 1895, and the appearance of some Latin fragments and a complete Ethiopic translation in subsequent years. An Egyptian origin for this writing is most probable. Internal evidence suggests the second half of the 2d century as the date of its composition. The gospels of the New Testament are freely used, but not quoted as Scripture; Paul is known, especially in the image in which he is pictured in the Acts of the Apostles; allusions to Pauline epistles occur several times, though these letters are never quoted as authoritative words of the apostle. Thus the *Epistula Apostolorum* relies on writings that the developing catholic churches in other provinces used and honored.

The genre and content of the *Epistula Apostolorum* reveals its anti-Gnostic intent. Its genre imitates the literary form of the Gnostic revelation discourse, in which the risen Jesus transmits heavenly wisdom and teaching to his disciples. Against the claim of various Gnostic writings circulating under the authority of a particular apostle, the *Epistula Apostolorum* adopts for its message the authority of all apostles, whose eleven names are given as John, Thomas, Peter, Andrew, James, Philipp, Bartholomew, Matthew, Nathanael, Judas, and Cephas. This list is a bit surprising since three names from the Synoptic gospels' lists are missing (James son of Alphaeus, Thaddeus, and Simon the Canaanite) and in their stead Nathanael, Judas Zelotes, and Cephas (in addition to Peter!) are added; most remarkable is the fact that not Peter but John and Thomas are heading the list—because

Bibliography to §11.3b: Text

Carl Schmidt, *Gespräche Jesu mit seinen Jüngern nach der Auferstehung* (TU 43; Leipzig: Hinrichs, 1919). First edition of the *Epistula Apostolorum*.

Hermann Duensing, *Epistula Apostolorum* (KlT 152; Berlin: de Gruyter, 1925). German translation of the Ethiopic and Coptic texts.

Cameron, *Other Gospels,* 131–162.

C. Detlef G. Müller, "Epistula Apostolorum," in Schneemelcher, *NT Apoc.,* 1. 249–84.

Bibliography to §11.3b: Studies

Manfred Hornschuh, *Studien zur Epistula Apostolorum* (PTS 5; Berlin: de Gruyter, 1965).

Julian V. Hills, *Tradition and Composition in the Epistula Apostolorum* (HDR 24; Minneapolis: Fortress, 1990).

Charles E. Hill, "The *Epistula Apostolorum*: An Asian Tract from the Time of Polycarp," *Journal of Early Christian Studies* 7 (1999), 1–53.

they were the preferred authorities in Gnostic circles? Before reporting the appearance of Jesus to the disciples, the *Epistula Apostolorum* includes a section that corresponds to the creed of the church, speaking of God the creator and preserver of the world, and describing the earthly appearance of Jesus with the use of materials from the gospels of the New Testament and the *Infancy Gospel of Thomas*. In the narrative about Jesus' resurrection, the physical appearance is emphasized (*Epist. Apost.* 1–12). The second part of the book could be called an anti-Gnostic theology, which treats all important topics of Christian theology in systematic fashion. Questions of christology are dealt with first: Jesus' way through the heavens in his coming, the incarnation, the Passover as remembrance of his death, and his second coming (13–19). Questions of eschatology follow: the resurrection of the flesh, together with the spirit and the soul, and the last judgment (21–29, including an excursus about the descent into Hades and preaching and baptism for Abraham, Isaac, and Jacob in chap. 27); then the preaching to Israel and the Gentiles (30). The last topic leads to an excursus about Paul, the apostle to the nations (31–33), defending Paul as a legitimate apostle of the catholic church against the claims to Paul as the authority of Gnostic theology, but also against his rejection in Jewish-Christian circles. The last part of this theological disquisition deals with the tribulations of the endtime, the fate of the sinners and the righteous, and their relationship to each other (34–40).

The final chapters of the *Epistula Apostolorum* are related to the genre of church order. The three orders are unusual and deviate from the offices as they were established in the catholic churches: father (=preacher of the revelations), servant (*diakonos,* charged with baptizing), and teacher (41–42). The teaching of the Christian virtues is presented as an interpretation of the parable of the ten virgins (43–45). The anti-Gnostic polemic is evident in the designation of the foolish virtues as Insight, Knowledge, Obedience, Endurance, and Mercy (perhaps the last three are directed against Jewish Christians), whereas the wise virgins are called Faith, Love, Joy, Peace, and Hope. Following this exposition are instructions about the rich, church discipline, and excommunication (46–49). The conclusion is a warning against false teachers (50). With the description of Jesus' ascension the author returns to the framework of the genre that he had adopted.

This book is an extremely important document because it responds directly to the challenge of Gnosticism. Gnostic Christianity in Egypt had identified "revelation" with the presentation of mysterious knowledge, usually transmitted in secret books in which Christ (or some other revealer figure) disclosed the reality of the transcendent world, thus revealing to the spiritual persons their origin, identity, and destiny. The *Epistula Apostolorum* fully adopts the genre of the Gnostic discourse. But it is an open book, written "for the whole world" (chap. 1). As in Gnostic books, what Jesus says in this book is the discourse of the messenger from heaven, but this messenger is at the same time the one who has become flesh and whose earthly life can be described in a biographical sketch. While the Gnostics relied on the sayings of Jesus, the *Epistula Apostolorum* relies on the narrative materials that, including the miracles, prove the true human presence of Jesus. What the believers are told about their true existence does not concern their heavenly origin but their earthly life. This earthly experience is defined by an eschatological expectation that permits the understanding of the essence of Christian faith in terms of the teaching of virtue and church order. The creed of the early catholic church as well as the gospels, understood as providing the narrative reality of this creed, furnished the materials for the forging of a new type of revelation discourse that could be used as a weapon in the fight against Gnosticism. The later church, however, did not develop this genre of anti-Gnostic polemic further but checked the continued growth of revelation through discourses of Jesus by canonizing the gospels of the New Testament. Thus the *Epistula Apostolorum* was soon forgotten.

(c) The Establishment of an Ecclesiastical Organization

The ecclesiastical organization envisioned in the *Epistula Apostolorum* (fathers, deacons, teachers) deviates from the leadership structure that was emerging in the catholic churches elsewhere (bishops, presbyters, and deacons). The institution of ecclesiastical offices that brought Egyptian Christianity into the mainstream of the universal catholic church of Syria, Asia Minor, Greece, and Rome lies beyond the scope of this book; it belongs to the end of the 2d century. *2 Clement* and the *Epistula Apostolorum* witness the strengthening of non-Gnostic Christianity of Egypt. These writings also demonstrate that, in addition to the Gospel of John, other New Testament writings such as the Gospel of Matthew and the Lukan writings became known in Egypt and that the letters of Paul began to be read not only in the schools of Gnostic teachers like Valentinus but also in communities of vernacular Christianity. Both used the same early Christian writings. The battle was no longer about the question of the legitimacy of any of those writings but about their interpretation. Clear decisions about their interpretation were difficult. At the end of the 2d century, Clement of Alexandria accepted the gospels of the New Testament canon and the Pauline corpus as authoritative but remained ambiguous about the relevance of some of the Gnostic books; the *Secret Gospel of Mark* was acceptable as long as it was used only in the special circles of the "perfect" Christians. Both Clement and the great 3d-century theologian Origen shared the allegorical method with the Jewish philosopher Philo of Alexandria and the genius of Gnostic theology Valentinus. Demetrius of Alexandria, bishop in the last two decades of the 2d century, was the first ecclesiastical leader who rigorously tried to enforce episcopal authority, but it is unlikely that he met with immediate success. His contemporary Clement of Alexandria, an open-minded philosopher, fought the Gnostics but proclaimed his ideal of the Christian as "the true Gnostic"; he also cared little for episcopal authority. At the beginning of the 3d century, Origen, who far surpassed the Gnostics in his skill as an exegete and his insights as a theologian, was defeated in his battle with the orthodox bishop of Alexandria and was forced to move to Caesarea in Palestine, where he reestablished his theological school. Even a hundred years later, the monks of Pachomius, founder of cenobite Christian monasticism, read and copied Gnostic writings for their own religious edification. Thanks to this Christian monastic activity, the writings of the Nag Hammadi Library have been preserved: members of the Pachomian monastery hid these precious books in order to protect them from the officially sanctioned heresy hunters. Thus orthodoxy and heresy continued to exist side by side in Egypt for centuries.

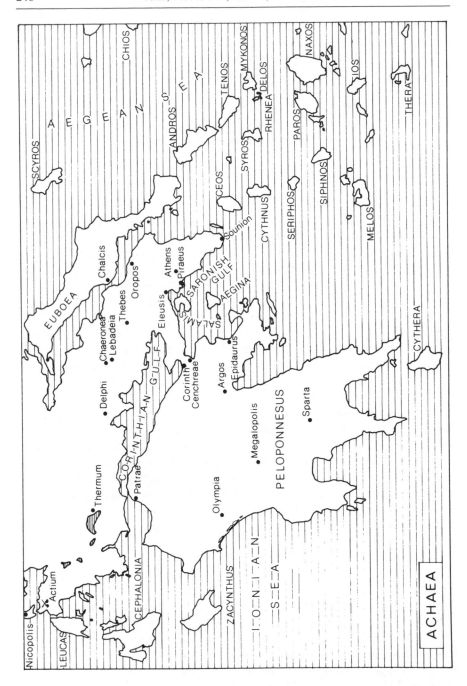

ASIA, MACEDONIA, GREECE, AND ROME

1. The Renewal of Apocalypticism

(a) Apocalypticism in the Pauline Churches:
The Second Letter to the Thessalonians

In the period after the Pauline mission, the churches of Asia Minor, Macedonia, and Greece developed in a direction that was quite different from most of Syria and Egypt. Rome was soon associated with the further history of these churches, and so was Antioch, which had in fact been related to the Pauline mission from the very beginning. The particular features that characterize the history of these churches were not due exclusively to the effectiveness of Paul's missionary efforts, although this must have been a significant factor. The Pauline letters demonstrate that Paul and his associates paid special attention to the founding of new congregations and to their consolidation, continuation, and growth, establishing them as centers of continuing missionary activity. However, the social and economic structures of the area of the Pauline mission must also be considered, since they were markedly different from Egypt and the inland areas of Syria. Greece, Macedonia, and the western parts of Asia Minor were dominated by a large number of cities that experienced a period of considerable prosperity under imperial Roman rule. In Syria, similar city cultures existed along the Mediterranean coast, with Antioch as the largest and leading city; in Egypt, Alexandria remained the only significant city.

Bibliography to §12.1

Philipp Vielhauer and Georg Strecker, "Apocalypses and Related Subjects: Introduction," and "Apocalypses in Early Christianity," in Schneemelcher, *NT Apoc.,* 2. 542–602.
Adela Yarbro Collins, "Early Christian Apocalyptic Literature," *ANRW* 2.25.6 (1988) 4665–4711.
See also the literature under §5.2b.

Bibliography to §12.1a: Commentaries

Beda Rigaux, *Les épîtres aux Thessaloniens* (EtBib; Paris: Gabalda, 1956).
Wolfgang Trilling, *Der zweite Brief an die Thessalonicher* (EKKNT 14; Neukirchen-Vluyn: Neukirchener Verlag, 1980).
Willi Marxsen, *Der zweite Thessalonicherbrief* (Zürcher Bibelkommentare NT 11, 2; Zürich: Theologischer Verlag, 1982).

Bibliography to §12.1a: Studies

R. F. Collins (ed.), *The Thessalonian Correspondence* (BETL 87; Leuven: Peeters, 1990).
William Wrede, *Die Echtheit des II. Thessalonicherbriefes* (TU NF 9, 2; Leipzig: Hinrichs, 1902).
Walter Schmithals, "The Historical Situation of the Thessalonian Epistles," in idem, *Paul and the Gnostics,* 123–218.

The domination of urban culture in the Pauline missionary areas meant that a comparatively large proportion of the population enjoyed at least a modest prosperity, had access to education, and had the freedom to travel or to settle elsewhere. Of course, there was slave labor, but slaves employed in households and industries were often better educated and had more freedom than slaves in rural areas. Some of these slaves were even wealthy and blended into a restless and unstable urban class of craftsmen, merchants, and employees with its own code of moral conduct. There were Roman administrators and a few Roman soldiers, but the internal administration of the cities was largely left to the local aristocracies, who were allied with Rome through the patronage system and by no means unwilling to support the most visible symbol of Roman presence, namely, the cult of the emperor. Urban culture also brought with it not only considerable economic opportunities but also a larger supply and demand in the religious market. The city of Rome, which possessed all these things in large measure, was the capital of the world and seat of a usually benevolent government, and it loomed large on the horizon of the cities in the East, be it as the "Great Babylonian Whore" (Revelation of John) or as the final goal of the victorious course of the gospel (Luke-Acts). From its first beginnings, the Christian church in Rome was a vital partner of the churches of Asia Minor, Macedonia, and Greece, though for a long time the leadership lay with the churches of the eastern Greek cities.

Among the various developments in the post-Pauline era until the turn of the 1st century, the renewal of apocalyptic expectations is particularly striking. Paul himself had expected Jesus' return in glory during his own lifetime, although he refused to engage in speculations about "times and seasons" (1 Thess 5:1). There is no evidence from the genuine Pauline letters that the problem of the delay of the parousia ever arose as long as Paul was still alive (not even 1 Thessalonians provides such information; see §9.2d). But Paul had criticized the foreshortening of the apocalyptic expectation in a realized eschatology (see 1 Corinthians, §9.3c). If the expectation of Jesus' return in glory continued to be a vital element of faith in the churches of Paul after his death, the question of the delay had to arise soon; in fact, it was aggravated by the death of Paul. There were three options: the eschatological expectation had to be revitalized, the delay had to be explained, or the eschatological expectation had to be translated into a new language. The first two options clashed very soon; this is evident in the Second Letter to the Thessalonians.

Some scholars see 2 Thessalonians as a genuine letter of Paul. If this were the case the letter would have come from the same situation as 1 Thessalonians, written to Thessalonica perhaps only a few weeks after the first letter due to an unexpected change of the church's situation. This new situation is characterized by the reference to opponents who claim that the day of the Lord is at hand (2 Thess 2:1–2). Such a situation, however, is hardly thinkable just a few weeks after the first letter. It fits better in the time after the apostle's death, when the letters of Paul had received new significance as his legacy to the church. Only by assuming a later date for the composition of the letter is it possible to explain the difficulties in the interpretation of 2 Thessalonians. The letter's frequent references to 1 Thessalonians are striking: as much as a third of 2 Thessalonians consists of sentences and phrases from 1 Thessalonians; but exactly in these contexts terms and words occur that Paul never used elsewhere or that he employed with a different meaning. Typically

Early Roman Coin from Macedonia
The obverse (above) shows the head of the goddess
Artemis in a circle of Macedonian shields. The reverse
(below), a cast of the same coin, shows a club (symbol of Heracles) in an oakwreath with the thunderbolt
of Zeus on the left. The inscription reads: "Of the First
(Region) of the Macedonians."

Pauline thoughts, often using almost the exact same words as 1 Thessalonians, are modified in a way unparalleled in the genuine Pauline letters. In 1 Thess 1:6–10 the experience of tribulation is understood as a confirmation of the certainty of election; in 2 Thess 1:4–10 tribulations prove that God will give just retribution to both the persecutors and to those who are persecuted. 1 Thess 3:8 speaks about the firm standing of the church "in the Lord"; 2 Thess 2:15 defines the firm standing of the church as holding on to the traditions that have been taught in the words and letters of the apostle. 1 Thess 1:5–7 relates the concept of imitation (of Paul and of the Lord) to the acceptance of the proclamation in much tribulation, making the congregation an example for the acceptance of the word in other congregations; and that Paul had worked night and day with his own hands was not an example to be imitated, but an expression of his love (1 Thess 2:8–9); but in 2 Thess 3:7–10 "Paul" says that he had worked day and night in the sweat of his brow so the church would have an example to imitate, with all the people working eagerly with their own hands: "Those who do not work should not eat!" That the dedicated work of the apostle to the Gentiles is no longer understood as a service on behalf of the gospel but rather as an admonition against laziness should leave no doubt that 2 Thessalonians was written in a situation completely different from that of Paul's life. It is a situation in which the proclamation of the Lord's arrival in the immediate future would disturb the habits of a hard-working class of church members that had adjusted its life to the ways of the society in which the congregations exist. This is the topic of the letter.

It is not quite clear what thoughts the opponents connected with their announcement of the immediate arrival of the day of the Lord. They certainly were not Gnostics who proclaimed the constant presence of eschatological salvation. Their refutation would not have required the presentation of a specific, though mysterious, eschatological timetable. The author of 2 Thessalonians agrees that the coming of the day of the Lord will put an end to the course of the world; he disagrees with the opponents' announcement of the date. If the congregation took that announcement seriously, the entire order of the life of the church and its members would be endangered. However important eschatology might have been to the author, the present time should not be understood from an eschatological perspective. The present experience of tribulation is therefore not a sign of the coming of the Lord in the near future. The author separates the present tribulations from the timetable of eschatological expectations and relates them to future retribution and judgment (2 Thess 1:4–10). Having clarified this issue at the beginning of the letter, he is ready to quote the dangerous eschatological message of his opponents, which they apparently justified with a reference to 1 Thessalonians (2:1–2), and to explain his own eschatological schedule in order to refute their message (2:3–12). According to the author's timetable, the valid sign of the nearness of the parousia is the appearance of the Antichrist, who is described in traditional terms of Jewish apocalypticism as "the man of lawlessness" and "the son of perdition." He will assume the posture of divinity and seat himself in the temple of God (since these are traditional concepts, this does not imply that the temple in Jerusalem was still standing). Furthermore, 2 Thess 2:8–12 presents a juxtaposition of the Antichrist and Jesus that, through the use of antithetical formulations and alliterations, for the first time develops an "antichristology" with exact correlations to christology.

In the exposition of the eschatological timetable an important argument is the mysterious reference to "that [or, he who] still restrains" the adversary of Christ (2:6–7). Some have suggested that the Roman state is the restrainer of the chaos that will arise when the Antichrist arrives, but it is more likely that the author is pointing to a mythological figure of the apocalyptic tradition, such as the angel who binds Satan for a thousand years (Rev 20:1–3). The author intentionally gives no hint as to the identity of this mysterious power because the purpose of the reference is to keep the reader mystified, just as Mark 13:14 refers to the mysterious "desolating sacrilege set up where it ought not to be." Matthew, to be sure, knew that this was a quotation from the Book of Daniel (Matt 24:15) because he was a biblical scholar. But neither the average reader of Mark 13 nor the recipient of 2 Thessalonians 2 was expected to know the exact solution of this mystery; rather, the reader should notice that the coming of the Antichrist was not yet at hand and that therefore the day of the Lord lay well in the distant future. That alone was important, and the author had no intention of giving his readers any clue for the calculation of the date of the parousia. The readers should simply learn that the opponents' radicalized eschatology lacked any insight into sound apocalyptic thinking.

2 Thessalonians wants to lead into a better understanding of Paul's letters, specifically Paul's first letter to Thessalonica. Paul should not be used in order to justify radical eschatological messages; rather, Paul is the originator of a Christian tradition (2 Thess 2:15) that points the church to obedient and responsible living in this world. Apocalyptic concepts are indeed renewed, but it is done in such a way that eschatological expectations are transformed into doctrines about future events, which do not determine the present time in any way—in contrast to Paul, who understood the present situation of the community as eschatological existence, in which the expected future coming of the Lord was operative in the conduct of those who were already now "children of the day and of the light" (1 Thess 5:4–5). For 2 Thessalonians, the conduct of the community is determined by moral admonitions that extol the values of a respected citizenship within the established society, admonitions that are set forward with explicit reference to Paul's command and example (2 Thess 3:6–13).

(b) Apocalypticism and Gnosticism: The Epistle of Jude

The renewed interest in apocalyptic traditions was useful not only in the struggle against a radicalized eschatology, it also proved to be an effective weapon in the

Bibliography to §12.1b: Commentaries

J. N. D. Kelly, A Commentary on the Epistles of Peter and Jude (Black's New Testament Commentaries; London: Black, 1969).

Walter Grundmann, Der Brief des Judas und der zweite Brief des Petrus (ThHK 15; Berlin: Evangelische Verlagsanstalt, 1974) 1–51.

Richard Bauckham, Jude, 2 Peter (WBC 50; Dallas: Word, 1983).

Henning Paulsen, Der Zweite Petrusbrief und der Judasbrief (KEK 12/2; Göttingen: Vandenhoeck & Ruprecht, 1992).

J. H. Neyrey, 2 Peter, Jude: A New Translation with Introduction and Commentary (AB 37C; New York: Doubleday, 1993).

Anton Vögtle, Der Judasbrief, Der Zweite Petrusbrief (EKKNT 22; Neukirchen-Vluyn: Neukirchener Verlag, 1994).

controversy with Gnosticism. In fact, Paul had already made recourse to apocalyptic concepts in his debate with the Corinthian spiritualists, who denied the reality of a future resurrection (1 Corinthians 15). The Epistle of Jude is a witness for the continuing recourse to apocalyptic traditions against Gnostics. Date and place of origin of this brief writing are uncertain. The first witness to its existence is the Second Epistle of Peter, which reproduces a revised version of Jude in its entirety in chapter 2 (§§7.3e; 12.2f). But in contrast to 2 Peter, Jude reveals a more naive attitude in its use of apocalyptic materials. It thus belongs to an earlier period and may have been written as early as the end of the 1st century. A relatively early date is also required because of the use of the pseudonym "Jude, the brother of James," referring without doubt not to the apostle Judas (Luke 6:16; Acts 1:13) but to a brother of Jesus (Mark 6:3; Matt 13:55). The author attaches this "Jude/Judas" to James, the brother of the Lord, which presupposes the existence of the Epistle of James (§10.1c.1). The use of a pseudonym from the family of Jesus would have made sense only as long as there was still some memory of the significance of members of Jesus' family (see Hegesippus in Eusebius *Hist. eccl.* 3.19–20). Even so, the use of this name remains somewhat puzzling and, at the same time, intriguing. Considering the obviously anti-Gnostic character of the writing, the name may have been chosen in view of the claim of Gnostic circles to the authority of Judas Thomas (§10.1b), who was also known as the brother of Jesus. The author of this pseudonymous epistle may have chosen Jude/Judas in order to denigrate the Gnostics' claim to this name, and "brother of James" was meant to deflate their boast that their tradition was authorized by Jesus' very brother. Syria would then be the most likely place of composition of the epistle.

The Epistle of Jude is not a real letter, but a small polemical tractate that lacks any specific addressee. It refers in general to the "faith" that has been transmitted to the saints and to the authority of "the apostles of our Lord Jesus Christ" (Jude 3 and 17). Both have become fixed traditional authorities that are simply presupposed without further explanation. The author does not characterize the opponents in any detail. That they were Gnostics is clear from the polemical reversal of the Gnostic claim to true spirituality in Jude 19: "worldly (*psychikoi*) people, devoid of the spirit (*pneuma*)." Many biblical examples employed by the author belong to the typical equipment of Gnostic speculation: Sodom and Gomorra (Jude 7), Cain (v. 11), the fallen angels (v. 6). But this does not exhaust the polemical arsenal of the author. For his exorbitant abuse of the opponents, although written in rather good Greek, he draws also on Jewish apocalyptic materials, specifically written sources, of which only the *Assumption of Moses* (Jude 9) and the *Apocalypse of Enoch* (Jude 14–15) can still be identified. In each case the purpose of the invective is the threat of punishment in the last judgment, interrupted several times by a disapproving

Bibliography to §12.1b: Studies

Frederik Wisse, "The Epistle of Jude in the History of Heresiology," in *Essays on Nag Hammadi Texts in Honor of Alexander Böhlig* (NHS 3; Leiden: Brill, 1972), 133–43.

Bibliography to §12.1b: History of Scholarship

Richard J. Bauckham, "The Letter of Jude: An Account of Research," *ANRW* 2.25.5 (1988) 3791–3826.

characterization of the opponents, whom the author castigates mercilessly. Such uncompromising polemic can only be explained on the basis of an apocalyptic view of past and present that divides all humanity into the two groups of the elect and the wicked. This view reveals that the rise of apocalypticism was one of the strongest motivations for the enforcement of an increasingly sharp division between orthodoxy and heresy. The author hopes that such a division will eventually be accomplished, although for the time being the Gnostics still participate in the meetings and common meals of the community (v. 12). But since the coming final judgment will bring the ultimate separation of the elect from the wicked, the author of Jude wants to bring an end to any peaceful coexistence with heretics in the present life of the church.

(c) Criticism of the Apocalyptic Expectation: The Revelation of John

The Revelation of John demonstrates that the renewal of apocalypticism was not an isolated phenomenon in the continuing history of the Pauline churches of Asia Minor at the end of the 1st century. The Revelation of John, however, is often misunderstood as a book of apocalyptic propaganda. Its intention is rather to present a critical discussion of already existing apocalyptic views and speculations. Although apocalyptic concepts and traditions are widely used in the writing, the designation "apocalypse" was poorly chosen for this Christian book, which, contrary to its original intentions, has been used repeatedly throughout the history of Christianity as a source and inspiration for apocalyptic and chiliastic (millennarian) movements.

Apocalyptic books were usually written under the pseudonym of some ancient biblical authority such as Enoch, Ezra, Baruch, or Daniel. But the Revelation of John is not pseudepigraphical, nor does it locate its visions in some fictitious place. There is no reason to doubt that the book was in fact written by "John" (Rev 1:1, 9) and that the place of composition was indeed the desolate Aegean island of Patmos, to which the author had been exiled. The recipients of the book would have known quite well who he was. Unfortunately, however, we no longer know anything else about him. He cannot be identified with the author of the Gospel of John or any of the Johannine letters. Language and terminology and the modes of theological argument are completely different. While the author of the Gospel of John belongs in the area of Syria and Palestine, the prophet of the Book of Revelation had a good knowledge about the churches in the cities of western Asia Minor to which he directed his work. He must have been one of the leaders of those churches, and Ephesus, the addressee of the first of his seven letters (2:1–7), was most likely the city

Bibliography to §12.1c: Commentaries

R. H. Charles, *A Critical and Exegetical Commentary on the Revelation of St. John* (2 vols; ICC: Edinburgh: T&T Clark, 1920, and reprints).

Wilhelm Bousset, *Die Offenbarung Johannis* (KEK; 6th ed.; Göttingen: Vandenhoeck & Ruprecht, 1906).

Heinz Kraft, *Die Offenbarung des Johannes* (HNT 16a; Tübingen: Mohr/Siebeck, 1974).

Elisabeth Schüssler Fiorenza, *Invitation to the Book of Revelation: A Commentary on the Apocalypse with Complete Text from the Jerusalem Bible* (Garden City, NY: Image Books/Doubleday, 1981).

David E. Aune, *Revelation* (3 vols.; WBC 52; Dallas: Word, 1997, Nashville, TN: Nelson, 1998).

Head and Arm of the Statue of a Flavian Emperor (Titus?)
Found in Ephesus in the vaults of the support structure for a large temple for the Flavian Augusti from the time of "the Lord and God" Domitian, which was built in that city while the prophet John was in exile on the island of Patmos.

of his own church. The memory of this "John of Ephesus" may have survived in a Papias fragment quoted by Eusebius (*Hist. eccl.* 3.39.4), which mentions in addition to John, the Lord's disciple, a second John, whom he calls a "presbyter." Eusebius (not Papias!) identifies this second John (with some caution) as the author of the Book of Revelation. Another piece of memory of this John possibly survives in a story that Clement of Alexandria (*Quis div. salv.* 42, quoted in Eusebius *Hist. eccl.* 3.23.5–19) tells about a young man, whom John entrusted to the bishop (or presbyter) of Smyrna (the young man later became the leader of brigands but eventually repented). Since this story must be dated before the time of bishop Polycarp of Smyrna, the John of that story could be the John of Ephesus who wrote the Book of Revelation. In any case, some memory survived that its author was not identical with the John of the Fourth Gospel. It was apparently the reputation of this John of Ephesus that later attracted the tradition of the Johannine Gospel and Epistles to Ephesus and eventually merged the two figures. For the understanding of Revelation it is important to note that its author makes no attempt to construct a fictitious situation as the framework of his writing, whether for himself or for the churches to which he writes. The fact that he was "on the island of Patmos on account of the word of God and the testimony of Jesus" (Rev 1:9) indicates that his ministry as a Christian prophet and as an officer of the church had led to his exile.

Bibliography to §12.1c: Studies

Austin Farrer, *A Rebirth of Images* (Westminster: Decre, 1949).

Günther Bornkamm, "Die Komposition der apokalyptischen Visionen in der Offenbarung Johannis," in idem, *Studien zu Antike und Christentum* (3d ed.; München: Kaiser, 1969) 214–22.

Elisabeth Schüssler Fiorenza, *Priester für Gott: Studien zum Herrschafts- und Priestermotif in der Apokalypse* (Münster: Aschendorff, 1972),

Dieter Georgi, "Die Visionen vom himmlischen Jerusalem in Apk 21 und 22," in *Kirche, Festschrift Bornkamm,* 351–72.

J. Lambrecht (ed.), *L'Apocalypse johannique et l'apocalyptique dans le Nouveau Testament* (BETL 53; Gembloux: Duclot, and Louvain: Leuven University Press, 1980).

Adela Yarbro Collins, *The Combat Myth in the Book of Revelation* (HDR 9; Missoula, MT: Scholars Press, 1976).

Eadem, *Crisis and Catharsis: The Power of Apocalypse* (Philadelphia: Westminster, 1984).

Eadem, "Pergamon in Early Christian Literature," in Helmut Koester (ed.), *Pergamon: Citadel of the Gods* (HTS 46; Harrisburg, PA: Trinity Press International, 1998) 163–84.

David L. Barr, "The Apocalypse as Oral Enactment," *Int* 40 (1986) 243–56.

David E. Aune, "The Apocalypse of John and Graeco-Roman Revelatory Magic," *NTS* 33 (1987) 481–501.

Idem, "The Form and Function of the Proclamations to the Seven Churches (Revelation 2–3)," *NTS* 36 (1990) 182–204.

Richard Bauckham, *The Climax of Prophecy: Studies on the Book of Revelation* (Edinburgh: T&T Clark, 1992).

Idem, *The Theology of the Book of Revelation* (Cambridge: Cambridge University Press, 1993).

Steven J. Friesen, *Twice Neokoros: Ephesos, Asia, and the Cult of the Flavian Imperial Family* (Religions in the Greco-Roman World 116; Leiden: Brill: 1993).

Bibliography to §12.1c: Bibliography and History of Scholarship

Robert L. Muse, *The Book of Revelation: An Annotated Bibliography* (New York: Garland, 1996).

Otto Böcher, "Die Johannes-Apokalypse in der neueren Forschung," *ANRW* 2.25.5 (1988) 3850–98.

Frederick J. Murphy, "The Book of Revelation," *CRBS* 2 (1994) 181–225.

The book thus had its origin in a time of persecution that seemed to threaten all Christians and of which the first signs were already visible (see, e.g., 2:13, and especially the references to a general persecution in 3:10; 6:9; etc.). According to Revelation 13 and 17, the general persecution is expected to be unleashed by the Roman state: the animal from the abyss is the Roman emperor; Babylon is the city of Rome. Before the middle of the 2d century there were only two periods in which the Christians, as well as many other people, might have believed that the Roman emperor was indeed the destroyer of a just order of the state and a blasphemer of God: the second half of the reign of Nero (54–68 CE) and the last years of the emperor Domitian (81–96). But the persecution of the Christians by Nero was limited to the city of Rome, and although Nero had a morbid desire to celebrate himself in public, he did not promote the emperor cult systematically and, moreover, was not hated in the eastern provinces (§6.2a). There are difficulties also with respect to the time of Domitian (§§6.2b; 6.5b). To be sure, he wanted to be addressed as "Lord and God" (*dominus et deus*), the philosophers were driven out of Rome, possibly also the Christians suffered persecution (§12.2e), and even some members of the imperial family were executed, perhaps because of their inclination toward Christianity. But the effects were not strongly experienced outside Rome, where it was particularly the Roman aristocracy that hated him; there was certainly no worldwide persecution under his rule. But the situation in Ephesus at that time was not comparable to the situation of cities in other provinces. Ephesus had for a long time desired to become the warden (*neokoros*) of a provincial temple for the cult of the emperor. This wish was finally granted by the emperor Domitian, and the construction of a large temple, dedicated to the "Augusti" (*Sebastoi*), was in progress during the latter years of Domitian's reign. It became an impressive monument; the massive supporting vaults that raised this temple high above the state agora of Ephesus can still be admired today, and the more than life-size head and arm of a temple statue that was believed to be Domitian's (it is more likely from the statue of Titus) are exhibited in the Ephesus museum at Selçuk. At the same time, western Asia Minor with its fast-growing Christian population suffered some economic difficulties (possibly reflected in the remark of Rev 6:6). This could well have provided the conditions for a situation in which existing tensions would deteriorate into a direct confrontation with the authorities of the Roman government.

That such a situation, for the first time in the history of Christianity, created the alternative "Christ or Caesar" may not exclusively have been due to the actions of the Roman authorities. Even the threat of a persecution would have forced the Christians to clarify what their talk about the rule of Christ really meant in relation to a particular political situation and shatter the time-honored formula, inherited from diaspora Judaism, that "one should be obedient to any government authority that comes from God" (Rom 13:1–7). For the prophet John, the Gnostic alternative was not acceptable. He would not agree that the entire visible world, together with its political institutions, was just a nightmare, nothing more than the world of error, terrible as it might seem, but ultimately without reality or substance. From his perspective, all of the history of the world was directed by God and was moving toward a goal designed by God. It was therefore necessary to find an answer that would make the experience of the troubled and fearful Christian church meaningful.

The prophet John sets out to give this answer and to reinforce the vision that
Christ and not Caesar was the destined ruler of the world and the fulfillment of
all hopes.

The difficulties in the understanding of this book arise from its pervasive apocalyptic and mythological language, images, concepts, and metaphors, which often
conceal for us today the political and historical references of the writing. The general mythological worldview of the time cannot by itself explain the extent of
apocalyptic mythology used here. There were alternatives: Josephus, for example,
a contemporary of John, used the linguistic medium of apologetic history. In the
tradition of apocalypticism, its language had served as an instrument to interpret
the world and its history in such a way that future events were set into a proper distance, thus allowing the community of the elect to be confident and hopeful without being disturbed by the bewildering events of the present times. This was how
the author of 2 Thessalonians used the traditions of apocalyptic language; in the
same fashion, it functioned in the Jewish apocalypses *4 Ezra* and *2 Baruch,* both
composed after the destruction of Jerusalem. This, however, is precisely what the
prophet John is fighting against and it is for this reason that he employs the exact
same language that was in use by those who employed the apocalyptic timetable in
order to move the ultimate confrontation of good and evil into the distant future.
John, however, is a prophet rather than an apocalypticist. His message is a call to
understand the present time as the beginning of the final eschatological events, which
are triggered by the confrontation with the cult of the emperor. Those who resist
the enforcement of the imperial cult, present in Ephesus at the time in a gigantic
construction project, are already involved in the final eschatological battle.

The language of the book is shaped by the author himself, not by any particular
written source or sources that he has employed. Of course, he has drawn into his
language materials from a variety of writings and traditions. Foremost is the Hebrew
Bible—phrases from the Bible often reflect the Hebrew text more closely than the
Greek translation of the Septuagint—and here the Book of Ezekiel played a special role, next to it the Book of Daniel. There are no explicit quotations, but the
allusions are often clear enough so that a reader who is familiar with the Bible will
understand what particular biblical prophecy is renewed in John's message. Parallels can also be found in pseudepigraphical apocalyptic books, but they are less
explicit and perhaps often accidental. In addition, John draws from contemporary
Hellenistic mythology and astrology. Poetic sections (hymns, doxologies, prayers)
are derived from the Semitic-style poetry of the Christian community or formed by
John in analogy to such materials. All this together emerges as a composition that
seems to fit the rules of good Greek literary style only very poorly. This, however,
does not imply that John did not know any better, because his mother tongue was
Aramaic. Nor does it indicate that he had not yet learned to speak and write well
in Greek, since he apparently knew Hebrew and Aramaic and was of Jewish origin. The language of the book rather is the result of a deliberate choice. It wants
to be archaizing, because the Book of Revelation is biblical prophecy. This language
is also needed for another reason: The arguments of the Book of Revelation do
not follow the rules of rational sequences, logical progression, and judicious
conclusions; they advance in images and metaphors that can stand side by side with-

out rational connections, until a final image moves the reader to a new level of insight, only in order to introduce another sequence of pictures that repeats the cycle on a higher level of awareness and wisdom. Traditional and familiar materials can be reproduced without explicit commentary until the reader notices striking omissions or additions that indicate the direction of the interpretation. The message of the author will not always find expression within the various images and visions themselves, but rather in their order, sequence, and numbers, in sudden interruptions of the context, and in hymnic, liturgical, or parenetic additions.

The prophet John uses as a primary ordering device an arrangement of seven scenes of visions in each section of the book. The introduction (Rev 1:1–20) leads into a sequence of seven letters to the churches Ephesus, Smyrna, Pergamon, Thyatira, Sardis, Philadelphia, and Laodicea (2:1–3:22). This designates the whole book as a circular letter to the church at large. But even if the communities that are addressed here are representatives of generally applicable settings, the author refers to real, not fictitious, situations; the parenetic sections of the letters are specific. All seven letters are formulated according to a schema derived from the biblical formula of covenant as it was modified in early Judaism: a basic statement, in which Christ introduces himself in his authority of saving activity, is followed by a narrative of the history of the church in question, then a call for repentance, and finally an announcement of curses and blessings. Heretical teachers in the communities are repeatedly mentioned (2:6, 9, 14–15, 20–24; 3:9) and variously identified as adherents of the teachings of Balaam, as disciples of the prophetess Jezebel, as Nicolaitans, and as the Synagogue of Satan. Since the author refers twice to those "who say that they are Jews" (2:9; 3:9), and the opponents are called those who learn "the deep things of Satan" (2:24), they were perhaps Jewish-Christian Gnostics. But it is not possible to be certain about the character of the heresy or heresies attacked here. Apocalyptic admonition is styled as a general request to separate from the heretics (cf. Jude).

The cycles of visions are introduced by a throne vision, which draws upon materials from Isaiah 6 and Ezekiel 1 (Rev 4:1–11). The appearance of a scroll with seven seals (5:1–2) should, according to the pattern of traditional visions, point to a following scene of disclosure, including the opening of the scroll, proclamation of its content, and commissioning of the prophet. At this point, however, John radically departs from the traditional pattern and, contrary to the intention of an apocalyptic book, introduces a novel interpretation. Instead of a disclosure and commissioning scene, John introduces a new figure, the Lion of Judah, the Lamb "as though it had been slain" (5:5–6). The following hymns and doxologies reveal who this figure is: the savior, "who by his blood has ransomed humanity for God" (5:9). His task, however, is by no means—as would be expected—to disclose the content of the scroll. Rather, the authority of universal rule is now transferred to him, and this is acknowledged by the entire celestial court. Everything that is said in the following chapters is not a revelation in the style of an apocalyptic book, but a description of this universal rule of Christ in historical perspective.

The following cycles of seven visions repeatedly demonstrate a similar procedure in John's revision of traditional materials. The vision of the seven seals (6:1–8:1) is not simply a description of the course of the world until its end, but John

inserts several other events (the four riders, sealing of the elect). The opening of
the seals does not bring forth scenes of disclosure but demonstrates the authoritative
rule of Christ. As one seal after the other is opened, the issuing events (war, hunger,
death, cosmic catastrophe) seemingly move toward a climax, namely, the final eschatological event. But the opening of the seventh seal (8:1–2) is intentionally anticlimactic: it simply introduces (8:3–5) a new series of seven visions, namely, the
seven trumpets (8:6–11:19). The reader of the seven seals is guided to learn that
all the terrible events of the past and the present demonstrate that Christ is ruling
and that the martyrs are protected in his hands (6:9–11; 7:7–17). The vision of the
seven trumpets is interpreted in an analogous fashion, but the terror of the ensuing
events is intensified (8:6–9:21). Once more, with the sixth trumpet the description
of these events ends abruptly without having reached its final climax. The seventh
trumpet, which appears in 11:15–19, like an appendix, simply grants a view of the
heavenly temple. Between the sixth and seventh trumpet, John has inserted a report of the commissioning of the prophet (10:1–11) and, for the first time in the
book, references to events of the recent past Christian history, namely, the fall of
Jerusalem and the martyrdom of the two witnesses (11:1–14; their identity remains
obscure). It is absolutely clear at this point of the sequences of visions that so far
everything spoke about the history of humankind in the past, not yet about the future, a past, however, that has not been under the rule of Satan but under the rule
of Christ. This is a deliberate criticism of traditional apocalyptic routine as is also
the fact that this past history is told in very vague terms without allusions to known
historical events with only one exception, the fall of Jerusalem and the martyrdom
of the two witnesses. That the prophet is commissioned only after the sixth trumpet—not much earlier at the opening of the seven seals— tells that only from this
point on his own prophetic ministry is about to begin with a disclosure of the meaning of present and future events.

    The visions of the second part of the book (12:1–22:5) are also arranged ac-
cording to the schema of "seven." With the exception of 16:1–21, however, they
are no longer explicitly numbered. There are three cycles. The first cycle begins
with the vision of the woman clothed with the sun (12:1ff.) and ends with the
vision of the sea of glass (15:2–8); the second comprises the vision of the seven
bowls of wrath (16:1–21); the third begins with the enthronement of the Logos
(19:11ff.) and ends with the vision of a new heaven and a new earth (21:1ff.). The
large excursus about Babylon (=Rome) appears between the second and third cycles (17:1–19:10). The contrast with the cycles of the first part of the book is evident: in the second part each cycle begins with the recent past or an event of the
future (19:11ff.). While the first part of the book described past history under the
rule of Christ, in the second part of the book the prophet tells what is happening
now and shall happen in the future. Under the perspective of universal history the
reader is made to understand that the rule of Christ is now entering the final conflict of this rule with the Roman state, the culmination of the divinely ordained
course of history.

    The first cycle of the visions of the second part of the book (12:1–15:8) includes
the events from the birth of the Messiah and the founding of the church (12:1–18)
to the parousia (14:14–20) and the eschatological adoration (15:2–4). In the vision

of the woman dressed with the sun, pagan mythological and astrological materials are used (note that Roman copies of the Artemis statue of Ephesus show her with a necklace of the zodiac, the twelve stars). In contrast to pagan mythology, which depicts the victory of the gods over the powers of chaos as the symbol of the establishment of order on earth under the rule of the divine king (as, e.g., in the famous sculpture of the Altar of Pergamon), here the battle against chaos, Michael fighting with the dragon, tells that order has been restored in heaven but that chaos is now ruling on earth. The presence of chaos on earth sets the scene for the first appearance of an enemy of divine rule on earth: the Roman state (13:1–10) and its ruler (13:11–18). For the first time in this book, John ascribes the occurrence of evil in the world to a power opposed to God. This enemy of God exercises his power of evil through worship, the cult of the emperor, which perverts and destroys the life of all nations (13:6–10, 15–17). The only alternative is faithfulness to the Lamb (14:1–5). John does not castigate the evil in the world in general but derives this evil from one single cause, namely, worship of the emperor. Rome is therefore the central theme, to be discussed later in 17:1–19:10, introduced by the vision of the seven bowls of wrath (15:1, 5–8; 16:1–21). In the extensive interpretation of the vision of the beasts (13:1ff.) and the Whore of Babylon (17:1–18), specific historical references appear repeatedly, though not all of them are still clear for the modern reader. It is plausible that the number 666 (13:18), the number 8 (17:11), and also the interpretation of the animal (13:3; 17:10–12) refer to the expected return of the emperor Nero, the *Nero redivivus*. $1 + 2 + 3 + \ldots + 8 = 36$ and $1 + 2 + 3 + \ldots + 36 = 666$, which is the equivalent of the letters CAESAR NERON in the Greek numerical system. The *Nero redivivus,* who is rejected by John, is not the evil persecutor of the Christians but the beloved figure of widespread popular beliefs, a kind of pagan messianic figure. In the statements about Rome, and especially in the lament of the merchants after the fall of Rome, criticism of the world-ruling economic power of Rome is the central point. The lament of the merchants and shipowners that recounts all the precious items that they can now no longer ship and sell (18:11–20) reveals a good knowledge of the trade of the time, especially in luxury items; the list of these items in the Book of Revelation resembles an inscription found in Ephesus listing customs duties imposed on shipments from Asia Minor to Rome. It is perhaps important to note here that John shows his good information about matters of economy also in Rev 6:6, where the outbreak of a famine is related to an increase in the price of wheat, while the price of olive oil and wine remained stable. It is well known that in the early imperial period the increasing production of expensive olive oils and wines for profit resulted in the reduction of available agricultural areas for the growing of wheat, with repeated famines as a consequence. The author of this book, the prophet John, had a good knowledge of Rome's grip on the economy of his time.

The last cycle (19:11–22:4) speaks about the future but also resumes earlier topics with the vision of the enthronement of the Logos (19:11–16) and Rome's military defeat (19:17–21). Traditional apocalyptic materials used in these last visions are primarily interpreted in terms of pastoral theology, especially the vision of the binding of Satan and the thousand-year kingdom (20:1–6). John wants to show that the martyrs and other faithful Christians will receive an immediate reward that is independent of the last judgment (20:11–15). After the appearance of a new heaven and a new earth (21:1)—the disappearance of the sea signifies the end of the chaos monster—the concluding vision of the heavenly Jerusalem that is coming down to earth (21:9–22:5) is the counterpart of the vision of Babylon; Jerusalem is the "bride," as Babylon was personified in the "whore"—elements of the traditional topic of the woman "virtue" and the woman "vice" are used here. This new super-city of huge dimensions combines Hellenistic concepts of the ideal democratic city with paradise motifs. There is no temple in the new Jerusalem, and also an impe-rial palace is missing. Its main feature is the central avenue, accessible to all, with the throne of God and the Lamb set in its center. Life-giving fruits are produced in the city itself on trees growing at the stream of paradise. Although the names of the twelve tribes of Israel are written on the gates of the city, all nations are invited to enter (21:3, 24) so that God can be the light of all people.

This concludes the cycles, in which the history of the world was presented in a series of images as history that is supported by faith in the sovereignty of God. No secret knowledge has been revealed and therefore the sealing of the book is ex-plicitly prohibited (22:10). Whatever events took place and will take place is not told to the wise person, who meditates on the secrets of another world, but it is made known to the entire community. The key for participation is therefore not the learning of divine insights, but the hymns and songs of the church that are intro-duced into the text at decisive points of the composition of the book. Even the first adoration of the Lamb as ruler of the universe is explicitly designated as the offer-ing of "the prayers of the saints," that is, the Christian community (5:8). In fact, almost all of the decisive statements about the rule and victory of God or Christ are presented in the form of hymns or doxologies of the martyrs or the faithful be-lievers (see 15:2–4, and especially the invitation to praise God, which is issued "to all his servants who fear him, small and great," 19:5). The hymns thus have an im-portant function in the formulation of the message that the book wants to convey. They unite the announcement of Christ's victory with the confession and hymnic praise by the church.

The Revelation of John is directly focused upon the events and problems of its own time and can only be understood once it is realized how closely it is tied to its particular historical situation. The acceptance or rejection of the book, however, in the history of the Christian churches was always based upon its understanding as a writing about the future and about heavenly realities. In the 2d century, Papias of Hierapolis, Justin Martyr, Irenaeus, and Melito of Sardis spoke about the Revelation of John in approving terms. But in the 3d and 4th centuries, the Greek-speaking Eastern churches became increasingly critical (Dionysius of Alexandria, Eusebius of Caesarea). The Book of Revelation is missing in several later lists of the canon-ical books, and while the major 4th- and 5th-century uncial manuscripts include it, it is missing in the majority of medieval Greek manuscripts of the New Testament. The book fared better in the West, where the Latin Vulgate ruled. Here the crit-icism begins at the time of the Reformation (Luther doubted its canonicity) and continued in the Enlightenment. On the other hand, beginning in antiquity, Chris-tian sects have employed the Book of Revelation with great frequency, especially for the announcement of the coming of the thousand-year kingdom of Christ. For this expectation, and in general for the renewal of the belief in an imminent end of the world and the second coming of Christ—once more trumpeted about at the end of the second millennium—Revelation has provided inspiration and, against its own intentions, has been the cause of much confused agitation. Only through a critical interpretation, however, which pays close attention to the relationship of tradition and redaction and to the function of the individual sections within the total composition in the light of its historical situation, can it receive the hearing it deserves. It is especially in the discussion of the relationship of Christianity to the state, the society, and the economy that this early Christian book could be a significant voice.

(d) Apocalyptic Ordering of Christian Life: The Shepherd of Hermas

The central message of the seven letters to the churches in the Revelation of John was the call to repent, based upon the expectation of Christ's coming in the near future. But there was no detailed exposition of the order for moral conduct under an eschatological perspective. In fact, individual morality seemed of little concern, in view of the prophetic interpretation of the historical events of the present, which placed the integrity of the community over against the evils of state and economy. Only a nonpolitical apocalyptic perspective would allow a call for repentance to provide an opportunity to focus on the problems of individual morality and Christian conduct. It would also open the door again for an influx of moral teachings

Bibliography to §12.1d: Text

Molly Whittaker, *Der Hirt des Hermas* (GCS, Die apostolischen Väter 1; Berlin: Akademie–Verlag, 1956).

Martin Leutzsch, "Hirt des Hermas," in Ulrich J. Körtner and idem, *Papiasfragmente, Hirt des Hermas* (Schriften des Urchristentums 3; Darmstadt: Wissenschaftliche Buchgesellschaft, 1998) 107–497.

Lake, *ApostFath,* 2. 1–305.

Bibliography to §12.1d: Commentaries

Carolyn Osiek, *Shepherd of Hermas: A Commentary* (Hermeneia; Minneapolis: Fortress, 1999).

Norbert Brox, *Der Hirt des Hermas* (KAV 7; Göttingen: Vandenhoeck & Ruprecht, 1991).

Martin Dibelius, *Der Hirt des Hermas* (HNT.E 4; Tübingen: Mohr/Siebeck, 1923).

Graydon Snyder, *The Shepherd of Hermas* (Grant, *ApostFath* 6).

Bibliography to §12.1c: Studies

Erik Peterson, "Beiträge zur Interpretation der Visionen im Pastor Hermae," "Kritische Analyse der fünften Vision des Hermas," "Die Begegnung mit dem Ungeheuer," and "Die Taufe im Acherusischen See," in idem, *Frühkirche, Judentum und Gnosis* (Freiburg: Herder, 1959) 254–332.

Lage Pernveden, *The Concept of the Church in the Shepherd of Hermas* (STL 27; Lund: Gleerup, 1966).

J. Reiling, *Hermas and Christian Prophecy: A Study of the Eleventh Mandate* (NovTSup 37; Leiden: Brill, 1973).

David Hellholm, *Das Visionenbuch des Hermas als Apokalypse,* vol. 1: *Methodische Vorüberlegungen und makrostrukturelle Textanalyse* (CB.NT 13.1; Lund: Gleerup, 1980).

Carolyn Osiek, *Rich and Poor in the Shepherd of Hermas: An Exegetical Investigation* (CBQMS 15; Washington, DC: Catholic Biblical Association, 1983).

John Christian Wilson, *Five Problems in the Interpretation of the Shepherd of Hermas: Authorship, Genre, Canonicity, Apocalyptic, and the Absence of the Name 'Jesus Christ'* (Lewiston, NY: Mellen, 1995).

from diaspora Judaism into the instruction of the Christian community. A most interesting witness for this process is the work that is preserved under the title *Shepherd of Hermas*.

The manuscript tradition shows that the *Shepherd of Hermas* was used in the Western churches, and its complete text is preserved only in two Latin manuscripts. The original Greek text was not known until its discovery in 1855 in a manuscript from the 15th century on Mt. Athos, in which the end of *Similitude* 9 and *Similitude* 10 are missing. The famous Bible codex Sinaiticus, discovered by Tischendorf (§7.2c), provided a second witness for a portion of the Greek text, which, however, breaks off with *Vis.* 4.3.6 (*Hermas* is the last manuscript in this codex). But the book was known early in Egypt, as is shown by a Greek papyrus fragment from the end of the 2d century (*Pap. Michigan* 130), several quotations in Clement of Alexandria, and a more extensive Greek papyrus from the 3d century, which contains the text of *Sim.* 2.9–9.5.1 (*Pap. Michigan* 129).

In contrast to the Revelation of John, *Hermas* provides almost no information about the time and situation of its origin. To be sure, Rome is named as the author's city of residence (*Vis.* 1.1.1); places from the vicinity of Rome also appear (*Vis.* 1.1.3; 4.1.3), although a later vision is located in Arcadia (*Sim.* 9.1.4). The *Muratorian Canon* also points to Roman origin, and a certain Clement is mentioned in *Vis.* 2.4.3, which may establish a connection with the Roman author of the *First Epistle of Clement* (see §12.2e). It is thus difficult to argue against Roman origin.

External evidence for the book proves that it was written no later than the middle of the 2d century, but a more precise dating is difficult. The author never quotes other early Christian writings. This, however, may not tell anything, since he also never quotes any part of Israel's Scripture although he knew it well. Only once does he quote anything explicitly, the lost writing *Eldad and Modad* (*Vis.* 2.3.4). Parallels to parables of the Synoptic Gospels, especially the parable of the good servant (*Sim.* 5.2; 5.4–7), are best explained as reflecting a knowledge of the parables of Jesus from the oral tradition. *Hermas* knows the Christian offices of apostle, bishop, teacher, and deacon (*Vis.* 3.5.1); prophets are also mentioned (e.g., *Mand.* 11). *Sim.* 9.16.5 speaks about the descent to Hades of the apostles and teachers for the preaching of baptism to the dead. None of these elements, however, are clear enough to allow a more precise dating. If the Clement mentioned in *Vis.* 2.4.3 is the secretary of the Roman church to whom we owe *1 Clement,* a date about the year 100 would be in order. In any case, the date should not be moved too far into the 2d century.

A precise date is made more difficult by the author's use of extensive source materials and traditions for the composition of this rather extensive writing. The first part, the five *Visions,* though no doubt written by a Christian author, never uses the name of Jesus Christ! The "Church," a female figure appearing in the first three visions as an old woman who becomes younger with each appearance, is borrowed from the Jewish figure of Wisdom. According to *Vis.* 2.4.1 she is the first creature of God, the one through whom the world has been created. The vision of the building of the tower (*Vision* 3) is composed from materials that originally depicted the creation of the world; the six young men who build the tower "are the holy angels of God, who were created first, to whom God delivered all his creation to make it increase, and to build it up, and to rule the whole creation" (*Vis.* 3.41). The interpretation of the tower as the church is secondary. The animal vision (*Vision* 4) also has no original Christian components. The animal symbolizes the coming tribulations, and the four colors symbolize this aeon, its destruction, the salvation of the elect, and the coming aeon. All this is pre-Christian apocalyptic material. Finally, the "Shepherd," who appears to Hermas in order to reveal the commandments to him (*Vision* 5), has not been sent by Christ, but by "the most revered angel," and only a very careful reader of the book can discover that this angel is identical with "the Son of God." The Christian interpretation that was secondarily attached to this originally Jewish material is closely connected with the commission to proclaim a final chance for repentance before the building of the tower (i.e., the church) is completed. Note the charge to preach repentance (*Vis.* 2.2), the interpretation of the stones for the building as different categories of believers (*Vis.* 3.5–7), the presentation of the Christian virtues (*Vis.* 3.8), and the explanation of the three different appearances of the "Church" (*Vis.* 3.10–13). Improvement of the moral conduct of the individual members of the church is the intent of the book.

The second part of the writing, the *Mandates,* is also mostly composed of traditional Jewish materials. *Mandates* 2–10 and 12 treat a series of virtues and vices, often in appropriate juxtapositions (e.g., truthfulness/lying). The material is taken from the doctrine of the two ways and is closely related to the *Didache* 1–6 and the Epistle of James (§10.1c), but Hermas is not speaking about the two ways, but about the two spirits seeking abode in the human heart, the holy spirit and the evil spirit. This section of moral teaching is introduced by the primary commandment to believe in the one God who has created and preserves everything (*Mand.* 1). From faith comes fear of God, from fear of God comes self-control, which leads to the virtue of righteousness (*Mand.* 1.2). This terminology points to the realm of Hellenistic Jewish moral teaching. Specifically Christian issues rarely occur. *Mand.* 4.2–3 is an insertion that expresses the primary interest of the author, namely, repentance offered as a single and unrepeatable opportunity to those who have been baptized earlier in life. The instruction about the distinction between the true and the false prophet (*Mandate* 11) is also a Christian addition to the essentially Jewish materials of the *Mandates.*

The third part of *Hermas,* the *Similitudes,* is based upon a collection of parables of certainly Jewish origin. The parable of the man living in a foreign city (*Similitude* 1) treats the topic of human life in the world as a sojourn in an alien world, something that is frequently discussed by the Jewish philosopher Philo of Alexandria. The parable about the elm tree and the vine that the tree supports illustrates the relationship of the rich and poor in the community (*Similitude* 2). Whether of Jewish or pagan origin, it fits any diaspora community, for which the support of its poor members was of vital concern. The parables of the dry trees (*Similitude* 3) and of the sprouting trees (*Similitude* 4) aid in discussing the situation of the righteous and the unrighteous in this aeon, and how the righteous who belong to the coming aeon should bear fruit. A christological interpretation appears for the first time with the parable of *Sim.* 5.2 about the good servant (*Sim.* 5.4–7)—the sections on fasting (*Sim.* 5.1 and 3) appear to be later interpolations and do not belong in this context. The Son of God who, together with the angels, aids the master of the vineyard in planting (and also gives the law to the people) is the Holy Spirit; the servant who works in the vineyard is "a flesh" in whom the Holy Spirit dwells, thus making the servant the Son of God and fellow heir. The christology of this, the only passage in the whole writing that alludes to Jesus, is adoptianist. The author has once more inserted a reference to the topic of repentance: the Lord of the vineyard delays his return in order to provide an opportunity for repentance. The same theme appears at the end of the parable of the evil shepherd (*Similitude* 6) by way of introducing the angel of punishment (*Sim.* 6.3–4) and through an admonition for repentance directed to the house of Hermas (*Similitude* 7).

The parable of the willow tree (*Similitude* 8) shows the Jewish origin of the material most clearly: the angel who cuts off the branches from the tree and gives them to the people is Michael, who sets the law into the hearts of the people; the tree itself is the law, which is proclaimed to all nations (*Sim.* 8.3.2–3). It is an eschatological parable that speaks of the general validity of the law for Israel and for the nations in the coming rule of God. A secondary Christian interpretation explains the parable in terms of repentance and conversion (*Sim.* 8.4–11). The last parable, *Similitude* 9 (*Similitude* 10 is a final admonition of the Shepherd) has been expanded by the author into an elaborate allegory that constitutes almost a quarter of the entire writing. Older materials have been used in the vision of the twelve mountains (*Sim.* 9.1), which originally referred to the twelve tribes of Israel (*Sim.* 9.17.1), and which the author then explains in a long-winded allegory as "the tribes who inhabit the world," to whom the Son of God was preaching through the apostles (*Sim.* 9.17–31).

Between this parable and its interpretation the author placed a vision of the building of the tower *of the church (Sim.* 9.3–4) that is reminiscent of the vision of the tower of *Visio* 3, but departs from it in many points of detail. This is the central part of the book. Its allegorical interpretations are complex and repeatedly contradict each other. For example, not only the rock on which the church is built, but also the door through which the believers enter into the kingdom of God, and finally also the lord of the building are explained as the "Son of God" (*Sim.* 9.12). On the whole, the figure of the "Son of God" is removed into such cosmic dimension that it is difficult to see in him the Jesus Christ who is the center of salvation for the believers. Even a direct relationship between the Son of God and the prophets who are charged with the preaching of repentance is consciously avoided; mediators are introduced instead. The highest angel sends the Shepherd, who in turn instructs the prophet with his message of repentance. Twelve heavenly virgins are sent to the prophet on behalf of the practice of virtue: Hermas spends a night with these virgins "like a brother, not like a husband" (*Sim.* 9.11). Because of the distance to which Christ has been moved in the fullness of his power, which transcends time and world, Christian existence becomes completely moralized, especially in view of the urgency of the message of repentance. To be sure, the author can use phrases that are reminiscent of Paul to describe the unity of the church as "one spirit, one body" (*Sim.* 9.13.5). This unity, however, presupposes an individualistic moral appeal; unity will come about if every single Christian fulfills the same moral commandments. The order for the life and conduct of the members of the community is mirrored in an apocalyptic image, the building of the tower of the church, which has such cosmic dimensions, transcending all earthly experience, that the thought of a historical and organic mutual responsibility as the basis for the building of community cannot even arise. Consistent apocalypticism—in contrast to the prophetic message of the Revelation of John—thus leads to a denial of communal historical responsibility of the Christian church in favor of a morality of personal sanctification.

2. THE TRANSFORMATION OF PAULINE THEOLOGY INTO ECCLESIASTICAL DOCTRINE

(a) The Conflict with Syncretism: The Epistle to the Colossians

In the radical apocalypticism of the *Shepherd of Hermas,* the problem of christology is most acute. The cosmic dimensions of the Son of God as the eschatological world ruler, drawn from apocalyptic mythology, left no space for the human Jesus who died on the cross. In the Revelation of John, Christ—in spite of his appearance as the ruler of the universe—always remained the Lamb that was slain. It seems that the only limit to the rise of cosmological speculations in christology was set by the recourse to the suffering, death, and resurrection of Jesus. Belief in the cosmic figure of Christ also appears early in the Pauline churches. Paul himself had indeed presented Christ as the eschatological ruler of the cosmos (see 1 Cor 15: 25) and as a heavenly figure whose origin was that of a divine being (Phil 2:5–6), in each case using apocalyptic or Gnostic mythologoumena. In the interpretation

Bibliography to §12.2

Hans von Campenhausen, *Ecclesiastical Authority and Spiritual Power in the Church of the First Three Centuries* (Stanford, CA: Stanford University Press, 1996).

Ernst Käsemann, "Paul and Early Catholicism," in idem, *New Testament Questions,* 236–51.

Ulrich Luz, "Erwägungen zur Entstehung des 'Frühkatholizismus,'" *ZNW* 65 (1974) 88–111.

Hans-Martin Schenke, "Das Weiterwirken des Paulus und die Pflege seines Erbes durch die Paulus-Schule," *NTS* 21 (1975) 505–18. A good exposition of the problem with relevant bibliography.

Andreas Lindemann, *Paulus im ältesten Christentum: Das Bild des Paulus und die Rezeption der paulinischen Theologie in der frühchristlichen Literatur* (BHTh 58; Tübingen: Mohr/Siebeck, 1979).

Ernst Dassmann, *Der Stachel im Fleisch: Paulus in der frühchristlichen Literatur bis Irenäus* (Münster: Aschendorff, 1979).

Hans Conzelmann, "Die Schule des Paulus," in *Theologia Crucis—Signum Crucis: Festschrift für Erich Dinkler* (Tübingen: Mohr/Siebeck, 1979) 85–96.

William S. Babcock (ed.), *Paul and the Legacies of Paul* (Dallas: Southern Methodist University Press, 1990).

Bibliography to §12.2a: Commentaries

Eduard Lohse, *Colossians and Philemon: A Commentary on the Epistles to the Colossians and to Philemon* (Hermeneia; Philadelphia: Fortress, 1971).

C. F. D. Moule, *The Epistles to the Colossians and Philemon* (CGTC; Cambridge: Cambridge University Press, 1957).

Joachim Gnilka, *Der Kolosserbrief* (HThK 10/1; Freiburg: Herder, 1980).

Petr Pokorny, *Colossians: A Commentary* (Peabody, MA: Hendrickson, 1991).

Jean-Noël Aletti, *St. Paul: Épitre aux Colossians: Introduction, traduction et commentaire* (EtBib, NS 20; Paris: Gabalda, 1993).

of Paul's legacy, the question of the significance of the death of Jesus on the cross, crucially important for Paul himself, would play a central role for the further development of christology and, by implication, of ecclesiology.

The discussion of this development is part of a complex problem in early Christian history that is known as "deutero-Paulinism" or, more recently, "the Pauline school." The question of the redaction and publication of the letters of Paul is, of course, closely related, although it is not necessarily the case that, in the generation after Paul, the reference to "Paul" was a reference to his letters. After his death Paul was primarily remembered as a missionary and martyr. The legend of the great apostle preceded the knowledge or use of the letters he had written. These letters were not immediately published as his authoritative legacy but were at first apparently used in the spirit in which they were written, namely, as writings for particular occasions. As such they were read by those to whom he had written.

Some interesting hypotheses about the eventual publication of Paul's letters have been advanced, but the beginning of this process is not yet fully understood. The earliest use of a letter of Paul appears in 2 Thessalonians, but here only one single letter, namely, 1 Thessalonians, has been used, probably by the church to which this first letter of Paul was directed (see §12.1a). The motivation for the use of a Pauline letter in this case is clearly the need to refute opponents who had used that letter to strengthen their arguments. The combination of several letters written to one and the same church into one single letter (see §7.3d on 2 Corinthians and Philippians) reveals the desire to produce more readable units and perhaps also the wish to announce the claim of a particular church to the possession of Paul's legacy. The Philippians may have published their letters as an epistle of the martyr Paul because they wanted to be remembered as the church that guarded the place of Paul's martyrdom. The collection of Paul's letters into an authoritative corpus of literature, however, is still a different process, and it is not possible to say with any certainty, when and why such a collection was made. The developments to be discussed here and in the following chapters belong in this process. The fact that the Pauline school engaged in such an endeavor is quite extraordinary in view of the continuing impact of the image of Paul as a powerful apostle and martyr, and

Bibliography to §12.2a: Studies

Wayne Meeks and Fred O. Francis (eds.), *Conflict at Colossae: A Problem in the Interpretation of Early Christianity, Illustrated by Selected Modern Studies* (SBLSBS 4; Missoula, MT: Scholars Press, 1973).

Hans-Martin Schenke, "Der Widerstreit gnostischer und kirchlicher Theologie im Spiegel des Kolosserbriefes," *ZThK* 61 (1964) 391–403.

James E. Crouch, *The Origin and Intention of the Colossian Haustafel* (FRLANT 109; Göttingen: Vandenhoeck & Ruprecht, 1972).

Carolyn Osiek and David L. Balch, *Families in the New Testament World: Households and House Churches* (Louisville: Westminster John Knox, 1997).

Angela Standhartinger, *Studien zur Entstehungsgeschichte des Kolosserbriefes* (NovTSup 94; Leiden: Brill, 1999).

Bibliography to §12.2a: History of Scholarship

Wolfgang Schenk, "Der Kolosserbrief in der neueren Forschung (1945–1985)," *ANRW* 2.25.4 (1987) 3327–64.

in most of the deutero-Pauline letters that image plays some role. Why it was important to collect and publish Paul's letters is best understood through the consideration of the deutero-Pauline letters, because the very fact that more letters in the name of Paul were produced testifies to the significance of Paul's legacy in the continuing history of the churches he had founded.

The Epistles to the Colossians and to the Ephesians are witnesses to the first stage of the history of Pauline churches after his death. Some scholars still presume that both letters were written by Paul himself, while others agree that Ephesians is deutero-Pauline but would still maintain that Colossians is a genuine letter of Paul. The latter position is understandable, because Ephesians was composed on the basis of, and in controversy with, Colossians. The type of the numerous, sometimes word-for-word agreements of the two letters, makes dependence of Ephesians upon Colossians more plausible than the assumptions of a common source for both letters. (A dependence of Colossians upon Ephesians is excluded because the latter often comments upon, corrects, and expands the materials of the former.)

Yet, even Colossians was hardly written by Paul himself. The letter contains a large number of words that occur in none of the certainly genuine Pauline letters (a total of 48; of these 33 are *hapax legomena,* i.e., words that occur nowhere else in the New Testament). In contrast to Paul, the style of the author of Colossians differs markedly from Paul's own style. There are long sequences of genitive constructions, like "the kingdom of the son of his love" (Col 1:13), "the word of the truth of the gospel that is among you" (1:5–6), "putting off the body of the flesh" (2:11). The author loves to combine parallel terms: "bearing fruit and growing" (1:6), "prayers and petitioning" (1:9), "for all endurance and patience" (1:11). He also constructs long periodic sentences that are difficult to understand (paragraph 1:9–20 is all one single sentence!).

Those linguistic features are rare in Paul's genuine letters. More important, however, for the question of authorship is the theological intention of those statements in Colossians that closely resemble Paul's own terminology. Col 1:13 says that God "has transferred us to the kingdom of his beloved Son," using the past tense. Paul always speaks of the "kingdom of God," never of the kingdom of the Son, and he always makes clear that one's participation in that kingdom is a matter of the future (e.g., 1 Cor 15:50). According to Col 1:18 and 2:19, Christ is the head of the church, which is his body. In 1 Cor 10:16; 12:12; and Rom 12:4–5, however, the concept of Christ as the "head" does not appear, while the church as a whole is Christ's body—head, members, and all. In the interpretation of baptism, Col 2:12 and 3:1 state that the Christians have not only already died but also already risen with Christ, while Paul explicitly rejects this interpretation of baptism and carefully avoids speaking about the rising with Christ as an event of the past (Rom 6:1ff.; 1 Thess 4:14ff.). Analogous observations can be made in the detailed exegesis of Colossians in many more instances. The conclusion leaves little doubt about the authorship of Colossians: a student of Paul, who was quite familiar with Paul's language, wrote this letter after Paul's death in order to address some urgent problems that were facing the churches of Paul at this moment.

One of the problems that the author of Colossians is addressing is the danger of false teachings and practices. It is difficult to know, however, whether the author is describing one particular group of opponents or is warning in more general terms of acute or possible dangers, drawing on, in this process, the controversies described in Paul's letters. In any case, his warnings are specific and concern dangers that are real and not just imagined. The attacks describe people who present a "philosophy" based on traditions (Col 2:8). According to the remarks that follow, these traditions point to a Jewish origin, because they include the observance of dietary rules, festivals of new moons and sabbaths (2:16), as well as circumcision (this must have been the cause for the polemical formulation in 2:11; on the dietary laws, see 2:21). This is reminiscent of the opponents of Paul in Galatians and Philippians 3 (§9.3b and e); but in the case of Colossians, the cosmic dimensions of such observations of the law are more explicit. Did the author fear that the Pauline concept of the "body of Christ" could be misunderstood in such a way that Christ became the head of a cosmic hierarchy, of celestial principalities and powers (2:10; cf. 1:16)? In that case, to be united with Christ would require the mediation of angelic powers so that the believer could be incorporated into the true body of Christ; this is indicated in the reference to "humility" and the service of angels (2:18). It is striking that in this context a term appears that is otherwise attested as a designation for the initiation into a mystery, "as he has had visions during the mystery rites" (2:18). What the author has in mind is the practice of rites that have their analogies in the mysteries and culminated in the "vision" of cosmic powers. Such practices were widespread at the time, and they were probably at home in some of the developing Gnostic sects. The author of Colossians shows familiarity with religious practices through which human beings tried to establish their unity with the cosmic Christ by using the mediation of cosmic realities, although nothing is said about the overcoming of hostile powers, which would be a typical indication for Gnosticism.

In the refutation of such doctrines and practices, the author of Colossians adopts some of the speculations about celestial realities for his own teaching. The hymn of Christ as the first-born and the creation of the cosmic powers through him, which he uses in 1:15–20, is essentially an adaptation of a wisdom hymn. Colossians here accepts the concept of Christ as the head of the powers (2:10), but for him the body of Christ is the church, and he argues that with the death of Christ on the cross the powers were disarmed and publicly exposed in disgrace (2:15). It is thus the author of Colossians, not the opponents, who assigns some negative attributes to the powers and places them in the lower regions of the cosmic realm: the Christians are requested to "seek the things that are above, where also Christ is, seated at the right hand of God" (3:1). The redemption is already accomplished for the believers, and Colossians can say, just like a Gnostic theologian, that they have already been raised with Christ (3:1) and have already entered into the kingdom (1:13). This is the case because Christ has abolished the law, "the bond that stood against us with its legal demands" (2:14). For those who have been redeemed by Christ, the commands of the law are only human precepts and doctrines, related solely to the earthly body (2:22–23). While the author of this letter is here renewing Paul's thesis that Christ is the end of the law, he accepts, at the same time, the position of the opponents of 1 Corinthians, spiritualizing the concept of already realized eschatology. Through Christ's death the church is already holy and without blemish (1:22) and needs no further purification through ritual acts, because it is exactly this church that is the "body of Christ" (1:18, where "the church" is the author's addition to the traditional hymn), related directly to the head, Christ, without any mediation through the powers of the cosmos (2:19).

This move away from the future eschatological perspective and expectation of the return of Christ in the near future, which is evident in all genuine letters of Paul, has been explained in a recent work of Angela Standhartinger as a response to the death of Paul. Paul's churches had been created as eschatological communities expecting the return of Christ during the life of the apostle. Paul himself had begun to address the problem of his impending death, when he wrote to the Philippians from his Ephesian imprisonment (§9.3e.2). But now Paul's churches had to face the fact that the apostle had died and Christ had not returned. Why did Paul have to die, and what about the understanding of the church as the community that was expecting Christ's return? The author of Colossians tries to give an answer to both questions. Paul had to die because he had to fulfill what was still missing in the sufferings of Christ on behalf of Christ's body (1:24). This has now been accomplished and therefore the work of Christ, his death and resurrection, has become fully available to the believers. They have died and have been raised with Christ— to be sure, their life is now still hidden but it will be revealed when Christ becomes "revealed" (3:3–4). Since the believers are in full possession of their life, there is no longer any concern about the time at which this revelation of Christ will happen. The delay of the parousia is no longer a problem, and Colossians makes no attempt to update the eschatological timetable.

This view of a salvation that is already fully realized leaves open the question of the conduct of Christians in this world. Is the Gnostic answer correct that exempts the Christian community from any further responsibility in this world and its society and institutions? Through his criticism of the powers, however, the author of Colossians has exorcised the demons from the world in which the believers live. Christian conduct owes nothing to the demons and is capable of meeting the challenge of accepting the moral values of the society. Avoiding vice and accepting virtue are called in theological terms "putting on the new human being" (3:10). The table of household duties (*Haustafel*, 3:18–4:1) appears here for the first time in Christian literature. It would become a rather popular feature in Christian parenesis; Ephesians (5:25–6:9) reproduces Colossians' household table with major modifications, and it is also used in 1 Peter (2:13–3:7). It was taken over from Stoic popular ethics, had already been accepted in Hellenistic Judaism (cf. *Didache* 4.9–11), and is essentially a secular instruction for conduct within the existing structures of the society. Its purpose is to show, and perhaps even to advertise, that special religious communities do not intend to disturb these structures. As it is used by Colossians, the insertion of the phrase "in the Lord" makes the exercise of these duties a Christian moral obligation. The greater emphasis upon the mutuality of obligations is also a result of the Christian adaptation of this table: wives should be obedient; but husbands also have obligations to their wives, parents to their children, and masters have duties toward their slaves. The hierarchical order of the society is thus modified but not fundamentally questioned. A similar adjustment of Christian morality to that of the Roman social structures is perhaps also visible in Colossians' omission of the phrase "neither male nor female" in the repetition of Paul's "neither Jew nor Greek" (compare Col 3:11 with Gal 3:28). This may have been motivated by the emancipation of women in sectarian groups, who also practiced asceticism (Col 2:21–22). Colossians promotes an ethical behavior that takes a positive view of life in this world, although the true life of the church "is hid with Christ in God" (3:3). Paul's eschatological and, therefore, critical view of life in this world (1 Cor 7) is missing. What the further direction of this development, which eliminated both the eschatological and the general religious motivation for conduct, would be will be learned from Ephesians, which presents a new version of Pauline theology, including a new religious motivation for conduct, in a critical discussion with Colossians.

In its external features, Colossians presents itself as a letter written by Paul. The prescript names the apostle Paul and Timothy as authors, the saints and faithful brothers and sisters in Christ in Colossae as addressees, and gives the normal Pauline greeting (1:1–2). It is difficult to say how much the names that appear in the final greetings of the letter (Col 4:10–14) relate to historical reality. Of the ten names, seven also appear in Paul's letter to Philemon and are probably borrowed from that letter, which the author of Colossians used as his model. But Tychicus (4:7) appears elsewhere only in the list of the members of the delegation bringing the collection to Jerusalem (Acts 20:4; this list seems to be reliable and genuine). It is therefore possible that at least some of these names in Colossians derive from a firsthand knowledge of Paul's fellow workers. This would argue for a relatively early date after Paul's death for the composition of Colossians, but it raises the difficult question of whether the additional designations that Colossians adds to almost all of the names (e.g., Mark "the cousin of Barnabas," 4:10; Luke "the beloved physician," 4:14) are trustworthy. Problematic is also the command to exchange this letter with the one written to Laodicea (4:16; by Paul? —but why does Paul then send greetings to Laodicea via Colossae? 4:15). The search for this "Laodicean Letter" has been in vain (that it is the letter now known as "Ephesians" is not possible), although much later such a letter was fabricated. It is probably better to assume that this entire concluding section of Colossians is a somewhat clumsy fictional expansion of the names borrowed from the genuine letter of Paul to Philemon.

(b) The Struggle against Gnosticism: The Epistle to the Ephesians

While Colossians might still be considered a true letter, directed to a particular community, the Epistle to the Ephesians never alludes to concrete problems or situations of a community or circle of churches. The words "in Ephesus" (Eph 1:1)

Bibliography to §12.2b: Commentaries

Ernest Best, *A Critical and Exegetical Commentary on Ephesians* (ICC; Edinburgh: T&T Clark, 1998).
John A. Allan, *The Epistle to the Ephesians: Introduction and Commentary* (Torch Bible Commentaries; London: SCM, 1959).
Rudolf Schnackenburg, *Der Brief an die Epheser* (EKKNT 10; Neukirchen-Vluyn: Neukirchener Verlag, 1982).
Michel Bouttier, *L'épître de saint Paul aux Éphésiens* (CNT, 2d series 9b; Geneva: Labor et Fides, 1991).
Petr Pokorny, *Der Brief des Paulus an die Epheser* (ThHK 10/2; Leipzig: Evangelische Verlagsanstalt, 1992).

are missing in the best and oldest manuscripts; the letter was thus directed to "the saints who are also faithful in Christ Jesus" in general. It is also possible that it was designed to be sent to a number of churches and that the name of the addressee was left blanc in the original, to be inserted in the copies that were then dispatched to these churches. According to Marcion, the letter was directed to the Laodiceans. Although there is no manuscript evidence for this assumption, Marcion's copy may have been the copy that had been sent to Laodicea. However, that it was the letter to the Laodiceans mentioned in Col 4:16 is impossible, because Ephesians was written much later than Colossians and, in fact, used Colossians extensively; the direct quotation about the sending of Tychicus (Eph 6:21 = Col 4:7), for example, can be explained only on the basis of literary dependence. Already this excludes Pauline authorship. Moreover, in addition to Colossians, Ephesians knows all or most of the genuine letters of Paul and employs them repeatedly (only the pseude-pigraphical Second Letter to the Thessalonians never appears). Ephesians also looks back to a time, now past, of the "holy apostles" (Eph 3:5). The preaching to the Gentiles, which had been Paul's office, is part of the events of salvation that took place in the past and upon which the church was founded (3:1–13). All this places Ephesians into a time that was quite distant from the apostolic period, most likely not earlier than the very end of the 1st century.

Ephesians further elaborated the theological language of the post-Pauline period, which had appeared in its beginning stages in Colossians. The literary style of Eph-esians is even more laborious and ornate than that of Colossians. Long sequences of combinations of nouns, connected through prepositions or by the use of geni-tives, are even more frequent (such as, "to the sonship through Jesus Christ to him according to the purpose of his will for the praise of the glory of his grace," 1:5–6). Synonyms are often accumulated ("according to the working of the power of his greatness," 1:19; "fellow heirs and members and partakers," 3:6). Sentences be-come so extended that the translator is often faced with great difficulties. (The following sections are made up of only one single sentence in each instance: 1:3–10; 1:15–21; 3:1–7; 3:8–12; 3:14–19; 4:11–16; the first of these sentences

Bibliography to §12.2b: Studies

Edgar J. Goodspeed, *The Meaning of Ephesians* (Chicago: University of Chicago Press, 1933).

Ernst Käsemann, "Das Interpretationsproblem des Epheserbriefes," in idem, *Exegetische Versuche,* 2. 253–61.

Idem, "Ephesians and Acts," in Leander E. Keck and J. Louis Martyn (eds.), *Studies in Luke-Acts: Essays Presented in Honor of Paul Schubert* (Nashville, TN: Abingdon, 1966) 288–97.

Petr Pokorny, "Epheserbrief und gnostische Mysterien," *ZNW* 53 (1962) 235–51.

Idem, *Der Epheserbrief und die Gnosis* (Berlin: Evangelische Verlagsanstalt, 1965).

Nils A. Dahl, "Cosmic Dimensions and Religious Knowledge (Eph. 3:18)," in E. Earle Ellis and Erich Grässer (eds.), *Jesus und Paulus* (Göttingen: Vandenhoeck & Ruprecht, 1975) 57–75.

Andreas Lindemann, *Die Aufhebung der Zeit: Geschichtsverständnis und Eschatologie im Eph-eserbrief* (StNT 12; Gütersloh: Mohn, 1975).

Idem, "Bemerkungen zu den Adressaten und zum Anlaß des Epheserbriefes," *ZNW* 67 (1976) 235–51.

Bibliography to §12.2b: History of Scholarship

Helmut Merkel, "Der Epheserbrief in der neueren exegetischen Diskussion," *ANRW* 2.25.4 (1987) 3156–3246.

contains no fewer than 130 words!). Yet it is not only the style, but also the theological terminology that is very different from Paul, despite many borrowings from Paul's genuine letters. This terminology shows some similarities with the writings from Qumran (§5.3c), while there are, on the other hand, numerous parallels with other Christian literature produced about the year 100 (such as *1 Clement* and the letters of Ignatius; see §§12.2d and e). This also confirms the date of the writing at the end of the 1st century; but since Ignatius used Ephesians, it cannot have been written many years after the beginning of the 2d century.

What kind of document is this book that is conventionally known as "Ephesians"? Several solutions of the problem of its genre have been proposed. Some suggest that it may have been a real letter written to a large number of churches, but then one would expect to find some traces of the various addressees in the manuscript tradition (only Marcion's address of the latter would confirm this). According to another suggestion, it was produced as a cover letter for the first collection of the Pauline letters; but Ephesians already presupposes the existence of such a collection, as did *1 Clement,* which was written at about the same time. Furthermore, such a cover letter would normally be much less weighty than Ephesians (cf. the cover letter of Polycarp for the collection of the letters of Ignatius, Pol. *Phil.* 13–14; see §12.2h). Could it have been a baptismal sermon? This hypothesis might come closer to a definition of its genre, but we know too little about the baptismal liturgy of that time, and sermons in early Christianity probably did not employ such an ornate style.

In order to explain the intention and genre of Ephesians one must answer the question of what the author wanted to achieve theologically. He was not trying to intervene in the specific problems of any particular church, nor did he discuss any specific ecclesiastical matter such as baptism. What he had in mind was rather a word about the general situation in the post-Pauline period, in view of the churches that had grown out of the Pauline mission and that knew and used the letters of Paul, especially the letter to the Colossians. But it is not only a knowledge of Paul's letters that sustained these churches: they were also bound to traditions that were established in the context of their founding and to the continuing use of Scripture and the interpretation of key scriptural passages. They were the churches of the converted Gentiles, but there were also Jewish members in their midst, and the problem of the relationship between Jews and Gentiles had by no means been solved. The latter is in particular one of the issues addressed by Ephesians.

The author of Colossians had discussed similar problems, but he had done this almost as if he were still living in Paul's time, summarizing, for example, arguments against ritual observance of the law in a way in which, he thought, Paul would have done it. The author of Ephesians had recognized that this was no longer possible, and he was especially convinced that Colossians' solutions were very problematic, to say the least. The situation was different, not because one could no longer fight Jewish-Christian propaganda with such arguments, or because of a great influx of members of the Essenic sect into the Christian church after the destruction of their monastery at the Dead Sea—we really do not know whether that was the indeed the case. There was a much deeper reason. The churches that derived from the Pauline mission had meanwhile been deeply affected by a cosmological interpretation of Scripture, by apocalypticism as the message of arranging the church's position within an eschatological timetable, and by syncretistic Gnosticism. Ephesians presupposes that many religious concepts to which Paul would have objected vehemently had become accepted. These included the understanding of Christ's death and resurrection, and of the gospel that proclaimed these events, as a "mystery" (Eph 3:3–4); the interpretation of baptism as the accomplishment of the resurrection with Christ, so that the Christians could understand themselves as already being raised and transferred into the heavenly regions (2:5–6; cf. Col 3:1–3!); the concept of Christ as the heavenly *anthropos* to whom the church is linked as his heavenly *syzygos* (Eph 2:14ff.; 5:25–32); and finally the transformation of the eschatological expectation of the parousia into a hope for personal salvation after death (6:10ff.). Colossians had anticipated some of these developments. The concept of Christ as the head of the body, the church (Eph 5:29), had been created by Colossians as a corrective to the view that Christ was the head of a cosmological hierarchy.

As a Pauline theologian, the author of Ephesians became the advocate of a new universalistic view of Christianity. This universalism entails both cosmological perspectives and the question of the Jews and Gentiles. Both dimensions belong together and form a unity; the question of the Jewish law also plays a role in this endeavor. For Paul, the law had come to an end since its time had run out due to the eschatological act of God; now the Gentiles had access to the divine promises of Scripture without the law. Paul understood the end of the law in terms of eschatological time. Ephesians, however, understands the law in terms of space: it is a dividing wall, not only a wall that separates Jews and Gentiles, but also a cosmic wall between the heavenly realms and the human sphere on earth. By tearing down this wall through his flesh in his death on the cross, Christ has created out of Jews and Gentiles a new corporate being (*anthropos*), who has access to God (2:11–22). For Paul, the participation of "Israel according to the flesh" was part of the eschatological hope that God would finally fulfill the promises given to Israel (Romans 11). For the author of Ephesians, who was a converted Jew (note his use of "you" when he is speaking to the Gentiles; Eph. 2:11, 17), the direction of this statement is reversed: the Jews are the first to be included, the Gentiles are then incorporated by the process of salvation that is built on the foundation of the prophets and apostles (2:19–20). All this, however, is no longer the object of eschatological expectation; it is already a reality, though a reality that can be described only in Gnostic terms.

Ephesians does not offer a definition of the unity of the church of Jews and Gentiles in sociological or political categories. Paul had made great efforts to document the unity of the church of Jews and Gentiles through a collection of money from the Gentiles for the church in Jerusalem (§9.3f). In Ephesians this unity is a divine process transcending time and space. Apostles, prophets, preachers, pastors, and teachers are appointed in order that the church might grow into this preordained unity "through faith and knowledge" (4:11–13). Insofar as the bond of Christ's body is understood as love, the church is protected from false teachings because truth documents its presence not through any particular doctrines, but in the increase of love (4:14–16). In the end, however, faith is nothing but knowledge, wisdom, and insight into the divine mystery (1:8–9, 17–18; 3:3–5, 18–19). This also explains the superabundance and pleonasm in the description of the cosmic dimension of salvation. Gnostic universalism has provided the language for this continuation of Pauline theology.

There is also a corrective to Gnosticism in Ephesians, namely, its moralism. Salvation is grace for those who were "dead" in sin and are "being made alive together with Christ" (2:3–5), "by grace saved through faith, . . . not through works" (2:8–9). This formulation sounds very much like Paul's own statements, but the continuation is different: "Created in Christ Jesus for good works, which God prepared beforehand, that we should walk in them" (2:10). Through such conduct the believers show that they are worthy of the heavenly call (4:1); through works one proves that one does not belong to darkness but to the light (5:8ff.). This conduct is described both in elaborately interpreted catalogs of virtues and vices that were taken over from the doctrine of the two ways (4:17–5:20) and in the table of household duties that the author took from Colossians (Eph 5:22–6:9). In its interpretation, Ephesians understands the duties of married partners as a copy of heavenly realities. The relationship of husband and wife corresponds to the relationship of the heavenly figures Christ and Church. This exposition is pointedly anti-Gnostic, because Gnosticism usually understands the rejection of married life as proof of one's membership in the heavenly world. With this anti-Gnostic justification of the institution of marriage, Ephesians provided a metaphysical foundation for the sanctioning of the social institutions of marriage, family, and slavery. This would become a significant encumbrance for Christian ethics.

Ephesians does not really enter into a theological controversy with Gnosticism, but simply draws from Gnosticism the categories for the construction of his universalism. The line of demarcation between church and Gnosticism was drawn in the realm of morality. This was a step with momentous consequences for the Pauline churches in their development toward early catholicism, which committed the church to a traditional morality and eventually commended moral defamation as an instrument in the fight against heretics. What Ephesians said in its characterization of pre-Christian pagan sinfulness and immorality (4:17–19) would soon reappear as a characterization of opponents in polemical writings against the Gnostics (§12.2g). For the future of Pauline theology in the early catholic church, Ephesians' failure to meet the challenge of Gnosticism theologically became a heavy burden, because the Gnostics learned very soon to utilize Ephesians' universalism in order to show that they were the true interpreters of Paul. Ephesians made a Gnostic interpretation of Paul's letters a legitimate enterprise. For the early Catholic church, however, Paul came under the suspicion of being a Gnostic. Though Paul would still be claimed as an authority, the theology documented in his letters was avoided, and it took a long time before the power and insight of his theological arguments were rediscovered. But at the time of the writing of Ephesians efforts to reinterpret Paul's theology for new challenges were still continuing. Evidence for this can be found in the Epistle to the Hebrews and in the letters of Ignatius of Antioch.

(c) Apocalyptic Gnosis as Legacy of Paul

(1) *The Epistle to the Hebrews* is witness for a different manner of developing the Pauline legacy in the generation after his death. Hebrews must be dated well

before the end of the 1st century, because two passages from this letter are quoted in *1 Clement* (36.2–5; 17.1). At the end of the 2d century, Hebrews is known in Egypt as a letter of Paul, and in the churches of the East it became part of the canon of the New Testament from the beginning. The writing was also known in the West, but Irenaeus, Tertullian, and Hippolytus did not consider it a genuine letter of Paul; it was not accepted into the canon of the Western churches until the 4th century. The origin of the title "To the Hebrews," which was added at a later time, is not known. The ancient theory that it was a translation of a letter that Paul had written in the Hebrew language "To the Hebrews" is certainly wrong. Language and style of the writing prove that it was originally written in Greek, in fact, in a cultivated Greek that shows familiarity with the training of Atticistic rhetorical schools (Paul was instructed in the very different rhetoric of the diatribe). In his scriptural interpretation, the author follows the Alexandrian allegorical method as it is known from the writings of Philo of Alexandria (§5.3f; Paul was also acquainted with this method, but used it rarely; see 1 Cor 10:1–13). Together with the allegorical method, Hebrew also shares with Philo a Platonic worldview: earthly transitoriness is the shadow and copy of the heavenly reality.

Hebrews does not even claim to be written by Paul. It lacks an epistolary prescript and thus gives no indication of its sender and addressee. It is striking, however, that the conclusion of the writing is given in the form of a letter nonetheless:

Bibliography to §12.2c (1):   Commentaries

Harold W. Attridge, *The Epistle to the Hebrews: A Commentary* (Hermeneia; Minneapolis: Fortress, 1989).

Jean Hering, *The Epistle to the Hebrews* (London: Epworth, 1970).

Herbert Braun, *An die Hebräer* (HNT 14; Tübingen: Mohr/Siebeck, 1984).

Harald Hegermann, *Der Brief an die Hebräer* (ThKNT 16; Berlin: Evangelische Verlagsanstalt, 1988).

Hans-Friedrich Weiss, *Der Brief an die Hebräer* (KEK 13; Göttingen: Vandenhoeck & Ruprecht, 1991).

Erich Grässer, *An die Hebräer,* vols. 1–2: *Heb 1, 1–10, 18* (EKKNT 17/1–2; Neukirchen-Vluyn: Neukirchener Verlag, 1990–1993).

Bibliography to §12.2c (1):   Studies

Ernst Käsemann, *The Wandering People of God: An Investigation of the Letter to the Hebrews* (Minneapolis: Augsburg, 1984). Classic monograph, first published in German in 1938, which gave direction to modern research.

Sidney G. Stowers, *The Hermeneutics of Philo and Hebrews* (Richmond: Knox, 1965).

Erich Grässer, *Der Glaube im Hebräerbrief* (MThSt 2; Marburg: Elwert, 1965).

Idem, *Aufbruch und Verheißung: Gesammelte Aufsätze zum Hebräerbrief* (BZNW 65; Berlin: de Gruyter, 1992).

L. K. K. Dey, *The Intermediary World and Patterns of Perfection in Philo and Hebrews* (SBLDS 25; Missoula, MT: Scholars Press, 1975).

Günther Bornkamm, "Das Bekenntnis im Hebräerbrief," in idem, *Studien zu Antike und Christentum* (3d ed.; München: Kaiser, 1969) 188–203.

Helmut Koester, "'Outside the Camp': Hebrews 13, 9–14," *HTR* 55 (1962), 299–315.

Ulrich Luck, "Himmlisches und irdisches Geschehen im Hebräerbrief," *NovT* 6 (1963) 192–215.

August Strobel, "Die Psalmengrundlage der Gethsemane-Parallele Hbr. 5, 7ff.," *ZNW* 45 (1954) 252–66.

Simon Kistemaker, *The Psalm Citations in the Epistle to the Hebrews* (Amsterdam: van Soest, 1971).

Bibliography to §12.2c (1):   History of Scholarship

Craig R. Koester, "The Epistle to the Hebrews in Recent Study," *CRBS* 2 (1994) 123–45.

here the author speaks about himself, expressing his hope to see the addressees soon (13:19) and indicating that he would come for a visit "together with our brother Timothy," who had been released from prison (13:23). This is apparently part of a pseudepigraphical frame that points to Paul's fellow worker Timothy and alludes to a Roman imprisonment (note the greetings of those who come from Italy, 13:24). These remarks have no bearing on the question of the author of this writing, but show that Hebrews belongs to the writings that resume the Pauline tradition.

The content of Hebrews is also related to the continuation of the tradition of Paul's churches, although this does not seem to imply that its author was familiar with a corpus of Paul's letters. But he refers repeatedly to basic religious concepts that were native to the churches that had been founded by the mission of Paul and his associates. It is a matter of course that Christian existence is based on faith; the fundamental quotation about justification by faith from Hab 2:4 (Rom 1:17) also appears in Hebrews (10:38). The understanding of conversion as forgiveness of sins, prominent in other deutero-Pauline writings (Eph 2:1ff.; Col 1:21ff.; cf. the formula quoted by Paul in Rom 3:25), is as current in Hebrews as is the emphasis upon Christ's expiatory death, especially in connection with the concept of the new covenant (Heb 1:3; chaps. 8–10; for Paul, see 1 Cor 11:24–25). Also among the foundations of faith is the expectation of the resurrection of the dead and the last judgment (Heb 6:1–2). All this points to a familiarity with fundamental religious concepts of Paul's churches—often found in materials quoted by Paul—but does not reveal a specific knowledge of Paul's theology as it is developed in his letters. Like Ephesians, Hebrews does not speak to the situation of a specific church, nor does the treatise deal with an immediate threat from heretical teachers. Rather, this epistle presents, in the form of a theological treatise, an interpretation of the ecclesiastical tradition within the general situation of the churches after Paul's time.

Apart from the conclusion, the author does not use any constitutive part of the literary genre of the letter, and the literary genre and its relationship to the content and purpose of the writing are not immediately clear. The suggestion that Hebrews was a sermon or homily is too vague in terms of literary genre, although it certainly contains a good deal of homiletic material in the style of Jewish diaspora preaching. The designation "theological tractate" also needs further clarification. One striking feature of the work is the intimate connection of theological argumentation with interpretation of Scripture. Furthermore, the author states explicitly that he intends to lead the readers beyond the foundations of faith to a deeper knowledge (5:11ff.). Accordingly, this "epistle" belongs to the same category as those writings of Philo of Alexandria that are esoteric and seek to mediate deeper insight into Scripture for the perfect. The interpretation of Scripture is the key for understanding Hebrews, and its outline can be explained as a sequence of pieces of scriptural exegesis under the heading of certain theological topics. The author, however, does not want to speak to only a limited circle of elect people, but to the whole Christian church (it would be entirely wrong to think that he wants to address only Christians of Jewish origin). The question of why the specific genre of esoteric scriptural "gnosis" was chosen for this writing is best answered by a reference to Gnosticism. For the continuation of the Pauline legacy, especially in the understanding of Scripture, Gnosticism offered the most convincing alternative, as Ephesians had already demonstrated.

Gnostic concepts are indeed found frequently in Hebrews and are crucial for the understanding of its arguments. Although using philosophical terminology related to Philo (Heb 1:3), Hebrews not only emphasizes the preexistence of the redeemer, it also speaks about his descent (9:1ff., 24). The common origin of the redeemed and the redeemer is presupposed (2:11). Another Gnostic concept is the understanding of the believers as those who are on the way to their heavenly home, a thought that occurs repeatedly throughout the entire work. But in contrast to Ephesians, Hebrews enters into a critical theological controversy with Gnosticism, refuting the Gnostic understanding of the redeemer and of the process of salvation. Two important elements, both basic in the Pauline proclamation, are used as criteria in this controversy: first, the recourse to the suffering of the redeemer on earth and, second, adherence to an apocalyptic view of the future (10:27). Such eschatology does not appear, as in Ephesians, as an individualistic expectation of salvation after death (Eph 6:10ff.); rather it appears as a hope that binds all the people of God together as a totality. The instrument of the theological criticism of Gnosticism is therefore both Hebrew's christology and its ecclesiology. The scriptural passages used here deal mostly with the exodus, the wandering people of God on their way to the promised land, and the priesthood and sacrificial cult of the wilderness tabernacle of Israel; but numerous other passages are also used. For the primary scriptural passages concerning the exodus and the tabernacle, the author was able to draw on a long tradition of interpretation. The closest parallels for his exegetical statements and for his interpretive method are found in the writings of Philo of Alexandria, but no direct dependence upon Philo can be demonstrated. Hebrews' two main themes are christological (Christ as the heavenly priest who has offered himself as a sacrifice) and ecclesiological (the church as the wandering people of God on the way to its heavenly rest).

The introduction (Heb 1:1–2:18) is based on a collection of passages from Scripture about the angels and polemicizes against the identification of Christ's position with that of the angels. The author obviously wants to exclude from the very beginning any mediation of salvation through angelic powers (cf. Colossians and the *Shepherd of Hermas;* §§12.1d; 12.2a). The connection of salvation with the "Son," and only with him, is important because only the Son is united with God himself (1:3; 2:10) and yet was made lower than the angels through the experience of death (2:8–10), thus participating fully in humanity's fate. The first major section of scriptural interpretation is presented under the theme of the wandering people of God (3:1–4:13) and uses Ps 95:7–11 ("Do not harden your hearts as at Meribah"), Num 14:21–23 (the wilderness generation shall not enter the promised land), and Gen 2:2 (God rested on the seventh day). The promised rest is still open, but it is not the goal for a celestial journey of the soul (an important theme of Gnostic theology) rather, it is the goal of the wanderings of an historical people on earth. The interpretation of the biblical passages is therefore not allegorical as in Gnosticism, but typological. It compares the old with the new people of God as historical entities and can thus speak about disobedience, hardness of heart, hope, and faithfulness. At the same time, the historical promises given to Israel are opened up so that the new wandering people of God can look forward to receiving their fulfillment.

The second major section discusses the christological foundation (4:14–7:28).

In this part the interpretation is based on Psalm 110 and Gen 14:17–20, which are the two scriptural passages that speak about Melchizedek. An excursus, Heb 5:11–6:20, urges progress in theological insight: at stake is a fresh approach to christology. For this endeavor, the author does not refer to the concept of cross and resurrection but to the pattern of humiliation and exaltation. (Hebrews does not mention the resurrection of Christ even once in this long tractate!) The basic thesis for the christological argument is, on the one hand, the complete identity of Christ with human beings in the experience of temptation (4:15), suffering, and death (5:7–8). On the other hand, the Melchizedek typology both demonstrates the complete divinity of the redeemer (note especially 7:2–3) and proves that the order of salvation represented by Melchizedek is superior to the order of Abraham, Levi/Aaron, and the law. In this way, Hebrews renews Paul's thesis of freedom from the law and bases that claim on his christology: Christ as the high priest of the order of Melchizedek has sacrificed himself once and for all, while the priests of the order of Levi must offer sacrifices repeatedly for others as well as for themselves.

The third section of scriptural proof discusses the superiority of the heavenly reality over its earthly copy, thus establishing the validity of the new covenant (8:1–10:18). The basic scriptural passages are Jer 31:31 (promise of the new covenant), Exodus 25–26 (description of the tabernacle in the wilderness), and Ps 40:6–8 ("Sacrifice and offerings you do not desire"). To the ritual offerings of the tabernacle, which are merely copies of heavenly realities, Hebrews contrasts the cosmological and anthropological dimensions of the way and the sacrifice of Christ, who has passed into the real heavenly sanctuary. This section would be completely misunderstood if it were interpreted as a criticism of the Jewish temple cult. To be sure, the material and temporary limitations of the sacrificial cult are pointed out (Heb 9:9–10), but the argument is not a polemic against the temple cult of Jerusalem (which did no longer exist at that time). Rather, the author of Hebrews uses the Platonic schema, arguing that the old covenant with its tabernacle sacrifices was but the shadow of the heavenly reality; whereas Christ's sacrifice, which established the new covenant, was his entry into the real heavenly temple. Therefore the new covenant now stands firm (9:15–17). This entry into the reality of the heavenly temple, however, was accomplished by Christ through his own flesh, that is, his real physical human death. Thus the argument is not directed against Judaism but against Gnosticism, which denies the reality of the death of Christ. It is no accident that Hebrews stresses in the same context the apocalyptic expectation of the coming judgment (9:27–28).

The final major section of the writing (10:19–12:29) continues the anti-Gnostic argumentation with the criticism of the idea of the soul's celestial journey. The terms "freedom of entrance" and "new and living way" (10:19–20) at the beginning of this section allude to this idea. Just as the opening passage speaks of the flesh and blood of Jesus, that is, of the sacrifice that he offered through his death on earth, the "way" of the community is described as a way of faith in its earthly experiences. Entrance into the promised heavenly rest is accomplished through the steadfastness of faith of the community in its earthly human experience. This is shown by the remembering of the famous examples of faith that are presented in Hebrews 11. The chapter is introduced by a well-known definition of faith (Heb 11:1) that has become a notorious *crux interpretum.* The definition explains "faith" as the "real presence" (this is the correct translation of the Greek term *hypostasis,* not "conviction" or something like that in all modern translations!) of things hoped for. The list of examples of faith ends with the mention of the witnesses who were persecuted (11:35–38). In this sense, Jesus is the forerunner of faith, because he endured the cross of shame (12:2). The final section (13:1–17), after a short parenesis (13:1–8), once more enjoins the criterion for the understanding of the community's existence. Christ died "outside of the camp," which means outside the realm of religious security. It is exactly because Christians have no abiding city in the world that their place is there where Jesus suffered. This is the challenge of the Epistle to the Hebrews to the pious of all times who seek their place in a heavenly salvation.

(2) *The Epistle of Barnabas.* Another example for the interpretation of the Bible in the genre of scriptural gnosis is the *Epistle of Barnabas.* Its interpretive method is closely related to Hebrews. *Barnabas* also strives for a scriptural interpretation of the soteriological understanding of Jesus' death, all the while holding on to an apocalyptic expectation. Like other works of the Apostolic Fathers, the Greek text of *Barnabas* is transmitted in several biblical manuscripts as part of the New Testament (it is complete in the 4th-century Codex Sinaiticus) and it is also extant in Latin translation. The book is quoted for the first time by Clement of Alexandria. The date of its composition is problematic. Other New Testament writings are never used in *Barnabas,* neither explicitly nor tacitly, which would suggest an early date, perhaps even before the end of the 1st century. On the other hand, some scholars have argued that *Barn.* 16.4 is a reference to the building plans of Hadrian for a temple of Jupiter Capitolinus in Jerusalem that triggered the Bar Kochba insurrection (132–135 CE); but that is just as hypothetical as the recourse to *Barn.* 4.4–5 for a date during the government of Vespasian (60–79 CE). The use of the doctrine of the Two Ways in *Barnabas* 18–20 provides no arguments for a date because it cannot be demonstrated that there was a literary relationship between *Barnabas* and the *Didache* (§10.1c); it is more likely that both used a common source.

Nothing is known about the author of the *Epistle of Barnabas.* The suggestion that Barnabas, Paul's fellow missionary in Antioch, wrote this book is not impossible but highly unlikely because of its radical rejection of the old covenant. It is also difficult to assume a date for this writing as early as the middle of the 1st century. The place of origin cannot be determined with any certainty. Alexandria has

Bibliography to §12.2c (2):   Texts

Robert A. Kraft, *Épître de Barnabé* (SC 172; Paris: Cerf, 1971).
Bihlmeyer, *ApostVät,* xx–xxiv, 10–34.
Wengst, *Didache, Barnabas, 2. Klemens,* 103–202.
Lake, *ApostFath,* 1. 335–409.

Bibliography to §12.2c (2):   Commentaries

Ferdinand Prostmeier, *Der Barnabasbrief* (KAV 8; Göttingen: Vandenhoeck & Ruprecht, 1999).
Robert A. Kraft, *Barnabas and the Didache* (Grant, *ApostFath,* 3).
Hans Windisch, *Der Barnabasbrief* (HNT.E 3; Tübingen: Mohr/Siebeck, 1920).

Bibliography to §12.2c (2):   Studies

Klaus Wengst, *Tradition und Theologie des Barnabasbriefes* (AKG 42; Berlin: de Gruyter, 1971).

been suggested because of the use of the allegorical method, but this method was well known in other places. The epistolary framework is only an external dress. The prescript contains a greeting to "the sons and daughters," but lacks both a sender and an addressee. In the conclusion, the unnamed author asks to be remembered and gives a final blessing (21.7–9). Actually, the writing is not a letter, but a treatise of scriptural gnosis, just like Hebrews. *Barnabas* provides valuable insights into the techniques and results of the scriptural exegesis employed during the same period by writers such as Matthew and somewhat later by Justin Martyr.

It is the explicitly stated intention of the writing to communicate a deeper knowledge (*gnosis,* 1.5). The author upholds the basic commandments of hope, justice, and love (1.6), and he grants that fear, patience, long-suffering, and self-control are helpers to faith. But he insists that it is necessary also to gain wisdom, insight, understanding, and knowledge (2.3). His aim is the demonstration of the deeper understanding of Scripture, as becomes evident in the repeated references to *gnosis* in the introductions to several sections of scriptural interpretation (6.9; 9.8). The basis of the interpretations offered by the author is apparently an older collection of biblical passages that was put together according to certain topics and that may have been of Jewish origin. This older collection showed an interest in a rationalistic and allegorical-spiritual understanding of the ritual law (cf. Philo of Alexandria). This interest is still visible in several sections of *Barnabas:* sacrifice and fasting (2.4–3.6), circumcision (9.1–9), dietary and purity laws (10.1–12), sabbath (15.1–8), and temple (16.1–10). Occasionally the author has altered his source and inserted Christian interpretations, for example, with the rationale for the sanctification of the Lord's day (15.9). But the chief contribution of the author appears in the additions that deal with the scriptural proof for the coming of Jesus, for his cross and resurrection (5.1–8.7; 11.1–12.9), and for the new covenant (13.1–14.9; cf. 4.6–8). He also expanded the collection of testimonia for the topic of circumcision by an allegorical interpretation referring to the cross (9.8–9): the 318 servants circumcised by Abraham point to the cross of Jesus, since the Greek writing of that number is ΙΗΤ, representing the first to letters of the name of Jesus (ΙΗ-ΣΟΥΣ) and the letter T as the symbol of the cross. The scriptural allegories of *Barnabas* often treat the same topics as those found in Hebrews.

A particular outline of the treatise as a whole is not recognizable. Much of the writing obviously follows the order of the topics of the source used by the author, into which additional collections of biblical materials have been inserted, such as those used in the formation of the passion narrative. *Barnabas* indeed provides interesting insights into the way in which Scripture was explored in order to form materials for the telling of the passion narrative, such as the detail that Jesus was given gall to drink with vinegar (7.3, 5; see §10.2a on the *Gospel of Peter*). *Barnabas,* of course, was familiar with some story about Jesus' suffering as well as with other gospel materials (see 5.8–9 and the criticism of the titles Son of David and Son of Man, 12.10–11); but it cannot be shown that he knew and used the Gospels of the New Testament. On the contrary, what *Barnabas* presents here is material from "the school of the evangelists." This demonstrates how the early Christian communities paid special attention to the exploration of Scripture in order to understand and to tell the suffering of Jesus. *Barnabas* still represents the initial stages of this process, which was continued in the *Gospel of Peter,* the Gospel of Matthew, and half a century later by Justin Martyr, who presented a systematic treatment of the relevant scriptural passages. Justin, however, knew the Gospels of Matthew and Luke (probably also Mark), using the written forms of their narratives, and was thus able to establish a certain order in the technique of writing scriptural proofs.

In addition to the scriptural proofs for the suffering of Jesus and the new covenant, the apocalyptic perspective is another concern that *Barnabas* shares with Hebrews. The extensive exploration of Scripture for the question of Jesus' suffering is introduced by an eschatological admonition (4.1–14) that quotes the books of *Enoch* (*1 Enoch* 98.61–64) and Daniel (7:24; 7:7–8). The expectation of the parousia was also incorporated into the allegorical treatment of the Jewish sacrificial rite with reference to the death of Jesus (*Barn.* 7.6–9). Moreover, the final admonition of the book (21.1–3) emphasizes the parousia. With this eschatological perspective *Barnabas* connects the Two Ways with the first part of his writing (*Barnabas* 18–20; cf. *Did.* 1–6; see §10.1c), which he calls "another gnosis." While *Did.* 1.1 designates the Two Ways as the way of life and the way of death, they appear in *Barnabas* as the way of light and the way of darkness, which are ruled by the angel of God and by the angel of Satan. This agrees with the source of *Did.* 1–6 that is preserved in the Latin *Doctrina.* In general, *Barnabas* shows fewer traces of a Christian revision of this Jewish catechism than the *Didache,* and is thus more closely related to the Jewish original. The reproduction of the Two Ways rounds out the picture of typical representatives of post-Pauline churches. The same basic features appeared in the other witnesses, though one or the other element may have been less clearly present in any particular case: scriptural exploration for the understanding of Jesus' death, forgiveness of sins through his death, regulation of Christian conduct according to the moral teachings that were inherited from diaspora Judaism, and expectation of parousia and last judgment. These essential elements were further established as foundations of Christian faith by 1 Peter and *1 Clement.* That *Barnabas* recommends such faith as true "gnosis" (21.4) indicates the anti-Gnostic orientation of this ecclesiastical piety.

(d) Ignatius of Antioch

We do not know the name of a single Christian from the decades that followed the death of the first-generation apostles, from the period of about 60–90 CE. The first postapostolic generation is thus completely nameless for us. All Christian writings from this period were either anonymous or written under the pseudonym of an apostle from the first generation, although this pseudonymity may appear in a veiled form, as in the Epistle to the Hebrews. This situation changes in the next generation. The first book written under the true name of the author, the Revelation of John, was produced at the very beginning (ca. 90 CE) of the second generation

Bibliography to §12.2d: Text

Bihlmeyer, *ApostVät,* xxxi–xxxvi, 82–113.
Fischer, *Die apostolischen Väter,* 109–225.
Lake, *ApostFath,* 1. 165–277.

after the apostles. But other names appear now suddenly, though only within the circle of the Pauline communities, in Rome, in Antioch, and in western Asia Minor. To be sure, even now and for several more centuries to come, one still finds a continuation of pseudepigraphical literature, but it is no longer the dominant phenomenon. On the other hand, in Syria (with the exception of Antioch) and in Egypt, pseudepigraphy under the name of an apostle or a biblical figure still continues unabated for at least another generation, until one learns the names of the first Gnostic founders of schools in Egypt, like Basilides and Valentinus. The first names of authors from eastern Syria are those of Tatian and Bar Deisan (Bardesanes) from the second half of the 2d century.

One of the factors related to the partial termination of pseudepigraphical writing, again in the areas of Antioch, western Asia Minor, Greece, and Rome, was the desire of churches or individuals to exercise ecclesiastical-political influence in their own right. Clement wrote in behalf of the Roman church to Corinth in order to set things right in that church. Ignatius, bishop of Antioch, wrote from Smyrna and Troas to other churches in Asia Minor and to Rome in order to leave his testament for the ordering of the churches and of ecclesiastical offices before his expected martyrdom. Polycarp, bishop of Smyrna sent the Ignatian letters to the church in Philippi and later wrote to that church to settle the case of a presbyter who had embezzled funds. Eusebius of Caesarea also preserves information about letters of the Corinthian bishop Dionysius (ca. 150 CE) dispatched to the Spartans, the Athenians, the churches of Gortyna and Cnossus on Crete, to Nicomedia in Bithynia, to Amastris in Pontus, and finally to Rome. In his letter to Rome, Dionysius reports that the letter of Clement to the Corinthians was still read in their church (Eusebius *Hist. eccl.* 4.23).

Bibliography to §12.2d: Commentaries

William R. Schoedel, *Ignatius of Antioch: A Commentary on the Letters of Ignatius of Antioch* (Hermeneia; Philadelphia: Fortress, 1985).

Lightfoot, *Apostolic Fathers,* vol. 2, parts 1–2.

Walter Bauer, *Die Briefe des Ignatius von Antiochien und der Polykarpbrief* (HNT.E 2; Tübingen: Mohr/Siebeck, 1920).

Robert Grant, *Ignatius of Antioch* (Grant, *ApostFath,* 4).

Henning Paulsen, *Die Briefe des Ignatius von Antiochia und der Brief des Polykarp von Smyrna* (HNT 18; Tübingen: Mohr/Siebeck, 1985).

Bibliography to §12.2d: Studies

Cyril Charles Richardson, *The Christianity of Ignatius of Antioch* (New York: Columbia University Press, 1935).

Heinrich Schlier, *Religionsgeschichtliche Untersuchungen zu den Ignatiusbriefen* (BZNW 8; Giessen: Töpelmann, 1929).

Virginia Corwin, *Saint Ignatius and Christianity in Antioch* (YPR 1; New Haven: Yale University Press, 1960).

Rudolf Bultmann, "Ignatius and Paul," in idem, *Existence and Faith,* 267–88.

Heinrich Rathke, *Ignatius von Antiochien und die Paulusbriefe* (Berlin: Akademie-Verlag, 1967).

W. M. Swartley, "The Imitatio Christi in the Ignatian Letters," *VigChr* 27 (1973) 81–105.

Henning Paulsen, *Studien zur Theologie des Ignatius von Antiochien* (FKDG 29; Göttingen: Vandenhoeck & Ruprecht, 1978).

Allen Brent, "Ignatius of Antioch and the Imperial Cult," *VigChr* 52 (1998) 30–58.

Another important factor in the decrease of pseudepigraphy and in the use of the letter as a political instrument was briefly mentioned above: the collection and publication of the letters of Paul, which became highly significant for the churches discussed in this chapter. Colossians and Ephesians were soon included in this collection, in addition to the genuine letters of Paul, but 2 Thessalonians seems to have been missing, perhaps also 2 Corinthians, because there are no traces of these two letters in the first attestation of this collection by *1 Clement* and Ignatius of Antioch. The collection may have been put together in Asia Minor, but it was known also in Rome and in Antioch before the turn of the 1st century. The further history of these churches is not conceivable without Paul, even for those who were critical of his theology. It is important to remember that a number of churches possessed copies of Paul's letters before anyone ever got the idea to refer to the gospels as written authority.

The letters of Ignatius of Antioch (on the question of the genuine letters of Ignatius, see §7.3f) will be discussed first, although *1 Clement* and perhaps 1 Peter were written a few years earlier. But Ignatius presents another attempt at a theological elaboration of Pauline concepts. He therefore belongs together with Ephesians and especially with Hebrews. The church of Antioch, where Ignatius was bishop, was perhaps more typical for Petrine Christianity in Syria after Paul's departure from that city (§9.2a). Matthew could have been written in Antioch—a writing that expresses some criticism of a Gentile mission that claims to be free from the law (§10.2c). The Gospels of Mark and Matthew, to be sure, rely upon the kerygma of the cross and resurrection and in general agree with Christian tenets that could be subsumed under the general category of the "Pauline gospel." But this may not mean much more than the proclamation of Christ's death and resurrection, the worship of Christ as Lord and Son of God, and the expectation of the parousia, articles of faith that characterized Antiochean Christianity from the beginning, even before Paul's arrival in that city (§8.3c). Ignatius, however, was deeply influenced as a theologian by the letters of Paul. The information from Eusebius (*Hist. eccl.* 3.22) that Ignatius was bishop of Antioch around the turn of the 1st century and was martyred under the emperor Trajan seems to be trustworthy, especially since the report of Ignatius's martyrdom, preserved independently of Eusebius (the *Martyrium Colbertinum*), confirms this date. Polycarp, bishop of Smyrna, to whom Ignatius wrote one of his letters, was martyred in 167 (according to Eusebius *Hist. eccl.* 4.14.10, 15.1), or perhaps already in 156 (this date derives from the less reliable information of an addition to the report of his martyrdom; see §12.3f). He was then 86 years old, and was therefore born in either 69/70 or 80/81. Since Polycarp was already bishop when Ignatius wrote to him, the martyrdom of Ignatius is best dated in Trajan's last years, that is, 110–117 CE.

The occasion for Ignatius's writing of the letters is complex. Various remarks in the letters show that, as bishop of Antioch, Ignatius had experienced strong opposition from a group in his church before his arrest. As a bishop destined for martyrdom, he left a church behind that was divided and apparently not fully appreciating the magnitude of his journey. Ignatius is therefore concerned that the church of Antioch is fully reconciled (of which he receives information in Troas; *Phld.* 10.1; *Smyrn.* 11.2; *Pol.* 7.2). At the same time, he understands his journey to

Rome as prisoner in terms of a triumphant procession in behalf of Christ and for this needs the churches of Asia Minor, both for support and publicity. Extensive preparations had to be undertaken by Ignatius, together with his friends. Messengers are sent ahead to announce his arrival, to arrange meetings with delegations from churches that he was unable to visit, to carry his letters to various churches, to send information back to Antioch, and to bring the letter written in Smyrna to the church in Rome (the Romans had already been informed of Ignatius' arrival by messengers sent from Antioch). Moreover, all of this could only be accomplished through substantial financial support to pay for the necessary expenditures. Support from the churches and a willing audience, however, presuppose that the churches are united under a gospel that proclaims Christ's suffering and death, without which Ignatius's martyrdom would mean nothing. Some of the letters show that there was opposition to the entire endeavor; controversy with such opponents is therefore a constitutive part of the letters.

The soldiers who guarded him led him through the southwestern regions of Asia, but did not continue to the coast at Ephesus, instead turning north from the upper Maeander to Philadelphia, where Ignatius had the opportunity to meet with members of the church, then traveling on to Smyrna. There Ignatius received delegations from the churches of Ephesus, Magnesia on the Maeander, and Tralles. A longer delay in Smyrna enabled Ignatius to establish a close friendship with the church and its bishop, Polycarp, which assured full support from here on. From Smyrna Ignatius wrote to the three churches, which had sent delegations (*Ephesians, Magnesians, and Trallians*) and to the *Romans*. He was then led to Troas, where he wrote to the *Smyrnaeans*, to *Polycarp*, and to the *Philadelphians*. No more information is available about the martyr's travel from Troas, which probably continued by ship to Neapolis and Philippi in Macedonia, then across northern Greece to the Adriatic on the Via Egnatia and, after landing in Italy, along one of the many roads to Rome.

All letters of Ignatius are true correspondence, introduced by a prescript with sender, addressee, and greeting, and concluded by final instructions and greetings, which are often specific. Ignatius will sometimes refer to special situations in the churches addressed and, of course, mention individual persons when discussing such questions as the sending of messengers. But on the whole, the content of the letters is of a more general character. Like a testament, they are the instruction and bequest of someone who is facing death. Fundamental statements about the soteriological significance of the cross of Christ, the office of the bishop, and the conduct of the members of the churches are repeated in most of the letters. Even the warnings about false teachers are sometimes, but not always, directed to the church in whose letter they occur. The writing to Polycarp, despite its personal note, is at the same time a generally valid instruction for the office of the bishop. The letter to the Romans occupies a special position. It is focused upon Ignatius's personal hope of attaining perfection through a martyr's death and thus establishes the authority of his writings as a testament (see below). It is therefore justified to treat the letters as a unity insofar as they refer to the same theological and ecclesiastical concerns.

The style and language of Ignatius's letters belongs to what has been called "Asian" rhetoric, manifestly different from both the vernacular spoken Koine and the Atticistic language of the literary purists of the time (see §3.2b). This "Asianism" wants to express pathos by an often bombastic terminology, repetitions, accumulation of synonyms, parallel sequences of short phrases, images, metaphors, and alliterations. While the external form of the prescripts of the letters superficially resembles the Pauline prescripts, they are richly ornamented with fancy titles for Ignatius himself as well as for the churches addressed. In addition, Ignatius makes use of kerygmatic, hymnic, and liturgical formulations or imitates their diction. All this results in expressions and appeals that invite the reader into a realm of religious experience, rather than rational reflection. This language is intensified by a sense of inescapable destiny, as these words are those of one going to martyrdom in order to demonstrate that Christ's work was indeed accomplished through suffering and death.

In his interpretation of Paul, Ignatius seems closer to Ephesians—which he knew and used—than to those interpreters of Paul who were concerned with biblical exegesis and clung to the apocalyptic expectation of the parousia. Ignatius's own eschatological expectation is reduced to the concept of martyrdom, which is the perfection of Christian existence. The Scriptures of Israel do not play any role in his thoughts or arguments; all that is explicitly quoted are two passages from Proverbs in *Eph.* 5.3 and *Magn.* 13.1. The controversy he describes with opponents in Philadelphia (*Phld.* 8.2) is characteristic for Ignatius's view of the Scriptures, to which the opponents referred in order to prove their point. Ignatius was not willing to enter into a discussion of the fine points of scriptural interpretation, but simply pointed instead to his own decisive authority, the gospel of Jesus' cross and resurrection. Ignatius does not use concepts of time and history, promise and fulfillment, but rather employs categories of space and cosmos that have closer affinity to Gnostic thought. In this respect, he also stands in proximity to the Gospel of John and shows many similarities to Johannine language (but it cannot be demonstrated that he knew and used this gospel). Occasionally, Ignatius makes mythological statements about a cosmological drama, describing the ascension of the redeemer as the cosmic victory over the powers of the stars (*Ephesians* 19). But in general, he prefers to speak about the heavenly and earthly worlds not in dynamic but in the static categories of spirit and flesh. These categories not only serve to describe his christology, but also his statements about the Eucharist, the church, and the existence of the believer. He uses the same language in the interpretation of the traditional kerygma about the coming of the redeemer, his death, and his resurrection. His primary witness for these statements is Paul, to whom he refers frequently. Ignatius considers Paul to be the theologian who had most truly understood the salvation proclaimed in Christ's cross and resurrection, although for Paul the categories of spirit and flesh were part of a dynamic understanding of eschatology.

The kerygma of his church, repeatedly quoted and reformulated by Ignatius and referred to as the "gospel," is greatly expanded when compared with the Pauline gospel formula (cf. 1 Cor 15:3–4). It begins with the statement about the birth of Jesus from Mary the virgin, which is used to underline the real and true humanity of Jesus (*Eph.* 18.2; *Trall.* 9), and adds the name of Pilate to the statement of Jesus' suffering and crucifixion (*Trall.* 9; in *Smyrn.* 1.2 Herod is also mentioned). This development of the kerygma was most likely one of the reasons for a similar expansion of the written Gospels, which began with the passion narrative, were expanded by an introduction resuming the story of Jesus with his baptism (Mark), and eventually included also narratives of Jesus' birth (Matthew and Luke). Ignatius interprets the kerygma according to the dualistic scheme of flesh and spirit. They are understood as fundamental metaphysical opposites, whereby "flesh" is not so much the sphere of sin (as in Paul) but rather the sphere of corruptibility. In the coming, dying, and rising of Christ the impossible becomes reality: flesh and spirit are united. Christ is the paradoxical realization of the unity of the spiritual and divine world with the earthly and human world of the flesh. Christ "is nailed to the cross in the flesh and in the spirit" (*Smyrn.* 1.1); after the resurrection his disciples touch him "in the flesh and the spirit" (*Smyrn.* 3.2). In *Smyrneans* 1, a kerygmatic formula is expanded by a phrase from Paul's letter to the Romans: "from the tribe of David according to the flesh, Son of God according to the will and power of God" (cf. Rom 1:3–4). In many instances, Ignatius simply inserts the word "truly" in order to underline the unity in Christ of the divine and earthly realities: "truly born, truly persecuted, truly crucified and dead, truly risen from the dead" (*Trall.* 9.1–2). Or he employs paradoxical juxtapositions of opposites to describe the presence of both spheres in Christ: "fleshly and spiritually, born and unborn, in the flesh becoming God, in death true life, from Mary and from God, first capable of suffering, then incapable of suffering" (*Eph.* 7.2).

That much already describes Ignatius's christology, because for him salvation is dependent on nothing but God's presence in the human Christ. This Christ becomes effective for the congregation in the gospel and in the Eucharist: as there is *one* flesh of Christ, there is also one bread, one cup, and one gospel (*Eph.* 20.2; *Smyrn.* 7.2; *Phld.* 4). The gospel itself is the arrival of the savior, his suffering, and his resurrection (*Phld.* 9.2). In the same way, the bread of the Eucharist is the present Christ, the medicine of immortality (*Eph.* 20.2). This formulation, however, does not imply that Ignatius thinks that the sacrament works like an impersonal, mechanical power. On the contrary, he repeatedly emphasizes the harmony and mutual love of the living congregation, in which gospel and Eucharist are effective (*Eph.* 4.1–5.2). While Ignatius may indicate that the participation in the Eucharist guarantees participation in the resurrection, the immediate effect of the Eucharist is the love and obedience of the Christians. As the Eucharist cannot be understood without the Christ who became flesh, neither can it be thought of without the Christian church. The worship service is the center of the congregation's life (*Eph.* 13.1), and whoever is outside the "altar," used as metaphor for the assembled congregation, is outside the bread of God (*Eph.* 5.2; *Trall.* 7.2).

The church has the same religious qualities as Christ, the gospel, and the sacrament. The Christians are "in Christ" (*Eph.* 11.1; 20.1), "in God" (*Eph.* 13.5), or imitators of God or Christ (*Trall.* 1.2; *Phld.* 7.2); and everything that the church does "in the flesh," that is, in the realm of earthly life, is "spiritual" (*Eph.* 8.2). The unity of spirit and flesh is visibly documented in the actions of the church (*Magn.* 13.2). The church is the "building of God" (*Eph.* 9.1; the cross of Christ is the machine for this building!), but the emphasis is not, as in the *Shepherd of Hermas* (§12.1d), upon the individual purity of the members as building stones, but upon the shaping of the life of the congregation through mutual love (*Eph.* 14; *Magn.* 1; and elsewhere). Elements from the Pauline letters are consciously adopted in these passages, and the many allusions to the Pauline correspondence demonstrate that Ignatius repeatedly returned to those letters for guidance and instruction. Ignatius learned from Paul that the Christian church is a living body that is constantly nourished and edified by gospel and Eucharist for mutual love and common tasks in a concrete social interaction; he thus avoids a moralizing view of Christian conduct. But like Paul, who turned to a topic of Stoic civic ethics for the description of the organic unity of the church as the body of Christ (1 Cor 12), Ignatius also draws on Hellenistic themes that are popular in the description of the harmony of the society (e.g., *Eph.* 4.1-5.1).

Ignatius goes beyond the more democratic ideals of Paul, when he recommends a hierarchical order for the offices of the church. Thus Ignatius has become known as the earliest advocate for a "monarchic episcopate," though this term is often misunderstood as implying the establishment of a lofty office with unlimited powers. Ignatius calls himself "Bishop of Antioch" and presupposes that each of the churches to which he writes is headed by a bishop. To what degree this structure was a reality at his time is an open question. There are no earlier testimonies to the institution of the monarchic episcopate, and the assumption of the appointment of the first bishops by the apostles of the first generation is clearly a later fiction. But it was indeed the case that the monarchic episcopate came to be widely accepted during the first decades of the 2d century in the cities around the Aegean Sea and in Rome, a bit later also elsewhere in western Syria, but only toward the end of the century in Alexandria and eastern Syria.

Although Ignatius sees the bishop as equipped with important powers and authority, he understands himself and the office of bishop more in charismatic than in institutional functions. The bishop represents what God is thinking (*Eph.* 3.2–4); he must be received like God (*Eph.* 6). He guarantees Christ's presence in baptism and in the community meals of the church, which must therefore never be held without him (*Smyrn.* 8.2). The congregation should act only in unanimity with the bishop; unity with the thought of God presupposes unity with the bishop (*Eph.* 3.2; *Phld.* 3.2). Whoever does something without the bishop violates Christian existence (*Magn.* 4; 7; *Phld.* 7.2; *Smyrn.* 8; in *Smyrn.* 9.1 actions without the bishop are even called the work of the devil). Such declarations must be understood in the light of statements about the church as representing Christ in its conduct and actions. The authority assigned to the bishop is not derived from concepts of power and control, but from the idea of Christ's unity with the church. Moreover, the bishop is not the only officer of the congregations, but shares his responsibility with the presbyters and the deacons. All three are frequently named together (*Magn.* 13.1; *Trall.* 2; 3; 7; *Phld.* 7.1; 10.2; *Smyrn.* 8.1). Obedience toward the bishop and the presbytery stand side by side (*Eph.* 2.2; 20.2; *Magn.* 2–3; *Trall.* 2.1). The deacons should be considered as Christ, the bishop as the Father, and the presbyters as God's council (*Trall.* 3.1). These, however, are metaphorical phrases of Ignatius's rhetoric and do not imply that the bishop has taken the place of God. The instructions for the bishop that Ignatius wrote for Polycarp demonstrate that Ignatius thought of the office of bishop in terms of authority but not in terms of power. The bishop's authority is grounded in his service and care for others. The bishop is asked to bear the illness of all people (Pol. 1.3), to devote his love not to the good people but to the difficult disciples (*Pol.* 2.1), to care for the widows (*Pol.* 4.1), and he should not be haughty in his dealings with slaves, whether male or female (*Pol.* 4.2). Cooperation and collegiality is the key for a successful conduct of office (*Pol.* 6.1).

There is a final and very important factor to be considered for the need and the eventual successful establishment of the office of the one bishop in each city, namely, the proliferation of Christian groups, especially in the major cities. Christians were restricted to assemblies in houses. As the congregations grew, it was obviously no longer possible for all members of the church of a city to meet in one and the same place. A central organization, however, was needed not so much for the establishment of unity of doctrine, but—which was much more important—for the administration of services and the supervision of the necessary finances. As is evident from the Ignatian correspondence, and especially from the letter to Polycarp, care for the widows and orphans, hospitality for visitors, in rare cases the payment for the manumission of a slave (in *Pol.* 4.3 Ignatius advises against this practice), and the support for travelers and messengers required considerable expenditures, which were possible only through the establishment of a centralized administration. The suggestion that the term "bishop" was borrowed from the usage of some secular associations, in which the title "bishop" (*episcopos*) was the designation for the treasurer, has some merit. In any case, there is no question that the churches that adopted the office structure of the monarchic episcopate, surrounded by trustworthy and faithful presbyters and deacons, were able to establish structures that withstood the adversities of centuries to come.

The office of the bishop also became significant in connection with the problem of heresy. Discussing this problem, Ignatius frequently refers to the office of the bishop (*Trall.* 7; *Pol.* 3; and elsewhere). It is difficult to get a clear picture regarding the character of these heretics, because Ignatius alludes to them only casually. In some instances he accuses them of "Judaism" (*Magn.* 8.1; *Phld.* 6.1); both the Sabbath and circumcision are mentioned (*Magn.* 9; *Phld.* 6.1). To confess Christ and to "Judaize" are mutually exclusive (*Magn.* 9). In addition, *Phld.* 8.2 mentions the controversy in which he was engaged about the interpretation of Scripture ("the archives"), to which Ignatius responded that his true "archives" are the cross and resurrection of Christ and immediately afterward contrasts, quite unexpectedly, "the priests and high priests" with Christ and the gospel (*Phld.* 9). Does Ignatius here allude to a Scripture-based understanding of Christ's priestly office of salvation, and were these opponents identical with those who preached circumcision? Moreover, it is not clear whether these Jewish-Christian opponents, who based their thoughts on the exegesis of Scripture, were different from the heretics that are attacked in the letters to the Smyrneans and Trallians. Here, docetism is rejected repeatedly in no uncertain terms; these opponents denied the true humanity of Jesus Christ (*Trall.* 10; *Smyrn.* 2; 4.2; 7.1), which may imply that they were Gnostics. This agrees with the observation that both letters reject speculations about angels and cosmic powers: even the angels and archons will be judged if they do not believe in the blood of Christ (*Smyrn.* 6.1; cf. *Trall.* 5). All that can be learned from these fragmentary references is the fact that Ignatius knew about Jewish-Christian as well as Gnostic separatists and the fact that they threatened the unity of local churches, especially as they despised his own zeal for martyrdom (*Smyrn.* 4.2) and did not contribute to the support for widows and orphans (*Smyrn.* 6.2).

Ignatius is obviously not interested in a systematic refutation of their teachings but attacks them for one reason only, namely, that they endanger the unity of the church. The refutation of the heretics is intended to warn the church and urge it to stand together in the unanimity of faith under the leadership of the bishop. Only in this way can the problem of heresy be solved and the congregation be preserved from disintegration into splinter groups. To fight heretics, the *one* local congregation must be strengthened, held together through its regular worship services, and through mutual love and obedience to the bishop. The criterion for the distinction between true and false belief is the "gospel," in which the reality of Jesus' coming, death, and resurrection is clearly stated. At the same time, Ignatius uses the letter as an instrument of ecclesiastical polity, as Paul had done half a century earlier. However, Ignatius does not have the patience to advise individual congregations in detail but prefers to provide general guidelines that would serve to strengthen congregations everywhere in the same way.

Ignatius was just a bishop of a local church. Why should he feel that he was called to give this sort of instruction in letters to other churches? The answer to this question involves the topic of Ignatius's self-consciousness as a martyr. Ignatius emphasizes repeatedly that he is not just speaking as a bishop but as one who is on his way to martyrdom, a way that Ignatius describes as a triumphant procession—never commenting on the miserable conditions he has to endure as a prisoner. Rather, he fulfills the honorable function of the "bearer of God" (*theophoros*) in the procession to the capital of the empire. The self-designation "bearer of God" must be understood almost literally. Ignatius's way to Rome is a religious procession in which he carries God triumphantly to the capital of the empire. This is described in a language that mirrors the language of the procession of the triumphant emperor. The God, however, whom Ignatius, the martyr, brings to Rome is the crucified Christ. Because he is writing as one who is on the way to his death as a martyr, his letters therefore take on the character of a testament. His calling to martyrdom gives him his authority. As bishop he would be nothing more than a voice of God, while as a martyr, he is the divine Logos (*Rom.* 2.1); in his martyrdom he will become like Christ and "attain to God" (*Rom.* 1.2; 4.2; 5.3; and elsewhere). This view is closely connected with his concept of the gospel and christology. The unity of divinity and humanity is perfected through suffering and death. Thus only in martyrdom can one fully participate in Christ's cross and resurrection (*Rom.* 6.1). The entire eschatological expectation of early Christianity is condensed into the idea of martyrdom—without denying that the regular members of the church are Christians in the full sense. But martyrdom, next to the gospel and the Eucharist, becomes the visible and tangible presence of salvation for the entire church, because it accomplishes the ultimate goal of Christian existence: in it one becomes a disciple (*Eph.* 1.2; *Rom.* 5.3); it is a call to the Father (*Rom.* 7.2); freedom from slavery (*Rom.* 4.3); the bread of God (*Rom.* 7.3). Ignatius's desire to win life in his own death, "to sink to the world in order to rise toward God" (*Rom.* 2.2), must be understood against the background of the renewal of the Pauline proclamation of cross and resurrection, against all Gnosticizing spiritualization and docetism. For Ignatius, Paul is therefore the blessed martyr in whose discipleship he wants to go to his death. Yet, Ignatius does not hesitate to call all Christians "fellow-initiates of Paul" (*Eph.* 12.2).

(e) Peter and Paul as the Authorities of Ecclesiastical Order: The First Epistle of Clement

Clement of Rome, to whom we owe the writing known as *1 Clement,* was one of the political leaders of the church who was active in that period by writing letters in his own name, not under the pseudonym of an apostle. The text of his letter to the church of Corinth was first discovered in the 5th-century biblical Codex Alexandrinus (§7.2c), where it follows upon the Revelation of John; however, one leaf that contained the text of *1 Clem.* 57.7–63.4 is missing. The complete Greek text became available through the discovery of Codex Hierosolymitanus (the same codex to which we owe the Greek text of the *Didache;* see §10.1c.2). In addition, two Latin, one Syriac, and two Coptic manuscripts have been published. There are also numerous quotations from *1 Clement* in Clement of Alexandria. Furthermore, the letter was used by Polycarp of Smyrna and is mentioned by Dionysios of Corinth in the middle of the 2d century. *1 Clement* must have been distributed widely quite

Bibliography to §12.2e: Text

Bihlmeyer, *ApostVät,* xxiv–xxviii, 35–70.
Fischer, *Die apostolischen Väter,* 1–107.
Lake, *ApostFath,* 1. 3–121.

Bibliography to §12.2e: Commentaries

Lightfoot, *Apostolic Fathers,* part 1, vols. 1–2.
Robert M. Grant and Holt H. Graham, *First and Second Clement* (Grant, *ApostFath* 2).
Andreas Lindemann, *Die Clemensbriefe* (HNT 17, Die Apostolischen Väter 1; Tübingen: Mohr/ Siebeck, 1992).
Horacio E. Lona, *Der erste Clemensbrief* (KAV 2; Göttingen: Vandenhoeck & Ruprecht, 1998).

Bibliography to §12.2e: Studies

Adolf von Harnack, *Einführung in die alte Kirchengeschichte: Das Schreiben der römischen Kirche and die korinthische aus der Zeit Domitians* (Leipzig: Hinrichs, 1929).
Werner Jaeger, *Early Christianity and Greek Paideia* (Cambridge, MA: Harvard University Press, 1961).
Karlmann Beyschlag, *Clemens Romanus und der Frühkatholizismus: Untersuchungen zu 1 Clemens 1–7* (BHTh 35; Tübingen: Mohr/Siebeck, 1966).
Barbara E. Bowe, *A Church in Krisis: Ecclesiology and Paraenesis in Clement of Rome* (HDR 23; Minneapolis: Fortress, 1988).
Gerhard Schneider, *Clemens von Rom: Epistola ad Corinthios, Brief an die Korinther* (FC 15; Freiburg: Herder, 1994).

Bibliography to §12.2e: Peter and Rome

Oscar Cullmann, *Peter: Disciple, Apostle, Martyr: A Historical and Theological Essay* (Philadelphia: Westminster, 1962).
Daniel Wm. O'Conner, *Peter in Rome: The Literary, Liturgical, and Archaeological Evidence* (New York: Columbia University Press, 1969).
Erich Dinkler, "Die Petrus-Rom-Frage," *ThR* NF 25 (1959) 189–230, 298–335; 27 (1961) 33–64.
Idem, "Petrus und Paulus in Rom," *Gymnasium* 87 (1980) 1–37.

Bronze Coin of Domitian
The inscription reads: CAES[AR] DIVI AUG[USTI] VESP[ASIANI] F[ILIUS] DOMITIANUS CO[N]S[UL] VII = "Caesar, Son of the divinized Augustus Vespasian, Domitian, consul for the seventh time." Domitian expelled the philosophers from Rome; in this context, the Christians also suffered persecution (95–96 C.E.).

early. It is a true letter, which names the Roman church as its sender and, also in the prescript, the church in Corinth as the recipient. According to well-attested ancient tradition, the letter was written by Clement, who was commissioned by the Roman church. This Clement was probably the secretary of the Roman church, and it is possible that the reference in *Herm. Vis.* 2.4.3 speaks of the same person (§12.1d). There is no indication that Clement was the bishop of the Roman church, as was claimed by later tradition, although there is little question that members of the church who were learned and literate moved to positions of leadership during those years. But *1 Clement,* who speaks about bishops in the plural (*1 Clem.* 42), does not contain any reference to the monarchic episcopate, which appears less than two decades later in Ignatius of Antioch and Polycarp of Smyrna. The most plausible date for the writing of *1 Clement* is 96–97, that is, immediately after the persecution of the Stoic philosophers and probably also of the Christians by the emperor Domitian. The letter points to persecutions in Rome that had hit the church only recently.

The occasion for writing the letter to Corinth was the removal of the presbyters by a number of younger members of the Corinthian church (*1 Clem.* 47.6). We are told very little about this rebellion, which the author calls foreign and unholy (*1 Clem.* 1.1). Clement reveals repeatedly that this rebellion had disturbed the church in Corinth very deeply, but he never informs the reader about its causes. It is tempting to assume that the troubles were caused by heretical teachers who had come to Corinth. The Revelation of John and Ignatius of Antioch show that Judaizing and Gnostic teachers were active at that time in Asia Minor, and it is not difficult to believe that such teachers had also come to Corinth and had been able to divide the church. In his response to the disturbances in Corinth, Clement emphasizes traditional Jewish-Christian teaching and morality, the creation of the world by God, the resurrection of Christ, and the future resurrection of the Christians. All these topics would be appropriate in a writing directed against Gnostic heretics. But the letter does not contain any polemical remarks about false teachers, and Clement shows no interest in any theological controversy. Rather, he repeats in great detail what he considers to be the foundation of Christian faith, teaching, and conduct, and he expects that careful and faithful attention to these matters will reconstitute the unity of the Corinthian church.

As Clement shares with Ignatius the interest in establishing the unity of a local church, they also have in common that they mention Peter and Paul side by side (Ign. *Rom.* 4.3; *1 Clement* 5). In both instances, Peter and Paul are introduced as apostles, and in both passages they are referred to as martyrs. It is by no means natural that these two apostles should be named together in the light of the conflict between Paul and Peter in Antioch (§9.2a) and the independent development of traditions under Peter's name in Syria (§10.2a). As we have seen, an anti-Pauline tradition of Peter (and James) was even developed in Syria at this time or at the beginning of the 2d century (§10.4c). The fact that these two apostles are reconciled with each other and named together reflects an important development in the ecclesiastical-political situation. Christian churches that had first formed their traditions independently under the name of a single apostle began to form alliances. The tradition of Peter certainly derives from Syria. Peter himself may have come to Rome toward the end of his life, as the later story of his Roman martyrdom claims; but there is no certain evidence for this, because for the years 60–90 no testimonies from the Roman church have been preserved. That Peter, however, was accepted as an authority not only in Antioch, but also in the "Pauline" churches from Asia Minor to Corinth eventually opened the way into the West for such typical "Petrine" Syrian writings as the Gospel of Matthew. Thus the alliance of Peter and Paul and the various writings under their authority became the most important foundation for the formation of the early catholic church.

The context in which both apostles are mentioned in *1 Clement* 5 is noteworthy. Clement says that he wants to add some examples from more recent times to those taken from Scripture. First, he points in general to the most righteous "pillars" (of the church) who have endured sufferings (5.2). With the remark, "Let us set before our eyes the good apostles" (5.3), he introduces a short reference to the martyrdom of Peter (5.4) and continues with a long enumeration of the sufferings and martyrdom of Paul (5.5–7). In neither case does he try to establish a special relationship of the events to the Roman church. This is remarkable in view of *1 Clement* 42, in which Clement says that the apostles, having preached the gospel in many countries and cities, everywhere appointed the earliest converts as bishops and deacons. Since in neither passage do any references appear concerning the relationship of individual apostles to specific churches, it follows that Clement is not interested in the doctrine of apostolic succession, but wants to speak generally about the continuance and stability of offices in the Christian churches. Thus Peter is not named as the founder of the legitimate church office in Rome, nor is Paul given that function for Corinth. Rather, both apostles together are quoted as authorities and examples for all churches.

In terms of the character of its materials, *1 Clement* is a parenesis. The materials used by the author in the parenetical sections are easily recognized: the teaching of the Two Ways, especially catalogs of virtues and vices, tables of household duties, and rules of the community. From the Scriptures come the collections of examples for virtues and vices; from the Christian tradition a collection of sayings of Jesus is quoted twice (13.2 and 46.8). To Christian sources used in the writing also belongs a collection of the letters of Paul (including the Epistle to the Hebrews) as well as kerygmatic and liturgical materials from his church, among these an extensive intercessory prayer (59.3–61.3). But Clement also relies on pagan traditions, most notably a description of the creation of the world through the wisdom of God (20.1–11), which may have come to the author by way of diaspora Judaism, as well as popular materials of illustrations like the story of the Phoenix (25.1–5). Throughout the parenesis, it is evident that Clement is also dependent upon the philosophical ideals of civic order and good citizenship.

An analysis of this rather long writing is difficult, but the literary procedures of the composition are evident. The actual occasion for the writing is mentioned only briefly (1.1). The formerly famous piety of the Corinthians is then described in the form of a catalog of virtues and a table of duties (1.2–2.8). A catalog of vices follows (3.2), and the first vice from this catalog (jealousy) is illustrated with materials from Scripture (4.1–13), from the Christian tradition (5.1–7), and from the Greek world (6). Clement proceeds in a similar way in the following chapters with a series of virtues: repentance (7–8), obedience (9.2–10.6), faith and hospitality (11–12), and humility (13–17). Almost all examples are drawn from Scripture, which is quoted extensively and often verbatim. A number of names and examples of behavior from Scripture appear more than once, each time illustrating a different virtue, and many examples have parallels in Hebrews 11. This demonstrates that the author is drawing on collections of scriptural examples, which can then be used to illustrate various virtues or vices. Traditions of different origin are occasionally inserted, such as a short catechism of words of Jesus (13.2) that was not drawn from any written gospel, but shows close affinities to the Synoptic Sayings Gospel (that is also the case for the quotation in *1 Clem.* 46.8).

After concluding remarks (17.1–19.1), a new section is begun that follows the outline of the Christian kerygma, though it contains many digressions. The section 19.2–20.12 speaks about the creation. Upon the mention of the Lord Jesus Christ, "whose blood was given for us" (21.6), the author quotes a table of household duties (21.6–8), and an admonition of Christ in the form of a citation of Ps 33:12–18 (*1 Clem.* 22.6–8) warns of double-mindedness (23) and introduces a discussion of the resurrection (23.4–25.5). For this Clement cites as an example the story of the Phoenix and alludes to parables that are reminiscent of Matt 24:32–33 and Mark 4:3–9. A warning of the coming judgment (*1 Clem.* 28.1) introduces admonitions concerning sanctification and good works (29–34.6) and a reminder of the promise (34.7–35.12). The statement, "this is the way in which we found our salvation, Jesus Christ" (36.1) looks back upon the whole first part of the letter, which is indeed an extensive description of Christian teachings, namely, the "way."

Special instructions begin only at this point of the letter. Material about the order of the church comes first, with many examples and quotations. The description of Christian offices and their foundation is important (42). *1 Clem.* 44.1–6 finally refers to the specific situation in Corinth. The admonition to restore unanimity, obedience, and subordination (45–58), in addition to more references to Scripture, uses specifically Christian materials more widely, some of which are drawn from the Pauline letters. The concluding intercessory prayer (59.3–61.3) abounds with allusions to Scripture and is dependent on prayers from the Jewish diaspora.

1 Clement provides important insights into the general piety of Christian churches in that period. What is found in this letter must have dominated the liturgy, teaching, and preaching of the church. Clement is convinced that this kind of piety and conduct should be the foundation for the unanimity of each individual congregation and for the unity of the church at large, rather than specific doctrines that could be identified as the theological position of one single Christian apostle like Paul. In the context of this Christian piety, nobody could have understood what the actual issues were in such controversies, as was the case, for example, in the showdown between Peter and Paul in Antioch. Clement was clearly not prepared to enter into a discussion of theological issues that might have been controversial in the Corinthian church to which he was writing. As long as the Corinthians were seriously ready to follow the "way" as described in this letter, such controversies would become irrelevant and in any case not important enough to cause a division in the congregation.

(f) The Letters of Peter and the Legacy of Paul

(1) *The First Epistle of Peter.* The piety propagated by Clement made it possible to refer in general to the authorities of the venerable martyrs Peter and Paul. The

letters of Paul, as *1 Clement* illustrates, could be understood as documents supporting this piety. This explains how it was possible that a deutero-Pauline letter could be written in Rome at about the same time, but be issued under the authority of Peter: the First Epistle of Peter. Except for the name of the sender in the prescript (1:1) nothing in this writing points to Peter. Everything is either Pauline or attributable to general Christian tradition, specifically Christian tradition as it had become established at the end of the 1st century. The beginning of the proem, "blessed be the God and Father of our Lord Jesus Christ," presupposes the identical formula of the proems in 2 Cor 1:3 and Eph 1:3, and although passages from letters of Paul are not explicitly cited, general familiarity with these letters, especially Romans and Ephesians, is not unlikely. Silvanus, who is mentioned as the amanuensis of the letter in 1 Pet 5:12, is known as the coauthor of a Pauline letter (1 Thess 1:1) and is otherwise attested as an apostle from Paul's staff (2 Cor 1:19; Acts 15:22ff.). Mark, who sends greetings in 1 Pet 5:13, appears in the list of greetings in Phlm 24 and Col 4:10 (note also Acts 13:5, etc., where "John Mark" is mentioned as a travel companion of Paul and Barnabas). The author calls himself a "witness of the sufferings of Christ" (1 Pet 5:1); this, however does not point to an eyewitness of Jesus' crucifixion, but to a Christian who had experienced the suffering of Christ in his own tribulations and will therefore, like all other Christians, "partake in the glory that is to be revealed" (1 Pet 5:1).

The good Greek style of 1 Peter also makes authorship by the Galilean disciple impossible. The author had a relatively high level of Greek literary training, was familiar with the formal styles of Greek rhetoric, and throughout uses the Greek translation of the Bible, the Septuagint. All this points to a Gentile Christian, who wrote at a time when the perception of the two great apostles Peter and Paul as martyrs had been firmly established, that is, the time of *1 Clement* and Ignatius of

Bibliography to §12.2f: Commentaries

Paul J. Achtemeier, *1 Peter: A Commentary on First Peter* (Hermeneia; Minneapolis: Fortress, 1996).
Edwin Gordon Selwyn, *The First Epistle of St. Peter* (2d ed.; London: Macmillan, and New York: St. Martin's, 1947 and reprints).
Frank W. Beare, *The First Epistle of Peter* (3d ed.; Oxford: Blackwell, 1970).
Henning Paulsen, *Der Zweite Petrusbrief und der Judasbrief* (KEK 12/2; Göttingen: Vandenhoeck & Ruprecht, 1992).
Anton Vögtle, *Der Judasbrief, der Zweite Petrusbrief* (EKKNT 22; Neukirchen-Vluyn: Neukirchener Verlag, 1994).

Bibliography to §12.2f: Studies

Rudolf Bultmann, "Bekenntnis- und Liedfragmente im ersten Petrusbrief," in idem, *Exegetica,* 285–97.
Ernst Käsemann, "An Apologia for Primitive Christian Eschatology," in idem, *Essays on New Testament Themes* (SBT 41; London: SCM, 1964) 169–95.
John H. Elliott, *A Home for the Homeless: A Sociological Exegesis of 1 Peter, Its Situation and Strategy* (Philadelphia: Fortress, 1981).
Birger Pearson, "The Apocalypse of Peter and Canonical 2 Peter," in Goehring, *Gnosticism,* 67–74.

Bibliography to §12.2f: Bibliography

Edouard Cothenet, "La Première de Pierre: bilan de 35 ans de recherches," *ANRW* 2.25.5 (1988) 3685–3712.
Richard J. Bauckham, "2 Peter: An Account of Research," *ANRW* 2.25.5 (1988) 3713–52.

Antioch. Models for pseudepigraphical letters under the name of one of these great apostles could be found in the Pauline corpus (see especially Ephesians). For the author of 1 Peter it was apparently no longer of special concern, whether such a pseudepigraphical letter would appear under the name of Peter or Paul. Peter was probably chosen as the author because the letter was written in Rome. Roman origin of 1 Peter is implied by the mention of "Babylon" (1 Pet 5:13), certainly a symbolic name for the capital of the empire (cf. Rev. 14:8; §12.1c). The First Letter of Peter therefore probably indicates that the Roman church now claimed Peter as its local martyr (Rome's claim to be the place of martyrdom also of Paul does not appear until the end of the 2d century); Rome's appropriation of Peter as its special apostolic authority was later fixed in the tradition that Peter was Rome's first bishop.

    1 Peter was apparently written for a specific situation. The address "to the sojourners of the diaspora of Pontus, Galatia, Cappadocia, Asia, and Bithynia" (1 Pet 1:1) is not necessarily a fiction, but indicates that the letter was sent to those churches as a circular letter in order to strengthen them in a situation of persecution. It is difficult, however, to say with any degree of certainty to which particular persecution the author refers. The Domitian persecution, which provided the date for *1 Clement,* was primarily a Roman affair. The Book of Revelation, written at that time, is not necessarily a witness for a general extension of that persecution to the provinces of Asia Minor, because its situation may have been closely connected with the building of the imperial temple in Ephesus. A more general persecution took place in Bithynia, one of the provinces mentioned in the address, caused by the measures that were taken by Pliny the Younger, when he was governor of that province in 111–113 CE (§12.3d). But whatever is said about persecution in 1 Peter does not necessarily refer to official actions of the Roman government but may simply address a mood of hostility of the population against their Christian neighbors. In any case, a more widespread hostility against Christians in a large geographical area is hardly possible much before the end of the 1st century, when the existence of larger Christian communities had become more visible in the public sphere. As Polycarp of Smyrna apparently knew 1 Peter, the letter cannot be dated later than the first two decades of the 2d century.

    Various hypotheses have been proposed with respect to the genre of 1 Peter. Because of the obvious allusions to baptism in 1:22–23 and 2:1ff. (note also "having been born anew to a living hope through the resurrection of Jesus Christ from the dead," 1:3) a baptismal liturgy as its life situation has been suggested. Some scholars have even tried to find in this writing an entire baptismal liturgy that was shaped secondarily into an epistle. Questions have also been raised with respect to an apparent ending of the letter in 4:11 and a new start in 4:12, especially since 4:12ff. seems to speak about suffering as a present reality, while the preceding chapter discussed suffering only as a possibility. Is 1 Pet 4:12–5:14 an appendix that was added, when the situation suddenly changed and the persecution intensified? Considerations of style, coherent diction, unity of the theological argument, and consistency in the treatment of traditional materials, however, argue against both the theory of an underlying baptismal liturgy and the appendix theory.

    The author of 1 Peter used diverse traditional materials, but incorporated them and made them serviceable to his primary topic in the same fashion throughout the entire letter. Such traditional materials are still recognizable in spite of the author's comments and additions. 1 Pet 1:20 and 3:18–19, 22 are drawn from established kerygmatic formulae that describe God's work of salvation; 2:21–25 quotes a hymn describing Christ's suffering that is not dependent upon the developed passion narrative, but shows how the Christian community employed Isaiah 53 in order to develop this narrative; 1 Pet 1:3–12 uses or imitates liturgical sentences for a fundamental description, imitating the examples set by Col 1:3–6 and Eph 1:3–14; 1 Pet 1:22–23 quotes an already fixed admonition for newly baptized Christians. In addition to these liturgical materials, the author uses parenetic traditions. 1 Pet 2:13–3:6 reproduces a table of household duties that contained not only the usual admonitions for slaves, women, and men, but was introduced by a request to be obedient to the governing authorities; 4:3–5 is based on a catalog of vices, 4:7–11 upon a catalog of virtues that was elaborated under the influence of passages from the Pauline letters. Eschatological admonitions like 1 Pet 1:13 (=Luke 12:35) show that the eschatological sections of the letter (1:13ff.; 4:12ff.; 5:6ff.) draw upon traditional eschatological parenesis. There are several instances in which sayings of Jesus are used, without being explicitly quoted (there is no evidence for the knowledge of the New Testament Gospels).

For the overall composition of the letter, the image of Israel controls the theology of 1 Peter. As the author draws on the Scriptures of Israel throughout, without explicitly quoting scriptural passages, it becomes clear that Israel is not a people of the past. Rather, "1 Peter has appropriated the language of Israel for the church in such a way that Israel in its totality has become for this letter the controlling metaphor in terms of which its theology is expressed" (Paul J. Achtemeier). The church is (the new) Israel. Whatever was promised is now present through the work of Christ so that Israel's Scriptures can speak directly about the church. It is a church, however, that should understand itself wholly as the eschatological people of God. 1 Peter thus renews the eschatological expectation of the parousia in the face of persecutions and therefore calls for joyfulness in suffering (1:6–7). The experience of suffering strengthens the confidence that the Christians are indeed the elect people of Israel and thus renews the hope in Christ's coming, though it also highlights the danger of apostasy (5:8–9). At the same time, the author enjoins regulations for Christian conduct that are not in themselves eschatological rules (compare the use of the household tables in Colossians and Ephesians), but now assume a new eschatological significance in order to assure that Christians are not caught suffering for wrongdoing but as righteous people (3:13–17; 4:14–16). 1 Peter is a call to the community to moral conduct according to the rules of the Roman society, so that Christian suffering in persecution can strengthen the communities' conviction that their suffering confirms their election as the Israel of the new ages.

(2) *The Second Epistle of Peter.* 1 Peter was still written from the perspective of a genuine eschatological expectation. This, however, is no longer the case with respect to the other New Testament letter under that name, the Second Epistle of Peter. This letter was also written to impress upon the mind of its readers the expectation of the parousia, but it does not proclaim that expectation as a hope and consolation for those who are persecuted; rather, it tries to defend it as theological dogma. 2 Peter is dependent upon 1 Peter and, in fact, refers to it explicitly (2 Pet

3:1). While most of the pseudepigraphical trappings are missing in 1 Peter, 2 Peter makes extensive use of them. The author introduces himself ceremoniously as "Symeon Petrus, servant and apostle of Jesus Christ," refers to the tradition that Jesus had predicted his martyrdom (1:14), emphasizes that he had been a witness of Jesus' transfiguration (1:16–18), and does not fail to observe that Paul is his beloved brother (3:15). The use of the Epistle of Jude (§12.1b) in chapter 2 could hardly be expected from Peter, the historical disciple of Jesus. Finally, the language of the writing is the elevated literary idiom of 2d-century Christianity, a thoroughly Hellenized literary language that uses such terms as "participants in divine nature" (1:4)—completely alien to early Christianity—and Greek proverbs, such as "the sow is washed only to wallow in its own mire" (2:22). Borrowings from Atticistic rhetoric distinguish 2 Peter from the Greek Koine of almost all other early Christian writings, including 1 Peter, a letter that is written in plain literary Greek.

The personal remembrances of "Peter" in 1:16–18 and the reference to the impending death of the assumed author (1:14) identify the genre of this letter as a testament, a genre borrowed from Jewish literature that became quite popular for Christian pseudepigraphical literature in the 2d century. The mention of Paul in this letter of "Peter" and the explicit reference to Paul's letters make it possible to classify 2 Peter with those early Christian writings that consider both Peter and Paul to be authorities of the church. But the situation is no longer the same as in Ignatius and *1 Clement,* because in 2 Pet 3:15–16 the author warns his readers about the difficulties in interpreting the Pauline letters and the distortions of Paul by the heretics, who were also perverting other writings. A very similar remark is found in a letter of bishop Dionysius of Corinth (quoted by Eusebius *Hist. eccl.* 4.23.12): "The apostles of the devil have filled my letters with tares by leaving out some things and putting in others.   Therefore it is no wonder that some have gone about falsifying even the Scripture of the Lord." Both statements presuppose that Christian writings that had achieved considerable authority were being edited and interpreted. The way that 2 Pet 3:2 puts side by side "the words said before by the holy prophets" and "the commandment of the Lord and Savior given through your apostles" suggests that not only the former but also the latter were accessible in writings of some authority. From such documents, namely, from written gospels, the author drew his information about Peter as an eyewitness of Jesus' transfiguration (1:16–18) and the prediction of Peter's martyrdom.

There can be little doubt concerning the identity of the people who are accused of twisting the Scriptures. Even Jude was arguing against Gnostic opponents. In his use of the Epistle of Jude, the author of 2 Peter reformulates the polemic against Gnosticism in order to aim it more directly against Gnostic interpretations of Genesis (see 2 Pet 2:4–10, the remarks about Gen 1:1–4, Noah as the preacher of righteousness, Sodom and Gomorra, and Lot the righteous), but avoids every passage in Jude that refers to apocryphal literature. With the term "cleverly disguised myths" (2 Pet 1:16) he attacks the Gnostics, to whom he further assigns the skeptical opinion regarding the expectation of the parousia ("Where is the promise of his coming? For ever since our ancestors died, all things continue as they were from the beginning of creation," 3:4) that had already been quoted in *1 Clem.* 23.2–4 (cf. *2 Clem.* 11.2) and was probably derived from an unknown (Christian?) book.

The new doctrine of the parousia of Christ that the author establishes against the Gnostics is anything but a renewal of the early Christian expectation. 2 Pet 3:5–13 presents an eschatological doctrine concerning the end of the visible world that demands recognition as a general truth also in the pagan world. The concept of the conflagration of the cosmos (3:12) is designed to make the Christian eschatological theories acceptable even to a Stoic philosopher. A relationship to earlier eschatological expectations is only superficially claimed by quotations from 1 Thess 5:2 and Rev 21:1 (2 Pet 3:10, 13). The Gnostic interpretation of Paul finally created a situation in which the alliance of the two authorities Peter and Paul had become questionable. While the letters of Paul were still quoted and used without hesitation around the year 100, a generation later the author of 2 Peter belonged to those orthodox Christians who named Paul as an authority of the church, but secretly wished that the great apostle had not written any letters—at least not such letters as those that were causing so many interpretive problems in the effort to defend true faith against heresy. All this, together with the use of written gospels, argues for a date of the writing of 2 Peter well after the beginning of the 2d century.

(g) Church Order in the Name of Paul: The Pastoral Epistles

The letters to the Colossians, Ephesians, and Hebrews, as well as Ignatius of Antioch, had been theologically engaged with Paul and with the continuation of theological reflection in Paul's name. But for *1 Clement,* Paul was little more than a teacher and counselor of the right conduct that would maintain the unity of the church. *1 Clement* thus pointed the way toward an "ecclesiastical" function of the heritage of the great apostle and martyr Paul. The type of Pauline letters that the au-

---

Bibliography to §12.2g: Commentaries

Martin Dibelius and Hans Conzelmann, *The Pastoral Epistles: A Commentary on the Pastoral Epistles* (Hermeneia; Philadelphia: Fortress, 1972).

Jürgen Roloff, *Der erste Brief an Timotheus* (EKKNT 15; Neukirchen-Vluyn: Neukirchener Verlag, 1988).

Bibliography to §12.2g: Studies

Hans von Campenhausen, "The Christian and Social Life According to the New Testament," in idem, *Tradition and Life,* 141–59.

Idem, "Polycarp von Smyrna und die Pastoralbriefe," in idem, *Frühzeit,* 197–252.

Martin Dibelius, "Ἐπίγνωσις ἀληθείας," in idem, *Botschaft und Geschichte,* 2. 1–13.

Robert J. Karris, "The Background and Significance of the Polemic of the Pastoral Epistles," *JBL* 92 (1973) 549–64.

Dennis MacDonald, *The Legend and the Apostle: The Battle for Paul in Story and Canon* (Philadelphia: Westminster, 1983).

Michael Wolter, *Die Pastoralbriefe als Paulustradition* (FRLANT 146; Göttingen: Vandenhoeck & Ruprecht, 1988).

Bibliography to §12.2g: History of Scholarship

Wolfgang Schenk, "Die Pastoralbriefe in der neueren Forschung," *ANRW* 2.25.4 (1987) 3404–38.

Bibliography to §12.2g: Text of *3 Corinthians*

Michel Testuz, *Papyrus Bodmer X–XII* (Cologne-Genève: Bibliotheca Bodmeriana, 1959).

Schneemelcher, *NT Apoc.,* 2. 254–56.

thor of 2 Peter would have appreciated were indeed being written during the first half of the 2d century, namely, "Paul's" letters to Timothy and Titus, usually called the Pastoral Epistles. These three letters, which are a unity in their language, theological concepts, and intention, and which were composed by the same author, differ remarkably from all other letters of the Pauline corpus. With the exception of Philemon, they are the only letters addressed to individuals. While Paul's letter to Philemon concerns a private affair, the manumission of Onesimus, Timothy and Titus are not addressed as private persons but as church leaders, entrusted with the organization and supervision of the life of Christian communities. They are official documents in behalf of the ordering of the churches, properly introduced by such presentations of the sender as "Paul, an apostle by the command of God our Savior and of Christ Jesus our hope" (1 Tim 1:1).

The external evidence for the Pastoral Epistles is not as good as that for the other letters of Paul. They were not included in the canon of Marcion (§12.3c), and it appears that Marcion did not know them at all. They are also missing in the oldest manuscript of the Pauline Epistles ($\mathfrak{P}^{46}$). But Irenaeus and Tertullian knew them as Pauline letters and they are also mentioned in the Muratorian Canon. Doubts about their authenticity were raised as early as the beginning of the 19th century; more recent scholarship has accumulated such an overwhelming number of conclusive arguments against the authenticity of the Pastoral Epistles that Pauline authorship can only be maintained on the basis of tortuous hypotheses and an amassing of historical improbabilities. I will mention only the most important arguments.

The language of the Pastoral Epistles shows many more striking departures from Pauline usage than the other pseudepigraphical letters of the Pauline corpus. Moreover, all these linguistic peculiarities, which lack analogies and parallels from the time of Paul, are part of the Christian language of the 2d century. Particularly striking is the terminology for the description of the event of salvation. The coming of Christ is described as "the epiphany of the Savior" (*soter:* Tit 2:13; cf. 2 Tim 1:10; Tit 3:4, 6, where this terminology is used for Jesus' appearance on earth). Paul himself uses the term "Savior" only once, and in this case for the future appearance of Christ (Phil 3:20). But there are numerous parallels for the description of the appearance of a divine being on earth with these terms in Hellenistic religious usage and in the cult of the emperor. The title "Savior God" (Tit 2:10) would be unique in the entire theological language of 1st-century Christianity. "The appearance of the goodness and loving-kindness (*philanthropia*) of our Savior, God" (Tit 3:4) is again paralleled by formulations from the emperor cult. True Christian conduct is called "religion" (*eusebeia*) throughout these epistles (1 Tim 2:2; 4:7; etc.); the Christian message is designated as "healthy doctrine" (1 Tim 1:10; 2 Tim 4:3; etc.), while the term "faith" is mostly used for the Christian credal formula (1 Tim 3:9; 6:10; etc.). All this is not only inconceivable for Paul, it is at the same time typical for the pagan religious language of the Roman imperial period, which was increasingly adopted by Christian writers during the 2d century. Occasionally the Pastoral Epistles attempt to resume Pauline phrases, but especially in these instances it is most evident that the writer was not Paul himself. A characteristic phrase of this type is Tit 3:5: "saved . . . not by deeds done by us in righteousness, but by virtue of his mercy" (see also 2 Tim 1:9). Even the author's attempt to let Paul speak about his own conversion reveals deutero-Pauline concepts; 1 Tim 1:13 says: "I formerly blasphemed and insulted him; but I received mercy because I had acted ignorantly in unbelief." "Ignorance" is the state typically assigned to the pagan convert, while Paul himself speaks proudly about the fact that, although his persecution of the church was an outrage, his righteousness under the law was perfect (Phil 3:4–6; cf. Gal 1:14).

The Pastoral Epistles cannot be placed in any situation of the ministry of Paul as it is known from his genuine letters or even as it is portrayed in the Book of Acts. At the end of Acts, Paul is under house arrest in Rome, but that Paul was martyred in Rome is not told. The only location of Paul explicitly mentioned in the Pastoral Epistles appears in Tit 3:12, where Paul says that he intends to spend the winter in Nicopolis (a major city on the west coast of Greece). The personal instructions in 2 Tim 4:9–21, which strongly seem to suggest the authenticity of the letters, point to a different place. Paul is here seen as imprisoned, expecting a final judgment and facing possible execution. In that situation he writes to Timothy, who is in Ephesus, to come to him and bring the cloak, the books, and the parchments that Paul has left in Troas (2 Tim 4:13); Demas had gone to Thessalonica, Crescens to Galatia, Titus to Dalmatia (4:10); Paul has sent Tychicus to Ephesus. In the greetings, Paul says that Erastus remained in Corinth and that he left Trophimus ill in Miletus (4:20). Although some later manuscript colophons say that Paul wrote this letter from Rome, there can be no question where the author of 2 Timothy locates Paul at this point of his ministry, shortly before his death. Any glance at a map will show that he thought of Paul as imprisoned in Philippi. Although these instructions and greetings belong to the pseudepigraphical armory of the author, they may well rest on a tradition that Paul was martyred in Philippi. Archaeological evidence has demonstrated that the Philippian church indeed later claimed to be the guardian of Paul's tomb. Ancient tradition also has it that Timothy was the first bishop of Ephesus and was martyred there. In order to construct a situation, the author of the Pastoral Epistles must have drawn on local traditions about the death of Paul and of his associates. Whether these traditions are trustworthy pieces of historical information is a another question.

Since the Pastoral Epistles were certainly not written by Paul himself, the question of their date in the history of early Christianity is still to be considered. That the authority of Paul's letters became problematic after the turn of the 1st century was already evident in 2 Peter. This problem became even more acute after Marcion had used an edited version of the Pauline corpus in his attempt to establish a canon of Christian Scriptures that would replace the Scriptures of Israel (§12.3c). How could Paul's letters still be claimed as a resource of apostolic authority for the Catholic churches? If one wanted to employ Paul, speaking on his own behalf in a pseudepigraphical letter as a defender of true teaching against Gnosticism, several alternatives were available. One of these alternatives was chosen by the author of *3 Corinthians,* which is a composite letter from the Corinthians and Paul's answer. They are now preserved as part of the *Acts of Paul.* It is most probable that these letters were not invented by the author of the *Acts of Paul,* but are a document written earlier in the 2d century and later incorporated into the *Acts of Paul. 3 Corinthians* begins as a letter sent by the Corinthian presbyters to Paul and enumerates the heretical teachings of the Gnostics: one should not make recourse to the prophets; the world and the human race were not created by God; Jesus was not born by the virgin and did not appear in the flesh; and there was no resurrection of the flesh. Paul, also here imprisoned in Philippi (!), responds with a letter in which he repeats and confirms the ecclesiastical confession of the creation of the world by God, the birth of Jesus from the seed of David through Mary, salvation through the body of Christ, resurrection of the flesh, and eternal punishment for all godless people. In composing this letter, the author used sentences from the Pauline epistles and from Scripture affirming the resurrection of the flesh. This letter, written at about the same time as the Pastoral Epistles—though the author apparently does not know them but also locates Paul in a Philippian prison—solves the problem of the Gnostic interpretation of Paul by quoting sentences from the genuine letters in defense of the catholic understanding of the theology of the great apostle.

The Pastoral Epistles choose a different alternative. The author resumes the tradition of Paul the martyr (§12.2e), but in doing so does not simply continue the tradition of the "letters from prison," a category to which *3 Corinthians* belongs. Rather, the author utilizes the prison situation to present the "Testament of Paul." By choosing this literary genre that had been developed in Judaism (§5.3c) and also determined the genre of 2 Peter, a prior decision was made that gives this type of defense of Paul its special character. Whoever speaks in his own testament no longer needs to be defended, because he is already one of the "ancient" people— in this case a revered martyr—whose authority is beyond question. The testament permits a recapitulation of the past, interpreted and summarized from the perspective of the present, and it thus becomes a signpost for the future. It also includes advice for the conduct in the present as a natural part of the genre, and it does not force the author to define and attack opponents systematically, but allows general warnings with respect to real but still unspecified present and future opponents. It is also typical that the testament is not addressed to people or congregations in general but to individuals.

The author of the Pastoral Epistles is a master in the utilization of the genre of the testament for the defense of the Pauline heritage. The Second Epistle to Timothy is the core of the testament. It is here that Paul looks back (2 Tim 1:3–18) to the past of the addressee (thus the mention of Timothy's grandmother and mother by name), which leads to the situation of the author, who is now imprisoned, forsaken by all. But Paul knows that his "heritage" (*paratheke*, the term appears only here in the New Testament) will be preserved. With the words, "But you, my child," 2 Tim 2:1 introduces the admonition of the testament. This address is typical for testament style. The admonition begins with a basic exhortation (2:1–13), which quotes traditional formulas of Christian faith twice (2:11 and 2:11–13); and admonitions for behavior toward heretics follow (2:14–21), then a personal admonition about correct conduct. Completely in accord with the genre of the testament, the next section provides a warning about the "last days" (3:1–17) that announces the coming of the false teachers (3:2–9), calls for steadfastness in persecutions (3:10–12), and refers to the Holy Scriptures as a source of strength (3:14–16). The warnings are concluded by an oath (4:1ff.) and a repeated reference to Paul's situation as a martyr facing death (4:6–8). The last section of the letter presents an apostle Paul who is occupied by the care for his churches into his very last days (4:9ff.). Forsaken by all, there is nothing left for him but to pass his legacy on to Timothy "through this testament." In contrast to Tit 3:12 (see also 1 Tim 3:14–15; 4:13) Paul makes no statements about his future plans; he only expresses his confidence "that the Lord will rescue me from every evil and save me for his heavenly kingdom" (2 Tim 4:18). In the original order of the three letters, 2 Timothy was probably designed to stand at the end (the canonical order placed the longest letter first and the shortest last).

The other two letters are closely and intricately connected with 2 Timothy and are by all means meant to be an integral part of Paul's testament. They explicate in more detail as Paul's legacy his statements regarding the ordering of the church and of Christian conduct and regarding procedures for the fight against heretics. 2 Timothy spoke about the heretics and about conduct only to the extant that was called for by the eschatological admonitions and parenesis appropriate for the testament genre. 1 Timothy makes room for detailed instruction by adopting a different genre, namely, that of a church order. The schema for the arrangements of the various topics stems from the traditional table of household duties, which has been modified and expanded to become a more appropriate table of ecclesiastical duties. The introductory chapter (1 Tim 1:3–20) leaves no doubt that the primary concern is the fight against false teachers, but these verses also make clear that the author is quite unwilling to get involved in a theological dispute with these people; rather, conduct according to faith and a good conscience will protect the church from such threats (see especially 1 Tim 1:18–19). The household/ecclesiastical duties begin with statements about the behavior over against political authorities, but is then expanded by a discussion of prayer (2:1–15), first the prayer of men, then the conduct of women in the worship service of the church (2:8–15). This leads more naturally into the subsequent instructions for officers of the church: bishops (3:1–7) and deacons (3:8–13). After a digression (3:14–4:10), the underlying table of duties is resumed with the discussion of "old people" and "young people" (5:1–2), returns to church officers with instruction for widows (5:3–16) and presbyters (5:17–20), then picks up the table of household duties once more with advice for slaves (6:1–2) and rich people (6:6–10, 17–19, apparently a modification of the traditional topic "masters"). The author has interrupted the underlying schema at certain points, in part with personal information (3:14–15), and in part with references to false teachers (4:1–5) and personal instructions for "Timothy," which are actually general instructions valid for all officers of the church (4:6–16; 6:3–5, 11–16).

The structure of the letter to Titus is similar. An instruction for presbyters (Tit 1:5–9) is followed by admonitions for old men, young women, young men, and slaves (2:1–10), and finally a remark about obedience to the government (3:1–2). Interruptions once more offer exhortations about false teachers (1:10–16; 3:9–11), personal information (3:12–14), and an admonition to "Titus" (2:15). In all three letters the author has inserted kerygmatic and hymnic traditions (e.g., 1 Tim 3:16; Tit 2:11; 3:4–5).

For the details of the instructions and admonitions, the Pastoral Epistles use catalogs of virtues and vices that are at times expanded by explanations and comments. It is remarkable that the same virtues are expected of the various church officers, bishops, deacons, presbyters, and widows, but appear at the same time as general criteria for the conduct of all Christians. Indeed, such virtues would have been completely acceptable for Christians, Jews, and pagans alike. Christian behavior that is requested here is fully identical with the general social and moral duties and virtues that were expected of any upright citizen at that time, and they actually appear in pagan lists of requirements for such professions as the general or the actor. In a summary formulation, they are stated thus: "Renounce impiety and base desires, and live prudent, upright, and religious lives in the world" (Tit 2:12). For the details of such morality, the author mentions faithfulness in marriage, care for one's children and homes, hospitality, avoidance of quarrelsome behavior, care for the weak and those in need, and satisfaction with one's worldly status and possessions. Because of this, the morality of the Pastoral Epistles has been correctly characterized as the ideal of good citizenship. A specifically eschatological motivation for Christian ethical behavior is completely missing. One finds instead only very general references to the Christian hope in the appearance of Christ in the future (Tit 2:13). Even when 1 Tim 6:7 says, "we brought nothing into this world, and we cannot take anything out of this world," the author is simply stating what pagan citizens of this time would have accepted, as they would also agree with the statement that "the love of money is the root of all evil" (1 Tim 6:10).

The Pastoral Epistles mark the end of Christian eschatological ethics and thus prepare the way for Christian apologetics (§12.3e). Christianity no longer looked upon itself as the community of the new ages that promised to break down social barriers, as those between men and women, free and slaves, at least as far as its own interior organization and order was concerned. Rather, the church had become obligated to the world and society at large and had to fulfill the general social norms and moral demands in an exemplary fashion. If Christians are still admonished to distinguish themselves in their moral actions from the rest of the society, such distinction would now be achieved through a more dignified and faithful observance of the generally accepted rules for good behavior. For a group of letters found in the Pauline corpus, this is a surprising turn. Paul himself had founded his ethics upon an eschatological perspective. He was even willing to accept radical consequences for conduct as legitimate (see, e.g., 1 Cor 7:25–35). On the other hand, he had refused to make such behavior the norm for his churches' morality, criticized excesses (see the criticism of the "strong people" in Corinth), and had explicitly emphasized the legitimacy of rational moral decisions after prudent consideration of the alternatives (see 1 Cor 7:2–7; 7:36–38; Phil 4:8–9). Was either the radicalization of eschatological ethics in the form of an ascetic denial of the world, or the prudent acceptance of the best moral standards of the secular society the true continuation of Pauline ethics? The false teachers attacked in the Pastoral Epistles had chosen the former alternative, while the author of the Pastoral Epistles chose the latter. A price had to be paid either way. Instead of the Gnostic alternative that expected the coming of the kingdom when women stopped bearing children, the Pastoral Epistles proclaims that women will be saved by bearing children.

The identity of the heretics attacked in the Pastoral Epistles has been a difficult problem for the modern interpreter. The genre of the testament does not require the author to enter into a theological controversy with false teaching. As ethics and moral conduct are the criteria for the distinction between true and false beliefs, a precise description of the teaching of the heretics is superfluous anyway. That does not mean, however, that the dangers from the false teachers were simply imagined or that the casual characterization of their teaching was freely invented. Whether a coherent picture of their teachings will emerge is a problem. The opponents want to be teachers of the law (1 Tim 1:7); they come from the "circumcision" (Tit 1:10) and preach "Jewish myths and human commands" (Tit 1:14). That they demand abstention from certain foods points to ascetic practices (1 Tim 4:3), especially since here and in Tit 1:14–15 the author emphasizes the purity of all things that God has created (see also the advice to drink some wine for the sake of the stomach, 1 Tim 5:23—red wine, I presume). Coupled with the dietary question in 1 Tim 4:3 is the prohibition of marriage, and in the same chapter the author rejects the "godless old wives' tales" (*mythoi,* 1 Tim 4:7). The reference to "myths and genealogies" (1 Tim 1:4; cf. "genealogies" in Tit 3:9) has a similar ring. All this could very well fit Gnostic teachers. This is confirmed by the explicit rejection of "the profane chatter and contradictions (*antitheses*) of what is falsely called knowledge" (*gnosis,* 1 Tim 6:20) and the quotation of the typical Gnostic claim that "the resurrection has already happened" (2 Tim 2:18). The reference to the *"antitheses* of the falsely called *gnosis"* could be understood as a specific rejection of Marcion, whose main work had the title "Antitheses" (§12.3c). But it is impossible to harmonize 1 Timothy's references to the opponents' teaching of the law with Marcion's radical rejection of the Jewish Scripture.

While such references are specific enough, other accusations do not help much. That all the false teachers want is money (1 Tim 6:5, 10; Tit 1:11) belongs to the standard arsenal of attacks against political, philosophical, and religious opponents. The statement that the opponents were especially eager to convert and recruit women (2 Tim 3:6–7) might fit known tendencies toward emancipation in Gnostic sects, but could also be an expression of the author's acceptance of the rules of decent behavior for women in Greco-Roman society, from which he derives the prohibition of public teaching by women (1 Tim 2:12)—a rule that was later interpolated into a genuine letter of Paul (1 Cor 14:33b–36). The ruling against a public ecclesiastical role of women by the author of the Pastoral Epistles does not mean, however, that this was the generally accepted practice in all churches from this time onward; there is evidence to the contrary well into the 3d and 4th centuries. Nevertheless, it had dire consequences for the future, because ever since Paul has been quoted as authority for such a ruling.

In view of the fact that the primary intention of the author is to strengthen the conduct of the churches according to the ideal of good citizenship, and considering that all his polemical remarks are fragmentary, the attempts to construct a coherent picture of the heretics that are mentioned in these letters are fundamentally and methodologically wrong. The author of the Pastoral Epistles did not intend to provide such a description but wanted to point to typical phenomena of heresy in general. This is especially clear in the predictions of the future that "Paul" gives in 2 Tim 3:1ff., but also in 1 Tim 4:1ff. The church leader must be equipped with the ability to identify heresies of whatever kind, for which the author has crystallized a variety of criteria from the tradition and from his own experiences. These criteria rarely describe the contents of heretical teaching but consist of formal categories: disputations, contradictions, and controversies, and the refusal to submit to the demands of a healthy Christian morality. The Pastoral Epistles are designed as a handbook, a manual for the church leader, enabling him to identify dangerous teachings and to reject them without having to enter into costly discussions of subtle theological arguments.

Adherence to the Pauline legacy has thus been removed from the uncertain realm of the interpretation of the letters of Paul. In theological terms, the "faith" has been cast into new formulations that are more appropriate to the religious language of the time and of society at large. The primary accomplishment of Paul is seen in the organization of his congregations—which was indeed a task to which he had once devoted considerable time and effort, and which had occupied a central place in his missionary activities. These congregations were, however, no longer experiments in the creation of the community of the new ages in view of Christ's return in the near future; they are, or should become, stable organizations with a firm place in society and well-established offices: one bishop or presiding presbyter (who should receive twice the salary of other officers, 1 Tim 4:17), under him presbyters, deacons, and widows; the latter are to be supported by the congregations, but should be thoroughly scrutinized so that they would not constitute an unnecessary financial burden for the community (1 Tim 5:3–16). The process of ordination should be orderly by the laying on of hands (1 Tim 5:22; cf. 4:14), so that the charisma of the office could be passed on in the proper way (2 Tim 1:6). The Pauline concept that gives all members of the church a share in the gifts of the spirit, thus qualifying everyone for one of the various offices of the congregation, has given way to the selection of specially prepared members for office. But moral qualifications are primary, and the members of the congregations are not reminded of their charismata, but of their duties as good citizens. The eschatological community has thus become a religion that can claim its legitimate place in society.

The time and place of the writing of the Pastoral Epistles should no longer be a question of debate. The geographical information points to the countries of the Aegean Sea. Places named explicitly include Ephesus, Troas, and Miletus in Asia Minor, Thessalonica in Macedonia, Corinth, Nicopolis, and Crete in Greece. The westernmost area is Dalmatia, in the east it is Galatia. Local traditions of Ephesus (Timothy as its first bishop) and Philippi (the place of Paul's martyrdom) are probably used. For the date of the Pastorals one must consider the following factors: a time of relative security from persecution, strong growth of Christianity among the artisans and tradespeople of the cities, organization of many congregations from Dalmatia to Galatia under the same church order, and a language that belongs to the 2d century and is not hesitant to borrow freely from the terminology of the imperial cult. The times of the emperors Hadrian and Antoninus Pius provided a relatively long period of freedom from persecution. Thus the years 120–160 would be most appropriate. The author was, no doubt, an influential and far-seeing leader of the church, who pointed the way toward a consolidation of Christianity as a well-organized religion acceptable to the culture of its time. He wanted to strengthen the defenses of this church against false teachers, whose propaganda sought to turn Christianity away from this world and from the prosaic and conservative morality of the society. From the first half of the 2d century, only one such church leader is known by name: bishop Polycarp of Smyrna. The hypothesis that Polycarp was in fact the author of these letters was proposed by Hans von Campenhausen and supported by a number of convincing arguments; but few scholars have been willing to accept this suggestion.

(h) Polycarp of Smyrna

Polycarp was bishop of Smyrna as early as the time of Ignatius of Antioch, and he suffered martyrdom after the middle of the 2d century. *The Martyrdom of Polycarp* (§12.3f) provides as the date of his martyrdom the year 154 or 155. The more reliable date, however, comes from Eusebius of Caesarea (*Hist. eccl.* 4.15.1), who gives the seventh year of Marcus Aurelius. At that time Polycarp was 86 years old. He was thus born ca. 80 CE). Since he was bishop of Smyrna at the time of Ignatius (110–117), the time of his office as bishop spans at least half a century. Polycarp was a towering figure and influential church leader for a long time. At a rather advanced age, he traveled to Rome (after 150 CE) to settle the dispute about the right date for Easter (the so-called Quartodeciman controversy) with the Roman bishop Anicetus. Though no agreement was reached, Anicetus is reported to have permitted Polycarp to celebrate the Eucharist in his church.

A document that survives as his *Letter to the Philippians* is not well preserved. All known Greek manuscripts derive from a Greek archetype in which the text of chapters 10–14 was missing. The Greek text of chapter 13 is quoted, almost completely, by Eusebius (*Hist. eccl.* 3.36.14–15), but only a rather poor Latin translation is available for chapters 10–12 and 14. It is quite likely that the letter as we have it was actually composed from two different writings to the church of Philippi. The first, consisting of chapters 13–14, was a cover letter for the sending of copies of the Ignatian letters to the Philippians upon their request. Here Polycarp refers to Ignatius as being still alive. In *Phil.* 9.1, however, Polycarp refers to Ignatius and two of his associates as blessed martyrs of the past, whose examples must be recalled. Thus the letter to which this remark belongs must have been written much later; *Phil.* 1–12 is therefore a different letter, which belongs to a

Bibliography to §12.2h: Text

Bihlmeyer, *ApostVät,* xxviii–xliv, 114–20.

Fischer, *Die apostolischen Väter,* 227–65.

Lake, *ApostFath,* 1. 279–301.

Bibliography to §12.2h: Commentaries

Lightfoot, *Apostolic Fathers,* vol. 2, part 2. 897–998.

William Schoedel, *Polycarp, Martyrdom of Polycarp, Fragments of Papias* (Grant, *ApostFath* 5).

Henning Paulsen, *Die Briefe des Ignatius von Antiochia und der Brief des Polykarp von Smyrna* (HNT 18; Tübingen: Mohr/Siebeck, 1985).

Bibliography to §12.2h: Studies

P. N. Harrison, *Polycarp's Two Epistles to the Philippians* (Cambridge: Cambridge University Press, 1936).

Hans von Campenhausen, "Polycarp von Smyrna und die Pastoralbriefe," in idem, *Frühzeit,* 197–252.

later time. This is confirmed by the use of other Christian writings in this letter. It not only knows and uses *1 Clement,* but also corrects the quotation of sayings of Jesus in *1 Clem.* 13.2 according to the text of the Gospels of Matthew and Luke (*Phil.* 2.3); a knowledge of the text of these two gospels is also evident in *Phil.* 7.2 and argues for a date of this letter some decades after the time of Ignatius, when the use of these gospels had been well established in Asia Minor, that is, after the year 130. Interestingly, there is no trace yet of a knowledge of the Gospel of John. The immediate occasion for the writing of this second letter was a case of embezzlement by the presbyter Valens in Philippi, which Polycarp discusses in chapter 11. That the Philippians appealed to Polycarp and sought his advice in this matter also argues for a date by which Polycarp had become famous and was well established (at the time of Ignatius, he was still a freshman bishop).

The language and theology of Polycarp's letter very closely resemble that of the Pastoral Epistles. Admonitions in the style of an ecclesiastical order that was developed on the basis of the older tables of household duties correspond closely to those of the Pastoral Epistles (cf. *Philippians* 4–6: women, widows, deacons, young people, presbyters). This is also the case with respect to catalogs of virtues and vices (*Phil.* 2.2; 4.3; 5.2; 12.2). Among the exhortations to prayer at the end of the letter, an admonition to pray for the government (*Phil.* 12.3) recalls 1 Tim 2.1–2. The warning against avarice is given in the same words as in the Pastorals (*Phil.* 4.1 = 1 Tim 6:10). Passages, however, that look like quotations from the Pastoral Epistles are rare in Polycarp's writing. In most instances, he makes the same statement in independent formulations, though using the same terminology. In addition, sentences and phrases from other letters of Paul occur frequently; and Polycarp also knew 1 Peter, although he never refers to Peter by name. The authority to which he appeals several times is the apostle Paul (*Phil.* 3.2; 9.2; 11.3). Indeed, for Polycarp there is no other apostolic authority but Paul, and the letter demonstrates how a bishop could conduct his office of directing and ordering the affairs of Christian churches in the spirit of Paul; yet it is the spirit of Paul as it had been recast by the Pastoral Epistles.

Polycarp is also concerned with the fight against false teachers; although, like the Pastoral Epistles, he does not enter into a discussion of their arguments. References to Jewish-Christian heretics are absent in his letter. The criteria established for the recognition of false teachers appear only in sentences directed against Gnostic teachers: "For everyone who does not confess that Jesus Christ has come in the flesh is an anti-Christ; and whoever does not confess the testimony of the cross is of the devil; and whoever perverts the sayings of the Lord to benefit his own desires and says there is neither resurrection nor judgment, that one is the first-born of Satan" (*Phil.* 7.1). Irenaeus, himself from Asia Minor and acquainted, as he claims, with the great bishop while still a child, tells an anecdote about the encounter of Polycarp with Marcion (on Marcion, see §12.3c): Marcion had said to Polycarp, "Recognize me!" whereupon Polycarp had answered, "I recognize you as the first-born of Satan" (Irenaeus *Adv. haer.* 3.3.4). Inasmuch as Irenaeus knew Polycarp's letter to the Philippians, it is quite doubtful whether this anecdote, as well as others that Irenaeus tells about him, can be used as historical evidence. But the possibility should be considered that when this letter (as well as the Pastoral

Epistles) was written, Polycarp knew Marcion and included him in the polemic against false teachers. Marcion's first appearance must be dated in the middle of Polycarp's tenure as bishop of Smyrna, and Marcion came from Pontus, from where he traveled to Rome ca. 130 CE. It is not impossible that Polycarp in this second letter to the Philippians (including *Phil.* 7.1) referred to Marcion with the remark about perverting the sayings of the Lord, since the Gospel of Luke, which Polycarp had come to know at that time, was published by Marcion in a thoroughly revised edition. As with the Pastoral Epistles, it could not be expected that all of Polycarp's remarks regarding the heretics should refer to the same heretical group. Thus, even if the Pastoral Epistles refer with statements about heretics to all sorts of false teachers, the warning of 1 Tim 6:20 against the "antithesis of the false gnosis" could still owe its formulation to the title of Marcion's primary work—especially if Polycarp was the author of that letter, about which the judgment must be left to the judicious reader of these ancient Christian writings.

3. CHRISTIANITY IN ITS ENCOUNTER WITH ITS SOCIAL WORLD

(a) Gospel and History as Victory in the World

Nearly all the early Christian writings mentioned thus far were written for use within the Christian community. Apologetic motifs occur occasionally, such as in the passion narrative of the Gospel of John. But Christianity could not address the Roman world until it had become more positive about that world and had decided that it had indeed a place in it and in the society of the imperial period—at least for the time being. Such a development presupposed an order for the church and for the life of its members that agreed with the generally recognized values of good-citizens' morality, a general diminution of the eschatological expectation of Christ's coming in the near future, and an unequivocal rejection of Gnosticism with its denial of the world and its order. All these requirements are displayed in the Pastoral Epistles in an exemplary fashion, though still in writings exclusively designed for internal Christian use. The first Christian piece of literature written from the perspective of apologetics that consciously appealed to pagan readership was the work of Luke. Although it was composed earlier than the Pastoral Epistles and some other writings discussed so far, Luke's work properly signals the beginning of attempts to present the essence of Christian faith to the outsider.

(1) *The Lukan Writings.* In the canon of the New Testament there are now two writings by Luke, one called the "Gospel of Luke," the third of the four canonical gospels, and the other, known as the "Acts of the Apostles." Both designations are secondary and were added only after the work of Luke was divided into two parts. Originally, however, Luke wrote only *one* single work, of which the title is lost, which spans the entire story from the announcement of the birth of John the Baptist in Jerusalem to the arrival and preaching of the apostle Paul in Rome. The prologue of Luke 1:1–4 is designed for the whole work, and it is briefly resumed in Acts 1:1–2, when the work was divided into two books. This division may have been necessary as a matter of convenience, because each of the two parts of this long

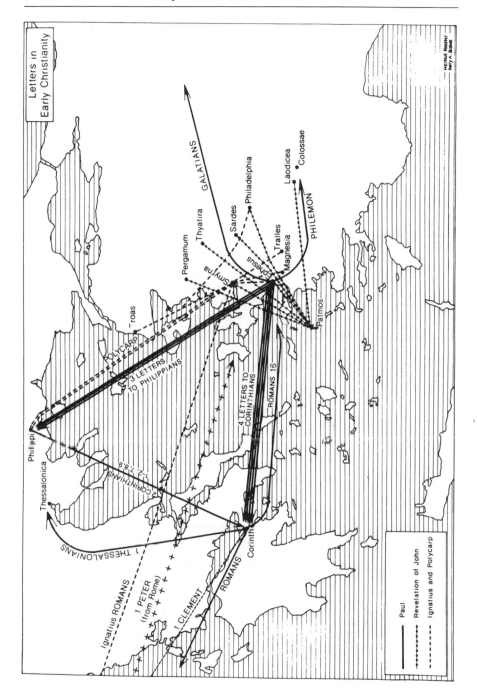

work—it constitutes about 27% of the entire New Testament—corresponds approximately to the largest possible size of a standard scroll. The two parts differ also insofar as Luke was able to use the Gospel of Mark as his main source for the first part, while in the second half of his work he was confronted with a much more complex and different situation regarding information and sources. Both parts, however, reveal one and the same language and style of literary composition.

In order to understand the purpose of Luke's work, the genre and intention must be determined for the entire work. It is difficult, however, to part with the familiar definition of the first part as "gospel" and the equally familiar, though much more questionable, view of the second part as the "history" of the earliest period of Christianity. Even the designation "gospel" for the first part is problematic, because in Luke's time this term was by no means known as the designation of a literary genre. "Biography" would be more appropriate, and Luke was certainly familiar with biographies and the requirements for composing books of this genre (§3.4d). Yet, the Gospel of Luke does not fulfill these requirements; although some biographical features are naturally present, there is little interest in the description of the development of character, or of the way in which the conduct of life shaped the political will of the individual. Again, as miracle stories are told throughout the gospel, one would rather have to speak instead of an "aretalogy." As far as the second part of Luke's work is concerned, the definition of the genre as "history" has been much debated in scholarship. Some features of the Acts of the Apostles superficially resemble what in antiquity was considered the writing of history as, for example, the insertion of speeches by one of the main actors at important junctures of the story. Other characteristics, such as the uncritical telling of miraculous stories and divine interventions, would not be permissible according to the standards of ancient historiography (§3.4c). The suggestion has therefore been made to consider the Book of Acts as a romance (§3.4e), in which delightful stories of wonders, marvels, and especially a story of a shipwreck are very appropriate. Thus we would be left with

Bibliography to §12.3a (1):   Studies

Henry Cadbury, *The Making of Luke-Acts* (2d ed.; London: SPCK, 1958).

Hans Conzelmann, *The Theology of St. Luke* (Philadelphia: Fortress, 1982).

Robert Maddox, *The Purpose of Luke-Acts* (FRLANT 126; Göttingen: Vandenhoeck & Ruprecht, 1982).

François Bovon, *Lukas in neuer Sicht: Gesammelte Aufsätze* (Biblisch-theologische Studien 8; Neukirchen–Vluyn: Neukirchener Verlag, 1985).

Idem, *L'oeuvre de Luc: Études d'exégèse et de théologie* (Lectio Divina 130; Paris: Cerf, 1987).

David L. Tiede, *Prophecy and History in Luke-Acts* (Philadelphia: Fortress, 1980).

Robert C. Tannehill, *The Narrative Unity of Luke-Acts: A Literary Interpretation* (2 vols.; Philadelphia/ Minneapolis: Fortress, 1986–1990).

Mikeal C. Parsons and Richard I. Pervo, *Rethinking the Unity of Luke and Acts* (Minneapolis: Fortress, 1993).

Marianne P. Bonz, *The Past as Legacy: Luke-Acts as Ancient Epic* (Minneapolis: Fortress, 2000).

Bibliography to §12.3a (1):   History of Scholarship

François Bovon, *Luke the Theologian: Thirty-Three Years of Research (1950–1983)* (Pittsburgh Theological Monograph Series 12: Allison Park, PA: Pickwick, 1987).

Idem, "Studies in Luke-Acts: Retrospect and Prospect," *HTR* 85 (1992) 175–96.

C. K. Barrett, *Luke the Historian in Recent Study* (London: Epworth, 1961).

the rather unlikely result that the first part of Luke's work is an aretalogy, the second part a romance—definitions that fail to explain genre and purpose of Luke's work as a whole.

The most illuminating thesis has recently been presented by Marianne P. Bonz. In an investigation of the genre of the epic story in the Greco-Roman world, especially of Virgil's *Aeneid* (§6.4b), she argues that, with the notable exception of its poetic form and the inclusion of minor literary elements drawn from a variety of other literary genres, Luke's narrative has nevertheless incorporated a number of stylistic and dramatic devices characteristic of Greco-Roman epic in general and emblematic of the *Aeneid* and its immediate literary successors in particular. Certainly nowhere outside the great foundational epics of antiquity is there the kind of fusion of prophecy and history that is found in Luke-Acts. The plot of Luke-Acts is structured around a central action in the form of a divinely willed mission to proclaim the kingdom of God and to gather its chosen people. The accomplishment of God's plan, which includes the death of the hero and the continuance of the mission by his followers, involves the pervasive use of divine guidance and supernatural intervention. Above all Luke appears to have been inspired by Virgil in his presentation of the church as the natural and, indeed, the only legitimate successor to ancient Israel. Seizing upon the divine origins of the Trojan people, long established in legend, Virgil's epic extends those claims to encompass Rome and its descendants. The promise of ancient Troy reaches its fulfillment in the creation of the Roman people, just as in Luke's narrative the promise of ancient Israel reaches its fulfillment in the establishment and growth of the new community of Christian believers. As Virgil's epic became the foundational story of the Roman people, Luke is writing the foundational story for the new Christian community.

Nowhere in Luke's work is the author explicitly named or in any way implied. Ecclesiastical tradition beginning at the end of the 2d century reports that "Luke" was the author and identifies him as the Luke mentioned in Phlm 24 as one of the associates of Paul who send greetings, and whom Col 4:14 calls "the beloved physician" (see also 2 Tim 4:11). This tradition has found further elaboration in a portion of the so-called *Anti-Marcionite Prologue* to the Gospel of Luke that may have been written at the end of the 2d century (though the *Prologues* date to the fourth century). Also here Luke is a physician, a Syrian from Antioch, who became a travel companion of Paul, remained unmarried, and died at the ripe age of eighty-four years in Boeotia. It is hardly believable, however, that the author of Luke-Acts was a member of Paul's missionary staff and a person once closely associated with Paul. That he was a physician cannot be demonstrated (he makes no more extensive use of medical terms than any other ancient writer), and the most likely date for the composition of this work (see below) clearly puts its author into a later generation. Either the name of the author was indeed Luke, but not the Luke mentioned as Paul's associate, or the name "Luke" was attached to the work at a later date, perhaps on the basis of 2 Tim 4:11 ("only Luke is still with me"). The author of Luke-Acts is no longer interested in Paul's theology; Paul's letters are not relevant for the intent of his work, which wants to present Paul's mission as the fulfillment of the divine plan initiated by Jesus. Paul is simply the chosen instrument for defining the claims of the "true Israel" and carrying this message to Rome. Luke therefore does not see a problem in presenting a picture of the great missionary Paul that conforms to some degree with the ideal of the missionary propagated by Paul's opponents of 2 Corinthians.

Nonetheless, a bit more can be said about the author of Luke-Acts. He was a Gentile, who must have had a good education and wrote Greek in a good literary style. His acquaintance with the Greek Bible (Septuagint) is thorough, and his language was deeply influenced by it, so that he sometimes writes in a "Biblical Greek," which may well have been intentional. He was raised and educated as a Christian, unless he had been associated formerly with a Jewish synagogue as a "god-fearer." For him Peter and Paul are the two great figures from the period of the earliest Christianity. This points to those segments of the early catholic church in which these two apostles were together considered as an authority (§12.2d) and thus suggests a place of origin somewhere in the geographical realm of these churches, namely, Antioch, Ephesus, Macedonia, or Rome. The author knows Ephesus well and is also acquainted with the administrative structures of Macedonian cities, while his knowledge of the geography of Palestine is very poor. It is thus most likely that his place of origin or residence was in the area of the Aegean Sea rather than in Syria. As far as the date of his writing is concerned, it is obvious that he does not belong to the first or second generation of Christianity. In the prologue of the Gospel (1:1–4), he speaks of the first generation as that of the eyewitnesses and ministers of the word, then points to the next generation when many had "undertaken to compile a narrative." His own efforts of giving an orderly account, "having followed all things closely for some time past," therefore belong to the third, rather than the second generation. On the other hand, in the fourth decade of the 2d century, Polycarp of Smyrna apparently knew Luke-Acts (cf. *Phil.* 1.2 with Acts 2:24), and Marcion used the Gospel of Luke for the edition of his canon of Scriptures. By about 150 CE, Justin Martyr had composed a gospel harmony on the basis of Matthew, Mark, and Luke. The Lukan work therefore must have been composed no later than the beginning of the 2d, but certainly not earlier than the very end of the 1st century.

Luke writes as if he is speaking primarily to the pagan world and dedicates his work to a certain Theophilus, who may have been a Gentile sympathizer, from whom he expected to receive financial support for the publication of his work. On the other hand, like all apologetic literature, Luke-Acts is also designed for the Christian churches. Luke's epic story is a story of the fulfillment of promises of old and therefore reaches back into the past of Israel and its prophets, to whom John the Baptist still belongs. His proclamation is the turning point from prophecy to fulfillment. From here on, it is the story of the gospel that is destined to conquer the world as it is finally proclaimed in the capital Rome. At the same time, Luke wants to demonstrate that Christianity—the term "Christians" appears here for the first time in any early Christian writing—and not Judaism is the legitimate heir of the promises of Scripture. Luke's work is a foundational epic for the church, which replaces the venerable epic of Israel, namely, the story of the exodus from Egypt, by a new story, which seals the separation of the Christians from the Jews. At the same time, Luke adds an apologetic feature: Christianity is a religion without any elements that could possibly constitute a political problem for Rome. It has been unjustly persecuted; Jesus' death on the cross was a miscarriage of justice. Roman officials are repeatedly introduced in order to certify that the Christian proclamation poses no danger to Rome's government. Paradoxically, however, Luke insists that it is the story that began in Jerusalem and arrived victoriously in Rome, not the story that brought Aeneas from the ruins of Troy to the shores of Italy, that determines the future of humankind according to the will of God.

(2) *The Gospel of Luke.* Although this is but the first part of a larger work, the different subject matter as well as the existence of older writings of the type of the "gospel" justifies a separate discussion of this first half of Luke-Acts. For the composition of this first part, which we now call the Gospel of Luke, the author was able to use the Gospel of Mark for the general outline of his composition. To this framework he added materials drawn from the Synoptic Sayings Gospel (Q) as well as numerous stories, sayings, and parables from a special source (see §7.3b on the Synoptic problem). Some scholars believe that there was a "protogospel of Luke," in which a story parallel to Mark's account was already combined with special Lukan materials. However that may be, the general framework resembles Mark's Gospel and often follows Mark's sequence of pericopes.

That Mark was Luke's major source is evident in Luke 3:1 to 9:50 (=Mark 1:2–9:41), from the ministry of the Baptist to about the second prediction of the passion. Most striking here is the relocation of a few passages from Mark (see below). The section from Mark 6:45–8:26 is not reproduced by Luke, either because it was missing in his copy of Mark, or because it was left out deliberately due to the many doublets contained in this section (§10.2b). With Luke 9:51, however, the author leaves Mark's story aside and begins the so-called Lukan travel narrative. He returns to Mark's framework only in 18:15, and then more or less follows Mark to the story of the finding of the empty tomb (Luke 24:12 = Mark 16:8), though he often treats his source rather freely. In addition to the travel narrative, another new feature is the birth narrative (Luke 1:5–2:51), which begins with the announcements of the births of John the Baptist and Jesus, tells stories of the births of both men, the circumcision of Jesus, and ends with the story of the twelve-year-old

Bibliography to §12.3a (2):   Commentaries

François Bovon, *The Gospel According to Luke,* vol.1: *Luke 1–9* (Hermeneia; Minneapolis: Fortress, 2000).

Idem, *Das Evangelium nach Lukas, Lk 1, 1–14,35* (2 vols.; EKKNT 3/1–2; Neukirchen-Vluyn: Neukirchener Verlag, 1989–1996).

Julius Wellhausen, *Evangelienkommentare* (Berlin: de Gruyter, 1987; first published 1904–1911).

Joseph A. Fitzmyer, *The Gospel According to Luke* (2 vols.; AB 28A; Garden City, NY: Doubleday, 1981–1985).

Wolfgang Wiefel, *Das Evangelium nach Lukas* (ThHK 3; Berlin: Evangelische Verlagsanstalt, 1988).

Bibliography to §12.3a (2):   Studies

See the Bibliography under §12.3a (1).

Bibliography to §12.3a (2):   History of Scholarship

Martin Rese, "Das Lukasevangelium: Ein Forschungsbericht," *ANRW* 2.25.3 (1985) 2258–2328.

Walter Radl (ed.), *Das Lukas-Evangelium* (WdF 261; Darmstadt: Wissenschaftliche Buchgesellschaft, 1988).

Jesus in the Temple. New materials added at the end of the gospel include the appearances of the risen Christ (on the Emmaus Road and to the Eleven) and Jesus' ascension (24:13–53). The latter (Luke 24:50–53) may have been added to the end of the Gospel after Luke's work was divided in two books, since the story of the ascension of Jesus is more properly told at the beginning of the Book of Acts (1:6–11). Materials drawn from the Synoptic Sayings Gospel have been inserted into the Markan framework at various points, usually in the form of major compositions of sayings found in the source. These include the "Sermon on the Plain" (Luke 6:20–49) and the speech about the Baptist (7:18–35). Other Q materials are used, together with Luke's special source in the travel narrative, for example, the discourse about the sending of the missionaries (9:56–10:15) and the speech against the Pharisees (11:37–52); smaller Q units are here often combined with special traditions. Unlike Matthew (§10.2c), Luke did not attempt to compose the sayings into major speeches of Jesus according to specific themes.

There is much special material in Luke's Gospel that is not paralleled in the other two Synoptic Gospels. Luke may have drawn these materials from one or several special sources and traditions. That all special materials are derived from one single writing (gospel?) is not likely. The character of these special materials is easily discerned from the following survey listing the most important units (including a small selection of sayings unique to Luke):

Miracle stories:

- The raising of the young man of Nain (the widow's son), 7:11–17
- The healing of a woman with a spirit of infirmity, 13:10–17
- The healing of a man with dropsy, 14:1–6
- The healing of ten lepers, 17:11–19

Apophthegms:

- The woman that was a sinner, 7:36–50
- Mary and Martha, 10:38–42 (cf. the serving women, 8:1–3)
- Blessedness of Jesus' mother, 11:27–28
- Dividing the inheritance, 12:13–14
- Answer to Herod, 13:31–33
- Zacchaeus, 19:1–10

Sayings:

- Social teaching of John, 3:10–14
- Woes against the rich, 6:24–26
- Eschatological sayings, 10:18–20; 12:49–50; 17:20–21
- Order of dignity at a meal, 14:7–14
- Friends with the unjust mammon, 16:9
- Sayings about the destruction of Jerusalem, 19:39–44
- The call to repentance, 13:1–5
- The two swords, 22:35–38

Similitudes, parables, example stories (all within the travel narrative):

- The good Samaritan, 10:29–37
- The friend at midnight, 11:5–8
- The rich fool, 12:13–21
- Servant's wages, 12:47–48
- The barren fig tree, 13:6–9
- Building a house and waging a war, 14:28–33
- The lost coin, 15:7–10
- The father who had two sons (Prodigal Son), 15:11–32
- The unjust steward, 16:1–13
- Dives and Lazarus, 16:19–31
- Servant's reward, 17:7–10
- The unjust judge, 18:1–8
- The Pharisee and the tax collector, 18:9–14

Insertions into the passion narrative:

- Words for Peter, 22:31–32
- Jesus before Herod, 23:6–16
- The women of Jerusalem, 23:27–31
- The two crucified criminals, 23:32, 33b, 39–43

Legends:

- The promise of the Baptist's birth, 1:5–25
- The annunciation, 1:26–38
- The birth of John the Baptist, 1:57–66, 80
- The nativity of Jesus, 2:1–20
- The circumcision of Jesus, 2:21–40
- Jesus at twelve years in the Temple, 2:41–52

Epiphany stories:

- The miraculous draft of fishes, 5:1–11
- The road to Emmaus, 24:13–35
- The appearances of the risen Christ, 24:36–49
- The ascension, 24:50–53

Hymnic materials:

- The Magnificat, 1:46–55
- The Benedictus, 1:68–79
- The Song of Simon, 2:29–32

Most striking among these special materials is the large number of parables, which obviously derive from a trustworthy tradition. In these parables as elsewhere,

Luke shows his art as a storyteller; although some of these materials may originally have existed in Aramaic, Luke succeeds in recasting them in a natural Greek narrative style. Remarkable are also several pericopes that deal with the question of rich and poor, and apophthegmas in which women play a role.

Luke's Gospel is carefully composed as the first act of the epic story. Through the interlacing of the stories of the announcements and the births of John the Baptist and Jesus, Jesus' appearance is closely connected with the appearance of the last of Israel's prophets. With the ministry of John the Baptist, the story of Israel's salvation reaches its climax and merges immediately into the story of Jesus. The contrast between the two figures is clearly stated in the definition of their different functions. John fulfills the prophetic office of Israel (1:15–17); Jesus, as the king on the throne of David over the house of Jacob, fulfills the messianic expectation of Israel (1:32–33). The two eschatological psalms (1:46–55 and 1:67–79; either hymns from the tradition of the Baptist's community or Lukan compositions) once more summarize the hope of Israel. The announcement of the angel and the angelic chorus in the story of Jesus' birth, however, signal a more universal horizon for the story that will be told. Jesus is the "Savior" (2:11; this is a typical Hellenistic title, which had also been used as a designation of the emperor), and his coming will bring peace on earth to all people of the divine pleasure. But the birth still takes place in the city of David, the circumcision of Jesus confirms that he was indeed a Jew, and when he first displays his wisdom, it takes place in the Temple of Jerusalem. But soon thereafter, Israel's prophetic function comes to an abrupt end. Luke reduces the Markan story of the end of John the Baptist (Mark 6:17–29) to a brief note about his imprisonment and places it before the appearance of Jesus for his baptism (Luke 3:19–20; Luke never tells about his death!) so that Jesus is baptized without John being present. Jesus' baptism in itself is no longer significant, nor is the divine voice signifying Jesus' appointment; rather the story is now told in order to demonstrate that the divine guide, the Holy Spirit, has arrived, who will guide not only the ministry of Jesus but the entire story, until it finds its culmination in Rome.

Jesus' ministry is told in a carefully designed composition. After the temptation the devil leaves him "until a certain time" (4:13); that time is indicated in 22:3 with the return of Satan into the traitor. This makes the story of Jesus' ministry a special period in which Satan is not present. The significance of this period is further illuminated in the story of Jesus' rejection in Nazareth, which Luke took out of its Markan context (Mark 6:1–6) and transferred to a place at the beginning of Jesus' ministry (Luke 4:16–30). Here Jesus appears in public empowered by the spirit (quoting Isa 61:1: "the spirit of the Lord is upon me"), but as it ends with the quotations of Elijah's mission to Gentiles and not to people in Israel (4:25–29), the story also points forward to the mission to the Gentiles. Jesus' ministry takes place in Israel as the "holy land," in which Galilee and Judea are the places of Jesus' preaching and healing, an undefined area the location of his travel, the Temple the place of his final teaching, and Jerusalem the city in which he suffers death. Every location has a religious significance. The mountain is set aside as the place of prayer (even in the story of the transfiguration; note 9:28), the lake for secret revelations to the disciples; thus there is no sermon "on the mount," nor a parable speech "on the lake shore." Luke does not have a realistic geographical concept of Palestine; it is for him a country full of locations that have religious meaning. While Mark had critically interpreted the motif of Jesus as the divine man by subjecting it to the criterion of the passion narrative (§10.2b), Luke revives this motif. Jesus is indeed the divine man who, empowered by the spirit, accomplishes miraculous deeds as he preaches the kingdom of God. With the beginning of Jesus' travel (Luke 9:51) his ministry enters a new phase. While the Twelve had still been sent "to preach the kingdom of God and to do miracles of healing" (9:2), the Seventy are now sent to preach the "nearness" of the kingdom (10:9), though not in power, but "like sheep among the wolves" (10:3). On the whole, the eschatological "now" becomes more prominent. Luke 12:2–59 and 17:20–37 are eschatological speeches, both concluding a segment of Jesus' travel narrative. It is not clear, however, whether such intensifying of the eschatological expectation is directed to the church at Luke's time and points the reader toward an important moment in the eschatological timetable as Jesus approaches Jerusalem and his death, while the city and its temple are facing their final demise.

In the last part of the Gospel, Luke resumes his earlier source, the Gospel of Mark. But instead of Mark's story of Jesus' entry into Jerusalem (Mark 11:1–11), Luke tells the story as Jesus' entry into the Temple, carefully avoiding the mention of Jerusalem (cf. Luke 19:45 with Mark 11:11). Every day Jesus teaches in the Temple (20:8; 21:37–38), and every night he returns to the Mount of Olives, but seemingly never enters the city. Luke here uses a pattern from Ezekiel: Jesus represents the divine "glory"; as long as he is present in the Temple, it functions as the place of God's presence, but when he leaves for the last time for the Mount of Olives, the Temple is without divine protection. Thus Luke adds the prediction of the Temple's destruction (19:41–44). In Luke, the Temple is not only the place of the debates about the census, the resurrection, and the question about the Son of David (20:29–44), but also the location for the apocalyptic discourse (21:5–36). Luke took this discourse from Mark 13, but in a thoroughly revised form so that it has become essentially a prediction of the fall of Jerusalem; into this discourse Luke has even introduced details from the siege of Jerusalem, now past history at the time of Luke's writing (21:20–24). Only at the end of the speech does one find some eschatological admonitions, reminiscent of Paul's terminology (21:34–36), which speak about the day of the Lord that will come upon the entire circle of the earth. That day is not preceded, however, by a cosmic catastrophe, but by terrifying astrological signs (*semeia*) that will cause fear among all people but signify to the believers that their salvation is near. When compared to that future event, the destruction of the Temple and of Jerusalem is nothing but an affair of past history. Jerusalem is no longer the place of promise but simply the historical place of Jesus' suffering, death, and resurrection. It is, however, significant in the progression of Luke's epic story, because Jesus' death in Jerusalem and its destruction set the stage for the move to the second phase of the story, the time of the proclamation of the gospel throughout the entire known world. To be sure, after the ascension (24:53; Acts 2:46; 3:1) the disciples once more return to Jerusalem and its Temple, but the geographical horizon of the events to come is no longer bound to the holy land.

Areopagus Speech of Paul

This bronze plaque inscribed with the Greek text of the so-called Areopagus Speech of Paul (Acts 17:22–31) was placed on the rock of the Areopagus Hill of Athens in modern times to commemorate the wedding of Greek culture and the Pauline mission.

(3) *The Acts of the Apostles.* In the first part of his work, Luke had been able to take advantage of the use of readily available written sources and other traditional materials. He was also able to concentrate his presentation, supported by the framework provided by Mark, upon the biography of one central figure. In the writing of the second part of his work, the Acts of the Apostles, Luke confronted an entirely different challenge. Though some materials and written sources were available, they were not uniform in character nor did they provide a structure for a coherent narrative. Moreover, they gave only very scanty information at points that were important for the continuation of the epic story. To portray the biography of a central figure was not suggested by the character of Luke's sources, nor would it have accorded with his intention to describe the victorious course of the proclamation

Bibliography to §12.3a (3):   Commentaries

Foakes Jackson and Lake, *Beginnings,* vols. 3–5.

Heanchen, *Acts.*

Hans Conzelmann, *Acts of the Apostles: A Commentary on the Acts of the Apostles* (Hermeneia; Philadelphia: Fortress, 1987).

C. K. Barrett, *A Critical and Exegetical Commentary on the Acts of the Apostles* (2 vols.; ICC; Edinburgh: T&T Clark, 1994–1998).

Gerhard Schneider, *Die Apostelgeschichte* (2 vols.; HThK 5; Herder: Freiburg, 1980–1982).

Rudolf Pesch, *Die Apostelgeschichte* (2 vols; EKKNT 5; Neukirchen-Vluyn: Neukirchener Verlag, 1986).

Bibliography to §12.3a (3):   Studies

Martin Dibelius, *Studies in Acts.*

Rudolf Bultmann, "Zur Frage nach den Quellen der Apostelgeschichte," in idem, *Exegetica,* 412–23.

J. C. O'Neill, *The Theology of Acts in its Historical Setting* (London: SPCK, 1961).

Leander E. Keck and J. Louis Martyn (eds.), *Studies in Luke-Acts: Essays Presented in Honor of Paul Schubert* (Nashville, TN: Abingdon, 1966).

Christoph Burchard, *Der dreizehnte Zeuge: Traditions- und kompositionsgeschichtliche Untersuchungen zu Lukas Darstellung der Frühzeit des Paulus* (FRLANT 103; Göttingen: Vandenhoeck & Ruprecht, 1970).

Petr Pokorny, "Die Romfahrt des Paulus," *ZNW* 64 (1973) 233–44.

Jacob Kremer (ed.), *Les Actes des Apôtres: Tradition, rédaction, théologie* (BETL 48; Gembloux: Duculot, 1979).

Richard I. Pervo, *Profit with Delight: The Literary Genre of the Acts of the Apostles* (Philadelphia: Fortress, 1987).

Idem, *Luke's Story of Paul* (Minneapolis: Fortress, 1990).

M.-É. Boismard and A. Lamouille, *Les Actes des Deux Apôtres* (3 vols.; EtBib 12–14; Paris: Gabalda, 1990).

Frans Neirynck, "Le texte des Actes des Apôtres et les caractéristiques stylistiques lucaniennes," in idem, *Evangelica II: 1982–1991: Collected Essays* (BETL 99; Leuven: Leuven University Press, 1991) 243–78.

Bibliography to §12.3a (3):   Bibliography

A. J. Mattil and Mary Bedford Mattil, *A Classified Bibliography of Literature on the Acts of the Apostles* (Leiden: Brill, 1966). Includes literature published until 1961.

Watson E. Mills, *A Bibliography of the Periodical Literature on the Acts of the Apostles: 1962–1984* (NovTSup 58; Leiden: Brill, 1986).

Idem, *The Acts of the Apostles* (BBRNTS 5; Lewiston: Mellen, 1996).

Joel B. Green and Michael C. McKeever, *Luke-Acts and New Testament Historiography* (IBR Bibliographies 8; Grand Rapids, MI: Baker, 1994).

from Jerusalem to Rome. Paul, to be sure, becomes the central figure in the story but, in order to set Paul on his course, Jesus himself appears to him in a vision; whatever Paul does thereafter is commissioned by the people who have received the divine spirit, and it is this same spirit who provides the guidance to the very end. The way in which this story is driven by repeated divine interference through actions of the spirit, visions, and angels reveals the author's intent to continue the epic story that he had begun in the first part of his work.

It is very difficult to retrieve from the Book of Acts useful historical information. Since the author does not write a history but an epic story, he has not subjected any of the traditional materials used in the book to the historian's critical scrutiny. There is no question that Luke used sources and traditions in the composition of the book. But these sources were often stories of miraculous events, healings, visions, and dreams—in short, the kind of stories that would be transmitted in a religious community for edification and spiritual instruction. How popular such stories were is demonstrated by the apocryphal acts of the apostles (§12.3b). On the other hand, wherever Luke seems to work like an ancient historian, he actually composed these passages himself. This is particularly true in the summary accounts and the speeches. The summary accounts (Acts 2:42–47; 4:32–37; 5:12–16; cf. 9:31–32), and thus also the information about the ideal life of the Christian community in Jerusalem, are Lukan compositions. Luke might have learned the technique of inserting these accounts from the Gospel of Mark (compare Luke 6:17–19 with Mark 3:7–12). The speeches of Acts are all composed by Luke as well, although traditional materials, such as christological formulas and fixed units of biblical exegesis, were frequently employed. There are no substantial theological differences between the speeches of Peter, Stephen, and Paul, which is in itself a historical improbability. Moreover, the theology of Paul's speeches in Acts cannot be harmonized with the theology of Paul as it is known from his letters. Paul could hardly have given a speech like the famous Areopagus speech (Acts 17:22–31), in which he ascribes divine origin to all human beings in the manner of a Stoic philosopher (17:28–29; this does not mesh with Rom 1:18ff.). Neither is it credible that Paul affirmed repeatedly in his trial that he had always lived as a law-abiding Jew, nor that in his missionary activities he had proclaimed anything other than the recognized Pharisaic doctrine of the resurrection (Acts 22:1ff.; 26:2ff.). The insertion of speeches, composed by the author and delivered by one of the important actors of the story, is a widespread technique that was not only used by ancient historians but also by authors of a romance or an epic in order to highlight the significance of important events.

Historically useful information, however, may have been incorporated by Luke into some of the narratives of Acts. Such materials include a number of individual pieces of information, for instance, about Barnabas (Acts 4:36–37—though this may be an edifying story) and about Stephen (6:8–9; 7:54, 57–58a); the list of the Hellenist missionaries (6:5) and the list of the prophets and teachers of Antioch (13:1–2); the report about the dispersion of the Hellenists and the mission of Philipp in Samaria (8:1–2, 5) and of the church in Antioch (11:19ff.); the martyrdom of James the son of Zebedee (12:1–2); and the apostolic decree (15:28–29). In Acts 13–14 and 16–21 (also 27–28?) Luke used one or several travel diaries that may ultimately derive from associates of Paul; he may also have extrapolated some of the details of the apostle's travel from Paul's letters. The character and extent of these sources, however, cannot be determined with any certainty, since Luke sometimes imitates the style of such sources. But some specific data from these itineraries could be trustworthy, such as Paul's expulsion from Corinth under the proconsul Gallio (18:12), the length of Paul's stay in Corinth (18:11) and in Ephesus (19:8, 10), and the presence of Apollos and disciples of John in Ephesus before Paul's arrival (18:24; 19:1–3).

All sources and materials used by Luke were revised according to his projected plan for his whole work. The story he tells could not have been derived from any one of the sources he employed. Frequently he also often contradicted the information contained in his sources. Since Luke wanted to describe the divinely guided, victorious course of the gospel from Jerusalem to Rome, he needed a circle of persons who would guarantee that this gospel was indeed the continuation and proclamation of the events that had begun in Bethlehem and Galilee. For this purpose Luke used the fiction of the "Twelve Apostles," something that must have been traditional at the time, and makes them the apostles chosen by Jesus and the leaders of the Jerusalem church. In 1 Cor 15:5–7, however, the "Twelve" were not identical with the "apostles," nor were they the leaders of the Jerusalem community when Paul visited the city for the Apostolic Council (the leaders were Cephas, John, and the Lord's brother James, Gal 2:9). For Luke, the Twelve Apostles are the eyewitnesses for the revelation in Jesus "beginning from the baptism of John until the day when he was taken up from us" (1:22; cf. 1:8; 10:37–41; 13:23–31). Because Judas the traitor no longer belonged to the circle chosen by Jesus, Luke inserts a story about the election of a new twelfth eyewitness (1:15–26). Consequently, Luke avoids the title "apostle" whenever he is speaking about Paul (the only exception is Acts 14:14, where the title seems to have slipped in inadvertently from Luke's source). The horizon for the continuation of the epic story is indicated by the story of Pentecost (2:1–13). The enthusiastic experience of the pouring out of the spirit and the speaking in tongues—most likely an overwhelming actual event at the beginning of the churches after the death of Jesus—received a new interpretation by Luke: it became a language miracle of universal significance, the counterpart of the universal confusion of tongues in Babylon (Gen 11:1–9). The event concerns the whole world; therefore all peoples are represented in a traditional list of nations (2:9–11, not a list of languages!). On the other hand, Luke also resumes older traditions of the interpretation of Pentecost when he describes it as an event in which the promise of Joel is fulfilled (Joel 3:1–5 = Acts 2:17–21). The speech of Peter that follows (2:14–36) is directed to the reader of the book, who is invited to understand that everything in the following story is the eschatological work of the Holy Spirit and thus divinely legitimized.

Luke carefully interwove apologetic motifs with his epic story. One of his special interests was to show that the activities of the Christian missionaries were in fact the actions of God. The trial of Peter and John before the Jewish sanhedrin demonstrates this point. The apostles say that they "must obey God rather than human beings" (Acts 5:29), and Gamaliel, the famous Jewish sage, says exactly what Luke wanted to emphasize to his pagan audience: "For if this plan or this

undertaking is merely human, it will fail; but if it is of God, you will not be able
to overthrow them. You might even be found opponents of God" (5:38–39). To
oppose the proven purpose of the divine will—every pagan and every Roman
knew this—would not only be impious presumption, it could be dangerous folly.
The proof for the presence of God is provided through the telling of stories of the
apostles' divinely empowered miraculous deeds (3:2ff.; 6:8; etc.). The story of
Ananias and Sapphira belongs to the same category (5:1–11; note that a summary
of miraculous healings follows this story, 5:12–16).

Luke idealizes the very first beginnings with his emphasis upon the unity and
unanimity of the Christian congregation, exemplified in the accounts of the church
in Jerusalem (2:36; 4:32). It is unlikely that Luke used sources for these accounts.
Where Luke used sources that spoke of conflicts within the church, he minimizes
problems and controversies. The traditional report about the Jerusalem apostles
and the Hellenists—powerful preachers in their own right as the information about
Stephen still shows—was therefore rewritten into a story of the election of persons
to serve at table during community meals (6:1–6). To be sure, Luke did not completely suppress the information from his source that Stephen was a preacher and
faith-healer (6:8), because Stephen's martyrdom would have been incomprehensible had he been nothing but a waiter. The report of his martyrdom was important
for Luke; he wanted to show why Christians could not avoid getting into a conflict
with an established, traditional religion. The speech of Stephen, written by Luke
(7:1–53), is an extensive interpretation of Scripture demonstrating that the entire
history of Israel from Abraham to Solomon justifies the Christian proclamation:
the almighty God does not live in temples made by human hands (7:48–50). This
thesis appeals to an enlightened pagan audience, but it also shows that the Christian message is the essence of the ancient and venerable tradition of Israel's Scriptures. Thus the Christians are the legitimate heirs of an ancient tradition, not its
scornful despisers or some kind of revolutionary new people. They are persecuted
only by those people whose fathers had already persecuted the prophets (7:51–52)
and who do not even themselves observe the law to which they appeal (7:53). The
apologetic intent of the report of this martyrdom is evident in the fact that Luke
reports only martyrdoms for which he can ascribe the responsibility to Jewish
authorities (note also Acts 12:1–2). He was careful not to raise equivalent accusations against the Roman authorities, or even to assign to them the responsibility
for the death of Jesus. The guilt is exclusively that of the Jewish authorities (see,
e.g., 13:27–28)—though not of the Jews in general!

From the beginning of Acts to the martyrdom of Stephen, the central figure in
the narrative has been Peter. At this point, however, Paul is introduced, still under
the name "Saul" (7:58; 8:3)—certainly unhistorical; if Paul/Saul had been present
as a witness at Stephen's martyrdom he would not have been able to say that he
"was still unknown by sight to the churches of Judea" when he visited Jerusalem
for the first time three years after his call (Gal 1:22). The fact that Luke positioned
Peter and Paul in the center of Acts reveals his dependence upon the ecclesiastical
tradition for which these two apostles and martyrs were the guarantors of the
church's beliefs (see *1 Clement* and Ignatius). Both, however, are presented in a
fashion that scarcely satisfies the curiosity of the modern historian. Peter is men-

tioned in Acts 15 for the last time. We hear nothing about his whereabouts at the time of Paul's final return to Jerusalem, and Luke fails to tell whether Peter finally traveled to Rome and was martyred there. Paul, who elsewhere in early Christian literature is both apostle and martyr, is not accorded any of these titles in the Book of Acts. Moreover, did Luke not know that Paul wrote letters? It has been suggested that Luke did not know about these letters—which is hardly credible, because everyone else between Antioch and Rome knew them at that time—and that the original ending of the Book of Acts that told Paul's martyrdom has been lost. Such assumptions, however, miss the point. Had Luke written this book as a historian, he would certainly have included all he knew about these two apostles. But the images of Peter and especially of Paul are wholly shaped by Luke's intention to present an epic story, in which Paul is guided by the Holy Spirit to bring the gospel to Rome. Since the Holy Spirit is the primary agent of the story, it does not matter whether Paul deserved the title "apostle" and whether he wrote letters. To conclude his work with Paul's martyrdom—wherever Paul was martyred—would have been anticlimactic. At the same time, the fiction of the "Twelve Apostles" as leaders of the Jerusalem community is maintained only as long as it is needed, namely, to demonstrate that the Hellenists and Paul as the apostle to the Gentiles are legitimately authorized by the Twelve Apostles and endowed by them with the Holy Spirit. Contrary to Paul's own statements in Gal 1:9ff., his commission to preach to the Gentiles is conveyed to him by an authorized agent (Ananias, Acts 9:10–19), and he has to go to Jerusalem after "some days" to meet the Twelve Apostles (9:23–30; but see Gal 1:17!). Moreover, Luke makes sure that the Gentile mission is inaugurated by Peter, one of the twelve original witnesses (Acts 10:1–11:18), and Paul does not begin his own mission until Peter has successfully defended the Gentile mission in Jerusalem (Acts 11:1–18 is deliberately placed before 11:25–26). On the other hand, since Luke's source did not say anything about the Twelve Apostles, or for that matter about Peter, at Paul's last visit to Jerusalem, Luke did not bother to introduce them once more nor did he bother to tell the reader what happened to them. They were no longer needed and their further exploits did not matter any more with respect to the epic story that Luke wants to tell.

It is not surprising, then, that the image of Paul's missionary activity is tailored to fit the purpose of Luke's work. Paul is designated to represent the continuation of the victorious course of the gospel to Rome. It is for this reason that the Pauline letters with their emphasis upon the presence of Christ's death in the fate of the apostle are excluded from playing any role in Luke's image of Paul. Nor could Luke have made any use of the reports of Paul's controversies with various opponents because he wanted to demonstrate the unity of early Christianity, which should not appear to be disturbed by the quarrel between law-abiding Jewish Christians and Gentiles rejecting the observance required by the law. For Luke, there is no longer a Pauline or Petrine tradition but only one united Christianity—Luke is the first writer to use the term "Christians" (Acts 11:26). The Apostolic Council and the Apostolic Decree (Acts 15:29) document this unity between Jews and Gentiles: Also the Gentile members of the church abide by the law because they abstain from sacrifices to idols, blood, and unchastity. "Paul" quotes this decree once more in the context of the accusation that he was no longer abiding by the law (21:25). When the problem of circumcision was raised at the Apostolic Council, it was solved by pointing out that the Holy Spirit had already solved the problem by purifying the hearts of the Gentile believers (15:8–9); the signs that God had accomplished through Barnabas and Paul serve as further proof (15:12). The problems that arose when Paul came to Jerusalem with the collection from the Gentile churches (Luke knew about the collection and preserved the names of members of the delegation in 20:4) are minimized. Another piece of the memory of the collection is used to insert a fictional trip of Paul and Barnabas to bring aid from Antioch to Jerusalem (11:27–30). Thus all suspicion is erased that there might have been serious conflicts between the Jewish and Gentile parts of the Christian church.

Paul is the great and restless itinerant preacher, endowed with the divine spirit, accomplishing awe-inspiring signs and miracles, as Peter had done before him. An exemplary documentation for this activity is presented in the missionary journey of Barnabas and Paul in Acts 13–14. Like Peter in his earlier speeches, so too Paul, in his speech in Pisidian Antioch (13:22–31), refers to the tradition of Israel and positions Jesus into a series of salvific acts that God has done in Israel. But Luke was also able to present Paul as delivering a speech that is connected with the tradition of Greek religion and philosophy (Areopagus speech, 17:22–31). Luke knew from Christian missionary practice that either point of departure could be impressive and convincing to a pagan audience. Throughout, Luke remains faithful to the view that the entire course of the preaching of the gospel is the eschatological event determined by the activity of the Holy Spirit. Under that perspective, Paul's troublesome toil over so many years in the building of his churches is transformed into a travel adventure of almost breathtaking speed (15:40–21:14). A somewhat longer stay in any of the major cities is mentioned only casually in pieces of information deriving from Luke's source (18:11; 19:10). Travels, the performance of miracles, and speeches, interrupted by an occasional stay in prison, fill most of the pages. Controversies never arise from within the Christian churches but are always caused by outsiders, especially by the Jews.

This same Paul, the greatest of the early Christian missionaries, was the divinely chosen vessel to carry the gospel to Rome, the capital of the world. Luke knew from his source that Paul had been arrested during his last stay in Jerusalem, information that enabled him to treat the position of Christianity toward the Roman authorities at some length and to contrast the almost respectful way in which Paul as a Roman citizen is treated by the Roman officials (22:24–29), with the hostile Jewish crowd in the Temple. On the other hand, Paul is given the opportunity to point out that his entire activity, the founding and establishment of a worldwide Christian church among the Gentiles, is due to divine initiative and direction. For this purpose, the readers of Acts see Paul repeat the story of his call twice (22:3–21; 26:9–20). On the other hand, Paul's speeches in these last chapters of the book leave no doubt that Christianity is by no means a novel invention designed to disturb the religious peace of the Roman empire. Luke is here defending Christianity against accusations of disrespect for ancient religious traditions; on the contrary, it is the legitimate culmination of the venerable tradition of Israel. Paul has to emphasize several times that he was indeed a Pharisee, a member of the most distinguished group of believers in Israel, and that he had never done anything against the religion of his fathers (22:1ff.; 23:1, 6; 24:14ff.; 25:8; 26:2ff.). Throughout Luke's work, the Pharisees are treated more positively than other Jewish groups or the Jews in general, and they do not participate in the trial of Jesus. A the same time, Paul is also depicted as a law-abiding Roman citizen. In the appeal to the emperor on his own behalf (25:10), he is also making a general appeal to the official Roman position in matters of religious policy, since he can portray himself as the prototype of a pious Roman subject who has never offended "against the (Jewish) law, or against the temple, or against Caesar" (25:8). Paul's trial is designed to demonstrate that his conviction (and thus the conviction of any Christian) would be a violation of the principles of Rome's policies in matters of religion. Also for this reason, it was not in Luke's interest to end his work with the story of Paul's condemnation and martyrdom. On the contrary, during the long and eventful travel to Rome, even though a prisoner, Paul remains in full possession of the powers of the spirit (27:1–28:16), and after his arrival to Rome he is able "to preach the Kingdom of God and teach about the Lord Jesus Christ quite openly and unhindered" (28:31)—an appropriate conclusion of the epic story that began in Jerusalem, as it is told in Luke's work.

(b) The Miracle-Working Apostles in Conflict with the World: The Acts of Peter and the Acts of Paul

While Luke forced the traditions and stories about Jesus and the apostles into a major literary work of grand design that was written for the Gentile sympathizer, the works known as the "apocryphal acts of the apostles" are more or less random collections of stories that were told and transmitted—and repeatedly altered—within the Christian communities. They reflect more closely than Luke's work the

Bibliography to §12.3b: Texts

Lipsius-Bonnet, *ActApostApoc,* 1. 1–111, 235–72. Latin and Greek texts of the *Acts of Paul* and *Acts of Peter.*

James Brashler and Douglas M. Parrott, "BG, 4: The Acts of Peter," in Douglas M. Parrott (ed.), *Nag Hammadi Codex V,2–5 and VI with Papyrus Berolinensis 8502, 1 and 4* (NHS 11: Leiden: Brill, 1979). Coptic fragment of the *Acts of Peter.*

Wilhelm Schneemelcher and Rudolphe Kasser, "The Acts of Paul," in Schneemelcher, *NT Apoc.,* 2. 213–70.

Wilhelm Schneemelcher, "The Acts of Peter," in idem, *NT Apoc.,* 2. 271–321.

Elliott, *Apocryphal NT,* 350–89.

Bibliography to §12.3b: Studies

Rosa Söder, *Die apokryphen Apostelgeschichten und die romanhafte Literatur der Antike* (Stuttgart: Kohlhammer, 1932; reprint 1969).

Dennis MacDonald, *The Legend and the Apostle: The Battle for Paul in Story and Canon* (Philadelphia: Westminster, 1983).

Gérard Poupon, "Les 'Actes de Pierre' et leur remaniement," *ANRW* 2.25.6 (1988) 4363–83.

Christine M. Thomas, "Word and Deed: The Acts of Peter and Orality," *Apocrypha* 3 (1992) 125–64.

Eadem, "The 'Prehistory' of the Acts of Peter," in François Bovon et al. (eds.), *The Apocryphal Acts of the Apostles* (Harvard Divinity School Studies; Cambridge, MA: Harvard University Press, 1999).

Jan N. Bremmer (ed.), *The Apocryphal Acts of Paul and Thecla* (Kampen: Pharos, 1996).

Idem (ed.), *The Apocryphal Acts of Peter: Magic, Miracle, and Gnosticism* (Leuven: Peeters, 1998).

reality of the religious experience of Christian people during the 2d and 3d centuries. In Luke's work, the apostles are primarily divinely inspired miracle workers and preachers of the gospel; they are not presented as fighters against heresy or as martyrs. The *Acts of Peter* and the *Acts of Paul* did not appear in written form until the end of the 2d century, but both books still used stories and traditions that were told many decades before they were finally written down. Their literary model is the Hellenistic romance, which implied a reduction in the apologetic elements and a dominance of the aretalogical features.

The transmission of these two books of apostolic acts is scanty; though reconstruction is possible to a certain degree, lacunae and uncertainties remain. Of the *Acts of Peter,* a manuscript from Vercelli contains a Latin translation of the last part of the book, the *Actus Vercellenses.* This work reports the controversies of Peter with the magician Simon in Rome and the martyrdom of Peter. The latter has also been transmitted independently and is preserved in a large number of Greek manuscripts and numerous translations. There are only two fragments of the first part of the *Acts of Peter:* the narrative of Peter's daughter in a Coptic papyrus, and a summary of a story called "The Daughter of the Gardener" in the apocryphal *Letter of Titus.* It is therefore difficult to obtain a clear picture of the first part of the work, which was apparently largely located in Jerusalem, since *Act. Verc.* 5 reports that Peter stayed in Jerusalem for a period of twelve years.

There are two manuscripts of the *Acts of Paul* that can be seen as witnesses of the entire work: a Greek papyrus written about 300 CE and a Coptic papyrus from the 4th century. Both manuscripts are fragmentary but allow conclusions about the composition of the entire work. In addition, several Greek and Coptic fragments survive. Three parts of the *Acts of Paul* were transmitted separately and are therefore better attested: (1) the *Acts of Paul and Thecla,* (2) the *Martyrdom of Paul,* and (3) a correspondence between Paul and the Corinthians (*3 Corinthians,* §12.2g). Of the first two, there exist several Greek manuscripts as well as translations; *3 Corinthians* became part of the canon of the Bible of the Armenian church and was probably also included in the corpus of the Pauline letters in the first Syrian canon, because the Syrian church father Ephrem wrote a commentary on it. Recently the original Greek text of *3 Corinthians* was discovered and published as *Papyrus Bodmer X.*

It seems that the *Acts of Paul* is dependent upon the *Acts of Peter.* The famous "Quo vadis" episode from the martyrdom of Peter is used in the *Acts of Paul.* In *Act. Verc.* 35, Peter is persuaded to leave Rome in order to escape martyrdom; on the way he meets Jesus, who is on his way to Rome. Upon Peter's question, "Where are you going, Lord?" Jesus answers, "I am going to Rome to be crucified." In the *Acts of Paul* (chap. 10) Jesus appears to Paul, who is on a boat traveling to Rome, and says to him the same words; but it makes little sense since Paul is not fleeing martyrdom anyway. If this dependence is acknowledged, both apostolic acts must have been written before the end of the 2d century, because Tertullian (*De baptismo* 17) knew of the *Acts of Paul* and reports that it was written by a presbyter from Asia Minor "out of love for Paul." A more precise dating is not possible. The Gospels of the New Testament are presupposed and are occasionally used, and at least the *Acts of Paul* reveals a knowledge of the Pauline letters, yet neither writing seems to be aware of anything like a "New Testament canon."

It is very difficult to determine the relationship of these two apocryphal acts to Luke's Book of Acts. Extant manuscripts cannot be considered to be faithful copies of the original, because these books are "oral literature." The stories were not only read, they were also told, and scribes who copied these books were likely to make changes accordingly. Moreover, the storytellers as well as the later copyists would also have some knowledge of the canonical Book of Acts. Despite this possible knowledge, however, these books present completely different images of Peter and Paul, on the basis of a considerable store of legends, from which also Luke drew some of his stories. For the authors of both apocryphal acts, Peter and Paul belong together. The *Acts of Peter* reports that Paul had worked in Rome before Peter's arrival; and the *Acts of Paul* introduces the captain of the ship that brought Paul to Rome as a Christian who was baptized by Peter (*Act. Verc.* 1; *Act. Paul.* 10; cf. *Act Verc.* 2). Most of all, the two apostles stand together as martyrs. The tradition of the two martyrs Peter and Paul that had appeared for the first time in *1 Clement* and in Ignatius of Antioch (§12.2d–e), apparently suppressed by Luke, was brought back through these apocryphal acts. The composition of the reports of these martyrdoms is dependent upon older narratives, which perhaps already existed in written form, just as Luke used a written source for the story of the martyrdom of Stephen in Acts 6–7. Such martyrdom stories were told and were circulated in the interest of piety and religious edification and were written down only after the oral tradition had added legendary and miraculous elements. In the cases of the martyrdoms of Peter and Paul, they were also promoted by the leadership of the Roman community in order to enhance the fame and reputation of the Roman church. In these cases, it is impossible to discover a kernel of historical truth in the martyrdom reports. The interest in writing down the story of a martyrdom immediately after the event begins to emerge only after the middle of the 2d century with the *Martyrdom of Polycarp*. And even here miraculous features are by no means lacking (§12.3f). Alongside the formation of the stories of the martyrdom of the apostles, other legends about them were not just transmitted individually, but also soon composed into cycles of stories. In composing the Book of Acts, Luke may already have used for his work collections of stories about Peter and Paul. The existence of such cycles of stories is also evident in the apocryphal acts of Peter and Paul; these traditions—not the canonical Book of Acts—were the primary sources of the *Acts of Peter* and the *Acts of Paul.*

The *Acts of Peter* employs a cycle of legends about the competition between Peter and Simon Magus. The use of this source does not fit the general purpose of the writing too well, since it ends with Peter's victory in a contest on the Roman forum at which the prefect of the city presides: Simon Magus dies after a crash while demonstrating his magical power of flight through the air, and Peter is recognized by all as the victor. Thus the author has to go to great lengths to find a reason for the subsequent execution of Peter by that same prefect of Rome. Since the magical stories of this originally independent cycle include a talking dog, a dried fish that swims happily in the water as though alive, and a flying magician, it is not surprising that it abounds with stories of healing of the blind and resurrections from the dead. Some of these were popular folktales that were incorporated into the cycle of Peter and Simon the Magician. The treasure of freely circulating stories, especially with magic as their topic, was very rich during the Roman period;

the romances drew their materials from this same source (see, e.g., the *Metamorphoses* of Apuleius, a work written at about the same time).

The *Acts of Paul* also uses an older cycle of legends about the heroine Thecla. It was with great difficulty and crowned with only partial success that the author tried to introduce his hero Paul into this older work. Though thoroughly legendary, it is a remarkable work, as it extols the ascetic virtues and independent activities of a female missionary and martyr. The narrative of Paul's martyrdom also existed independently before it served to form the conclusion of the *Acts of Paul;* the introduction added by the author, with a motif borrowed from the *Acts of Peter,* in which Jesus tells Paul that he was going to be crucified (see above), does not fit the following narrative of Paul's decapitation. These apocryphal acts thus give numerous indications of the formation of Christian legends at an earlier date that were not limited to the primary apostolic figures, but also included such figures as the virgin Thecla. It is therefore highly improbable that these legends were primarily developed on the basis of canonical writings. To be sure, the canonical Book of Acts also tells about the Samaritan magician Simon (Acts 8:9–24), but this Lukan report already presupposes the existence of the Simon legend that the *Acts of Peter* used. The encounter with Simon in Acts 8:14ff. names Peter and John, who meet Simon in Samaria; according to *Act. Verc.* 8, Peter and Paul meet Simon in Jerusalem. This was probably what Luke also found in his source, but he had to replace Paul with John, because the calling of Paul would not be told until the next chapter (Acts 9:1ff.).

But it is not only the legends and martyrdoms of the apostles that these apocryphal acts seek to preserve. Both the *Acts of Paul* and the *Acts of Peter,* as well as the *Acts of Thecla,* are strongly interested in the propagation of ideals of encratism, especially sexual abstinence. This lifestyle and attitude toward existence was either played down or opposed in the early Catholic literature, but must have been rather popular in the Christian churches of the 2d century. Even Luke reveals that he inclined toward sexual asceticism. In his reproduction of Jesus' answer to the question of the Sadducees he introduced a significant alteration: those who are worthy of the age to come neither marry nor are given into marriage (compare Luke 20:34–36 with Mark 12:25). In the Book of Acts, none of the apostles are married—contrary to Paul's report that the other apostles, the brothers of the Lord, and Peter "are accompanied by a believing wife" in their missionary travels (1 Cor 9:5). Luke also separates Philipp "the evangelist" who has four prophesying virgin daughters (Acts 21:8–9; cf. 6:5; 8:5–40) from Philipp the apostle (1:13). In contrast, the Pastoral Epistles explicitly reject false teachers who forbid marriage (§12.2g). But the *Acts of Paul* and the *Acts of Peter,* both by no means "heretical" writings, repeatedly emphasize the ideal of virginity. They are not interested in an accommodation of Christian ideals to the general morality of the good citizen, nor are they excluding women from the apostolic office. With such an attitude, they were probably closer to the religious outlook of many earnest Christians of their time than were the Pastoral Epistles. This must not be overlooked if one chooses to call this attitude "encratite." It was not necessarily the moral conviction of a special heretical group, but part of a widespread morality of Christians in churches that insisted also upon the other Christian responsibilities such as mutual help and care, providing for the poor, and communal responsibilities for the widows, which are all recommended in these apocryphal acts. They were in complete agreement with early Catholic writings about the need to reject Gnosticism and to preserve the "faith" handed down by the apostles. This is especially evident in the *Acts of Paul,* which includes in the reproduction of *3 Corinthians* (*Act. Paul* 8), a detailed report on the correspondence of Paul with the Corinthians about false (Gnostic) teachers, thus taking a position against Gnosticism that was completely in accord with the Pastoral Epistles (§12.2g).

It has been argued that these apocryphal acts are more closely related to the Hellenistic romance, because they succumbed more than the canonical Acts to the desire for edification and entertainment. But this judgment is only partially justified. Religious edification was certainly an important feature, and what is missing in comparison to the canonical Acts is the apologetic motif. The apocryphal acts are not willing to sacrifice the early Christian ideal of moral rigorism to apologetic interests, and the examples of the great martyr apostles were more significant for their piety than the argument that Christianity was a religion that did not threaten the Roman state. To be sure, the flowers of pious fantasy bloom more richly in these writings—which are not lacking in Luke, though he refrained from introducing baptized lions and talking dogs—but the *Acts of Paul* and the *Acts of Peter* still express a Christian vision that is not satisfied with the limitations of a society determined by the prudent morality of the good citizen. "Blessed are those who for the love of God have departed from the fashion of the world, for they shall judge angels and shall be blessed at the right hand of the Father" (*Act. Paul* 3.6). The divinely sanctioned protest against the existing world order is thus renewed with an explicit reference to the eschatological beatitudes of Jesus.

(c) The Pauline Gospel as Renunciation of the World: Marcion

At the beginning of the 2d century the heirs of the churches that had been founded by Paul had developed a theological position that made it possible for Christianity to establish itself in the world and culture of its time as a morally respectable religious community. This also opened the opportunity of conquering that world through its propaganda and the moral example of its communal life. This Christian position was deeply indebted to the Scriptures of Israel. The Christians understood themselves to be the legitimate heirs of the promises given to Israel, which had been fulfilled in the coming of Jesus, in his resurrection, and in the founding of the church by the workings of the Holy Spirit. They could proudly look back upon Paul as one of the founders of this church, and it was also possible to use his letters in parenesis and for the further development of church order. But Paul's letters were no longer significant as a norm of theology; some even seemed convinced

Bibliography to §12.3c

Adolf von Harnack, *Marcion: Das Evangelium vom fremden Gott* (Darmstadt: Wissenschaftliche Buchgesellschaft, 1996; first published 1923 and 1924).

Idem, *Marcion: The Gospel of the Alien God* (Durham, NC: Labyrinth, 1990).

R. Joseph Hoffmann, *Marcion: On the Restitution of Christianity. An Essay on the Development of Radical Paulinist Theology in the Second Century* (AARAS 46; Chico, CA: Scholars Press, 1984).

that the church would do better without them. To be sure, there were false teachers, but nothing indicates that any Christian group, Gnostic or Jewish-Christian, possessed an organization that could seriously threaten the unity of the early catholic churches from Antioch to Rome, which were led by bishops and cultivated close connections with each other through letters and personal visits. While the false teachers propagated theological teachings that promised deeper religious insights to the initiate, the strength of early catholicism was not to be found in the appeal and unity of its theology. In fact, a unified theology did not exist and there was no ideological coercion. Rather, the pillars of faith were the adherence to the Scriptures and to the gospel of Jesus' cross and resurrection, as well as the commandments to participate in the life and worship of the church, particularly in the Eucharist, to submit to the bishop, to care for the poor, the widows, and orphans, and to strive for respectable conduct in one's life and affairs.

In this situation, Marcion, a theologian who was deeply influenced by the theology of Paul's letters, called the foundations of this ecclesiastical position into question and caused a crisis for the church that was overcome only through a theological renewal, and finally through the creation of a new Holy Scripture, namely, the New Testament. Marcion would later become the archheretic of the catholic church. Unfortunately, none of his writings are preserved. The earliest testimony to his appearance may be the anecdote about Marcion's encounter with Polycarp that is told by Irenaeus (§12.2b). By the middle of the 2d century, Marcionite churches existed in many places all over the Mediterranean, as is attested by Justin Martyr (*1 Apol.* 26.5; 58.1–2). Before he wrote his *First Apology* ca. 150 CE, Justin had already written a treatise against Marcion (which is lost). Later witnesses are a large number of antiheretical writers, who cite various passages and fragments from Marcion's works. Adolf von Harnack was the first scholar who accomplished a critical examination of all the relevant materials and reconstructed Marcion's career and theology (published in the year 1920). All further research is based on Harnack's monograph.

Marcion was probably born shortly after the year 100 in the province of Pontus in northern Asia Minor. Thus he was a somewhat younger contemporary of Polycarp, and a little older than the apologist Justin Martyr. He grew up in a Christian home and was educated in the church. It is also known that he was quite wealthy and owned a shipping business. This information about the occupation and social position of a Christian of that period demonstrates that the stories about wealthy women and men who made major donations to Christian churches were by no means the result of wishful thinking. Marcion was active at first in Asia Minor as a church member. (The story that he was excommunicated by his own father because he had seduced a virgin is a malicious polemical invention; its symbolic meaning should not be overlooked.) Between the years 135 and 138 he came to Rome, joined the Christian church there, and donated the enormous sum of 200,000 sesterces; according to Tertullian's report, this money was returned to him when he was excommunicated. The date of his departure from the Roman church has been preserved in the tradition of the Marcionite churches as the year 144 CE. It is not possible to know whether Marcion was formally excommunicated or left of his own free will. His two major works must have been written in Rome before he left the church, that is, between 135–138 and 144. They became the basis for the organization of a new church that rapidly spread in the East and in the West. Marcion probably died after 160, and thus his activity coincides almost precisely with the peaceful years of the rule of Hadrian and Antoninus Pius.

Marcion's point of departure was Paul, more specifically, the Paul of the letters. Marcion was particularly interested in the theological statements of these letters, most of all of Galatians. It was there that Marcion discovered the insurmountable and radical opposition of law and gospel as described by Paul. Marcion concluded that Paul was the only true disciple of Jesus, because Jesus had also broken the law. But what had the church made of this Paul? It had falsified Paul into a teacher of legalistic morality and into an interpreter of the law and the prophets, who had used allegorical tricks to show that there was no difference between the actions of God as attested in the Scripture of Israel and the Father of Jesus Christ. Since such statements appeared in the letters of Paul themselves as Marcion had found them in use in the churches, it was evident to him that the churches had not preserved their original text.

From the Gnostics, Marcion could receive neither aid nor advice, although he must have been familiar with Gnostic teachings. His own view that the God of love, the Father of Jesus Christ, could not be identical with the God of the law who had created the world could scarcely be explained without the assumption of Gnostic influence. This, however, does not make Marcion a Gnostic theologian, because he rejected the use of the speculative allegorical method of scriptural interpretation employed by the Gnostics, as well as the formation of mythological constructs that claimed to derive from special revelation. If Valentinus was a mystic and poet, Marcion was a pragmatist and scholar, both men must have known each other because they were in Rome at the same time. Marcion did not want to be a prophet proclaiming a new revelation, nor did he ever try to publish his thoughts in the form of a pseudepigraphical book under the name of Paul. He did not even understand himself as an exegete in the sense of that time; in that case he would have engaged the allegorical and typological methods of exegesis. It was exactly these methods that Marcion blamed for the terrible obfuscation of the fundamental opposition of law and gospel. There was only one path open to him: he had to attempt a critical reconstruction of Paul's original writings as a textual critic, philologian, and reformer. The result of that work was what is known as "Marcion's canon," the first attempt to create a Christian Holy Scripture that would replace the Scriptures of Israel. It was not new in the sense that it replaced a canon of New Testament writings that the church already possessed—there is nothing to indicate that such a canon existed at that time—rather, it was new because it was designed to supersede and replace the Holy Scripture used by the churches, namely, what later became known as the Old Testament.

Marcion had to make a selection from among all the Christian writings that were in circulation, many of them under the name of an apostle. That the letters of Paul would be included was obvious. Among the Gospels, his choice fell upon Luke. He also knew Matthew, but this writing had to be rejected because of its position with respect to the law. The Gospel of John, never quoted or referred to by Polycarp of Smyrna or by Justin, was apparently not yet known in Asia Minor and in Rome.

For his edition of the Pauline letters, Marcion established an order not attested any-where else: Galatians stands at the head of the collection, followed by 1 and 2 Cor-inthians, Romans, 1 and 2 Thessalonians, Ephesians (called "Laodiceans" by Marcion), Colossians, Philippians, and Philemon. The Pastoral Epistles are miss-ing; Marcion probably did not know them (or were they not yet written?), since an appropriate redaction would not have presented major difficulties for him. There is no trace of Hebrews; if Marcion knew that writing, it would be no surprise that he did not use it.

The basis of the Marcionite edition of Paul's letters was the so-called Western Text (§7.2a), which was the most widely used popular text of the 2d century. A number of special features that later writers noticed in Marcion's text were not the result of his own revision but part of the text that he used. Marcion's method of redaction must be called philological, and he never claimed that the results of his work should be considered sacrosanct or final. The vast majority of all the textual changes that he introduced were deletions, ranging from the omission of a single word to the elimination of entire paragraphs. Additions are rare, but in a number of instances Marcion modified the text through transpositions in order to restore what he thought must have been the original sense. Among the deletions one finds quotations from Scripture or passages that speak positively about the relationship of Christ or the Christians to the world and history created and ruled by the cre-ator God of the Scriptures of Israel. Marcion revised the Gospel of Luke in an anal-ogous way: among the passages he eliminated are the birth narratives, the baptism of Jesus and his genealogy (Luke 1:1–4:15), all quotations from Scripture, the parables of the fig tree (13:6–9) and of the Prodigal Son (15:11–32), and the entry into Jerusalem and the cleansing of the Temple (19:29–46).

Marcion's second major work, the *Antitheses,* is lost and cannot be reconstructed as a whole. Tertullian, Irenaeus, Origen, and Ephrem still knew it, but nothing is preserved apart from quotations and polemical references. The book apparently contained a number of antitheses about the fundamental difference between the creator God of Israel's Scriptures and the Father of Jesus Christ. Its main content was exegetical, presented in the form of commentaries on individual passages from Luke and the Pauline letters. Passages from Matthew are occasionally referred to, and Marcion never mentions any apocryphal writings. In these exegetical anti-theses, Marcion regularly quotes and critically interprets passages from the Scrip-tures and juxtaposes passages from Luke or Paul; for example, Exod 12:11 ("your loins be girded, your sandals on your feet, and your staff in your hand") and Luke 9:3 ("take nothing for your journey, no staff, no bag"); or Exod 21:24 ("eye for eye, tooth for tooth") and Luke 6:29 ("to him who strikes you on the cheek, offer the other also"). The radical opposition between law and gospel was thus demonstrated even in small details.

On the basis of the information about the *Antitheses,* as well as from the way that Marcion revised the texts of Luke and Paul, it is possible to reconstruct a rather clear picture of his theology. Its central concept was the sharp contrast between the "foreign" God and the God of Israel's Scriptures. Marcion's message has rightly been called "the gospel of the foreign God." This foreign God is the highest God and the Savior; he has no relationship whatsoever to the creation of the world. His essence is goodness, and he shows only love and mercy. The creator God, on the other hand, is not evil—in this respect Marcion's thought is clearly distinguished from Gnosticism—but is utterly just and thus punishes transgressions mercilessly. Salvation comes only through the dissolution of the power of the creator God. Insofar as he wields his power by means of the law and the prophets, it has already come to an end for the believer who rejects the Scriptures of Israel. Jesus came in order to invalidate those Scriptures. Jesus is the son of the foreign God and indeed God himself, distinguished from the Father only by name. Since the created world of human bodies is part of the creator God's dominion, Jesus accepted the human body in appearance only because it would have been impossible for him to be united in reality with the creator God's material body. In the technical language of christology, such a concept would be called "modalistic docetism," since Marcion considered Jesus to be completely identical with God in all respects, who took human form in appearance only but not in reality. It was also in appearance only that Jesus took the name of Christ/Messiah, which is taken from the Hebrew Scriptures, because he wanted to deceive the creator God. Marcion's christological modalism is related to a Christian belief that was very widespread at the time, which saw Christ as the full and replete presence of God, particularly in the Eucharist. This view was not really challenged until later, when Tertullian and other fathers began to criticize the propagation of this sort of modalist christology that obliterated the trinitarian distinctions. On the other hand, the explicit docetism of Marcion must have been suspicious from the outset and meant that Marcion could be accused as a Gnostic (see Ignatius's attacks on his docetist opponents, §12.2d). In his understanding of Jesus' message, Marcion followed the kerygma of the church: Jesus preached the gospel for the salvation of sinners. Out of his pure and inexplicable love for humanity, the foreign God sent his son as a sacrifice for sin through which he purchased them from the creator God. In agreement with the kerygma of the church, Marcion also spoke of Jesus' descent into hell, though not in order to redeem the righteous of Israel, but rather to save Cain and the Sodomites. Modifications of the church's beliefs were necessary in his eschatology because the good foreign God does not judge or punish anyone. Marcion assumed that he would simply remove the nonbelievers from his sight. Simultaneously with the final salvation of all believers, the creator God would destroy himself and his whole creation.

The salvation, however, has not yet been accomplished in the present, and there is no trace in Marcion's thought of a renewal of the early Christian expectation for an immediate end to the world. But in contrast to the catholic church's morality of the pious citizen, Marcion emphasizes the tension arising from the believers' existence in a world in which they no longer have any share: as long as they are in the flesh, they will suffer and experience persecution. Although these ideas have their roots in Pauline theology. Marcion goes beyond Paul in his prohibition of marriage and his demand for abstention from meat and wine, thus clearly accepting the encratite tendencies of his time (cf. the *Acts of Peter* and the *Acts of Paul,* §12.3b). Teachings of this kind, however, could be found elsewhere, and need not have posed a threat to the early catholic church. The real threat arose for a different reason. Marcion was not only a theologian and exegete, he was also a gifted and successful organizer, who systematically created and firmly established religious communities, designed to stand as the sacred new creation of the foreign God in this world. In that respect, Marcion had learned much from the early catholic church. His own churches had bishops, deacons, and presbyters. Each office was open to all members, women as well as men, because the new creation had made distinctions of gender irrelevant. Sanctification and renunciation of the world had thus found a stable form of ecclesiastical organization. The Marcionites possessed another powerful weapon: they had a sacred book that was a Christian creation, the first-ever canon of the New Testament, which contained the pure words of Jesus and the unadulterated teachings of Paul. As a result, for the first time in its history, Christianity was divided into two churches, both strictly organized and competing with each other. The Marcionite church indeed survived for many centuries, and it took several decades before the defenders of early catholic Christianity began to understand how they could meet Marcion's challenge. It is not impossible that the Pastoral Epistles were a first answer to Marcion (§12.2g). That sort of response did not grasp the real issue, however, because it simply reinforced the same understanding of the Pauline letters that Marcion had so vehemently criticized. In order to defend itself against Marcion, the church first had to create its own canon of Christian writings, and it had to rediscover the theological inheritance of Paul in an attempt to redefine the relationship between Christianity and the world; this endeavor did not begin until Irenaeus and Tertullian. Meanwhile, the situation of the Christian churches changed drastically, as the time of relative peace between church and state came to an end, and the catholic Christians were forced to compare themselves with the Marcionites in their readiness to suffer martyrdom.

(d) The Position of the Roman Authorities

No official decision of the Roman authorities concerning Christianity is known from the 1st century, and it cannot be assumed that during this period members of churches or their leaders were ever persecuted or punished because of their Christian faith as such. Convictions were apparently based upon such accusations as causing public unrest, forming illegal and secret associations, and refusing to sacrifice to the emperor (the latter is first attested by the Revelation of John, §12.1c; for the problem as a whole, see §6.5a–b). The Acts of the Apostles, however, reveals a situation in which even the Roman authorities began to show an explicit interest in the question of the existence and character of this new religious movement, an interest to which Luke responds, especially in his description of the trial of Paul (§12.3a). It must be noted that Luke is here describing the situation at his own time at the turn of the 1st century—not at the time of Paul! Also Luke's story of the riot of the silversmiths at Ephesus reflects the situation of Luke's time:

Bibliography to §12.3d: Text of the Letter of Pliny

Betty Radice (ed. and trans.), *Pliny: The Letters* (LCL; 2 vols.) 2. 284–93.

J. Stevenson, *A New Eusebius: Documents Illustrative of the History of the Church to A.D. 337* (London: SPCK, 1947, and reprints) 13–16.

Kee, *Origins,* 51–53.

Cuiras of the Emperor Hadrian
(from a statue found in the Athenian agora)
In upper center the goddess Athena, flanked by her
symbols, snake and owl, and crowned by two Nike
figures (Victories). She is standing on the back of the
symbol of Rome, the she-wolf nursing Romulus and
Remus. Below, the horned image of Zeus-Ammon,
recalling the divinity of Alexander the Great.

Christians had become so numerous that the silversmiths had begun to fear for their business. The same situation is attested in the first extant report of a Roman administrator about the Christians, namely, a letter of the younger Pliny to the emperor Trajan that is preserved, together with Trajan's answer, in Pliny's published correspondence. Pliny had been sent by Trajan as governor to Bithynia in order to settle the affairs of that difficult province in the northwestern part of Asia Minor. He arrived in Bithynia in the year 111 and remained there until he died in 113. As his correspondence demonstrates, and as he himself says, he wrote to Trajan whenever he was faced with difficult cases in order to obtain the emperor's decision. In one of these letters (10.96) he describes what he had found out about the Christians and gave an account of his method of conducting trials whenever accusations were submitted against them.

As Pliny relates, the number of Christians in the province of Bithynia had increased dramatically; "the contagious disease of this false religion (*superstitio*)" had spread not only in the cities but also in the villages, and included people of all ages and social classes. As a consequence, many temples had already become deserted, regular sacrifices had been largely discontinued, and it had become difficult to sell sacrificial meat. Pliny had not taken measures against the Christians in his capacity as governor until several people had been denounced as Christians and even an anonymous accusation listing many names had come to his attention. Pliny had not yet come to a clear understanding as to whether the name "Christian" as such was in itself sufficient cause for conviction, or whether it was necessary to find evidence "of crimes connected with the name." In any case, in the trial he had sentenced people to death who insisted even after repeated interrogation that they were Chris-

Bibliography to §12.3d: Studies

Henry J. Cadbury, "Roman Law and the Trial of Paul," in Foakes Jackson and Lake, *Beginnings,* 5. 297–338.

W. H. C. Frend, *Martyrdom and Persecution in the Early Church* (Oxford: Blackwell, 1965) 104–235.

Rudolf Freudenberger, *Das Verhalten der römischen Behörden gegen die Christen im 2. Jahrhundert* (München: Beck, 1967).

Joachim Molthagen, *Der römische Staat und die Christen im zweiten und dritten Jahrhundert* (Hypomnemata 28; 2d ed.; Göttingen: Vandenhoeck & Ruprecht, 1975).

Antonie Wlosok, "Christliche Apologetik gegenüber kaiserlicher Politik," in Heinzgünter Frohnes and Uwe W. Knorr (eds.), *Die Alte Kirche* (München: Kaiser, 1974) 147–65. Excellent summary with comprehensive bibliography.

Dominique Cuss, *Imperial Cult and Honorary Terms in the New Testament* (Paradosis 23; Freiburg/ Schweiz: Freiburg University Press, 1974).

Kurt Aland, "Das Verhaltnis von Kirche und Staat in der Frühzeit," *ANRW* 2.2.23 (1979) 60–226.

P. Keresztes, "The Imperial Roman Government and the Christian Church, I: From Nero to the Severi," *ANRW* 2.2.23 (1979) 247–315.

Idem, "Nero, the Christians and the Jews in Tacitus and Clement of Rome," *Latomus* 43 (1984) 404–13.

Robert L. Wilken, *The Christians as the Romans Saw Them* (New Haven: Yale University Press, 1984) 1–30.

Glen W. Bowersock, *Martyrdom and Rome* (Cambridge: Cambridge University Press, 1995).

Bibliography to §12.3d: History of Scholarship

Richard Klein (ed.), *Das frühe Christentum im römischen Staat* (WdF 267; Darmstadt: Wissenschaftliche Buchgesellschaft, 1971).

tians, "because in any case obstinacy and unbending perversity deserve to be punished." There is no question that Pliny considered being a Christian a punishable crime. On the other hand, those who denied that they were Christians or said that they had only formerly been Christians were requested to make a supplication to the gods, an offering to the emperor's statue, and to curse Christ, and were then freed; a statue of the emperor had been brought into the courtroom just for this purpose.

In his answer, Trajan confirms Pliny's procedures, but notes that nothing final should be laid down with regard to a regular procedure in this matter. He adds two extremely important instructions: first, Christians should not be sought out, but should only be convicted and punished if accused; second, anonymous accusations should not be admitted in court because "this is not worthy of our time" (*non nostri saeculi est*). In other words, Christians were safe as long as they were not denounced by someone bearing ill will against them. It is clear that this is the situation presupposed by the Pastoral Epistles' admonition to lead a blameless life, to exercise the virtues of good citizenship, and to apply strict standards regarding the moral qualifications of people in ecclesiastical office.

The Christians, however, might in this case have some success in persuading their neighbors not to inform against them, but they were far from able to convince a Roman governor of their innocence simply by leading a morally irreproachable life; this is evident from Pliny's letter. He readily recognizes that in their meeting, as reported by some "former" Christians, the Christians bound themselves by an oath "not to commit theft or robbery or adultery, not to break their word, and not to disavow a debt when repayment was demanded." This clearly reflects the catalog of vices that was so frequently used in the parenesis of Christian letters. Yet, there remained too much that the Roman governor had to view as potentially dangerous. Problematic was the formation of private associations (*hetaeria*); this Pliny had forbidden on the basis of an earlier instruction from Trajan. Private meetings at night (before sunrise) were always suspicious, no matter how many "hymns to Christ as a god" (*carmina Christo quasi deo*) the Christians sang, and no matter how harmless and ordinary the food that the Christians ate together. For Pliny, Christianity still remained a movement that lacked all the elements appropriate for true religion and piety. This was evident in the Christian refusal to sacrifice to the gods and to the emperor, not because of the Romans' opinion that emperor cult and Christ's cult were irreconcilable opposites, but because it seemed obvious to them that there could be no true and useful religion unless its public character and the worship of the gods of the Roman people were part of its observances. Since the Christians did not want to hear of that, they were not really "pious." Pliny found his judgment confirmed in his questioning of two maid-servants who were deacons of a church (not "deaconesses" but "ministers"; the instructions of 1 Tim 2:11–12 were evidently not observed in this church). In their statements, obtained under torture, he found nothing but "a perverse and extravagant false religion" (*superstitio prava, immodica*). In his measures against Christians, Pliny was not out to punish criminals; his intention was rather to convert people who had gone astray. As an enlightened administrator, he hoped to achieve a reformation of these people and wanted to give an opportunity for repentance (*penitentiae locus*). Trajan confirmed this approach saying that those who are converted should receive "pardon on the basis of their repentance" (*venia ex penitentia*). The Roman official's dilemma was obvious. The generous offer of forgiveness to people who had been accused, if they promised to turn away from their unsavory conduct, was rejected by the faithful members of the church. What should one do with people who confessed their faith stubbornly in the face of such generosity? It was therefore deemed advisable to stay out of the way of the Christians rather than to spy them out.

This policy remained in effect under Trajan's successors. A document from Hadrian (117–138) discussing the treatment of the Christians is extant. The document was preserved in its original Latin text in Justin Martyr *1 Apol.* 68; according to Eusebius, however, in the known manuscripts of Justin's works, the document appears in a Greek translation, which Eusebius provided in *Hist. eccl.* 4.9.1–3. The governor (proconsul) of the province of Asia had written to Hadrian to learn what he should do about the Christians (this letter is not preserved). Hadrian directed the answer to the governor's successor in Ephesus, Minucius Fundanus, instructing him that only such accusations of Christians be permitted that could be brought to public trial, and that the Christians should be punished whenever they had done something illegal. Those who accused Christians, however, solely intending to slander them without being able to prove any crimes, should themselves be subject to punishment. Doubts about this document's authenticity have been raised, because it does not mention that a stubborn insistence upon the confession of Christ is in itself punishable. This was the position confirmed in the correspondence between Pliny and Trajan, and it would reappear later in trials against Christians beginning in the time of Marcus Aurelius (after 161) (according to the witness of later Christian reports of martyrdoms; note also the repeated statements of Tertullian). However, the fact that there were very few, if any, martyrdoms during the reigns of Hadrian and Antoninus Pius affirms the authenticity of the rescript of Hadrian to Minucius Fundanus. Not only did these emperors believe that they were ruling the Roman world in an enlightened age, also the political situation of the Roman empire in this period, both in its domestic and external affairs, as well as the unprecedented economic prosperity, did not warrant the persecution of a religious group that otherwise observed the rules of public peace and order and that was eager to prove its fulfillment of a good citizen's morality. In this respect, the Pastoral Epistles, written in Ephesus or Smyrna at the time of Hadrian's rescript, were absolutely correct in their admonitions to the Christian communities. After the middle of the 2d century, however, when the time of peace and prosperity ended, the Roman authorities were increasingly forced to take measures against the Christians because public opinion blamed them for several misfortunes and calamities. Under Marcus Aurelius, when the empire was involved in continuous wars and when the soldiers brought the plague from the eastern battlefields, the time of the martyrs began. The battle between state and church that was fought out on the basis of fundamental controversial issues belongs, however, to the 3d and 4th centuries.

(e) The Earliest Christian Apologists

(1) *Beginnings and the Apology of Aristides.* The peaceful time of the emperors Hadrian and Antoninus Pius (117–161) is also the period of the formation of

Pergamon: Altar of Zeus

The Altar of Zeus was excavated by a team of German archeologists before World War I and reassembled in Berlin. The picture shows the flanked staircase leading to the entrance through the stoa at the top of the staircase. The altar itself was situated behind that stoa in an open peristyle court.

Christian apologetic literature. The work of Luke already demonstrated an apologetic interest (though most scholars date this work somewhat before this period; see §12.3a). Another fairly early apology already mentioned is the *Kerygma of Peter* (§10.2a). In both works, the exposition of scriptural proof appeared as a central element of the apologetic argument, and this would also play a considerable role in other apologetic writings. In order to understand the importance of this genre of literature, it is necessary to refer to the model that ultimately shaped the writings of the early Christian apologists. They were not primarily interested in the defense of Christianity against accusations that had been raised by the pagan world and by the Roman state, even though this motif played a considerable role. But the primary model of apologetic works was the Greek *protrepticus,* that is, a literary genre designed as an invitation to a philosophical way of life, directed to all those who were willing to engage in the search for true philosophy and make it the rule for their conduct of life. The *Protrepticus* of Aristotle was most influential for the formation of this genre; although it is now lost, its influence extended as far as St. Augustine's *City of God* (by way of Cicero's *Hortensius,* which is also lost but was known to St. Augustine).

To be sure, in the earliest apologetic writings one does not find literary standards that are comparable to these protreptic writings. Moreover, there is no direct dependence upon the Greek prototype. The fist Christian apologists take their immediate point of departure from Jewish apologetics (§5.3e). But the motif of invitation to the true philosophy was still determinative for Christian apologetics. The following themes were therefore dominant: (1) Christianity is a philosophy, that is, a doctrine of correct living and conduct that can be taught; (2) this philosophy serves not only to build the individual moral personality, but also the community and thus the state; (3) since Christianity is the true philosophy, its truth can be documented on the basis of the wisdom of ancient traditions; (4) the philosophical doctrine of

---

Bibliography to §12.2e: Texts

Edgar J. Goodspeed (ed.), *Die ältesten Apologeten* (reprint: Göttingen: Vandenhoeck & Ruprecht, 1984). Greek and Latin texts of the 2d-century apologists.

D. Ruiz Buebo (ed.), *Padres Apologistas Griegos* (BAC 116; Madrid: La Editorial Catolica, 1954).

Miroslav Marcovich (ed.), *Iustini Martyris Apologiae pro Christianis* (PTS 38; Berlin: de Gruyter, 1994).

Idem (ed.), *Iustini Martyris Dialogus cum Tryphone* (PTS 47; Berlin: de Gruyter, 1997).

A. Lukyn Williams, trans., *Justin Martyr: The Dialogue with Trypho* (Translations of Christian Literature, Series 1; Greek Texts; London: SPCK, and New York: Macmillan, 1930).

Bibliography to §12.2e: Studies

J. Geffcken, *Zwei griechische Apologeten* (Leipzig und Berlin: Teubner, 1907).

Hans von Campenhausen, "Justin," in idem, *The Fathers of the Greek Church* (New York: Pantheon, 1959) 12–20.

Erwin R. Goodenough, *The Theology of Justin Martyr* (Amsterdam: Philo, 1968).

E. F. Osborn, *Justin Martyr* (BHTh 74; Tübingen: Mohr/Siebeck, 1973).

Demetrios Trakatellis, *The Pre-Existence of Christ in the Writings of Justin Martyr* (HDR 6; Missoula, MT: Scholars Press, 1976).

Robert M. Grant, *Greek Apologists of the Second Century* (Philadelphia: Westminster, 1988).

Christianity is superior to all other philosophies and exceeds by far all superstitions of traditional religions and beliefs in divinities. All these themes, though to different degrees in each case, played an essential role in the formation of Christian apologetic writings.

Unfortunately, the works of the oldest Christian apologists, Quadratus and Aristides—both directed to the emperor Hadrian—are preserved only very poorly. From the apology of Quadratus only a single sentence is known, quoted by Eusebius (*Hist. eccl.* 4.3.2). Nevertheless, even this meager evidence reveals that Quadratus discussed Jesus' miracles of healing and raising people from the dead. As for the *Apology* of Aristides, Eusebius says merely that it was addressed to Hadrian and was still read by many in his time (*Hist. eccl.* 4.3.3). But a Syriac translation has been discovered (where the writing is addressed to Antoninus Pius) and subsequently a Greek text in a speech of the medieval monastic romance of *Barlaam and Josaphat.* The two texts exhibit considerable differences, causing substantial difficulties for any attempt at a detailed reconstruction of the original.

On the whole, however, the apologetic arguments are still clearly recognizable. The author begins with a proof for the existence of God that tries to reflect philosophical arguments and, in fact, shows influence from Aristotle: God is the one who moves everything, but is himself without beginning, the one who encompasses everything, but is not contained in anything. A list of the nations introduces refutations of the various conceptions of deities. The division into the polytheistic nations of Chaldeans, Greeks, and Egyptians, who are contrasted to the Jews as the monotheists, is traditional and derived from Jewish apologetics. This division, however, has been revised by the author. He assumes three peoples: Jews, Christians, and polytheists; the last are then divided into those three polytheistic nations (*Arist.* 2). Against the Chaldeans, the author argues that the elements heaven, earth, water, and sun are not gods because they can be explained as natural phenomena. Therefore, human beings also are not gods, since they are composed of these elements (*Arist.* 3–7). The arguments in these chapters are derived from the popularized natural sciences of the Hellenistic period. In the next section, Aristides repeats arguments from philosophy, both traditional and popular, against traditional religious beliefs (11). For the Egyptians, he uses the widely favored arguments against the Egyptian worship of animals as if they were gods (12). Up to this point, Aristides' apology is nothing more than a collection of arguments against polytheism that would find immediate agreement from nearly any educated Jewish or pagan reader. Quite different is the following polemic against the Jews, who are, of course, recognized as a nation that knows the one true God. The arguments here are drawn from the Christian polemic against Jewish-Christian syncretism. For Aristides (14), the falsehood of the Jewish worship of God is evident, because their observation of the Sabbath, the festivals, and circumcision is nothing but service of the angels (compare the polemic of Colossians, §12.2a). The teaching of the Christians and the true worship of God are described in terms of the Christian creed. It comprises the confession of Jesus as the Son of God, his coming from heaven, his birth by the virgin, his crucifixion (by the Jews!), his death, burial, resurrection on the third day, and ascension, and finally the proclamation to the nations. Thus Aristides simply quotes "the faith" without feeling any need for further explanations

(15.1–2). The citation of the Christian creed is followed by quotations of *Didache* materials (15.3–9); the Decalogue, golden rule, the command to love one's enemies, even loving one's slaves (this last borrowed from tables of household duties), care for the widows, orphans, and the poor. The conclusion stresses the Christian preparedness for martyrdom. In the final remarks (16–17) occurs the statement that the prayer of the Christians is what maintains the continued existence of the world.

(2) *Justin Martyr.* While the apology of Aristides was a somewhat pedestrian though clearly arranged composition of traditional materials and established arguments, the apologist Justin Martyr, writing in the middle of the 2d century, thoroughly reworked the traditional materials of philosophical protreptic and Jewish apologetic arguments in the interests of Christian theology. Justin came from the eastern regions of the Roman empire (Samaria), stayed for some time in Ephesus, and then established his school in Rome, where he was martyred between 163 and 167. In the extensive *Corpus Justinum,* only three writings can be claimed as genuine works of Justin: two apologies and a dialogue with the Jew Trypho. The *First Apology* is directed to Antoninus Pius and his two adopted sons Lucius Verus and Marcus Aurelius. It must have been written soon after the year 150. The *Second Apology* may have been written at about the same time, the *Dialogue with Trypho,* Justin's most extensive writing, not long thereafter. All three writings are preserved in only two manuscripts, written in 1364 and 1541 CE, respectively, the latter being a copy of the former. Their text must be corrected in a number of instances, but it is more reliable than formerly believed, especially in its biblical quotations. There is, however, a major lacuna in the *Dialogue with Trypho* in both manuscripts. On the basis of the gospel quotations of the *First Apology* and the *Dialogue with Trypho* one can conclude with great certainty that Justin also had composed a harmony of the Gospels of Matthew, Mark, and Luke (he did not know the Gospel of John), which is lost but was used by his student Tatian for the composition of his famous and influential four-gospel harmony known as the *Diatessaron.*

The *First Apology* and the *Dialogue* are not of one piece, but include several smaller tractates composed by Justin previously for different purposes. One good example is the commentary on Psalm 22 in *Dialogue* 98–106. The psalm is first quoted in its entirety, then interpreted sentence by sentence, while in each instance corresponding texts from the gospels are quoted verbatim. In such works, Justin discloses valuable information about the activities of Christian schools. Their work included not only detailed interpretations of passages from the Bible but also critical work on its Greek text. It has been demonstrated persuasively that numerous details in Justin's quotations derive from a Jewish tradition of textual revisions, in which the Greek text of the Septuagint was brought into closer agreement with the continuing revisions of the Hebrew text. In resuming this tradition of text-critical work in his school, Justin was a predecessor of the extensive text-critical work on the Greek Bible in Origen's *Hexapla* (§5.3b). Impressive beginnings of Christian scholarly work are clearly visible here. Such work extended also to the text of the gospels, which Justin usually calls the "Remembrances of the Apostles," thereby relating them to the oral tradition of the sayings of Jesus, which had been conventionally quoted and referred to as what was remembered from what Jesus had said (*1 Clement,* Papias). In a few instances, Justin also refers to them as "gospels" (*euangelia*). This term is here used for the first time in Christian literature for the written documents that later were generally designated in this way. It is very likely that Justin learned this usage from Marcion, who had found in Luke's work the written "gospel" of Paul. It is also possible that in his time readings from these documents in the context of Christian worship were called "readings of the 'gospel.'" In any case, there is no earlier evidence for the use of this term as a designation of written documents. These "gospels" were, however, not yet sacrosanct "Holy Scripture." On the contrary, Justin had no problem when he revised and harmonized their texts systematically so that it would agree as closely as possible with the words of biblical prophecies. In this effort, the gospels were transformed into historical records, in which the prophecies of the Bible are attested as fulfilled in an historical event.

The systematic theological work of Justin's school is also evident in a fundamental reconception of the specifically apologetic productions. Justin was a Platonist and represented a position that is generally called "Middle Platonism" (§4.1a). He was a Gentile convert to Christianity who had worn the mantle of the philosopher before his conversion. To be sure, the description he gives at the beginning of the *Dialogue* of his philosophical inquiries from the Stoics via the Peripatetics and Pythagoreans to the Platonists closely follows a traditional schema and cannot be understood as a personal biographical report. Justin's Middle-Platonic concepts are particularly evident in his doctrine of the Logos. Christ as the divine Logos was a power that existed with God from the primordial beginnings; this power then appeared in the world through its birth by Mary. This "dynamistic" christology, developed under Middle-Platonic influence and shared by other apologists, stands in sharp contrast to the more widespread beliefs of the Christian churches called "modalism," according to which Christ is simply God, who appeared in the world in another "mode" (a christology that is also found in Marcion, §12.3c).

Justin also went a decisive step ahead in his development of the traditional polemic against pagan beliefs in many gods. For him the pagan belief in gods was neither foolish nor ridiculous, but a deliberate imitation of the scriptural prophecies of Christ's coming, inspired by evil demons in order to lead people astray into the worship of false gods (see, e.g., *1 Apol.* 21ff.). The proofs that Justin adduces for this theory show that his school had systematically collected pagan beliefs about the appearances of gods and religious cults and had matched them with appropriate passages from Scripture. But how can it be demonstrated that the fulfillment of these predictions fabricated by the evil demons is merely a delusion? And how is it to be distinguished from the true fulfillment? In order to answer these questions, Justin was able to draw on the accomplishments of his exegetical school. The basis for his demonstration is his principle of his apologetic proof: "It is the work of God to speak before something is taking place, in order to show that it [the true fulfillment] happens exactly as it was predicted" (*1 Apol.* 12.6). The detailed demonstrations follow the legitimate and established principles of the allegorical method, which are handled with precision, as is evident in Justin's distinction between "type," "symbol," and "parable." As a scholar, Justin can thus understand in his methodical analysis of the prophecy the exact features of the fulfilling event, while the evil demons have only a vague notion and therefore always make mistakes when they produce their fake fulfillment.

But in order to establish in detail that the fulfillment of the prophecies in Christ indeed corresponds precisely to the prophecies of Scriptures, Justin is able to draw on trustworthy historical documents that have recorded the fulfilling events, namely, the "Remembrances of the Apostles." In his scriptural proof, Justin does not seek to prove the truth of the written gospels—that is simply presupposed. Rather, he wanted to demonstrate the truth of the Christian creed, "the faith." After a reference to the trustworthiness and inspiration of the Greek translation of the Bible—note that the Septuagint, not its Hebrew original, is seen as inspired!—(*1 Apol.* 31.1–5), this Christian creed is quoted in full: "In the books of the prophets have been predicted the coming of our Lord Jesus Christ, his birth through the virgin, his growing up, his healing of all diseases and raising of the dead, that he would be mocked, his crucifixion and death, resurrection and ascension, that he would be called the Son of God, and the proclamation to all nations." A comparison of this creed of Justin with that of Aristides shows that it has been expanded in its middle section in a manner revealing the influence of the story of Jesus as told in the written gospels. The following chapters (*1 Apology* 32ff.) provide the evidence in detail. Isa 7:14 predicted the birth of Jesus: Justin shows the fulfillment by quoting sentences from Luke 1:31–35, Matt 1:21, and the *Protevangelium of James* 11. Jesus' birthplace was predicted in Micah 5:2 (Bethlehem); the fulfillment is reported in Matt 2:1 and Luke 2:2 (*1 Apology* 33–34). In the same way Justin argues the case for almost every sentence of the Christian creed in the remaining chapters of the *First Apology,* and even more extensively in his *Dialogue.* Though the latter is ostensibly directed against the Jews, it becomes clear that the apologetic argument from Scripture, once it was fully developed, was suited for a work against the Jews as much as for a writing to the Gentiles.

It is important to note that this method of demonstrating the truth, despite the seeming artificiality of its arguments, is not just a clever trick. It is rather the expression of a new consciousness of history that had deep roots in Justin's worldview. He firmly believed that there were indeed visible actions of God in the world and its history, and that it is both possible to understand these actions of God and necessary to respond to them in faith. The inclusion of Greek philosophy and religion into this view of history as the story of salvation is extremely significant. It may be difficult to accept Justin's assurance that Plato learned from Moses; but it was exactly that view that made it possible to include the entire Greek tradition, which had become so important in the Roman world, into the dimension of God's saving history. Justin here also begins to distinguish critically in the Greek tradition between opportunities for the true recognition of God and pseudoreligious falsifications (i.e., those inspired by the evil demons). In this way, Justin avoids a demonization of the entire pagan world.

This type of apologetic literature, though ostensibly addressed to the pagan world, had a profound effect upon the Christian church and its theology, which should not be underestimated. It enabled the church to leave the confines of a history of salvation that was exclusively informed by Israel's Scripture and history and to revitalize the process of Hellenization by including the Greek world and its tradition. At the same time retaining these Scriptures as a book of revelation and prophecy opened the way to appropriate the entire cultural tradition of the ancient world, of which the heritage of Israel remained the most distinguished element. In this process, the words of Jesus received new significance. In order to illustrate the demands of Christian conduct, Aristides had still used *Didache* materials, but Justin discontinued this traditional dependence upon the teaching of the two ways and substituted a catechism composed of sayings of Jesus. Jesus thus assumes a new role; his words establish him as the true teacher of right philosophy, since in brief words of rich meaning he explains how one should conduct one's life. Jesus' sayings perform an important function in the protreptic purpose of the apologetic literature: they present an invitation to a philosophical life (Justin says that his words were brief because he is not a sophist; *1 Apol.* 14.5). Jesus' sayings commend temperance, love of all people, care for others, serving everyone, avoidance of oaths, even praying for one's enemies, and doing good works. All these are presented as virtues of a true philosophical life (*1 Apology* 15–16). The Sermon on the Mount has here become a philosophical protreptic. It is noteworthy, however, that Justin does more than quote Jesus' words in order to demonstrate that Christians are good citizens and reliable taxpayers (*1 Apol.* 17.1–2); he also reminds the emperors that Jesus had exhorted the Christians to suffer or even die for their faith (*1 Apol.* 19.6–8). When the peaceful period of the empire ended with the beginning of the reign of Marcus Aurelius, the philosophical emperor, Justin himself earned martyrdom through his willingness to confess his faith publicly. The report of the martyrdom of Justin and his associates is extant, and it quoted the answers that Justin gave in the interrogation that brought death upon him.

(f) Martyrs: The Martyrdom of Polycarp

The end of the "golden age" of Rome shortly after the middle of the 2d century not only forced the Christians to come out from behind the screen of good citizenship that had protected them for a while and to defend their faith publicly in Roman

Bibliography to §12.2f: Text

Bihlmeyer, *ApostVät,* xxxviii–xliv, 120–32.
Herbert A. Musurillo (ed.), *The Acts of the Christian Martyrs* (2d ed.; Oxford: Clarendon, 1979) xiii–xv, 2–21.
Lake, *ApostFath* 2. 307–45.

Bibliography to §12.2f: Commentaries

Lightfoot, *Apostolic Fathers,* vol. 2, part 2. 935–98.
Gerd Buschmann, *Das Martyrium des Polykarp* (KAV 6; Göttingen: Vandenhoeck & Ruprecht, 1998).
William Schoedel, *Polycarp, Martyrdom of Polycarp, Fragments of Papias* (Grant, *ApostFath* 5).

Bibliography to §12.2f: Studies

Hans von Campenhausen, "Bearbeitungen und Interpolationen des Polykarpmartyriums," in idem, *Frühzeit,* 253–301.
Hans Conzelmann, *Bemerkungen zum Martyrium Polykarps* (NAWG.PH 1978.2; Göttingen: Vandenhoeck & Ruprecht, 1987).
Gerd Buschmann, *Martyrium Polycarpi—Eine formkritische Studie: Ein Beitrag zur Frage der Entstehung der Gattung Märtyrerakte* (BZNW 70; Berlin: de Gruyter, 1994).

courts; it also demanded that they ponder again the destiny of Christian existence, as they began to preserve the memory of their leaders, sisters, and brothers who had suffered martyrdom. At this time, the memories of the great apostles Peter and Paul were crystallized into mostly legendary stories of their martyrdom, but also new reports of martyrdoms were now written down and distributed widely to other churches for consideration and encouragement. The oldest and most famous of these reports is a letter of the church of Smyrna reporting the martyrdom of their bishop Polycarp. This writing, drawn up immediately after Polycarp's death, is still a moving testimony to the early Christian courage in public witness. The extant report, however, raises some troubling problems for the critical scholar with respect to the thoughts and desires of those who repeatedly revised this report during its transmission in the subsequent centuries. The *Martyrdom of Polycarp* is preserved in six Greek manuscripts, all deriving from the *Corpus Polycarpianum,* which was written at the beginning of the 5th century. But Eusebius, at the beginning of the 4th century, copied almost the entire text available to him (*Hist. eccl.* 4.15.3–45). On the whole, Eusebius's text must be judged as more reliable than that of the later manuscripts deriving from the *Corpus Polycarpianum.* The latter contains several passages, sentences, and phrases not included in Eusebius's text. But even Eusebius' text must have been the result of some revisions of the original, as Hans von Campenhausen has demonstrated in a convincing analysis. The following picture of the historical development of this venerable document thus emerges.

The letter of the church of Smyrna originally ended with *Mart. Pol.* 20. Chapter 21 was added because of an interest in the hagiographic calendar—evidence that a special festival in memory of the famous bishop's martyrdom was being instituted. But a criticism of such veneration of martyrs has also been interpolated: "Christ we worship as the Son of God, but the martyrs we love as disciples and imitators of the Lord" (*Mart. Pol.* 17.3). Nevertheless, biographical curiosity and interest in the memorial celebration for the dead led to the addition of several names (17.2), a note that it was not possible to obtain the body and the relics (17.1), and information concerning the memorial celebration (18.3). In order to exalt the famous martyr, his holiness was augmented in a description of his behavior and experience: 9.1 contains a reference to a voice from heaven encouraging Polycarp; but it is an interpolation because it interrupts the context unnecessarily. From his mortal wound emerges not only blood but even a dove (16.1—Eusebius did not read that in his text). A polemical interpolation is also recognizable: 5.1 directly continues what was said in 3.2; but chapter 4 includes a remark about a Phrygian, that is, a Montanist (the movement did not yet exist at the time of Polycarp's death), who first volunteers for martyrdom, but is then persuaded to sacrifice. Also the remarks about the participation of Jews seem to be later interpolations.

The secondary development of the text also shows an increasing interest in interpolating features from the passion narratives of the Gospels into the description of the martyrdom. Even before Eusebius, a reader who knew the Gospel of John

Bibliography to §12.2f: History of Scholarship

B. Dehandschutter, "The Martyrium Polycarpi: a Century of Research," *ANRW* 2.2.27 (1993) 485–522.

added the phrases that "the hour had come" (John 17:1) in *Mart. Pol.* 8.1, that "they sat him on an ass" (John 12:14), and that everything happened "on a Great Sabbath" (John 19:31)—but in *Mart. Pol.* 8.3 the ass is forgotten and Polycarp walks humbly on foot. Influence from the passion narratives is especially evident in the recension of the writing that took place after Eusebius. Eusebius did not read in his copy that Polycarp's martyrdom happened "according to the Gospel" (1.1b–2.1), that martyrs do not really feel any pain (2.2b–3), that there were traitors in Polycarp's house, and that the police captain had "the same name, being called Herod" (6.2–7.1). The concept of the imitation of Jesus (19.1b–2) is also missing in Eusebius's text; the reference to the "Gospel" in 22.1 belongs to the same redactor.

But the original letter written by the church in Smyrna—minus all later interpolations—is no less impressive. It also described the suffering of the other martyr who dies with Polycarp (Eusebius *Hist eccl.* 4.15.4). After Germanicus had been thrown to the wild beasts (*Mart. Pol.* 3.1), the crowd cried out, "Away with the atheists! Let Polycarp be searched for!" (3.2). Polycarp had been persuaded against his will to leave the city and was staying with friends not far away (5.1). While there, he had a dream in which he saw the pillow under his head burning with fire, and told his friends that he would be burned alive (5.2)—quite remarkable, since beforehand the Christians had been thrown to the wild beasts. He decided not to flee any further (7.1); thus the police found him and brought him to the stadium. Despite his advanced age, Polycarp refused to swear by the genius of the emperor (9.2): "For eighty-six years I have served Christ, and he has done me no wrong. How can I now blaspheme my king who saved me?" (9.3). Since the interrogation was in vain, and Polycarp steadfastly continued to confess his faith, he was condemned to death by fire (chaps. 10–11) and was finally stabbed with a dagger, since the fire miraculously did not touch him (16.1). When the crowd had cried out, "This is the teacher of Asia, the father of the Christians, the destroyer of our gods!" the reasons for the hostility against the Christians was formulated in a pregnant fashion (12.2). Polycarp died because he refused to deny what the governor of the Roman province called "atheism," and because, looking at the crowd that fanatically called for his death, he had waved his hand at them and said, "Away with the atheists!" (9.2).

Agora: The central square of the Greek city, surrounded by public buildings, temples, and open halls with stores (stoas), but with open access from several sides. People went here for business, leisure, and shopping. It also served for assemblies of the people and was considered a sacred place. See I 73–74.

Amanuensis: A secretary who would draft letters and take dictation. It is likely that the apostle Paul used an amanuensis for the composition of his correspondence.

Anacoluthon: An incomplete sentence (e.g., without a predicate). Sometimes an anacoluthon results from carelessness; often, however, an *anacoluthon* is deliberately constructed for rhetorical effect.

Anthropos: The Greek word for "human being." In philosophical and theological speculations, it is often used to describe the celestial or spiritual prototype for the creation of human beings. The *Anthropos* is thought of as bisexual or asexual and is sometimes identified with the redeemer, thus identified with the heavenly Christ.

Apocalypticism: Disclosure of the events of the past, the present, and especially the future in mythological language (restitution of Israel, cosmic catastrophe and a creation of a new heaven and earth). Such disclosures usually appear with the claim that they have been received through visions and are propagated through books, often considered mysterious and secret. Apocalypticism implies that the course of future events can be calculated. See I 246–54; see also under *Eschatology.*

Apophthegma: A brief story, usually transmitted orally, in which a traditional saying of a famous person (Diogenes, Jesus, and others) forms the conclusion. In most cases, the saying is more original, while the narrative part of the apophthegma is secondary and subject to variation. Sometimes such traditions are also called *Paradigm,* a very brief *apophthegma* is designated as *chrie.*

Aretalogy: The enumeration of the great deeds of a god or goddess (e.g., Isis) or of a divinely inspired human being (a "divine man"). An aretalogy can appear in the form of a sequence of brief sentences, each describing a different *arete* ("virtuous quality" or "powerful act"), or in the form a series of stories, such as miracle stories, as they are told of the god Asklepios or of Jesus.

Colophon: A subscript to a work often found in ancient manuscripts; it gives the title of the work, sometimes also information about the author or the place of composition. Colophons are not original parts of such works, but rather additions of the scribe.

Cosmogony: Mythical descriptions of the birth or the creation of the universe, either by a process of divine evolution or through the interaction of various divine powers or substances, usually resulting in the creation of heaven and earth.

Covenant formula: A genre of literature or oral literature that presents the making of a covenant between God and Israel, mirroring the suzerainty treaties of the ancient orient. It consists of a historical introduction (e.g., the story of the Exodus), a basic command, individual stipulations (e.g., the decalogue), and curses and blessings. See I 252.

Diaspora: Part or all of a nation living away from its homeland in various other cities and countries. Especially used of Israelites (Jews and Samaritans) living in the many cities of the Hellenistic world and the Roman empire. See I 210–17.

Divine Man: A human being endowed with divine powers, thus transcending in accomplishments the range of normal human abilities. Poets (e.g., Homer), philosophers, rulers, and miracle workers were considered divine men, sometimes also called "Son of God."

Docetism: The belief that Christ could not really become a human being because of the insurmountable difference between the divine and the human world. It was therefore thought that Christ only "seemed" (Greek *dokei*) to be human, but actually never gave up his divine nature and essence. See II 203, 289, 335.

Encratism: Abstention from sex, marriage, certain foods and drinks for religious reasons in order to avoid contamination from natural and earthly things. See the General Index under "Asceticism."

Eudaimonia: Usually translated "happiness." But the term expresses much more: the status of complete peace and imperturbability in this life. It is often commended as the ultimate goal of a philosophical or religious life.

Eschatology: The understanding of the present under the perspective of a coming or impending divinely guided renewal of the world and society. Signs of such renewal may be seen as appearing already in the present time (realized eschatology). Eschatological beliefs may expressed in terms of apocalyptic mythology or in political terms or in the form of individual piety. See the General Index.

Etymology: The method used to explain the meaning of a term or a word on the basis of its assumed literal sense of linguistic roots, contrary to its understanding on the basis of the context of its actual usage.

Form: In form criticism the structure of a unit transmitted in the oral tradition, such as the form of a saying or of a miracle story or an apophthegma. See below under *Genre* and II 61–65.

Forum: The central square in a Roman city. Like the Greek agora, it is surrounded by administrative buildings and temples and also serves as a market place. But while the Greek agora is a square surrounded by a variety of different buildings, the forum is one unified building enclosing with its peristyle an interior rectangular space with access gates allowing easy control of entry.

Genre: The structure of particular types of literature, such as letters, gospels, biographies. See above under *Form* and II 61–65.

Gymnasium: Gymnasia were the primary facilities for athletic activities and schooling in Greek and Roman cities. A gymnasium was normally a large court surrounded by stoas and various rooms serving as places for exercise, dressing, oiling, washing, and as lecture halls; one of these spaces was usually reserved for worship.

Ithyphallic: "with raised phallus," that is, with erect penis. Satyrs and donkeys in the company of the god Dionysus are usually presented in this way as well as some other gods such as Priapus.

Kerygma: "Proclamation." Technical term for fixed formulations of the early Christian proclamation, such as "the kerygma of the death, resurrection and exaltation of Jesus," sometimes also used in a more general sense for the preaching of the gospel.

Leitourgia: The term for certain public offices in Greek cities, such as "president of the gymnasium." A *leitourgia* was considered a special honor, but also involved the expenditure of considerable amounts of money, for example, providing animals for regular sacrifices or financing athletic contests.

Manumission: The legal procedure for the freeing of a slave. It required the supervision of a public official or of a temple, the payments of certain sums of money, and the filing of the appropriate document, which was sometimes published in the form of an inscription.

Modalism: A christological belief that fully identified God and Christ in their divine nature so that Christ became a "mode" of the being or presence of god. Later modalists were accused of saying that God the Father suffered on the cross.

Onomasticon: A method used in the composition of psalms, or hymns, or wisdom lists; the first letter in each succeeding line or verse would be made to correspond to the order of letters in the alphabet or in a divine or magical name.

Parenesis: "Admonition." The word is used to designate certain traditional types of admonition and exhortation aimed at proper religious and moral life. Most early Christian letters contain parenetical sections.

Parousia: Originally "coming" or "presence" of a person (like the apostle Paul) or of a divine being. Later it was specifically used to designate the second coming of Jesus.

Pericope: Technical term for a segment of a biblical text, as it was "cut out" for liturgical reading in worship service. Pericopes are usually small, self-contained units, comprising not more than a part of the chapter of a biblical book.

Prescript: The opening of a letter, comprising the name(s) of the sender and the addressee as well as a greeting. See the General Index.

Proem: The second section of a letter, following upon the prescript. It is formulated either as a thanksgiving prayer or as doxology and may include lengthy descriptions of the situation of the sender and of the status of the addressee. See the General Index.

Protrepticus: An invitation to enter upon a truly philosophical or religious life, a defense of the qualities and virtues of such a life, and a description of the basic philosophical concepts by which it should be guided. See II 5, 342, 347.

Stichometry: A list in which the number of lines in each of the books in question is given. Ancient stichometries help us to estimate the length of writings that are lost or only preserved in fragments.

Stoa: A public building in an ancient city consisting of a long hall with a single or double colonnade, open on one side and often with a line of shops on the other side, Stoas did not only serve as shopping malls; they were also used as courthouses, picture galleries, lecture halls (like the Painted Stoa in Athens where Zeno, the founder of the "Stoic" philosophy, gave his lectures), and as places for general business and leisure. Often of large dimensions (several hundred feet long), they lined many squares, streets, and courts.

Syzygy: Mostly used with respect to mythical speculations in which the celestial, divine world is described as consisting of pairs, for example, of male and female in each cosmic aeon; it is also sometimes applied to the reconstruction of history, in which pairs occur, such as Cain and Abel, Paul and Peter. See the General Index.

Technitai: "Craftsmen." The term is used for the members of any profession that requires a skill, be it bakers or actors or shipbuilders. They were usually organized in associations, such as the "Dinoysiac Technitai" (the association of professional actors and dancers related to the theater under the protection of the god Dionysus).

Testament: A genre of literature. It is a modification of the covenant formula (see above) in which the historical introduction is replaced by the biographical description of an individual (patriarch or apostle). This individual, who may be already dead at the time of writing, then gives instructions and pronounces blessings and curses. See I 252–53; II 138, 285, 290, 303–4. Note that the use of the term "testament" for each of the two parts of the Christian Bible dates from a later period.

Theogony: A mythical description of the evolution of the world of the gods in a primordial time, describing their origin, function, and powers. Theogonies often recount dramatic celestial struggles, and they precede cosmogonies in many ancient myths.

Thiasos (pl. *thiasoi*): A term for an association with a particular religious commitment. The term is also used for secular associations under the protectorate of a deity.

GENERAL INDEX
(NAMES, PLACES, SUBJECTS)

Bold Roman numerals refer to the volumes, bold page numbers indicate specific discussion of frequently cited names and subjects.

BIBLICAL, JEWISH, AND EARLY CHRISTIAN WRITINGS

Alphabetical Index
(bold print indicates specific treatment of a writing)

Authors Discussed in the Text